RESTORATION STUDIES III

RESTORATION STUDIES III

A Collection of Essays About the
History, Beliefs, and Practices
of the
Reorganized Church of Jesus Christ of
Latter Day Saints

Maurice L. Draper, Ph.D.
Editor

Debra Combs, B.A.
Assistant Editor

TEMPLE SCHOOL

The Auditorium

Independence, Missouri

1986

Herald Publishing House

Library of Congress Cataloging in Publication Data
(Revised for vol. 3)
Main entry under title:

Restoration studies.

   Vol. 3: Debra Combs, assistant editor.
   Includes bibliographical references.
   1. Reorganized Church of Jesus Christ of Latter Day Saints—Addresses, essays, lectures. I. Draper, Maurice L. II. Lindgren, A. Bruce. III. Combs, Debra, 1952-
BX8674.R46 1983   289.3'33   82-23375
ISBN 0-8309-0362-3   (v. 2)

Printed in the United States of America

90 89 88 87   2 3 4 5

BOARD OF EDITORIAL ADVISERS

The members of the Board of Editorial Advisers have provided significant guidance in the selection of the essays. The manuscripts were circulated anonymously for editorial review. Most of those approved for publication received the affirmative recommendation of at least a majority of the advisers, but few had unreserved unanimous approval. For this reason, among others, responsibility for the final selection became the responsibility of the editor. No doubt there will be similar differences in judgment and response by the various readers. This volume is submitted in the hope that it will enrich those who read, despite, or perhaps even because of, differences in understanding and point of view.

Independence, Missouri
April 15, 1985

Maurice L. Draper, Ph.D.
Editor

CONTENTS

PREFACE

With the publication of *Restoration Studies III* we are well on our way to establishing a significant and, it is hoped, an enduring tradition. A healthy and vital forum for the expression of ideas and positions concerning the history, beliefs, and practices of the Reorganized Church of Jesus Christ of Latter Day Saints has been established. Through the three volumes of *Restoration Studies* a serious and meaningful relationship has taken root which bears fruit in investigation, inquiry, and dialogue.

Each essay within this volume stands alone on its own merit and is representative only of the author. There is no implied intention that these essays represent the views or beliefs of the editors, the editorial board, or the general church. The integrity of diversity in thought and opinion which is encouraged is reflected to the degree that some readers may find the concepts exciting while others may find them uncomfortable. It is hoped that in both cases the results will be greater knowledge, wider understandings, and new vision.

During the past eighteen months, since the acceptance of Section 156 of the Doctrine and Covenants, church members have been involved in the significant process of giving definition to their individual response to the Restoration message. This inquiry has been reflected in many of the essays in this collection.

It is with a degree of excitement and anticipation that we at Temple School recommend this volume for your reflection and enlightenment. We commend Maurice Draper, Debra Combs, and the editorial board for their fine work. Our hope is that this volume will be another stepping-stone in a continuing dialogue between reader and author.

Paul M. Edwards
President, Temple School
1985

I
CHURCH MISSION AND PROGRAM

I

CHURCH MISSION AND PROGRAM

Editor's Note:

Howard S. Sheehy, Jr., Independence, Missouri, is a member of the First Presidency of the Reorganized Church of Jesus Christ of Latter Day Saints. He has a master of science degree in education from Kansas University, where he is also a candidate for the doctor of philosophy degree. "The Church: Structure, Function, and Unity" was delivered at Park College February 24, 1983, as part of the W. Wallace Smith lecture series.

Harry J. Fielding of Auckland, New Zealand, is assigned to the Australia-New Zealand Region of the Reorganized Church of Jesus Christ of Latter Day Saints and serves as an assistant to the apostle for the South Pacific area. His master of arts degree from Auckland University was granted with honors.

Currently serving as a "contractual assignee" for the Reorganized church in Kirtland Stake, Kirtland, Ohio, Galen Worthington received his B.A. in elementary education from Graceland College in 1985.

Richard P. Howard, M.A. (history), of Independence, Missouri, is the church historian for the church. He is also currently the president of the John Whitmer Historical Association.

Pastor of the Willoughby, Ohio, congregation of the Reorganized church, Kenneth D. Sowers, Jr., B.S. (education), is a middle school teacher.

Lois Taylor Braby is a staff executive in the Christian Education Commission of the Reorganized church at its World Headquarters in Independence, Missouri. She has master of science degrees in both sociology and counseling.

Assistant to the Administrator of the Northern Plains and Prairie Provinces Region of the Reorganized church, Vivian Collins Campbell, Ph.D. (family ecology), is also the wife of a bishop in the church. The Campbells reside in Great Falls, Montana.

Levi S. Peterson's article is a reprint from *Sunstone*, May–June, 1982. It was originally delivered as the presidential address at the general meeting of the Association for Mormon Letters, January 1982. Dr. Peterson is a professor of English and director of the honors program at Weber State College in Ogden, Utah.

THE CHURCH: STRUCTURE, FUNCTION, AND UNITY
Howard S. Sheehy, Jr.

During the presidency of W. Wallace Smith, the Reorganized Church of Jesus Christ of Latter Day Saints experienced its most rapid expansion in non-Western cultures, predominantly black nations, and non-Christian societies. It may be too early yet to assess fully the impact of this expansion on the long-term development of the church, but I would certainly agree with the implied thesis of the doctoral study of President Maurice L. Draper that the impact has been in both directions: that is, the church theology as well as its policies and leaders have been affected at least as much as have been the converts in the Third-World countries. The giving and receiving principle in development has been fully active in our experience.

In some ways this paper may be considered a companion to the one in this series presented in 1980 by my teacher and friend, Apostle Clifford A. Cole, entitled "The Dilemma of the Church in Christian Mission." The preparation of this paper has been focused on a conference of African church leaders held in Nairobi, Kenya. Unforeseen circumstances gave me an opportunity to "field test" the concepts presented here at a similar conference held in Mexico City with leaders from Latin America and the Caribbean area.

In the early history of religious experience God instructed his servant Moses to gather the people in Horeb (Deuteronomy 4:10) and God made a covenant with the children of Israel, "If ye will obey my voice indeed, and keep my covenant, then ye shall be a peculiar treasure unto me above all people; for all the earth is mine; and ye shall be unto me a kingdom of priests, and a holy nation" (Exodus 19:5, 6). The people responded, "And it shall be our righteousness, if we observe to do all these commandments before the Lord our God, as he hath commanded us" (Deuteronomy 6:25). At Mount Sinai, after the people were sanctified (that is, after they agreed and were prepared to be set apart to the service of God), they received the Ten Commandments and were witnesses to God's power on the mountain manifest by "thunderings, and the lightnings, . . . and the mountain smoking" (Exodus 20:18).

This event was for the Hebrew nation the highest expression of *qahal* the Hebrew word used in the Old Testament that is translated "church" but which has a literal meaning: a "people gathered or summoned together for a purpose." This is the early historical scriptural origin of the church concept.

Two separate ideas of the church have emerged from this Old Testament and found their place in early Christian writings. The first is *The People of God*.

The People of God. The church continued through the biblical era to be viewed as a covenant community. In the New Testament it saw its roots as being among those who from the beginning had lived by faith in God's covenant promises (see especially Hebrews 11). This particular title identifies with emphasis those whom God has chosen and created and brought into being. God's initiative is primary. The relationship with God is possible by his gracious forgiveness of sin, and it is maintained by the remembrance of his act of deliverance and the promised hope of inheritance. It is seen as a covenant without end because it shall never be denied by God. The extension of the community comes about by God's continuing invitation to all to be his people, so that the covenant community will eventually include those from every nation, tribe, language, and people. It is unlike any other community because it is designed to bring about reconciliation with the Creator and thus the church becomes the source of our redemption. The focus of this idea is on what God has done and is doing.

The response of the church member is to accept and obey God's law. The future belongs to God and he will in justice and mercy bring all of life's elements to their intended purpose.

The contrasting view we shall call *The Kingdom and the Temple.*

The Kingdom and the Temple. This concept of the church as a "gathering of the people" calls on two of the central symbols of the Old Testament. The society is referred to as a holy nation and a royal priesthood (I Peter 2:9). The faithful are spoken of as kings and priests (Revelation 1:6 and 5:10), rulers and divines. Here the emphasis is on the authority of the people. Just as God ruled the universe, the earthly kingdom was to have dominion and sovereignty. At the center of the kingdom is the city of David: Jerusalem. This was the place to receive Messiah. Central to this city and the Messianic reign was the temple, the place of God's presence. Here at the temple the priesthood served, making sacrifices and seeking to effect for the people reconciliation with God. These concepts are broadened in New Testament thought to make of all the believers "lively stones" (they are the substance of the church), with Jesus the chief cornerstone of the temple, the standard to which all measurements and relationships are determined. The self-sacrifice of Christ becomes the call for the priesthood or the disciples to present themselves, their bodies, as living sacrifices for the sake of establishing the kingdom. The future belongs to the people. Their application of their faith to the institutions of society will bring about God's purposes.

The Reorganized Church of Jesus Christ of Latter Day Saints attempts today to blend these images in a way that bears witness to the interaction between God and the people. Similar language can be noted in this theological statement of "The Church and Mission."

The Church and Mission Through the life and ministry of Jesus Christ, God created the church (John 1:14). God draws people into the church through their faithful response to the Holy Spirit. Thus, the church is God's reconciling community in the world (II Corinthians 5:15-21). As the people of God, the church is called to transcend all human barriers in every culture where it is planted. Since all are sinners, all are called into the church. By God's grace, it is within the nurturing community of faith, the Body of Christ, that salvation occurs.

The faith of the church is in God, who is at work in the Body of Christ, reconciling the world unto himself. In faith the church perceives and bears witness of God's reconciling ministry within its fellowship and structure. Persons are renewed in this community of love and faith. Through this process of renewal the church is strengthened and enabled to penetrate the world in the spirit of reconciliation. The activity of the church is always in response to God's initiative. While ministering in boldness, the church humbly confesses that its power is in the One who called it into being. Form and structure must never become substitutes for this central call to be God's people in leading the world into faith and repentance. As God's people, the church relates to the world in a quality of relationship which bears witness of the reconciling power of the Lord of the church.

The church has a faith in God to share with the world. While the church has no inherent power to develop that faith in others, it has the firm testimony and assurance that the Holy Spirit is revealing God's reconciling power to those who will receive the ministry of the church. It is this faith that God is in Christ reconciling the world unto himself which sends the church into mission (II Corinthians 5:17-19).

The mission of the church is, like that of Jesus, to stand *in* the world rather than *against* the world. The principle of incarnation informs our ministry—"I called you servants for the world's sake, and you are their servants for my sake" (Doctrine and Covenants 90:8b). The church does not isolate itself from the world or exert power over or against the world. It gives its life in witness to the saving power of Jesus Christ in the midst of the world. The church is characterized by its obedience to God rather than being noted for any inherent power to compel others to obedience.*

In addition to these broad scope models of the church, the function of the church, in what we call the pastoral unit, is richly described by other analogies in the Bible. Jesus called on the people's agricultural understanding to communicate what he had in mind. He referred to the "vineyard" and the "flock."

These analogies evoke thoughts of the rural life of the people and their recognition that they were entirely dependent on God. They lived with the knowledge that it was necessary to produce a harvest, and that judgment of quality productivity was ultimately beneficial to the quality of life. We are familiar with the stewardship message of the rented vineyard. There is a parallel development in the gospel of John regarding the symbol of Jesus as the vine, and the disciples or the church as branches dependent on the vine and judged by their ability to produce similar fruit. The strongest analogies of this category, however, develop around the church as the flock of God. The nature of the ministry of Jesus and subsequently

the role of the church is described prophetically and poetically in Isaiah 40:11: "He shall feed his flock like a shepherd; he shall gather the lambs with his arms, and carry them in his bosom, and shall gently lead those that are with young." John identifies Jesus as the Good Shepherd, using the Old Testament image of the psalmist but enriching the personal dimension by his being the one who knows the sheep and whose voice is known by the sheep. Included in the gospels are also various emphases on sheep and goats, sheep lost and found, sheep and wolves, and sheep with or without a shepherd. There is also the comparison of shepherds, strangers, hirelings, wolves, and good shepherds.

The universal church is described by Jesus in terms of "other sheep...which are not of this fold; them also I must bring...and there shall be one fold and one shepherd" (John 10:16). The essence of this promise is extended more broadly in the Book of Mormon (III Nephi 7:24-26). Jesus frequently used the "flock of God," in describing the pastoral care and as the evangelistic tasks of the church. The commission to Peter to "feed the sheep and lambs" further identifies the pastoral, shepherding function of the disciple among the membership of the church.

Building on the words of Jesus, early New Testament writers continued to define the church. The Apostle Paul referred to it primarily as *ecclesia*, the "called out ones—those who are summoned or belong to the Lord," a very similar meaning to its Old Testament origins. The *ecclesia* often refers to God's action toward his children who are called, chosen, gathered, justified, and sanctified the people of God. In contrast to the earlier kings and priests images, other New Testament writers introduce themselves as slaves of God. This is their em-

---

*The First Presidency, "The Church and Mission," January, 1979.

phasis on personal motivation, obedience, and allegiance. To be a slave of Christ is to imitate his lowliness, his humiliation, and suffering. In this connection the Greek term *diakonia* became a description of the church. Christ serving the church and the church serving the Christ—this mutuality of responsibility constitutes the church as *diakonia*. An early statement of the giving and receiving principle and a blending of the two separate Old Testament concepts.

Many other analogies describing the church can be found in the New Testament scriptures: the household and the family (Ephesians 2:19), the bride of Christ (Ephesians 5:27), the pillar and the ground of the truth (I Timothy 3:16), and perhaps the most familiar of all used by the Apostle Paul, the body of Christ (Romans 12:5 and Ephesians 1:23).

The complete dependence and interrelatedness of differing functions and responsibilities within the church is clearly communicated by the language "the eye cannot say unto the hand, I have no need of thee; nor again the head to the feet, I have no need of you" (I Corinthians 12:21). All of these inform and enrich our understanding of the nature of a divine institution, organized to facilitate and enable God's love to be active in our lives, and to help us fulfill the commission of our Savior to call others to discipleship by the power of witness of his presence in our world.

The Book of Mormon also uses a mixture of these same analogies to describe the establishment of the church during the time of Alma, approximately 150 years before the birth of Jesus. Alma addresses those who have been oppressed in the kingdom of Noah and gathered together in secret because they have witnessed the martyrdom of Abinadi. In telling about God's purpose for them, Alma says,

If you are desirous to come *into the fold of God*

and to be called *his people,* and are willing to bear one another's burdens that they may be light, and are willing to mourn with those that mourn, and comfort those that stand in need of comfort, and to stand as witnesses of God at all times, and in all things, and in all places. . . . If this be the desire of your hearts, what have you against being baptized in the name of the Lord, as a witness before him that you have entered into a covenant with him that you will serve him and keep his commandments (italics mine).—Mosiah 9:39-41

This charge was accepted by the people as they clapped their hands with joy. Following this initiation and covenant-making ceremony by baptism of its members the church was established by the designation of priests whose function it was to preach and teach the words of Alma and the prophets. These priests were self-supporting and the membership imparted physical and spiritual resources to one another. This account further contributes to the universality of both the imagery of the church and its primary commission.

We are appreciative today of the scriptures with regard to the structure, function, and nature of the church. The imagery is rich in substance and stimulates creative thought and application in circumstances that are now vastly different, and yet at times, surprisingly similar. The simplicity of the analogies allows for multicultural implementation and encourages periodic renewal of former established traditions that may have lost their significance. Their universality enables the church to be faithful to its purpose in a divergent economic, political, and social world. Unity is made possible by the establishment of a foundation that is inherent in human experience. There is commonality in our perceptions of family, farming, and fellowship.

Drawing on the vineyard and vine analogies of Jesus, we can explore the relationship of the church with the Christian world, the relationship of the church headquarters with the field administration, and the role of the local church.

The parable of the workers in the vineyard may best describe our relationship to the Christian faith. As a church we have come relatively late to the labor. We must recognize that many churches have been engaged in the Christian task for centuries: they were at work long before we were even established. While we have entered into the vineyard and engaged ourselves in similar tasks, we have largely chosen, at least to this date, to do our work independently. Especially on the American scene, it seemed necessary for us to sharply identify our "distinctives" in order to establish our identity. More recently, however, we have seen the value of cooperation with some U.S. national organizations of an ecumenical nature in areas of stewardship education and church school methodology. We have participated in a few state organizations seeking to address certain moral/economic issues. There is minimal participation in ecumenical organizations by our national churches. The action of the 1980 World Conference represents a forward-looking official stance in this regard. World Conference Resolution No. 1157–Participation in Interdenominational Christian Ministries states the following:

Resolved, That the World Conference hereby endorses the participation of the World Church in interdenominational Christian ministries where such participation does not require the World Church to (1) alter or abandon any of the traditional beliefs and practices of the church, (2) endorse any creeds or theological positions which are inconsistent with any of the traditional beliefs and practices of the church, or (3) commit a disproportionate share of the church's resources of time, money, or personnel...Resolved, That the World Conference hereby affirms the right of each field jurisdiction to determine the nature of its own participation in interdenominational Christian ministries and to determine the level of commitment of its resources of time, money, and personnel where such participation does not require any field jurisdiction to (1) alter or abandon any of the traditional beliefs and practices of the church, or (2) endorse any creeds or theological positions which are inconsistent with any of the traditional beliefs and practices of the church.[*]

We are finding identification with other Christian bodies and are gaining mutual respect.

The parable of the vine may be used to describe the relationship of the World Church structure (denominational headquarters) to the local field supervisory jurisdictions: (stakes, regions, districts, national and tribal churches) as well as the pastoral units (congregations, branches, and missions). The various elements of the vine are made cohesive by the priesthood function. The president is charged with "presiding over the whole church" in his role as president of the High Priesthood. By the delegation of authority, and identification of responsibilities of various priesthood offices, both the administrative and functional tasks are coordinated. Within the priesthood structure are offices which primarily relate to the local church, others with supervisory roles of larger areas, and still others with international responsibility.

Ordination to the priesthood is determined by the identification of a divine call for an individual by the administrative officer, acceptance of the call by the candidate, and approval of the call by a legislative body of the members. The blending of God's action and human responsibility is again the principle. Only such persons may be selected as presiding officers. In sustaining, approving, or electing jurisdictional officers the right of nomination always rests with the administrative leadership. In legislative conferences this right may also rest with the members, but those nominated to presiding functions should be from the leading priesthood members as may be appropriate to the level of organization. Here the balance of

---

[*]Rules and Resolutions (Independence, Missouri: Herald House, 1980), 257-8.

authority rests between priesthood leadership and the membership's voice and vote, in what is frequently referred to as a theocratic-democracy. The legislative rights of the local church are also circumscribed by the actions or rules of the World Conference to the degree that the lesser body is prohibited not only from imposing its will upon the larger body but also from acting out of harmony with the approved rules and resolutions of the larger body. The First Presidency are the "leading interpreters of the law" regarding procedure and doctrine and become final authority in these matters for the whole church. The unifying elements of the church are contained in the "vine," that is, individual and group authority to act does not exist independent of the body, and the ebb and flow of administrative direction through priesthood officers serves to maintain the church as an integral organization. It should be remembered, however, that the moral authority for management or administration of the church, what we call "presiding," is ultimately in response to the Christ. A paraphrased comment from the *Interpreters Dictionary of the Bible* is helpful here (Vol. I, p. 626). The church in the New Testament was not a democracy in the sense that the power was in the hands of the people, who would then delegate it to ministers freely elected. Neither was the church in the New Testament an oligarchy (ruling few) in the sense that the apostles, and often their appointed ministers, were authorized to designate their successors.

The original church order had its source in the idea of the church. Christ was the head of the church, which he ruled through his Spirit. Power in the church belonged neither to the minister nor to the community itself, but to Christ.

Early instruction in the Restoration movement (1830) echoes this understanding: "The elders are to conduct the meetings as they are led by the Holy Ghost, according to the commandments and revelations of God" (Doctrine and Covenants 17:9, 1830).

If "workers in the vineyard" describes our relationship to other Christian bodies, and "vine and its branches" describes the relationship of the church headquarters to field jurisdictions, then the local church may best be described as the fruit or the flower of the vine. It is in the local church that the fruit is developed and the harvest is garnered. The function of the vine is to nurture, impart strength, and determine certain inherent characteristics. The fruit, however, is also influenced by the environment in which it grows. The soil or culture in which the plant has roots, the length of the growing season or maturity achieved, the climate, the presence of disease entities or the migration of plant pests—all have their effect and must be coped with by the local church. The tastes and needs of the surrounding community also have their say about the culinary treatment of the produce. With respect to the sacraments of the church, for example, it is the vine (World Church) that determines the essence or essential meaning to be conveyed in the performance of the ordinance and, within certain limits, the form to be followed in performing the ordinance. It is the local church, however, that determines the exact procedure. This includes the elements used to insure that the essence of the ordinance is accurately conveyed in the culture (for example, the specific items used to represent the body and blood of the Christ). It may be that the traditional grape juice will be replaced with water or coconut milk, the "bread" may be leavened or unleavened, made of wheat, rice, corn, or perhaps a tuber. Similarly, the worship setting and the manner of service will reflect cultural patterns and practices.

Another application of this decentralization principle may be seen in the identification of the ministry of the Holy Spirit with respect to the calling of local members to priesthood responsibility. The priesthood offices are delineated and defined at the World Church level in the Doctrine and Covenants. Within these guidelines, local officers are free to initiate calls as they are directed by the Spirit to the Aaronic priesthood and the office of elder, recommending them to the field apostles for administrative approval. The ordinations are then authorized by local legislative bodies. It is anticipated that generally these priesthood members will serve in their own culture, among members who know them, and in the case of deacons and teachers, they are not considered "traveling ministers." Despite the provincial nature of the process, in the event of a change of residence, even to another nation or culture, the priesthood authority is recognized churchwide. This justifies the administrative clearance of the apostle.

In the instance of priesthood calls to World Church orders, councils, or quorums, however, the initiative rests with general officers and approval is requested from legislative bodies that are more inclusive than the local unit. In the case of local priesthood calls the standards of education, literacy, social standing, and competence are locally determined and usually culturally derived. Those who serve in the World Church orders, councils, and quorums must be sensitive to cultural or social arrangements and be open to diversity or plurality that necessarily exists in an international body.

Summary: The church is first and foremost an expression of the creative power of God. It is described as being made up of those people who are in a covenant relationship with God as well as one another to achieve divine purpose. Organizers and leaders are acceptable both to God and to the people. The church has always had the same fundamental task: witnessing the gospel to the world and maintaining the spiritual lives of believers. The witnessing function may range from evangelistic preaching to social/economic services and may include the demonstration of comprehensive community building which we have often referred to as the Zionic enterprise. The maintenance of members' spiritual lives is perhaps best accomplished when those persons who have become a living part of the body of Christ accept or are given the opportunity to become responsible to make a distinctive contribution to the functioning of the body. We all need to offer the gifts of our lives for the benefit of others and the achievement of the divine purpose. The form of equality of ministerial service is a major question facing the church.

It may be said that twenty years after the resurrection of Jesus, the church achieved "universality"; that is, Jews and non-Jews were admitted with equality into the fellowship. By the middle of the first century the church was "one." Since that time the church has struggled to make the theoretical, the ideal, become an experienced reality. At times the very nature of the church will need to stretch to maintain unity among what seem to be polarities of expression and practice. There is always unequal maturity as well as the cycle of traditional ritual and subsequent renewal periods. When all levels of the church as previously described in the vine and vineyard workers analogies are in proper balance, the church may also be seen as a sailing vessel. The policies and procedures of the World Church serve as the keel. It both stabilizes the ship and gives thrust to the force factors of the wind. The local church members crew the ship, provide its services, and when it is under way their presiding officers control the rudder and guide the journey. The local church is in company with other vessels, and must observe the "rules of the road" respecting their course. Navigational aids are available to all who learn to read them. Some, like the sun and stars, are inherent in the universe; others are of human origin but have also proved reliable. As we continue to ask ourselves about the nature of the church we will be helped if we remember it is the stormy sea which makes the best sailors. We live in the hope that the process of our laboring together qualifies us for our commission and the fulfillment of our journey. It is in Christ and in his church that we are reconciled with our Creator.

THE CHURCH AND THE SACRAMENTS—TOWARD A FUNCTIONAL INTERPRETATION

Harry J. Fielding

Introduction

Throughout its history the Christian church has struggled to resolve an inherent tension produced by preserving historical traditions and customs and concomitantly seeking to introduce innovation. Christ himself, while working mostly within the social and religious structures of his time, did not hesitate to challenge the *status quo* when he deemed it necessary. This was also true of several early apostles. The martyrdom of Stephen (explained in Acts 6 and 7), for example, happened at least partly because he was perceived to be threatening the traditions of his ancestors. He paid the ultimate price: death.

The Apostle Paul probably ranks as the greatest pragmatist in the early Christian church. His willingness to dispense with Jewish tradition when working in other cultures caused great contention at the "Council of Jerusalem" in the middle of the first century (Acts 15). Fortunately for Christianity, a consensus emerged which largely preserved the integrity of Jewish Christians and Gentile Christians alike. Had this not happened, it is quite likely that, as Wayne Ham wrote, "Christianity could have become just another Jewish sect."[1]

In its relatively brief existence the Christian church has carried with it past traditions, but it has also adapted many of these customs, forms of worship, and re-ligious observances. The fact that such adaptations have occurred underscores a vital but often unstated premise: religion does not occur in a vacuum, but is intertwined with the wide culture of which it is a component part. Thus, in attempting to analyze contemporary trends in the Christian church and to suggest certain adaptations within the context of the Saints church, it is necessary to recognize the complex interplay of culture and religion and of present and past. It is not a simple linear process in which an outmoded form is replaced by a modern, complex form, but rather, this involves a process of *dialogue* in which social, ideological, and technological/economic forces all play a part.

Christianity in the twentieth century has been characterized by a multiplicity of forms and approaches. The remarkable spread of Christianity in the Third World countries in this century and the previous century has raised some searching questions for the church as it has attempted, not always with a great deal of success, to develop truly "indigenous churches" in Third World situations. The soul-searching has not only been in terms of Third-World Christianity; questions as to the relevance of Christianity in First- and Second-World situations have also been raised. There has arisen what Langdon Gilkey terms "the present ferment in theology." And the questions Gilkey raises regarding "the mode of their [the churches'] practical existence to their theoretical self-understanding"[2] have profound implications for the Christian church today.

The Saints church has not escaped the "theological ferment." Indeed its inception was in just such a setting and the ferment has continued in various ways until the present. Section 156 of the Doctrine and Covenants in many ways epitomizes this fervor. In some ways, though, the concentration on the issue of the ordination of women, while vital and timely, nevertheless obscures a much deeper and fundamental issue.

Form and Function in the Sacraments

There is a clear emphasis on service and commitment expressed in Section 156. The instructions regarding both temple and priesthood suggest that these areas are means of bringing about "spiritual awakening," "great blessing," and various "ministries." The emphasis is on *function* rather than the specific forms that are yet to be developed. Indeed, verse 4 specifically states that the *"functions"* of priesthood offices " . . . will be expanded and given additional meaning" and verses 7 and 8 further emphasize the importance of priesthood function. The concept of *function* as opposed to outward appearance or *form* is of great significance in developing a holistic appreciation of the sacraments of the church. Such an appreciation is particularly important as issues such as "open" and "close" Communion are debated. It is far more productive and less emotionally threatening to examine the *functions* sacraments play in the life of the church and to develop ways to enhance these functions, than to merely concentrate on the *forms* in which the sacraments are expressed.

Although there is more diversity and freedom of expression being exercised with the sacraments than is generally perceived by the membership at large, some areas still need liberating. This essay does not provide a detailed examination of the philosophy and practice of the various sacramental ordinances in the Saints church; that has already been done in a thorough fashion by Peter A. Judd.[3] Instead it is an examination of three of the sacramental ordinances—baptism, confirmation and the Lord's Supper—and shows how *form* rather than *function* in certain aspects of these sacraments has led to what is, in my opinion, a rather inadequate understanding by a great many church members of the relationship of these sacraments to each other and to the sacramental life of the church.

The sacramental ordinances, represent the "basic stuff" of the gathered community of the church. In the sacramental ordinances, "symbols are used to signify the covenant relationship between God and the human creation."[4] The symbols used (bread, wine, water, human hands, etc.) are the keys to unlocking a whole range of human relationships and values. It is important to note that the symbols themselves

are not of primary significance and that the key to an understanding of their symbolic quality lies in circumstances to which they refer or of which they are a part. It is not their particular nature but their relationships which account for their selection as symbols.[5]

Unfortunately, too often in the life of the church when the sacraments are considered, there has been a tendency to focus on either the symbols themselves or upon the form of expression in the particular ordinance. This has led to a diminished consideration of the relational aspects of the sacraments—the particular functions that the sacraments represent in the development of covenant relationships. This may be illustrated by reference to the sacrament of baptism.

Contemporary Saints church authors

point to two major components in the sacramental ordinance of baptism.[6] The first has to do with an attitude of *personal commitment* in which persons being baptized enter into a *covenant relationship* with God. The second aspect, *belonging,* deals with the institutional nature of the church. In this aspect there is a symbolic initiation of new members into the life of the church; they announce their intention to join with a community of persons who espouse similar ideals and beliefs. Once having been baptized and confirmed by the laying on of hands, initiates are entitled to all the privileges and responsibilities of membership. The sacrament of baptism thus has two different *functions* and it is important to clearly recognize and distinguish between these. It is my belief that failure to distinguish effectively has placed the church in the position of demanding of many persons an unnecessary and sometimes degrading rebaptism.

In times past, it appears to me, there has been a great deal more emphasis on the first aspect of baptism (the "covenant" aspect) than the second. No doubt this is as it should be—the primary functions of the sacraments are, after all, *relational;* that is to say, they are concerned with assisting persons in developing quality relationships with God and fellow humans. If this is true, and fellow Christians have entered into a covenant relationship with God through the waters of baptism, although in the institutional setting of another Christian denomination, it is surely not a very affirming experience to demand rebaptism of those persons. In effect, we are saying to these people that their previous relationship with God was of no account, or at the very most of minimal importance. Such persons may have spent a lifetime serving God effectively and sincerely.

Through an insistence on rebaptism we seek to welcome initiates to our fellowship and yet ironically at the same time we are unconsciously degrading their previous Christian commitment. The problem is particularly acute in predominantly non-Christian countries where there is little or no recognition of denominational differences—one is simply a Christian. To insist on rebaptism in such circumstances is, I believe, nonsense both culturally and doctrinally. Such insistence grows out of an inadequate and outdated model of the church in which concepts such as "authority" and "the one true church" are paramount. In an age of ecumenical co-operation and enrichment, such a model is neither desirable nor viable. We are called to join with many other persons and organizations in affirming that God is creator and sustainer of the universe and that Jesus Christ is Lord.

If the covenant function of baptism is to be given primary emphasis, then we must recognize the validity of that covenant for any particular individual, even when the covenant has been made within the institutional framework of another Christian denomination. Some readers will no doubt object to this view, on the grounds that the person of whom we are demanding rebaptism has now reached a higher level of understanding and commitment than when the previous covenant was made. Such an argument, however, could be (or should be!) applied to every member of the Saints church who renews his/her covenant periodically at the sacrament of the Lord's Supper. No, that is not reason enough to cling to a rigid insistence on rebaptism.

On the other hand the second function of the sacrament of baptism (that of affirming corporate identity) is also extremely important in the life of the church. It is essential that we welcome new members into our fellowship and add their ideas and labors of love to those similarly committed to the highest Christian ideals. Every society and group has ways of announcing that people "belong" to that group and the church is no exception. It is important for the ongoing life of the church that this function be performed. However, it is my contention that the sacrament of baptism is not the most appropriate sacramental expression in which to embody this function of belonging.

A more appropriate vehicle is the prayer of confirmation and the accompanying laying on of hands. This symbolic act could be used to welcome into the fellowship of the Saints church all those who have previously made a covenant in the waters of baptism, either in the Saints church or in another Christian denomination. Thus the second function of baptism as presently understood and practiced in the Saints church would be expressed through the confirmation prayer, and the sacrament of baptism in the Saints church would be freed to concentrate upon the covenant relationship aspect for all those who had not previously made such a covenant. Indeed, the confirmation experience is already understood to "complete(s) a person's initiation into the church"[7] so the approach suggested above is hardly introducing radical change in our approach to the sacrament of confirmation.

In any meaningful examination of the sacrament of baptism and its functional application in the Saints church today, one is led inevitably into a concomitant examination of the sacrament of the Lord's Supper. There is an undeniable link between the two in Latter Day Saint thought which is well summarized by Peter Judd:

It is usually claimed that the Lord's Supper as practiced in the Saints church has a significance for Latter Day Saints that it is unlikely to have for anyone else. This is based on interpretation of the Lord's Supper as renewal or reaffirmation of the baptismal covenant. In recent years there have been discussions in the church over the pros and cons of discontinuing the practice of close communion. The issue hangs centrally on whether the Lord's Supper is seen primarily as a distinctive mark of Latter Day Saint identity, being closely tied to an understanding of baptism as membership in the Saints church, or as a mark of commonality shared by all Christians, being tied closely to an understanding of baptism as membership in the wider "body of Christ.[8]

The dual functions of baptism are discussed in the above quotation, but it is, in my view, highly significant that Judd identifies the central issue in the debate over open and close Communion as having to do with *membership* rather than *covenant*. On the other hand, another Saints church author, George Njeim, in his meticulously researched and clearly written book[9] places a great deal of emphasis on the covenant aspect of the Lord's Supper. In particular, he feels that the reference to keeping Christ's commandments in the Communion prayers is directly related to the concept of covenant and the commandments in the Sermon on the Mount as recorded in the Book of Mormon (III Nephi 5). He argues that while the wording in the Book of Mormon account is almost identical to that used in the gospel of Matthew, the setting is vastly different.

In Matthew the sermon is given early in the ministry of Jesus, before he has established his authority and the nature of the sermon is to present "teachings" rather than "commandments." Njeim contends that in the Book of Mormon account, Jesus is clearly identified as redeemer and he gives a series of commandments before launching into his Sermon on the Mount. Furthermore, and of great significance to Njeim, the sermon is followed soon after by the sacrament of the Lord's Supper. This sacrament is linked, in Njeim's view, to that which has preceded it. A standard has been established in the principles, instructions, and commandments outlined in the Sermon on the Mount and it is this standard that the Lord wishes us to live by as we celebrate his supper.

I have no quarrel with Njeim over linking the covenant function of baptism with the sacrament of the Lord's Supper. On the contrary, I would agree that this is the central affirmation of the Communion meal. It is far more than simply a meal of remembrance, although it obviously includes that element. I quite happily concur that a vital part of the covenant relationship established at baptism is the obligation to keep Christ's commandments and would see the sacrament of the Lord's Supper as being an appropriate aid to facilitate the fulfillment of that obligation. However, I do have a great deal of difficulty in agreeing with Njeim's assertion that "It is the linking of the commandments of Jesus to the Lord's Supper in the prayer of consecration which compels the church to observe close Communion."[10]

In my view, an adequate basis for understanding the commandments of Christ and the development of a significant covenant relationship does not founder simply because some people (regardless of whether they are Latter Day Saints or not) are not familiar with the Book of Mormon. There are many non-Latter Day Saints with whom I am personally acquainted who have a profound sense of covenant with the Lord Jesus and whose lives exemplify their perceived obligation to keep Christ's commandments. I have shared with some of these fine people in partaking of the emblems of the Lord's Supper both in their churches and in mine, and have felt immeasurably enriched in doing so. Their baptismal covenant is as meaningful to each of them as mine is to me and their allegiance is to the same God and the same Lord I profess to serve.

Form and Function in the Church[11]

The deeply felt emotions over such issues as the ordination of women and re-interpretation of the nature of the sacraments arise out of the "inherent tension" referred to at the beginning of this essay. Such tension is somewhat inevitable, given the dynamic nature of social conditions and the reciprocal influence that religion and society have on each other. However, the tensions between old and new forms both within faiths and between faiths, may be resolved, or at least diminished, if the admonitions of Paul Tillich, the twentieth-century Christian existentialist theologian, are heeded.[12] Tillich suggests that the church should not become bound by its past ("sometimes we might ask if the Christian Church hasn't carried with it too much of its past and left behind too little");[13] nor should it disregard its past. There is a vast difference between forgetting and being forgotten. The inability to remember is just as destructive as the inability to forget. The church should never forget its foundation. But "if it is unable to leave behind much of what was built on this foundation, it will lose its future."

Another theologian who has warned against blindly clinging to tradition and custom is Lloyd Geering. In an article in which he elaborates on the overwhelming trend of the church toward "religious pluralism"[14] Geering notes the continuing decline of the mainstream Christian denominations and sees the future trends being toward "the proliferation of small religious groups."[15] The emphasis, in Geering's view, will be an increasing movement toward individual choice, which tends "to militate against the formation of either large or permanent religious organizations." Geering laments that too many church leaders refuse to recognize the reality of the situation and try to solve the problem by adopting methods designed to "regain lost ground," whereas, in Geering's view, "the nature of the present social and religious change is so deep-seated that none of these measures can do any more than bring a minor and temporary relief." Even the trend toward ecumenism will not be enough, he believes, to rescue the situation. Perhaps the only form of ecumenism which is "permanently viable" is that "which arises out of the humanity which men of all races and cultures share."[16]

As mentioned in the introductory section of this essay, the Saints church "has not escaped the theological ferment." It was stated that "Section 156 of the Doctrine and Covenants in many ways epitomizes this fervor" and in the following section I went on to examine some of the implications of Section 156 in terms of form and function in the sacraments of the church. My central thesis was that the *functions* or purposes that the sacraments play in the gathered life of the church are far more important than the particular *forms* in which they may be expressed. I drew attention to the clear emphasis that is placed upon the *function* of priesthood and various "ministries" in Section 156. I now wish to extend my thesis and suggest that the concepts of form and function have implications beyond the sacramental ordinances to the very nature of the church itself.

There is a real danger, in my opinion, of regarding Section 156 in isolation. Such an approach could interpret it as being an "institution-centered" document whose major concerns have to do with priesthood function and the establishment of a church temple. There are signs within this section, however, suggesting that such conclusions should not be hastily drawn. For example, in 156:1 Charles D. Neff is commended for his leadership which "has been of particular value *in a*

time of expanding witness of my gospel." The temple ministries (functions) deal with such things as expanded priesthood functions, the "pursuit of peace," "reconciliation and for healing of the spirit," "leadership education," and "a stengthening of faith and preparation for witness" (Doctrine and Covenants 156:5). Above all, the passage goes on to emphasize, "it shall be a place in which the *essential meaning of the Restoration as healing and redeeming agent* is given new life and understanding, inspired by the life and witness of the *Redeemer of the world"* (italics mine). The final verse comes squarely as a challenge to the Saints to devote themselves "completely to the work of the kingdom" and to "go forth to witness of my [God's] love and my concern for all persons."

The implications for the church are profound. The church is portrayed as existing to bring ministry and blessing to the world. Even "the power of this priesthood" is not designed for the institutional life of the church, but is "for the blessing and salvation of humanity" (Doctrine and Covenants 156:7). There is a clear undergirding theme of emphasizing the purposes (functions) of the church in Section 156. This should not be altogether surprising, for it is a recurrent theme in the ministry of the current prophet-president of the church. In 1978 he drew the church's attention to reaching out to "the bruised and the brokenhearted as well as those who are enmeshed in sin" (Doctrine and Covenants 153:9a), and urged the church to "bear affirmative testimony of my [God's] love and my desires for all to come unto me" (Doctrine and Covenants 153:9b). In 1980 there is particularly clear instruction given to the Council of Twelve and the Presiding Bishopric regarding pursuing "strategies and methods" which will help to promote missionary work and outreach, and in the same document the members at large are admonished to "move out in faith and confidence to proclaim my gospel" (Doctrine and Covenants 154:7a).

There is abundant evidence in the above to show the intense concern felt by the prophet-president that the church should begin to fulfill its basic purpose (function) of bearing witness and bringing ministry to a world in need. But if any doubt remains, it is dispelled by the instruction which came to the church in 1982 (Doctrine and Covenants 155):

6. Some of you have felt confusion as you have sought to labor in the midst of the many voices which are competing for a following, claiming to know my will. *At a time when my word has clearly sent you forth to witness of my gospel, there are many who are still temporizing, looking for further confirming signs of the truth of those instructions which have already been given.*

7. Know, O my people, the time for hesitation is past. The earth, my creation, groans for the *liberating truths of my gospel which have been given for the salvation of the world.* Test my words. Trust in my promises for they have been given for your assurance and will bear you up in times of doubt. *Be not overly concerned with method as you go forth to witness in my name. There are many techniques for proclaiming my word which may be used as needs and circumstances dictate* (italics mine).

Set against the background of the three previous revelations, Section 156 reminds the church that it exists to bring ministry to the world. The church's institutional life needs to be examined and upgraded so that its ministry is relevant to the present age. Simply stated, Section 156 emphasizes both the growth and expansion elements which provide the basic thrust of the church's Faith to Grow program.[17]

Because the church is called to minister in the world, and because there is diverse cultural expression in the world, the Saints church is faced with a difficult question: Is it possible to allow widespread diversity in the expressive activities (including the sacraments) of the church and yet at the same time retain a sense of unity and World Church identity? We might ask: Is it possible for the church to identify particular functions that may be part of its universal calling or mission?

At an RLDS conference I attended in August 1983 (the Fifth Asia-Pacific Conference), representatives from eleven countries struggled with this basic issue. During the discussion, Wayne Ham suggested a model comprising five specific functions of the church, and there seemed to be fairly general agreement that such functions were applicable in each of the countries represented. Later, a sixth element was added, which I have placed as the central element (see Fig 1, following) in the model.

Figure 1. Functions of the Church

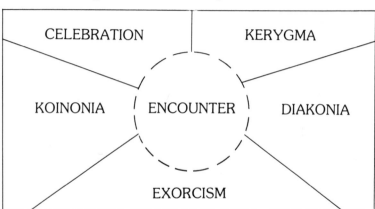

CELEBRATION   KERYGMA

KOINONIA   ENCOUNTER   DIAKONIA

EXORCISM

The undergirding purpose of the church, in my opinion, is to provide the climate for people to encounter God's presence. I have placed "encounter" as the central reference point because I feel it permeates each of the other five functions. Intersecting this are other basic functions the church is called to express. A brief explanation of these functions follows:

Celebration involves the community in praise and joy. This will occur through many different activities such as worship, play, and recognition of rites of passage. It is not just a specific activity, but an attitude that permeates the entire life of the church.

Kerygma may be interpreted as the proclaiming function of the church. This may take traditional forms such as preaching and teaching, or it may be expressed on a more personal level by individual members of the church.

Diakonia involves the church in servant ministries. It is here that the church seeks to bring reconciliation and wholeness through redemptive ministries to individuals and groups within society.

Exorcism may be loosely defined as the casting out of those aspects of culture which are dehumanizing and which inhibit the spiritual potential of the church, society, and individual lives.

Koinonia describes the fellowship function of the church. The church is called to be God's demonstration for humanity.

This model represents, perhaps, an ideal church. In actual practice, it is unlikely that the church would fulfill all of these functions (or even a majority of them) adequately. The life of the church, and the forms that it adopts to live out that life, must be related to the particular situations in which it finds itself. Each congregation must seek the most appropriate

ways to perform basic functions to which the church is called. This is similar to the process employed by Eskimo ivory carvers, as described by Renè Dubos:

As the carver held the raw fragment of ivory in his hand, he turned it gently this way and that, whispering to it, "Who are you? Who hides in you?" The carver rarely set out consciously to shape a particular form. Instead of compelling the fragment of ivory to become a man, a child, a wolf, a seal, a baby walrus or some other preconceived object, he tried subconsciously to discover the structural characteristics and patterns inherent in the material itself. He continuously let his hand be guided to the inner structure of the ivory as it revealed itself to the knife. The form of the human being or the animal did not have to be created; it was there from the beginning and only had to be released.[18]

Elizabeth O'Connor also writes of the relationship between "inner and outer forms" and suggests that creativity in our inner lives is directly related to creativity in the world. The task of the church is to "call forth gifts" and this covenant relationship is extended to the whole world. The church enriches and is enriched by the "mysterious law of reciprocity" at work in the universe.[19] The mission of the church, in this view, is one of "enabling" or evoking "the treasure of personality." The church is called to establish groups of persons who, by the power of the Holy Spirit, become "small initiating centers of life at work in the world," O'Connor continues.

Both O'Connor and Dubos are pointing to a "release model" of ministry which I believe the Saints church must embrace if we are to adequately fulfill our mission. We must identify our basic calling or functions and then find appropriate forms (programs, materials, ordinances, etc.) in which to express our purpose. The possibilities for the church to encourage the release of this creative power are limitless. Such ministries are indeed universal and not limited by time or cultural setting. The entire world is seen as God's domain, and God's power is discerned at work in a complete range of human activities and relationships. Such a view encompasses not only other cultures, but also other religions. It gives rise to a view of the church as a "continuing process" which is "in constant interaction with its environment. . . . The *form* of the church, therefore, is not fixed forever in a preexistent pattern, but is dynamic and flexible, responsive to circumstances and conditions of human experience."[20]

The challenge before the church today is to build relational ministry in today's cultures. We must guard against the tendency to attach permanence to the church's forms of expression. Today's church should release the resources which allow persons to enjoy a contemporary experience—indeed, a contemporary lifestyle—empowered by the living presence of the Holy Spirit. It is in this sense that Hendrik Kraemer describes the church as an "*apostolic* body." It is apostolic not in terms of authority, "but because in all its words and actions it ought to be a bearer of witness to God and his decisive creative and redeeming acts and purposes."[21]

Summary and Conclusion

The history of the Christian church has been characterized by its continuing struggle to find appropriate ways of bringing ministry relevant to its age, while at the same time seeking to preserve traditions. A reciprocal influence has always existed between church and society, but at many points the church has chosen either not to recognize this or to minimize its importance. In so doing, the church has become locked into various *forms* or models and has seen the maintaining of these as its primary calling, rather than seeking to discover the basic functions or ministry it is called to perform.

This has been true of the Saints church also, and recent debate over the efficacy of the sacramental ordinances, particularly centered on the sacrament of the Lord's Supper, has grown from the "maintenance background" described above. What is crucial for us to recognize is that the sacraments do not belong to the church. We sometimes talk of the sacraments *of* the church as though these are somehow the prerogative and possession of the church institution.

I believe that it gives a far more accurate representation to see the sacraments as being instituted by God and practiced within the confines of the church institution. I use the word "confines" with great deliberateness, because I feel that for the present the church provides the most suitable climate in which to express the sacramental ordinances, but this may not always be the case. The sacraments exist as part of a holistic complex of relationships; they exist to assist persons in developing the quality of their relationships with God and with each other.

If we fail to see that the sacraments exist as *means of assistance* and not as *end products in their own right,* then we effectively close ourselves off from avenues of insight and rich resources that would aid us in our task of ministry. The sacramental ordinances exist as "helps" or "crutches" for our covenant relationships, and I believe that *ultimately* the sacraments as we now know them will disappear from the life of the church and will be replaced by the living and empowering presence of the Holy Spirit.

The church itself has, in my opinion, fallen into the trap of maintaining institutional forms at the expense of functioning effectively in the world. I earlier drew attention to how Section 156 of the Doctrine and Covenants helps to bring this into focus. Indeed, the church itself must never be regarded as an indispensable institution; it too exists as a means of assistance for promoting growth in our covenant relationships and for allowing others to enter into such relationships. The church exists, as Stephen Neill expresses it, as a "provisional arrangement"[22] and must be regarded as "expendable":

Herein is the genius of Christian witness: the disciple and the chruch are expendable. They are instruments—means and not ends. When the doctrine of expendability is taken seriously, the church becomes a distinct organization. In contrast to many organizations, it does not exist primarily for the benefit of its members. Rather, it enlists ordinary people in its fellowship to give them a job—to witness. The church exists to further the mission of Jesus Christ.[23]

The "incarnational thrust" of Section 156 and the few sections preceding it is not new in Latter Day Saint thought.[24] However since the mid-1960s there has been an increasing philosophical emphasis upon the incarnational approach. For example, in 1965 the First Presidency issued a powerful statement on the relationship of the church to the social order[25] which spells out the need for acquiring a wide range of political, economic, and vocational skills in order to build effective "kingdom communities."

In 1973, one of the "foundation stones of faith in the Restoration"[26] was placed under close scrutiny with the publication of a series of essays on Zion. It is perhaps rather fitting that this essay should conclude with extracts of the First Presidency's Preface from that book, because I am aware that the views in this essay will not be "equally acceptable to every reader." But if it should serve to stimulate thought and discussion and perhaps contribute in some small way to a growing understanding of the dynamic nature of the church and society, then I shall be well satisfied. For

in the light of continuing revelation the "cause of Zion" has become increasingly rich in meaning. Indeed, we have come to see in it the integrating principle of history, the challenge of the ages. It is incarnational in spirit and method. It is the process of giving form and substance to the purpose of God in human life. Its resources are those of the universe, for the Lord himself has said in the inspired word that spirit and element belong together. . . .

Students of this book will find many concepts and numerous points of view. Not all are acceptable to every reader. It is proper, however, to explore each other's minds in the spirit of faith. Zion is a human expression which involves the whole realm of divine creation. We can all be enriched if we will listen to each other. We can all be enlightened by the Holy Spirit as we study and reflect upon each other's ideas, hopes, and testimonies.

Zion the beautiful beckons us on.[27]

Notes

1. Wayne Ham, *Yesterday's Horizons: Exploring the History of Christianity* (Independence, Missouri: Herald House, 1975), 18.
2. Langdon Gilkey, *Naming the Whirlwind: the Renewal of God-Language* (Indianapolis: Bobbs-Merrill Co., 1969), 5.
3. Peter A. Judd, *The Sacraments: An Exploration into Their Meaning and Practice in the Saints Church* (Independence, Missouri: Herald House, 1978).
4. Peter A. Judd and A. Bruce Lindgren, *An Introduction to the Saints Church* (Independence, Missouri: Herald House, 1976), 110.
5. Raymond Firth, *Symbols Public and Private* (London: George Allen and Unwin, Ltd., 1973), 18.
6. See, for example, Peter A. Judd, chapter 2; Judd and Lindgren, 101, 102; Maurice L. Draper in *Credo: I Believe* (Independence, Missouri: Herald House, 1983) treats these aspects in some depth in chapter 10.
7. Judd, *The Sacraments*, 55.
8. Ibid., 91.
9. George A. Njeim, *The Sacrament of the Lord's Supper in the Fullness of the Gospel* (Independence, Missouri: Herald House, 1978).
10. Njeim, 220.

11. Much of the material in this section was published previously in an essay I wrote for *Exchange*, vol. 1, no. 4 (Winter, 1983-84) entitled, "Missions/mission?" Drummoyne, N.S.W.: Australia-New Zealand Region, Reorganized Church of Jesus Christ of Latter Day Saints.

12. Paul Tillich, *The Eternal Now* (New York: Charles Scribner's Sons, 1956).

13. Ibid., 29.

14. Lloyd Geering, "The Pluralist Tendency— Pluralism and the Future of Religion in New Zealand," in *Religion in New Zealand Society*, ed. Brian Colless and Peter Donovan (Palmerston North: Dunmore Press. 1980).

15. Geering, 176.

16. Ibid., 183.

17. For a concise definition of these terms, see *Leader's Handbook* (Independence, Missouri: Herald House, 1984), 10.

18. Rene Dubos, *A God Within* (London: Angus and Robertson 1973).

19. Elizabeth O'Connor, *Eighth Day of Creation* (Waco, Texas: Word, Inc., 1971), 9.

20. Maurice L. Draper, *Credo: I Believe* (Independence, Missouri: Herald House, 1983), 89-90.

21. Hendrik Kraemer, *The Christian Message in a Non-Christian World*, third edition (London: James Clarke, 1956).

22. Stephen Neill, *The Unfinished Task* (London: Edinburgh Press, 1972), 72.

23. Joe Serig, "Church and Mission," in *Evangelism - The Ministry of the Church* (Independence, Missouri: Herald House, 1981), 34.

24. For developments in Latter Day Saint thought see some of the excellent essays in *The Restoration Movement: Essays in Mormon History*, eds. Alma R. Blair, Paul M. Edwards, and F. Mark McKiernan (Independence, Missouri: Herald House, 1979).

25. The First Presidency, *The Church and the Social Order* (Independence, Missouri: Herald House, 1965).

26. Paul A. Wellington, ed., *Readings on Concepts of Zion* (Independence, Missouri: Herald House, 1973), 9.

27. Ibid., Preface.

CRISES IN THE RLDS TRADITION: NEW GRASPS OF ESSENTIAL/INSTRUMENTAL FAITH

Galen Worthington

We are living in an age of rapid change. This is true whether we wish it or not. It is true whether we are ignorant of it or intensely conscious of it. The extent to which an individual lives is determined by the extent to which he is able to make adjustments necessary to meet the changing conditions. The extent to which an institution lives will be determined by the extent to which it can adapt itself to the ever-changing environment in which it finds itself.

The lives of saints as individuals offer no exception to this rule. Neither the Church as a whole or any of its departments are exempt from this. Safety. . .lies not in hiding our heads ostrichlike but in a recognition of the changes coming and intelligent and prayerful effort to utilize them in the realization of our aims.

—F.M. McDowell (The First Presidency)
Saints' Herald, *Jan. 30, 1924, 99*

Instruction which has been given in former years is applicable in principle to the needs of today and should be so regarded by those who are seeking ways to accomplish the will of their heavenly Father. But the demands of a growing church require that these principles shall be evaluated and subjected to further interpretation. This requisite has always been present. In meeting it under the guidance of my Spirit, my servants have learned the intent of these principles more truly.—Doctrine and Covenants 147:7

What is it that can be considered unchanging in our faith? What part of it is subject to change over time? What do we mean by saying that one aspect of faith and belief is *essential* while another is *instrumental?* Patriarch Maurice Draper, formerly a member of the First Presidency of the Reorganized Church of Jesus Christ of Latter Day Saints, has stated in his book *Credo: I Believe* that "in dealing with religious experience and the objects and processes thus involved, we may perceive categories of essential and instrumental truth."[1] Essential truths involve principles which individuals and organizations hold to be true in all ages and circumstances. Instrumental truths are interpretations and applications of essential truth. Except when we separate these two ideas for academic study, they are like two sides of a coin, each interdependent with the other.

In the development of the Christian church there were periods of crisis which, when resolved, led to fundamental shifts in theology and practice. An example of this would be Peter's experience with Cornelius, a Roman centurion. Up to this point the Christian community had limited its evangelistic thrust to the Jews. Perhaps this was due in part to the scriptural record where Jesus at one time had stated, "Go nowhere among the Gentiles, and enter no town of the Samaritans, but go rather to the lost sheep of the house of Israel" (Matthew 10:5, 6).* After Peter had received his vision and heard the testimony of Cornelius, he remarked that "truly I perceive that God shows no partiality, but in every nation any one who fears Him and does what is right is acceptable to Him" (Acts 10:34, 35). As an individual Peter underwent a change in essential thought. He took his testimony to the Saints in Jerusalem saying,

If then God gave the same gift to them as he gave to us when we believed in the Lord Jesus Christ, who was I that I could withstand God? When they heard this they [the apostles and saints] were silenced. And they glorified God, saying, "Then to the Gentiles also God has granted repentance unto life"—Acts 11:17, 18.

This new comprehension of the gospel reflected a fundamental change for the saints. Undoubtedly many struggled very hard to accept the new doctrine, particularly those of the "circumcision party" who had a strong conviction to the contrary. For the Christian church, this was a crisis in coming to grips with what was essential and what was instrumental to their faith.

Why was it so difficult for them to see something that seems obvious to us today—that every human being needs to

_____
*All Bible references are to the Revised Standard Version.

receive the Gospel? Like us, they grew accustomed to a tradition which at an earlier time was probably wise and appropriate, *but had reached a point where its continued application was hindering the work.* Why is there this struggle?

I believe the answer lies in the idea that for God to prepare a people for his purposes of redemption, they must be forever open to fresh insights of his word. They must possess an attitude that leaves them open to the directions pressed by continuing revelation. People's habits must be broken periodically to free them to realize what is essential and what is instrumental for their time. God always will be bringing something new to his people which, ultimately, encourages them to rely on him and the guidance of the Holy Spirit, rather than on forms, traditions, and doctrines which each generation develops.

There are evidences of this in the RLDS faith. There have been incidences where people were forced to grasp new dimensions of essential/instrumental faith and realize what was thought to be essential was really only a *method* for accomplishing the fundamental purposes. We will explore two such examples experienced by RLDS members and the institution that governs this community of believers. The first is the "supreme directional control" crisis of 1924-25, and the second is the Seventy's struggle to accept and implement the direction given in Doctrine and Covenants, Section 143 (1954).

I. Supreme Directional Control

Section 104 given by Joseph Smith, Jr., in 1835 and Section 122 given by Joseph Smith III, in 1894, had clearly established the First Presidency's right to govern the affairs of the church. However, the relationship of the quorums at the turn of the twentieth century could be described as independent. Joseph

33

Smith III's leadership had been quiet, gentle, and unassuming. Each of the quorums of the Council of Twelve, the Presiding Bishopric, the Seventy, and High Priests enjoyed the freedom to operate in their own area of responsibility as they saw fit, in consultation with the First Presidency.

Then in 1914 Frederick M. Smith brought a totally different leadership style. His vigorous, progressive personality set forth new ideas that the other quorums at times found hard to accept. He saw the need for the First Presidency to have greater influence in directing the affairs of a growing organization, if for no other reason than to make for smoother, more efficient administrative functioning. He did not always get his wish. On February 17, 1971, in a letter addressed to J. F. Mintun, the Secretary of the Council of Presidents of Seventy, President Smith suggested that nominations for the office of Presidents of Seventy might well come from the Presidency and be submitted to the Twelve, Presidents of Seventy, and the Seventy before being sent to the General Conference.[2] For the Seventy, Doctrine and Covenants 124:5 was very clear and on April 18, 1919, at Conference, a resolution was accepted "That the Presidents of Seventy shall not be restricted or prevented from making such selections in harmony with the said provisions. . . ."[3] To this day the seventy select their own presidents to establish the council of their choice. It was becoming clear by the 1920s something had to be done to clarify the relationships and interdependency of the quorums with the authority of the First Presidency clearly understood.

A joint council of the Presidency, Twelve, and Order of Bishops met for a series of meetings April 15-25, 1924, mainly at the suggestion of the Presiding Bishopric to discuss the financial condition of the church. It appeared to some officials that the decrease in church income was attributed to "differences which have existed between various quorums, especially the First Presidency and the Presiding Bishopric, and an attempt was made to crystallize the opinion of the council in regard to what these relations should be."[4]

. . . In the discussions and deliberations . . . a better understanding has been reached . . . a long step has been taken towards a restoration of the complete unity and confidence so essential to the success of the work of the Church.[5]

The long step taken referred to a document adopted by the council about an issue that eventually came to be known as "supreme directional control," an administrative control to be exercised by the First Presidency. The adoption of this document was not without opposition.

It would be beneficial to recount some of the history involved in the development of church publications. Since May 1865, there had been a member of the First Presidency in editorial control. The Board of Publication was created in 1870 by Conference action, and Joseph Smith III was designated the president of the board. A year later the board was allowed to elect its own president. In 1872 the Presiding Bishop was given the responsibility of nominating board members; the Conference of 1879 designated him a standing member. The church president still functioned as editor in chief.[6] Then the 1891 Conference Resolution 351 shifted the burden of publication management more fully to the Council of Twelve and the Presiding Bishopric. It should be stated that Joseph III voted against GCR 351, but only because he believed that the responsibility should have been shifted solely to the Bishopric.[7] At close inspection it would appear that the intent of the resolution was to free the president from excessive administrative detail while in practice he would continue to exercise editorial control. So we see how the bishopric came to oversee church publications. It was perhaps a bit of bad luck on the part of Frederick M. Smith that his relationship with the bishopric began to deteriorate.

Some months prior to the April 1924 council, the Board of Publication was concerned with "getting more subscribers to...Church publication...Realizing that the people of the church are the final judges as to whether they want the church papers...in an effort to obtain a fair cross-section of the opinion of the saints...(a) questionnaire was sent..."[8] The response to the survey was used to develop a new five-point editorial policy at a May 23, 1924, meeting (see Appendix A). Most of it revolved around an "open Church press" to "allow free and frank discussions of any church problem," giving the news "without bias."[9] On May 29 the First Presidency met with the board to discuss the new policy. The results of that meeting set the stage for a conflict in church leadership that would last until the 1925 Conference. The board would not change its new policy and then proceeded to elect new editors for church publications. This action was announced in the June 4 *Saints' Herald.*

It soon became apparent that far more than a policy toward publications was involved. Immediately following the board announcement came an article entitled "An Open Letter," addressed to the church at large (see Appendix B). It was signed by eighteen church leaders, and included the Presiding Bishopric, two apostles, the presiding patriarch, the senior President of Seventy, and the church secretary, recorder, publicity agent, and historian. The letter specifically stated the following:

The controversy regarding church government, which began several years ago among the leading quorums, has now spread throughout the membership, and a crisis has been reached which demands serious consideration....we believe that the

organic law...has established certain definite and abiding principles which are essential to progress.[10]

At least six of the church leaders who signed the open letter were members of the newly elected Board of Publication, with the most obvious connection being the Presiding Bishopric. (It was perhaps no small coincidence that the "open letter" was signed June 2, 1924, the same day the Board of Publication had met and approved the new editorial policy.) The church publications had in effect been seized by a certain group and it was this same group that had objected to the April Joint Council policy of supreme directional control. This conclusion is verified by the *Herald* editorials that followed the June 4 issue. The June 11 *Herald* had an article by T. W. Williams entitled "Faith of Our Fathers."

This is what was in the minds of those who formulated this "Open Letter..." We felt...we could define certain principles of government in keeping with the mind of God and in agreement with the experiences of His people....The principles of government in the church never change....Unity cannot be brought about by mandate or decree, or ultimation of either group or individual. It is the sequence to common understanding. And common understanding is impossible without free discussion....*And free discussion predisposes a free press....We cannot afford to make any radical departures from the plan on church government which has met with divine approval* (italics mine).[11]

The First Presidency's reaction to all of this came the very next week. F. M. Smith declared,

I regret to find it necessary to denounce the action of the Board of Publication . . . (It) has assumed unwarranted powers in the matter . . . the church must now be informed that the Presidency has not only disapproved the action of the Board but has made formal protest.... For the first time since 1865 the editorial columns of the *Herald* do not represent the Presidency.[12]

He went on to explain the Joint Council's action in April and how "we had hoped that the almost unanimous vote in the adoption of this held some promise of the settlement of what has for some time been a vexatious matter."[13] President Smith presented the complete text of the adopted policy (see Appendix C) and mentioned that those in disagreement had led "organized opposition" and "have chosen to join a group not offically constituted a council of the Church. . . . Feelings. . . have been shattered by the apparent and active unwillingness of those of the council signing the 'Open Letter' to act in harmony with the large majority decision of the council."[14] The board responded to the president's charges, more or less stating that normal procedures had been followed and that the president had nothing to complain about.

We have sought no powers not hitherto freely acknowledged as belonging to the Board, nor have we adopted a policy unfair to a single individual group or quorum. We have acted as we believe . . . and are content to leave the decision to the coming General Conference.[15]

Not all of the men elected by the board on May 29 were opposed to the document. True to their word, the "attempt was made to choose men of recognized standing, and selecting them from groups of varying opinions so that all angles of Church problems might be effectively presented. . ."[16] For instance, Elbert A. Smith, a member of the First Presidency, was elected a contributing editor for the *Herald*. he stated:

Under normal conditions the appointment tendered me would have been accepted without hesitation. . .However. . .the late action of the Board. . .[relieved]. . .the Presidency of editorial control. This has made it difficult for me to accept the position of contributing editor without danger of being misunderstood. However, after careful and prayerful thought I have decided to accept.[17]

My conclusions are that certain Joint Council members, and a number of church leaders who were not present at the April meeting, were deeply disturbed by the supreme directional control (SDC) document. They believed it represented a "radical departure" from previously established church government. In order to make the SDC document an issue before the church they had to bring it to the attention of the membership. There had to be opportunity for Saints to openly debate the issue. This they accomplished by seizing control of the church publications in May 1924. By doing this they must have felt that common consent would be achieved and the essential pattern of church government preserved.

General Conference convened on Monday, April 6, 1925, in the Stone Church. The First Presidency was given the right to preside. The delegate credentials were approved. On April 7, President Smith opened the discussion on church government. The council document was distributed among the delegates.

At the same session a substitute for the original document was introduced from the Presidents of Seventy. The most prominent change was from the phrase "with supreme directional control resting in the First Presidency. . ." to "with general oversight invested in the Presidency. . . ." T. C. Kelly, who was of the Council of Presidents of Seventy, had been one of those who signed the "Open Letter" of June 4, 1924. It can be safely said that the substitute document was regarded as coming from those in opposition to the SDC document.

Debate on the conference floor resumed April 8, 1925, with quorum reports coming in from the Council of Twelve, the high priests, and the elders. From the quorums there was a two to one ratio for approval of the SDC document. The seventy were almost equally divided over the issue.[18]

At the same time "opposition

meetings" were being held on the Temple Lot across from the Stone Church. From these meetings another document was produced and read to the conference by Bishop McGuire (see Appendix D). That the opposition felt SDC, as they understood the First Presidency to mean it, represented a fundamental change, became clear through this document.

The document on Church Government... would fundamentally change the established order of the church....[T]his change...strikes at the very heart of the principles of church government contained in our Standard books....Should this document be endorsed it would be tantamount to apostasy—a departure from the accepted principles and practices of this Reorganized Church.[19]

Here we see that for many Saints the SDC document was interpreted to mean an essential change in church government, breaking with the established traditions to which they had grown accustomed. For President F.M. Smith there was no essential change. He had, from the beginning, introduced SDC for relations between the quorums, not for the church as a whole. If there was conflict between quorums and departments, there had to be one head to make decisions. In a speech to the conference President Smith declared that the document on church government applied only to the administrative affairs of the church. He argued that

If this body's will is to be carried out, there must be...proper machinery that does not allow of its work being frustrated by a contention between two heads....That is where our trouble has been, in independence of departments.[20]

The vote was taken and SDC passed by a 65 percent majority. In other related matters, a resolution was passed so that "no one should be removed from the Board of Publication...without the approval of the First Presidency."[21] Section 135 released the Presiding Bishopric from their duties.

It appears that in church government,

each area functioned almost autonomously, and that this freedom was considered essential for the Reorganized church. One reason for this might have been that RLDS members had seen the development of what was to them an authoritarian government in the Utah Mormon church. They wanted to avoid having too much power concentrated in the hands of a single person. As the church progressed, though, President Smith realized that for it to continue functioning there had to be someone with more definitive authority and according to the Joint Council action of April 1924, that final authority would rest in the First Presidency. The measure was just a move to make administrative operations run smoother. Yet, due to extreme interpretations, the council action was seen as a chance for the president to assume dictatorial powers over all the church. This whole crisis was primarily a division over what was considered essential church law and instrumental church procedures for accomplishing the law.

II. Struggle of the Seventy

In the Reorganized church the first ordinations to the office of seventy were in 1853. More complete organization occurred with the ordination of the Presidents of Seventy in 1860. The second quorum was organized in 1892. Growth in the number of seventies allowed the third quorum to come into existence in 1905.[22] In revelations given by Joseph Smith III, several distinctions about the ministry of the seventy developed. The greatest primary understanding, based on Section 122, was that the seventy were to be traveling ministers, free from local responsibilities to be able to devote themselves full-time to missionary activity. The traveling ministry became equated with full-time church appointment. On the initiative of the High Priests Quorum and of the Seventy at the September 1880 Conference action was taken stating

the twelve and the Seventy, as the especial witnesses of the Church to the world, should first go as missionaries.

. . . moneys shall only be paid out of the Church treasury to members of the Quorums of Twelve and of the Seventy . . . if there be any Elders laboring in distant fields who are not members of the above quorums . . . they shall . . . return home.[23]

Missionary activity was not only exclusively the work of the Twelve and the Seventy, but we see that the Seventy would be supported financially by the church.

With the economic problems that developed in the 1920s and 1930s, many of the Seventy were released from appointment. In a 1953 *Herald* it was reported that the number of seventies dwindled until the third quorum was disbanded and the second quorum was merged with the first. Another observer reported it this way:

With the coming of the great Depression and the subsequent inability of the Church to financially sustain the missionary work, the Seventy began to decrease in number and *likewise in their ability to function as God had directed* (italics mine).[24]

To the seventies, full-time appointment was the way "God had directed." This was considered to be church law. There could be no substantial deviation from this essential understanding. The Council of Presidents of Seventy were only calling new seventies from among men already appointees, such as missionary elders.

A problem had now developed. The church was limited in how many appointees it could support. Even today the RLDS church has less than two hundred full-time families under appointment. The work was being held back and an alternate solution was needed. Section 143, given in 1954, provided that alternate solution. President Israel A. Smith presented an inspired document which called for changes in the way that seventies were

called. Specific instruction included "my servants of this council should not be overcareful in selecting elders . . . to occupy as Seventies. . . . [T]here are many who . . . desire to do missionary work who are called to be Seventies." This was interpreted to mean that self-sustaining men could meaningfully fulfill the office of seventy.

The minutes of the April 10 business session record that all of the quorums accepted the document, without qualification, save one: the Quorum of Seventy.

We approve the document in so far as it pertains to the call and ordination of Donald V. Lents and request that the remainder of this document be referred to the Councils of Presidency, Twelve, and Seventy for consideration during the period before the Conference of 1956.[25]

For the Seventy, the document represented a change so great that they could not, as a group, support it as the mind and will of God. Following the vote that approved the document for inclusion in the Doctrine and Covenants, the Senior President of Seventy, Z.Z. Renfroe, made a statement pledging support for implementation of the new doctrine.[26] That promised support did not materialize. A year and a half later, in a series of articles about the history, calling, and function of the seventy, the *Saints Herald* reported, "it is not sufficient that a man be qualified to serve in the office of Seventy; he must also be in a condition to use his qualifications."[27] The article quoted scripture and Joseph Smith III's philosophy:

Though the words "travel constantly" . . . have in recent years been interpreted more freely than the interpretation given by Joseph Smith III, we feel that some heed should be given to his instruction as there was undoubtedly some divine inspiration motivating his advice.

While it is possible for a period of time the church may not be able financially to meet its obligations to permit all Seventies to depend upon their ministry for their support . . . it seems clear that in the ultimate organization of the Church, as God has planned it, all Seventies are to be free to devote their entire effort to the work . . . (italics mine).[28]

The seventy could not grasp this new perspective of faith which was saying that they could be self-sustaining and still fulfill God's intent. The struggle of the seventy went on until "...in 1962 President W. Wallace Smith told them they were impeding the progress of the Church." One of the Presidents of Seventy was Russell Ralston who felt depressed over the situation until, at a Wednesday night service, he had an experience that helped him to grasp the new perspective. "When he [Ralston] humbled himself, these words appeared to him: 'The letter of the law killeth; the Spirit giveth life...what is the letter of the law?' Ralston answered, 'the Seventies will travel continually.' '...And what is the spirit of the law?' And Ralston answered again, 'The Seventies are a special witness unto me.'"

Ralston discovered the true essence of the seventy's calling to be special witnesses. The idea of being able to travel full-time, he realized was instrumental. His own change in faith allowed him to go on to help other seventies to accept the new understanding.

Today the Seventy are over two hundred strong, with many of them fulfilling their calling in self-sustaining ministry. The revitalization that began in the 1980s to respond to God's command to "complete their organization" was made possible by those who struggled to see "the wisdom of the prophetic leadership which led us from the narrow structures of the past to a fuller implementation of God's purposes."[29]

What Does It All Mean?

Jesus came that humankind might have life and have it more abundantly (John 10:10). My understanding of Christian history with regard to apostasy is that the people who believed in Christ labored for so long under a heavy load of tradition, form, and ritual, that they could not experience abundant life. This was why there was the Restoration...not a movement to reinstante some ancient church organizational pattern, but God's movement to create a people who would seek new depths in realizing human potential. God wanted a group of people that would be ever-growing, struggling with the nature of an essential and instrumental faith.

It is true that without form or tradition we cannot function in the present or learn from the past. Faith, then, becomes that dynamic process of balancing tradition and present-day guidance from the Holy Spirit. It is a forging of old and new understandings into a coherent base from which we can experiment with new directions. Faith forms a base of affirmations which gives individuals the security to explore newness. History lessons teach us that we are not alone in our struggle to grasp new understandings of essentials. Just as the "faith of our fathers [and mothers]" met the challenges of their day, so can we be assured of meeting ours. Surely our posterity will look back and wonder why we had to fight with the new revelations of our day. What of the future? I believe that God is working through the RLDS community to lay the foundation for the creation of a whole new humanity—a people that will be free to have more abundant lives.

> Saints with vision of the future
> Need foundations strong and true;
> As they seek new revelation,
> God's intent is born anew.
> —*Hymns of the Saints* (Independence, Missouri: Herald House, 1981), Hymn 386

Appendix A. Board of Publication Policy*

Whereas the Board of Publication, acting for the church in the direction and management of the publishing interests,

---

Saints Herald (June 4, 1924): 530

sent a questionnaire throughout the church asking for frank criticism of the church publications;

And whereas the consensus of opinion as reflected in over six hundred answers unquestionably indicates a desire on the part of the members that certain definite policies be established in the conduct of the HERALD;

Therefore, be it resolved by the Board of Publication that the following policy should govern in the editing of the HERALD.

First: Insure an open church press.

Second: Accord space in HERALD columns freely to all general officials on equal and impartial terms.

Third: Allow free and frank discussion of any church problem, only attempting to confine arguments to the affirmative and not permitting destructive or altogether negative criticism.

Fourth: Give the news of the church as fully as possible and without bias.

Fifth: Balance the editorial content of the HERALD so that the educational, doctrinal, departmental, and spiritual factors may each be given emphasis. The HERALD should be broad enough to appeal to the membership as a whole, and an earnest effort be made to edit it so that it may minister to the varying groups within the church.

To facilitate the carrying out of the above program and policies to reduce expenses and to rally the support of all the Saints to the church publications, resolved that the HERALD, *Ensign,* and *Autumn Leaves* be placed under the direction of a managing editor, and that contributing staffs of six representative church men be chosen for the HERALD and for the *Ensign,* and a staff of three for the *Autumn Leaves.*

Saints Herald (June 4, 1924): 531

Appendix B. An Open Letter*

The controversy regarding church government, which began several years ago among the leading quorums, has now spread throughout the membership, and a crisis has been reached which demands serious consideration. There are fundamental issues which must be decided before peace can come to the church.

We believe that the organic law, supplemented by the experience of more than half a century on the part of the Reorganization, has established certain definite and abiding principles which are essential to progress. We issue this open letter so that a frank consideration of them may be had throughout the church.

We believe that the coming General Conference, in full possession of the facts, should speak and settle this controversy in a definite, constructive manner. Only in such conference settlement can our people be reunited, confidence be reestablished, and the cause of the Master advanced.

We affirm our belief in the following principles and pledge our adherence thereto:

1. General Conference, the enactments of which combine both the inspiration of God and the will of his people, is the highest authority in the church.

2. To obtain the common judgment, and to insure the cooperation and support of the people, all general church programs and policies must be submitted to the General Conference for consideration and decision before being initiated.

3. The law recognizes two general divisions in the administrative work of the church—spiritual and temporal, and specifies "that the temporalities of the church are to be under the charge and care of the Bishopric." In temporal affairs, the bishop acts as trustee-in-trust for the church and

is directly responsible to the General Conference.

4. All quorums, departments, and institutions within the church shall operate on budgets appropriated by General Conference. The Bishop shall limit expenditures to such budgets and General Conference appropriations.

5. We accept the Bible, Book of Mormon, and Doctrine and Covenants, which contain the constitutional law of the church, and recognize the rights and powers of the priesthood as therein defined. We declare for government in the church by lawful and orderly processes and hold that General Conference enactments are binding without exception upon members, officials, and quorums.

JOHN W. RUSHTON, *Apostle.*

T.W. WILLIAMS, *Apostle.*

BENJAMIN R. McGUIRE, *Presiding Bishop*

JAMES F. KEIR, *Member of Presiding Bishopric.*

I.A. SMITH, *Member of Presiding Bishopric.*

FREDERICK A. SMITH, *Presiding Patriarch.*

R.S. SALYARDS, *General Church Secretary.*

F.A. RUSSELL, *General Church Recorder.*

ARTHUR E. McKIM, *General Publicity Agent.*

S.A. BURGESS, *General Church Historian.*

T.C. KELLEY, *President of Council of Seven Presidents of Seventy.*

E.A. CURTIS, *Member of Council of Seven Presidents of Seventy.*

G.E. HARRINGTON, *High Priest.*

W.R. PICKERING, *High Priest.*

T.J. ELLIOTT, *High Priest.*

U.W. GREENE, *Patriarch and Evangelical Minister.*

RICHARD BULLARD, *Patriarch and Evangelical Minister.*

JOSEPH LUFF, *Former Member of Quorum of Twelve Apostles and Church Physician.*

INDEPENDENCE, Missouri, *June 2, 1924.*

Appendix C. Supreme Directional Control Document*

This church, as defined by the late Joseph Smith, is a theocratic-democracy—not man-made, but of divine appointment and origin. (Matthew 16:18; Doctrine and Covenants 1:5; 17:7; 1 Nephi 3:221; 3 Nephi 10:1.)

The government of the church is by divine authority through priesthood. (Doctrine and Covenants 68:4; 104; Acts 20:28). The government in its objective is beneficent, and its purpose is betterment of human conditions. The divine authority becomes operative through the consent of the governed—the common consent indicated in the law (Doctrine and Covenants 25:1; 27:4). It is divine government among the people, for the people, and for the glory of God and the achievement of his purposes towards ideal conditions.

God directs the church through clearly indicated channels (Doctrine and Covenants 43:1, 2; 27:2); and his voice is the directing power of the church; but to this the assent of the people must be secured.

In organic expression and functioning there must be recognized grades of official prerogative and responsibility (Doctrine and Covenants 104; 122:9), with supreme directional control resting in the Presidency as the chief and first quorum of the church (Doctrine and Covenants 122:2, 9; 104:42). This control it is presumed is beneficent. Protection against prostitution of this power is amply provided in the law.

To carry into effect the purposes of the church, effective administration is im-

---

Saints Herald (June 18, 1924): 579

41

perative, and organic solidarity is maintained only by effective discipline, which is in consonance with the beneficent purposes of the church, but yet strongly enough administered to prevent the purposes of the organization being frustrated by individual caprice and rebellion. Authority to be effective must be respected.

This view of the organization of the church affirms the interdependence of departments and coordination of action and holds General Conference as the instrument of the expression of the will of the people.

Appendix D. Opposition Document *

Whereas, the document on Church Government, now before the General Conference of the Reorganized Church of Jesus Christ of Latter Day Saints, grants to the First Presidency supreme directional control over all the affairs of the church, spiritual and temporal; and

Whereas, because of the irregularities attending the introduction and development of the doctrine of supreme directional control, together with the threat of "elimination" made by the President of the Church against some of leading church officers who are opposed to the document on Church Government, and because of the illegal selection and instruction of certain delegations to the General Conference; and

Whereas, this document on church government limits the legislative rights of the General Conference to assenting or consenting to the proposals of an autocratically controlled priesthood; and

Whereas, the existing unhappy division in the church growing out of the attempt to force upon the church this doctrine threatens its very existence; and

Whereas, this demand for a completely centralized government with supreme directional control, which would in fact rest in the President, would fundamentally change the established order of the church; and

Whereas, this change from a theocratic-democracy to an autocracy or a hierarchy with final and supreme directional control in the hands of one man strikes at the very heart of the principles of church government contained in our Standard books (the Bible, the Book of Mormon, and the Book of Doctrine and Covenants) and the General Conference enactments, by which the Reorganized Church in the Temple Lot Suit established its rights and claim to be the true church in succession; and

Whereas, should this document be endorsed it would be tantamount to apostasy—a departure from the accepted principles and practices of this Reorganized Church;

Therefore, we solemnly declare that we will not support nor countenance this attempt to change the fundamental principles of government given of God, and will consider ourselves justified in taking such steps as will protect the constitutional rights of the officers and the members of the church against this insidious departure from the faith.

Further, as a group holding allegiance to the faith and principles established from the beginning of the Reorganized Church, we pledge ourselves to carry on the work of God in harmony with His law.

History of the Reorganized Church of Jesus Christ of Latter Day Saints (Independence, Missouri: Herald House, 1973), vol. 7; 632-33.

Notes

1. Maurice L. Draper, *Credo: I Believe* (Independence, Missouri: Herald House, 1983), p. 81.
2. *History of the Reorganized Church of Jesus Christ of Latter Day Saints* (Independence, Missouri: Herald House, 1973), vol. 7:174. (Hereafter indicated as *CH*.)
3. *Rules and Resolutions* (Independence, Missouri: Herald House, 1980), p. 70.
4. *Saints Herald* (hereafter indicated as *SH*) June 18, 1924, vol. 71:578; October 24, 1924, vol. 71:1009 ff, *CH*, vol. 7:598.
5. Ibid., April 30, 1924, vol. 71:409.
6. Ibid., July 2, 1924, vol. 71:626.
7. *CH*, vol. 5:99 ff.
8. *SH*, June 4, 1924, vol. 71:530.
9. Ibid.
10. Ibid.:531.
11. Ibid.:553-54.
12. Ibid.:578.
13. Ibid.:579.
14. Ibid.
15. Ibid.:605.
16. Ibid.:531.
17. Ibid.:626.
18. *CH*, vol. 7:631.
19. Ibid.:632-33.
20. Ibid.:636, 638.
21. Ibid.:643.
22. *SH*, April 13, 1953, vol. 100:341.
23. *CH*, vol. 4:321-22.
24. *SH*, November 7, 1954, vol. 102:1079.
25. *Conference Daily* (reports and minutes of the World Conference of the Reorganized Church of Jesus Christ of Latter Day Saints), April 11, 1954:115.
26. Ibid.:116.
27. *SH*, December 12, 1955, vol. 102:1191.
28. Ibid.
29. Russell F. Ralston, as reported by Elbert A. Dempsey, Jr., *SH* 129 (April 1, 1982):12, 34.

THE EMERGING RLDS IDENTITY
Richard P. Howard

Theologians, philosophers, historians, and countless unidentifiable disciples of religion through the centuries have sought useful identities around which to explain the meaning of religious faith. This same quest has characterized religions which have had a relatively short history and yet have experienced many changes in belief, structure, and purpose. Latter Day Saints of the Reorganization have experienced varying mixtures of pain and joy in assessing the contours of their shifting identity. This paper explores aspects of the RLDS identity under four main topics: Revelation, Theodemocracy, Authority, and Zion. There would be others, perhaps of equal importance. The aim here is two-fold: to suggest the emergent, processual nature of the RLDS identity, and to stimulate serious reflection on its historical development and future possibilities.

A. Revelation as a Source of Identity in the Latter Day Saint Experience

1. Records of Revelatory Events: Meanings and Implications

The early Latter Day Saints during the days of Joseph Smith, Jr., viewed revelation as propositional. This means that the prophet Joseph Smith, Jr., was considered the recipient of divinely communicated information and instruction for launching the church and setting it in order. Smith's early followers made no distinction between the revelatory encounter and its ensuing written record. That the record *was* was the revelatory event is seen in the descriptive titles given to those records by the scribes who wrote them from Joseph's dictation: "revelations, covenants, and commandments, given to Joseph the Seer." Revelation was seen as God's verbal messages to Joseph Smith, Jr., and recorded verbatim by various scribes.

Numerous studies have demonstrated Joseph Smith, Jr.'s extensive, substantive revision and editing of many of those same documents in 1834–1835, when preparing them for publication in the Doctrine and Covenants. This fact alone points to a different conception of LDS revelation: *revelation as encounter, from which the prophet draws inferences, interpretations, and instructions, to be recorded for the guidance of the church.*

2. Problems in Historical Analysis and Interpretation

One primary problem of identity is the difficulty of analyzing fragmentary records of revelatory events. The task is formidable, since the revelatory events themselves have vanished. Consider the uncertainties of diagnosing illnesses of living people who cooperate fully in detailed examinations of all the factors possibly related to their symptoms. Often there is need for a second, or even a third, diagnosis. This illustrates the plight of the historian, whose work is done in the knowledge that the past is beyond full recall. The records are partial and fragmentary, and those who left them behind are nearly always unavailable to cast light on our questions.

Events are central to the meaning of history. Events are more than isolated happenings in time and space. The importance of an event or a cluster of events lies in patterns of development discerned in connections established with other events. In any case, events are largely "out of sight." Persons related to their occurrence and initial interpretation, whether dead or alive, have left only partial records. And these are filled with diverse memories and understandings of the events and their significance.

Now, if this is true for events generally, the truth becomes all the more pointed in confronting *revelatory* events. In the case of Joseph Smith, Jr.'s encounters with God, only he—or at most very few others—actually witnessed those primal moments of his religious history. Beyond the formal, written manuscript records (inferences, instruction, and information) derived from those encounters, Joseph Smith communicated very little of substance about the nature and content of the encounters themselves. This lack of information magnifies the problems of historical reconstruction, and requires modesty in any claims to "historical knowledge." Such claims must rest on reliable historical and theological principles, and be guided by sound methodology. Historical interpretation and reinterpretation, then, are essentially a process—a never ending endeavor. In any investigation, final certainty about the past is unattainable. The dream of complete answers yields to the process of building and testing theories and hypotheses. This dynamic enterprise proceeds in the light of faith and under the demands of intelligence and obedience to the Christian mission. It may be that a healthy sense of identity (in terms of historical awareness) emerges *in that process,* not from some absolute, final conception of the meaning of history.

3. *Latter Day Saint Revelation and Scripture*

One issue of RLDS identity, emerging from the concept of revelation as encounter, relates to the meaning of LDS scripture. In *Exploring the Faith* the World Church's Basic Beliefs Committee in 1971 described scripture as the human response to, and record of, revelation—the divine/human encounter. This represented a radical shift in meaning from early Latter Day Saintism, wherein revelation and its record (scripture) were thought to be synonymous. The first generation of Latter Day Saints viewed the "fullness of the gospel" as embodied in its scriptures. However, the incarnational theology of recent RLDS experience identifies the gospel in terms of the revelation of God in the lived-out life of Jesus. This definition implies that the reconciling activity of the gospel in all its fullness of power and meaning is central to the human experience, and is seen as the work of the Holy Spirit in the church's life.

The immensity of that shift in the church's theology of scripture calls for a broader identity, in terms of *how scripture is to be used in our church's ministry in the world.* By Conference resolution of 1878 the RLDS church identified scripture as the Bible, the Book of Mormon, and the revelations of God contained in the Book of Doctrine and Covenants. Scriptures so defined were to be used

. . . as the standard of authority on all matters of church government and doctrine, and the final standard of reference on appeal in all controversies arising, or which may arise in this Church of Christ. [*]

That sharply focused definition and purpose did not encompass all the uses of

---

[*]*Rules and Resolutions* (Independence, Missouri: Herald Publishing House, 1975), Resolution 215, pp. 41-42

scripture then prevailing. However, the meaning seems clear: anything about the gospel of possible relevance in settling controversies was presumed to be lodged in one of the three "standard" books of Latter Day Saint scripture. It was but a simple matter to find the proper text and use it to resolve any dilemma. Using scripture in this way has produced mixed results. Some cases were readily settled, and that was a strength; but many situations arose in which it was clear that the scriptures did not agree. For example, by comparing Isaiah 2:4 and Micah 4:3 with Joel 3:10, one must decide: shall it be swords into plowshares and spears into pruning hooks, or the other way around? Scriptures often say very different things on a given issue, and have long been used to "prove" conflicting positions.

To me, this means that the best use of scripture flows from an unending quest for the essential nature and purpose of scripture in terms of informing the RLDS identity—of what it means to be the church in today's world. From that journey could come, it seems to me, a better grasp of the dynamic ties between revelation and scripture, and of the power of those ties in the church's life of faith and service.

4. Continuing Revelation and Historical Precedent

Human life robbed of continuity with the past would cease to make sense. There *must* be significant personal and corporate memories if the community is to move meaningfully into the future, and if the members of that community are to have a strong sense of personal identity and worth. However, the church cannot focus its whole energies and life toward the past. Why should the church seek to relive the past, as if there were no present or future, as if the early Saints somehow demanded a replication of their history by

later generations? The fragmented lenses of human memory, imagination, and perception make this impossible anyhow, even if it were desirable.

At best, Latter Day Saints offer the world the vision of a people living on the boundary between history and revelation, with one foot in the past, and the other moving in faith into the future. By the gift and power of continued revelation the church fashions a sacred history from which it draws courage and compassion to live toward the future. However, a lifestyle pointed toward the future inevitably has its foundations in an *understanding of the past*. This is a paradox to be confronted if the church is to accept the challenge of living by continued revelation. Should the church demand that all new revelation be consistent with every finite inference drawn and recorded from previous revelation? If so, the fullest possibilities of continued revelation will not be realized. For, by revelation the living God, from the future-in-process, bids the covenant people to walk together in the bonds of faith. In that "faith journey" can be discerned the essence of the emerging RLDS identity.

B. Identity in Terms of Theodemocracy

1. Theocracy: The Reign of God

Early LDS history set the stage for a dynamic tension between theocratic and democratic polarities. By theocracy is meant that the decision-making process in church life is at the initiative and under the control of God. In 1829 a pattern emerged whereby in response to earnest pleas for divine guidance for their lives, persons received counsel from Joseph Smith, Jr. Sections 4-6 and 8-15 of the Doctrine and Covenants indicate this pattern. On the day the church was organized—April 6, 1830—the membership were informed that they were to live by the inspired words given to them by the prophet Joseph Smith, Jr.:

...the church...shalt give heed unto all his [Joseph Smith, Jr.'s] words, and commandments, which he shall give unto you, as he receiveth them, walking in all holiness before me; for his word ye shall receive, as if from mine own mouth, in all patience and faith; for by doing these things, the gates of hell shall not prevail against you.—Doctrine and Covenants 19:2a, b

During the summer of 1830 this interpretation of theocracy was challenged by the so-called "revelations" to Hiram Page, of Fayette, New York. By then he was influencing Cowdery and the Whitmers to some differing ideas about church government. Soon Joseph Smith, Jr., instructed Cowdery through revelation on how to deal with this threat to theocracy:

Verily I [God] say unto thee, No one shall be appointed to receive commandments and revelations in this church excepting my servant Joseph Smith, Jr., for he receiveth them even as Moses; and thou shalt be obedient unto the things which I shall give unto him, even as Aaron, to declare faithfully the commandments and revelations, with power and authority unto the church.—Doctrine and Covenants 27:2a, b

Theocracy was again affirmed in the case of one Sister Hubble, who in early 1831 was "giving revelations" to the church. In response to that challenge, the following instruction was recorded:

I [God] say unto you, that ye have received a commandment for a law unto my church, through him whom I have appointed unto you, to receive commandments and revelations from my hand. And this ye shall know assuredly, that there is none other appointed unto you to receive commandments and revelations until he be taken, if he abide in me. But verily, verily I say unto you, that none else shall be appointed unto this gift except it be through him, for if it be taken from him he shall not have power, except to appoint another in his stead; and this shall be a law unto you, that ye receive not the teachings of any that shall come before you as revelations, or commandments.—Doctrine and Covenants 43:1-2b

This meant that theocratic power extends to include the prophet's unconditional right to appoint his successor in office.

Even were the incumbent to lose his prophetic status due to transgression, he still had authority to appoint his successor. Clearly, theocracy was central to the experience of early Latter Day Saintism, and was personified in the prophetic leader.

2. Democracy: The Reign of the People

Born at a time of a great democratic surge in American history, the Restoration reflected that dimension of its culture in its early experience. Sections 25, 27, and 58 of the Doctrine and Covenants embody the democratic dimension. Note the following excerpts:

And all things shall be done by common consent in the church, by much prayer and faith; for all things you shall receive by faith. Amen.—Doctrine and Covenants 25:1b

Neither shall anything be appointed unto any of this church contrary to the church covenants, for all things must be done in order and by common consent in the church, by the prayer of faith.—Doctrine and Covenants 27:4c

It is not meet that [God] should command in all things, for he that is compelled in all things, the same is a slothful and not a wise servant; wherefore he receiveth no reward. Verily I say, Men should be anxiously engaged in a good cause, and do many things of their own free will, and bring to pass much righteousness; for the power is in them, wherein they are agents unto themselves.—Doctrine and Covenants 58:6c, d

These three citations convey the reality of the tension between unquestioned obedience to the pronouncements of an oracle, and the exercise by the people of their right of choice. Both positions were clearly called for by theocratic fiat, and both were given full consent in 1835 when the Doctrine and Covenants was accepted as binding on the quorums of the church by their own vote.

3. A Blend: Theodemocracy

From the polarity thus far seen in the

early counsel given to the young church, the stage was set for the RLDS experience of trying to combine both the theocratic and democratic elements. In the midst of trying to work out the most useful equation the RLDS church has in effect been working at its basic identity. The quest has been to blend the theocratic and democratic polarities in ways that honor the claims of the kingdom of God (theocracy) on those who cherish their God-given freedoms.

An example of RLDS theodemocracy is seen in the following instruction to the General Conference of 1887. The context centered in disputes over procedures in the administration of the Lord's Supper.

And the Spirit saith further: Contention is unseemly; therefore, cease to contend respecting the sacrament and the time of administering it; for whether it be upon the first Lord's day of every month, or upon the Lord's day of every week, if it be administered by the officers of the church with sincerity of heart and in purity of purpose, and be partaken of in remembrance of Jesus Christ and in willingness to take upon them his name by them who partake, it is acceptable to God. To avoid confusion let him who presides in the sacrament meeting, and those who administer it cause that the emblems be duly prepared upon clean vessels for the bread and clean vessels for the wine, or the water, as may be expedient; and the officer may break the bread before it is blessed, and pour the wine before it is blessed; or he may, if he be so led, bless the bread before it be broken and the wine before it be poured; nevertheless both bread and wine should be uncovered when presented for the blessing to be asked upon it. It is expedient that the bread and wine should be administered in the early part of the meeting, before weariness and confusion ensue. Let him that partaketh and him that refraineth cease to contend with his brother that each may be benefited when he eateth at the table of the Lord.—Doctrine and Covenants 119:5

The theocratic aspects of this instruction are clear, as are those which leave decisions in the hands of the people. The largest aspects of theocracy here, in my view, entreat the people to cease contending, to stop questioning each other's scruples and motives, and to administer the sacrament with purity of heart.

Occasionally in RLDS history opposing views have been aired in the midst of the revelatory process. At such times theodemocracy has been central to the emerging RLDS identity. Historians find in the records of these struggles something of the reality of the theodemocratic relationship being worked at by people honestly differing with each other, but possessed by a fundamental mutuality of goodwill. That struggle has strengthened the RLDS identity of people aware of their basic loyalty, both to God and to one another.

C. Authority: Exclusive or Contingent?

1. Early Models and Problems of Historical Reconstruction

Many sources document early LDSism's claim to an exclusive authority to represent God on earth. Those evidences can be indicated under the following four categories:

A. **The Book of Mormon.** Early LDSism accepted the Book of Mormon as equal to the Bible in authority. Such a stance notified Protestantism that its supreme authority, the Bible, was insufficient. The Book of Mormon, for early LDSism, was its exclusive witness to God's redemptive action in the new world, both ancient and modern.

B. **Publication of the revelations of Joseph Smith.** In publishing "revelations" from their modern prophet-oracle, early Latter Day Saints were telling the world around them that God was speaking in this last generation before the end of time. To the early Saints, those messages were the exclusive, authoritative word of God, given especially to them to declare.

C. ***The kingdom of God.*** With the designation of Independence, Missouri, as the site for the New Jerusalem, the kingdom of God on earth, Latter Day Saints migrated to build a system encompassing both sacred and secular realms of life. The system was brick and mortar, hard-working people learning vocations, not just theory. The place had been chosen and renamed, people began moving there, high hope burst forth from their hearts and faces—hope of building the perfect kingdom of God. Early Mormons lived *for* each other, and found their personal identity in terms of the larger network of relationships and accountability structures. All of this they did in a larger culture of individualism, capitalism, and fierce competition for power and wealth. Early Mormonism differed greatly from its surrounding milieu. Its dream of a global kingdom of God headquartered in Independence, Missouri, cemented its identity as the true colony of God on earth, awaiting the second coming of Christ. Bitter persecution was soon to be the lot of the early Restoration. The hostility engendered reaction from the church people, who in process became all the more convinced of their exclusive authority.

D. ***Early missionary literature.*** The early missionary literature of the Latter Day Saints showed their conviction of exclusive authority. One example was Orson Hyde's flyer, published and distributed at Toronto, Canada, in 1836. In this broadside he warned the public of the awful fate in store if they did not respond to the gospel. He negated the pretensions to authority of all other churches of that time:

> Wo! Wo! unto them, saith the Lord, who preach for hire, and pervert the ways of truth. Wo! to them who suffer themselves to be led by the precepts of men, contrary to that which they know to be written in the oracles of truth; for they shall perish!. . .I am unwilling to dismiss this subject, without telling you your duty, in plain terms, that my garments may be clean from your blood in a coming day. The great body of the clergy are acting without authority from God at this time. My reasons for saying so, are these. 1st the sick are not healed under their hands. 2nd. They do not confirm those whom they baptize by the laying on of their hands for the gift of the Holy Spirit, and why? Because they are not authorised so to do.

Other similar writings from Parley P. Pratt, Orson Pratt, and others portray the view of the early Saints that theirs was the only church authorized to preach the gospel, to heal the sick, to administer the ordinances, and to build the kingdom of God.

To try to understand the early Saints' motives, their concepts, and their community building efforts, is to sense the impossibility of reconstructing historically the reality of their times. That cannot be done in any complete way. What can be done is to try to imagine, on the basis of incomplete records, what their situation might have been. To do this humbly is to take the first step toward understanding the complexity of their lives and their own perceptions of their task. That understanding can confirm a vital aspect of the emerging RLDS identity: great restraint in judging the words and the deeds of the early Saints, either as normative for today, or as inappropriate for their day.

2. Joseph Smith III, the Early RLDS Church, and Identity Beyond the Mormon Boundary

Many sects emerged after the deaths of Joseph and Hyrum Smith in 1844 and the break-up of Nauvoo in 1846. Nearly all of those groups but the new "Reorganizers" of 1852-1859 were led by one dominant figure claiming full authority to represent a continuation of early Mormonism. Many of the Reorganizers had earlier affiliated with some of the other sects in search of the most legitimate form of Latter Day Saintism. They began coming together in southern Wisconsin in 1851-52. In 1853 they chose interim leaders, against the time when a lineal descendant of Joseph Smith, Jr., might become their prophet-president. During that seven-year time of waiting and development, the growing membership came to expect to play a large role in the decision-making process. They were finished with the type of one-man rule which they felt had led to so many problems in the early church, especially during the years 1837-1846.

Joseph Smith III became the RLDS prophet-president on April 6, 1860, at the age of twenty-seven. Most of his fellow leaders were older than he, having been veterans of early church life in Missouri, Ohio, or Illinois. Joseph III differed greatly from his late father in temperament. It was not in his nature to gather power unto himself, and to wield it arbitrarily over others, as Joseph Smith, Jr., had done, especially during the Nauvoo years. Joseph III exercised care and restraint in making major decisions affecting his people. He leaned heavily on the views of others in that process. On becoming editor of the *Saints' Herald* in 1865 Joseph III opened its columns to the views of any wishing to express them. He was eager to learn from others, slow to rule unjustly, and firm in the conviction that historical precedent was only one of many factors in choosing a course of action. Even so, he made it known that he was in fact the church president, and that he would not be forced into hasty or arbitrary courses of action by any person or group.

This notable blend of courage and humility enabled Joseph III to promote the policy of "an open pulpit" wherever the RLDS church existed. He urged the Saints to allow other religionists free access to RLDS pulpits, hoping in part for reciprocity. From such mutuality, he reasoned, the Restoration stood to gain an advantage otherwise impossible from an isolationist stance. He sought for the RLDS church a legitimacy in the eyes of the larger communities in which the Saints were living. Joseph III repeatedly urged the branches of the church to bear strong Christian witness in their larger communities. He often expressed the view that if the Saints were ever to build Zion in Missouri, they must first learn to cherish and build up the communities where they lived, in goodwill and mutuality toward all.

However, such a lifestyle involved enormous difficulties. From day to day the Saints felt the need to tell neighbors and friends the many doctrinal differences between the RLDS and the LDS churches. This also meant proving that the RLDS church had exclusive authority to preach the Restoration gospel. It was but one step further to assert that the RLDS church had sole authority to represent God in the world. Living as they did for so many years on that "Mormon boundary," RLDS members often experienced great frustration in their attempts to nurture openness toward other churches. Even today the RLDS church has not fully overcome the unfortunate results of the deeply felt need to define itself in terms of its differences with the Mormon church, i.e., to permit Utah Mormonism to dictate the contours of the RLDS identity. The struggle continues to bear a unique Christian witness in a world closed off at times by the historical "Mormon boundary."

3. Authority in the Modern World

At the World Futurist Society meeting in Toronto, Canada, in July 1980 the following aspects of the world's dilemma were set forth:

- poverty amidst plenty
- deterioration of the natural environment
- loss of human faith in the institutions of society
- the alienation of youth
- rejection of traditional values
- erosion of world monetary systems
- global insecurity

These things had not happened overnight, but had been emerging in world history for several decades at least. Since World War II the RLDS church has increasingly begun to discern its prophetic role in relating to these problems in behalf of the world. Since 1960, it has sought to bring redemptive ministries in Eastern cultures, Latin America, Africa, and among American Indian peoples. In those efforts it has found that its authority as a reconciling force in the world does not derive solely from theory and doctrine. Instead, in the attempts to discern the meaning of the rapidly changing world, church leaders have found that authority is largely a function of how deeply the church shares, in line with its resources, in God's healing ministries on behalf of the world. To the extent of that sharing, the church has gained an authority of competence and compassion, lending hope to despairing persons, and enlisting them in ever widening redemptive processes.

Confronting the breadth and depth of the world's present dilemma in light of the church's limitations of imagination, money, personnel, skills, political power, and social status could easily bring despair. In that framework the RLDS church could atrophy to merely that of social critic, foretelling the apocalypse. However, that would be a denial of the recent RLDS experience of healing and bringing hope and courage to brokenhearted persons. In that process have come intimations of a new authority offering an identity linked as never before with the peoples of the earth.

D. Zion: Universals, Particulars, and Identity

1. The Early Latter Day Saint Experience

The early scriptural literature of the Latter Day Saint movement built a strong case for community life based on altruistic sharing among members. The "golden age" in the Book of Mormon, the city of Enoch in Joseph Smith, Jr.'s "New Translation" of the Bible (Genesis 8), and the early documents in the Doctrine and Covenants all expressed the vitality of community as central to the gospel's meaning. Each of those scriptural sources pointed to a universal principle: the gospel draws diverse peoples together in many ways, among them geographic and economic.

Early Latter Day Saint history is in one sense the story of people determined to live and work together in close physical proximity. Together they bought and cleared lands, helped one another build homes, shops, and stores. They worked together to educate their children. Of one thing they were sure: Zion was the basic expression of the gospel, not merely a theoretical ideal. Such expression had to thrive there and then in that place, otherwise the gospel could have had little meaning to them.

There was a vigor and an urgency in their community building, for they were sure that Jesus was going to return to the earth at any moment, to usher in the New Age of peace and goodwill. This meant that they must move to Zion right now, at any cost, in hope of sharing in the great winding-up scene of history. So eager were they for this goal that they became an offense to those around them. Under intense persecution they reacted militantly; in the end they were forced from five communities in less than sixteen years.

2. Early RLDS Efforts

In the early history of the RLDS church the desire to return to Missouri grew right along with the membership rolls. By 1870 the United Order of Enoch was formed in Lamoni, Iowa. During the next decade several RLDS families moved back to Independence. Their dream of the New Jerusalem still flourished, although their objective and the conditions under which they sought to achieve them were to change greatly. From that day forward many RLDS members conceived of Zion mostly in those tangible, material, and geographic dimensions, though they tended not to emphasize the much earlier millennial expectation as a fundamental motivating force. Numerous groups of them since those early days of RLDS history have sought to express their convictions by gathering together to build specific stewardship communities. To them, they have built Zion, or at least pilot communities representing a vital response to the historic commission to build up the kingdom of God.

3. Twentieth-Century Transitions

Zionic objectives, concepts, and procedures have changed with the transition from the nineteenth century to present times. The millennial expectation (a feature of early nineteenth-century American culture) has receded, a fact shown by patterns in RLDS literature.

The image of Zion as leaven—a social change agent at work in secular cultures, and in a more protracted historical process—has little in common with earlier apocalyptic approaches. Appeals to church members in the U.S.A., Canada, Great Britain, Scandinavia, other European nations, and the Pacific islands, to gather to Zion as soon as possible were once commonplace. However, such an approach no longer seems either urgent or wise. Changing social, economic, and political conditions and structures have vastly complicated Zion building processes. The church's theological horizons have widened, heightening the felt need to grasp essential historical and theological principles and to apply them as foundational to any physical, geographic Zion. We seek the universals of Zionic endeavor in order to capture the imagination and commitment of the Saints everywhere. Universals are elusive, because no culture or people is identical with any other; no one culture can speak for all.

Given these complex factors, the church presses toward the twenty-first century projecting some new signals to one another regarding the Zionic commission. This fact has aroused both discouragement and hope, and also indicates the magnitude of the kingdom-building process. The church's Zionic identity depends partly on its capacity to confront the ambiguities of the task, as well as the courage and humility to admit its limited vision and its lagging commitment. Whenever the church has conceived of the Zionic task as finishable, frustration, guilt, and despair have plagued its efforts. Like so many other things done in church life, the meaning, the identity, has emerged *in the midst of the journey*, not at some fancied "end." For the Saints, there has never been an end to God's work in the world—only an eternal round of new beginnings.

E. Summary.

I have sought in this paper to set forth some of the dimensions of the emerging identity of a unique religious community. In all four areas—Revelation, Theodemocracy, Authority, and Zion—can be discerned the processes of continuity and change in the corporate and individual experiences of Reorganized Latter Day Saints. In the midst of radical transformations have appeared the unbroken threads of continuity. Revelation, though viewed differently now than 150 years ago, is still a central distinctive expression of RLDS history. Theodemocracy is perhaps more vibrant today than ever before—certainly more than in the 1830s. The present world dilemma and recent theological ferment have combined to change the basis and nature of the church's authority. However, the claim to ample divine authority to magnify the unique mission of the Restoration in and for the world still stands on a solid historical foundation. And Zion, whether in terms of particulars or universals, has always claimed the energies, imaginations, and life commitments of Restoration adherents, from 1830 to the present time.

The RLDS identity, though ever in a state of flux, and for that reason exhibiting some rather confusing attributes through the decades, offers a fruitful arena for historical description and analysis. The emergent character of that identity from the beginning has marked the Restoration as a people willing (if not always comfortable in the process) to risk much in order to examine, to discern, to debate, to proclaim, and to live out the essentials of its faith.

GROWING PAINS
Kenneth D. Sowers, Jr.

The RLDS church is focusing its attention during this decade of the 80s on the theme "Faith to Grow." Many lively and pleasant images are associated with growth, but a real part in most growth is something we link with disease (dis-ease), namely, pain. And while the presence of pain testifies to the reality of living, it also conjures up in the mind many unpleasant thoughts and is often not seen as a natural companion of growth. This paper will concentrate on the types of growing pains that are felt as an orgranization makes the transition from sodality to modality, from sect to denomination, from ignobility to respectability.

Growing pains are confusing to most, uncomfortable to all. The only apparent way to avoid these types of pains seems to be to opt for non-growth and ultimately, death. Let us instead consider these growing pains a part of the natural process in the path to maturity and learn to cope with the pain maturation brings.

Sociologists and certain church growth writers[1] use the terms sodality and modality to describe organizational types. In many cases the organization that begins its existence as a sodality develops into a modality. The RLDS church is traveling on this journey. It is a journey that has carried with it some distressing moments as the church struggles to rightly divide cultural and theological elements of its faith in a determined effort to keep it on the path to becoming a broad-visioned church, a modality.

Many of the issues that surfaced at the 1984 World Conference reflect not only the urgency among the leadership to move in this direction, but also show that these concerns are being faced at the grassroots level in the congregations. Issues such as the nature of priesthood and the ordination of women, open Communion, decentralization of authority and decision making, diversity in religious worship, and efforts at truly becoming a World Church rather than merely an American institution clearly show that the RLDS church is rapidly moving from a sodality to a modality in its organization.

The fact that these issues crop up at various levels of church life further illustrates that the church exhibits a readiness for growth never before seen. The painful reactions experienced by many warn that there is need to explore these changes and deal with them both courageously and sensitively.

In understanding growing pains it is, first of all, important to recognize that they are normal. They happen in individual lives—they happen in corporate systems. Some pains are more critical than others. Growing pains associated with life or death crises cannot be ignored or wished away. As we examine the characteristics of growth relating to modality and sodality we can better cope with the natural discomfort that is associated with such growth. Organizations and their changes may be better seen by examining their distinctives of modality and sodality. Certain groups in the Catholic church chose the term sodality because it comes from the Latin word meaning *brotherhood*. In the French, it means *comrade*.[2]

We can appreciate these two words and the way the relate to one another in observing how they function in society.

The school is one such example. Because of mandatory education laws, a child between the ages of six and sixteen is enrolled in a school district. No particularly crucial decision had to be made and few requirements had to be met to join this system. Within that school system there exist several groups which the child may or may not join. He is not regarded a member of the drama club simply because he is a member of that school.

To stay in school, the child must obey the most basic of rules—he doesn't even have to perform well in his studies. In fact, if he performs poorly, he may be invited to attend an additional year! Only if he disregards the taboos of the school system is he expelled. If he wants to join the debating club or a sports team, he is then involved in a much more specific task; should he fail to perform adequately, he risks being dismissed. Typically, there will be a greater demand in terms of time, money, and commitment in order to remain a member in good standing in that organization.

The school system is a modality. It is characterized by being inclusive. It is easy to join and relies heavily on biological or transfer growth. There are few requirements to maintain membership. Members are seldom expelled from the ranks of a modality. Modalities are people organizations, often oriented toward maintenance, but with a vision broad enough to meet the needs of many types of persons.

The school club is a sodality. It is exclusive. It is less easy to join, relies heavily on convert growth, and places greater requirements on its members. If a member doesn't contribute to the group's function, then that member is expendable. It is not primarily a people organization, and it is noted for its narrow vision that enables it to focus clearly on a task and successfully relate to that task.

Ernst Troeltsch was probably the first to relate these terms to church and call a sect a sodality and a church a modality.[3] And when using sodality and modality to describe religious groups, other traits become apparent.[4]

Modality	Sodality
Decisions made by common consent	Decisions made by a leader with "vision"
Stresses "being"	Stresses "doing"
Relies on biological growth	Relies on conversions
Seldom excommunicates	Uses excommunication as a disciplinary measure
Maintenance oriented	Mission oriented

Religious sodalities are task oriented and in so doing are able to reach out in specific directions more effectively. Sodality members perceive a need and then work to meet it. They don't always bother with complete organization before getting started, but out of sheer urgency dive into the task at hand. As a rule, sodalities do not have broad vision; in fact, the reason they are effective depends a great deal on their ability to focus in on one area. Church sodalities with this narrow scope of vision are often noted for their attitude of being the purest or truest of their kind. "The one and only church" which is pleasing to God is one example. Also noteworthy is the strong group solidarity that exists. This is followed by heavy demands that seem to be cheerfully borne.

The most important factor in any sodality is the leadership. In many cases, the people will follow a person who has great personal charisma without careful consideration of their own agency. In today's world, this is usually considered a leading characteristic of a cult. If the leadership has vision, especially related to the means of accomplishing a specific task and the recruitment of new members, the sodality will sustain a respectable level of growth. Many of these traits can be seen in the history of the Restoration.

Churches that are modalities are usually larger and make attempts to relate meaningfully to a wide variety of persons. They see themselves as mutually dependent on culture, while most sodalities (especially sects) are smaller and seek identification apart from or over against the prevailing culture, often transplanting a foreign culture that is "better." This took place in the New Testament church when the increasing number of Gentile believers forced the Jewish Christians to decide whether cultural aspects of their faith (i.e., circumcision) were part of a pure religious culture or not. There is a rise in this attitude among fundamental Christians who push for a return to Hebrew cultural distinctives. Because of the very different viewpoints in this area alone, modalities are often accused of "selling out" their faith by those in the sodalities.

It is surely wrong to try to classify a religious group as either a sodality or a modality because we are dealing with a continuum rather than absolute categories. And too, "there is a sense in which the local church itself . . . is often a consensus group within a pluralistic denomination" and this makes the local church a kind of sodality.[5] Because of this, it is more helpful to examine the traits of an organization, and see if those traits tend to be more in one direction than the other.

While a healthy modality will breed sodalities to accomplish mission-minded tasks, all too often these sodalities lose track of the big picture and break off from the parent group. Catholic monastic orders were the sodalities of the "universal church." When Martin Luther, once part of a monastic order, introduced the concept of the priesthood of all be-

lievers and broke away from the church, he failed to create a mission-minded sodality for his new organization.[6] There was no group within the new church that dealt primarily with the idea of mission. The concept of "priesthood of all believers" was more acurate in placing the responsibility for mission on the whole laity, but it ignored the human dilemma that occurs when "everyone is responsible, no one responds." Each reformer in turn saw a missing element in the modality, and accordingly tried to stress that missing element in the church group he led. Rather than offering a cure for the problem, it just twisted the problem in a different way.

In all of this a pattern emerges which is not good or bad; it is merely a pattern of human behavior. Some personality types are basically inclusive and tolerant; others are more exclusive and intolerant. Heritage plays an enormous role in shifting the balance from one side to the other. Neither modality or sodality are entirely sufficient in meeting human needs. And so the pendulum swings. "Both Evangelicalism and Catholicism exhibit, in many practical matters, the influence of a 'natural' law of human organization. Max Weber spoke of it as the 'routinization of charisma.' Catholic sociologist Thomas O'Dea spoke of the problem of the second generation."[7] We see it as the journey back and forth from modality to sodality.

Sodalities almost always mature into modalities. This is seen in the classical Pentecostal churches who grew from sects in the early part of this century to respected denominations of today. We also know that

the second and third generations of New England Puritans lacked the religious zeal and conviction of their immigrant forebears. They had not experienced the persecution which led to the *Mayflower* crossing, and they had to understand their Puritanism in the light of a new world and a distinctly colonial experience.[8]

It should come as no surprise that there is a lack of fervor in the members of the RLDS faith to proclaim the "old Jerusalem gospel" our forefathers told. The church started by Joseph Smith, Jr., never matured into a modality before his death. His son Joseph III actually launched a new sodality, very different from the intent of the church his father left in Nauvoo. The RLDS church is just now going into the modality stage because it had not one, but two full generations of people in different sodalities to grow from. It has spent years struggling with the question as to whether it must try to duplicate the New Testament church, the Restored church, the Reorganized church, or none of the above.

We can identify some of the traits of the early Restoration (pre-1844) that mark it as a sodality. First of all, the church had no room for nominal faith. Persecution helped this along, but it is also true that the church attracted those who were intensely interested in a mission (sodality) type of faith. Many of them felt betrayed by the lack of urgency toward mission they felt in the mainline churches they had recently left, and consequently, attacked those very institutions. The idea of apostasy in a very limited sense appealed to their situation, and existing churches received more attention than those without the Christ. The church attracted those who needed a dynamic and moving faith, and those kinds of people often brought on persecution.

Second, Joseph Smith did not actually govern by consensus or even common consent, in its truest meaning. He governed by unanimity—and where he found it lacking, there often followed censure, excommunication, or at least greatly reduced responsibility. He sometimes shared what his perception of the Lord's will was, and at times people must have felt that to disagree with Joseph was

essentially dissent with God. People also allowed Joseph Smith to significantly alter their faith and goals because he was a charismatic individual, a man of spiritual giftedness and vision that inspired followership. If Joseph had asked his people to file an accounting, such as we are asked to do, he would have found a positive response, possibly in the 70 to 80 percent range. But Joseph would have been asking a people (committed to a sodality) who assumed that any response he asked for directly built up the kingdom. And so, because of the highly organized sodality that existed, the early Saints were able to establish communities in several areas, build temples, and evangelize beyond ordinary means.

How does a charismatic leader, such as Joseph Smith, find an equally charismatic replacement? Usually, this is impossible. One wonders if the presence of an equally capable successor would not threaten current leadership sufficiently to eliminate any chance of such a replacement. Sodalities are so sensitive to strong leadership that they may not be able to tolerate two strong leaders. This seems to explain to some degree the friction between Sidney Rigdon and Joseph. It also supports the apparent situation that while Joseph was still alive, no individual could replace his leadership. Even in death, there was no one who could replace him with the unity needed to avoid schism. In order for a sodality to amount to more than a flash in the pan, it must deal effectively with the issue of successorship. No one could continue the movement Joseph began, nor the momentum with which he moved it. Considering the pace of change experienced by Mormonism in the first fourteen years, it would hardly have been desirable to continue at that rate. At the death of the prophet, there seemed to be at least two choices.

One choice was to expand vision,

broaden the mission, and become more eclectic—allow the church to meet the needs of a wider variety of persons. This type of church may have been able to unite many of the splinter groups under a moderate leadership. Obviously, this did not happen. The right leadership may not have been available or else the sodality Joseph began was not yet mature enough to develop into a modality at such an early age.

The other option, which eventually occurred, was to rally around various charismatic leaders and raise a banner of distinctiveness from which others could gain identity. Those who waved each banner claimed it to be identical to that of their founder, but in reality each was a separate, spawning sodality. Each began the process anew.

While various schisms would rise and fall in popularity, the bulk of the leadership would move West, along with the greatest following. There they would establish a new sodality, bolstered by the gradual acceptance of Nauvoo's most infamous doctrine, polygamy. Even though most people were not directly involved with polygamy, it did offer the Utah Saints a counter cultural element that soon symbolized the new sodality.

It was several years later that young Joseph finally joined a group of the "true Latter Day Saints" and the rally point of that newly formed sodality seemed to be a reaction to public opinion of the more widely known Utah church. These Saints, who now followed the far less charismatic leadership of Joseph III, concentrated their efforts more on mission than personality, and among other things, that mission seemed to inform the world that "we are not polygamous, Utah Mormons."

All of the previous information has been simplified to keep this work within the bounds of a somewhat reasonable length. It has attempted to illustrate this theme: The Restoration was born as a sodality, in response to the missing elements of the existing religions. It was then apt to develop into a modality as it matured, or spawn a new sodality. The latter happened. We can use this information to help us better survive the growing pains we experience today and to avoid schism that will renew the process all over again.

The RLDS members grew weary of defining themselves in terms of who they are not. Today, in looking at the many areas of growth, we can see the church stretching out and becoming a modality. This might have happened a generation ago if things had gone differently. The early years of the Reorganization were spent like the "new kid on the block." The fights to establish credibility were with words rather than with fists. Debaters, especially a few gifted men, sought to gain identity in a religious world that was hostile to Mormonism. In these debates, particularly in the defense of Joseph Smith, we found ourselves canonizing church history. Critical research and examination were discouraged. As a result, emphasis was on the telling of the story, rather than the story itself. Joseph Smith's story began to be substituted for the gospel story which "everyone already knew." People began to search for a testimony of the truth of the "first vision" and the "coming forth of the Book of Mormon" as a prerequisite for membership. As a result, we deepened our attributes of a sodality and limited the opportunity to broaden our scope of ministry for years to come.

It is not altogether wrong to be a sodality. There is a mixture of sodality and modality that can capitalize on their individual strengths and yet still coexist.

The growing pains mentioned earlier are an indication of the development toward modality and also the frustrated cries of those who fear having their sodality torn from them. Ordination of women is a continuation of the modality process. At the same time, the call to greater commitment on the part of those already ordained is representative of the responsible discipleship seen in effective sodalities.

The question of Communion is more difficult to resolve. From a sodality's point of view, it would strengthen unity and distinctiveness to continue close Communion and perhaps even increase membership requirements. The challenging theology of the modality recognizes God's hand reaching out in many areas and in many churches—with significant power *and* authority. Since the issue of close Communion was first decided by a World Conference that represented a sodality, the time will come when Conference representation will be made up mostly from the modality part of the church and the Communion will be "open" to others in the Christian faith. This will require careful and deliberate implementation, as in the case of ordination of women, so that members of the sodality will not be unduly offended.

Decentralization will eventually benefit both sides of the spectrum. It will improve the efficiency of the organization and will increase ownership of programs by those in the local congregation (sodality). It will also provide for greater diversity that will accent our individuality throughout the world, without sacrificing the unity of the greater body.

In a similar light—diversity of religious worship is necessary in a worldwide church. By gaining acceptance of the many worship styles in other cultures, the church at large will be more willing to accept alternate worship styles in their own culture (a far more difficult task). In a modality, there is room for the traditional as well as the innovative, for the solemn as well as the charismatic. Looking at other mainline churches (modalities), we see this has already happened time and again.

Finally, one of the most encouraging signs of a healthy modality is the greater awareness of the world scope of the church. World Conferences as well as church publications emphasize the fact that the RLDS church is far more than an American church. The early Restoration sent missionaries to other lands. Many, if not most, of those new converts saw the land of Joseph as their destination. This was mainly a reaction to a very limited concept of Zion. The Reorganization's expansion into other countries did not begin in earnest until the late 1950s. This expansion was of a different nature, and it established fellowships that remained in those countries. In the past twenty-five years more missions have been planted than in the 125 years prior to that. This outreach to other nations and cultures is an indicator that the church is growing toward a modality-type faith and at the same time building an appreciation among Western members of the church for the vast potential in other lands. This trend, if it continues, soon will make the "domestic field" smaller than the so-called "foreign field!" Churches require diversity and flexibility to adapt to such a marked shift.

As we move toward a modality structure, we need to look closely at the elements of our past history as a sodality that were strong and worth retaining. There needs to remain a healthy identification with the church, the *World Church*. This is somewhat different from the attitude that limits the Restoration to America or even to Joseph Smith. A positive characteristic of a sodality is that members are proud of their organization, not merely satisfied. It is this attitude that leads to another exceptional quality of sodalities: outreach. Mission is the central core of Christianity. And still, this has been the most neglected part of the domestic field. The church in the United States and Canada is nearly at a standstill regarding evangelism.

The reasons for this are legion, but most are related in some way to this painful process of transition from a sodality to a modality. The change has been too traumatic to concentrate on mission. Recognizing the source of this pain (i.e., the transition process) helps to get back on the path of outreach. One final indispensable aspect of strong sodalities needs mentioning. That is the emphasis on discipleship. There is always danger that strong discipleship groups can become ingrown and exclusive; however, any Christian group that lacks discipleship veers away from the power that justifies its existence.

We will continue to find sodalities and modalities in every healthy organization. They are tendencies in people that God uses to accomplish his purposes. There need to be a greater awareness of the difficulties in living together and a surge of mutual acceptance. A dynamic church needs broad vision and understanding alongside mission and discipleship. In addition to honest and sensitive inspection of heritage, there needs to be place for firm convictions and loyalty. Modalities and sodalities need to stop fighting one another and work together to build up the kingdom of God.

Notes

1. Especially helpful in this area, see C. Peter Wagner, *Leading Your Church to Growth* (Ventura, California: Regal Books, 1984). See also Richard G. Hutcheson, Jr. *Wheel within the Wheel: Confronting the Management Crisis of the Pluralistic Church* (Atlanta, Georgia: John Knox Press, 1979).
2. Hutcheson, 113-116.
3. Wagner, 155.
4. Ibid., 157.
5. Hutcheson, 113.
6. Wagner, 153-155.
7. Bob Moran, CSP, "Reflections on the Way We Are: A Priest in Evangelical Land," *The Journal of the Minister's Personal Library*, vol. 5, no. 2, 4.
8. Ibid., 4.

BEYOND EQUALITY...TO JUSTICE

Lois Taylor Braby

New Dimensions of Stewardship

Stewardship is the response of my people to the ministry of my Son. —Doctrine and Covenants 147:5a

Stewardship is a basic principle of the Restoration faith. It may be defined as the response given to the ministry of love which permeates all life. This response carries with it the promise of a creation empowered to fulfill the reason for its being. As persons affirm a loving presence in the universe, they look within, accepting themselves as children of God and co-creators, endowed with purpose and potential. This affirmation calls persons not only to be responsible stewards over their own life but to stand as just and loving stewards in their society and culture. It calls persons to "embody the divine intent in the midst of the world."[1]

The church has recently been admonished to

seek ways of effecting a greater understanding of the meaning of the stewardship of temporalities as a response to [God's] grace and love so that the understanding of the principle may stir the hearts of the people as never before...all to the end that the people may come to provide more fully and joyfully for the great work to which all are called. —Doctrine and Covenants 154:5a, b

A greater understanding of the principle of stewardship may be derived by a study of the philosophical view of David L. Norton which has been termed Normative Individualism. The following is a précis of Norton's philosophy as it relates to the principle of stewardship. This philosophy, outlined in his book *Personal Destinies: A Philosophy of Ethical Individualism*, is a statement of challenge to all who would respond to the ministry of Jesus Christ within a needy world. It is a call to go beyond comfort to commitment, to go beyond equality to justice.

Self-actualization Ethics

The worth of souls is great in the sight of God. —Doctrine and Covenants 16:3

The foundational ethic of Normative Individualism is self-actualization. Norton has derived his contemporary system of self-actualization ethics from the classical Greek philosophy of eudaemonism.

Eudaemonism was formulated from the writings of Socrates, Plato, and Aristotle and is the term for the "ethical doctrine that each person is obliged to know and to live in truth to his [her] daemon (or inner genius), thereby progressively actualizing an excellence that is his [hers] innately and potentially."[2] Both classical eudaemonism and contemporary Normative Individualism share these premises: (1) Know thyself (as inscribed on the temple of Apollo at Delphi), and (2) Become what you are (from Pindar, Pythian Ode II, line 72). According to these ethics, it is every person's primary responsibility to discover the "daemon" within and to live in accordance with it.

Norton brings the self (individual) into the social (normative) realm when he contends that the work of actualizing the inner self or daemon is not only vital to the search for personal fulfillment but is a moral necessity, and thus a social responsibility.

This challenge to a life of stewardship integrates self with society. Here lies the promise of Zion as a community which can personify the dynamic power of God's enabling love for all. As Christian stewards develop their personal giftedness, they will reach out lovingly to others that all might fulfill the "measure of their creation." Justice becomes manifest in this stewardship response for the foundation of justice is the "presupposition of the unique, irreplaceable, potential worth of every person and the source of justice is found in the essential nature of the person as an individual."[3]

Intrinsic Justice—a New Social Framework

The question of justice appears in the world with persons . . . as integrity is the cardinal virtue of personal life, justice is the paramount virtue of society.[4]

Throughout human history there has been a consistent cry for "equality" resounding from all those who have seen or who have experienced the effects of injustice within society. Violence in every form has erupted in those societies where inequities have existed as accepted modes of social life. Persons frustrated by the apparent gulf between the privileged and the deprived have resorted to every sort of action to narrow that gulf.

Social reformers search for structures of community which will unlock the potential within all persons, allowing them to move from social systems described as "survival of the fittest," to those described as "life in the fullest." Designers of the ultimate community seek for means to allow all persons "equal opportunity," "equal treatment under the law," "equal access to resources," holding the ideal of equality in community as the highest form of justice. This social ideal may, indeed, be misguided.

The theory of intrinsic justice, as developed by David Norton, lays bare the restrictive nature of the concept of equality. Equality connotes equivalence (=) and is termed comparative or *inter-individual* justice. Comparative justice, that social equality for which human beings have historically struggled, is revealed as a justice of equivalence and uniformity. (If you have two cars in your garage, I have the right to have two cars in my garage.) This type of justice, according to Norton, is "make-believe" justice. It is, in fact, *unjust* as it allows no place for the individual.

Diversity Is the Strength of Zion

All are called according to the gifts of God unto them.—Doctrine and Covenants 119:8

In the society which is built on the concept of equality or comparative justice, all persons will be treated the same, all will receive the same type and amount of resources, and the same input to society is expected from all. All are expected to act the same and, in some societies, attempts are made to force all to think the same. Since uniformity and equivalence are the rule in this type of society, it is not only unjust but constitutes a form of slavery to the human spirit. In this type of setting, equality destroys creative thought and thus creative activity. Our modern world has witnessed examples of this type of human devastation. The individual is considered of no worth. Worth is counted only to the group. The group actually becomes parasitic, feeding off the life of the individuals within it. Though this kind of society may exemplify equality in its purest form, the seeds of its own destruction are implanted within it—*the injustice of the diminishing worth of the individual.*

The intrinsic justice of Normative Individualism rejects social equality, with its foundation of comparison to others, and grounds its system of justice on the cornerstone of the "presupposition of the unique, irreplaceable, potential worth of every person."[5] Intrinsic justice is termed noncomparative or *intra-individual* justice. Since the question of justice appears in the world with persons and remains so long as there are persons in the world, the source of justice is in the essential nature of the person as an individual. The premise is that all persons, by virtue of their human be-ing, are *entitled* to the necessities for the actualization of their unique potentiality. This noncomparative, intrinsic justice goes beyond the sameness of equality and touches the human need for the uniqueness of diversity.

The Stewardship of Productive Living

It is required of the Lord, at the hand of every steward, to render an account of his [her] stewardship. —Doctrine and Covenants 72:1c

Norton contends that social equality which grants the same benefits to all is built on the "economics of scarcity." The justice applied in this type of society is grounded in distributable goods rather than in the worth of persons. The ultimate goal in this society would be that all persons should receive identical benefits regardless of individual difference in need. Norton maintains that "distributable goods are not independent variables in the matrix of justice, but are the products

of life and work. And it is in terms of the individual 'productive life' that the problem of justice originates."[6]

In the system of intrinsic justice the productive life is not defined as one that *produces* the most distributable goods (goods, products, money, etc.) to society, but the one that *utilizes* the goods of life, whatever they might be, which are essential to that person's development of life potential. As these persons actualize their potential by productive living this actualized good returns to society in the form that is a result of their unique gift (art, music, agriculture, invention, human service, business development, etc.). There are as many forms of society "goods" as there are persons.

In the realm of Christian life the activity of developing personal potential for the benefit of others has been termed *stewardship*. In the realm of secular life this activity has been termed *productive citizenship*. In both instances, as in the philosophical system of Normative Individualism, it is the highest form of self-social ethics.

Within this philosophical framework, injustice becomes two-dimensional. First, it abounds when persons are deprived of their "entitled claims" to life sustenance or to life goods which allow them to develop their unique potential. Second, it abounds when persons advance "unentitled claims" to that which is not necessary to their life sustenance nor to the development of their potential. These unentitled claims are based on the unjust concept of the "maximizing principle of material benefits." This principle calls for the "proliferation without limit of the material holdings of persons on the grounds that of such goods 'each person prefers a larger to a lesser share.'"[7] Both the principle and the alleged preference are questionable and neither are acceptable in the life of the Christian steward.

The Injustice of Superabundance

Unto the church assembled and at large . . .both in private and in public expenditure carry into active exercise the principle of sacrifice and repression of unnecessary wants. —Doctrine and Covenants 130:7a, d

The principle of the maximization of material benefits encourages persons to dream of and seek for superabundance. This of course is not possible for all persons.

Unlimited acquisition is institutionalized in societies which operate from this foundation, granting moral self-satisfaction to the enormously wealthy together with the moral impetus for others to do as well for themselves.[8]

Even in Christian societies righteousness has often been measured by the amount of material goods which persons have maximized. We can see the influence of this principle in the American culture as we recall the Protestant work ethic, the great American dream, the Horatio Alger ideal and such story themes as "rags to riches," "pauper to prince," and the ever-present European influence of the "Cinderella story."

Normative Individualism supports the principle of *entitled claims* which is the foundation of intrinsic justice. Individuals are thus entitled, not to *all* kinds and *unlimited* amounts of distributable goods, but only goods of certain kinds; and only the amount of these goods which they can utilize in the process of actualizing their self-potential. Norton suggests that persons without knowledge of their own identities will endorse the maximization of benefits without limits for they are not aware of their own nor others' "intrinsic, irreplaceable, potential worth."

Persons thus unaware, claim entitlement to *everything* without determining its value to their self-actualization nor concern for its value to others' need. This undisciplined misuse of material goods constitutes gross waste and is in itself immoral for in its waste it denies self and others. Society loses the contribution which could be made by those denied as well as an actualizing, moral contribution by those who deny.

These are portentous times. The lives of many are being sacrificed unnecessarily to the gods of war, greed, and avarice. The land is being desecrated by the thoughtless waste of vital resources. You must obey my commandments and be in the forefront of those who would mediate this needless destruction while there is yet day. —Doctrine and Covenants 150:7

Those persons who are aware of their worth and potential, those who have chosen to be concerned stewards over their total lives, claim only those goods which they can use in their process of self-actualization. They recognize that to live by the maximization of benefits principle is to *waste* what could be available for others, and at the same time, to amass fortunes and goods which have no value to their own personal development but indeed may be *distractions* which become destructive to their lives. These persons choose not to waste resources nor to waste themselves. They choose to live in the realm of intrinsic justice, using only the goods to which they are entitled. Their choice is a moral one for society and for self. They have become faithful and wise stewards, responding to the urgings of the divine in them.

The Justice of Love

What doth the Lord require of thee, but to do justly, and to love mercy, and to walk humbly with thy God? —Micah 6:3

It is an underlying principle of Norton's philosophy that as persons come to appreciate their uniqueness and worth, self-love enters their lives empowering them to develop their potential excellence. Out of the value of this actualizing experience, their love is expanded and is offered freely to all, supporting the unique worth of others.

The theory of intrinsic justice as described here is not to be conceived as a model of positive law for

even in a democracy, the intuitive meaning of positive law is that of a regulation imposed upon individuals by an authority external to themselves . . . but the model upon which [intrinsic] justice is properly conceived is not positive law but love, and its regulations are not externally imposed, but immanent with the individual.[9]

Love, as defined in this model, is aspiration to higher value. It affirms the Socratic idea that to love is to prossess in potential what one lacks in actuality and that which incomplete actuality requires for its completion and its worth. Justice can be manifest only where love dwells. Where love dwells justice will abound.

And thou shalt love the Lord thy God with all thy heart, and with all thy soul, and with all thy mind, and with all thy strength. This is the first commandment. And the second is like this, Thou shalt love thy neighbor as thyself. There is none other commandment greater than these. —Mark 12:35, 36

Normative Individualism pushes us beyond the concept of comparative justice—the justice of social equality. It is not equivalence that we, as Christians, seek.

It is not sameness we desire. It is the affirmation of our individual uniqueness, of our potential offering to society in the form of our productive, meaningful work. We do not seek to actualize our potential because "someone else has so we must also." We seek to actualize our potential excellence because it is an inner need, a natural entitlement which comes to life with us. In truth, we seek more than equality, we seek justice—a justice grounded, not in positive law, but in love, a justice that comes, not from external sources, but from within and operates out of the overflow of a reverence for life and for the "unique, irreplaceable, potential worth of all persons."

The justice of which we speak can be attained only as our lives are disciplined to the principle of stewardship. The challenge for this day which calls us to respond to the need for justice in our world is found in these words,

You who are my disciples must be found continuing in the forefront of these organizations and movements which are recognizing the worth of persons and are committed to bringing the ministry of my Son to bear on their lives. —Doctrine and Covenants 151:9

Notes

1. Basic Beliefs Committee, *Exploring the Faith* (Independence, Missouri: Herald House, 1970), 175.
2. David L. Norton, *Personal Destinies: A Philosophy of Ethical Individualism* (Princeton: Princeton University Press, 1976), 1x.
3. Ibid., 313.
4. Ibid., 310.
5. Ibid., 313.
6. Ibid.
7. Ibid., 315.
8. Ibid., 323.
9. Ibid., 343.

KOHLBERT'S THEORY OF MORAL REASONING AND IMPLICATIONS FOR FUNDING CHURCH PROGRAM BY MOTIVATING STEWARD RESPONSE

Vivian Collins Campbell

Introduction

For many years there has been need in the Reorganized Church of Jesus Christ of Latter Day Saints to broaden the base of contributors to tithing and the general fund. A current World Church goal is to achieve 21 percent of members as accounting stewards. Why is it that less than one in five are accounting stewards and one in three are contributors? Probably multiple factors need to be considered. The purpose of this essay is to explore one possibility: i.e., challenges presented by leadership may not be readily comprehended by many of the members. This lack of understanding may be causing confusion and lack of positive response.

In turn each of Kohlberg's Stages of Moral Reasoning will be briefly described followed by comments about what possibly motivates and is understood by a maturing member. Because of the complexity of the material, it is very difficult to select neat and short examples of the different stages. In fact, the neater and shorter the examples the more ambiguous the task. Nevertheless, for the sake of illustration, isolated segments have been selected from scriptures, *Saints Herald* articles, and stewardship publications. Examples that appear questionable to the reader could provide stimuli for further discussion. No attempt was made to do a comprehensive content analysis of adult or children's stewardship materials. This author's purpose is to illustrate and suggest possible motivating factors for stewards in each of Kohlberg's Stages of Moral Reasoning. It is hoped that this will be helpful to those responsible for implementing programs, guiding members to more mature responses.

Key Points About Kohlberg's Stages

Kohlberg's six Stages of Moral Reasoning were developed after much longitudinal research based on the theory of Piaget. However, Kohlberg's work is more comprehensive and highly refined. His study focused on a sequence of stages which revealed that persons restructure their thinking about moral questions as they develop.

In considering the stages, It is essential to remember the following points:

1. The stages of moral development appear to be the same for all persons, regardless of culture or social class.

2. Stages cannot be skipped. Each stage is built upon the one before.

3. Change is gradual. At any one time, about half of a person's thinking is at one stage, and the remainder at adjacent stages. Most persons can comprehend

one stage above their predominate one.

4. Stage and age cannot be equated. Nor can stage and intelligence be equated. Some persons develop faster than others. Also some persons develop further than others. Development can be arrested at any stage or age.

5. How a person reasons morally does influence behavior. However, understanding reasoning in terms of principles does not guarantee moral action.

Kohlberg said that logic is to the cognitive domain what justice is to the moral domain. The stages he describes are the underlying principles of justice from the lowest stages of maturity to the most mature. In order for a person to think justly, the development of what Piaget called reversibility is essential. Reversibility is being able to look at an action or idea forward and backward: to be able to retrace steps and see an issue from all sides. With increasing moral maturity comes the ability to understand and consider other persons' points of view.[1]

Kohlberg divides moral development into three periods he calls levels. Each level is divided into two stages, for a total of six stages. The stages are the *structure* and not the *content* or solutions to particular problems. Each stage is a reintegration of the stages that go before it. Persons go through them at different rates and may cease to develop beyond the lower stages. The age ranges that go with the stages are not timetables for normal development but rather are given as general guidelines.[2]

Kohlberg's Stages and Implications for Motivating Steward Response.

Stage 0

The beginning of a child's life Kohlberg calls level 0 or the *premoral period*. At first the premoral children's actions are their judgments, but later they begin to think about their actions, though not in a social sense. The children at this premoral stage decide what is good or bad on the basis of what they like and want or on what they do not like or what hurts them. They have no conception of rules and feel no obligation to obey them.

Level 1: Preconventional Morality. Stage 1

The broad general age range for this stage is from about five or six to about ten or twelve. Children are unable to see another's point of view. They see rules or authority as needing to be followed in order to avoid punishment or because they lack power, rather than out of respect. Motivation is from fear of getting caught and avoiding punishment. It is assumed might makes right. Fairness is an eye for an eye, a tooth for a tooth. Retaliation is an automatic response to an act committed, regardless of intention or motive.[3]

Although many children are in Stage 1 as a normal part of development, probably few adult members are permanently arrested in this stage. A Stage 1 adult could understand and be most apt to respond to an appeal to avoid punishment. An example is the scriptural admonition, "For he that is tithed shall not be burned (at his coming)" (Doctrine and Covenants 64:5a).

Stage 2

The broad general age range for this stage is from about seven to eight to about twelve to fourteen. The people at this stage are basically hedonistic and see what is right as what satisfies their own needs and occasionally the needs of others. Human relations are interpreted in terms of reciprocity or fairness; however, at this stage emphasis on reciprocity is in terms of equality, not loyalty, gratitude, or justice. Motivation is out of self-interest; "What's in it for me?" It is assumed that you have to look out for yourself and are obligated to help only those who help you. The orientation is "you scratch my back and I'll scratch yours." Fairness is "coming out even." The law of expiatory justice, an eye for an eye, a tooth for a tooth, is still present. Stage 2 sees people as having a right to do what they want with self and possessions even if it conflicts with the rights of others. The attitude is, "What I do is my own business."[4]

Defensive Stage 2 adults may insist that personal finances are no one's business but their own, and therefore would not believe in accounting. Since for Stage 2, relationships are interpreted in terms of reciprocity or fairness, a challenge to participate in a partnership with God could be motivating. The adult or child could appreciate the question, "How would you like it if you didn't get your share? And since we receive help from God it is only fair for us to help in return." With the strong self-interest of "What's in it for me?" Stage 2 persons would likely respond to testimonies about blessings received and the scriptural promise,

Bring ye all the tithes into the storehouse, that there may be meat in mine house, and prove me now herewith saith the Lord of hosts, if I will not open you the windows of heaven, and pour you out a blessing, that there shall not be room to receive it.—Malachi 3:10

This Presiding Bishopric's statement about saintly response could be easily appreciated by persons with Stage 2 understanding. "We believe all will be blessed in sharing their resources as a personal response to the needs of God's people."[5]

Level 2: Conventional Morality
Stage 3

The age range is from about ten or eleven on. This stage is more common at the age of twelve or thirteen. Many adults never get beyond this. In Stage 3, one can readily understand the Golden Rule. The person in this stage understands sharing and sees the necessity of cooperating. Good is defined as what helps others or is approved by them, and approval and disapproval of others is tremendously important. Behavior is often judged by intention: for example, "She means well." Intentionality becomes very important and tends to be overworked. Imitation, identification, and the use of moral clichés are quite common.

Children at this stage can understand what it means to have others count on them. Approval is earned by being nice. Adults at this stage might be unduly concerned about what the neighbors think. Motivation is based on desire for approval by living up to good-girl, good-boy stereotypes. There is much emphasis on conformity and it is assumed that good behavior equals social conformity. Fairness is trying to make everyone happy, but those considered are only the ones directly involved. Justice is embedded in concern for the approval of others and in social conformity. A crucial point that separates Stage 3 from Stage 4 is that, Stage 3 persons lack the ability to see society as an integrated system.[6]

In the Kohlberg framework children would not be baptized until they were in Stage 2 but capable of understanding Stage 3. They would be past the point of following authority out of fear and could understand sharing and cooperation. They would have desire for approval and want to live up to good-boy and good-girl stereotypes. Probably about the time of baptism would be an appropriate time to begin stewardship accounting while desire to cooperate and share is prominent.

Since desire for approval is tremendously important, adults with Stage 3 understanding might be motivated by an approach using peer pressure or encouragement with emphasis on being a "good member."

The following statement by the Presiding Bishopric appealing for cooperation would be readily appreciated by persons with Stage 3 understanding. "Success in temporal response to the needs of the church requires a spirit of unity and mutual purpose among the Saints."[7]

Stage 4

Some twelve- to fourteen-year-olds are beginning to move into this stage, but it is more likely to occur around ages fifteen to seventeen. This is the terminal stage for many adults and is the modal stage in the United States. The person at this stage is oriented toward authority, fixed rules, and the maintenance of the social order. An important point to keep in mind about Stage 4 is that its orientation is to maintain the existing system as it is and not toward creating an ideal social or legal system. Right behavior is doing one's duty and maintaining law and order for its own sake. Respect is earned by performing "dutifully." The justice perspective of Stage 4 is that when resolving conflicts one should do what is best for the average rather than for the ideal. It is an operational morality in terms of the utilitarian principle of the greatest good for the greatest number. The morality of Stage 4 persons leaves no clear answer to issues involving obligation to persons outside one's own social order, or to persons who do not accept the rules of the social order, or to the creation of social change.[8]

Since according to Kohlberg more adults in the United States are in Stage 4 than any other stage, it is fairly safe to assume that there are a significant number in the church as well. Persons in this stage would likely be concerned about maintaining the institution of the church as it is and be resistant to change. A positive aspect of this characteristic could be that once adults with Stage 4 understandings are motivated to be accounting and contributing members there would be strong inclination to continue.

Emphasis on one's duty and being obedient to God's laws could be motivating to persons with Stage 4 understanding. The following scripture could be appreciated. "Stewardship is the response of my people to the ministry of my Son and is required alike of all those who seek to build the kingdom" (Doctrine and Covenants 147:5a).

The following statement by the Presiding Bishopric could be understood. The presenting of the tithing statement "is a symbolic reminder of the baptismal covenant to love God, to keep his commandments and to serve him."[9]

At this point Kohlberg describes what he calls Stage 4½. It is not a true stage because only a minority of people go through it. Some youth who reach Stage 4 in high school while they are living in an environment where they are not really required to test their own beliefs and values, may enter a moratorium experience when they leave home and enter college. At this time they are exposed to many conflicting viewpoints.

There is a tendency at this point to become very cynical and relativistic about beliefs and values. The combination of moratorium and cognitive conflict about one's own values leads to the belief that all values are relative, that all societies have equal claim to validity, and that no one can really say that anyone's values are superior to anyone else's.[10]

Stage 4½, then,

involves people who reach the highest form of conventional morality, step outside it, question it, reject it, but have no adequate resolution to the conflict. They are beyond conventional morality, but have not yet developed principled morality. The question is whether or not this is a transitional stage that leads to Stage 5. Apparently it may be, but not necessarily. Kohlberg says that in many it does lead to principled morality, but that in others it does not, and that people can remain at Stage 4½ permanently. He cites as examples of adults who remained at Stage 4½ Hitler, Stalin, and possibly some of the people involved in the Watergate scandal, in reference to the sorts of behavior and rationalizations that have been attributed to Haldeman, Erlichman and the President.[11]

Level 3: Postconventional, Autonomous, or Principled Level
Stage 5

According to Kohlberg an adult is not likely to reach this stage until middle or late twenties. He says the earliest he has seen Stage 5 was twenty-three. Cognitive development required is full formal thought and deductive reasoning. Kohlberg believes that a person reaching this stage must have had personal experience involving responsibility for the self, values conflict, identity questioning, and crises, along with the understanding of a need for commitment. A person at this stage emphasizes the legal point of view, but also considers the possibility of changing law for the good of society, rather than rigidly maintaining law and order as in Stage 4. Stage 5 is the level of the United States Constitution and Bill of Rights. At Stage 5 universal moral principles define right and wrong. There is dissatisfaction with rules because they are prescriptive, concrete, and apply only in specific situations. Principles allow for exceptions; rules do not.[12]

The reasoning of each stage resolves the conflicts of the preceding stage. For example, the utilitarian principle of the maximization for the greatest good is discarded because the rights of the minority are ignored. Persons in Stage 4 adopt the perspective of the average moral agent, and in Stage 5 the impartial moral agent. Rather than taking the perspective of the average moral agent, the Stage 5 person would attempt to resolve a conflict in terms of what is right for the individual and the greatest good for the greatest number.[13]

The following statements from the Presiding Bishopric would not be fully appreciated until persons develop Stage 5 understanding.

We need to be aware of the inherent worth and dignity of each person as we try to live out what it means for the church to be the body of Christ in today's world.

Giving ourselves to others helps to fulfill the meaning of our existence.

As disciples of the Lord Jesus Christ and stewards of the kingdom we are challenged to use our resources to meet the needs of people in fulfilling individual and corporate potential.

When the identity and worth of souls is discerned, we will respond by upholding each person's dignity.[14]

Even though individual enterprise is to be recognized as the crux of essential freedoms in stewardship relationships, individual stewards are to be reborn to a sense of social awareness that will cause them to "lose themselves" in service to others.[15]

Maturing stewards would not really appreciate the need for commitment until they develop Stage 5 reasoning. The following statement from the Presiding Bishopric could be motivating by emphasizing a need for commitment. "If we can respond through the total giving of our lives, to the demands of stewardship, the future holds undreamed-of possibilities."[16]

Stage 6

Kohlberg says that only a few people reach this stage. Some cultures have no Stage 5 or Stage 6 people. Development of Stage 6 is not likely before the late twenties; and is more likely in the thirties or later. Cognitive development requires that formal operations are complete. Also Kohlberg believes that advancement to the stage

requires personal experience involving sustained responsibility for the welfare of others; irreversible moral decisions in actual situations; and high level cognitive stimulation, conflict and reflection.[17]

A person in this stage defines what is right by a decision of conscience in accordance with self-chosen ethical principles according to logical comprehensiveness, universality, and consistency. The principles are abstract and not concrete moral rules as are the Ten Commandments. They are abstract guidelines that can be universalized and applied to many situations in decision making. The person at this level is concerned with universal principles of justice, equality of human rights, and respect for the dignity and worth of all persons. The ultimate principle is justice which is the core of morality. While Stage 5 is an impartial moral agent, Stage 6 is an ideal moral agent.

These excerpts from Presiding Bishopric articles are probably fully appreciated only by the ideal moral agent.

There is a divine plan to help man in the process of sharing possessions with the cause of the kingdom. Sometimes called the spiritual Law of Temporalities, it is a plan conceived of God which is designed to help man utilize the temporal aspects of life to achieve spiritual objectives in harmony with God's purposes. It is a law of spiritual undergirding, primarily intended to assist man to develop spiritually into an unselfish being after the image of God. Thus the stewardship of temporalities becomes the privotal point about which the total stewardship of life revolves.[18]

"Go ye into all the world and, whatsoever place you cannot go into, ye shall send, that the testimony may go from you into all the world, unto every creature" (Doctrine and Covenants 83:10). It is the self-forgetful spirit of the law of tithing that enables us to minister to many beyond the immediate concerns and needs of our local branches and congregations. Our tradition to tithe is the true spirit of benevolence—the disposition to do good without thought of return or reward. It is giving with no strings attached that is at the heart of Christian stewardship.[19]

While the concept of commitment is not fully understood and appreciated until a person has Stage 5 understanding, it is likely that the concept of consecration of surplus is not fully understood and appreciated until Stage 6. In calling all to be stewards the Presiding Bishopric made the following statement about motivation which is possibly incomprehensible to many.

We are to be motivated to respond in these specific ways not because of a sense of duty or obligation, but because of love, which we comprehend in its greatest dimension, as we bow humbly at the foot of the cross of him who gave himself for all. It is in this spirit of consecration expressed in the life of our Lord that we're called to respond as stewards under him.[20]

Implications for Practice

Research indicates that persons cannot be led into higher levels of reasoning. However, development of moral maturity can be encouraged, not by indoctrination, but by providing a conducive atmosphere. Important conditions appear to be as follows:

1. Exposure to the next higher stage of reasoning
2. Exposure to situations posing problems and contradictions for a person's current moral structure, leading to dissatisfaction with that person's current level
3. An atmosphere of interchange and dialogue combining the first two conditions, in which conflicting moral views are compared in an open manner.[21]

Research also indicates that children were confused and failed to advance when presented with moral reasoning two stages above their measured levels.[22]

We can only speculate that adults also may become confused and fail to respond when presented with moral reasoning two stages above their predominant levels. It may be that trying to guide persons to be selfless and altruistic before they are developmentally ready might be only guilt-producing. This guilt rather than being productive could be destructive in that persons could suffer from illusive feelings that they should be doing better but be unable to find concrete reasons for these feelings.

It is likely that typical congregations would have some members in each of Kohlberg's six Stages of Moral Reasoning. It may be possible to design approaches for motivating steward response specifically for each developmental stage. An awareness of the stages could help leaders to assess the relationship between the probable stage of a member and which approach would be most motivating and thus help broaden the base of contributors to fund church program.

Notes

1. Lawrence Kohlberg, "The Cognitive-Developmental Approach to Moral Education," *Readings in Human Development*, ed. Bradley B. Glanville (Dushkin Publishing Group, Inc., Guilford, Connecticut 1978), 144.
2. Ibid., 145.
3. John S. Stewart, *Values Development Education*. Final Report An Evaluative Study of the High-School Use Film Program of Youth Films, Incorporated (T.W. Ward and J. S. Stewart, East Lansing, Michigan, July 1973), 11-84, 85.
4. Ibid., 11-86, 87.
5. *Saints' Herald*, 29:317.
6. Stewart, 11-89, 90.
7. *Saints' Herald*, 29:365.
8. Stewart, 11-95.
9. *In the Manner Designed of God* (Independence, Missouri: Herald House), 6.
10. Stewart, 11-95.
11. Ibid., 11-96.
12. Ibid., 11-97.
13. Ibid., 11-98.
14. *Saints' Herald*, 29:461.
15. *Surplus and the Storehouse Principle* (Independence, Missouri: Herald House), 11.
16. "The All Encircling Word," *Reflections on Stewardship* (Independence, Missouri: Herald House).
17. Stewart, 11-100.
18. *In the Manner Designed of God*, 5.
19. "Ministry to Many," *Reflections on Stewardship*, 9.
20. *Saints' Herald*, January 1984.
21. Kohlberg, 149.
22. Gail Beaton Peterson, Richard N. Hey, and Larry Richard Peterson, "Intersection of Family Development and Moral Stage Frameworks: Implications for Theory and Research," *Journal of Marriage and the Family* (May 1979).

THE CIVILIZING OF MORMONDOM
Levi S. Peterson

(Reprinted by permission of the author from *Sunstone*, May-June, 1982)

Many Mormons see little value in the process of civilization. Some of them tend to regard the Church as a culture which *gives to* but does not *take from* its sister cultures in the world, particularly in such essential matters as theological insight and moral understanding. Such things, in their view, come strictly through revelation, and it is the role of the Church to dispense them to the world through missionary work. It is inconceivable that an increased understanding of perfection might come to the Church from the wisdom which slowly accumulates through the civilized development of the human conscience in many cultures.

Certain other Mormons are even more militantly conscious of their disesteem for civilization, which they express by rejecting the world at large as the symbolic Babylon from which the Church, as God's specially anointed society, is to keep itself unspotted. This view tends to take on a doomsday color, for the changes occurring in non-Mormon cultures are often seen as totally corrupt and retrogressive, tainted by sin and worthy of destruction. Everywhere are wars and rumors of wars without end and perversities and whoredoms beyond calculation. Armageddon looms on the horizon, and the fearful settle into the fortress of their righteousness to await the imminent end of the world—something like Jonah, who supposed there was nothing in the city of Nineveh worthy of salvation.

This cynical view of civilization is unfortunate. The Church is not a detached and isolated island; it has a symbiotic, interdependent relationship with numerous other cultures, with whose people its members commingle on a daily basis. Civilization is a social process which flourishes most dramatically precisely when such interaction takes place. A new insight, a new value, a new tool passes from person to person, crossing boundaries and domesticating itself in various cultures, stimulating among its recipients further inventions and discoveries.

Given the fact of proximity and interaction, the Church has inevitably influenced its sister cultures, not merely by proselyting converts from among them but also by the example it gives of Christian living. But one does no dishonor to the divine mission of the Church by admitting that, in its turn, the Church is highly influenced by the world, sometimes even in matters relating to Christian living. Evidence for this assertion may be seen in events preceding the revelation of 1978 which extended the priesthood to Mormon men of all races. That revelation was an immense relief to numerous Mormons, whose united concern and questioning about the inequality of the former policy had moved the prophet to seek a revelation on the matter. But why should Mormons of the 1970s have been so concerned when Mormons of the 1920s were not? The reason is that they had been influenced by the growing racial equality in other cultures. Seeing other Americans, white as well as non-white, endorsing racial equality, Mormons gradually became sensitive to its value and became more and more uncomfortable with the former priesthood doctrine. This was civilization at work. The Church, being a conservative society, may change more slowly than some other particular culture and in a differing order and proportion, but it nonetheless changes in rough correspondence to the large, collective changes affecting the totality of the civilized world.

Furthermore, not even the problems of civilization justify Mormons in holding a cynical view of it. Admittedly, some civilized developments, like advances in Olympic skiing techniques or in high fashions of dress, seem trifling and inconsequential. Other developments, like industrialism and environmentalism, are mutually contradictory; although people value the wealth and leisure afforded by the development of industry, they deplore the pollution and environmental disfigurements which accompany it. Another form of civilized development, warfare, is downright destructive. Even certain benign developments create problems: for example, scientific medicine, applied with an admirable humanitarianism over the entire earth, has fostered an ominous growth in population.

Nonetheless, Mormons—along with all other human beings—should desire, work for, and expect the survival of civilization. They should assume that its processes will continue, carrying humanity further in many categories of development. If at present violence, anxiety, and moral uncertainty abound in the world, it is all the more important that we not confuse the substantive achievements of civilization with its disorders and that we confront its problems rationally, trying our best to harmonize contradictory developments, to subordinate lesser values to greater, and to master our destructive energies. Civilization, whatever

its disorder, is what humanity was born to. It implies the fruition and fulfillment of the individual person; it illuminates, rounds out, and justifies mortal experience, and it offers human beings a lifetime odyssey into discovery, growth, and satisfaction.

Those within the Church most aware of the civilized changes going on in the world are the intellectuals. They are instinctively attracted to the expanding edge of civilization, where the old is constantly transformed into the new in science, art, morality, and dozens of other categories. Thus they become agents of civilization, indispensable catalysts who serve an important function. Many writers have used the term *Mormon intellectual,* yet so far as I am aware no one has bothered to define it in detail. I propose the following characteristics. First, Mormon intellectuals are liberal rather than conservative. More tolerant of the innovative and the unusual than most other Mormons, they associate change with a flourishing, fulfilled life. An even more crucial trait is an alert, active, and questioning intelligence. Curious and adventurous in temperament, they develop their mental gifts by exploring the world around them. They are well read, and they keep themselves versed in national and international issues. They prefer art and entertainment of an aesthetic rather than of a popular quality and are likely to be as interested in the form and technique of art as in its content and message. They respect reason and base their convictions upon evidence and logic.

Even if they are not scientists, they accept a scientific view of the world and are interested in the social consequences of science. They interpret the scriptures allegorically rather than literally and try to harmonize them with science. Although they are committed Christians, they are likely to question and analyze many

Church doctrines which their brothers and sisters in the Church accept without question. They do not discount the Holy Spirit as a source of truth but recognize that the *experience* of the Spirit varies from individual to individual and must itself be subject to the arbitration and evaluation of reason. Accepting that the Holy Spirit provides the elemental revelations upon which Mormon theology is based, they may nonetheless doubt that it concerns itself with the trivia of daily living. Intellectuals tend to be well educated, but advanced formal learning alone is not a sure criterion. Such a mind is often found among persons without extensive formal education, as in the case of a self-cultivated businessman, an artistic housewife, and a rancher with a shelffull of philosophy books.

Particularly useful for understanding the impact of this personality type upon the Church is Father Thomas O'Dea's sociological study *The Mormons,* published in 1957. O'Dea devotes a chapter to the internal conflicts and tensions of the Church, among which the most prominent and threatening is the conflict between tradition and education. Through its esteem for education the Church has, O'Dea points out, paradoxically exposed its members to the militant ideas of secular culture. The Mormon intellectual is at the center of this conflict because he is, by O'Dea's implicit definition, an educator—a university professor or an institute or seminary teacher. "As creator and preserver," O'Dea writes, "the intellectual is esteemed; as critic and questioner, he is suspect."[1] In O'Dea's treatment, the role of critic and questioner far outweighs the role of creator and preserver. O'Dea sees the tension raised by intellectuals as potentially destructive to the Church and he thinks of them as unhappy people caught in a state of spiritual estrangement from an organization that,

for emotional reasons, they cannot abandon: "Torn between a loyalty to the Mormon tradition and a commitment to modern thought, affected by both a genuine attachment to their own group and its way of life and the intellectual dispositions of the modern temper, these men find their own Mormonism a great problem to themselves."[2]

O'Dea accurately points out that Mormon intellectuals exert a pressure for changing the Church in terms of a worldly pattern, and he accurately stresses the disequilibrium and tension which this pressure creates. He is unwilling to predict the outcome of the encounter between the Church and secular culture and does not discount the possibility of radical, destructive change. My own view, however, is that this tension is healthy and productive. Certainly it is possible that the worldly changes proposed by intellectuals could prove damaging; if, for example, imported ideas led to an official abandonment of the doctrine of the Restoration, something vital would have departed from Mormonism. But this is not likely. It is more probable that the Church will decide it cannot tolerate the tension raised by its intellectuals and will simply eradicate them through excommunication.

These extremes need not occur. Generally speaking, Mormon intellectuals are neither alienated from the Church nor bent upon its destruction. Implicit among the traits which I attribute to them is a *commitment to,* an *engagement with,* the Church. They constitute a loyal opposition, a body of critics and questioners who desire not to destroy but to improve the Church. Writing articles, preaching sermons, making comments in Sunday School lessons, and conversing with friends, they spread new ideas and suggest new practices. And as intellectuals persist in propounding changes, the

75

Church slowly becomes prepared to accept many of them. The service intellectuals render the Church may be illustrated by a specific consideration of three contemporary issues.

The first issue concerns the age of the earth and the origin of life. Although this matter became an issue in the Church not long after the publication of Darwin's *The Origin of Species* in 1859, it remains unsettled today. The most prominent Mormon position on this issue, which I will call the literalist position, derives from a literal reading of Genesis; it holds God created the earth only a few millennia ago, that he created species in a literal Garden of Eden through distinct acts of creation, and that the first man, Adam, brought death for the first time not only upon humanity but upon all other species as well. The intellectual position is that organic evolution, as understood by modern biology, is God's mode of creation; the earth is therefore ancient and life forms, including humanity, have evolved from earlier, more primitive life forms. This view arises from the need of thoughtful Mormons to harmonize their rational belief with that of the preponderance of other thoughtful people and from their conviction that the theory of evolution does not contradict the essentials of Christianity.

However, if one wishes to throw a pall of shocked silence upon the members of a typical Mormon Sunday School class, one has only to declare a belief in evolution. A great many in the Church agree with the denunciation of evolution made by Joseph Fielding Smith. Elder Smith describes his book, *Man: His Origin and Destiny*, as a refutation of "the most pernicious doctrine ever entering the mind of man: the theory that man evolved from the lower forms of life. For its source we must go beyond the activities and research of mortal man to the author of evil, who has been an enemy of truth from the beginning before the earth was formed."[3]

Although official statements of the Church have often seemed to favor the literalist side of this issue, a surprising number of General Authorities have over the years spoken or written in favor of evolution. These include B. H. Roberts, John A. Widstoe, and David O. McKay. The result is that the Church has officially endorsed neither position. Strictly speaking, a good Mormon may believe in either a recent, instantaneous creation or in an ancient, evolutionary creation.

The inconclusive struggle between the two positions has been well documented in a number of recent essays. Richard Sherlock chronicles a furor which arose in the Church educational system in 1911 when four professors at BYU persisted in openly declaring the harmony between the Gospel and evolution. The dismissal of the professors demonstrated that the Church university was not to be the public forum for such an idea.[4] Sherlock documents another episode involving the refusal of the General Authorities in 1931 to approve the publication of B. H. Roberts's speculative work, *The Truth, The Way, The Life*, which postulated the existence of pre-Adamic men.[5] In an excellent essay tracing the Mormon conflict over evolution from its beginnings, Duane E. Jeffery details another dispute, perhaps less spectacular but equally crucial, which arose among the General Authorities upon the publication in 1954 of *Man: His Origin and Destiny*. Although President McKay did not denounce the book in sermon or in publication, he quietly assured anxious inquirers that Joseph Fielding Smith's work did not represent the official position of the Church.[6]

Unfortunately, the Church seems at the present moment to be edging toward an official endorsement of the literalist view of creation. Ironically, the discovery of DNA—the basic molecule of all living matter—and the resultant new technology of biological engineering make organic evolution more certain than ever. However, a close acquaintance with the facts upon which the theory of evolution is based is absent among even many well educated Mormons because in the crowded curriculum of modern universities they get little exposure to the life sciences. Many Mormons take license for believing evolution to be false in the objective candor with which scientists admit that evolution is a theory—a view accepted for all practical purposes as factual, yet admittedly subject to change should new facts emerge. Speakers in General Conference allude to the literalist interpretation of the creation without the slightest recognition that another interpretation exists, and recent lesson manuals propound it with a total confidence. Similarly, the dictionary published in the new LDS edition of the King James Bible defines the word *death* in a literalist way. The definition reads: "Latter-day revelation teaches that there was no death on this earth for any forms of life before the fall of Adam. Indeed, death entered the world as a direct result of the fall." Such a definition, placed in such a sensitive spot, is indeed alarming, for it comes close to being an official disavowal of the theory of evolution.

The vital function of intellectuals for the present is to influence the Church to maintain its traditional policy of non-alignment. The advantages to the Church of such neutrality are great. For one thing, it can thereby continue to shelter a greater variety of personality types. An official stand against evolution not only would alienate many existing members but would obviate the possibility of converting other thoughtful, science-oriented people. Perhaps even more important, the present policy of tolerance allows the Church to exercise an influence upon the course of scientific civilization. At present, Mormon scientists are accepted members of scientific communities and make notable contributions in many areas. A prominent example at BYU is one of the most energetic and colorful paleontologists in the United States, Professor James A. Jensen, affectionately known as Dinosaur Jim. This indefatigable prober into the fossil record of ancient life has unearthed a new species of giant dinosaur and has clarified the nature of the flying reptile, *Archaeopteryx*.

A different kind of contribution to the scientific world is made by three BYU biologists, James Farmer, William Bradshaw, and Brent Johnson, in an essay where they ponder the moral and theological perplexities of biological engineering. Among the problems they note is the test tube baby. They describe the process by which a physician implants in a woman's uterus only one of a number of her previously extracted ova, all of which have been fertilized externally by her husband's sperm. The authors wonder whether the discarded ova, quickened with life, are to be considered human souls. They also ponder the spiritual and ethical problems of the woman who, unable to carry a fetus in her uterus, rents the uterus of a surrogate mother, into whom the fertilized ovum of the first woman is implanted. These authors end their essay on an optimistic note: "Although the new biology may alter the way in which Mormons think about some ethical problems, it will not fundamentally change the need to live by faith in a world that we do not fully comprehend. The Lord may have placed very few constraints on us in our search for knowledge and understanding. It seems rather that he allows us much freedom in this world.

As a result, science moves inevitably towards synthesis of living things, as it has already achieved the ability to alter species."[7] Although these Mormon biologists raise far more questions than they answer, one can only admire their intelligent, courageous effort to accommodate, rather than to retreat from, an expanding scientific civilization. Their essay, slanted towards Mormons, could as easily have been slanted towards non-Mormons. Because they are respected members of a broad scientific community, they are in a position to inject Latter-day Saint values into the world-wise discussion over the problems of biological engineering. Regardless of their private beliefs concerning evolution, their respectability in the scientific world would be lessened if the Church were to officially denounce the theory of evolution.

A second large issue raised by Mormon intellectuals is the liberalization of sex. Mormons retain an immoderate degree of the old Christian assumption that sexual passion is of itself repugnant to God. As a reminder of the conscious commitment of traditional Christianity to mortification of the flesh, consider a letter from St. Jerome to Laeta, a Roman mother who had consecrated her infant daughter to the life of a nun. It is replete with suggestions for shielding the little girl from a knowledge of her own appetites and desires. Thinking ahead to the time of her maturity, Jerome even warns against her taking baths, which may arouse, he fears, too much sensual awareness in a woman consecrated to virginity: "Such an one should blush and feel overcome at the idea of seeing herself undressed. By vigils and fasts she mortifies her body and brings it into subjection. By a cold chastity she seeks to put out the flame of lust and to quench the hot desires of youth. And by a deliberate squalor she makes haste to spoil her natural good looks. Why, then,

should she add fuel to a sleeping fire by taking baths?"[8] St. Jerome was by no means unique. For centuries, traditional Christianity taught that, although sexual exchange between married partners was legitimate and necessary, those Christians who desired to excel in godliness had to maintain total chastity.

Mormon intellectuals are not likely to have much sympathy with such a repressive attitude, having been influenced by what is appropriately called the sexual revolution. During the past century, there has been in the civilization surrounding Mormondom a remarkable freeing of inhibition and anxiety about sex. The physiological facts of reproduction are widely disseminated, and the human body is more openly displayed. Sexual pleasure has become a widely accepted value, and techniques for arriving at it are abundantly discussed in books and manuals. For many Mormons, the sexual revolution has been a large scale renewal of Sodom and Gomorrah; throughout the world they see a multiplication of X-rated movies, pornographic book stores, uncloseted homosexuality, pre-marital sex, and partner swapping among couples. Such persons, having taken account of the fringe excesses, fail to take account of the fact that sexual liberalization has a legitimate focus in the committed married couple. Intellectuals, on the other hand, are more likely to recognize that fact. For them, the sexual revolution, despite its disorders, is a civilized development toward a more complete fulfillment of the instincts and desires God gave to humanity.

The Church has long taught that sex is sacred rather than inherently evil. Evidence of this appears in *Ensign* articles and in conference sermons which express, along with the usual admonitions against fornication, adultery, homosexuality, and masturbation, the belief that sex is something to be controlled not because God hates it but because it is holy. An enlightened statement of this point of view, one which the Mormon intellectual might readily accept, is Carlfred B. Broderick's essay "Three Philosophies of Sex, Plus One."[9] Broderick considers as equally erroneous the notion that sex is inherently evil and the notion that sex may be indulged in extra-maritally. The correct view, he says, is that sex is sacred and is the center of a happy, successful marriage. The rules against extra-marital sex exist simply because such sexual experience militates against a fulfilling marriage. Broderick does not explicitly endorse a vigorous and passionate sexual exchange between married partners, but his language is so positive that one can at least suppose that he is no advocate of restraint and inhibition.

Unfortunately, there are yet many in the Church who do advocate restraint and inhibition between married partners. Many speakers and writers, impressed by the Apostle Paul's analogy between the body and a temple, interpret the sacredness of sex to mean that it should be cautiously and timorously practiced. The logic of the analogy, one can only suppose, goes thus: just as one does not play basketball in the temple, so one does not engage in sex for mere pleasure. A notable expression of this attitude is Steve Gilliland's essay "Chastity: A Principle of Power." Gilliland's concern is with chastity not for the unwed but for the married. He notes that President Kimball has declared that sex between married partners need not be limited strictly to procreation, but Gilliland goes on to extol and scripturally explicate chastity in such detail that one wonders why he bothered mentioning President Kimball's statement. "The chaste couple," Gilliland writes, "is concerned about strengthening each other. Their feelings of responsibility prevent them from doing anything that would weaken or tempt each other. Modesty in speech and dress are as much for the protection of others and one's partner as for one's self."[10]

It is the role of Mormon intellectuals to dissuade their brother and sister Mormons from such an excessive self-punishing notion of chastity, which is nothing other than an unwitting adumbration of the early Christian hostility toward sexual pleasure. There is nothing admirable about asceticism; it is a primitive and uncivilized attitude. Surely they are wrong who rationalize restraint and inhibition through an analogy between the human body and the temple. A healthy accession of pleasure is not a desecration of the human body. Mormons do not think it a desecration of the body to eat and drink for pleasure as well as for nourishment. A free, frank, and abundant sexual expression is both proper and desirable between husbands and wives—not only for procreation and affection, but for the simple pleasure of passion. Lust is not an appropriate word for any mutually fulfilling exchange between a husband and wife. Passion is God's gift to marriage and needs no apology.

A third large issue raised by Mormon intellectuals is the status of women. The crux of the issue is that venerable civilized value, equality. In the freeing of slaves and serfs, in the raising of the standard of living for the working class, in the extension of suffrage to all adults, we see the steady progress of equality in our civilization. Now women are asking for further equality, it being only natural in an advanced society, where simple physical strength does not determine competency. According to the Victorian novelist George Meredith, one may judge the level of civilization in a society by the degree of equality which it extends to women.[11]

By that standard, Mormon culture is lacking. The Church actively discourages women from seeking a professional parity with men by emphasizing a single important role for them as homemakers. It has, in fact, gained a national notoriety for its militant campaign against the passage of the Equal Rights Amendment, which it sees as a theat to family life. Furthermore, the Church has forthrightly persisted in its policy of denying the priesthood to women. This policy is defended in an abundant literature, of which Rodney Turner's *Woman and the Priesthood*[12] is an egregious example. With a scarcely veiled condescension, this book asserts that God has ordained man to be over woman in spiritual matters. In more conciliatory tones, the General Authorities have tried to mollify women by emphasizing the dignity and beauty of the homemaker and by admonishing women to cultivate their private relationship with God.

Paradoxically, numerous faithful women hold jobs outside the home, some because they are single or widowed, many others because they wish to supplement their husband's income. Nonetheless, the large majority of Mormon women support the Church in its opposition to women's liberation. If asked, most of them would assert that they have no desire to hold the priesthood. Believing their restricted role to be ordained of God, they accept it with good will.

Their acquiescence may change in the near future. A native Mormon protest movement is clearly underway. Its most spectacular proponent has been Sonia Johnson, whose excommunication for publicly opposing the Church's stand on the ERA has brought national exposure to the status of Mormon women. Less sensational but ultimately more potent for change within the Church is a growing number of speakers and writers who,

without defying the Church, relentlessly keep alive the idea that Mormon women suffer from an unjustifiable inequality. Although this loyal protest has been raised chiefly by women, men too are now participating in it. Sensitive, liberal, and aware of trends in the world, these women and men are intellectuals. However, the constituency for whom they speak includes all Mormon women; these intellectuals detect, even in those women who courageously accept their present status, a subliminal sense of deprivation.

One particular deprivation clarified by Mormon intellectuals is the lack of a pattern of feminine deity. An essay by Linda Wilcox documents the history of the Mormon concept of a Heavenly Mother and calls attention to the recent appearance of a worship directed toward her. "At the present," writes Wilcox, "the nineteenth-century generalized image of a female counterpart to a literal male Father God is receiving increased attention and expansion and is becoming more personalized and individualized."[13] Wilcox's low-keyed, objective historical study corroborates what many people already know from informal conversations: many Church members, women and men alike, are addressing prayers to the Heavenly Mother and believe themselves to have received a response from her. Though lacking in polemic intent, this essay reminds us that behind this new form of worship, particularly among women, is the need for an enhanced esteem for femininity. Without question, many Mormon women have hitherto been unable to visualize themselves as complete religious persons because the traditional Christian image of deity is so overwhelmingly masculine.

Another deprivation to which intellectuals are calling attention is the denial to women of the priesthood. This denial is conspicuous because, without exception, worthy males are ordained at age twelve and remain in the priesthood all their lives. Their participation in the priesthood is understood by all to be a high privilege. Women may seek inspiration for the conduct of their private lives and may engage in Church callings, but they do not engage in the administrative work of the Church nor in the performance of most of its rituals. To a growing number of sensitive Mormons, this seems anomalous, for in the world at large women are proving successful in executive and professional positions. It is evident that Mormon women possess the spiritual and administrative competence to function in the priesthood. All that lacks is permission.

This prohibition is all the more difficult to bear as women become aware, through recent historical writing, that they have lost former rights to the exercise of spiritual gifts. Mormons reading the journals of their pioneer grandmothers are likely to be aware that women in the nineteenth century practiced the gifts of the Spirit—attending prayer circles, anointing with oil, healing the sick, and receiving revelation in behalf of others—much more abundantly than do their granddaughters in the twentieth century. The loss of the right to exercise these gifts is poignantly traced in Linda King Newell's essay, "A Gift Given, A Gift Taken." For example, Newell notes 1946 as the termination of the right of women to anoint and administer to sick sisters; the "official death knell" came in the form of a letter from Joseph Fielding Smith who asserted that "it is far better for us to follow the plan the Lord has given us and send for the Elders of the Church to come and administer to the sick and afflicted."[14] The simple historical facts are astonishing, and Newell sets them forth in language which is touched, not by anger or protest, but by delicate grief.

The most consequential question now before the Church is whether women will be permitted to hold the priesthood. It is a question so fraught with misgivings and perturbations that only very recently has it been openly aired. A decade ago, a woman seemed bold if she simply declared her independence from the priesthood in spiritual matters relating strictly to herself. For example, in a 1971 essay, Cheryll Lynn May indicates that the priesthood is only a supplement to her private efforts to approach God: "For me, the central core of the Gospel is the individual personal relationship between God and man. In most cases, priesthood authority acts to promote and enrich this relationship; when it does not, it must, for me, take second place."[15]

Indicative of a new frankness in the 1980s is an essay by Anthony A. Hutchinson, "Women and Ordination: Introduction to the Biblical Context." Hutchinson examines the primitive Christian church and fails to find there a precedent forbidding the priesthood to women. "In terms of the New Testament evidence, there is no reason to deny ordination to women; there are, instead, compelling reasons to recommend it."[16] Even more assertive is a personal essay in which Laurel Thatcher Ulrich traces her own evolution as a Mormon intellectual. Beset by the fear that a woman should not exert herself as a writer and thinker, she has nonetheless grown into a constructive religious critic. Of particular interest is her obvious confidence in the propriety of the priesthood for women:

For me, learning to question the present structure of the priesthood has been a positive as well as a negative experience. With feelings of anger and betrayal has come a new sense of responsibility; with recognition of discrimination has come renewed conviction of the essential message of the gospel of Jesus Christ. I am convinced that an effective challenge to male dominance can only be built upon "principles of righteousness." Trusting the spirit of the priesthood in the Church,

81

Mormon women must recognize the potential for priesthood in themselves.[17]

What of the future? I predict that the Church will extend to women a larger participation in spiritual things. Ultimately, that participation will include the priesthood. I believe this will happen because of the civilizing process. Part of that process involves Mormon intellectuals, who have been influenced by the extension of equality to women in the world at large. They discuss, question, challenge, and in general keep the issue of equality alive. That is how the more important part of the civilizing process can work. As other Mormons are forced to think about the status of women, the great civilized value of equality works in their hearts. Implying the absolute worth and dignity of individuals, equality requires that no person or class of persons be arbitrarily precluded from the rights and privileges that make life worthwhile. Perhaps it will eventually touch the hearts of so many Mormons that the prophet will inquire of God. Perhaps then, when the members of the Church are ready to accept women in the priesthood, they will discover that God also is ready.

Mormon intellectuals do not lead an enviable life. Often they sense keenly the distance between themselves and the rest of the Church. Isolated from one another, they may suffer guilt and doubt; at times they may well wonder whether their evolving values, seemingly unpalatable to other Mormons, are not perverse or insane. For this reason, it is important that they form their own communities, both for comfort and for enhancing their effectiveness as agents of change. They should gather as friends in discussion groups and readings. They should join professional and cultural organizations. Above all, they should maintain *voices*. Independent presses, liberal journals and magazines, symposiums and conferences are all vital. *Sunstone, Dialogue, Exponent II* and similar publications are crucial. It does not matter that the analysis and criticism offered through their pages seem to go unnoticed. These publications give a concrete, durable form to expanding ideas, which enter thousands of homes and hundreds of libraries. Printed ideas are potent for change; at unexpected moments they come alive and declare the future.

Above all, intellectuals should not apologize but take pride in their contribution to the Church they love and wish to see flourish. In particular, they may be proud of their part in the process by which the Church is growing into an international religion. A Church that takes seriously its duty to be a religion for all nations, for all classes, temperaments, and mentalities, cannot fail to change. It must further its own perfection by keeping pace with the revolving civilization around it.

Notes

1. Thomas F. O'Dea, *The Mormons* (Chicago: The University of Chicago Press, 1957), 224.
2. Ibid., 236.
3. Joseph Fielding Smith, *Man: His Origin and Destiny* (Salt Lake City: Deseret Book Co., 1954), 133.
4. Richard Sherlock, "Campus in Crisis: BYU, 1911," *Sunstone* 4 (January-February 1979):10-16.
5. Richard Sherlock, "'We Can See No Advantage to a Continuation of the Discussion': The Roberts/Smith/Talmage Affair," *Dialogue* 13 (Fall 1980):63:78.
6. Duane E. Jeffery, "Seers, Saints and Evolution: The Uncomfortable Interface," *Dialogue* 8 (1973):41-75.
7. James L. Farmer, William S. Bradshaw, and F. Brent Johnson, "The New Biology and

Mormon Theology," *Dialogue* 12 (Winter 1979):75.

8. St. Jerome, "Letter CVII (To Laeta)," *The Intellectual Tradition of the West*, I, eds. Morton Donner, Kenneth E. Eble, and Robert E. Helbling (Glenview, Ill.: Scott, Foresman and Co., 1967), 260.

9. Carlfred B. Broderick, "Three Philosophies of Sex, Plus One," *Dialogue* 2 (Autumn 1967):97-106.

10. Steve Gilliland, "Chastity: A Principle of Power," *Ensign* (June 1980):18.

11. George Meredith, *An Essay on Comedy and the Uses of the Comic Spirit*, ed. Lane Cooper (Ithaca: Cornell University Press, 1956), 118-119; first published, 1877.

12. Rodney Turner, *Woman and the Priesthood* (Salt Lake City: Deseret Book Co., 1972).

13. Linda Wilcox, "The Mormon Concept of a Mother in Heaven," *Sunstone* 6 (September-October 1981):15.

14. Linda King Newell, "A Gift Given, A Gift Taken: Washing, Anointing, and Blessing the Sick Among Mormon Women," *Sunstone* 6 (September-October 1981):23.

15. Cheryll Lynn May, *Dialogue* 6 (Summer 1971):52.

16. Anthony A. Hutchinson, "Women and Ordination: Introduction to the Biblical Context," *Dialogue* 14 (Winter 1981):71.

17. Laurel Thatcher Ulrich, "The Pink Dialogue and Beyond," *Dialogue* 14 (Winter):38.

II
PRIESTHOOD

PRIESTHOOD

Editor's Note:

Alan D. Tyree, Phi Beta Kappa scholar, B.A. (music and education), is a member of the First Presidency of the Reorganized Church of Jesus Christ of Latter Day Saints, Independence, Missouri. "Divine Calling in Human History" was delivered as the 1984 W. Wallace Smith Lecture at Park College.

Professor Velma Ruch, Ph.D. (English literature), Lamoni, Iowa, delivered her essay at Graceland College in Lamoni on April 18, 1985, as part of the lecture series jointly sponsored by the John Whitmer Historical Association and the History Department of the college in 1984–85.

L. Madelon Brunson, M.A. (history), is archivist for the Reorganized church at its World Headquarters in Independence, Missouri. Her essay is reprinted from *Dialogue: A Journal of Mormon Thought,* vol. 17, number 3 (Autumn, 1984).

DIVINE CALLING IN HUMAN HISTORY

Alan D. Tyree

At the present day in the history of the Reorganized Church of Jesus Christ of Latter Day Saints, there are no questions more pressing than the questions which relate to priesthood. What should be the place of priesthood in the church's servanthood? Do women have any role in priesthood functions and structures? These and similar questions are being discussed and debated in virtually every congregation in North America, and in many other places throughout the world.

This paper will not attempt to answer these questions, but it is my hope that some data and historical perspectives offered will be of some use to the leaders and members of the church as they wrestle with such questions and their implications. I will first briefly touch on some of the philosophical aspects of the nature of priesthood. Is it eternal, existing in its essence in God, apart from its human expression, only intermittently being granted by God to deserving and qualified men? Or is priesthood's essence only existent in human history, in the particular individuals who carry its functions in the context of culture? Subsequently, I will review superficially the history of priesthood in the Old Testament and New Testament periods, then offer a review of some historical perceptions from the recent past in the Reorganized church.

I must acknowledge my indebtedness to Paul Edwards, Wayne Ham, Peter Judd, and Geoffrey Spencer for their major contributions to this paper in the form of essential research. Without their expertise in reviewing the necessary literature, this paper could not have been prepared. However, at the same moment I laud their valuable assistance, I free them from responsibility for the actual contents of this presentation, lest I find myself in the position of Jonah's whale in the apocryphal account of the story. You will recall that somewhere near Nineveh, the beached whale "barfed" Jonah out on the sand. The whale was still green around the gills (never mind that mammals don't have gills), and Jonah himself was somewhat the worse for wear due to the whale's gastric juices. In an Oliver Hardy style, Jonah says to the whale: "We wouldn't be in this fine mess if you had only kept your big mouth shut!" Herewith I grant therefore my valued colleagues complete dissolution of marriage to this text, no matter how closely or distantly it may seem to be related to their excellent research.

I

As far as the Judeo-Christian tradition is concerned, from the earliest times when humanity has experienced a sense of the Divine moving and acting in our world, Deity has elicited a response of awe and an awareness of mystery. There has always been the feeling that the Deity *surprised* humans by self-disclosure or by some display of divine power—it was not as if someone consciously set about to create God, or through personal effort invented a means to discover God. Jews and Christians alike testify that it was always the Divine which apprehended the human rather than the human apprehending the Divine.

With that divine self-disclosure came an awareness on the part of the recipients of revelation that they were somehow *favored* to have this new correspondence with God. Whether it was generally recognized by their tribe or family or village or culture, or whether no one else at all was aware of it, the individual *knew* that God had intervened in a way that was uncommon. They thus became a chosen person or people, called out from the ordinary stream of their peers. This concept of vocation, of calling, was and is implicit in any apperception of the Divine.

Priesthood is a natural result of human society's attempts to socialize and institutionalize this apperception. Priesthood developed as a means of dealing with the varieties of religious experiences operating subjectively among a people, and dealing with it in an organized way that authenticated divine experience, and authorized its intermediaries.

Priesthood as a concept is inextricably related with the human experiences of the Divine, and, in the minds of the believers, it partakes of some of the same attributes as the Deity possesses. Thus to perceive a Deity which is seen as eternal, absolute, and universal often gives rise to a perception of a priesthood which is eternal, absolute, and universal. God's intermediary is perceived by the common folk to possess some of God's attributes. This is so because of the *way* in which Deity breaks into one's awareness, causing at one and the same time (1) an understanding of some sort about the nature of God, and (2) an awareness of one's unique favor in having been chosen as an intermediary for this experience and for its future consequences.

It makes little difference that an anthro-pologist may be able to document the scientific influences, both physical and psychological, which may have had a part in creating the experience or illusion of an experience. The supreme fact is that the person experienced as real whatever the person *thinks* he or she experienced.

Simply stated, God is perceived as *acting* in the human world, whereas humans *react* to the divine initiative. When that action is felt personally, one feels personally favored and called by God. This sense of calling is analogous to a perception of the Divine because of the way in which it arises from experience with God. Some of the qualities of holiness thought to exist in the prophecy also are thought to dwell in the prophet. This leads naturally to the assumption that the qualities of priority and universality which inhere in God or God's will also inhere in the "favoredness" of priesthood as a key of access to God. Thus priesthood may be thought to be eternal, preexistent, absolute and universal, because God is so perceived, and priesthood is conceived as our closest tie to God.

However, it is appropriate for us to ask if we are warranted in holding such perceptions. Does such a concept of priesthood square with all else that we know about reality, and about Deity? From another perspective, is priesthood categorically different from all other human experiences and categories, dwelling in an ethereal realm that only occasionally catches up the human into a mystical relationship with the Divine? Or is priesthood a category of human experience, set apart from all others, perhaps, but nonetheless fully integrated into the totality of life? Is priesthood what priesthood does, functionally (nominalism)? Or is priesthood what priesthood is conceived to be (realism)?

Joseph Smith, Jr., left some scriptural indications which may be interpreted to suggest that we are warranted in holding a belief in a priesthood which exists as universal essence, eternal and absolute, and therefore existing independent of human manifestations of priesthood. In the Inspired Version, Hebrews 7:3 reads ". . . which order [of priesthood] was without father, without mother, without descent, having neither beginning of days nor end of life. And all those who are ordained unto this priesthood . . . [abide] a priest continually." A passage in the Doctrine and Covenants (Independence, Missouri: Herald House, 1983), Section 83:2g and 3a also reads "which priesthood continueth in the church of God in all generations, and is withoiut beginning of days or end of years . . . which priesthood also continueth and abideth forever."

But may it not be that the "order of priesthood" exists without father, mother, and descent, and without beginning or ending, due to the fact that it does not at all exist independent of the particular priests who collectively comprise priesthood? The priests obviously do have father and mother and descent and do have a beginning and an ending. But the sum of them does equal more than an adding of finite persons together with other finite persons, for they may succeed one another, providing priesthood with a quality of transcendence. Priesthood may have patterns of succession that exceed finitude, permitting a continuity of succession so that the priesthood may "continue and abide forever" as long as humans exist to carry the lineage. Furthermore, believing in eternal life for humans also establishes a continuity of priesthood in the priests who partake of eternal life, thus imparting eternal qualities to priesthood itself through the priests who are bearers both of eternal life and priesthood.

Moreover, if it is held that priesthood is "eternal," then it may also be argued that it is so by virtue of its *particularity*, not its universality, because its particularity is in the embodiment of priesthood in individual men. Joseph Smith also brought to the church the scripture which says that "the elements are eternal" (Doctrine and Covenants 90:5). Thomas Aquinas said that if universals exist in things as their essence, then things are made individual by their matter. That is, if the universal idea of priesthood exists in individual members of priesthood as their essence, then the priesthood members are made particular manifestations of universal priesthood by virtue of their material nature. However, Joseph Smith, Jr.'s statement that "the elements are eternal" would suggest the contrary, that due to the individual priest participating in human life and therefore partaking of physical and material existence, the elements of matter, being eternal, foresee an eternal quality to the individual's priesthood. Thus priesthood's particularity is cause for its universality and eternal qualities.

Inasmuch as priesthood is described by Joseph Smith, Jr., in several scriptures as being "without father or mother," it may be presumed that he is suggesting that priesthood is universal, and that individuals may share temporarily in the essence of the universal as they are divinely called and ordained. They are born of father and mother, but priesthood is not, and continues without them. Yet when taken in the context of Joseph Smith's other scriptural statements, such as "the elements are eternal," we are exposed to a different facet of his thinking. If priesthood is "without father or mother, beginning or ending," does it necessarily follow that it is *in itself* preexistent, eternal, and universal? It might rather be that priesthood is without beginning or ending due to it always and only existing in humans. If its essence can only be found in the particular then it is as eternal as the particular is. Joseph Smith, Jr., said that not only does the human spirit continue after death, but that the elements comprising the material universe (hence the human embodiment) are also eternal. Thus if humans are eternal, and if priesthood is found only in humans, then it may be that priesthood continues because of its expression in individual humans. Particularity and nominalism are as logical an interpretation for Joseph Smith's scriptural expressions as may be realism and universalism.

There are some compelling reasons why it is difficult for us to accept the idea of priesthood existing absolutely or universally, independent from any particular expression. First, the concept of universals and absolutes seems to have had its origin in Greek thought, not in Judeo-Christian developments. This requires us to look to a cultural rather than revealed source for even the concept of the universal/absolute itself.

Second, the evolution of priesthood historically has been related pragmatically to circumstances of culture and exigency. This will be explored in some detail later in this paper, documenting the impact of cultural considerations on the evolution of priesthood from Old Testament and New Testament times, and from the more recent history of the Restoration movement.

Third, we must take into consideration that the authoritarian churches which espouse a polity grounded in theism and operating through a priesthood hierarchy (such as the Catholic, Orthodox, and Mormon churches) are dependent on the universal view for support to much of their theology, for example, doctrines of the fall, sin, salvation, moral law, the church, etc.[1] Although it may not be necessarily so, in practice it appears that most (or perhaps all) such churches wed government by the clergy with a universalistic or realistic view of priesthood. It becomes questionable, therefore, whether a church which identifies itself as a "theocratic democracy," as does the RLDS church, can accept a universalistic position and remain a balanced theocratic democracy, because it may bring in its train a polity which is more theistic (that is God and priesthood directed) and less democratic (direction by the people) than the church perceives itself to be.

The weight of the evidence seems to require us to look at priesthood as being particular, rooted in human history, evolving in human culture, serving divine and universal purposes (as best these may be perceived) but within a context of human society. For Latter Day Saints, it is the bringing together of the divine intent into the affairs of the human social order for the redemption of society, which is "the cause of Zion" or the kingdom of God on earth. For our faith to be consistent, this suggests a nominalistic view of priesthood as existing in the particular individuals who are called to be priests.

II

In ancient times, priesthood was not necessary for the performance of sacrificial functions. Although sacrifice was an important form of worship, anyone could offer sacrifices. Not only is this the viewpoint of scholars of Old Testament and Hebrew history, it also appears that Joseph Smith, Jr.'s Inspired Version of the scriptures supports this point of view. In Genesis 4:4-10, Adam's first sacrificial offerings appear to have been made early in his life experience prior to the development of priesthood. Further support to this understanding appears in the insight which Joseph Smith brought in Doctrine and Covenants 104:18-28, which indicates that priesthood was instituted sometime during Adam's extraordinarily long lifetime, spanning more than nine centuries. However, there appears no suggestion either in Genesis or the Doctrine and Covenants that priesthood was necessary for the offering of sacrifice during the earliest times.

Originally, there was no requirement that Levites or priests or a special family or tribe should provide for this function. These requirements came later. When priesthood appeared as a functioning authority, it came into the context of a society which was already patriarchal. Consequently, priesthood originally was conferred only on males. The earliest forms of priesthood had to do more with caring for and guarding the sanctuary and its appurtenances (after they had been related to the worship of the people), and for consulting the prophetic oracle. The Urim and Thummim, along with the Ephod, were used as a means of consulting the oracle for answers that would establish right from wrong, yes from no, true from false, guilty from not guilty. Thus, criminal cases were appealed to the priest for decision as being "brought before God," inasmuch as the priest could consult the oracle, the Urim and Thummim.

Priesthood began to be inherited and passed from generation to generation during this same early period when a chief function was to consult the oracle. Perhaps this had to do with the necessity of learning the art of using and interpreting the Urim and Thummim, and thus it naturally involved passing on a skill from father to son. In any event, early established priesthoods are noted historically at the sanctuaries of Shiloh and Dan during the time of the Judges. But apparently they did not serve sacrificial functions. Continuing down through this period (the fourteenth through the twelfth centuries B.C.), it appears that all participants in the covenant had the privilege and responsibility of offering sacrifice.

During the time of the Monarchy (from the eleventh to the seventh century B.C.), the priests continued to use the Urim and Thummim (Deuteronomy 33:8), served the important function of preserving the faith, traditions, and teachings of the nation (Deuteronomy 33:9-10), served as criminal and civil judges (Deuteronomy 17:8-11, 21:5), and began to serve as officiants in offering sacrifices on behalf of the people.

By the eighth century B.C., although the judicial functions were continuing, there was little mention of the prophetic role being integral with the priestly role. Instead, separate isolated individuals arose as prophets. In time, the use of the Urim and Thummim disappeared altogether. Now the greatest emphasis in the function of priesthood was on the ritualistic aspects of their acts, with great attention to purity requirements and to isolation of the sacred from the profane. (See chapter 44 of Ezekiel.) By this time, the role of the priest as officiant in the sacrifices was well established, and the teaching of tradition was equally emphasized. Indeed, it begins to appear that their ritual functions, not their judicial functions, were the focus of many regulations governing the priests. With the development of the "priestly code" and the formation of the priesthood as a holy order (see Numbers 16:1-5, 18:7 and Leviticus 21:6-8), ritualism seems to have preoccupied the attention of the ministers. Only the priests could now serve at the altar and guard the sanctity of the sanctuary. Furthermore, trespass of the sanctuary carried the penalty of death. Many prescriptions and proscriptions now governed the daily activities of the Levites and priests.

In Chronicles, the division of the priests into twenty-four classes is described. This was necessary because of the proliferation of their numbers. Apparently there was a popular saying at the time in Jerusalem that there were as many priests and Levites in the Temple as there were stones in its walls. Estimates of their numbers reached as high as 20,000. With growth in numbers and with the evolution of time, political aspects of their condition became apparent. Discrimination occurred on the basis of one's tribe, particular family, temple-centered or dispersed service, service in high places, et cetera. This was particularly critical at the time of Ezekiel, when he declared that the priesthood was henceforth to be reserved for the descendants of Zadok. In spite of this, however, the descendants of Ithamar exerted enough political influence to maintain their right to officiate as well. (See I Chronicles 24:1-6 and Driver,[2] page 154-155.) From time to time, the priestly environment was highly politicized.

Further evolution of the functions of the priesthood came to include the blowing of the trumpets (to signal the alarm of war or at the time of the new moon), but it also eventually developed into a separate class whose function was to provide music at the temple.

Given all of the foregoing, it is interesting to note the evolution of service functions in the sacramental office. Beginning with the right and responsibility to offer sacrifice resting upon all the faithful, changes gradually were incorporated which not only limited who might have the right and authority to so function, but also where such sacrifices should occur, and with what attention to purity they should offer sacrifice. We also note that the prophetic function, which originally inhered in the priests, eventually evolved into a separate class of ministers, whose designation was more mystical than formal, and whose function often seemed to be to reform the excesses of the priests.

These changes occurred as a result of growing sociological complexity, and were in response to the thrust of the perceived divine will in the context of human history. With greater numbers of priests, it became necessary to find something distinctive for them to do, permitting specialization and prerequisite qualifications to multiply.

III

With the advent of Christ, new concepts of the roles of leaders were both taught and exemplified. Whereas in the traditional Hebrew pattern, the leaders were priests of a particular lineage who were chosen to serve as intermediaries between God and humanity, now *all* were called to serve as ministers to one another in Jesus' stead. This universal call to membership in the body of Christ was in contrast to the patriarchal society in which the church appeared, and at variance as well with the usual norms of Roman social organization.

Jesus' lifestyle was contagious. It was the role of a self-sacrificing servant, and others were not only *called* to emulate him, they *wanted* to. There is, therefore, a major distinction between the leadership roles found in the Old Testament, of a priesthood which stood between God and humanity, and the New Testament image of leaders who were from among the people and who stood with them. It has been historically a problem for Christian churches to determine which of these two traditions they would prefer to institutionalize in their own experience, with the Catholic, Orthodox, and Mormon positions appearing primarily to be oriented toward the Old Testament intermediary model for priesthood, and the New Testament servant role being the preferred model for much of Protestantism.

In addition, the New Testament church saw priesthood develop from the traditional Old Testament model into altogether new images and functions for ministry.[3] This ministry originally was performed without priesthood office by all members of the body, but by the time of the later New Testament writers, already there were traces of the institutionalization of some functions into priesthood office. To acknowledge the truth of the situation, we need only to be aware that the very names used to identify the priesthood roles were themselves *functionally descriptive.* Whereas they have been adapted into English in most cases rather than translated, we may simply return to the original Greek to learn that they are less of the nature of *offices,* and more appropriately *functions.* For example, the term *deacon* comes from the Greek word *diak'onos* which means *servant.* The term *teacher* (*didas'kalos*) has been translated into English, and therefore denotes one who serves the function of teaching.

The English word *priest* in fact comes from the Greek word *presbu'teros,* from which we get the word *presbytery* and which is translated *elder* in English. As a result, in the Restoration movement there is confusion of the terms *priest* and *elder* by virtue of their translation from the same Greek word into the English language. The word used to denote the priest who served in the Jewish temple is the Greek word *hiereus',* which literally means an officiant of the temple. The term *bishop* comes from the Greek word *epis'kopos,* which means *overseer,* and thus the New Testament bishops were those who had the oversight of the congregations of the church. The term *apostle* comes from the word *apos'tolos,* which means *messenger,* or "those who are sent." The term *evangelist* comes from the word *euanggelistes',* which denotes one who shares the gospel. The term *prophet* comes from the word *prophe'tes,* which means one who tells forth the word of God. It, therefore, could appropriately be translated in English to mean either one who foretells or one who preaches.

In each case, these words are descriptive of the roles and functions they were to serve. Consequently, due to the increased amplitude of ministry occasioned by the Christian gospel outside of the temple or synagogue, most of these are functions which were not thought of or foreseen in the traditional Jewish religion. We ought not, therefore, to be surprised that there is little office-related resemblance between the Old Testament priesthood and New Testament ministries. After all, the call of the Christ was to enter into relationships of ministry to others which had not been a part of the experience of Judaism. Much that Jesus represented was disjunctive with their history and tradition and current practices. He frequently said, "Ye have heard it said of old . . . but I say unto you . . ." His gospel was a new departure, and the Good News was to be carried by persons of different authority to serve in different functions.

Because the functions were to be served for the sake of people in the midst of life as they lived it, these priesthood innovations were directly related to the culture and lifestyle of the people. In the New Testament, we do not see a concept of priesthood which came out of eternity or even as a legacy from Judaism and which seemed to have little relevance to life as it was lived by the current generation. On the contrary, although it may have had its origin in the eternal love of an eternal God who holds forth the promise of eternal life for humanity, nevertheless the actual functioning of the priesthood, and consequently its structures, were directly related to the salvation process for people in the midst of human life.

It is interesting to note that the equality which was announced in Jesus' gospel had implications for differences of national origin, race, sex, and slavery. The New Testament clearly identified the Gentile as well as the Jew for calling to priesthood service. The slave as well as the free was to be permitted to serve, though subject to permission by the slave's master.[4] It is also noteworthy that the New Testament writers used the same Greek word (only modified by the feminine ending) as a label for the functional service of women who served as prophetesses (*prophe'tis*), and they included female elders (*presbu'tera*) as a regular part of the body of the saints.[5]

However, while the early New Testament church was open, spirit-directed, and led by gifted people who freely used their giftedness without restrictions of polity and hierarchy, the post-apostolic church soon had to deal with the problem of a growing institution. False doctrines and their proponents were requiring some decisive action by administrators. Oppression from opposing cultures and governments created a necessity for solidarity in well-integrated congregations. The need for stability, security, and permanence virtually forced the church to move into more structured models, with authority figures empowered to act for the good of the body.

Quite naturally, the organizational models chosen were Old Testament ones, modified with elements from the Greco-Roman world. Once again, the ability of the common people to have direct access to Deity in forms of worship became subordinate to the intermediary of a clergy. Once again, the officers of the religion began to function as rulers, judges, and mediators of the Word. Eventually, they held virtually all the keys of access to Divinity. Thus the hierarchy of the church could be appropriately compared with the Jewish hierarchy, as Clement of Rome did. By the second century, the ecclesiastical hierarchy was established, and a sharp line of delineation between the laity and the clergy was apparent. Increasingly the ministers were seen as standing in the stead of Christ, and as God's representative on earth. These symbols and images reinforced the earlier male dominance already present in Judaism, and which was further supported by the militant Roman image of Christianity conquering the world in the sign of the cross.

The concept that "ye are all one in Christ Jesus—there is neither Jew nor Greek, there is neither bond nor free, there is neither male nor female" (Galatians 3:28) had now given way to the practice that "you are in fact divided into the clergy and the laity, the leaders and the followers, the powerful and the powerless"—no matter how necessary nor how culturally determined the division was. Once again, we see the people of God, so soon after the freshness of their immediate revelatory experience with the Christ, adapting the institutional church and its structures to the exigencies of life in the real world confronting them, and entering into the give-and-take of dialogue with God, with one another, and with the world.

To see priesthood in this light of Old and New Testament history frees us to examine the question of who may hold priesthood in the light of cultural considerations. This had been the historical experience of the church. Joseph Smith III, in bringing spiritual guidance to the church on the question of the ordination of black men, did not hesitate to place it in the context of the American Civil War and its aftermath. The attitudes of people and the laws of the land had a direct bearing on the content of the message and thus on the availability of priesthood to some categories of man and the effective scope of their ministry. The document said: "Be not hasty in ordaining men of the Negro race to offices in my church, for verily I say unto you, All are not acceptable unto me as servants. . . and *there are some who are chosen instruments to be ministers to their own race*. [italics mine]. Be ye content, I the Lord have spoken it" (Doctrine and

Covenants 116:4). The view of priesthood shown here is not of some universal essence which may be universally applied, but rather an opportunity and privilege which is extended to some who are favored with divine call, to serve the purposes of God in the current historical situation, and in light of the many crosscurrents within the social order.

Some blacks were to be called, not to partake of the essence of priesthood in offering ministry to all persons because they were possessors of an authoritative, divine, universal priesthood, but rather to share a functional, ministerial role within a limited population drawn from their own racial type. Were blacks to have access to the priesthood? Yes, but. . . . And with that "but," all of the possibilities of interpretation and application and accommodation came into play. Priesthood does not exist in an idealistic vacuum. It is interrelated with society in culture. Priesthood is not to be applied universally; it is contingent on many factors, not the least of which is the experience of the earthly, human church with the divine revelation. For, as Joseph Smith III also said in revelatory instruction to the church, "All are called *according to the gifts of God* [italics mine] unto them" (Doctrine and Covenants 119:8). Factors of giftedness, divine call, cultural approbation, personal choice, the general support of the people who are to be recipients of the ministry—all of these and many other factors have a direct bearing on priesthood and its particularity.

In résumé, we observe these things about the history of God's action toward humans through priesthood:

1. God takes the initiative in revelation.
2. Humans react to God's initiative.
3. A part of that reaction is to feel favored, to experience a call.
4. Resulting from God's initiative in

such a call, elaborations of priestly function began to develop early in Hebrew history.
5. The earliest functions were to consult the oracle, thus a prophetic function, as an addition to the primary function of maintaining the faith and traditions.
6. The function as officiants in sacrificial offerings became identified with priesthood after having originally been a non-priesthood responsibility. A particular segment of the population was identified for priesthood call.
7. Ritual became more important after the priesthood became primarily responsible for sacrificial offering. Ritual purity was rigorously required.
8. Priesthood practices evolved culturally in differentiation and proliferation of function on an arithmetic progression with increasing priesthood population and complexity of the social order.
9. The cultural context is clearly intertwined with priesthood roles, functions, and offices in the history of Old Testament Judaism.
10. The New Testament offers a continuation of the principle of cultural effect on priesthood. Christianity emerged within a Jewish culture, under Roman domination, in a patriarchal society.
11. The impact of the new revelation in Jesus Christ and the relatedness of his ministry (and thus the church's) with culture resulted in a new differentiation and proliferation of ministerial roles.
12. In a corollary way, the traditional Jewish church hierarchy was deemphasized and virtually ignored by the New Testament church.
13. The roles in the New Testament

church structures were named and functionally described by their name in the stream of culture.

14. As had been observed in early Hebrew tradition, access to priesthood was no longer limited to a chosen family, tribe, or nation.

15. Priesthood was not confined to those who were qualified by a rigorous process of ritual purification.

16. The opportunity to serve was not limited by race, sex, age, slavery, etc.

17. Inasmuch as priesthood roles were originally only identified by function and not clearly delineated as offices in the New Testament church, we are left with a linguistic puzzle to know if the female prophets and elders were also functionally employed (and ordained) in a ministerial context as were the ordained male counterparts.

18. The post-apostolic church evolved with institutional development similar to that which evolved in Judaism, from a general, open call and responsibility placed on all, to a restricted, self-regulated, authoritarian clergy.

19. In Christianity as in Judaism, institutional religion found itself in dialogue with God and with culture.

20. In the Restoration movement, scriptures which at first may be thought to suggest a universalistic view of priesthood on closer scrutiny seem to support nominalism and particularity.

21. This is true on a philosophical basis in light of the views of Joseph Smith, Jr., on the continuity of life and the conservation of matter and life beyond the grave.

22. It is also observed in Joseph Smith III's application of nominalistic views in regard to the calling of blacks to priesthood responsibility.

23. He reaffirmed in modern times that "all are called," and that their God-given gifts are to be respected in the scope of their ministry.

What may we project from such a review of history? Does it suggest a nominalistic approach in considering the call of women to priesthood in our day? What significance does it have when we view the many cultural differences present in the various world missions of the modern Restoration church? Is priesthood so particular that some may be called to function according to giftedness which may be appropriate only to their own cultural context? If so, what are the implications for priesthood authority within a world church? If priesthood is particular, what are the implications for an individual who becomes inactive in all priestly roles and functions? Does the injunction that "all are called according to the gifts of God unto them" suggest a calling for all who are willing to respond to God's call? Does it also suggest an accountability for either their use or disuse of the gifts of God to them? If so, how are they to be held accountable?

Or, to rephrase all these questions in one: Is the Restoration church of today shackled to an interpretation of priesthood that is found only in the past histories of God's relations with humanity? Or does the dialogue between God, the church, and the world continue?

Only the church of today, blessed with revelatory insight from God, can continue the struggle to resolve these and similar questions.

Notes

1. All are universally condemned under the one man's fall; all are sinners; all are saved through Christ's atonement; all are subject to a universal moral law; Christ established one universal church; etc.

2. S. R. Driver, *An Introduction to the Literature of the Old Testament* (New York: Merriam Books. 1960), 154-155.

3. Although the writer of the letter to the Hebrews seems to develop bridges between the Old Testament priesthood and New Testament ministerial roles and functions, it is clearly in the context of a major departure from the established Jewish forms and functions of priesthood.

4. Ephesians 6:5-9; Colossians 3:22-23; Titus 2:9-10; I Peter 2:18-21.

5. Luke 2:36; I Timothy 5:1-2. There is a linguistic problem with regard to *presbu'teros/presbu'tera*, in that the same word is used both in its masculine and feminine forms. It could always be translated to mean *elderly man* and *elderly woman*, or *male elders* and *female elders*, or according to context occasionally one way and then the other. However, the last alternative is ours only if it was so currently used in the cultural context of the new church. If one were to suppose that the male term *elders* usually or always meant a priesthood office, then we are left with a dilemma of knowing how to interpret the female form of the noun.

The deaconesses were also known in the New Testament church, with corroborating historical reference in the letter of Pliny to Trajan, A.D. 109. From this early tradition, deaconesses have continued in the Greek Orthodox church down to the present day. Although the term *deaconess* is used in Canon 19 of the Nicene Council (A.D. 325), and by the Archbishop of York (732-766), and by the Bishop of Exeter (1050-1072), the consecrated office of deaconess did not survive in the Roman church, and hence was generally lost to early Protestantism.

We have another puzzle left to us by the New Testament writers and translators: Phoebe is referred to as *servant* in Romans 16:1. However, the masculine form of the word is used: *diak'onos*. Since the same word is also translated *deacon* and *minister* in other places in the New Testament, we would be just as warranted in translating this passage to read *deaconess* as some translators have done. It is the masculine form of the word which is most puzzling, for whether "servant," "minister," or "deacon," the feminine form would have been more appropriate.

TO MAGNIFY OUR CALLING: A RESPONSE TO SECTION 156

Velma Ruch

On Tuesday, April 3, 1984, a document, destined to have far-reaching influence on the church and the world it serves, was presented to the membership of the RLDS church by President Wallace B. Smith. On Thursday, April 5, it was accepted by the delegates in conference assembled as the word and will of God and became Section 156 of the Doctrine and Covenants.[1] Probably no revelation since the early revelations of Joseph Smith, Jr., has had the potential for greater impact both within and without the church than this one. And yet, the primary topics with which it dealt—the temple, the functions of the holy priesthood, and the extension of ordination to women—were not new. Even while engaging in the complex task of developing a structure for the fledgling church and attempting to achieve orderly progression amidst misunderstanding from within and persecution from without, the prophet and the people were attempting to seek light and further insight into the role and purpose of the temple, the call and responsibilities of the priesthood, and the relationship of women to ordination and their larger role in the church. Section 156 is in the tradition of developing understanding and continuing revelation which has been one of the major distinctives of the Restoration movement.

Historically, from ancient times to the present, the role of the prophet has always been a difficult one. Prophets are called to be spokespersons for the Divine and as such must have both a vertical relationship, to be sensitive to divine impulsion, and a horizontal relationship, in close kinship with humanity to be deeply involved with issues of the day. These issues must always be perceived under the mantle of eternity and be focused on matters of ultimate significance. For the good of the people, prophets are often called on to speak uncomfortable truths necessary for repentance and to project a vision, not always understood, of a future that will lead to the release of our potential as sons and daughters of God. Not surprisingly, many prophets were sources of contention. They were often reviled and some were even put to death because the recipients of the prophet's words did not wish to hear. Not all had the courage as did Micaiah to stand out against the prevailing opinion and say, "As the Lord liveth, what the Lord saith unto me, that will I speak" (I Kings 22:14). Even Jeremiah, a prophet who never lacked courage, laments, "Woe is me, my mother, that thou hast borne me a man of strife and...contention" (Jeremiah 15:10). But he could not resist the power of the Lord, "His word was in mine heart as a burning fire shut up in my bones; I was weary with forbearing, and I could not stay" (Jeremiah 20:9).

Perhaps one of the most difficult problems of the prophetic office is the necessity for the prophet to struggle with his own integrity, to be certain that he truly is speaking the word of the Lord and not in subtle ways altering that word through personal pride or through the desire to speak soothing words to the people. Reinhold Niebuhr who writes of Jeremiah's struggle observes the following:

It is instructive that the same Jeremiah who spoke so uncompromisingly against the false prophets tried to return his prophetic commission to God. He was not certain that he was worthy of it, and he doubted his courage to maintain the integrity of the word of God against the resistance of a whole generation which demanded security from religion and rejected the prophet who could offer no security on this side of repentance. His commission was returned to him by the Lord with the demand that he "separate the precious from the vile" in himself, so that he might be worthy to be a prophet.[2]

President Wallace B. Smith before presenting the 1984 document to the church as "the mind and will of God" apparently experienced some of the same struggles as the ancient prophets. "The burdens of [the] office," he wrote in the preamble, "have not become easier. In seeking to address some of the difficult and potentially divisive issues facing the church today, I have found myself spending much time in prayer and fasting, importuning the Spirit on behalf of the church." He, too, was concerned with his own integrity, with desiring to truly know that the words were not his own. "Because of the nature of that which I am now presenting," he wrote, "I have sought over and over for confirmation. Each time the message has been impressed upon me again, consistently and steadily. Therefore, I can do no other than to bring what I have received, in all humility, and leave it in your hands, believing with full assurance that it does truly represent the mind and will of God."[3]

But revelation involves a two-fold process: the experience of the prophet must find answering response in the spirits of the people. Revelation is an unveiling and as such calls for the best intellectual response of which we are capable. But it is more than that. It is an experience, a spiritual endowment. Knowledge is quickened by power and we, too, with "full assurance" know that we "can do no other" than to follow its guidance. Discernment is a gift of the Spirit and with it we can discern between that which is right and that which is wrong. It is our responsibility as members of the church of Christ to live in such a way that our response to the work of the Spirit can be true and that, so fortified, we never need fear the powers of falsehood and deception.

The people by overwhelming vote declared the document presented by President Smith to be a revelation.[4] The power accompanying its delivery and the many individual experiences both at the conference and later testify to the fact that this was no ordinary presentation. Because the issues with which it dealt were controversial and altered the firm beliefs of many, it was indeed "divisive." Such divisiveness is not all bad. So many times we take our beliefs for granted and forget to "experiment" on the word of God. A full and frank discussion of differing points of view when done in brotherly and sisterly love and with a desire to become more aware of the foundations of our beliefs can only lead to greater understanding. That which was dead and half-forgotten comes alive and the church and the world both profit.

As I read the revelation it seemed to me that latent in its every word was the impulsion "to magnify our calling." Our understanding of who we are and what God has in store for us is progressive. "God fills every person according to the measure of his vessel," Saint John of the Cross once wrote. But as our vessels are filled we develop the wherewithal to expand. We allow the potter to create a larger vessel. Words, too, are like vessels.

They must be filled with experience to have meaning; the greater our experience, the greater the meaning. Section 156 put new meaning into old words. The problems and the dreams it addressed, though of long standing in the church, were for *our* day, for *our* individual and social circumstances. If we read with understanding, and creatively explore its admonition, we will, both individually and collectively, grow toward greater understanding of that to which we are called.

As we have seen, the three-fold concern of the document, beyond the instructions regarding personnel, dealt with the acceleration of planning for the building and ministries of the temple, the awakening and continuing commitment of the priesthood, and the provision for calling women to priesthood responsibilities. Each of these has a history and, as a result of the revelation, fairly detailed plans for the future.

From the very beginning of the church, the dream of the New Jerusalem and the relationship of the temple to that dream, was an important part of the revelations of Joseph. The concept of an ideal society appears to be as old as humanity itself. It is related to our innate desire to find fulfillment, to be what we were created to be. It was the ancient dream of a golden age. It was "Thy kingdom come. Thy will be done on earth, as it is done in heaven." It was Zion. The temple, or temple complex, was to be an instrument in bringing that dream to fruition. It was envisioned as a center of education for heart and mind, and the center from which an endowed ministry could move out into the world in reconciliation and benediction. But the movement is not conceived of as one way. The ministry of church and world would be interrelated. Temple ministries need the expertise and understanding engendered in a multitude of fields

and its ministers in turn must be knowledgeable enough concerning world problems and global concerns that appropriate response and ministry become possible.

The temple, or temples, though their outward structure may sometime be complete, in function will always be progressive. The kingdom within us and among us which the ministries of the temple seek to promote is both a present fact and a future development. Growth, renewal, reconciliation are ongoing processes. In our finite state and amidst ever changing social conditions we must be open to expanding understanding and differing applications of Zionic principles to the world scene. It is significant that closely related to the first revelation concerning the temple (Doctrine and Covenants 57:1d) was another incorporating the principle of growing in light and wisdom: "Ye cannot behold with your natural eyes, for the present time, the design of your God concerning those things which shall come hereafter and the glory which shall follow, after much tribulation" (Doctrine and Covenants 58:2a). The truth we glimpse in moments of power requires that we embody that which we have seen. To *know* is not complete without to *be* and that is a lifelong and generations-long endeavor. To simultaneously have and not have is the challenge of the unfolding mysteries of the kingdom.

Though we speak of the temple, the vision that Joseph apparently had was of a temple complex consisting of as many as twenty-four buildings, each with special functions. Most of them were referred to as "Houses of the Lord," but there was a precise designation of office-specific priesthood ministries attached to many of them. They were all functional in nature. Some of them carried administrative value, others evangelistic and apostolic import, others civic and social implications, while still others focused on pastoral ministries. As the Saints were driven out of Missouri, it became impossible to put this plan into operation. Now, a century and a half later we are urged to let the "work continue at an accelerated rate, according to the instructions already given, for there is great need of the spiritual awakening that will be engendered by the ministries experienced within its walls" (Doctrine and Covenants 156:3). These ministries almost of necessity involve a complex of buildings all related to a central temple sanctuary.

In Joseph's first revelation regarding the temple he designated "a spot for the temple," a place "lying westward upon a lot which is not far from the courthouse." But the revelation also directed the people to buy every tract lying westward up to a particular point. When Joseph Smith, Jr., purchased a plot of land for the temple site, he purchased 63.27 acres of virgin land. Someplace on this plot, prior to its purchase, the elders met and dedicated the general area for the temple site. Although some have thought that the original site where the blessing occurred is the property now owned by the Hedrickite faction, there is no conclusive evidence to substantiate this. It is, however, likely that the blessing would occur somewhere on the highest ground of the plot. The RLDS church does have access to a significant portion of the Temple Lot, including the high ground lying northeast of the Auditorium—the same land Joseph described as lying westward from the courthouse. It is therefore on the original Temple Lot purchased by Joseph Smith, Jr., that the temple will be built. No doubt the first building wil be the temple sanctuary, and, if the consecration of the people permit, may become a reality within one or two decades. The whole complex could well take a century or more to develop.

Section 156 charged the First Presidency with the responsibility of developing the details of the ministry of the temple. Though the general direction of temple activities is quite clear—and that direction has nothing to do with secret rites or ceremonies—the details are still in process of formulation. The thoughts which follow are primarily from President Alan Tyree, and are designed not as a final word on temple function but as a point of departure in our further exploration of the temple concept and its relationship to the Zionic process.

The theological base of temple ministries would be related to the life and ministry of Jesus. Central to that ministry was self-sacrifice, the giving of self to others. Thus the spirit of everyone who enters the temple should be one of dedication and desire for meaningful commitment. How best to express that commitment would be part of the ministry available in the temple. Counselor-ministers would be on hand to assist individuals, families, or groups to come to a clearer understanding of the nature and extent of their offering. A small chapel where such consecrations and dedications could be made before God, the assisting minister, and perhaps others of similar concern could well be an important part of temple structure.

In terms of activity, Jesus' ministry was characterized by teaching, preaching, and healing. All three of these should be part of temple ministries. The Restoration movement from the beginning set great store on the teaching aspect of ministry. The establishment of a schoolhouse was always a major concern as the Saints moved from place to place. The two elements of education and worship were primary considerations in the original plan for the House of the Lord. We know of the importance of the School of the Prophets at Kirtland. As a matter of fact, the committee in charge of building a schoolhouse at Kirtland evolved into the temple-building committee. The one thing common to both buildings was educational purpose. It was on March 18, 1833, that the School of the Prophets was organized in Kirtland "to provide insights in language, history, and customs for the advancement of the priesthood." (See Paul M. Edwards, "Historical Relationships of Higher Education to the RLDS Church.") Later there were dreams for a University of Nauvoo. Because of the problems of sheer survival at Nauvoo, the dream faltered. Almost immediately after the reorganization of the church in 1860, the idea of a university was resurrected. After extended discussion over many years, Graceland was established in 1895. In 1974 the Temple School came into being. It emerged as the church's in-house educational organization and became a part of a developing plan for temple ministries. Whether their work will ever be of seminar status is open to question. There are, however, plans for developing advanced courses of university quality.

Though formal educational degrees have never been a requirement for priesthood office or lay ministry, the leaders of the church have constantly emphasized the importance of combining intellectual discipline with spiritual consecration. In the world in which we live devout ignorance will fall short of meeting human need and has always been a betrayal of our call to stewardship over our intellectual resources. To further emphasize the need for study, in the future every person called to priesthood office will be expected before ordination to complete preordination training and education. Following ordination, persons holding priesthood office will be asked to be involved in continuing education. The Temple School will promote and supervise these activities, but the educational pursuits sponsored through the Temple School will be directed to the entire membership and friends of the church and will not be limited to members of the priesthood. The call to "the office of member," assumed at baptism, carries stewardship responsibility and is of vital importance. All members should be encouraged to develop the Zionic skills which will enable them to go forth in ministry as workers who "needeth not to be ashamed." Educational ministries of the temple are dedicated to this end.

Teaching as conceived in the temple must be related to the healing, reconciling, saving ministry that was part of Christly teaching. The abundant life involves the total person and whether the needs of individuals are physical, psychical, or spiritual, specialized ministry should be available. The temple "shall be for reconciliation and for healing of the spirit," the revelation states. "By its ministries an attitude of wholeness of body, mind, and spirit as a desirable end toward which to strive will be fostered" (Doctrine and Covenants 156:5a, c). No part of human need would be overlooked. Counselors would be available to assist in the "healing of the spirit" but such ministry would also recognize the importance of "wholeness of body." Persons would be guided to an understanding of the principles of physical health. For those physically ill, there would not only be an opportunity for administration but also, as needed, a referral service to medical specialists. All would be done in the context of spiritual ministry.

Persons would go to the temple to be reconciled to the Lord, to the church, to others, and to themselves. The ministry of patriarchs would be particularly useful in this regard, though professinally qualified counselors would also be available. The reconciling ministry would sometimes be person to person or family to family, but it could well be extended to groups to help relieve tension between component parts of society. Such ministry, of course, would not be totally encompassed within temple walls but would be of the nature of outreach. It is a vision of a group of workers and ministers who have combined intellectual and spiritual discipline and who can in their various capacities touch, awaken, and reillumine the lives of persons who have grown indifferent and who suffer from conflict and distress.

The public worship and preaching ministry of the temple will be important. The temple may become the First Presidency's pulpit. To not interfere with regular congregational worship, services might be scheduled for Sunday afternoons with speakers invited from within and without the church. To further extend this preaching ministry to the world, the sermons preached in the temple could be assembled and published in annual volumes. The temple, though walled and centered in a specific location, must never be thought of simply as a structure. The emphasis is on function.

Temple ministries, inspired by the central location, can take place anywhere in the world. These would include not only the sharing of sermons, but the ministries of reconciliation, of counseling, of healing, of peace. The qualities of ministry developed at the temple by the various priesthood orders and quorums would extend throughout the church through the ordained representatives of these offices, wherever they may be. The only limitations may be more in the nature of quantity rather than quality, and the potential for equivalent quantity is limited only by the evangelistic achievements of the local church. The ministries which are "temple" in quality cannot be contained within four walls, but radiate forth throughout the church. Temple ministries are seen therefore as having a worldwide scope and are not confined to the Center Place only.

Central to all statements about the temple in the revelation was the one, "The temple shall be dedicated to the pursuit of peace." That peace must be inner, interpersonal, and international in scope. The call to peace requires that we align our individual lives in harmony with a personal vocation and in creative interaction with our fellow human beings promote the New Jerusalem. For this work the temple will be one major focus from which influence can radiate to all the world. The promotion of peace will happen in a variety of ways, but the ministry of specialists in a multitude of fields will be needed to write books, to develop symposia, institutes, and workshops, to move into areas of distress and, in humility as did the Wise Men of old lay their gifts of understanding before the Christ. Even though we anticipate the added blessing which will come to ministries of peace that occur in the temple, we cannot, nor should we attempt to, do them alone. Cooperation with other organizations dedicated to human welfare would be mandated but always with the recognition that ministry to physical needs becomes barren unless accompanied by spiritual imperative. The temple is conceived to help us "learn the joyful communion of Saints"—not a communion limited to a select few, but rather that from a center we may go to all the world to receive and give and make the places we occupy shine as Zion, the redeemed of the Lord.

Temple ministries predicate a dedicated and knowledgeable priesthood. Though nothing can ever replace the ministry of the member—"the symphonic richness" of a diversity of gifts—as a group grows more complex, the more its productivity depends on structural efficiency. The early Christian church found it to be so as did the early Restoration. In each case, structure developed gradually as function dictated but always with divine impulsion. Priesthood offices came into being and persons were designed for such offices as they prepared themselves for specialized ministry, the need of the group for such ministry became evident, and the divine call and blessing were assured. This did not, nor does it today, occur without the approval of the people. If ministry is not accepted, it might as well not be.

Ecclesiastical structure, though necessary, is not without its dangers. Often it leads to a centralization of power and decision making that is inhibiting to the proper development and ministry of the membership. Christ attempted by the footwashing ceremony to demonstrate to his apostles what it meant to be a servant. The Restoration also saw the footwashing ceremony as significant but often did not penetrate to the depth of its meaning. Thus we have "pride" and "personal aggrandizement." The challenge that comes to the contemporary church is to instill in all a concept of servanthood and to recognize that though some serve in specialized ways, the call is to all.

The purpose of priesthood, as the revelation states, is "for the blessing and salvation of humanity" (Doctrine and Covenants 7a). Since it is designed to facilitate the witnessing, revealing, redeeming ministry of the gospel, it must be composed "of those who have an abiding faith and desire to serve me with all their hearts...and with great devotion" (Doctrine and Covenants 8a). The call is demanding; it requires the willingness to give all. It does not require perfection—weaknesses will always be present in the most devoted of servants—but it does require love and humility without which no one can assist in the work. It requires repentance for failures and continuing commitment. It requires the

recognition of one's gifts and the discipline to develop them for effective ministry.

In the history of the Christian church there have always been those who have failed, who have become corrupt clergy. That failure was never simply personal. Influence, both conscious and unconscious, infected those who lost ministry, who lost faith, who became bitter, who were persuaded to go and do likewise. The most serious offense was not heresy or active evil but passivity, indifference, the failure to be sufficiently active in pursuit of the good. Of the seven deadly sins, sloth may be the most insidious. In a world desperate for ministry and where the workers are few, sloth is a luxury we cannot afford. Section 156 recognized the dangers of a disinterested, inactive priesthood and called for "inquiry" to be made "by the proper administrative officers, according to the provisions of the law, to determine the continuing nature of their commitment" (Doctrine and Covenants 156:8b).

The committee on priesthood appointed by the First Presidency to make recommendations for carrying out the spirit of the revelation dealt with this issue as with several others raised by the revelation. Their recommendations as reviewed and modified by the Joint Council and field administrators are published in a booklet, *Guidelines for Priesthood*. As already indicated, one major recommendation was educational in nature and reflected the desire of the people for priesthood of excellence. To enhance the effectiveness and authority of the ministry, preordination training is carefully prescribed as is ministerial education following ordination. No such specific requirements for all priesthood have been made in the past. Though priesthood ministry in the Reorganization is still predominantly a lay ministry and does not require seminary training, devotion to individual development and a willingness to constantly "seek learning by study and by faith" must be present in those who accept priesthood responsibility. These qualities are more important than formal educational degrees, though for some ministries, particularly those emanating from the temple, academic recognition by the professional community will be important. Such scholarly competence, of course, must be matched by equivalent spiritual competence.

To further assure a prepared and active priesthood, the new guidelines call for regular evaluation of priesthood performance. Though "priesthood is of a continuing nature, priesthood authority is granted by the church as a privilege." The license to officiate in office is given by the church and under proper procedure can be withdrawn. Such withdrawal is not done lightly, but until now there was no effective way of limiting activity or of giving up authority of office for a time without a certain stigma. The new rules allow for categories of priesthood activity: Active, for the majority of functioning priesthood; Superannuation, an honorable release from the responsibility of office; Inactive, a status recognizing the lack of ministerial activity for personal and/or situational conditions; Silence, revoking of license for cause; Release, relinquishing of priesthood license for reasons of conscience, life's circumstances, or personal desire; Suspension, a short term, usually voluntary, relinquishment of duty occasioned by personal difficulty, such as divorce. To assist priesthood in the evaluation of their performance and to promote accountability, a triennial review will be conducted. This review will involve the priesthood member's self-evaluation and plan for future service and a meeting with the pastor or immediate supervisor in which current status and future opportunities for service are discussed.

Section 156 indicated that some priesthood offices would be "expanded and given additional meaning as the purposes of temple ministries are revealed more fully" (4b). That statement was taken seriously by the authors of the guidelines and new position descriptions were developed for the various offices. It was a freeing of the offices to an awareness of endowments awaiting our ready response. The hierarchical conception of priesthood has, over the years, been promoted by inadequate understanding of the high calling of each office. As a consequence the feeling developed that one was not truly worthful unless one progressed up the priesthood ladder. The reason for expansion of the current conception of the duties of office is to emphasize that a highly specialized and demanding ministry is required in each calling. For a person to remain a deacon, for instance, might suggest approbation of the kind of meaningful service being given. No doubt some persons will be called to different offices, but such change, initiated by divine-human recognition, might be in response to awareness that individuals have developed in ways that call for a different approach to service, not that they now have been awarded a position of greater honor. Often the persons called may not feel qualified for the new responsibilities—it is more comfortable to stay in predetermined grooves—but such are the promises of God that as they move out, they discover a latent giftedness of which they have been insufficiently aware. The spirit that leads to such discovery is part of the call to divine-human partnership.

Though the revelation provided for the extension of priesthood to women, it is not likely that the numbers of persons called to priesthood responsibility will substantially increase. For a long time church officials have considered the possibility of establishing some kind of ratio for the number of priesthood in each office. Because there were so many variables—not the least of which was the thought that we should not tell God who should be called—attempts at establishing ratios never got off the drawing board. The committee was charged with the responsibility of at least suggesting some kind of model that could be used as a guide. After some distress at the seeming impossibility of the task, a tentative model was developed. Its purpose is not to restrict but rather to suggest a hypothetical number needed in each office to provide balance in congregational and community ministry.

No statement in the revelation was more controversial than the one regarding the ordination of women. Women have been a "vexed" question for the Christian church since the beginning. Christ attempted to show the way in his relationship to women. Paul, despite some of his strictures growing out of local situations, depended on women. Some of the greatest mystics of all time have been women. All this was not lost on Joseph Smith and the women of the early Restoration. In many of his writings Joseph Smith indicated his personal quest for understanding. In the revelation given to Emma (Doctrine and Covenants 24:2c) she was called to "be ordained under his hand to expound Scriptures, and to exhort the church, according as it shall be given thee by my Spirit." When Emma became president of the Nauvoo Relief Society her two counselors were ordained for their ministry. This, of course, was outside of priesthood structure but was in a sense parallel. As Madelon Brunson points out in her book *Bonds of Sisterhood*,[5] the women took their ordinations seriously. Among other

things, they administered to the sick, and several women testified of the benefits received. Such activity was abruptly terminated when it was thought by some that women had no right "to usurp priesthood duties."

The women of the early church did not wish to step outside the law, but they had no clear view of how they could most effectively serve the church. They were amazingly adjustable as they sought one organization after another as an outlet for their work. Almost without exception, momentary success was blocked by criticism and disorganization. The more successful an organization was, the more likely it was to be disbanded. It is not surprising that Marietta Walker, after the highly successful Prayer Union came under heavy criticism, asked in her Home Column in the *Herald* whether the church had any need for the services of women at all or if the church would sustain them in their work. The question of what that work should be sooner or later came back to the possibility of priesthood for women. The subject was frequently raised in the pages of the *Herald* and eventually came to the Conference floor. Since 1970 the ordination of women has been a major issue at World Conference. The issue was resolved by Section 156 when women were called "to share the burdens and responsibilities of priesthood in my church" (9a).

Plans for the first ordinations of women are set for November 17, 1985. Ordination services will be conducted on that day throughout the church though not necessarily in all jurisdictions. World church officers, wherever possible, will participate in the ordinations. The ordination services will not be restricted to women. Wherever men have been called and approved for office, they, too, will be ordained. All women ordained on that day will have been approved by the First

Presidency. This is not designed to restrict but rather is done in recognition of the sensitivity of these first calls and in an attempt to assure geographical distribution.

Though the opening of priesthood to women has been less divisive throughout the church than at first expected—the numerous testimonies of change of heart have been remarkable—nevertheless time will be needed in many places before either pastor or congregation can receive priesthood ministry from women. No division is so hard to heal as the religiously inflamed. The threat is to the center of our being and the source of our commitment. The most pain has been experienced where pastors have problems. A few have resigned rather than deal with the issue. To date, a couple of dozen persons, a very small percentage, have given the ordination of women as a reason for dropping their church membership. The revelation takes cognizance of the burdens of those who find themselves in uncertainty and confusion and admonishes that "considerable labor and ministerial support" should be provided. "This should be extended with prayer and tenderness of feeling, that all may be blessed with the full power of my reconciling Spirit" (156:10).

The call for ordination of women in the Reorganization is not simply following the lead of other churches. The main distinction of the calls provided for in Section 156 is that they are for lay priesthood. Most ordinations of women in other churches have looked toward professional ministry. Serving in this manner these women have often felt powerless and overlooked. Women called to the priesthood in the Reorganized church, as close a part of the congregation as they are, can forge a new way both in their relationship to the group and in the ministry of men and women together blessed by the Holy Spirit. It was Joseph Smith, Jr., who in his revelations emphasized the importance of lay ministry. It was Wallace B. Smith 150 years later who, under the impulsion of the Holy Spirit, extended the opportunity for such ministry to women and thus completed the concept of men and women with different gifts working together in equality before God and within the church.

With changing social circumstances we need to transcend past bitterness and alienation through understanding of ourselves and others and get on with the work to which we are called. The promise of the church can be achieved only when every part of the membership is enabled to participate fully in its work. For us to get our full stride as a church will take time. For many women it will require a discipline and dedication not expected of them before. It will require the readiness of Mary who responded to the angel, "Behold, the handmaid of the Lord, be it unto me according to thy will." It will require the pioneering of both men and women in a new relationship and the willingness of a congregation to grow in understanding of the sources of ministry. It will require responsiveness to spiritual power and commitment to "the work entrusted to all." A favorite hymn of the Restoration, "The Spirit of God Like a Fire Is Burning" sets the tone for the new day:

The knowledge and power of God are expanding,
The veil o'er the earth is beginning to burst.[6]

The revelation known as Section 156 of the Doctrine and Covenants is destined to be one of the most significant of the Restoration. In its essence it calls us to "be prepared in all things when I shall send you again, to magnify the calling whereunto I have called you, and the mission with which I have commissioned you" (Doctrine and Covenants 85:21e). The call involves us all and is an open door to a higher level of ministry than we have yet known.

Notes

1. Doctrine and Covenants (Independence, Missouri: Herald House, 1983).
2. Reinhold Niebuhr, *Beyond Tragedy* (New York: Charles Scribner's Sons. 1937), 110.
3. Preface to Section 156.
4. *World Conference Bulletin* (Independence, Missouri: Herald House), April 5, 1984, 333.
5. L. Madelon Brunson. *Bonds of Sisterhood* (Independence, Missouri: Herald House, 1985).
6. *Hymns of the Saints* (Independence, Misouri: Herald House, 1981), no. 33.

STRANGER IN A STRANGE LAND: A PERSONAL RESPONSE TO THE 1984 DOCUMENT

L. Madelon Brunson

(Reprinted by permission from *Dialogue*, vol. 17, no. 3)

Every RLDS Conference since 1970 has entertained legislation or discussion respecting ordination of women or expansion of their role. A review of the conferences from 1970 forward will be helpful background in understanding the persistency of this issue.

Delegates of the 1970 Conference moved to adopt a resolution which stated that women constituted a majority of the church membership but had limited opportunity to act as representatives. The legislation recommended that female participation on committees and commissions be more in keeping with their proportion of membership. When the item reached the floor, individuals in the Australian delegation presented a substitute motion which called the Conference to affirm the acceptance of the leadership of women. It advocated an end to discrimination on the basis of gender and asked the presidency to clarify the church's stand on the ordination of women. One delegate objected to consideration. The chair ruled against objection, but the Conference voted to table the entire matter.[1]

Looking toward the 1972 World Conference, the Portland, Oregon, Metropolitan branch passed a resolution on expanded female participation in church life. The preamble cited scriptures on equality and the church's confirmation of the principle. It called the church to reaffirm its belief. The last paragraph specified: "Resolved, That all those in administrative positions within the church be encouraged to appoint, hire and nominate women for positions not scripturally requiring priesthood so that women, who constitute over half of the church membership, may be more adequately and equally represented in the administrative decision-making of the church."[2] This resolution resembled the 1970 attempt, which had lost when eclipsed by the more radical substitute regarding ordination of women. During a 1972 World Conference business session, discussion of this "Opportunities for Women" resolution called attention to the fact that the U.S. Senate had, only the month before, overwhelmingly passed the Equal Rights Amendment. A motion to refer to the First Presidency and the Council of Twelve failed when a delegate pointed out that referral would leave the issue in an all-male domain. An amendment requesting the presidency to bring a progress report to the 1974 Conference was also unsuccessful. The body voted down a substitute asking for a study of positions which would not infringe on priesthood responsibilities. The original motion passed.[3]

The 1974 World Conference legislative body received the presidency's report suggesting implementation of the "Opportunities for Women" resolution. "This would include (a) employment of more women in paid staff positions; (b) appointment of more women to advisory commissions, committees, and boards; (c) moral and ethical leadership in the quest for full equality of women." They concluded with a pledge to continue searching for ways to move affirmatively toward equal participation.[4]

Pre-1976 Conference distribution of upcoming business included a resolution of the First Presidency regarding the ordination of women. Some unrest over this anticipated legislation resulted in counter proposals, and the Conference faced legislation hostile to the concept. The presidency's intention was to rescind General Conference Resolution (GCR) 564 as "no longer responsive to the needs of the Church." GCR 564 had been in the *Book of Rules and Resolutions* since 1905. It originated when Will S. Pender, a seventy assigned to the Seattle and British Columbia District, appealed to the Zion's Religio Literary Society on behalf of his wife, Fannie. He explained that she was in charge of the home class Religio work in Idaho and traveled at her own expense for the organization. Railroad companies offered reduced fares for ordained ministers traveling on church business, and he asked the Religio to request the General Conference to "set apart all such laborers, (Male or female) appointed by the Religio for that class of work by laying on of hands."[5] On April 8, 1905, the Religio Society presented this communication to the Conference without recommendation. The 1905 assembly promptly referred the issue to a joint council of the First Presidency and the Twelve with instructions to report their considerations before adjournment of the current conference body. In summary, the 1905 enactment stated that since no rules or

provisions by revelation existed on the ordination of women, and since the request was based on economic measures, the committee could not see its way clear to approve the setting apart or ordination.[6]

In the 1976 request for rescission of this old resolution, the Presidency noted that several women's names had been submitted for ordination and that the 1905 decision precluded the processing of these calls. While another clause confessed that there was "no ultimate theological reason why women . . . could not hold priesthood," the final enactment paragraph stated that "consideration of the ordination of women be deferred until it appears in the judgment of the First Presidency that the church, by common consent, is ready to accept such ministry."[7] The 1976 World Conference voted to rescind GCR 564.

The 1978 Conference heard legislation which claimed that an organizational approach in effect for several years at the congregational level, and as set forth by the *Congregational Leaders Handbook, 1978*, tended to blur the traditional role of priesthood and unordained members. This was ruled out of order and therefore not discussed. However, other business entitled "Utilization of Unordained Men" was considered by the legislative body. The resolution urged the Conference to recommend that the Presidency study ways to more "effectively utilize the talents and abilities of unordained men."[8] A motion to amend by changing the word "men" to "persons" failed and the original resolution passed.

Legislation at the 1980 Conference requested endorsing the idea that women should never hold priesthood office in the RLDS church. Objection to consideration was sustained. Two other measures, at the same Conference, suggested that the New Zealand National Church and Adelaide District of Australia were ready to ordain women. The rationale was that various stages of cultural development existed throughout the church and that national churches should be free to determine the ordination issue for themselves in consultation with the First Presidency. This was ruled out of order since the chair interpreted it as conflicting with the 1976 Conference action, and since priesthood authority extended beyond national boundaries. Another enactment enjoined the Conference to work toward the end of injustice and any social conditions which limit human freedom. Objection to consideration failed and the resolution passed. A motion calling for an annual progress report regarding the nondiscrimination in employment of women in the church failed.[9]

Finally, the 1982 Conference entertained two resolutions pertaining to the ordination of women. One stated that as there was no scriptural basis for ordaining women, the Conference should wait for prophetic guidance. The other contended that there was no scriptural basis for limiting God in the matter and resolved that the church should affirm that there be no "barriers to ordination based on race, ethnic or national origin, or gender."[10] The Chair called these two items to the floor with a report of the First Presidency reviewing the history of the issue as handled by past Conferences. The narration also included the "Recommendations on the Role of Women" as endorsed in 1974. After the recounting of this brief history, the statement requested that the two items be laid on the table.[11] However, rather than table the legislation, the delegates chose a motion of referral. This motion recommended that a task force, under the guidance of the First Presidency, make a survey to determine the attitude of members throughout the church and report to the 1984 Conference.[12]

The task force reported the survey results in the February 15, 1984, *Saints Herald* as well as the *World Conference Bulletin,* April 1, 1984, pp. 244-58; 49 percent of the respondents opposed women being eligible for priesthood call, while approximately one-third approved.

Nearly 2,800 delegates attended the first day's business session on Tuesday, April 3, 1984, with the task force's information in hand. They had heard the document, now Section 156, only an hour earlier. Legislative consideration of the message was scheduled for Thursday. About 40 percent of the 1984 Conference body was female. As a member of the legislative group, I heard the document with a complex mixture of emotions and thoughts. A general feeling of depression settled in as I faced the dilemma of deciding how to vote on the pronouncement.

I spent Wednesday evening alone examining my response and listing what I perceived as my responsibilities to God, the church, and myself. When I entered the Conference Chamber the next day, I knew I could *not* vote no and align myself with those who believe that women are somehow inferior. Abstention seemed the only alternative to supporting the act of bringing women into participation in a hierarchical system. As Patriarch Duane Couey prayed prior to consideration of the document, quiet words entered my mind to go forward in trust. I voted yes on behalf of the women who believe this is an answer to the discrimination problem.

What were the reasons for my feelings of depression? I certainly believe women are capable and competent and should be able to choose ordination. Was I depressed because the guidelines were not included, though preferably separate from the document? Somewhat. Was I depressed because I might not be called; or, that I might be tempted to conform in order to be called? Perhaps. Because of the divisions which will undoubtedly occur among many? Probably. Because the structure seemed destined to remain the same? Certainly. Because of the pain which will ensue with the execution of the process? Assuredly. My depression was accentuated as I listened to others and felt utterly alone in my response. But perhaps the ultimate cause for my depression was being compelled to face the reality that unless I was willing to accommodate and accept the system, I would never perform the ordinances. This is a loss, and I grieve.

Were there some aspects of this change which I could celebrate? Wallace B. Smith was certainly bold in bringing such a controversial proclamation. Many women with whom I have talked have a feeling of relief or release, a general feeling of peace that somehow the institution at least affirms their equality and worth as persons. A few concerned men feel a lessening of the pressure caused from the knowledge that they participate in a discriminating system. I am glad for them, but I do not celebrate this. Relaxation may postpone necessary examination of a structure which still discriminates. The excluded ones have not been the system's sole victims. Eliminating the hierarchical order, the paternalism (maternalism?), which curbs growth and separates us is, to me, imperative. We deserve a time for relaxation and renewal if the resting time motivates us with increased energy toward justice and equity.

I personally feel a sense of urgency to proceed with explorations into what it means to be a church. While I respect President Smith's courage, I yearn for a maturity among our people and our leadership that will allow us to deal with issues openly and honestly. A document is considered by the legislative body under the aura which is absent in resolution deliberations. Are we only a cult with bureaucratic trappings?

The problems of discrimination in all our cultures are so systemically deep that our grasp of the proper questions in this transition is tenuous, let alone the potential solutions. Psychologists are only now discovering differences in the moral development of men and women. "The disparity between women's experience and the representation of human development, noted throughout the psychological literature, has generally been seen to signify a problem in women's development," says psychologist Carol Gilligan. "Instead, the failure of women to fit existing models of human growth may point to a problem in the representation, a limitation in the conception of human condition, an omission of certain truths about life."[13] In short, we operate out of two different realities.

A high percentage of women who choose to accept ordination will probably adapt, rather than bring their own individual femaleness to redefine ministry, office, and authority. Women will be *assimilated*, and this coalescence will be male-defined and male-determined, since administrative decision-makers at every level will continue to be male for long into the future. If women were *integrated* this could begin the necessary changes in the structure because of their different reality.[14] This would mean involving a variety of confident women in very substantial ways in the planning and decisions regarding the effectuation of those plans. The equality I hope for is not "sameness" but equality in our right to individuality and autonomy.

I have heard some men express their hope that women entering the priesthood will change the structure. This seems an unrealistic expectation when the same men are already in the system, some even in positions of power, and have not been able to effect these hoped-for changes. However, the execution of the new directive may cause such a wrenching that changes of structure will become more conceivable. Traditionally all-male professions and trades have been devalued when women enter those fields. This disposition has possibilities for leading us into a long-delayed examination of ordination and organization.

The design of RLDS priesthood calls, which Paul Edwards has described, is capricious in my view and will result in problems unique to our denomination. I say capricious because there are no clear-cut qualifications, and total responsibility for the "call" is in the hands of individual administrators. The pain involved in the struggle to implement this action will illuminate the existing misogyny. I agree with Beverly Harrison when she says, "it is never the mere presence of women, not the image of women, not fear of 'femininity,' which is the heart of misogyny. The core of misogyny, which has yet to be broken or even touched, is that reaction which occurs when women's concrete power is manifest, when we women live and act as full and adequate persons in our own right."[15] Women will be perceived out of a different perspective now that they are ordainable, and this "core of misogyny" will emerge from the darkest and most unexpected corners. If this bigotry is recognized and overcome, it could result in growth, and this is heartening.

The problem of language could involve another paper, if not a book. Our denomination has not yet been able to deal with the predominant use of male imagery relative to God. The inclusive language policy adopted in 1978 did not confront this aspect of sexism in language. Will women in the priesthood help us deal with the predominant male imagery relative to God, or will our predominant male imagery relative to God deter us from accepting female ministry?

In the dualistic system of thought, ordination of women was the only answer. There will be pain for everyone. We now have a broader base of discrimination. But there will also be joy for the women set free to touch people at the essence of their being through the symbolic acts of the ordinances.

The priesthood-of-all-believers philosophy still claims my attention. Our over-emphasis on ecclesiastical authority prevents us from perceiving as "ministers" those who act authoritatively through their caring and presence to human need. Acceptance of the "all are called" (Doctrine and Covenants 119:8b) quote cited in the 1984 document signifies the priesthood-of-all-believers attitude. Yet the very act of ordination separates us. There are those who are ordained, and there are the "others."

My primary concern is that resolving the enactment of the ordination of women, which is already so long overdue for those of us who call ourselves prophetic, will consume the energies needed in answering our greater call. My lament is that we seem unable to make a leap of faith which would carry us beyond concern over who shall sit on the right and who shall sit on the left—who is the lesser and who is the greater. I feel a sense of urgency that we make this leap of faith that would carry us to resolute commitment to justice and equality in a hungry, nuclear-shadowed world where love and worth of persons is still conditional.

Notes

1. *World Conference Bulletin,* April 12, 1970, pp. 329-30.
2. *World Conference Bulletin,* April 9, 1972, p. 170.
3. "World Conference Transcript: 1972," pp. 355-62, RLDS Library-Archives.
4. "Report of the First Presidency," *World Conference Bulletin,* April 1, 1974, p. 208.
5. "Minutes of General Conference: 1905," *Supplement to Saints' Herald,* April 6, 1905, p. 755.
6. "Minutes of General Conference," *Supplement to Saints' Herald,* April 18, 1905, p. 804.
7. *World Conference Bulletin,* March 28, 1976, p. 181.
8. *World Conference Bulletin,* April 6, 1978, p. 256.
9. *World Conference Bulletin,* April 6-12, 1980, pp. 236, 239, 274, 294, 307, 309.
10. *World Conference Bulletin,* March 28 and March 31, 1982, pp. 268, 331.
11. Ibid., p. 335-337.
12. Ibid., p. 355; "1982 World Conference Transcript," pp. 234-242, RLDS Archives.
13. Carol Gilligan, *In a Different Voice: Psychological Theory and Women's Development* (Cambridge, Mass.: Harvard University Press, 1982), pp. 1-2; see also Anne Wilson Schaef, *Women's Reality: An Emerging Female System in the White Male Society* (Minneapolis, Minn.: Winston Press, 1981).
14. See L. Madelon Brunson, "Scattered Like Autumn Leaves: Why RLDS Women Organize," in *Restoration Studies* II (Independence: Herald Publishing House, 1983), pp. 125-32.
15. Beverly Wildung Harrison, "The Power of Anger in the Work of Love: Christian Ethics for Women and Other Strangers," *Union Seminary Quarterly Review* 36 (Supplementary, 1981):42.

III
CHURCH HISTORY

CHURCH HISTORY

Editor's Note:

Roger Yarrington is assistant to the First Presidency for communications in the Reorganized church in Independence, Missouri. His Ph.D. in American studies was preceded by a master of arts degree in journalism. For many years he was in Washington, D.C., as the editor of the official journal of the American Association of Community and Junior Colleges.

Wayne A. Ham, Ph.D. (education), also has a master of divinity degree. He is director of the Division of Program Services for the Reorganized church at its World Headquarters in Independence, Missouri.

Van Hale operates a business in Salt Lake City. He has published articles in *BYU Studies* and *Sunstone*. He also co-hosts the radio talk show, "Mormon Miscellaneous."

As curator of the Liberty Hall Historic Center in Lamoni, Iowa, Norma Derry Hiles, B.A. (history), shares insights about a "pluralistic" aspect of the history of the Reorganized church as related to Lamoni, Iowa, the church's headquarters for a number of years.

Richard P. Howard, M.A. (history), is church historian for the Reorganized church and is currently president of the John Whitmer Historical Association. His essay about the changing RLDS response to polygamy first appeared in the *John Whitmer Historical Association Journal,* vol. 3 (1983)

John Fredrick Glaser, B.A. (history), of McAllen, Texas, contributes a study of a little known aspect of the tensions in Nauvoo in "The Disaffection of William Law." It represents to a great extent the point of view of William Law and his supporters, an aspect of the Nauvoo story not widely known among the contemporary members of the Reorganized church.

CONTEXT OF THE RESTORATION
Roger Yarrington

We often forget how young the country was in 1820 when Joseph Smith had his vision in the grove. John Adams and Thomas Jefferson were still alive. Towns up and down the East Coast still had citizens who remembered life in the English colonies and men who remembered fighting in the Revolution.

Adams was living in Quincy, Massachusetts, enjoying the role of sage. Jefferson was living in Monticello, his estate outside Charlottesville. He had fulfilled a dream the previous year by founding the University of Virginia. He and Adams were healing a long political feud by friendly correspondence in their final years.

The country was feeling secure. It had weathered the Revolution and its first major test, the War of 1812. Politicians in Europe were occupied with revolutions in Spain and Portugal. Napoleon was still alive but in exile. James Monroe, fifth president of the United States, was ending his first term. In his second term he would proclaim the Monroe Doctrine, warning Europe not to interfere in this hemisphere. John Quincy Adams, who would succeed him as president, was secretary of state. Major General Andrew Jackson, hero of the War of 1812, was commander of the army's southern division where he had just subdued the Seminoles. He would be in the White House by the end of the decade, bringing with him "Jacksonian democracy" and new political power for working men and the West.

Population of the new nation was 9.6 million. New York was the largest city with 124,000 people. Boston's population was 43,000. About 200,000 immigrants had entered the country during the past thirty years. The number would soon increase dramatically.

Westward expansion was gathering momentum. The Erie Canal would be completed in a few years, speeding migration into the western lands Jefferson gained by the Louisiana Purchase. Those lands had just been made more secure from English influence on the Indians by the Treaty of Ghent and a new line of American forts along the Great Lakes and the Mississippi. John Jacob Astor was conducting a fur trade with the Indians around the Great Lakes and investing his profits in land on Manhattan Island in New York.

The line of western settlements ran to the Mississippi Valley and occasionally beyond. One place the frontier line stretched farther west was along the Missouri River, from St. Louis to a small settlement called Independence, a jumping-off place for trails to Santa Fe and Oregon. Nearby was Fort Osage, a frontier trading post.

Western Lands

Joseph said he went into the grove to pray in the early spring of 1820. At that time the Congress of the United States had as its main item of business the Missouri bill. The debate on the bill ran continuously through the spring months of March, April, and May. The question debated was whether the state would be admitted to the Union as a slave state or a free state. A compromise bill was passed, admitting Maine as a free state that year and Missouri as a slave state the next year. A census indicated 66,000 people lived in the territory. In September the frontiersman Daniel Boone died there.

The new state was on the frontier. There were no states of Michigan, Wisconsin, Minnesota, Iowa, or Arkansas. An army expedition led by Stephen Long was exploring the western territories between the Missouri River and the Rockies. Congress was debating how far west the expedition should go. Some saw no reason for it to go past Council Bluffs where Lewis and Clark had held conferences with the Indians. They pointed out in Congressional debate that the site was 200 miles beyond the nearest settlement.

Congress was debating also the need for a national currency, settlement of Revolutionary War claims, sales of government lands, and treaties with the Chippewas in Michigan Territory and the Seminoles in Florida.

Persons moving west were rapidly establishing new territories, new settlements. Community building was a common activity, familiar to all persons on the frontier. There was a feeling of new beginnings in the west.

The price of western lands was lowered by the federal government to $1.25 per acre and the minimum purchase required was lowered to eighty acres, making lands available to more persons. The *Washington Intelligencer* ran an ad in its early spring issues for bounty lands—lands given as bounties to veterans of the War of 1812, many of whom sold them to land speculators who, in turn, sold them to the public:

Every person who visits the Western Country, particularly those who intend settling there, should take with them a few quarter sections of these lands. Every man who has a young and growing family and can spare a few hundred dollars, should not miss the present opportunity of getting some of these lands, as it will ensure to his children a greater certainty than any other investment he can possibly make for their benefit.

A few years later Charles Dickens would parody the land-speculating, community-building fever in America with the story of the Englishman *Martin Chuzzlewit* and his attempt to settle on land he bought in the new frontier community of "Eden."

And later the historian Frederick Jackson Turner would develop the thesis that the frontier shaped the character of America. He described the movement of civilization across the continent and theorized that the experience of moving west, filling up unsettled land, developed the personal characteristics that Americans prized and made possible a continuing reinvention of the concept of community as new settlements were created.

This reinvention of civilization every few miles as the frontier line moved west was gathering momentum in 1820. The idea of colonization was even reaching across oceans. A colony of Negroes was being sent to Liberia by the Washington Colonization Society for the repatriation of Africans.

Pioneer and Farmers

Timothy Dwight, who had been president of Yale and died in 1817, had taken walking tours in the summers. He wrote essays reporting on his observations. In one published in 1821 he described the sorts of persons who had been settling the frontier. The first to move into previously unsettled lands he called foresters or pioneers. Those who followed immediately behind them he called farmers. In his essay, "Travels: in New-England and New-York," he characterized the foresters this way:

These men cannot live in regular society. They are too idle; too talkative; too passionate; too prodigal; and too shiftless; to acquire either property or

117

character. They are impatient of the restraints of law, religion, and morality; grumble about the taxes, by which Rulers, Ministers, and School-masters, are supported; and complain incessantly, as well as bitterly, of the extortions of mechanics, farmers, merchants, and physicians; to whom they are always indebted.

Such people, Dwight said, find they cannot live in settled towns and therefore, under pressure of public contempt and sometimes the threat of jail, go into the wilderness.

Here they are obliged either to work, or starve. They accordingly cut down some trees, and girdle others; they furnish themselves with an ill-built log-house, and a worse barn; and reduce a part of the forest into fields, half-enclosed, and half-cultivated. The forests furnish browse; and their fields yield a stinted herbage. On this scanty provision they feed a few cattle: and with these, and the penurious products of their labour, eked out by hunting and fishing, they keep their families alive.

Such men on the frontier, Dwight said, become increasingly uncivilized. He wrote: "Almost everything in the family, which is amiable and meritorious, is usually the result of her [the forester's wife] principles, care, and influence."

Dwight said there were many troubles in New England, "but we should have had many more, if this body of foresters had remained at home."

The farmer who followed the forester was another type, he said. The forester's farm, once cleared, promised immediate subsistence to a better husbandman who, with industry and spirit, changed the desert into a fruitful field.

Dwight acknowledged that some of the foresters became sober, industrious citizens, once they acquired property. After they sold their first cleared land, with its small improvements, they had a sum of money, perhaps for the first time. This awakened some hope and the wish to acquire more. It also made them realize the need for law to protect their property and the need for government.

Thus situated, he sees that reputation, also, is within his reach. Ambition forces him to aim at it; and compels him to a life of sobriety, and decency. That his children may obtain this benefit, he is obliged to send them to school, and to unite with those around him in supporting a School-master. His neighbours are disposed to build a church, and settle a Minister. A regard to his own character, to the character and feelings of his family, and very often to the solicitations of his wife, prompts him to contribute to both these objects; to attend, when they are compassed, upon the public worship of God; and perhaps to be in the end a religious man.

Compromise on Slavery

The spring 1820 issues of the *Washington Intelligencer* carried ads on runaway slaves, such as one for Charles, eighteen or nineteen years old. The owner said he would pay $200 reward for this missing slave who "will probably try to get to the Eastern Shore where I bought him." In other words, the young man would try to get back to his home, family, and friends.

The slavery issue facing Congress as it debated the Missouri bill was soon to consume the nation in a sectional confrontation. There were approximately 93,000 slaves in the country. Within a decade the number would rise to 156,000. King Cotton in the south was demanding more slave labor. As a result, in the north, the small antislavery movement would grow into an abolitionist political force.

One of the instruments to aid that force was about to come into being: low-cost daily newspapers for the urban Northeast. The industrialization of the region was beginning with the rising factory system. A new wave of immigration from Europe was ready to feed the urban growth. Newspapers were still mostly four-page weeklies, sold by annual subscription, paid in advance, the way modern subscribers are accumstomed to buying magazines. The price was typically eight dollars per year. Most subscribers were people of some means. Publishers were looking for ways to attract a broader audience.

The year the church was organized the

118

Boston Transcript began as a daily newspaper with a subscription price of only four dollars a year. It was a precursor of a new concept in newspaper journalism. Three years later the *New York Sun* was published by Benjamin Day as a daily to be sold on the streets for a penny, making the paper available to persons of limited means. Its success brought imitators. James Gordon Bennett began the *New York Herald* in 1835 and soon had as competitor Horace Greeley, the great proponent of the West, who used his *New York Tribune* to editorialize vigorously for abolition.

These developments were just over the horizon as the Restoration began. The best the long debates in Congress could do for Missouri in 1820 was a compromise on slavery.

A National Culture

Writers and artists were finding American themes for their work in the richness and diversity of people and land. A national culture was just beginning to emerge.

Washington Irving published his *Sketch Book* that year with its stories of "Rip Van Winkle" and "The Legend of Sleepy Hollow." James Fenimore Cooper was writing the first of his "Leatherstocking Stories," *Pioneers*, and James Audubon was working on his *Birds of America*. Gilbert Stuart was living in Boston where he was admired. S.F.B. Morse, Thomas Sully, and John Vanderlyn were painting in New York. Rembrandt Peale displayed his latest painting at his gallery in Baltimore. John Trumbull, artist of the Revolution, was painting four large Revolutionary scenes for the rotunda of the capitol in Washington. Edward Hicks was painting his numerous versions of "The Peaceable Kingdom," depicting his interpretation of the Isaiah prophecy about the lion and the lamb.

Americans were proud of their land, its beauty, openness, and promise. They were fascinated by the potential in the continent they saw stretching westward. Irving, in his *Sketch Book* essay "The Author's Account of Himself," felt impelled to explain, almost excuse, his interest in traveling abroad. Apparently he was afraid his countrymen, already impressed with the vastness, richness, and beauty of their own land, would not understand why he would want to go abroad. He was fond of visiting new scenes, he said. And, having become acquainted with his own country, he wished to see those from which his civilization had come. But first he felt it necessary to pay his respects to his own country:

I visited various parts of my own country; and had I been merely a lover of fine scenery, I should have felt little desire to seek elsewhere its gratification, for on no country have the charms of nature been more prodigally lavished. Her mighty lakes, like oceans of liquid silver; her mountains, with their bright aerial tints; her valleys, teeming with wild fertility; her tremendous cataracts, thundering in their solitudes; her boundless plains, waving with spontaneous verdure; her broad deep rivers, rolling in solemn silence to the ocean; her trackless forests, where vegetation puts forth all its magnificence; her skies, kindling with the magic of summer clouds and glorious sunshine; no, never need an American look beyond his own country for the sublime and beautiful of natural scenery.

Other writers sounded the same themes, becoming equally carried away by the beauty of the land—and by their own words—apparently not pausing to reflect that the same skies, clouds, sun they were praising were seen also in other countries.

There were about forty colleges in the country. The curricula were heavy on the study of classical languages—Latin, Greek, Hebrew—which were studied by everyone in all four years of college. French was expected of anyone who traveled abroad. A few travelers and statesmen were learning German, but only a few. It was not yet considered a tongue for learning. But that was to change shortly. John Quincy Adams, representing America in Europe in his earlier years, felt obliged to learn Dutch and Russian, as well as the other languages everyone of learning knew.

Charles Anthon was named adjunct professor of Greek and Latin at Columbia College in New York in 1820. He rose in professorial rank and was recognized as one of the very best classical scholars and teachers in America. It was there that Martin Harris would seek him out in 1828 to look at some characters Joseph Smith had copied from the Book of Mormon plates.

John Lloyd Stephens was a student at Columbia. In 1843 he would publish his *Incidents of Travel in Yucatan* with marvelous drawings by Frank Catherwood, describing traces of ancient civilizations being uncovered in Central America.

A tremendous expansion of higher education was taking place. The churches were losing their hold on the older universities and were concerned that the states were setting up public institutions. Church people feared the secularization of higher education. The Baptist convention of 1820 decided education was a basic part of the church's responsibility and pledged that every state would have its own Baptist college. Four years later the Methodist conference voted to put a college in each of its jurisdictions.

Religious Movements

In his 1842 account of his own early experiences, Joseph Smith described the religious environment in and around Palmyra, New York, in 1820. He said there were many revival meetings. The second Great Awakening was drawing to a close. Alexander Campbell was follow-

ing in the footsteps of his revivalist father, Thomas, working from his headquarters in western Virginia.

At Cane Ridge, Kentucky, revivalists and their followers from the Baptist, Methodist, and Presbyterian churches were gathering regularly for extremely emotional revivals with persons barking and rolling on the ground. The Methodist revivalist Peter Cartwright said,

The news spread through all the churches, and through all the land, and it excited great wonder and surprise; but it kindled a religious flame that spread over all Kentucky and through many states.

The revivalist message also caused many internal controversies, resulting in schisms, losses of members, and shrill rhetoric. Joseph said the Methodists, Presbyterians, and Baptists were all active near his home. The "lo here and lo there" he said he heard from these revivalists and their converts was part of the "news" spreading out from Cane Ridge. Perry Miller, the historian, wrote that "there can be no doubt that in the 1820s the area in which the revivals grew to the rankest luxuriance was the state of New York." The religious flame referred to by Cartwright reached Joseph's neighborhood with great force. Afterwards it was called the "burnt-over district."

In New England the descendants of the Puritans were more conservative. But changes had been taking place there, too. The Episcopalians and then the Congregationalists had become uneasy with concepts of the Trinity. References were struck from the order of service in some Episcopal churches. A movement toward unitarianism gathered force at the turn of the century. Then, in 1805, Henry Ware, a Unitarian, was named Hollis Professor of Theology at Harvard and influenced a generation of New England ministers.

In 1819 William Ellery Channing preached a sermon on the oneness of God at the installation of Jared Sparks as minister of a Unitarian Church in Baltimore. He clarified the theology of the movement and established himself as its doctrinal leader. The following year, Channing published his essay, "The Moral Argument," which was against the old Calvinism and expressed the growing American belief in the possibilities for human development and the perfectability of human beings. That same year, 1820, the Massachusetts Supreme Court ruled in the Dedham case how church property should be divided to give the Unitarians their fair share as they withdrew from Congregationalist affiliations.

For most people in New England the old church habits went on. Missionaries were sent out as far as Hawaii. Isaiah Thomas, the old printer who had begun his patriot paper, *The Massachusetts Spy*, the same year as the Boston Massacre, was going to church twice each Sunday in Worcester, listening to learned sermons by the Rev. Dr. Aaron Bancroft, father of George who would write a ten-volume *History of the United States.*

At about the same time other New Englanders, according to Ralph Waldo Emerson, were beginning to feel an inner stirring. In his essay "Historic Notes of Life and Letters" Emerson said there was "a reaction of the general mind against the too formal science, religion and social life of the earlier period." There began to be "a certain sharpness of criticism, an eagerness for reform." What he was describing was the beginning of a new movement, transcendentalism, which he said began in 1820, the year Edward Everett returned from several years in Europe where he visited with scholars and philosophers. Everett was to become professor of Greek at Harvard and George Ticknor, his traveling companion with whom he studied languages and philosophy in Germany, would become Harvard's professor of belles-lettres,

teaching Latin, French, Spanish, and Portuguese. Everett and Ticknor opened the eyes of New England scholars to the work being done in Germany and they opened their friends' minds to new lines of critical thought from Gottingen and other centers of German culture. "The rudest undergraduate found a new morning opened to him in the lecture-rooms of Harvard Hall," Emerson said.

Transcendentalism—as it developed through countless discussions, debates, and lectures in Boston, Cambridge, Concord, and other Massachusetts towns—taught that human knowledge is not limited by experience or observation, but is enlarged also by reason, an intuitive capacity to know what is true. One can find the truth within oneself, the transcendentalists said. They emphasized the importance of the individual. The churches impeded the search for truth, they said, because they emphasized form and creeds rather than self-reliance. This was a theme, a way of looking at life, that would guide Emerson, Thoreau, and a circle of followers during the next several decades as they wrote essays and poems and gave lectures which would affect leading thinkers more than the organized religious activities of the common people.

Joseph Smith probably did not know much about the intellectual ferment surrounding him as he walked into the grove, nor would he—a boy of fourteen years—understand it well if he had known. But he acted in an environment aswirl with new ideas, new beginnings, opportunities for growth, movements, and changes. Historians Henry Steele Commager and Richard Morris said, "It was, in many ways, the most dynamic period of American history." The message Joseph brought back from the grove would fit the times which were ripe for visions, especially ones that could be carried west.

References

Billington, Ray Allen. *Westward Expansion*. New York: Macmillan, 1960.

Brooks, Van Wyck. *The Flowering of New England*, 1815-1865. New York: E.P. Dutton, 1936.

Craven, Avery, Walter Johnson, and F. Roger Dunn. *A Documentary History of the American People*. New York: Ginn, 1951.

Cunliffe, Marcus. *The Nation Takes Shape*. Chicago: University of Chicago Press, 1959.

Miller, Perry. *The American Transcendentalists*. Garden City: Doubleday, 1957.

Miller, Perry. *The Life of the Mind in America*. New York: Harcourt, Brace & World, 1965.

Nye, Russell B. *The Cultural Life of the New Nation, 1776-1830*. New York: Harper & Row, 1960.

Sweet, William W. *Religion in the Development of American Culture, 1765-1840*. New York: Scribners, 1952.

Sweet, William W. *The Story of Religion in America*. New York: Harper & Row, 1930.

Thomas, Isaiah. *The Diary of Isaiah Thomas*. Worcester: American Antiquarian Society, 1909.

Turner, Frederick Jackson. *The Frontier in American History*. New York: Holt, Rinehart and Winston, 1962.

Washington Intelligencer, 1820.

CENTER-PLACE SAINTS *
Wayne A. Ham

From the beginning of Christianity until now, there have been centrifugal forces operating in the Christian community, divisiveness rising out of theological and sociological impulses. As a result of this tendency toward fragmentation, Christianity is an extremely complex movement composed not only of the mainline denominations, but also of sects and cults including snake handlers, holy rollers, and para-church organizations such as the PTL Club, 700 Club, Wycliffe Bible Society, etc.

This macrocosm, which is Christianity, is reflected in the microcosm which is Latter Day Saintism. Fragmentation has been ever present.

The first off-shoot of the Restoration church sprouted in 1830, the year the church was organized. Wycan Clark organized the Pure Church of Jesus Christ at Kirtland. It appears the six members held three or four meetings, then disbanded.

During Joseph Smith's lifetime there were at least eight different off-shoots, but no one seemed to have the charisma necessary to challenge the authority of the prophet and set up a rival faction that would endure. A massive defection of the church leadership occurred in 1837-1838, with several apostles, counselors to the presidency, and Book of Mormon witnesses leaving the fold. Yet no one seemed able to put together a church organization that persisted. But once Joseph Smith died—now that was a different story.

And so out of the myriad of Restoration sects today, here is a brief roll call of some strange sounding names: Have you ever heard of the Zion's Order of the Sons of Levi? The Church of Christ at Zion's Retreat? The Perfected Church of Jesus Christ of Immaculate Latter Day Saints? The Church of the Body and the Spirit of Jesus Christ? The Congregation of the Jehovah's Presbytery of Zion? The Church of Jesus Christ of the Children of Zion? (That was Sidney Rigdon's church after the 1844 split.) Have you ever heard of the Reorganized Church of Jesus Christ—not the one we know, but the one that separated from the Church of Jesus Christ (Bickertonite) in 1909?

Steven Shields in *Divergent Paths of the Restoration* lists thirty Restoration groups that now exist, forty-six groups that existed for a while but no longer survive, and seven independent individuals who function like churches. New Latter Day Saint groups are constantly coming into existence. Three have made the news fairly recently. In Denver in 1972 the Homosexual Church of Jesus Christ; in 1980 in Hyden, Idaho, the Arian Christian Church (a church that combines Mormonism and Hitlerism so that prayers are said with the Hitler salute and the swastika is a predominant symbol) and the most recent one that has come to my attention is the Zion's First International Church organized by people offended by the Mormon's stand against the ERA. ie

In this paper I will focus on nine churches in Independence, Missouri. Eight of these are Restoration churches and one provides a historical footnote for the Restoration movement. My objectives are to share some of my impressions of their role and status in the Restoration

---

*Since this essay refers to movements in a dynamic situation, details are constantly changing. The intent of the essay is not to describe comprehensively the movements referred to, but to call attention to the phenomenon of diversity in the activity and form in the Restoration movement.

movement. Very little has been done by way of historical analysis concerning most of the smallest churches, thus providing a virgin field for research. My main sources were, first of all, personal interviews (I have gone to worship with each of these groups and I had some conversations with their representatives), and second, an independent researcher who lives in Independence, a fascinating fellow named Robert F. Smith, who works at odd jobs so that he is free for church history research in the church archives. Robert is very private concerning his own faith stance, but he is definitely not RLDS or LDS. *Divergent Paths of the Restoration* by Steven Shields provided some useful information, but it is sort of spotty, some of it is right on target, but other information is based on hearsay.

Let us begin with the Church of Jesus Christ of Latter-day Saints. Commonly called the Mormon church, it is currently undergoing a worldwide population explosion, currently claiming 4.8 million members around the world. In 1980 there were 211,000 adult converts, approximately the size of the RLDS denomination in total.

In 1970 Independence had one Mormon ward in the process of dividing into two, meeting in an inadequate chapel to which they had recently attached a gymnasium. Nearby there was a jello factory, the welfare project for the stake, and a mission president's home. Ten years later we find a vastly different situation—in addition to the former properties, there is a visitor's center attracting multitudes of in-town and out-of-town guests. Three Independence wards are meeting in a new stake center, with two additional wards, one from Kansas City and one serving the LDS members of Blue Springs, meeting in the older chapel down the street.

Are the Mormons picking away at the RLDS membership here in town? I asked the Independence stake president. He responded that they have not been as successful as they would like with the RLDS. He personally knew of only about a dozen in the stake that were former RLDS members. However, they are experiencing quite a harvest from the mainline Christian denominations.

I attended the Independence First Ward with Mayumi Yamada, who was a convert to Mormonism in Japan. Somebody told her that if she was a Latter Day Saint, she really ought to go to Graceland College. She showed up in Lamoni for first semester classes and discovered that, yes, there is a difference! Well, she is safely in Salt Lake City, now, but during the Thanksgiving holidays she visited in our home and we had an opportunity to go to a Sacrament meeting with her. The first thing that amazed me was that it was like going to church in Hawaii. About 50 percent of the ward were Polynesian. About 600 Samoans, some Tongans, some Tahitians, and some Hawaiians have gathered to the Center Place. Now if you think that the Mormon church runs its people's lives, note that in this case the church leaders have directed the Polynesians to go home but they won't go. Why? Because this is the Center Place where the Great Temple shall be built, the edifice to which Jesus Christ shall return. Also the affluence that "Joseph's land" provides gives some incentive to remain here.

The unique role of the Independence temple is discussed widely in Mormon circles. The Mormons are building smaller temples now in more widely diverse locations. Recently the church announced that there will soon be a temple in Chicago and a temple in Dallas. The central Midwest desperately needs a temple. LDS from around here go to the Manti, Utah, temple for their endowments. Why wasn't Independence selected for a new temple? My own theory is that when they build the Independence temple, they will pull out all the stops. It will be a magnificent edifice, not in keeping with the current impetus toward smallness.

Temples themselves are a tool for missionary work. When the Seattle temple was recently dedicated, nonmembers toured the building ahead of its dedication, as is the custom. There was some picketing done by ERA proponents, Ex-Mormons for Jesus, and other dissident groups. Even with that picketing, even with that negative attention, several thousands of converts resulted from contacts made by the dedication of the Seattle temple. When they open this wingding of a temple in Independence, you can imagine the abundant harvest in proselytes.

Why the delay when the Mormon church owns property on the original Temple Lot itself? Are they holding out for that one little spot where Joseph Smith placed the marker? It is going to be interesting to watch the ongong expansion of the Church of Jesus Christ of Latter-day Saints in Indpendence.

Let us look now to the Church of Christ (Temple Lot.) If the Mormons are reflective of what was going on in the Restoration movement at Nauvoo, if the RLDS church is more reflective of what was going on in the middle period of Joseph Smith's ministry at Kirtland, then the Temple Lot Church is reflective of what was going on in the early New York period and in the early Independence period. For Temple Lot members Joseph Smith became a fallen prophet—about the time he started introducing the High Priesthood and the First Presidency, his ego overcame his spirituality. And so the Temple Lot people accept the Book of Mormon and earliest revelations of Joseph Smith only up to about 1833.

After the death of Joseph Smith and the scattering of the Saints, Granville Hedrick pulled together six branches of the church in Illinois. This loose association of branches considered itself to be a remnant of the original Restoration. In 1867, prompted by revelation, they returned to Independence and purchased that much coveted Temple Lot. In the early 1900s the Temple Lot Church population stabilized at 3,000 members, but then in 1925 there was a big fracas in the RLDS church. A controversy referred to as Supreme Directional Control suggested to some RLDS that President Frederick M. Smith was becoming a dictator, assuming one-man control, refusing to share the power of administration with other quorums, and consequently there was a mass exodus to the Temple Lot Church. By 1929 the population of the Temple Lot Church was around 8,000. Buoyed up by that kind of population increase and renaissance and new funding, construction on the long-awaited temple was begun.

There was a widespread conviction in Independence in 1928 and '29 that 1930 was to be the Year of the Return. This was the year in which Jesus Christ would suddenly come to his temple. So there was a great surge of interest in digging the basement to prepare the foundation for the temple on the Temple Lot. Ah, but unfortunately schism reared its ugly head in the Temple Lot Church in the early part of 1930, and as a result by the end of the year the membership leveled off at 4,500. Today membership is back down to about 2,600. Most of the old-timers in the Temple Lot Church are former RLDS who came out during that very troublesome time of the Supreme Directional Control controversy. Could that church have survived had it not been for that renaissance experience in the 1920s at the expense of the RLDS?

Currently there are two Temple Lot

locals (branches) in Independence. I heard one referred to as the "liberal" local and the other called the "conservative" local, but that didn't make much sense to me, so I asked what had caused the two locals to be created. It seems that an RLDS doctrine concerning probation after death was the culprit.

The old-time Temple Lot people didn't believe that there was probation after death. When you died, that was it; you had had your chance! But the people coming in from the RLDS had the notion of a "prison house" to which Jesus and the elders went to preach to the spirits in captivity. The "probationers" meet east of town.

At the recent general assembly of the Temple Lot Church I watched with great interest because I can see the Temple Lot from my office window in the Auditorium. I noted the long hours of conferring and wondered what might be the focus of debate in the assembly. Apparently the problem this year concerned the type of wine used in the Communion. The tradition in the Temple Lot Church has been to have fermented wine. But apparently there is a convert now in the church from the Seventh-Day Adventist movement agitating for unfermented grape juice. The fermented-wine people won this battle, but apparently it was a very traumatic experience for some of the assembly-goers. This church has been rife with internal strife and doctrinal dispute over the years.

Now let us proceed to a church that resulted from that schism back in the 1930s. This group is now called the Church of Christ with the Elijah Message. Otto Fetting was a seventy in the RLDS church. During the upheaval over Supreme Directional Control, he went to the Temple Lot Church. In 1927 he reported to the Temple Lot Conference that John the Baptist had come to visit him and had brought a message for the church about building the temple. Several other messages were eventually provided by this angelic visitor. As the twelfth message was shared among the Temple Lot membership, controversy erupted. The Temple Lot people believed that they were a remnant of the original church but that there were also other remnants and that the priesthood of God was to be found intact in other remnants. The twelfth message of John the Baptist, however, stated clearly that those who came now to the Church of Christ had to submit themselves to rebaptism, a denial of priesthood authority in the factions. Out of the doctrinal controversy over whether those coming out of the RLDS should be rebaptized or not, the Temple Lot General Assembly by a very narrow vote rejected Otto Fetting and his messages, precipitating a walk-out by Fetting's followers who quietly formed the Church of Christ Established Anew.

Fetting died in 1933 after having given thirty messages. Four years later Wilhelm Draves announced that John the Baptist had returned to earth and come to him with yet another message. The validity of Draves' messages has led to yet another split. Sixty-nine messages have come through Brother Draves, and he is still receiving them. These messages encourage the saints and call the ministry of the church.

Today there are about 2,000 members in the church which now calls itself the Church of Christ with the Elijah Message. Several indigenous Christian churches in other lands such as Trinidad, Kenya, India, and Uganda have affiliated with this group. By the way, the same Articles of Faith and Practice used in the Temple Lot Church are used here as well. One item of information in the ninety-seventh message that really fascinated me is a listing of persons who should be added to the evangelists "when they come fully in this way." Sixteen names appear, including Julian E. Whiting, Eugene O. Walton, and John J. Schut. Brother Schut has been in correspondence with me. He lives in the Netherlands and is friends with people from different factions. The Temple Lot people had claimed him, the Church of Jesus Christ of Monongahela, Pennsylvania (Bickertonites), had claimed him, and now he shows up in one of Brother Draves' messages, so I assume then that the Church of Christ with the Elijah Message is claiming him. So I wrote to Brother Schut to find out where he stands, and it turns out that he is still with the Temple Lot Church, but he feels comfortable with everybody. Brother Whiting and Brother Walton will turn up later in our story.

The Church of Christ on East Gudgell (I'm adding on East Gudgell to distinguish it from another Church of Christ we'll talk about a little later) accepted the messages brought by Otto Fetting, thirty messages in all. They tentatively went along with Wilhelm Draves, but in 1943 some of the membership affirmed that Draves was proven to be a fraud. As the story is told, to see if John the Baptist was really coming to Draves, someone typed out a list of names and left it in Brother Draves' room. Then in the next message from John the Baptist, those very names appeared. As a result, there was a split in the church, with one group under Apostle S. Thayer Bronson calling themselves the Church of Christ, loyal to Fetting's messages but not to Draves'. In another split in 1953, the southern branch of the church, mostly in Mississippi under Apostle Holland Davis, went its own way.

In 1956 the Church of Christ on East Gudgell adopted the seventh-day Sabbath principle in response to revelation. With about 200 members on the books in Independence, there are about 2,000 members worldwide. One of their apostles is a Nigerian, a minister who was at one time affiliated with David L. Roberts, whom we will mention later. The 750 Nigerian members of the Church of Christ represent the now-familiar process of an indigenous church in a developing nation affiliating with a Restoration denomination. Those same Articles of Faith and Practice used by the Temple Lot Church and the Elijah Message folks is also the touchstone for determining the basic beliefs of the Church of Christ on East Gudgell.

The Church of Jesus Christ, a little white church on South Cottage Street, has an interesting story behind it. This church has a public assembly area on the ground floor, but on the second story is the temple-rite room. Here meet the faithful of Alpheus Cutler. Cutler had been with the church all the way through the Nauvoo days, but he did not follow Brigham Young. In 1852 he took a group off to Manti, Iowa, and established a United Order there. Just before he died, he had a vision of a beautiful land between two lakes in the far north country. He counseled his followers to go there, for one reason—among others—to escape from the marauding missionaries of the Reorganization who were picking away at the flock, including Cutler's own son. So shortly after Alpheus Cutler's death, the group headed out in the dead of winter toward Minnesota. After a migration of epic proportions, the Cutlerites found that spot between two lakes at a place now called Clitherall. In 1928 most of the young people of this group moved to Independence. Why? The temple was to be built by 1930 to which Christ could come, or so it was hoped.

In the 1950s there was a split in this small church, the Minnesota Saints calling themselves the True Church of Jesus Christ, and the group in Independence calling themselves the Church of Jesus Christ. The issue was who should be president.

Let me digress for a minute to mention Eugene Walton, his associate Jack Winegar, and his son-in-law Jim Rouse. Brother Walton was an RLDS seventy who became embroiled in the controversy over the "new curriculum." Associating for a time with Barney Fuller and his World Redemption Association, this trio joined the Cutlerites. You need to understand that the Cutlerites don't do missionary work; they feel that the Lord himself will build up the church in his own good time and primarily from among the Indian people. When Brother Walton arrived bearing revelations the Cutlerites hoped that he might be the "one mighty and strong" promised to rally the church. In the Church of Jesus Christ a system of joint ownership of property is in use. When a "revelation" came to Brother Walton appointing him to be the prophet, the older members of the group bolted, excommunicating Walton and his two friends. This trio will show up later in another church, but in the meantime there are about thirty members of this Church of Jesus Christ left in the world. What fascinates me about this group is that they appear to be a reflection of the public manifestations of the church at Nauvoo. Many doctrines and practices were being explored in secret councils during the Nauvoo era, but what someone coming to the city of Nauvoo would see in the church's public life is essentially what has been preserved in the Cutlerite movement.

You might think that they would get a little discouraged by the fact that the church seems to be dwindling away, but they are not discouraged. Why? Because Father Cutler issued a prophecy that the day would come when there would be seven members, maybe five, maybe even three but there would be a stem left, and the Lord would cause the work to grow again.

The present president of the Church of Jesus Christ is Julian E. Whiting, the same Whiting who is named in one of the Elijah messages to Wilhelm Draves. Very interesting, I think.

Now on to the True Church of Jesus Christ Restored (Hebrew Mormon) currently being reincorporated as the True Church of Jesus Christ of Latter-day Saints. An unusual syncretism is at work in this church. According to this group's story, there had been three prophets in this last dispensation of time—Joseph Smith, Jr., James Jessie Strang, and now David L. Roberts. David Roberts was baptized into the Church of Christ Established Anew after having been a Pentecostal Christian for a while. In 1967, however, the angel Nephi visited him, presenting a particular charge. This claim to angelic ministration was not well received among Brother Draves' followers, so Brother Roberts resigned from that organization. For a time he affiliated with the Church of Jesus Christ of Latter-day Saints (Strangite), a small group of about 200 members. The Strangites accepted him for a while, but seven years after that initial visit by Nephi, along comes Elijah. Elijah ordained David L. Roberts to be prophet of the church and king of the world. At this point the Strangites cast Brother Roberts out.

By now David Roberts had married a Seventh Day Adventist and converted her. The two together began the process of Hebrewizing the church by introducing Jewish customs and practices. The seventh-day Sabbath, all of the Jewish feast days, and the kosher laws are observed. And yet some other doctrines arise such as the "mighty miracle consubstantiation communion," a doctrine of the Lord's Supper that appears to be a restatement of Martin Luther's doctrine of consubstantiation.

Denise Roberts is now a member of the First Presidency, the co-bishop of the flock, the queen, and presiding patriarch to the church. What is the worldwide membership of this group? Brother Roberts reports 11,000 adherents. But almost all of them are in India, and are in fact "honorary members" that have not yet been baptized. In fact, Brother Roberts hasn't heard from them for over a year.

And so the question that must be asked is, When is a church truly a church? There are two members of this church in Independence, David and Denise Robers. I'm not sure how many other baptized members you will find anywhere, perhaps a few in Ohio and a few in Europe. And yet this group has a church structure that is very well formulated. It has an internally consistent theology—ask about *any* point of doctrine and you will be given an answer. One Friday evening, my wife and I attended Passover Service at Mount Zion Synagogue. The two of them sat up front on the rostrum, the two of us sat down below as the congregation. No one else showed up, but we underwent a fascinating service of worship nevertheless.

The next group I wish to single out is the Reorganized Church of Jesus Christ of Latter Day Saints, the largest of the Restoration churches in Independence. Forty-two different congregations meet on Sunday mornings representing an incredible span of theological diversity. If you want a super-fundamentalist congregation, try Enoch Hill in Center Stake. If you want a super-liberal congregation, at least by RLDS standards, try Walnut Gardens in Blue Valley Stake or the Santa Fe Stake Mission.

In our particular neighborhood we have three churches with three different feeling-tones—Walnut Gardens, East

Alton, and Beacon Heights. In true RLDS fashion our family drives past all three of these to go to East 39th Street congregation in another stake, mainly because my sixteen-year-old son tells me they have the prettiest girls in town and as an added bonus they have an excellent ministry of music.

With all this diversity, you would think that everyone would be contented, but such is not the case. There are dissidents in our midst, as for example in the Restoration Festival, Inc., the *Restoration Voice* group, the Restoration Information Center with its vitriolic *Watchman of Zion* newsletter, the School of the Saints, and others. There are also charismatics to be found in Zion—people who feel very much at home with born-again tongues-speakers at the local Full Gospel Businessmen's Association.

Some observers speculate that the dissidents will remain in the RLDS church only until they discover a compelling charismatic leader. But I am not sure that experience will bear that out. Look at Barney Fuller—he had much support while he stayed in the church, criticizing it. When he left the church to set up his own Church of the New Jerusalem, his support evaporated. And Eugene O. Walton had an active support network only until he left; then his following shriveled up. There seem to be a lot of RLDS in town who like to complain and gripe about the church establishment, but most deep-down-inside are probably loyal to the institution.

Let us now look at Restorationists United. Eugene Walton was a radio minister for the Baptist Church until he found the RLDS church. He became a self-sustaining seventy for the RLDS, but he didn't like what he perceived to be the liberalizing, protestantizing trend of the late 1960s. He joined with Barney Fuller in World Redemption, Inc., which later became the Church of the New Jerusalem, but that connection faded. His journey then took him to the Church of Jesus Christ (Cutlerite), and there he had his revelation which designated him to be the "one mighty and strong," the prophet. When the Cutlerites cast him out, he established the Restorationists United.

Brother Walton does a fantastic job of getting favorable publicity. When the Blessing Document came forth, one of the newspapers in Independence had a big spread on the front page; on one side was a photo of Wallace B. Smith saying how delighted the RLDS were to have the document, on the other side a photo of Eugene Walton contradicting everything that Wallace B. Smith was saying. Now how can someone who leads a group with a worldwide membership of twenty-five and a membership in town of ten command such media attention?

Eugene Walton has had five revelations. He has his First Presidency established—Walton, Jack Winegar, and Walton's son-in-law Jim Rouse. Unfortunately for them, there is no church over which to preside. Brother Walton maintains that the church has not yet been organized since they are waiting for the hand of the Lord to move.

Now let us turn to a group that used to be a Restoration church, but isn't any more. Nonetheless, it provides an interesting historical footnote to Latter Day Saintism in Independence. Pauline Hancock, daughter of one of the well-known RLDS seventies, became associated with the protest movement during the Supreme Directional Control controversy. Later she joined forces with Irvin Luke and Gene and Olive Wilcox from Englewood RLDS congregation. As they studied together, they came to some conclusions which created for them a church that was essentially Protestant in nature, and yet it retained belief in the Book of Mormon. They built a church on South Crysler but didn't finish the sanctuary. Locally they are known as the Basement Church. Then in 1973 this church rejected the Book of Mormon. Pastor Pauline Hancock had died by that time, leaving Gene Wilcox to be the new pastor.

Although no longer considering itself to be a Restoration church, it still had a mission to the Restoration—a mission of warning. The *Independence Examiner* on its Saturday church page often carries advertisements aimed against the Book of Mormon.

The current membership of this church is about thirty-five persons, mostly a few families with interlocking ties. They have considered closing down the operation on South Crysler and supporting a local conservative Bible-believing Protestant church. And yet their mission to inform the Latter Day Saints in Independence about the incorrect assumptions on which the Restoration faith is built keeps them going.

Those of you who are familiar with the anti-Mormon Modern Microfilm Company of Salt Lake City will be interested to hear about the relationship of Jerald and Sandra Tanner to this group. Jerald Tanner came to Independence to do historical research and discovered this church. He was baptized by Pauline Hancock, went back to Salt Lake City, and converted Sandra who was to become his wife. He had her fly back to Independence so that she could be baptized into this Church of Christ on South Crysler. The Tanners gave up the Book of Mormon and "found Christ" before this little flock on South Crysler, but now they are together in their resolve to expose Mormonism as a fraudulent movement.

We have looked at nine Restoration churches, but this isn't the whole story. If I were doing a more extensive work, I might want to include the pentecostal Living World Mission over in Kansas City. The pastor, Jean Burns, and her assistant Don Harsh are Book of Mormon believers. Then there is the Floyd Denham clan, who don't function as a church, but they have been "cut off" from the Temple Lot Church and they definitely have a mission. Every winter the whole clan, about thirty-five of them, travel in three campers into Mexico to preach the Book of Mormon. Then there is Forest Tony with his True Church of Jesus Christ of Latter Day Saints. His ads in the newspaper give the community cause to pause and wonder. His most famous ad prophesied that a mighty wind would arise to blow down the Auditorium and the city. Another group I'll mention, although they come to town only once a year, is the Church of Christ Restored, the group based in Mississippi that separated from the Church of Christ on East Gudgell. Every June they come to a rented hall on Crysler for their General Assembly. Then there's Doug Boyd, a self-proclaimed prophet, who was reared on a diet of World Wide Church of God ideas, so he celebrates all of the Jewish holy days. He comes to town for every major Jewish festival to stand on the Temple Lot and proclaim his prophecies. Then there is James R. Snell, an independent who wants nothing to do with any of the churches. But he is a Book of Mormon believer. Joseph did well in bringing forth the Book of Mormon, but he overstepped his bounds when he created the church. Snell publishes the newsletter, *An Open Book,* and a whole range of publications dealing with the Book of Mormon.

One of the reasons for some of this sectarian fragmentation in Zion involves charismatic leadership. Many early schisms of the Restoration resulted from personality cults. When the charismatic leader dies, often the organization they create collapses. Many of the church leaders mentioned in this paper obviously had charisma. I would consider Alpheus Cutler to have been such a leader. Even though he lived over a hundred years ago, Father Cutler's influence still lives on in that Church of Jesus Christ down on South Cottage Street. Otto Fetting obviously had the power to convince all those folks that John the Baptist was coming to his bedroom night after night dropping off messges. Wilhelm Draves has his own charisma. And certainly Pauline Hancock had it.

Another reason for schism is the doctrinal issue. For the early RLDS, plural marriage and presidential succession were divisive. For the Temple Lot folks the issue of rebaptism split that organization in two. The seventh-day Sabbath principle has functioned as a church-splitting issue for one group of Fettingites.

Another source of schism is the longing to return to sectarian foundations. Byron R. Ralston has given us some of the characteristics of sect. He describes them as exclusive, an elect gathered community, a remnant, with profound fear of social change and the resulting secularization. Strong lay participation and fear of professionalism marks the sect as well, in addition a very strict ideological stand. Where a denomination accommodates itself to the social and cultural values of its culture and reinforces a certain social consensus, a sect stands in opposition.

The process of the denominàlization of sects often engenders schismatic tendencies. As the "professionals" of religion come forward to assert leadership, whether it be in Christian education or in the hierarchy, some of the rank-and-file will feel threatened. This sense of loss of status, combined with the failure to have their charismatic needs satisfied, may result in fragmentation of the movement. This sect-to-denomination pilgrimage, I feel, goes a long way toward explaining the current unease of "dissidents" within the RLDS church.

Stephen Shields lists all of the Restoration churches that he could locate, and in the twentieth century alone he suggests that twenty-four schisms have come out of the Mormon church, eight schisms have come out of the RLDS church, and ten schisms have come out of the Temple Lot Church. We might want to note that most of these schismatic groups emerging out of the Temple Lot Church had their impetus in former RLDS members who "crossed over" during the Supreme Directional Control controversy.

While we have focused on schismatic churches, please note that in the Restoration movement the Mormon church accounts for 95 percent of all Restorationists and the Mormon church and the RLDS church combined account for 99 percent. So you can see what a negligible impact all of the schisms have made in terms of membership acquisition.

Let me now offer some predictions. I think that in the future the Mormon church in Independence is going to keep growing at a healthy rate. This is their day. Things have really come together for them. I am wondering if they might discover church history to be an RLDS Achilles heel. You see, we have never really come to terms with Nauvoo and the role of Joseph Smith, Jr., in that era. Our people could be very vulnerable if a new assessment of Nauvoo and the early Reorganization is not made. We now have rejoiced in the recent discovery of the Blessing Document. Historians realize that Joseph suggested about twelve different methods of succession at one time or another. We were lucky on that one, but what happens (this is all speculation, mind you) if an old document comes forth in Joseph's handwriting listing his plural wives? Mark Hoffmann, discoverer

in 1980 of the original Anton transcript and in 1981 of the Blessing Document, may be springing some other surprises on us in the future.

Second, I am going to predict that the RLDS church and the Temple Lot Church will continue to experience internal pressures and adjustments. I think most of the RLDS dissidents will remain in the church and will continue to agitate and protest change.

Third, I would like to predict that Elijah will keep on coming to Wilhelm Draves, to David L. Roberts, and maybe even to someone in the Church of Christ on East Gudgell since that group has been waiting in the silence of forty years. Even in the Temple Lot Church, the precedent is there to expect continuing revelation and visitations.

Fourth, I am going to predict that the Church of Jesus Christ (Bickertonite) of Monongahela, Pennsylvania, which is the third largest Restoration church, could find a harvest in Independence if they decided to proselyte here. There is a remarkably sweet spirit about this movement. Members speak in tongues and they prophesy in their meetings. Women are ordained deaconesses. The ordinance of footwashing is practiced—all in all a combination of features that would attract attention here.

Well, it's a fascinating story. And it is so open-ended. History is in the making every day in our city. Independence, in the hearts of Restorationists, is a very special place, not only for what has already happened here but also because of what has been promised for the future of the Center Place. And no one need go away unhappy—there is something here for every type of mentality and belief. And if you should happen *not* to find what you are looking for, well, that's easily remedied—just gather six people together . . .

WRITING RELIGIOUS HISTORY: COMPARING THE *HISTORY OF THE CHURCH* WITH THE SYNOPTIC GOSPELS

Van Hale

It has become popular in some circles to contend that, because of flaws in their written history, Mormons must discard their extra-biblical religion for an exclusively biblical one. Those who argue this position point out that, without any indication, many additions, deletions, and changes have been made in the official history of the church. The critics, Jerald and Sandra Tanner, for example, point out that in this *History* some prophecies have been added, and some deleted; contradictory statements have been harmonized, and exaggerations and crude statements have been dropped or changed. The reason for this, they claim, is that Mormon historians

were evidently trying to make Joseph Smith into a very saintly man. They do not dare let their people see the real Joseph Smith. They would rather falsify the *History of the Church* than allow Joseph Smith's true character to be known.[1]

In their discussion, the Tanners frequently employ such words as "falsify," "deceive," "doctored," "bogus," "forgery," "fraudulent," and "dishonest."[2] They come to the extreme conclusion that "The Mormon Church leaders have worked hard to destroy the truth concerning Joseph Smith and the Church."[3]

No student of Mormon history would challenge the Tanners assertion that changes have been made in the official history. The variants between the current

edition of the *History of the Church* and the known primary sources conservatively exceeds 100,000 words.[4] However, the vast majority of these changes are the result of generally accepted editorial procedure. It is common knowledge among students that the *History* is not simply an exact reproduction of all known original documents. It has passed through a number of editors over a period of at least one hundred years who have done what editors do.[5] They have made selections from available material which they have shaped, molded, and polished. While the Tanners are critical of all changes including even standard editorial changes, of greater interest and significance is the relatively small number of changes which reveal the editors' biased treatment of their source material. These changes are those which alter a point of doctrine or the image of a person or event. For me the evidence is conclusive that these editors have indeed made additions, deletions, and changes which improve the image of Joseph Smith and the church, remove contradictions, and harmonize earlier and later doctrine.

The impact of this on individual religious faith, of course, depends on the individual. The Tanners and other critics contend that these changes reveal a dishonesty among early and more recent church leaders of such magnitude as to devastate the entire religion. They are unwilling to make any allowance for what I believe is a widely acknowledged characteristic of religious histories. Not many students of religious history would challenge my claim that religious authors, charged with evangelistic fervor, have characteristically tended to write positive, faith-promoting histories by improving earlier portrayals of certain persons and events beyond what their sources justify. I believe the vision of the critics is so narrow they do not see that their standard is so rigid that by it all religions which have produced a written history stand condemned, including their own Bible-centered religion. Rather than attempt to support this generalization, I have chosen specifically to compare the *History of the Church* with the religious history most highly regarded by these critics—the Synoptic Gospels.

I have nothing new to present. In fact, my point—that it is unreasonable to expect devoted disciples of 130 years ago to write history in accord with the standards of current professional historians—may seem too obvious for discussion. However, the recent proliferation of books, tracts, tapes, and movies condemning Mormonism because of the nature of its official history demonstrates that there are many for whom this point is not obvious. My purpose here is to bring together two sets of observations: those pertaining to the writing of the *History of the Church*, and those pertaining to the writing of the four Gospels. While there is yet much to be said regarding changes in the *History of the Church*, the sampling presented by Jerald and Sandra Tanner in their several works[6] is sufficiently broad to suit my purposes. Nor do I have new observations concerning the Gospels. They have been discussed in minute detail by many fine scholars. My purpose is not to add to that discussion, but rather to glean from it

parallels to the writing of the *History of the Church.*

I will focus on the observations of New Testament scholars which reveal some characteristics of the relationship of the Synoptic Gospels—Matthew, Mark, and Luke—to each other.

During the past 150 years, a massive body of literature has been written on the topic of what has been termed the "Synoptic Problem."[7] The intent has been to account for the close harmony of much of the material in Matthew, Mark, and Luke. It has been calculated that "approximately 91 percent of Mark is paralleled in one of the other two gospels or in both."[8] Only thirty-one verses of Mark are not found either in Matthew or Luke. The most prevalent conclusion has been explained by Protestant author William Barclay:

the priority of Mark is one of the most widely accepted principles of the modern study of the gospels. . .among Protestant scholars, the generally accepted view is that Mark is the earliest of the gospels and that Mark was used as a basis by the other two gospel writers.[9]

Another eminent New Testament scholar, Bruce Metzger, has further explained that

Matthew and Luke followed Mark's historical narrative, making its language fundamental to their own accounts, arranging its material to conform to their own purposes in writing, and adding material from other sources oral and written.[10]

The evidence which has been amassed for this is very convincing, as it would need to be to obtain such wide acceptance among scholars.

But rather than present the evidence that Matthew and Luke incorporated Mark into their gospels, I offer some implications of this conclusion which have parallels to the writing of the *History of the Church.* My interest is in how Matthew and Luke used Mark. Considering the fact that these two works are widely separated in many ways including time, culture, writing, and editorial practices, and means of preserving and transmitting the text, it is certainly possible to carry the parallelism too far. However, the parallel does certainly exist that later devoted disciples did make use of earlier source material which they did not simply reproduce without alteration. I have already acknowledged that the editors of the *History of the Church* did have a bias, and did improve on their source material by making some additions, deletions, and changes, some even of theological significance.

I will now turn to New Testament scholars who have acknowledged that Matthew and Luke have done the same thing with their major source, Mark. First of all, "in style and language Mark is decidedly less polished than Matthew and Luke,"[11] who, with greater literary skills, improved his language and style. However, two other types of improvements made by Matthew and Luke are more interesting and more significant. These are Matthew's and Luke's improvement of Mark's portrayal of the apostles and of Jesus.

The portrait of the apostles, as found in the gospel of Mark, is considerably different from that of Matthew or Luke. Anyone reading Mark with this in mind will readily concur with William Barclay that

In Mark there is criticism of the slow minds and the dull understanding of the twelve. . . . Mark's is the picture of dull-witted men with impervious minds unwilling and unable to understand.[12]

Barclay further suggests that

Matthew and Luke made changes in Mark's narrative because they had a more respectful and reverential attitude to the story. We might say that they look at the facts much more theologically than Mark does. Mark is prepared to put things in a way from which Matthew and Luke shrink, because they are more aware of the theological implications than Mark is.

Matthew and Luke tend, so to speak, to "protect" the apostles. They tend to omit anything that might look like a criticism of the apostles, or anything that might show them in an unfavourable light.[13]

I will now present a few of the many examples of this. In chapter 4 Mark records Jesus' parable of the sower after which the Twelve ask him to explain it. Jesus replied, "Don't you understand this parable? How then will you ever understand any parable?" (v. 13).[14] Matthew and Luke both incorporate this incident from Mark into their gospels, but both delete this criticism of the Twelve. Again in the ninth chapter Jesus is teaching the disciples of his death and resurrection, "But," Mark writes, "they did not understand what this teaching meant, and they were afraid to ask him" (v. 32). Matthew deletes this and adds, "The disciples became very sad" (17:23).

Mark's description of the apostles as "amazed" and "afraid" (10:32; 6:51) is also deleted by Matthew and Luke. The story in Mark of Jesus calming the storm is copied point by point by Matthew and Luke except for the accusing question the disciples put to Jesus: "Teacher, don't you care that we are about to die?" (4:38). In Matthew this becomes "Save us, Lord, we are about to die" (8:25), and Luke alters it to read, "Master, Master! We are about to die!" (8:24).

Mark (10:51, 52) concludes his story of Jesus walking on the water this way:

And he went up unto them into the ship; and the wind ceased: and they were sore amazed in themselves beyond measure and wondered. For they considered not the miracle of the loaves: for their heart was hardened.

Matthew follows Mark's account, but replaces this ending with "Then they that were in the ship came and worshipped him, saying, Of a truth thou art the Son of God" (14:33). Matthew's picture of the disciples is that of a worshiping body of men. "Mark's is the picture of dull-witted men with impervious minds unwilling and unable to understand."

Mark 9 contains Jesus' answer to the question, "Who is the greatest in the kingdom of God?" The incident that raised the question was an unseemly dispute among the disciples as to who among them was the greatest. When Jesus asked what they were arguing about, they would not answer him. Matthew and Luke include Jesus' teaching, but from the pattern we see emerging, it is no surprise that they both omit this uncomplimentary argument among the disciples (9:33-37).

In the next chapter James and John come to Jesus with the ambitious request to sit on his right hand and on left hand when he sits upon his throne. This makes the remaining ten disciples angry. While Luke completely omits the incident, Matthew includes it, but changes the account to read James and John's mother made the ambitious request.

I believe this sampling is sufficient to support the conclusion of most New Testament scholars, as stated by Metzger:

In the early church there was an increase of respect for the apostles, who came to be regarded as the pillars of the church. Matthew and Luke often soften Mark's blunt and sometimes uncomplimentary statements regarding these leaders of the church.[15]

Of even greater interest are the changes made by Matthew and Luke which improve on Mark's picture of Jesus. Twice in Mark (3:5; 10:14) Jesus displays the human emotion of anger, which both Matthew and Luke delete (Matthew 12:12, 13; 19:14, and Luke 6:10; 18:16).

In several instances Mark makes statements which seem to limit Jesus. In one of the healing accounts Mark relates that "they brought him *all* that were sick...and he healed *many*" (Mark 1:32-34). Matthew changes this to read "they brought unto him *many*...and he healed all that were sick" (Matthew 8:16). Mark also writes that "Jesus *could* no more openly enter into the city" (Mark 1:45).

Again, Matthew and Luke omit the phrase (Matthew 8:4; Luke 5:15, 16). Mark tells of Jesus' journey to Nazareth where "He was not able to perform any miracles there, except that he placed his hands on a few sick people and healed them" (6:5). Matthew alters this to read "he did not perform many miracles there" (Matthew 13:58). To Mark he "could not"; to Matthew he "did not." According to Mark no one knows the time of the Second Coming, including the Son. But, Matthew and Luke omit the phrase which specifically declares Jesus' lack of knowledge (Mark 13:32; Matthew 24:36; Luke 21:33). In Matthew Jesus healed "with a word" (8:16), "instantly" (15:28; 17:18). In Mark there are two accounts of Jesus using spittle to effect a cure, one of which required two stages for results (7:32-37; 8:22-26). Matthew and Luke omit both incidents. Mark tells of Jesus cursing a fig tree, which withered the next day (11:20, 21). Matthew alters the account so that it withered immediately, causing his disciples to marvel (21:19, 20).

Mark refers to Jesus as "the Lord" only once, whereas Matthew uses the term nineteen times and Luke sixteen.[16]

The baptism of Jesus is of interest on several points. In Mark, John is baptizing "for the remission of sins" (1:4) and Jesus comes to him and is baptized. Matthew deletes the reference to John baptizing for the remission of sins (Matthew 3:1, 2), thus removing the possible inference in Mark that Jesus was baptized for a remission of his sins. Then Matthew (3:13-15) adds this note of explanation as to why Jesus was baptized:

John tried to stop him. "I need to be baptized by you," he said, "and are you coming to me?" For the present," Jesus answered, "let it be so, for the right thing for us to do is to do everything a good man ought to do." Then John let him have his way.

One final example is this startling account in Mark 3:20, 21, Barclay Translation:

Jesus went into a house, and once again such a crowd gathered that it was impossible for them even to eat a meal. When his own family heard what was going on, they left home to come and forcibly restrain him. "He has taken leave of his senses," they said.[17]

Mark here makes the remarkable admission that Jesus' own family thought he had taken leave of his senses. Neither Matthew nor Luke chose to include this.

The authors of the New Testament and the authors of the *History of the Church* were faithful evangelists writing history to promote faith. The result is that in them we have two histories which are defective according to current professional historical standards. The most prolific in their condemnation of this characteristic of the official Mormon history are evangelists for some other form of Christianity. On the one hand they claim that Mormons must deny their faith because of their flawed history, while on the other hand, they remain ignorant of, or deny, the same characteristic in the New Testament. They fail to acknowledge the two approaches to religious history—the evangelistic and the professional. To put it crudely, the "bring them to salvation" evangelist, and the "tell it all" professional historian are not likely ever to appreciate each other's approach to history. These critics of Mormon history will accept only the evangelistic approach to history when it comes to the New Testament, and only the professional approach when it comes to Mormon history. They thus conclude that the history they accept is perfect while Mormon history is seriously defective. I cannot resist concluding with this counsel of Jesus from the Sermon on the Mount (Matthew 7:3-5):

Why do you look at the speck in your brother's eye and pay no attention to the log in your own eye? How dare you say to your brother, 'Please let me take that speck out of your eye,' when you have a log in your own eye? You hypocrite! First take the log out of your own eye, and then you will be able to see clearly to take the speck out of your brother's eye.

Notes

1. Jerald and Sandra Tanner, *Changes in Joseph Smith's History* (Modern Microfilm), 3.
2. Ibid., 1-9.
3. Ibid., 3.
4. The Tanners count over 62,000 words added or deleted without counting the changes made from the manuscripts to the first printing. Of course, the Tanners are sensationalizing. They themselves have not been able to show any reasonable significance behind the overwhelming majority of the changes.
5. The editing began in 1838 and continued intermittently through the late 1940s when the current edition of the *History of the Church* was completed. See Dean C. Jessee, "The Writing of Joseph Smith's History," *BYU Studies* 11 (Summer 1971):439.
6. In addition to the one already cited, see *Falsification of Joseph Smith's History* (Salt Lake City, Modern Microfilm), and *The Changing World of Mormonism* (Chicago: Moody Press, 1980), ch. 13.
7. All major recent New Testament commentaries and introductions treat the subject.
8. George Buttrick, ed. *Interpreter's Dictionary of the Bible*, 5 vols. (Nashville: Abingdon, 1962) 4:492.
9. William Barclay, *Introduction to the First Three Gospels* (Philadelphia: Westminster Press, 1975), 86, 87.
10. Bruce M. Metzger, *The New Testament: Its Background, Growth, and Content* (Nashville: Abingdon Press, 1965), 83.
11. Ibid.
12. Barclay, 89.
13. Ibid., 90.

14. Most of the biblical quotations cited are from Today's English Version. Also cited are the King James Version and A New Translation by William Barclay.

15. Metzger, 81.

16. For a discussion of the doctrinal implications of the use of *the Lord* by the New Testament writers see Oscar Cullmann, *The Christology of the New Testament* (Philadelphia: Westminster Press, 1963), 193-237.

17. This passage has proved embarrassing to Christians throughout history. The result is that a number of early manuscripts altered the passage to read, "When the scribes and the others had heard about him, they went out to seize him, for they said, "He is beside himself." See Bruce M. Metzger, *A Textual Commentary on the Greek New Testament* (New York: United Bible Societies, 1975), 81.

LAMONI: CRUCIBLE FOR PLURALISM IN THE REORGANIZATION CHURCH

Norma Derry Hiles

For some time, I have felt drawn toward the idea that the personality and psyche of the current Reorganized church member reflects in many ways the early Lamoni settlement period. Often we are tempted to view recent diversities as a new and frightening or unhealthy phenomena when, in fact, this may be the most apparent personality trait of the Reorganized church from its inception. The differences of opinion in all aspects of our religious life have, for many years, found uncomfortable refuge under the RLDS umbrella. I suggest we need to view our diversified heritage more comfortably as a strength—not as a weakness. Experiences such as the settling of Lamoni should teach us that the seeds of our collective survival are strong among us.

Out of the pain and suffering of the Mormon Nauvoo experience, a number of strands of social and religious consciousness emerged which would forever change the complexion and behavior of those who would later meld into the Reorganized church. The Mormon population of Nauvoo dispersed after the death of Joseph Smith, Jr., into numerous groups. Each group came away with varying attitudes toward the cause for the Nauvoo debacle—most of them still clinging to bits of their Mormon legacy and most of them adopting a form of the prophet's Zion-building ideal. During the 1850s a number of lesser Mormon factions, among them the Strangites, the Thompsonites, the Cutlerites, and the William Smith followers coalesced into the Reorganized church with Jason Briggs and Zenas Gurley, Sr., as their spokespersons. This group was composed mostly of stalwart conservatives like William Marks, one of the earliest foes of polygamy, who nevertheless clung tenaciously to cherished values in American Christianity and yet had been bitten by the "vision of a perfect community to be established by the church."[1]

The status of the fledgling Reorganization church was greatly enhanced in 1860 when the Mormon founder's oldest son, Joseph Smith III, assumed leadership of the sect. To some it was a fulfillment of the revelation given to Jason Briggs in Beloit, Wisconsin, several years before. To others it verified their belief that young Joseph had been designated as his father's successor, a claim Joseph III never made for himself.[2]

Joseph III's letters reveal the very complex and diversified community for which he had agreed to provide leadership. From the first, the conflicts of interest, the dichotomy of attitudes and beliefs, the old wounds and hatreds, and the multiple theological attitudes were apparent. To try to meld this complexity of persons and their individuality into a workable group must have seemed to young Joseph a most formidable task.

Over the years, as I have read more and more of Joseph's papers and letters, I have marveled at his patience and tenacity and frequently have been amazed at his generous spirit and diplomatic skills. Now and then he wrote to Charles Derry, a cherished friend, of his weariness at the in-fighting and "pettifogging" as he loved to call it. He also expressed much anger at constantly being misunderstood.[3] However, for the most part he persevered, willing to compromise, to set short-term goals and work toward them with agonizing slowness. He seemed able to sustain himself with a dream of the Utopian society envisioned by his father, perhaps never attainable, but still worth the effort.

Convinced that his father's approach toward organizing Utopian communities was basically correct, Joseph III, however, believed that the early Mormons had tried to accomplish too much too quickly, with too few skills to achieve success. Because of their millennial beliefs they had unfortunately assumed they would be spared the pain of personal change. Joseph III, a realistic pragmatist, believed that the early Saints "had not been sufficiently prepared to overcome their fundamentally selfish human nature and were not able to accept an all-sharing Utopian society." He also noted that the Saints had never exhibited the respect for each other that made possible a communitarian community. He soon came to believe that the Reorganization's Zion-building experiences should be more liberal in nature and he urged members to live in the larger community not apart from it—a much different view from his father's. He believed that the millennial kingdom of God could be initiated only through personal righteousness and moral perfection. Therefore, the gathering philosophy that Joseph Smith III espoused during the early years was an emphasis on the spiritual nature of Zion, rather than its physical, community building aspect.[4]

Joseph's emphasis on the inner purity of the Saints and the necessity of effecting social changes in the world prompted him to immerse himself in social and political reform movements and to urge his followers to do the same. He wrote in the *True Latter Day Saint Herald*, the official newspaper of the church.

the church should begin to take a high moral ground in regard to the very many abuses in society, which can only be reached, to correction, by a strong setting upon them of the current of public opinion.[5]

He called for a church-wide crusade to eliminate sin. Joseph believed that even if the reform movements took decades or centuries to accomplish, the church would ultimately triumph if it moved in a cautious, steady, and unified manner.[6]

Not unlike other leaders before and since, Joseph III seemed often out of step with his followers. Most of them longed for and argued about the time when the church would establish a settlement modeled after the experiment in early Mormon years. They clung to the concept of the millennium. Charles Derry recorded in his diary, year after year, world events which he saw as apocalyptic. They viewed themselves as people who lived "daily as strangers and pilgrims on the earth, who look for a city which hath foundations, whose builder and maker is God." Joseph's move to Plano, the large church population there, and the operation of the Herald Publishing Company all seemed to satisfy the Saints for a time and served as an unofficial gathering for them.[7]

However, in the late 1860s the clamor for a gathering place began to haunt Joseph wherever he went and it came from all sides. He wrote in the *Herald* in 1866 that he heard from every quarter the constant pleading for a Zionistic experiment. He scolded the members for wanting Zion before completing the necessary self-perfection. Smith suggested

140

that the Saints continue to live justly in their diverse locations and not concern themselves with community building until they were worthy of the task.[8] It seems that the admonition of "being worthy" would have put an end to the discussion for some time—but Joseph was not so lucky.

Unlike the followers of Joseph Smith, Jr., the Reorganized Saints felt complete freedom, in fact some seemed to feel it was necessary, to disagree with Joseph III. The complaints increased concerning his reluctance to give concrete expression to the gathering concept. Joseph began to rethink his position about church-established settlements and he moved toward compromise. In late 1869, Joseph advanced a plan suggesting that the Reorganized church not sponsor a true communal experiment but instead form a joint stock company that would make land available to Latter Day Saint members in terms equitable to both settlers and the stock company. One purpose was to make land and homes available to members with very little means. In this way the church could indirectly sponsor a settlement of mostly church members and satisfy the pleas of many for a place to gather. At the same time the experiment would neither have official church management nor millenarian overtones, thereby saving itself from the destructive forces which Joseph III felt were inherent in the early Kirtland, Far West, and Nauvoo communities.[9]

The United Order of Enoch was formed at the October Conference of 1869 as a joint stock company and the seeds of the idea which later emerged as the Lamoni community began to grow. Joseph III made it clear that he did not intend the experiment as a Zionic community. He saw it as a means to an end, not as an end in itself.[10] Nevertheless his proposal received overwhelming support

from the Conference body and Joseph moved quickly to organize the land grant company.

The particulars of the Order of Enoch governance were drafted by February of 1870 and the Board of Directors was elected. During the spring, circulars were sent out urging the membership of the church to either buy shares or loan money, interest free, for the purchase of land. Many of the Saints believed that their dreams of a physical Zion would soon be realized!

Elijah Banta, a great amiable giant of a man from Sandwich, Illinois, Israel Rogers, Presiding Bishop from Plano, and David Dancer, a recent convert from Kewanee, Illinois, composed the Committee on Location. They traveled throughout Iowa, Illinois, and Missouri—their goal, inexpensive but productive land. Elijah Banta stumbled across a large tract of land in Decatur County while visiting Ebenezer Robinson in Pleasanton, Iowa. He believed, from the first, that it was exactly what they were looking for. Excited by his discovery and the possibilities it held, Banta made several trips to Decatur County between October and December of 1870. He conveyed his information and recommendations to the Committee on Location which met with the full board and Joseph on April 5, 1871.[11] The transaction was approved and Banta contracted on behalf of the United Order of Enoch to purchase 2,680 acres of contiguous farmland and several smaller parcels amounting to 3,330 acres in all. The purchase amount was approximately $8.00 an acre. Members of the Order of Enoch immediately began to make plans to develop the land. Some settlers arrived as early as July of 1871. From the inception of the Lamoni community, the Latter Day Saints settling there seemed to consider religious fellowship its most important advantage.[12]

141

Typically, however, all was not "a bed of roses." The membership was certainly not unified in their feelings about gathering and although Joseph and other leaders were respected and often loved, they were not always listened to or agreed with—a habit we seem to continue to this day! It was as though after Nauvoo, those of the Reorganization had vowed never to follow blindly and without questioning again. For Reorganized church members the settling of Lamoni seemed to unite them in their determination that the one thing they could agree upon was never to agree.

Elijah Banta recorded in his diary in February of 1870:

many of the bretherren in Plano are oposed to to the Co being called the first united order of Enoch they wish the man that has been industrious and saving to yeald up his earnings for them [meaning the Order of Enoch] to Spend or live on in ease.[13]

This was an obvious suggestion that some of the brethren did not trust others of the brethren. A great many of the people who did give or lend money to the Order of Enoch seem to have done so with a number of reservations. Typical of letters that came with pledges of money was one written by Robert Elvin, which included $50.00. He wrote,

A great deal of money has been kept from the committee through the influence of those who are opposed to the effort. I find that it dose not require as much wisdom to get the saints to refuse as it dose to render the necessary help.[14]

Another letter from James Drown, of the Sherman Branch in Michigan, seems a rather typical response.

I improve this opportunity to write you a few lines letting you know that we are willing to do what we can toward the redemption of Zion the saints here are hard up & there is but few of us that can get money to send at present. . . .I concicrate $1.00 for the purpose of helping to purchase land for the redemption of Zion. (I) James Drown, and Br. John Gulenbauk, sends $1.00 for the same purpose.[15]

Daniel Hougas in Macedonia, Iowa, wrote to Joseph III: "The following members of the Farm Creek Branch agree to give the sum opposite their names, for the purpous of the location of the church's headquarters." He then listed six names with varying sums opposite, ranging from one dollar to ten. He cryptically added at the end of the letter, "If the headquarters are settled we are willing to do more. If the location suits me, I am willing to do more."[16]

A more heartwarming response came from John Garver, Sr., in San Bernardino, California, to I. L. Rogers:

In response to the call, I send you $100 dollars as a donation for the purpose of purchacing land and considerit a privlige to aid in so good a cause. And the Lord guide his servants in all their acts.[17]

Jesse Seelye wrote from Savannah, New York, to Israel L. Rogers:

I Received of Joseph Smith a circular bearing date Nov 1875 in relation to a Site or location for the settlement of the Saints; calling upon the Saints to consecrate or donate of their means for that purpose. . . .I believe I have an interest in this work for I want an Inheritance with the Saints of god. I shall send you two hundred dollars the first of April.[18]

You will notice that even though Joseph and the Committee on Location had agreed to purchase land in Fayette Township, Decatur County, as early as 1871, the majority of the church membership was unaware that Joseph intended for the headquarters of the church and the Herald Publishing Co. to settle there as well.[19] All during the 1870s he continued to ask for and accept reports and suggestions for other alternative locations. In April of 1876 the final decisions by the CB&Q Railroad to run its line through Lamoni became a firm reality and, in June of that year, Joseph wrote to Charles Derry.

Present indications denote a locating of the Press in S.W. Iowa—and it will be wisdom as soon as you can do so consistently to get into that region. The fact is I see no other really eligible place. Please use

142

this information for your own guidance only.. . .[20]

During January of 1877 he wrote Brother T. Hindirks the following note,

I am quite certain that DeKalb County, Missouri is in the regions round about, and in the borders of Zion. If you, and your brethren, feel well to go in there and make homes, may the blessing of God go with you. I say Amen to it.

Make good, solid, permanant homes, do right and live in your homes as men of God.[21]

During the summer of that same year, Joseph III secured forty acres of land a mile west of the townsite in Fayette Township for the new home he anticipated building.

It was not until October of 1881, however, that Joseph III announced in the *Saints' Herald* that the printing office was moving and that the next issue would appear on November 1, as scheduled, from Lamoni, Iowa. Once moved, the *Herald* office set up temporary quarters in a frame building in Lamoni and later moved into its new brick office, almost in the center of town. Joseph's concerns and vacillating feelings as the Saints began to gather seem obvious.

There were advantages for the church members who moved into the Lamoni community as they helped one another settle the land and build homes. By 1881 there were about one thousand of them. The community became largely shaped by the moral and religious expectations of both the newly arrived Reorganized church population and the citizens (a majority were Methodists) who had lived in the area for some time. There were several instances recorded that in the early days the Saints seem to have voted as a bloc as in the 1883 election of Elijah Banta to the State Legislature.[22] The response in the Republican Decatur County *Journal* was highly critical. However, if these political activities antagonized some, it does not appear that the Reorganized church Saints ever presented a front united sufficiently to cause their neighbors the same alarm and concern as in Nauvoo.

Joseph Smith III seemed increasingly pleased with Lamoni. He thought the environment especially attractive because of the general upstanding nature of the society. He deemed it a fine place to raise children and wrote that the citizens of Lamoni demonstrated a concern and trust he had rarely seen before. He enjoyed the friendships and the genteel socialization. Moreover, he came to believe that Lamoni had filled its purpose well, it had become a business and church center for the Saints and was increasingly stable and upwardly mobile. Joseph's contentment with Lamoni and his love for his home there did not change his commitment to the spiritual perfection of the people, however. He saw Independence as the ultimate location of the church's headquarters.[23]

Some historians have viewed the years that the Reorganization had its printing company and church headquarters in Lamoni as insignificant. One has suggested that Lamoni was a way-stop on the road to Zion. I see early Lamoni as having served a rather different and perhaps more significant purpose. The successful settling of Lamoni taught the early Reorganized church Saints some important lessons, ones which some of us are still struggling to learn. The reality of our movement is diversity, pluralism, and individualism. These elements, used compassionately and well, are both strengthening and progressive. These very traits may in fact enable us to achieve the Christian character which Joseph III deemed a primary goal.

Notes

1. Clare Vlahos, "The Dissent of Jason Briggs and Zenas H. Gurley," DuRose Room, Frederick Madison Smith Library, Graceland College, Lamoni, Iowa, 1967, 2-4.

2. Joseph Smith III, *The Memoirs of President Joseph Smith III* (1832-1914) (Independence, Missouri: Herald House, 1979), 74. Original text appeared in the *Saints' Herald*, April 9, 1935.

3. Joseph Smith III to Charles Derry from Plano, Illinois, June 10, 1868. P15 f4, RLDS Library and Archives, Independence, Missouri.

4. Roger D. Launius, "The Mormon Quest for a Perfect Society at Lamoni, Iowa 1870-1900," *The Annals of Iowa*, vol. 47, no. 4 (Spring 1984):326-27.

5. Joseph Smith III, "The Location of Zion," *Saints' Herald* (April 1863): 138.

6. Joseph Smith III, "Pleasant Chat," *Saints' Herald* (June 1, 1866):68-69; *Herald* (August 1, 1867): 81; *Herald* (September 1, 1869):146.

7. Joseph Smith III and Heman C. Smith, *The History of the Reorganized Church of Jesus Christ of Latter Day Saints* (Independence, Missouri: Herald House, 1901), 297, 409.

8. Joseph Smith III, "Pleasant Chat," *Saints' Herald* (June 1, 1866):68-69.

9. Larry E. Hunt, *Frederick Madison Smith: Saint as Reformer, vol. 1* (Independence, Missouri: Herald House, 1982), 150-55.

10. Ibid.

11. Thomas W. Williams, "Elijah Banta," original in DuRose Room, Frederick Madison Smith Library. See also Elijah Banta Journals, Book B, beginning May 1868 for detailed account of Order of Enoch activities, plans, and land purchases.

12. Williams, "Elijah Banta."

13. Elijah Banta Journals (February 20, 1870), 80.

14. Letter to Israel Rogers from Robert M. Elvin, February 18, 1876, from Nebraska City, Nebraska. P24 f38, RLDS Library and Archives.

15. Letter to Israel Rogers from James Drown, Sherman, Michigan, branch, November 8, 1876, P24, RLDS Library and Archives. For other letters, see P24 "Location of Business Headquarters" folders 38, 39, 40, 41.

16. Letter to Joseph Smith III from Daniel Hougas, March 27, 1876. P24 f38, RLDS Library and Archives.

17. Letter to I. L. Rogers from John Garver, Sr., April 15, 1876. RLDS Library and Archives.

18. Letter to I. L. Rogers from Jesse Seelye, March 19, 1876. RLDS Library and Archives.

19. W. W. Blair, *Memoirs of W. W. Blair*, DuRose Room, Frederick Madison Smith Library, December 23, 1873.

20. Letter to Charles Derry, June 9, 1876, JSLB 1, p. 21, RLDS Library and Archives.

21. Letter to Temme Hindirks, January 4, 1877. JSLB 1, p. 59, RLDS Library and Archives.

22. Joseph Smith III, *Saints' Herald* (May 15, 1882): 152; (May 23, 1885): 333; Decatur County *Journal* (July 6, 1882), (October 11, 1883), (October 18, 1883).

23. Joseph Smith III, letter to Joseph Luff, February 22, 1881, JSLB 3, 300-308; *Saints' Herald*, January 15, 1887, editorial, RLDS Library and Archives.

THE CHANGING RLDS RESPONSE TO MORMON POLYGAMY: A PRELIMINARY ANALYSIS

Richard P. Howard

(Reprinted by permission from the *John Whitmer Historical Association Journal*, vol. 3)

A Diverse Response in the Early Reorganization

During the early years of the Reorganization opposition to plural marriage was one of the church's central concerns — second only to affirming the principle of lineal descent in church presidency. The first RLDS publication, *A Word of Consolation,* contained a strongly worded attack on polygamy, condemning it *per se* but making no attempt to either identify or exclude any proponents. This type of attack on Mormon polygamy from the press and representatives of the early RLDS movement continued into the 1860s, so that it became clear to the public that one of the chief distinctions between the RLDS and the LDS churches was their contrasting positions on polygamy.

Joseph Smith III's inaugural address at Amboy on April 6, 1860, seemed to call for a new, twin emphasis in the anti-polygamy stance of the RLDS church:

There is but one principle taught by the leaders of any faction of this people that I hold in utter abhorrence; that is a principle taught by Brigham Young and those believing in him. I have been told that my father taught such doctrines. I have never believed it and never can believe it. If such things were done, then I believe they never were done by divine authority. I believe my father was a good man, and a good man never could have promulgated such doctrines.[1]

If this was to be the start of a new approach — i.e., opposing polygamy, to be sure, but going beyond that to try to clear Joseph Smith, Jr., of any connection with its origin — such a shift in emphasis was rather slow in developing. Before Joseph III became president of the Reorganization three statements by two persons later to become leaders in the Reorganization had already reached public notice. These represented an alternative view to the 1860 Amboy statement of Joseph Smith III. The first one, by Isaac Sheen in 1852, was reprinted in the first number of the *True Latter Day Saints' Herald* in January 1860, from the October 9, 1852, issue of the *Saturday Evening Post:*

The Salt Lake apostles also excuse themselves by **saying** that Joseph Smith taught the **spiritual-wife doctrine,** but this excuse is as weak as their excuse concerning the ancient kings and patriarchs. Joseph Smith repented of his connection with this doctrine, and said it was was of the devil. He caused the revelation on that subject to be burned, and when he voluntarily came to Nauvoo and resigned himself into the arms of his enemies, he said that he was going to Carthage to die. At that time he also said, that if it had not been for that accursed **spiritual wife doctrine,** he would not have come to that. By his conduct at that time he proved the sincerity of his repentance, and of his profession as a prophet. If Abraham and Jacob, by repentance, can obtain salvation and exaltation, so can Joseph Smith.[2] (Emphasis added.)

Within a year after Sheen's statement had appeared in the *Saturday Evening Post,* William Marks published a letter in the periodical of C. B. Thompson, for whose faction Marks was then a representative. From that letter the following is quoted:

Joseph, however, became convinced before his death that he had done wrong; for about three weeks before his death, I met him one morning in the street, and he said to me, Brother Marks, I have something to communicate to you, we retired to a by-place, and set down together, when he said: "We are a ruined people." I asked, how so? he said: "This doctrine of polygamy, or Spiritual-wife system, that has been taught and practiced among us, will prove our destruction and overthrow. I have been deceived," said he, "in reference to its practice; it is wrong; it is a curse to mankind, and we shall have to leave the United States soon, unless it can be put down, and its practice stopped in the church. Now," said he, "Brother Marks, you have not received this doctrine, and how glad I am. I want you to go into the high council, and I will have charges preferred against all who practice this doctrine, and I want you to try them by the laws of the church, and cut them off, if they will not repent, and cease the practice of this doctrine; and" said he, "I will go into the stand, and preach against it, with all my might, and in this way we may rid the church of this damnable heresy."[3]

In the first issue of the *True Latter Day Saints' Herald,* Marks published a second statement on polygamy, similar in nearly every detail to his 1853 recollection. The following is excerpted from it:

About the first of June, 1844, (situated as I was at that time, being the Presiding Elder of the Stake at Nauvoo, and by appointment the Presiding Office of the High Council) I had a very good opportunity to know the affairs of the Church, and my convictions at that time were, that the Church in a great measure had departed from the pure principles and doctrines of Jesus Christ. I felt much troubled in mind about the condition of the Church. I prayed earnestly to my Heavenly Father to show me something in regard to it, when I was wrapt in vision, and it was shown me by the Spirit, that the top or branches had overcome the root, in sin and wickedness, and the only way to cleanse and purify it was, to disorganize it, and in due time, the Lord would reorganize it again. . . . A few days after the occurrence, I met with Brother Joseph.

He said that he wanted to converse with me on the affairs of the Church, and we retired by ourselves. I will give his words verbatim, for they are indelibly stamped upon my mind. He said he had desired for a long time to have a talk with me on the subject of polygamy. He said it eventually would prove the overthrow of the Church, and we should soon be obliged to leave the United States, unless it could be speedily put down. He was satisfied that it was a cursed doctrine, and that there must be every exertion made to put it down. He said that he would go before the congregation and proclaim against it, and I must go into the High Council, and he would prefer charges against those in transgression, and I must sever them from the Church, unless they made ample satisfaction. There was much more said, but this was the substance. The mob commenced to gather about Carthage in a few days after, therefore there was nothing done concerning it.[4]

These statements by Sheen and Marks agree in their view that Joseph Smith, Jr., was somehow involved in the inception of the spiritual wife doctrine which led to polygamy at Nauvoo, but that he renounced the doctrine as a mistake before his death. Joseph Smith III seemed to be answering such a position in his inaugural by saying that he had been told that such had been the case with his father, but that he, Joseph III, could never believe it. That stance seemed not to affect Marks's assessment of the situation, even though he became a member of the RLDS First Presidency in 1863. Two years later he wrote a letter to Hiram Falk and Josiah Butterfield, from which the following is taken:

Brother Joseph came to me about two weeks before he was kiled and sais Brother Marks I want to talk with you we went by our selves and he sais this poligamy business in the Church must be stopt or the Church is ruend and we cant stay in the United States I have been deceive in this thing and it must be put down I thoght it would be an advantage to Mankind but I find it proves a curse I asked him how it coul be dun he said I must go into the high Council and he would prefur charges against those in adultry and i must cut them off and he would go onto the stand and preach against it and thought buy so doing we might put it it down but the mob son commenced gathering and there was nothing dun.[5]

Earlier that year (May 2, 1865) a joint council of Twelve and Presidency had discussed the question of polygamy, with specific reference to Nauvoo:

The question arose as to whether Joseph the Martyr taught the doctrine of polygamy. President Marks said Brother Hyrum came to his place once and told him he did not believe in it and he was going to see Joseph about it and if he had a revelation on the subject he would believe it. And after that Hyrum read a revelation on it in the High Council and he Marks felt that it was not true but he saw the High Council received it.[6]

One can discern the basis for polarity emerging in the RLDS church leadership over whether the battle against polygamy should also include attempts to establish the founder's innocence with respect to its origin. Joseph III's stance, i.e., that his father had been a good man and therefore could not have promulgated such doctrines, was inconsistent with the recollections of others of his RLDS colleagues who had been adult members of the Nauvoo church. Two years later another joint council of Presidency and Twelve again confronted the issue:

The following resolution was put and tabled. Resolved, that we do not believe that the revelation, alleged to have come through Joseph Smith, the Martyr, authorizing polygamy, or spiritual wifery, came from God, neither do we believe that J. Smith was in any wise the author or excuser of these doctrines. J. W. Briggs, Z. H. Gurley, E. C. Briggs, and John Shippy defended the resolution; Wm. W. Blair, Josiah Ells and C. Derry opposed it on the grounds that its passage would be more injurious than good because of the almost universal opinion among the Saints that Joseph was in some way connected with it. J. W. Briggs moved it be tabled, and hence the resolution was lost. Pres. Smith then told us that the passage of the resolution would do more injury than good.[7]

I have unearthed no further statements by any of these discussants that would clarify the meaning of Joseph Smith III's remark that to pass such a resolution would do more injury than good. He,

along with the others on that council, probably felt that, given the general opinion then thought to be prevailing, such a measure would win little support within the RLDS church, and might even be disruptive. Whether Joseph III ever doubted the accuracy of the assumptions made about his father's innocence in his 1860 inaugural we cannot know for sure. However, his brother David appears to have had his own uncertainties, writing from Salt Lake City in 1872:

It is an unpleasant subject to me. If I knew in regard to the subject I would tell you the truth. You, I think know me well enough to know I never would deceive you in anything, cost what tears it would. I would tell you if I thought my brother was a deceiver. I would save you from deception. I know my mother believes just as we do in faith, repentance, baptism, and all the saving doctrines, in the books of the church and all, but I do not wish to ask her in regard to polygamy, for dear brother God forgive me if I am wrong. How can I tell you if I did not love you. I could not. I believe there was something wrong. I don't know it, but I believe it, the testimony is too great for me to deny. Now you may give up everything if you must and cease to regard me as your friend but I never did deceive you and never will. If my father sinned I can not help it. The truth to me is the same. He must suffer for his sin. I do not know that he did, and if I had not received such a convincing testimony of the gospel my faith might fail but it does not even though he did sin. . . . I hope you will burn up this letter, and not let it shock your faith, if I could tell you otherwise I would oh how gladly, if neglecting to answer the question would be right I would do that, I have prayed and suffered and can suffer no longer and so tell you what I think the truth is. . . . Trust me Sherman to tell you the truth hard or soft be my dear friend still and please write me a long and kind letter to hold me up. . . . When I was with you before I did not know as much as I do now in regard to my father's life. Even if he did wrong he repented and told the saints that polygamy was a false and wicked doctrine.[8]

With no misgivings about the integrity of Joseph Smith III, it can be noted that from the late 1870s on he was moved to try to clear his father's name of any connection with the inception of Mormon polygamy. This seems probable in view of two major factors which intervened and convinced Joseph III to take such a course. First, death had claimed the lives of William Marks (May 22, 1872) and Isaac Sheen (April 3, 1874). Disability had isolated David H. Smith's tortured questions from the arena of active debate over the matter. Second, the intensifying RLDS-LDS ideological warfare and strong anti-Mormon sentiment in the United States generally, led to a style of RLDS denunciations of the "LDS apostasy" with great fervor and detailed documentation. In that climate, Reorganization rhetoric identified the RLDS church as the one true successor to original, pure Latter Day Saintism. Now it seemed imperative to identify original Mormonism, the prophet Joseph Smith (represented now by his son Joseph III), and the RLDS church as standing on essentially common ground. In a practical sense this meant projecting as pure an image of Joseph Smith, Jr., as possible, one in keeping with the loftiest ideals of the gospel as perceived by RLDS leaders.

Therefore, for motives perhaps beyond historical analysis, Joseph Smith III launched his personal pilgrimage from the late 1870s on to try to establish his father's innocence. That pilgrimage led him twice on lengthy tours of Utah (1885 and 1889), to denounce polygamy and to clear his father's name. For to clear that name was to clear his own, his mother's, and that of any Smith family member remaining faithful to the gospel as promulgated by the RLDS church. Extending the rationale: to establish Joseph, Jr.'s innocence was to gain a legitimacy for the RLDS church to be had in no other way. So for several generations, defending Joseph, Jr., became both the style and aim of the antipolygamy stance of the RLDS church. As editor of the *Saints' Herald*, Joseph Smith III encouraged publication of views advocating the

"innocence" of his father by blaming Mormon polygamy on Brigham Young—and fixing its inception in a post-Nauvoo time frame. Several of these polemics appeared in the *Herald* early in 1879.[9]

However, there was a rather unsettling element in RLDS circles potentially threatening RLDS efforts to clear the Smith family name from the polygamous stigma. The prime symbol of that element was Zenas H. Gurley, Jr., a member of the RLDS Council of Twelve since 1874. Gurley's father had been a seventy at Nauvoo, and had served as an RLDS apostle from April 1853 until his death in 1871.

The younger Gurley had become embroiled with other church leaders, including Joseph Smith III, on various doctrinal themes. By 1879 Gurley was pleading with Smith to allow the use of the church press to air both sides of controverted issues. Gurley differed with Smith on the question of whether the latter's father had been involved in the inception of plural marriage at Nauvoo. Since the *Herald* had been advancing Smith's position on this issue Gurley urged that he and others be given space in the church paper to present the other side of the controversy. In his March 25, 1879, letter to Smith, Gurley wrote:

I have felt somewhat sore and chagrined at the attempts made through the *Herald* to establish the innocence of your father touching polygamy, as though the work of God depended in any sense upon his innocence or guilt, and I may say here that **many** others in the church have expressed similar feelings to me, but have and do feel too delicate to speak with you upon the matter because it's your father. I however have more confidence in your good sense and judgment to allow such feelings preventing me, will you open the columns of the *Herald* to the other side of the story? And have I not a right as a member of the Body to demand it? The impression is obtaining that the object of those statements and articles are to build up family name—hence selfish interests and is militating against you.

I believe firmly in your father's guilt and think it susceptible of proof, and have for years. I have frequently been asked to write upon the subject and I do think if one side of the story is continued that the other must have a hearing. If the *Herald* columns are not open upon this matter will you publish the names of those in the church who believe your father guilty? . . . all the assertions you have made relative to your father cannot change the facts one iota, nor benefit him nor you, but eternity **will reveal** them. I believe then that your mission is something higher than that, however I will not question your right to follow the bent of your own mind. But I ask equal privilege for myself and others; that of being heard.[10]

Joseph's response of April 2, 1879, indicated the complex position in which Gurley's demands were placing him. With compelling logic and appeals to Gurley's basic loyalty to the gospel, Joseph attempted to disarm him in the interest of the unity of the church:

What I have done, or tried to do; and this I have done conscientiously; was to deny that my father was the human author of the polygamy practiced by the Utah Saints, and the revelations claimed as its sanctioning, and authorization. If in this I have offended against honesty, and good, sound doctrine and policy I am not only regretful but deeply sorry; and shall where it is made manifest to me, make the amplest amends in my power.

Your belief in his guilt (how, or how much you hold him guilty of I do not know) as well as that of some others I have known for years; but yourself will bear me witness that I have not abated a single jot of manly esteem or brotherly regard for them or for you. So far as the opening of the columns of the *Herald* to a discussion of the guilt of Joseph Smith from your pen is concerned; were I to choose, I should much prefer to open them for Orson Pratt, John Taylor, or Joseph F. Smith for the obvious reason, that they hold that the dogma of polygamy is true, and that while Joseph Smith was its author he was innocent in so being; and to my mind the influence upon the church and upon the world would be infinitely less harmful by such a course; than would the presentation of the same discussion by you or others in the Reorganization who believe the doctrine to be evil, but believe him to have been its human author.[11]

Joseph III appeals here to Gurley's sense of fairness in light of Joseph's necessity to grapple not alone with honesty, but "good, sound doctrine and policy." He is not for a moment suggesting that Mormon advocates of polygamy should be given *Herald* space to advance their position. Rather, he skillfully juxtaposes that scenario with the much less palatable one (at least to Joseph) of opening the *Herald* to RLDS writers convinced of the need to fix the blame on his father. He is clearly saying no to Gurley, but in a way calculated to leave him without further cause to continue the fray in light of their larger, common allegiance to the gospel work. Joseph then continues:

I do not know what evidence you may be in possession of, different, or more direct than I have seen or heard; I know however, that you know personally, nothing about it; and therefore, that your belief is from secondary classes of evidences. These it is your privilege to receive as conclusive to you, I have the privilege to reject and disbelieve them; and this without lessening my respect and esteem for you, however much I may suffer in yours, for being indurate to what you deem not only plausible, but true.

As to what you state about the arbitrament of the future as to his guilt and that then I will be obliged to confess that he was so guilty, suppose we leave it right there. I am not positive nor sure that he was innocent; and as I have no means of deciding, not accepting evidence that seems clear and conclusive to you and others I am content to take my chances of defending the gospel upon the hypothesis that he was not the human author of that polygamic revelation, nor of Utah polygamy.[12]

Here Joseph reminds Gurley of the latter's status as mere secondhand witness to the origin of Nauvoo polygamy. He then returns to the matter raised earlier, i.e., the wisdom of an open *Herald* policy on the matter:

Are you of the opinion that a presentation of what you deem essential, in the *Herald* from your pen and as many others as might choose to write, would add to the advancement of the gospel cause; or strengthen the Reorganization? Do you think it necessary to the development of the gospel, and to the prosperity and success of the work, which you assure me you love, that my name should be further blackened, and the load of approbrium that I am already carrying, from the religious and irreligious world in and out of all churches; and from those who deem me apostate from the truth because of my hostility to polygamy and my method of showing that hostility, should be increased by an attack from you and others, of the kind proposed by you? I do not ask these questions in bad feeling, but as a matter of business, and that business the creation of a unity among the brethren.

. . . You must remember that Bro Sheen, the first editor of the *Herald*, and others in the early days of the Reorganization took the grounds that Joseph Smith was the author of polygamy, and defended the church and the truth from that stand point. With very few exceptions I stood alone in my opinion on the point. All that is now known touching his guilt in this regard was known then; and all that has so far been made known confirms me in my then opinion, with little alteration. If, for the success of the general cause it should be found that the body of elders should take other ground than has been taken; I of course must submit to the general verdict.[13]

Gurley's views persist despite Joseph's arguments, as is clear in his response of April 6. Gurley's appeal, like that of Joseph's of April 2, was to a sense of basic fairness to all parties to the controversy:

Now consider the facts that you are Pres. of the church, the *Herald* the "official organ" thereof, and your positions as editor are accepted by the world as the position of the church. And then calmly and with that justice you are wont to possess answer it. Moreover, is not this whole matter an individual interest? Can it be shown that the cause of Christ, the triumph of truth, depends upon your father's innocence or guilt? And if not, pray tell me what right have you or anyone else in placing the matter before the world as a part of church polity or church necessity for her cause. And does it not occur to you that we who hold the opposite view to you in this matter have had greatest cause (if any be admitted) to have our high esteem for you lessened because of your using the church organ to herald your views and to the exclusion of ours? . . . Polygamy tried to make its appearance (and did by conversation) into my father's household prior to your father's death and in the years '45-6 came nearly making a complete success of it, so much so that my father was led to believe conscientiously that two more wives were necessary for his salvation. His plans were thwarted by the firm resistance of my mother, but suffice to say that it proved the bane of my father's life afterward, his love for your father prevented his telling all he knew about the matter—at least I so think—but I confess that I am made of sterner stuff.[14]

From what has been stated so far, we can generalize that the RLDS church's stance against polygamy gradually changed over the years. At first it had been one of general condemnation. Then the lines between RLDSism and Utah Mormonism became more clearly drawn, and Joseph Smith III seemed increasingly intent on clearing his father's name. The RLDS position more and more became that of not only condemning polygamy, but also of intentionally trying to dissociate Joseph Smith, Jr.'s name completely from its origin. However, we are still faced with the question of the origin of Mormon polygamy, and we turn now to that question, admitting at the outset that, as Joseph Smith III contended, a final, comprehensive answer cannot be had on the basis of the evidences extant.

Factors Leading to Nauvoo Polygamy

When, how, and why did polygamy begain in Mormon history? Historiographically and polemically the Utah Mormon church has tried to document this event back to 1831, with a handwritten manuscript dated ca. 1859 and purporting to be "the essence" of a revelation from God to Joseph Smith, Jr., to some of the elders in Missouri, commanding them to take Indian women as wives along the "borders by the Lamanites." Since this was written many years later (1859), and in Utah, one takes this document at face value with great risk. On the other hand, the RLDS church produced numerous affidavits from persons during the 1880s and 1890s affirming that polygamy had never existed in Nauvoo, that Joseph Smith knew nothing of its advent in the church, and that it was wholly the invention of

Brigham Young in Utah. Both churches have created literally hundreds of pages of published and manuscript materials in defense of their respective points of view. Space permits no more than mere acknowledgment of these materials, since it is relatively fruitless to deal seriously with the flaws in these kinds of evidence.

This paper posits the theory that Mormon polygamy's inception came during the Nauvoo era, and was an outgrowth of the emerging system of temple rituals at Nauvoo from 1840 to 1844. In order to develop the theory I shall sketch in briefly certain developments that shaped the peculiar ritual usages associated with the Nauvoo Temple. This exploration goes back in time to the death of Alvin Smith, eldest son of Joseph Smith, Sr., and Lucy Mack Smith. He died unexpectedly on November 19, 1823. Due to his having died without confessing to Christ, the Presbyterian minister who preached his funeral consigned Alvin to everlasting torment in the fires of hell. This was to become a vexing burden to the Smith family, who brooded over Alvin's destiny for many years to follow.

The terms of Section 76 of the Doctrine and Covenants, recorded in February 1832, seemed not to help reconcile this plight of the deceased Alvin. However, some hope for a resolution came in 1836 in the Kirtland Temple, where, in a visionary experience, Joseph Smith, Jr., beheld Alvin in celestial glory. Even so, the final, definitive reconciliation came, according to Lucy Mack Smith's account, at the deathbed scene of her husband, Joseph, Sr. At that time Joseph, Jr., came into the room to announce to his father that the church would now be permitted to practice baptism for the dead. Joseph Smith, Sr., seemed pleased at this news, and requested that arrangements be made immediately for Alvin's baptism.[15] The elder Smith died on September 14, 1840, at Nauvoo. At the October 1840 conference of the church at Nauvoo Joseph Smith, Jr., and Lyman Wight instructed the Saints on baptism for the dead, and called for the building of a temple, presumably to accommodate the ritual.[16] At that time baptisms for the dead were being performed in the Mississippi River.

Workers immediately began excavations for the temple, and soon baptisms for the dead were being performed at other locations. For example, a report from Kirtland, Ohio, referred to a conference on May 22, 1841, at which baptisms for the dead totalling at least a dozen were performed.[17] It seems clear, then, that an ordinance emerging in September 1840 largely out of the Smith family's anxiety over the eternal welfare of their deceased Alvin won immediate acceptance, and was practiced in the church, both at Nauvoo and elsewhere.[18] This new departure portended a larger cultus of esoteric rituals soon to be in place in the Nauvoo Temple under construction from 1841 until its dedication on May 1, 1846.

Baptism for the dead awaited inspirational authentication. That occurred as part of a document recorded on January 19, 1841, and read to the General Conference by John C. Bennett the following April at Nauvoo.[19] The June 1, 1841, issue of *Times and Seasons* published most of what was to become Section 107 (RLDS Doctrine and Covenants), including the entire portion dealing with baptism for the dead. Finally codified in print, baptism for the dead was firmly established as a temple ritual, although the Saints were forced by lack of temple facilities to practice it wherever they could.

In October 1841 Joseph Smith preached on the necessity for salvation works for the dead, and told the church conference that there could be no further baptism for the dead until a temple font was in place to accommodate it.[20] Within two months a temporary font was in use in the temple basement. All of these developments point to the enthusiasm of the church's response to the directives of Joseph Smith, Jr., from September 1840 through the end of 1841, enjoining baptism for the dead as an essential gospel principle. Seeing the need for new instruction to further systematize the procedures relating to baptism for the dead, Joseph in September 1842 read two lengthy letters he had written on the subject to the church, later publishing them.[21] They were cast in language which clearly reflected the author's conviction of their inspirational stature.

To hold that baptism for the dead stemmed solely from the Smith family's anxiety over Alvin's future is to oversimplify the case. Another conditioning factor was the history of the persecution of the Saints, which began with their history as a religious movement. By 1839 they had become a beleaguered people, rootless and driven from one place to another with demoralizing repetitiveness. They had been forced from as many as four gathering locales in less than a decade. As they built Nauvoo they felt the need for structures that would promise longevity, security, and predictability beyond the transient experiences of earthly life as they had known it to that point. Also, just when the church theology seemed preoccupied with "establishing the ancient order of things" (biblical, especially Old Testament, forms and images), a new, double emphasis emerged—one on the exaltation of the priesthood with its exclusive authority, and the other on the plurality of Gods, epitomized in Joseph Smith's speculative *Book of Abraham,* begun in 1835 and published by him in early 1842.[22]

All these developments—the Smith family's grief over Alvin, the intense persecution of the Saints, the speculative theological propensities of church leadership—produced a milieu in which baptism for the dead came into focus as a means of sealing the deceased ancestors and relatives of the living Saints into the promises of the Mormon kingdom (celestial glory). Having resolved the dilemma of the deceased, Joseph Smith soon saw the need to preserve the present-tense Mormon family structure within the context of the exaltation of the priesthood elite. Therefore, during the summer of 1843, the doctrine of celestial marriage, or marriage for eternity, with direct implications for celestial—not *earthly*—polygamy, was introduced by revelation to the High Council at Nauvoo. (Both William Marks [p. 15] and Austin Cowles [p. 22], recalled this event.) Celestial marriage meant that a faithful Mormon elder could be sealed to his wife for eternity. A corollary was later added at Nauvoo: the practice of sealing parents to their offspring for eternity. Now the entire Mormon family system, both in terms of past nonmember ancestors, together with present living members, would be joined in one grand assembly in the celestial kingdom, in keeping with the evolving doctrine of the "endowment," soon to be embodied in temple rituals in Nauvoo.

By these things at Nauvoo the church arrived at the point where celestial polygamy became an inevitability. To illustrate, suppose that a Mormon elder is sealed to his wife for eternity. She dies suddenly, leaving the elder with a young family to care for. He soon remarries, again in the temple—for eternity. This means that he will have two wives in the celestial realm. It was then but a short step from that situation to the rationalization that what is valid in the celestial realm should surely be legitimate for time on earth, e.g., there at Nauvoo. So it was that by late 1843 a number of church officials at Nauvoo had become involved with celestial polygamy, by what might be referred to as an "accident of history." This means that polygamy was not consciously intended or foreseen when baptism for the dead was begun by Joseph Smith, Jr., in September 1840. However, by late 1843, with the other doctrinal developments and the emerging temple usages and theology, some certain members of the Mormon priesthood elite were, in effect, polygamists, at least in terms of their future arrangements in the hoped-for-celestial order. To illustrate, consider the following excerpt from a letter written by Jacob Scott, an elder of Nauvoo, writing to his daughter in Canada, on January 5, 1844:

Several revelations of great utility and uncommon interest have been lately communicated to Joseph and the church. One is that all marriage contracts or covenants are to be **everlasting,** that is, the parties if they belong to the church and will obey the will of God in this relationship to each other, are to be married for both **Time** and **Eternity:** and as respects those whose partners were dead before this **Revelation** was given to the Church; they may have the privilege to be married to their deceased husband, or wives (as the case may be) for eternity, and if it is a man who desires to be married to his deceased wife, a Sister in the Church stands as Proxy or as a representative of the deceased in attending to the marriage ceremony and so in the case of a widow who desires to be joined in an everlasting covenant, to her dead husband. . . . I intend to be married to the wife of my youth before I go to Ireland, I would be unspeakably glad to have you all here to witness our second Nuptials . . . many members of the Church have already availed themselves of this privilege and have been married to their deceased partners, and in some cases where a man has been married to two or three wives, and they are dead, he has been married to them all; in the order, in which he was married to them while living and also widows have been married to their dead husbands but only to one husband.[23] [Emphasis Scott's.]

As can be deduced from the above, Jacob Scott represents at least one elder

at Nauvoo in 1844 who enthusiastically endorsed the concept of marriage for eternity (celestial marriage) and its logical extension, celestial polygamy. It is not improbable that several Nauvoo citizens by early 1844 were also contracting plural marriages, both for the celestial realm and for earthly life there and then. After all, with an eye to eternity, to obey the implications of divine law took precedence over obedience to the letter of the law of the state of Illinois. They were indeed building for the eternal scope of their family-kingdom networks in celestial glory. The perpetuity of the Mormon kingdom, sought from the start in the face of recurring persecution and inner turmoil, would now be insured by the efficacy of the temple cultus.

Early Responses to Plural Marriage at Nauvoo

The rumors of polygamy at Nauvoo soon reached the public through such papers as Thomas C. Sharp's *Warsaw Message.* The February 7, 1844, issue contained a thirteen-stanza poem, "Buckeye's Lamentation for Want of More Wives," from which these stanzas are excerpted:

I once thought I had knowledge great,
But now I find 'tis small.
I once thought I'd religion too,
But now I find I've none at all—
For I have but ONE LONE WIFE,
And can obtain no more;
And the doctrine is I can't be saved,
Unless I've HALF A SCORE.

A TENFOLD glory—that's the prize!
Without it you're undone!
But with it you will shine as bright
As the bright shining sun.
There you may shine like mighty Gods,
Creating worlds so fair—
At least a world for every WIFE
That you take with you there.[24]

By April 1844 a small group of dissident leaders and members had separated from the church to form what they felt to be a more faithful expression of Latter Day Saintism. Among these were William Law, former member of the First Presidency, his wife, and his brother Wilson Law. Austin Cowles, Robert and Charles Foster (brothers), and Chauncey and Francis Higbee (brothers) also were among this group. On June 7, 1844, they issued the first (and last) number of a newspaper edited by Sylvester Emmons, under the title, *Nauvoo Expositor*. Its contents greatly distressed President Joseph Smith and other church leaders. For example, note the following three affidavits concerning plural marriage, authored by William Law, his wife Jane, and Austin Cowles, in that order:

I hereby certify that Hyrum Smith did, (in his office), read to me a certain written document, which he said was a revelation from God, he said that he was with Joseph when it was received. He afterwards gave me the document to read, and I took it to my house, and read it, and showed it to my wife, and returned it next day. The revelation (so called) authorized certain men to have more wives than one at a time, in this world and in the world to come. It said this was the **law,** and commanded Joseph to enter into the **law.**—And also that he should administer to others. Several other items were in the revelation, supporting the above doctrines.[25]

I certify that I read the revelation referred to in the above affidavit of my husband, it sustained in strong terms the doctrine of more wives than one at a time, in this world, and in the next, it authorized some to have to the number of **ten,** and set forth that those women who would not allow their husbands to have more wives than one should be under condemnation before God.[26]

In the latter part of the summer, 1843, the Patriarch, Hyrum Smith, did in the High Council, of which I was a member, introduce what he said was a revelation given through the Prophet; that the said Hyrum Smith did essay to read the said revelation in the said Council, that according to his reading there was contained the following doctrines; 1st, the sealing up of persons to eternal life, against all sins, save that of shedding innocent blood or consenting thereto; 2nd, the doctrine of a plurality of wives, or marrying virgins; that "David and

Solomon had many waives, yet in this they sinned not save in the matter of Uriah." This revelation with other evidence, that the aforesaid heresies were taught and practiced in the Church; determined me to leave the office of first counsellor to the president of the Church at Nauvoo, inasmuch as I dared not teach or administer such laws.[27]

With the now public presentation of such views as these by former leaders (Law, until January 1844, had been Joseph's counselor, and Cowles had been a member of the High Council), there were now firsthand witnesses to strange developments occurring at the seat of power. These were not merely remote persons reacting to hearsay evidence. The Laws, Austin Cowles, and others, because of their interpretations of matters relating to celestial marriage, placed no confidence in Smith's official published denunciations of deviant marriage doctrines and practices emerging in church life.[28] The dissidents' periodical, the *Nauvoo Expositor,* was public symbol of that loss of confidence. This development provoked those at the top of the hierarchy to seek ways immediately to rid the community of the paper and the press issuing it.

So it was that the city council met under the direction of Mayor Joseph Smith, Jr., and on June 10 passed a resolution declaring the *Nauvoo Expositor* a public nuisance. Its immediate destruction was called for, and the order was executed by the mayor through a unit of the Nauvoo Legion that night. Minutes of that meeting appeared in the June 19, 1844, issue of the church newspaper, the *Nauvoo Neighbor*. Significantly, the minutes represented Joseph Smith, Jr., as the author of a revelation on marriage, and the revelation itself as dealing with marriage in eternity and in biblical times, not plural marriage as such:

They [*Expositor* publishers] make [it] a criminality, for a man to have a wife on the earth, while he has one in heaven, according to the keys of the holy

Priesthood—and he [Joseph] then read a statement of William Law's from the *Expositor,* where the truth of God was transformed into a lie concerning this thing—He [Joseph] then read several statements of Austin Cowles in the Expositor concerning a private interview, and said he never had any private conversation with Austin Cowles on these subjects—that he preached on the stand from the bible, showing the order in ancient days, having nothing to do with the present times...said he would rather die tomorrow and have the thing [*Expositor*] smashed, than live and have it go on, for it was exciting the spirit of mobocracy among the people and bringing death and destruction upon us....H.[yrum] Smith proceeded to show the falsehood of Austin Cowles in the *Expositor,* in relation to the revelation referred to, that it was in reference to **former** days, and not the present time as related by Cowles. Mayor [Joseph Smith] said he had never preached the revelation in private, as he had in public—had not taught it to the anointed in the church in private, which statement many present confirmed, that on enquiring concerning the passage in the resurrection concerning "they neither marry nor are given in marriage," [Mt. 22:30] he received for answer, men in this life must marry in view of eternity, otherwise they must remain as angels, or be single in heaven, which was the amount of the revelation referred to, and the Mayor spoke at considerable length in explanation of this principle.[29]

These minutes, published in the church press while Joseph Smith, Jr., was yet alive and in Nauvoo, show him affirming the fact of a revelation dealing with both ancient marriage and present-day marriage for eternity. He chides the *Expositor* affiants for imputing criminal offense to Mormon leaders having a wife here while being sealed to former, deceased ones, in heaven, "*according to the keys of the holy priesthood.*" (Emphasis mine.) This shows Joseph's full endorsement of his revelation on marriage for eternity, tying it to priesthood authority, and revealing its direct implications for celestial polygamy. In light of those explanations it is *easy* for one to appreciate the city council's disposition to place little confidence in the efficacy of repeated denials of the truth of the *Expositor's* allegations. For, clearly,

such denials did not dispel the growing conviction, both in and out of the church, that polygamy was fast becoming a feature of the theological/temple system of Nauvoo Mormonism. Radical action was called for and taken, by a nearly unanimous vote of the city council.

Another witness of polygamy's origins at Nauvoo was Sidney Rigdon, who until 1844 was one of Joseph Smith's counselors in the First Presidency. Shortly after Rigdon's failure in his bid for guardianship over the church in August 1844, he established his following near Pittsburgh, Pennsylvania, and began his periodical, the *Messenger and Advocate.* Assessing the deteriorating situation in Nauvoo, Rigdon made the following observations:

It would seem almost impossible that there could be found a set of men and women, in this age of the world, with the revelations of God in their hands, who could invent and propagate doctrines so ruinous to society, so debasing and demoralizing as the doctrine of a man having a plurality of wives; for it is the existence of this strange doctrine—worse than the strange fire offered on the alter, by corrupted Israel—that was at the root of all the evils which have followed, and are following in the church,...The crime of the people was that they loved to have it so, they were not charged with introducing the corruptions, but having pleasure in them after the prophets, and leaders, had introduced them.

[*Rigdon then quotes and comments on II Tim. 3:1-9, charging that "...the Twelve and their adherents have entered into houses and led silly women astray,...having a form of godliness."... Ridgon's conclusion then is that they effected the ruin of silly females at Nauvoo through a form of godliness.*]

The Twelve and their adherents have endeavored to carry on this spiritual wife business in secret....and have gone to the most shameful and desperate lengths, to keep it from the public....How often have these men and their accomplices stood up before the congregation, and called God and all the holy angels to witness, that there was no such doctrine taught in the church; and it has now come to light, by testimony which cannot be gainsaid, that at the time they thus dared heaven and insulted the world, they were living in

155

the practice of these enormities: and there were multitudes of their followers in the congregation at the time who knew it.[30]

From this it can be seen that Rigdon credits the very top leaders for introducing the plural marriage system into Mormonism, and the Twelve for continuing its practice secretly after the assassinations of June 1844. To this exposition Rigdon added a dire prediction eight months later, as the time approached for the breakup of the church at Nauvoo:

To those who have corrupted their way before the Lord, we say, "Go to, now, and weep and howl for the miseries which are coming upon you," your corruptions are eating you "as doth a canker," your priesthood has "rotted as a garment," and your righteousness as rags, and as filthy garments that are moth eaten, and it cannot hide your shame. Ye adulterers and adulteresses, shame will cover you, reproach will follow you, "your refuge of lies" will not hide you, and your "agreement with hell will not save you."

God has looked upon you, and beheld your shame; your abominations are a stink in the nose of Jehovah; your "turning things upside down," will not avail you. The story of wrath is gathering, and it will burst on your heads as the whirlwind, and desolate you as the pestilence. Your city shall be desolated, for your inheritances are defiled under you.[31]

On receiving news of the demise of Nauvoo and the flight of the Saints, Rigdon issued his strongest rebuke of the Smiths and the Twelve, citing their introduction of polygamy as the prime cause of the Nauvoo debacle:

This system [plural marriage] was introduced by the Smiths some time before their death, and was the thing which put them into the power of their enemies, and was the immediate cause of their death.—This system the twelve, so called, undertook to carry out, and it has terminated in their overthrow, and the complete ruin of all those who follow their pernicious ways....We warned Joseph Smith and his family, of the ruin that was coming on them, and of the certain destruction which awaited them, for their iniquity, for making their house, instead of a house of God a sink of corruption. From them we received like treatment, as we did from the Twelve, and their followers....

The Smiths have fallen before their enemies, as the Lord said they would, and their families sunk into everlasting shame, and disgrace, until their very name is a reproach; and must remain so forever.[32]

[Rigdon then quotes verbatim the material he had written a year earlier, in which he had predicted the present misery of the church—quoted above.]

While there is some risk in taking Rigdon's statements at face value, without accounting for his bias born of his friction with Smith and the Twelve, one must remember that during this whole period he continued in the Latter Day Saint faith, sensing its claims on him as larger than the claims of any leader or leadership group. He stands as one of a company of Smith's sometime followers who connect him with the origin of Mormon polygamy at Nauvoo. That company included Sheen, Marks, the Laws, and Cowles— all of whom published statements to this effect. Add to these prominent members of the original church those referred to by Sidney Rigdon as the "multitudes of their followers in the congregation at the time who knew it," and one confronts some of that array of souls who, in the judgment of W. W. Blair, Josiah Ells, and Charles Derry, comprised the "almost universal opinion among the Saints that Joseph was in some way connected with it" (polygamy, or spiritual wifery at Nauvoo). For that reason, perhaps, the RLDS Twelve and Presidency in 1867, as shown earlier,[33] failed to sustain a resolution stating, "Neither do we believe that J[oseph] Smith was in any wise the author or excuser of these doctrines."

Summary and Conclusions

On the basis of the foregoing, then, the following conclusions seem appropriate to consider:

1. Polygamy began at Nauvoo as a consequence of Mormon history filled with
   • eclectic, speculative theological ferment;

- unrelenting persecution;
- strong emphasis on authoritarian control through a hierarchical power elite;
- an intricate temple cultus designed to guarantee the perpetuity of the Mormon kingdom in this life and the next;
  - a considered rejection of societal strictures and mores in the light of what Mormons felt to be divinely revealed principles transcending "man-made" laws.

2. In its first expression Mormon polygamy was meant for celestial life, in terms of the duty of widowed elders to marry their previous (deceased) wives for eternity, even while honoring present marital covenants for time and for eternity as well. The resulting polygamy, celestial in nature, apparently was seen by some as justifying its practice in this life also.

3. As the public became aware of rumors that some of the top Mormon leaders had begun to contract polygamous marriages in this life, the breakup of Nauvoo Mormonism and the punishment (even death) of some of its high leaders became more certain. The emergence of radical opposition within Mormonism at Nauvoo laid the groundwork, both for continued experimentation with polygamy by some of the schismatic groupings emanating from Nauvoo's disintegration and for bitter reaction by other groups which felt polygamy to be wrong.

4. While the early (1852-1859) stance of the RLDS church was violently antipolygamy in its rhetoric, the fact is that it made no attempt to dissociate the name of Joseph Smith, Jr., from complicity in polygamy's Nauvoo origin. It is not clear whether such dissociation was not attempted because no linkage was felt to exist or simply because it was not felt to be important. What was vital was that the early identity of the RLDS church be seen in terms of its opposition to polygamy.

5. The presence of Joseph Smith III from 1860 as the top RLDS leader gradually but greatly changed the RLDS strategy in opposing polygamy. Joseph III not only did not believe that his father could have been connected with polygamy, he stated that "he could never believe it." Increasingly the need was felt to clear Joseph Smith, Jr.'s name of any connection with the inception of Nauvoo polygamy. Also, if RLDSism was to be defended as the true successor to true Mormonism against the LDS apostasy, then the image of original Mormonism, as well as that of its founding prophet, would have to be consistent with the best gospel principles that RLDS leaders could frame. Such a gospel could neither be nor ever have been related in any way with non-Christian marriage customs.

6. Ascertaining the extent of Joseph Smith, Jr.'s responsibility for Mormon polygamy's origins at Nauvoo is impossible to do. The fact that several of his peers at Nauvoo, later identified with the RLDS leadership, remembered, wrote of, and openly discussed Joseph's involvement in—but also his rejection of—polygamy, is strong evidence that the evolution of Nauvoo polygamy was "accidental"; i.e., polygamy was not forseen at the start of the growth of the temple cultus, but was a natural consequence. Once Joseph Smith, Jr., came to see the harm being done to

the church, he sought the help of Marks to use all their combined power to put down polygamy in the church. However, by that time things had gone too far.

7. Emma Smith's 1879 defense of Joseph Smith, Jr.'s innocence is somewhat weakened by Joseph III's long delays in accepting William McLellan's 1861 and 1872 challenges (a close reading should be made here of note 8 at the end of this essay), and further by his delay (eight months after the interview, and six months after Emma's death) in publishing his interview with her.[34] These delays in and of themselves raise questions which are unanswerable on the basis of any known evidence regarding the amount of weight to give this line of argument.

8. In view of polygamy's "accidental" entrance into the church at Nauvoo in 1843-1844, the century-long campaign to clear Joseph Smith, Jr.'s name from any connection whatever with it has been unnecessary. The believable records extant indicate his direct responsibility for the eternal marriage covenant (celestial marriage— marriage for eternity), and for its logical consequence, celestial polygamy. However, only an indirect responsibility for earthly, Nauvoo polygamy in the 1843-1844 period can be documented as attributable to Joseph Smith, Jr.

9. Historical evidence and present program imperatives suggest that the RLDS church will in the long run gain a more accurate self-image by actively exploring a broader range of its historical development, with specific focus on the rapid transformations of church life, during the pre-Reorganization years.

Notes

1. Quoted by Joseph Smith III and Heman C. Smith, in *History of the Reorganized Church of Jesus Christ of Latter Day Saints*, vol. 3, 248, from its original publication in the *True Latter Day Saints' Herald* 1, no. 5 (May, 1860):103.

2. *True Latter Day Saints' Herald* 1, no. 1 (January 1860):24.

3. "Epistle of Wm. Marks,..." in *Zion's Harbinger and Baneemy's Organ*, July 1853, 53.

4. Letter from William Marks to Isaac Sheen, October 23, 1859, published in the *True Latter Day Saints' Herald* 1, no. 1 (January 1860):22, 23.

5. Letter, William Marks (Shabbona Grove, DeKalb County, Illinois) to Hiram Falk and Josiah Butterfield, October 1, 1865, RLDS Archives.

6. Minutes of the Council of Twelve, RLDS church, Wednesday, May 2, 1865, Book A, p. 11. Attending this meeting were Joseph Smith III and William Marks of the First Presidency, and W. W. Blair, James Blakeslee, Reuben Newkirk, John Shippy, and Charles Derry of the Council of Twelve.

7. Ibid., Tuesday, April 9, 1867, Book A, p. 34. Attending this meeting were Joseph Smith III of the First Presidency, and J. W. Briggs, Zenas H. Gurley, Wm. W. Blair, John Shippy, E. C.Briggs, Josiah Ells, and Charles Derry of the Council of Twelve.

8. Letter, David H. Smith (Salt Lake City) to "Bro. Sherman," July 27, 1872, RLDS Archives. That same summer William E. McLellan (early apostle of Latter Day Saintism, leader of several schismatic groupings after 1836, but one who nonetheless enjoyed Emma Smith's respect—expressed in her letter to Joseph Smith III in Feburary 1867), wrote to Joseph Smith III on the polygamy question:

   You said in your speech at Amboy April 6th 1860, "I believe my father was a good man, and a good man never could have promulgated such doctrines." You referred to Polygamy. Now let me tell you my dear Sir. I asked your Mother particularly upon this point. She said, one night after she and Joseph had retired for the night, he told her that the doctrine and practice of Polygamy was going to ruin the church. He wished her to get up and burn the revelation. She refused to touch it even with tongs. He rose from his bed and pulled open the fire with his fingers, and put the revealment in and burned it up. But copies of it were extant, so it was preserved. You say, "I have never believed it and never can believe it." Can you dispute your dear Mother? She related this to me, and will if you ask her tell you the same thing. It made a powerful impression on my mind at the time [1847—the year McLellan had spoken with Emma about this], and I've often reflected on it since. Now Sir suppose you could be convinced that your father not only believed in Polygamy but actually practiced it his individual self, then what would you say—and then do about it? Was he an adulterer so long ago [reference here is to McLellan's allegations, made previously in this letter, of Joseph Smith, Jr.'s illicit sexual encounters with two women at Kirtland—which he says Emma had verified to him in their 1847 conversation], and still a "good man." You say, "I believe in the doctrines of honesty and truth." So do I. But I can't believe your father continued to be a religiously honest man. No sir. I can't for if I should I would have to believe your Mother a liar, and that would be hard for me to do, considering my acquaintance with her.

[McLellan began this letter in July 1872, finished and mailed it on September 8, 1872, from Independence, Missouri. The letter is in the RLDS Archives, Independence, Missouri.]

It is likely that Joseph III never responded either to this letter or to McLellan's 1861 letter along the same lines. The reason for this statement is that in 1880, a year following the death of Emma Smith Bidamon, Joseph wrote that his only conversation with his mother on this subject occurred "near the close of her life" (E. W. Tullidge, *Life of Joseph The Prophet*, 1880 ed., 763). In his interview with her, she told him that there had never been such a revelation, and that there had never been any other women in Joseph's life than herself (see below). Emma died April 30, 1879, and Joseph Smith III waited until October 1879 to publish her responses to the questions he had put to her the previous February. Given these facts the force of Emma's final testimony is weakened in terms of its validity as primary evidence, for it is not possible to probe the hidden factors in the two long delays of Joseph III:

first in talking with Emma, and second, in finally publishing her statements.

9. For example, see William B. Smith's assessment of Section 132 (Utah Mormon Doctrine and Covenants—the section on polygamy attributed to Joseph Smith, Jr., dated July 12, 1843) as a "wicked forgery." (Smith, a younger brother to Joseph Smith, Jr., an uncle to Joseph III and an apostle and patriarch at Nauvoo, was later a polygamist and schismatic leader of sorts, but in April 1878 joined the RLDS church. He had pressed his nephew for the RLDS patriarchate, but finally chose to settle for the office of high priest.)—*Saints' Herald* 26, no. 1 (January 1, 1879):1; also see J. R. Lambert's reply to William Empey's letter challenging the authority of the RLDS church. Lambert uses most of the space defending Joseph Smith, Jr., against Empey's charge of having received the polygamy revelation of July 1843. *Saints' Herald* 26, no. 1 (January 1, 1879):5, 6; also see the editorial, "Out of their own mouths," *Saints' Herald* 26, no. 6 (March 15, 1879):84, 85, for a carefully arranged series of quotations from Mormon polygamists Parley P. Pratt and John Taylor, demonstrating the basic conflict between their Nauvoo statements denying polygamy and their much later Utah statements crediting Joseph Smith for having been the instrument through which the divine principle of polygamy had been given to the church. Since these conflicting statements negate their credibility, that settles the matter for the *Herald* editor: Joseph had never had anything to do with Nauvoo polygamy. It was this sort of reasoning and the printing of it in the *Herald* that upset Zenas Gurley, Jr., for to him its appearance in the *Herald* implied an official church position, not merely an editorial opinion.

10. Letter, Z. H. Gurley [Jr.] (Sedgwick, Iowa) to Joseph Smith III (Plano, Illinois), March 25, 1879. RLDS Archives, Independence, Missouri.

11. Letter, Joseph Smith III (Plano, Illinois) to Z. H. Gurley (Sedgwick, Iowa), April 2, 1879. RLDS Archives, Independence, Missouri.

12. Ibid.

13. Ibid.

14. Letter, Z. H. Gurley, (Sedgwick, Iowa) to Joseph Smith III (Plano, Illinois), April 6, 1879. RLDS Archives, Independence, Missouri.

15. Lucy Mack Smith, *Biographical Sketches of Joseph Smith, the Prophet, and His Progenitors for Many Generations* (Liverpool: S. W. Richards, 1863), 265, 266.

16. General Conference Minutes, October 3, 1840, Nauvoo, Illinois, in *Times and Seasons* 1, no. 12 (October 1840):186, 187.

17. *Times and Seasons* 2, no. 17 (July 1, 1841):460.

18. General Conference Minutes, April 7, 1841, Nauvoo, Illinois, *Times and Seasons* 2, no. 12 (April 15, 1841):386; See RLDS Doctrine and Covenants, Section 107:10-17 for the part dealing with baptism for the dead and the temple.

19. *Times and Seasons* 2, no. 15 (June 1, 1841): 424-429; see especially pp. 426, 427 for the instruction on baptism for the dead.

20. General Conference Minutes, October 3, 1841, Nauvoo, Illinois, *Times and Seasons* 2, no. 24 (October 15, 1841): 577, 578.

21. *Times and Seasons* 3, no. 22 (September 14, 1842):919, 920 (Section 109, RLDS Doctrine and Covenants); *Times and Seasons* 3, no. 23 (October 1, 1842):934-936 (Section 110, RLDS Doctrine and Covenants).

22. This appeared in three installments in *Times and Seasons* during Joseph's tenure as its editor: vol. 3, no. 9 (March 1, 1842): 703-706; vol. 3, no. 10 (March 15, 1842):719-722; vol. 3, no. 14 (May 16, 1842):783, 784.

23. Letter, Jacob Scott (Nauvoo, Illinois) to his daughter Mary Warnock (Streetsville, Upper Canada). RLDS Archives, Independence, Missouri.

24. As quoted in Fawn M. Brodie, *No Man Knows My History; the Life of Joseph Smith the Mormon Prophet* (New York: Alfred A. Knopf, 1946), 344.

25. *Nauvoo Expositor* 1, no. 1 (June 7, 1844):2.

26. Ibid.

27. Ibid.

28. Early in 1844 polygamy and other evils were staunchly denied and denounced in *Times and Seasons*. These were probably representative of all other official denials of polygamy's presence in Nauvoo:

   "NOTICE. As we have lately been credibly informed, that an Elder of the Church of Jesus Christ, of latter-day Saints, by the name of Hiram Brown, has been preaching Polygamy, and other false and corrupt doctrines, in the county of Lapeer, state of Michigan. "This is to inform him and the Church in general, that he has been cut off from the church, for his iniquity; and he is further notified to appear at the Special Conference, on the 6th of April, next, to make answer to these charges.

   JOSEPH SMITH, HYRUM SMITH, Presidents of said Church."
   (Vol. V. No. 3 [Feb. 1, 1844], 423)

   "To the brethren of the Church of Jesus Christ of Latterday Saints, living on China Creek, in Hancock County, Greeting:—Whereas brother Richard Hewitt has called on me to-day, to know my views concerning some doctrines that are preached in your place, and states to me that some of your elders say, that a man having a certain priesthood, may have as many wives as he pleases, and that doctrine is taught here: I say unto you that that man teaches false doctrine, for there is no such doctrine taught here; neither is there any such thing practiced here. And any man that is found teaching privately or publicly any such doctrine, is culpable, and will stand a chance to be brought before the High Council, and lose his license and membership also: therefore he had better beware what he is about.

   "And again I say unto you, an elder has no business to undertake to preach mysteries in any part of the world, for God has commanded us all to preach nothing but the first principles unto the world. Neither has any elder any authority to preach any mysterious thing to any branch of the church unless he has a direct commandment from God to do so. Let the matter of the grand councils of heaven, and the making of gods, worlds, and devils entirely alone: for you are not called to teach any such doctrine—for neither you nor the people are capacitated to understand any such principles—less so to teach them. For when God commands men to teach such principles the saints will receive them. Therefore beware what you teach! for the mysteries of God are not given to all men; and unto those to whom they are given they are placed under restriction to impart only such as God will command them; and the residue is to be kept in a faithful breast, otherwise he will be brought under condemnation. By this God will prove his faithful servants, who will be called and numbered with the chosen.

   "And as to the celestial glory, all will enter in and possess that kingdom that obey the gospel, and continue in faith in the Lord unto the end of his days. Now, therefore, I say unto you, you must cease preaching your miraculous things, and let the mysteries alone until by and bye. Preach faith in the Lord Jesus Christ; repentance and baptism for the remission of sins; the laying on of the hands for the gift of the Holy Ghost: teaching the necessity of strict obedience unto these principles; reasoning out of the scriptures; proving them unto the people. Cease your schisms and divisions, and your contentions. Humble yourselves as in dust and ashes, lest God should make you an ensample of his wrath unto the surrounding world. Amen.

In the bonds of the everlasting covenant,

I am your obedient servant,

Hyrum Smith."

(Vol. V, No. 6 [March 15, 1844], 474)

"TO THE ELDERS ABROAD. We very frequently receive letters from elders and individuals abroad, inquiring of us whether certain statements that they hear, and have written to them, are true: some pertaining to John C. Bennett's spiritual wife system; others in regard to immoral conduct, practiced by individuals, and sanctioned by the church: and as it is impossible for us to answer all of them, we take this opportunity of answering them all, once for all.

In the first place, we cannot but express our surprise that any elder or priest who has been in Nauvoo, and has had an opportunity of hearing the principles of truth advanced, should for one moment give credence to the idea that any thing like iniquity is practiced, much less taught or sanctioned, by the authorities of the Church of Jesus Christ of Latter Day Saints.

"We are the more surprised, since every species of iniquity is spoken against, and exposed publicly at the stand, and every means made use of that possibly can be, to suppress vice, both religious and civil; not only so, but every species of iniquity has frequently been exposed in the Times and Seasons, and its practisers and advocates held up to the world as corrupt men that ought to be avoided. . . .

"We have in our midst corrupt men, (and let no man be astonished at this for 'the net shall gather in of every kind, good and bad;') these corrupt men circulate corrupt principles, for a corrupt tree cannot bring forth good fruit: these spread their pernicious influence abroad, 'they hatch cockatrice eggs, and weave the spider's web; he that eateth of their eggs dieth, and that which is crushed breaketh out into a viper;' their words eat as doth a canker; 'the poison of asps is under their tongue, and the way of peace they have not known.' Such men not unfrequently go abroad and prey upon the credul[it]y of the people, probably have clandestinely obtained an ordination, and go forth as elders, the more effectually to impose upon the public. Some have got horses, and others money, under specious pretenses,

from the unwary and unsuspecting, among the newly formed branches who have not had the sagacity to detect them."

"There are other men who are corrupt and sensual, and who teach corrupt principles for the sake of gratifying their sensual appetites, at the expense and ruin of virtue and innocence. Such men ought to be avoided as pests to society, and be frowned down upon with contempt by every virtuous man and woman. . . . "If any man writes to you, or preaches to you, doctrines contrary to the Bible, the Book of Mormon or the book of Doctrine and Covenants, set him down as an imposter. You need not write to us to know what you are to do with such men; you have the authority with you. —try them by the principles contained in the acknowledged word of God; if they preach, or teach, or practice contrary to that, disfellowship them; cut them off from among you as useless and dangerous branches, and if they are belonging to any of the quorums in the church, report them to the president of the quorum to which they belong, and if you cannot find that out, if they are members of an official standing, belonging to Nauvoo, report them to us.

"Follow after purity, virtue, holiness, integrity, Godliness, and every thing that has a tendency to exalt and ennoble the human mind; and shun every man who teaches any other principles."

(Vol. V, No. 7 [April 1, 1844], 490).

These carefully written denials of doctrinal aberration at Nauvoo are subject to varying interpretations, because of their double meanings at many points. Both RLDS and LDS polemicists have sought to capitalize on that characteristic. These counsels against and denials of doctrinal heresies are therefore not as useful to either side of the controversy as has been thought by both contending parties in past decades.

29. *Nauvoo Neightbor* 2, no. 8 (Wednesday, June 19, 1844):3/239.

30. Sidney Rigdon, letter to Bro. J. Greig, *Latter Day Saints' Messenger and Advocate* 1, no. 1 (October 15, 1844):13.

31. *Latter Day Saints' Messenger and Advocate* 1, no. 15 (June 15, 1845):236, 237.

32. Ibid., vol. II, no. 6 (June 1846), letter from Sidney Rigdon to editor Ebenezer Robinson, 475.

33. Supra, 5

34. From Joseph Smith III's interview with his mother at Nauvoo in February 1879 the following is taken, as published in the *Saints' Herald* in October 1879, 289, 290:

"Q. —What about the revelation on polygamy?

Did Joseph Smith have anything like it? What of spiritual wifery?

"A. — There was no revelation on either polygamy, or spiritual wives. There were some rumors of something of the sort, of which I asked my husband. He assured me that all there was or it was, that, in a chat about plural wives, he had said, "Well, such a system might possibly be, if everybody was agreed to it, and would behave as they should; but they would not; and, besides, it was contrary to the will of heaven.' No such thing as polygamy, or spiritual wifery, was taught, publicly or privately, before my husband's death, that I have now, or ever had any knowledge of.

"Q. — Did he not have other wives than yourself?

"A. — He had no other wife but me; nor did he to my knowledge ever have.

"Q. — Did he not hold marital relations with women other than yourself?

"A. — He did not have improper relations with any woman that ever came to my knowledge.

"Q. — Was there nothing about spiritual wives that you recollect?

"A. — At one time my husband came to me and asked me if I had heard certain rumors about spiritual marriages, or anything of the kind; and assured me that if I had, that they were without foundation; that there was no such doctrine, and never should be with his knowledge, or consent. I know that he had no other wife or wives than myself, in any sense, either spiritual or otherwise."

Perhaps I have made too much of Joseph Smith III's inexplicable unresponsiveness in dealing with William McLellan's challenges of 1861 and 1872. However, a careful reading of these Emma Smith statements indicates caution in accepting them literally, at face value, without raising questions inherent in the dynamics of the 1879 situation in which Joseph Smith III interviewed his mother. Some of the questions worthy of note are: Did Emma's negative reference to the "revelation" on polygamy mean simply and only that there was never such a thing, or could it have meant that the document she in fact could have discussed had most assuredly NOT been a revelation, in her judgment? Or had Emma psychologically "blocked out" the painful distasteful memories of these things, so that in truth she could no longer call them to mind? Or, was Emma primarily protecting her son's crucial leadership situation, and feeling increasing freedom to do so in view of what she felt to be her own impending demise? Had she "leveled" with McLellan in 1847 — a time in which she may have felt that Mormonism was behind her — a time when she had no real hope or intention for her sons' possible future leadership roles in Mormonism? Or, was Emma trying to protect the good name of the church with which she had cast her lot on April 6, 1860, at Amboy, Illinois? Or, out of her deep antipathy towards Utah Mormonism, was she stating the case in 1879 so as to cause as much difficulty for the western Saints as possible, at a time when the U.S. government was intensifying its prosecution of polygamists in the Great Salt Lake Valley?

Or, was McLellan lying to Joseph III in 1861 and 1872 in those lengthy letters, and thus hoping that Joseph would not check out his story with his mother and find him out? Or, was McLellan so sure of the accuracy of Emma's 1847 statements to him that he wanted to pressure Joseph III into discovering the truth for himself? Or, was McLellan so sure that Joseph III already knew the facts as Emma had verified to him in 1847 that he wanted either to taunt Joseph III or to force him into an admission of Joseph, Jr.'s guilt?

At the very least the serious student of these matters must realize that the data currently extant does not deal with this type of inquiry. It is at the brink of "psycho-history," tried so many times by biographers and historians with but isolated examples of success. Perhaps the best thing to do is raise the hard questions that compel profound restraint in dealing with the evidences that are available.

THE DISAFFECTION OF WILLIAM LAW

John Fredrick Glaser

"The great mistake of my life is my having anything to do with Mormonism," wrote William Law forty years after his disaffection with Joseph Smith during the early 1840s.[1] His experience illuminates the circumstances under which Joseph Smith's leadership of Mormonism came to an end.

There were intense reactions to Joseph's activities both by outsiders, who saw the developing religion as a threat to their communities, and by church members who believed that the emerging doctrines and actions were contrary to the will of God. Joseph Smith appears to have been aware of both aspects of the growing intensity of these reactions.

His most effective opponent was his presidential counselor, William Law. After months of growing distress, Law funded and published the *Nauvoo Expositor*. In this newspaper he sought to inform the people of abuses by Joseph Smith and called for reforms within the church. Law accused Joseph of being above the law, mingling church and state, altering the judicial order of the church, controlling the finances of the church by ecclesiastical authority, and introducing false doctrines such as polygamy and the progression of gods.[2] Joseph responded by having the paper declared a nuisance and ordering its destruction. William retaliated by filing a complaint to authorities who issued a warrant for Joseph's arrest on charges of inciting riot. It was while awaiting trial on these charges that Joseph was murdered.

Although adequate consideration by historians of the last days of Joseph Smith must take into account the actions of William Law, many writers about this situation have found him to be an enigma. Conservative church historians have used hagiographic methods to depict Joseph as an uncorrupted saint and William as the "Judas" or "Brutus" of the Mormon Saga.[3]

According to Richard Price, a writer with an RLDS background and of fundamentalist persuasion, the *Expositor*'s charges were contrived in order to imprison the prophet; William Law then raised and provoked the mob who stormed the jail in Carthage, Illinois, and murdered the prisoner—Law's motive being to seize leadership of the church himself.[4] By contrast, Francis Gibbons, a Utah Mormon fundamentalist, relates Law's actions to the depletion of his personal wealth. He states, "His shrewd business judgment convinced him that once the doctrine of plural wives surfaced, Nauvoo was doomed, and with it, his wealth."[5] Lyndon Cook[6] and Kenneth Godfrey,[7] both professors of Mormon history at Brigham Young University, maintain that Law lacked the strength to adhere to the gospel that Joseph taught.

These and similar explanations may lack a proper focus because they are given by persons who have been associated with Mormonism as loyal members. It is this writer's opinion that we cannot ascribe the schism merely to differences of theology and disregard the human emotions involved. Mormon thought relies heavily on the life and teachings of Joseph Smith, in the belief that they are the wellspring of revelation in a special divine dispensation. Nevertheless, any theocrat, however enlightened or inspired, could, under certain circumstances, call for commitments which violate another person's ethical standards and sense of propriety. Joseph Smith was human and as such, even as a prophet of God, he was subject to error. This was the case in his relationship with William Law. The disaffection was due to a conflict with Joseph Smith over economics, moral questions, and political issues.

Who was this apostate who dared go against the prophet of God? Thomas Ford, the governor of Illinois, described William Law as "one of the most eloquent preachers of the Mormons, who appeared to me to be a deluded but conscientious and candid man.[8] This "deluded man" is reported to have led the movement that "set the prophet up without mercy."[9]

Little is known of Law's childhood, but we do know that at ten years of age he arrived in America, the youngest child of an Irish immigrant family that settled in western Pennsylvania. At the age of twenty-four he married Jan Silverthorn, a woman of some wealth, and settled in Churchville, Ontario.[10] Missionary efforts in that region by Parley P. Pratt had established Mormonism in Churchville. A contemporary minister recollected that the "village was for a time the stronghold of Mormonism. . . . They had frequent meetings both on Sabbath and weekdays, and a considerable number wre baptized by their preacher."[11] William and Jane entered into the fold in 1836. He recalled of his conversion, "John Taylor and Almon W. Babbit came to Canada as preachers where I lived, twenty-five miles south of Toronto."[12] Of his conviction at the time he joined, he wrote, "When I became a

member of the church, I did so upon the strength of scripture evidence and reason."[13] One year later he was ordained an elder. During this time political troubles plagued the area. The settlers demanded either responsible rule from the British or complete separation. William had amassed some weath and may have felt that his freedom was threatened. His brother already had been imprisoned for involvement in political activity.[14] In August of 1837, Joseph Smith visited the Saints in the politically divided area and "told his Canadian brethren . . . to sell while they could get out of the place or blood would be upon their heels."[15] By 1838 William Law had left the area and had written to Isaac Russell, "I believe we will have a rebellion in the lower Province [Quebec] and perhaps in this [area (Ontario)]."[16] His departure may have been encouraged by his respect for Joseph Smith and the Restoration movement.

It is interesting to note that through correspondence with Isaac Russell, William understood that Joseph was beset by problems and that the Missouri Saints had erred in their comportment during that time. Isaac, also from Ontario, had joined the church through Parley Pratt's work. After returning from a successful mission in Britain, he had lived for a time in Missouri and had begun to resist Joseph Smith himself. Prior to his leading his own schismatic, short-lived group into northern Louisiana, he had written to his congregation in Alston, England, about the problems in the church, claiming that Joseph was a fallen prophet.

On April 26, 1839, Russell was excommunicated. It is difficult to tell what was the ultimate effect of his allegations against Joseph, but William Law, a close friend of Russell's, defended Joseph in correspondence. To Russell he wrote,

Brother Joseph is truly a wonderful man. He is all

we could wish a prophet to be. . . . You will find that Joseph has not fallen, he has not done his work yet, and if he sins is there no room for repentance, can not God forgive him, and can not we forgive him very often in a day.[17]

Even after being in Joseph's company and having ample opportunity to observe him, William affirmed to Isaac Russell,

I have carefully watched his movements since I have been here and I assure you I have found him honest and honorable in all our transactions which have been very considerable. I believe he is an honest upright man, and as to his follies let who ever is guiltless throw the first stone at him, I shan't do it.

William also indicated that he was aware of the difficulites in Missouri and wrote,

I fear there has been wickedness in the camp, but I hope this chastisement will be for the good of all. . . . The evil reports which we hear did not discourage us, as we know in whom we trust, we are determined to hold out to the end though we may have to suffer all things.

By 1838 Law was gripped with a strong desire to gather with the Saints. Having left Churchville, he wrote from his temporary refuge in Pennsylvania, "As soon as I learn the fixed place of resting for the Saints I shall endeavor to move there, for I long to be with the Saints, to be gathered with the people of God."[18] He dreamed of happiness in Zion and wrote of the need to bear the ills of this present life with fortitude, to carefully observe the commandments, to walk humbly, to trust the Lord rather than human wisdom, and of the glory of Zion.

In September 1839, he left Pennsylvania for Nauvoo, leading a train of seven wagons, along with his brother Wilson, who was also to play a part in later developments at Nauvoo. On nearing Springfield they were met by Joseph, then on his way to Washington, D.C., to seek redress for the losses of the Saints in Missouri.[19] On arrival in Nauvoo the Law brothers quickly established themselves with a flour mill, a steam sawmill, and a general store at the corner of Water and Granger streets. They also bought land on the bluff in upper Nauvoo.

William's financial talents won the admiration of Joseph Smith. While destitute people came to Nauvoo to share in the inheritances of the kingdom of God, William was establishing badly needed industry in Joseph's "city beautiful." He had already demonstrated his financial support by having loaned Joseph one hundred dollars to help with the expenses of his trip to Washington, D.C., when the parties met near Springfield.[20] Additional responsibilities soon came to him: trustee of the Agricultural and Marketing Association, registrar of the University of Nauvoo, officer in the Nauvoo Legion. In January 1841 he was called to be a counselor to the president, one of the most prestigious positions in the church. At the same time, Joseph prophesied,

He shall heal the sick; he shall cast out devils, and shall be delivered from those who would administer unto him deadly poison, and he shall be led in paths where the poisonous serpent cannot lay hold upon his heel, and he shall mount up on the imagination of thoughts as upon eagles' wings; and what if I will that he should raise the dead, let him not withhold his voice.[21]

For the first three years William was totally devoted to the prophet in the same spirit in which he had earlier written to Isaac Russell, "He continues to bring forth the deep mysteries of the kingdom, and we feast upon them until our souls are made fat, and our hearts rejoice exceedingly."[22] Even years after his disaffection he could still look back on his experience at Nauvoo and claim, "I went from my home in Canada to Nauvoo and found a very poor, but industrious people; they appeared to be moral and religiously disposed; the saints and others preached morality and brotherly kindness every Sunday."[23] It appears that William Law was as faithful a member as could have been converted. His commitment seemed bonded in love and trust toward Joseph.

It was to be shaken, however, by developments that he found intolerable to his ethical standards. Who could have foreseen the animosity that led to an irreparable break in their relationship in December 1843? What were the causes of the disaffection?

The basis of William Law's most significant contribution to the church was his financial prowess. Looking back in later years at his Nauvoo experience, he stated,

We [William and his brother Wilson] had property to the amount of about 30,000 [dollars] which was [a] good deal in those days. We had farms in Nauvoo, city lots and our residences. . . . We had a large steam flour saw mill and a store.[24]

Prior to his arrival he had inquired about factors involved in his economic plans for Nauvoo.

As to the mercantile business I wish you could give me all the information you can on that subject as soon as possible. . . . Let me know how the people pay, what kind of goods is most suitable, how much capital would be needed, whether there are any stores there and where the best situation would be for doing business in that line. Would a first rate new horsepower for grinding and sawing be useful? There is a new invention come out that is excellent.[25]

He anticipated what he would like to do and began early to accumulate the necessary capital. He related, "I have some prospect of selling out in Canada as the Estate will be divided this winter, at all events I shall have enough to take us up in the spring and a little over."[26]

When Joseph returned from Washington, D.C., after the meeting near Springfield, he saw the Law brothers well established in business. At that time Joseph was in great financial difficulty. As the trustee of the lands at Nauvoo, he had indebted himself enormously. He had anticipated that immigrant Saints would buy land from him. Instead, many of them bought property on the bluff where land was cheaper and conditions healthier than in the marshy riverfront where Joseph had made the original purchase. His problems increased when he could not industrialize the city and currency was devalued to the extent that a bartering system was developed to compensate workers. Meanwhile, the continuing flow of destitute settlers flooded the area. Furthermore, great financial sacrifices were asked of the people in response to the instruction to build the temple, where new religious doctrines were to be practiced, and also to finance the Nauvoo House, a large hotel to house visitors and immigrants from all over the world.[27]

No doubt this financial stress contributed initially to the break between the two men. Perhaps William was reluctant to aid the prophet, seeing Joseph involve himself in unsound business practices. A debit and credit relationship between the two is recorded in the Day Book of William Law. According to it, Joseph owed William over five thousand dollars by 1842.[28]

In 1841 Joseph by the influence of the Spirit commanded William to invest his money in the erection of the Nauvoo House and to help in the publication of Joseph's revision of the King James Bible. (Editor's note: The commandment referred to here was part of a document that was never formally approved by the church as a revelation. The Reorganized church officially removed it from the book of Doctrine and Covenants in 1970.)[29]

The fact that William appears to have been less than enthusiastic in support of these projects may have added to the growing tension between the two men. It also seems that Joseph was becoming increasingly hostile to those who defied his orders. For example, Joseph harangued Robert Foster, who was, along with William Law, one of the chief contractors in the city. He called their buildings mammoth skeletons.

166

There is no flesh on them. . . . They are all for personal interest and aggrandizement. . . . I want the Nauvoo House built. It must be built. Our salvation depends upon it. . . . I will say to those who have labored on the Nauvoo House, and cannot get their pay—Be patient; and if any man takes the means which are set apart for the building of that house, and applies it to his own use, let him, for he will destroy himself. If any man is hungry, let him come to me, and I will feed him at my table. . . . I will divide with them to the last morsel; and then if the man is not satisfied, I will kick his backside![30]

Tension also grew among the people who had to be satisfied with payment for their labors through barter while those who worked for the independent businessmen were paid with money. The situation may have been further aggravated when Joseph built a new general store, which would no doubt compete with Williams' establishment.

Meanwhile, outside financial pressures on Joseph were mounting and he declared bankruptcy without naming William, to whom he owed considerable money, as one of his creditors. A final blow involving economic matters seems to have come during July 1843, the same month in which Law may have discovered the polygamy doctrine. (Editor's note: The Mormon Church in Utah has published since 1876 in their version of the book of Doctrine and Covenants that polygamy was either "given" or "recorded" on July 12, 1843, depending on which issue of the book is noted.) On July 8, William Law mortgaged the east half of the lot where his store was situated to Henry Buchwalter in the amount of $200. For reasons unknown, Buchwalter attached a note to the deed stating, "I hereby assign into the hand of Joseph Smith all my rights title and claim to this mortgage with interest thereon July 20, 1843."[31] By this time the relationships of Law and Smith must have reached a critical stage. William began a vociferous denunciation of Joseph on the basis of economic fraud. He appealed to the governor about an attempted land grab by Joseph, whose defense was that he had meddled with no property that did not belong to him and that he had purchased from a Mr. Hicks property which Hicks had previously received from Law in payment of a debt.

Law's campaign was militant, but he later stated:

It would have been the smart thing to do to remain quiet, sell our property without noise for what we could get and move away. . . . I wanted to do my duty and nothing else, and didn't care for the consequences. . . . Many friends advised me to be smart and remain quiet, but I would not hear of it and spoke my mind whenever an opportunity offered. . . . Secret orders went out that nobody could buy property without the permission of Joseph Smith, Hyrum or the authorities, as they called them, so our property was practically worthless.[32]

After the death of Joseph and Hyrum and William's disassociation with the Mormons and departure from Nauvoo, the financial problems that developed there continued to haunt him. Emma, Joseph's widow, along with Joseph Coolidge, the court-appointed estate executor, sued William and received a default judgment for two hundred dollars and a mortgage foreclosure on a lot in Nauvoo.[33]

Of his business dealings with Joseph, William wrote to Dr. Wyl,

One trait was his jealousy of his friends, lest any of them should be esteemed before him in the eyes of the Church or the public. He would destroy his best friend for the sake of a few hundred dollars. It was his policy to get away with a man's money, first because he wanted it, and second because he believed that in getting a man's money he deprived him of power and position and left him in a measure helpless and dependent.[34]

Although financial matters were important, the rupture of December 1843 seems to have hinged on a moral issue. The years at Nauvoo saw the rise of polygamy. Although the extent and nature of Joseph's involvement are difficult to determine, he appears to have participated in the speculations and experimentations. Evidence indicates that he was spiritually sealed to many women, but due to the extreme secrecy of the doctrine we do not know how many of these engagements were physically consummated.[35]

From a very early date, William held in high esteem the moral conduct of the Saints and the leader of the church. He defended them at great length and denounced efforts to tarnish the reputation of the Saints. In 1842, for example, when John C. Bennett was expelled from the church for adultery and later accused Joseph of having many wives, William wrote an affidavit that was published in the *Times and Seasons* in which he defended the moral rectitude of the Saints and condemned Bennett.[36]

Law's reaction to the polygamy speculation was expressed in rigorous terms. Brigham Young recollected that in a private meeting Joseph broached the issue of plural marriage and Law declared, "If an angel from heaven was to reveal to me that a man should have more than one wife, if it were in my power, I would kill him."[37] In the *Nauvoo Expositor* William claimed that he learned of the polygamy doctrine through Joseph, who gave a document to him to take home and read. In his later years he gave a more detailed account in which he said that instead of Joseph it was Hyrum who gave it to him:

Hyrum gave it to me in his office, told me to take it home and read it, then be careful with it and bring it back again. I took it home, read it and showed it to my wife. She and I were turned upside down by it; we did not know what to do. I said to my wife that I could take it over to Joseph and ask him about it. But she was not of my opinion. I did not believe that he would acknowledge it, and I said so to my wife. But she was not of my opinion. She felt perfectly sure that he would father it. When I came to Joseph and showed him the paper, he said, "Yes, that is a genuine revelation." I said to the prophet,

"But in the Book of Doctrine and Covenants there is a revelation just to the contrary of this," "Oh," said Joseph, "that was given when the church was in its infancy, then it was all right to feed the people on milk, but now it is necessary to give them strong meat." We talked a long time about it, finally our discussion became very hot and we gave it up. From that time on the breach between us became more open and more decided every day, after having been prepared for a long time.[38]

In this account William declares his final suspicions were confirmed that Joseph was a "rascal" and set out to "tread on the viper." But, according to his diary, which conflicted with statements of his later years, he had contemplated the "revelation" for some months. His judgment about the matter was settled when he wrote in his diary on January 1, 1844:

Through our religious zeal we hearkened to the teachings of man more than to the written word of God; yea, (for a short moment) even in the contradiction to the commandments of the most high; but his spirit prevailed and before the fearful step was taken . . . we saw and learned that justice and truth, virtue and holiness, could alone bring us into the presence of God.

Published reports indicate that Joseph made demands on his followers that included tests of their faith, one of which was an "Abrahamic" test in which he would ask a man if he could have his wife.[39] Heber C. Kimball underwent this test after his arrival from an overseas mission in England. In total confusion he fasted for three days, after which Joseph took the couple into the second story of his Red Brick store and declared to them it was all a test and proceeded to weep at the obedience, devotion, and faith of Heber.[40]

Evidently, Joseph Smith administered this test to William Law. But according to Joseph Jackson, Joseph Smith's bodyguard, Joseph had made many comments of his desire to have Jane Law. The validity of Jackson's report is questionable, but it implies that an adulterous affair was attempted.[41] Thomas Ford stated that the rupture between the men occurred when Joseph approached Jane Law.[42] John D. Lee also reported the same reason for the break.[43] William Law's own diary entry states that "[Joseph] ha[s] late endeavored to seduce my wife, and ha[s] found her a virtuous woman."[44]

As the rumor spread through Nauvoo, a counter accusation arose that it was Jane who approached Joseph. This rumor also claimed that Law was an adulterer and could not partake of the spiritual sealing with his wife. The journal of Alexander Neibaur, a Nauvoo dentist, records (uncorrected):

Mr Wm Law—wisht to be Married to his Wife for eternity Mr (Joseph) Smith said would Inquire of the Lord, Answered no because Law was a Adulterous person. Mrs Law wandet to know why she could not be Married to Mr Law Mr S said would not wound her feeling by telling her, some days after Mr Smith going toward his office Mrs Law stood in the door beckoned to him went across to inquire yes please to walk in no one but herself in the house. she drawing her Arms around him if you wont seal me to my husband Seal me unto you. he said stand away & pushing her Gentle aside giving her a denial & going out. when Mr. Law came home he Inquired who have been in his Absence. she said no one but Br Joseph, he then demanded what had pass[ed] Mrs L then told Joseph wandet her to be married to him.[45]

It is obvious that both of these rumors could not be completely true. There are several indications that the counter accusation was false. There are no names of witnesses nor of the persons involved in the adultery charges against William Law. In addition, he had received his "holy endowment" which persons accused of adultery could not do. Again, at the excommunication trial, Jack Scott, a Canadian convert, testified that to smooth things over between Joseph and William on this issue Joseph sealed the couple for time and eternity.[46]

In any case William endeavored to keep the matter out of the public eye. No-where in the *Nauvoo Expositor* is any mention of advances by Joseph toward Jane and while being interviewed in his later years William steered away from the topic and emphasized his wife's virtue. Dr. Wyl investigated the discord between William and Joseph and published his account in an anti-Mormon book. To him Law wrote,

Of my wife, however, your remarks were far from flattering. She, were she living, would consider them insulting. You said she was much "adored" and "desired" by Smith; that Smith admired and lusted after many men's wives and daughters, is a fact, no doubt; but they could not help that. They, or most of them, considered his admiration an insult and treated him with scorn. In return for this scorn, he generally managed to blacken their reputations—see the case of your friend Mrs. Pratt, a good virtuous woman. I will now take the trouble of showing you just how my wife and Joe Smith stood toward each other. For some time in 1843, I think, he ordered the Twelve to meet and cut off from the church William Law and his wife, also Dr. Foster, and to publish it in the *Times and Seasons* at once. They did so. A few days after I saw the notice in the paper, I think it was the same day, I met Elder John Taylor and remarked to him, "You have been cutting off my wife and me from the Church." I asked him what the charges were and who had made them. He said, "Brother Joseph ordered you cut off." He said further that Joseph had known for a long time that we were apostates, and further that my wife had been speaking evil of him for a long time; he had found it out, said she had slandered him and lied about him without cause. I said, "Elder Taylor, my wife would not speak evil of yourself or anyone else without good cause, Joseph is the liar and not she. . . ." He went on to say about his wife, "My wife is dead over four years and a truer, purer, more faithful wife never lived."[47]

In a final "epitaph" to polygamy, as an older man, he stated,

For you will find in the Book of Jacob, I think, a strong condemnation of polygamy. Read a little further and you will find, "if I, the Lord, will raise up a pure seed unto myself, I will command my people," or words to that effect. I have no Book of Mormon and may not quote correctly. This last passage opened a door for Joseph to command the priesthood to get all the wives they could and raise a pure seed to the Lord (I say to the devil).[48]

Another source of animosity by William Law toward Joseph Smith was the use of political power. From the outset of his arrival in Nauvoo, William was deeply involved in politics, supporting all of the prophet's desires. When Joseph was kidnapped, in an effort to take him back to Missouri, William was the first of the Mormons that "rescued" him. He was supported unanimously for a second term as counselor to Joseph Smith. William, however, had major disagreements with Joseph over political matters.[49] In Nauvoo the theocratic society demanded loyalty to the spiritual autocracy of Joseph Smith. The first instance of William's disagreement with Joseph was over the election of local candidates for the United States Congress soon after the introduction of polygamy.[50] As it happened, Joseph was securing legal help from Cyrus Walker, a defense lawyer, in exchange for the Mormon vote in the election. William knew of the plan and noted that "Joseph promised Walker that he should have nine out of every ten Mormon votes."[51] Two days before the election, on August 5, 1843, Hyrum Smith commanded the people of Nauvoo to elect Walker's opponent. William, dismayed over Hyrum's admonition, stood and spoke in opposition, describing the move as shameful. So forcefully did he speak that the people began to shout for Walker. Then Hyrum took the stand again and stated that his instruction was a revelation from God. The next morning William reported the event to Joseph, who then asked Hyrum about it. Hyrum insisted that he had received a revelation. "Oh, said Joseph, if this is a revelation, then it is all right and he went on the stand" and reassured the Saints to vote for Hoge.[52]

During this time the polygamy issue caused growing disenchantment for Law and he opposed it vigorously. On January 8, 1844, he was dropped without

warning from the presidency as Joseph's counselor. Being articulate in church law, William claimed that such a move without a trial was illegal, based on an earlier statement by the prophet that no action should be had before church councils without the parties having an opportunity to be present to defend themselves.[53]

Of his sudden dismissal Law wrote,

I confess I feel annoyed very much by such an unprecedented treatment for it is illegal, inasmuch as I was appointed by revelation (so called) first (and was sustained) twice after by unanimous voice of the general Conference.[54]

From this time on his anger seemed to mount. It is interesting to note that he still believed in the church polity and law and that it was Joseph who was fallen and ruining the work of the Lord. Of his removal from a position of authority Law wrote, "I feel relieved from a most embarrassing situation. I cannot fellowship the abominations which I verily know are practiced by this man, consequently I am glad to be free from him."[55]

The effect on Law's emotions is indicated in his diary entries. On January 13, 1844, he wrote:

What feelings have been I cannot relate, various and painful at times almost beyond endurance; a thousand recollections burst upon my burning brain, the past, the present, and the future, disappointed hopes, injured feelings, where they should have been held sacred....These things are as poisn'd arrows in my bleeding heart.[56]

William sought out other dissenters and they began to hold their own services. To each other they confessed their problems and nonconformity with the church leadership. The group included Robert Foster, who claimed that Joseph had tried to seduce his wife,[57] and the Higbee brothers, who claimed that Joseph had wronged their father.[58] This group planned to force debate on the polygamy issue at the conference in April 1844, but Joseph is reported to have said to the conference that it had been expected by some that the little petty difficulties which have existed, would be brought up and investigated before this conference, but it will not be the case; these things are too trivial a nature to occupy the attention of so large a body.[59]

It was at this conference that the "King Follett" sermon was presented, seeming to add another dimension to the celestial marriage doctrine.

On April 18 the group was excommunicated, allegedly without a trial. Law was outraged and wrote, "By the above the Church has as a body transgressed the laws of the Church and of God & every principle of justice and are under deep transgression."[60] In May 1844, embarking on a new strategy,[61] he proceeded to procure a printing press and produced the prospectus of the Nauvoo Expositor which was to be published the next week. Joseph then sought reconciliation through Sidney Rigdon, but Law's demands were too great, including withdrawal of the spiritual wife doctrine. On June 7 the Expositor appeared, creating general excitement both in Nauvoo and in neighboring communities. The Nauvoo City Council then declared the newspaper a public nuisance and ordered it destroyed.[62] The copy for the second issue was being prepared when the order was carried out. Law describes the action from his point of view:

There was a meeting at the court house. I think Stephen A. Douglas was present at the meeting. My friends urged me to come to Carthage with the press immediately. No conclusion was arrived at, however. The same evening we went home and when we came to Nauvoo we rode over our broken office furniture. The work of Joseph's agents had been very complete; it had been done by a mob of about 200. The building, a new, pretty brick structure, had been perfectly gutted, not a bit left of anything.[63]

William's plan had worked.[64] He immediately filed a complaint against Joseph for inciting mob action against the newspaper. The Warsaw Signal declared that it was time to declare open warfare on Joseph Smith and his people.[65] William, however, began to feel the ire of those who were loyal to Joseph and planned his escape.

Seeing what had been done, I took abode, for safety's sake, at my brother's. I left Nauvoo on a large new steam ferry-boat, which transported my family and my brother to Burlington, Iowa. While we had people packing our things in my house, we rode, my brother and I, through the city in an open carriage, to show that we were not afraid.[66]

Joseph's consternation is illustrated by a dream concerning the Law brothers, in which they had bound him and thrown him into a deep pit or well. Up above he perceived Wilson in the grasp of a tiger and William with a huge snake coiled around him, making him blue in the face and forcing green poison to seep out of his mouth. As the snake relaxed its grip, William cried out to Joseph, who responded that he couldn't help because they had bound him. Joseph is reported to have related this dream to his companions while he was incarcerated at Carthage.[67] The next day the prison was stormed by an angry mob and Joseph was killed.

Meanwhile, the Law brothers were seeking refuge. They heard of Joseph's death upon landing at Burlington. William's reaction was reported to Isaac Hill:

. . . as they brought it upon themselves, and I used my influence to prevent any outrage even from the commencement of the excitement, believing that Civil Law had power to expose iniquity, and punish the wicked. I say consequently I look on and while the wicked slay the wicked I believe I can see the hand of a blasphemed God stretched out in judgment, the cries of innocence and virtue have ascended up before the throne of God, and he has taken sudden vengeance.[68]

From Burlington the Laws traveled to Hampton, Illinois, where they settled temporarily. The Mormons were convinced of William's complicity in the murder and accused him of responsibility for killing the prophet. A warrant was issued for his arrest, but he was released for lack of proof.[69] On hearing of his connections with the slain prophet, the community began to ostracize him. In response to a slanderous report by a man named Jacques in a local paper, William wrote:

He wishes the public to believe that I represented myself and friends as Modern Mormons. I never intended to convey any such idea, but the very reverse. It was over opposition to Modern Mormonism, with its vile heresies and abominations, that caused the difficulty between Joseph Smith and us; . . . when I became a member of the Church I did so upon the strength of Scripture evidence and reason, the same powers of truth are still before me. Shall I then deny my religion because Joseph and others believed in it, and afterwards perverted it to evil purposes, or apostatized from it? No! I might as well deny the purity and righteousness of the acts of Solomon in building and dedicating the Temple—which God accepted—because Solomon afterwards became grossly wicked. . . . I am not ashamed of my religion, but believe I can successfully vindicate the truth and purity of it before any reasonable unprejudiced community, taking the scripture of the Old and New testament as a standard of faith.[70]

In 1846 they moved to Monticello Township of Lafayette County, Wisconsin, where they regained economic strength. On the banks of the Apple River they operated a mill and did some farming. Later they moved to Shullsburg, Wisconsin, where they settled permanently.[71] William became a doctor, developed a good reputation, and served on the local bank board.[72]

From then on William became more and more bitter. Later in life he denounced everything associated with Mormonism.

For more than forty years I have kept Mormonism all my past connection with it, out of my mind, and away from my friends and acquaintances so far as possible. Have never read any of the books published about Mormons; never read Bennett's book, have kept no papers published in Nauvoo; have not one scrap of any kind; the only number of the *Expositor* I had, someone carried off.

My wife (at an early day) burned up the Book of Mormon and the Doctrine and Covenants. She said no Mormon work could find a place in her house. We have lived down in a great measure of disgrace following our unfortunate association with the Mormons. We committed no crime. This is my consolation that we only erred in judgment.

The great mistake of my life is my having anything to do with Mormonism. And I feel it to be a deep disgrace and never speak of it when I can avoid it; for over forty years I have been almost entirely silent on the subject, and will so continue after this.[73]

Five years after writing this letter, William Law was laid to rest beside his brother. There has been speculation that the motivation for his actions was a desire to become the prophet of the movement. Another explanation is based on his democratic spirit, preventing a total commitment to the religion. Perhaps it was the conflict between the Nauvoo doctrines and his understanding of the scriptures and his reason.

In any case, the drama of disaffection embodied all of the dilemmas confronting the people in Nauvoo. Joseph's death and the end of Nauvoo centered in political pressures, economic problems, and the theological practices that conflicted with the moral background of the day. William Law was caught in these currents and his story gives us insight into how they affected the lives of the individuals involved in them.

Notes

1. Letter from William Law to Dr. Wylmeter (hereafter referred to as Dr. Wyl). One of three letters published in the Salt Lake City *Tribune*, July 3, 1887. Also in the archives of the Reorganized Church of Jesus Christ of Latter Day Saints (hereafter referred to as RLDS church), Independence, Missouri. Dr. Wylmeter was the author of *Joseph Smith the Prophet: His Family and His Friends — A Study Based on Facts and Documents* (Salt Lake City: Tribune Printing and Publishing Co. 1886).

2. Nauvoo *Expositor*, RLDS Library and Archives, Independence, Missouri. I am indebted to Alma Blair of Graceland College for my copy.

3. *History of the Church of Jesus Christ of Latter-day Saints* 2nd edition, rev. (Salt Lake City: Deseret News, 1932-51) vol. 5, 152.

4. Richard Price, *The Polygamy Conspiracies* (Independence, Missouri: Cumorah Books, Inc., 1983). Price is a voice in a conservative movement in the RLDS church which disavows theories of Joseph Smith's introducing polygamy.

5. Francis M. Gibbons, *Joseph Smith: Martyred Prophet of God* (Salt Lake City: Deseret Book Co., 1977), 230.

6. Lyndon W. Cook, "William Law, Nauvoo Dissenter," *Brigham Young University Studies*, vol. 22 (November 1, 1982): 47.

7. Kenneth Godfrey, "The Counselor, the Colonel, the Convict, the Columnist, a Most Unlikely Quartet" (Paper presented in 1982 to the Mormon History Association).

8. Thomas Ford, *A History of Illinois*, vol. 2 (Chicago: Lakeside Press, 1946), 160-2.

9. John D. Lee, *The Mormon Menace — Confessions of John D. Lee* (New York: Home Protection Publishing Co. 1905) 185.

10. Cook, 22:47.

11. *Christian Examiner*, December 11, 1838, Toronto.

12. "Interview with William Law," *Weekly Tribune*, Salt Lake City, August 4, 1887.

13. *Upper Mississippi Weekly*, October 5, 1844, Rock Island, Illinois, Library, RLDS Library and Archives.

14. Godfrey, 3.

15. Correspondence of Hepziah Richards, Kirtland, Ohio, January 28, 1838. Archives of the Church of Jesus Christ of Latter-day Saints (hereafter referred to as "LDS church"), Salt Lake City, Utah.

16. William Law to Isaac Russell from Churchville, November 10, 1837. See Lyndon Cook, "Joseph Is Truly a Wonderful Man, He Is All We Could Wish a Prophet to Be." *Brigham Young University Studies*, vol. 20 (November 2, 1980):212.

17. Ibid., 212.

18. Ibid., 216.

19. *History of the Church of Jesus Christ of Latter-day Saints*, 2nd ed., vol. 4, 20.

20. Cook, 22:53.

21. Doctrine and Covenants (Independence, Missouri: Herald House, 1983), Section 107:30.

22. Cook, 20:218.

23. *Upper Mississippi Weekly*, October 5, 1844.

24. Ibid.

25. Cook, 20:217.

26. Ibid., 213.

27. Robert B. Flanders, *Kingdom on the Mississippi* (Urbana, Illinois: University of Illinois Press, 1965).

28. Godfrey. The Day Book entries cover only a fifteen-month period. At that lending rate, Godfrey estimates that Joseph may have owed over $10,000.

29. Doctrine and Covenants, 107:27, 28.

30. *History of the Church of Jesus Christ of Latter-day Saints*, vol. 5, 285.

31. Hancock County, Illinois, book of Bonds and Mortgages, BM1 501, vol. 1, p. 502. Several days later William mortgaged the thirty-two entire lot (148) to Samuel Hoyt for $791.32 (August 4, 1843).

32. *Upper Mississippi Weekly*, October 5, 1844.

33. Hancock County, Illinois, Circuit Court Book D (May 21, 1845), 258.

34. Law to Wyl, January 20, 1887.

35. The RLDS church has traditionally held that Joseph Smith was never involved in the practice of polygamy. Regarding this see Richard Howard, "The Changing RLDS Response to Mormon Polygamy: A Preliminary Analysis," reprinted from *John Whitmer Historical Association Journal*, vol. 3 (1983), in this book.

36. *Times and Seasons*, Nauvoo, Illinois (August 1, 1842):872-73. See note 3, vol. 5, pp. 146, 160, 183.

37. Brigham Young Address, October 8, 1866,

Brigham Young Papers, LDS Church Archives, Salt Lake City.

38. *Upper Mississippi Valley*, October 5, 1844.

39. See for example, *Journal of Discourses*, vol. 2 (Liverpool: F. D. Richards, 1855): 13.

40. Stanley Bucholz Kimball, *Heber C. Kimball* (Urbana, Illinois: University of Illinois Press, 1981), 93.

41. Joseph Jackson. *A Narrative of the Adventures and Experiences of Joseph H. Jackson*, p. 19. Letter from Dan Jones to Thomas Bullock, January 20, 1855, archives of the LDS church, Salt Lake City. Jackson's account is a lurid one and its accuracy is open to question. He broke with Joseph and joined William's camp. It has been suggested that he circulated the questionable account that Emma wanted Law for a spiritual husband. Law later told a similar story about Joseph offering Emma the opportunity of choosing a husband in his own stead. William Law to Dr. Wyl, January 7, 1887.

42. Lee, *Mormon Menace—Confusions of John D. Lee*, 161. "Soon after these institutes were established, Joe Smith began to play tyrant over several of his followers. The first act of this sort which excited attention, was an attempt to take the wife of William Law, one of his most talented and principled disciples, and make her a spiritual wife."

43. Cook, 22:185. "There was trouble between Joseph and Brother Law, his second counselor on account of Law's wife. Law said that the prophet proposed making her his wife, and she so reported to her husband. Law loved his wife and was devoted to her, as she was amiable and handsome woman, and he did not feel like giving her up to another man."

44. William Law's Diary, "Record of Doings of Nauvoo in 1844." Entry for May 13, 1844. Private collection. All references to this diary in this paper are found in footnotes for Lyndon Cook. See note 6.

45. Journal of Alexander Neibaur, May 24, 1844. Original is in LDS Church Archives. See note 6.

46. Minutes of meeting on April 18, 1844, Brigham Young Papers. See note 38.

47. Law to Wyl, January 20, 1887.

48. William was referring to a passage in Wyl's book (see note 1): "The other intended victim who escaped the prophet's clutches was high-spirited Mrs. Sarah M. Pratt. She stoutly repelled his repeated approaches, though he had to pay the penalty for refusing to consecrate her honour. She has been ever since hated and slandered by the Mormon leaders. Joe threatened her, if she divulged to her husband or anyone else what he had proposed; adding if you do, I will ruin your character, I will deny everything, and the Church will believe me and not you. My standing in the Church must be upheld at any cost and sacrifice." P. 72.

49. Lyndon Cook makes a point of William's democratic spirit and independence. This is evidenced by William's probable earlier sympathy to the liberation of Canada.

50. William Law to Dr. Wyl, January 7, 1887. William's questioning of the political operation of Nauvoo may have begun earlier. "I saw nothing wrong until after the city charter was obtained. A change was soon apparent: the laws of the country were set at defiance, and although outwardly everything was smooth, the under current was most vile and obnoxious. Time revealed to me and to many others that we had not even suspected."

51. Journal of Alexander Neibaur, May 4, 1844.

52. *Upper Mississippi Valley*, October 5, 1844.

53. *Nauvoo High Council Minutes*, July 11, 1840, LDS Church archives.

54. Journal of Alexander Neibaur, January 8, 1844.

55. Ibid., January 8, 1844.

56. Ibid., January 13, 1844.

57. Fawn Brodie, *No Man Knows My History* (New York: Knopf, 1845).

58. Law to Wyl, January 20, 1887.

59. Andrew S. Ehat and Lyndon W. Cook, ed. *Words of Joseph Smith*. Copyright Religious Studies Center, Brigham Young University (Provo, Utah: Bookcraft, Inc.) 339.

60. Journal of Alexander Neibaur, May 24, 1844.

61. The months from January to May of 1844 saw these men grow increasingly hostile to each other even to the point of death. Joseph was constantly increasing his number of bodyguards and had the Nauvoo police stationed outside the home of the dissenters. William claimed that Joseph was making an attempt on his life. A court of inquiry was held to investigate the claims as recorded in the Journal of Wilford Woodruff, January 3, 1844. Immediately there arose a counter accusation that William was attempting to take Joseph's life. Porter Rockwell claimed that

while imprisoned in Missouri, he learned of William's complicity in the extradition attempts. Even his mother seconded the accusation by stating that on her visit to her imprisoned son, she read documents that stated William was the agent for the Missourians.

62. Lee, *Mormon Menace—Confessions of John D. Lee*, vol 2, 161-2. "The Mormons themselves published the proceedings of the council in the trial and destruction of the heretical press; from which it does not appear that any one were tried or that the owners of the property had notice to the trial or were permitted to defend in any particular. The proceeding was an ex-parte proceeding, partly civil and partly ecclesiastical against the press itself. No jury was called or sworn nor were the witnesses required to give evidence upon oath. The councillors stood up one after another, and some of them several times, and related what they pretended to know. In this mode it was abundantly proved that the owners of the proscribed press were sinners, whore masters, thieves, swindlers, counterfeiters, and robbers; the evidence of which is reported in the trial at full length. It was altogether the most curious and irregular trial that ever was recorded in any civilized country; and one finds difficulty in determining whether the proceedings were more the result of insanity or depravity. The trial resulted in the convicting of the press as a public nuisance. The mayor was ordered to see it abated as such, and if necessary to call the legion to his assistance."

63. *Upper Mississippi Valley*, October 5, 1844.

64. William Law to Dr. Wyl: "When I left Nauvoo, I left Mormonism behind, believing that I had done my part faithfully even at the risk of my life, and believing also, that the *Expositor* would continue to do the work it was intended to do. The Smiths thought they had killed it: whereas by destroying the press, they gave it a new lease on life and extra power to overthrow them and drive their followers from the state."

65. *Warsaw Signal*, June 12, 1844. "War and extermination is inevitable? CITIZENS ARISE, ONE AND ALL... Can you stand by and suffer such INFERNAL DEVILS! to ROB men of their property and rights, without avenging them? We have no time for comments; every man will make his own. Let it be made with POWDER AND BALLS..."

66. Cook, vol. 20.

67. Dan Jones to Thomas Bullock, January 20, 1855. LDS Church Archives. Also see Diary of Wilford Woodruff, July 14, 1844. LDS Church Archives.

68. William Law to Isaac Hill, July 20, 1844, LDS Church Archives.

69. Godfrey, October 5, 1844.

70. Ibid.

71. Alma Brookover, unpublished paper, RLDS Library and Archives.

72. William Law to Dr. Wyl, January 20, 1887. He stated of his livelihood, "I have prospered very much notwithstanding Joseph's curse; I have done a large medical practice, think I have been fairly successful; and am retiring from it as fast as I can."

73. William Law to Dr. Wyl, January 27, 1887.

IV
SCRIPTURAL AND THEOLOGICAL STUDIES

SCRIPTURAL AND THEOLOGICAL STUDIES

Editor's Note:

Don H. Compier, M.A. (religion), is assigned to the language staff of the Council of Twelve of the Reorganized church in Independence, Missouri.

A resident of Niagara Falls, Ontario, Canada, Shirley M. Stoner is completing work on a B.A. degree in philosophy as *Restoration Studies III* goes to press. She is librarian at the Niagara Falls Commission School of Horticulture after a thirty-year professional teaching career.

At Central Michigan University, Mt. Pleasant, Michigan, Donald J. Breckon, Ph.D., is professor and associate dean of Education, Health, and Human Services.

Assigned to the North Atlantic States Region for the Reorganized church, Dale E. Luffman, M.Ed. (counseling), is a candidate for the master of arts degree at Princeton Theological Seminary.

With degrees in history, philosophy, and sociology, Clare D. Vlahos is a doctoral candidate in American Studies and is an instructor at Kansas City, Kansas, Community College.

Larry W. Conrad received the B.A. degree in religious studies and is currently working toward a master of arts degree in the history of Christian thought at Vanderbilt University in Nashville, Tennessee. Co-author Paul Shupe's B.A. degree is in the fields of religious studies and history. He is presently studying for the Ph.D. degree in theology at Vanderbilt University.

The essay by James E. Lancaster, M.S., first appeared in the John Whitmer Historical Association *Journal,* Volume 3 (1983). He is a mathematician with Chrysler Corporation's Technical Computer Center, working on robotics and computer vision.

Bruce W. Clavey is nearing completion of study for a bachelor of science degree in computer science at Cleveland State University. He resides at Kirtland, Ohio, and holds a position in the computer operations field at SDS Biotech Corporation, a firm involved in research and development in agricultural and animal health chemicals.

G. St. John Stott, Ph.D. (English and American literature and history), is *Maitre de conferences* and teaches American literature and history at the University of Tunis, Tunisia.

C. Robert Mesle, Ph.D. (philosophy and religion), is an associate professor of philosophy and religon at Graceland College.

CANONIZATION IN THE REORGANIZED CHURCH OF JESUS CHRIST OF LATTER DAY SAINTS

Don H. Compier

The English word *canon* comes from a classical Greek noun meaning "straight rod" or "ruler," which was also used metaphorically in the sense of a rule or norm.[1] The process of canonization, then, is the way certain writings are accepted as normative or authoritative for a religious group, becoming "a standard for the faith and life of the church."[2]

For most Christian denominations, the process of canonization is a datum of ancient history. While many Christians still believe, at least theoretically, in an open canon, no new canonical writings have actually been accepted since the authority of the twenty-seven books of the new Testament was firmly established by conciliar authority late in the fourth century, A.D.[3]

The Reorganized Church of Jesus Christ of Latter Day Saints, however, has a procedure by which numerous additions to its canon have been made and continue to be made. In recent years, a new canonical document has been accepted at almost every biennial conference. The prophet-president of the church presents what he considers to be an inspired writing, and the Conference votes to accept the document as an expression of "the mind and will of God." Such acceptance automatically canonizes what the prophet has presented.

In the face of such a unique phenomenon, several questions present themselves. Some are of an historical nature: How did this process develop historically? Was canonization in the Restoration movement always carried out as it is today, or have there been procedural changes over the years? Other questions are theological: What is the theological justification of this procedure of canonization? What are its strengths and potential weaknesses?

The Historical Development

The Restoration movement began with the "coming forth" of a new book of scripture, the Book of Mormon. This work was evidently accepted unquestioningly by all of Joseph Smith's followers, so that it never appeared necessary to canonize it officially through the action of a conference held during the founding prophet's lifetime.

The revelations given by Smith were another matter, however. These were usually presented orally in response to a pressing problem, or as a result of the curiosity of the prophet or his followers, for example, about John the beloved disciple.[4] A sizable number of these experiences were recorded in writing, so that the desire eventually arose to publish Joseph's revelations as an addition to the canon of the new church. A conference held in Ohio during November 1831 decided that Smith should collect and "prepare" the revelatory documents and send them with Oliver Cowdery to Independence, Missouri, for publication there. It is reported that Joseph offered a prayer of dedication for this prospective "Book of Commandments."[5] Evidently the Saints expected and accepted a new book of scripture while being quite content to leave the specific content of that work to their prophet.

The destruction of the church's press at Independence by mob action prevented the completion of the Book of Commandments—though some galley sheets were apparently gathered up and bound. Thus a high council held at Kirtland, Ohio, in September 1834 authorized a second attempt to publish Smith's revelations. A committee was charged with this responsibility. The description of the committee's task is of interest. The council instructed them to "arrange the items of the doctrine of Jesus Christ, for the government of the church." These items were to be taken from the Bible, the Book of Mormon, "and the revelations which have been given to the church up to this date, or shall be until such arrangements are made."[6] Smith was one of the members of this committee.

It was the work of the committee—not the specific content of the Book of Doctrine and Covenants—that was considered by the quorums of the church meeting in general assembly at Kirtland on August 17, 1835. Their unanimous acceptance of the book that had not yet been published[7] was in effect a decision to include the forthcoming publication in the church's canon of scripture. It is interesting to note that their action thus "canonized" not only Smith's revelations (selected and worded as he chose) but also non-revelatory material, namely the "Lectures on Faith" and the articles on government and marriage.[8]

No further action of a canonical nature was taken by a church conference during the lifetime of Smith, but this does not mean that the Mormon canon did not continue to expand. It is evident that the basic principle of canonization in the Restoration movement was faith in the prophetic office of Joseph Smith, Jr. His recorded revelatory experiences were accorded authority even if they were published only in the church's periodical literature. It is not at all surprising, then, that no conference approval was considered necessary to authorize the inclusion of sections not in the Doctrine and Covenants of 1835 when the second edition of that book was printed in September 1844. In any case, the new material dealt with matters, such as the law of tithing (Section 106, RLDS editions), which had enjoyed the popular support of the church during the prophet's lifetime. Baptism for the dead, another subject of the material first included in 1844 (Sections 107, 109, 110), had been instituted by Smith in September 1840; if the church had felt it necessary to vote on this matter, it certainly had opportunity to do so.

Both of the chief factions of Mormonism would later act to formally canonize writings of Smith published only in the church's newspapers during the prophet's life. Thus the church in Utah would produce *The Pearl of Great Price*, while Isaac Sheen of the Reorganization felt at liberty to include the reported visions of Moses and Enoch as Sections 22 and 36 of the RLDS church's first edition of the Doctrine and Covenants (1864). Indeed, the veneration of Joseph even resulted in the publication of manuscript materials as part of the canon. Thus the Reorganized church would publish the so-called New Translation of the Bible, based on incomplete manuscripts, in 1867.[9]

Eventually the Reorganization had to struggle with the question of additions to the canon due to the revelatory experiences of Joseph's succesors in the prophetic office. At the spring Conference of 1873, Joseph Smith III presented a revelation to the body dealing with administrative concerns. The Conference voted to "endorse the Revelation as one sent from God."[10] The decision to include this document, along with others, in the church's canon was not made until 1878. The fall Conference of that year moved to accept "young Joseph's" revelations of 1861, 1863, 1865, and 1873 (subsequently Sections 114–117) "as being the word of the Lord to his Church . . . authoritative and binding on us as a body . . . that they be hereafter compiled with that book" (the Doctrine and Covenants).[11]

And in response to challenges from such persons as Jason Briggs and Zenas Gurley, Jr., the small Conference decided to carefully define the church's canon. A motion was approved to

recognize the Holy Scriptures, the Book of Mormon, the revelations of God contained in the Book of Doctrine and Covenants, and all other revelations which have been or shall be revealed through God's appointed prophet, which have been or may be hereafter accepted by the Church as the standard of authority on all matters of church government and doctrine, and the final standard of reference on appeal in all controversies.[12]

Three implications of this important action should be noted. In the first place, in light of a previous motion approved at the same conference,[13] it is clear that the conference was canonizing only the New Translation and not other versions of the Bible. In effect, then, only works that are the result of revelatory experiences of Joseph Smith, Jr., and his successors are here accepted as canonical for the Reorganized church. Secondly, those portions of the Doctrine and Covenants that are not revelations are explicitly excluded from the canon, reversing the acceptance of the "Lectures on Faith," the articles on marriage and government (Sections 111 and 112), and the minutes of the organization of the High Council at Kirtland (Section 99). Last, the revelations to the founder first included in the editions of 1844 and 1864 are specifically accepted as authoritative. That would include Sections 107, 109, and 110, with their teaching on baptism for the dead.

The procedure for canonization followed thereafter by the Reorganization was thus definitively established in 1878. The process required that canonical documents (1) originate with the president and prophet of the church, Joseph Smith, Jr., and his successors in office, and (2) be adopted by the vote of a General Conference of the church. In practice, this would lead to a tradition of "instant canonization": the prophet's document is immediately acted on by the Conference and speedily added to the Doctrine and Covenants. This is what occurred when Joseph Smith III received his next revelation in 1882,[14] and with only one exception [15] it has been RLDS practice ever since.

What happens, though, when later generations can no longer accept a doctrine articulated in a revelation given years ago? The Reorganization faced this issue of "decanonization" in the 1960s, when at least some members were troubled by the teaching on baptism for the dead so clearly espoused by Joseph Smith, Jr., in Sections 107, 109, and 110. The Conference of 1968 requested that the First Presidency study the possible preparation of a new edition of the Doctrine and Covenants placing all sections not accepted by conferences in a historical appendix.[16] The First Presidency reported its recommendations to the Conference of 1970, whose concurrence led to the creation of a historical appendix containing Sections 107, 109, 110, 113, and 123.[17]

Several comments about this action may be in order. First of all, the rationale for the relocation of Sections 107, 109, and 110 was, at least in part, articulated as due to the fact that these sections were never endorsed by a Conference. That contention is a historical fallacy. Section 107 was read to the Nauvoo Conference of April 1841; though this revelation was not voted on specifically, canonical endorsement is implied in the assembly's vote to sustain the Presidency of the church. Moreover, the Conference of 1878 clearly accepted Section 107, and probably 109 and 110 as well, since these letters do seem to result from what Joseph considered to be revelatory experiences.

Second, it is interesting that the Conference of 1970 did not feel free to explicitly decanonize these writings. They were not removed from the Doctrine and Covenants entirely—just moved to the back. This fact may indicate something of the difficulty of withdrawing canonical authority once that standing has been granted by previous conferences.

A Theological Evaluation

Now that we have seen the historical development of canonization in the Reorganized church, a few evaluative suggestions might be appropriate. The RLDS practice has the sanction of tradition. Is that sufficient, or are changes in the procedure of canonization justifiable?

Some writers of the Reorganization have defended the practice of the church by arguing for the benefits of an open canon. They stress that their procedure permits God to continue speaking, so that the benefits of increased insight and fresh responses to new situations are continually available to the church.[18]

While many Protestants and Catholics express similar beliefs, it does seem that the Restoration movement has taken the idea of an open canon seriously enough to actually add new writings to the Christian canon. If one believes in a God who is purposively consistent, and if one recognizes that human conditions shift constantly, it is clear that the idea of an open canon offers great theological advantages. But an argument for an open canon does not automatically and logically lead to support for the RLDS practice, since there are many ways other than the one chosen by the Reorganization to remain open to additional scriptural insights. The crucial question, then, is not Should we uphold the idea of an open canon? but, rather, What practice is best for implementing this idea? In the realm of apologetics, it is crucial that RLDS writers defend the current practice of the church, not the idea of an open canon in general. Thus, it is difficult not to conclude that Reorganized apologetics have been particularly weak at this point.

Another argument that might be presented is based on the necessary authority of the prophetic office. It might be said that our practice permits the church to be forcefully led by revelation, even when a rather sharp change of course is called for. As the most recently canonized document of the Reorganization (Section 156, permitting the ordination of women) shows, there is a certain cogency to this argument. However, all that is necessary to deflate this defense is to point to the obvious fact that there are many noncanonical ways by which the proper authority of the church's prophet both can be and is exercised. As the Conference of 1873 demonstrated, it is entirely possible to accept an inspired utterance as binding upon the church, without thereby making an immediate decision as to its canonical status. Moreover, the leadership of the church has always issued policy documents, etc., that the church considers authoritative; yet such documents are not canonized, even though they, too, at times show clear signs of inspiration and of enduring worth.

All in all, it is hard to escape the conclusion that the RLDS practice of canonization is based primarily on a traditional foundation—and a not very well articulated one, at that. Yet, on the other hand, there are several strong theological reasons that suggest that a revision of the process of canonization in the Reorganized church might well be in order. These reasons are based on the canonical procedure that produced the Bible, but they are articulated by RLDS authors, and have functional and theological criteria to recommend them also.

1. Scripture should have what Roy Cheville called "survival quality."[19] The Old and New Testaments were the result of long community usage. Over centuries, the community discovered which writings had enduring value for instruction, worship, or other things.[20] The results of this sifting procedure were by no means perfect, but the process did produce a body of quality literature that the faith community accepted as a normative "common denominator."

The RLDS practice does not allow "survival quality" to be tested. The problems faced by the Conferences of 1968-1970 are due precisely to this fact. The history of our community had not proven baptism for the dead to be a valid doctrine—yet it was enshrined in our canonical writings! We discovered that once something is in the canon, it is most difficult to remove. That problem is inherent if the current practice is continued.

2. Scriptures should be the result of a process of selection.[21] The works of many writers are considered by the community. All may have some inspirational value. But to function as a normative standard, their number cannot be too great. Hence selection is a necessity.

The New Testament, then, represents a kind of "best of . . ." collection of early Christian writings. A number of authors are represented, yet only twenty-seven out of the hundreds of works were included in the canon.

Restoration scriptures are, paradoxically, both too inclusive and too exclusive. They are too inclusive because every "inspired document" presented by the prophet to a conference is, after approval, printed in the Doctrine and Covenants. In that sense, the principle of selectivity is inoperative. Our scriptural record has thus become burdened with minutiae—names of persons, offices, and the like—that are of nothing but antiquarian interest to later generations. If this process continues unabated, our Doctrine and Covenants will someday be an exceedingly large and cumbersome volume!

On the other hand, they are too exclusive because only the writings of Joseph Smith, Jr., and his successors are considered for canonization—not even the Bible has really been accepted by us except as revised by Joseph Smith! Now certainly the prophets of the Reorganization have been varied personalities. Even so, they represent only one rather unique perspective, that of the presiding officer of the church, while many valuable writings by capable, "inspired" individuals cannot even be considered for canonization.

There may be powerful reasons, then, to be true to our motto of openness to the future by creating a new canonical tradition for the Reorganized church. If it is true that God challenges us to continually reinterpret our faith (Section 147:7), there may well be a divine imperative to reconsider the procedure by which documents become part of the canon of the RLDS church.

Notes

1. Brevard S. Childs, *Introduction to the Old Testament as Scripture* (Philadelphia: Fortress Press, 1979), 49.
2. Geoffrey F. Spencer, *The Burning Bush* (Independence, Missouri: Herald Publishing House, 1975), 118.
3. F. W. Beare, "Canon of the NT," in the *Interpreter's Dictionary of the Bible*, vol. I (New York and Nashville: Abingdon Press, 1962), 520-532.
4. Doctrine and Covenants, Section 7.
5. *The History of the Reorganized Church of Jesus Christ of Latter Day Saints*, vol. I: *1805-1835* (Independence, Missouri: Herald Publishing House, 1951), 225 and 228.
6. Quoted by F. Henry Edwards, *A New Commentary on the Doctrine and Covenants* (Independence, Missouri: Herald Publishing House, 1977), 33.
7. Since the articles on marriage and government were that day ordered to be included in it, and since the book was not back from the bindery and offered for sale until September 1835.
8. See the minutes of the general assembly, published in the introduction to current RLDS editions of the Doctrine and Covenants, and Richard P. Howard, *Restoration Scriptures: A Study of Their Textual Development* (Independence, Missouri: Herald Publishing House, 1969), 204-206. *The History*, 578, erroneously claims that the textual differences between the Book of Commandments and the Doctrine and Covenants have to do with the fact that only the latter's contents were endorsed by a conference.
9. Howard, *Restoration Scriptures*.
10. *Supplement to the True Latter Day Saint's Herald*, May 1, 1873, 284-286, 288-291.
11. *The Saint's Herald* (October 1, 1878): 296.
12. Ibid., 295-96.
13. Ibid., 295.
14. *The Saints' Herald*, October 15, 1882, 321.
15. Section 121, originating in 1885, was accepted years later.
16. *World Conference Bulletin*, 1968, 283.
17. *World Conference Bulletin* (1970): 141-143, 286.
18. Many examples could be cited so just a few will be mentioned here. See introduction to *A New Commentary on the Doctrine and Covenants; The Burning Bush; Exploring the Faith* (Independence, Missouri: Herald Publishing House, 1970), especially p. 214; and *An Introduction to the Saints' Church* by Peter Judd and Bruce Lindgren (Independence, Missouri: Herald Publishing House, 1976), 83-91.
19. *Scriptures from Ancient America* (Independence, Missouri: Herald Publishing House, 1964), 14.
20. See R. H. Pfeiffer, "Canon of the OT," *Interpreter's Dictionary of the Bible*, 498-520. Child's treatment of this subject is also worthy of study—his whole book is devoted to it. See also Beare's article, cited previously.
21. Spencer, 119.

THE PROBLEM OF GENDER AND IMAGERY IN RELIGION

Shirley M. Stoner

Reorganized Latter Day Saints share many beliefs with other Christians. Like others of the Judeo-Christian tradition, we have been conditioned to think that God and Christ are male. Thinking men and women have discerned in this belief discrimination against the female half of the human race and have begun to question the implications of this policy. The worth of the individual is basic to Latter Day Saint theology. In my experience in the church this belief has never been taken to mean that the worth of the male soul is greater than that of the female. Rather we have believed and taught that each person, whether male or female, is a child of God, with equal responsibility toward establishing the Zionic condition, and with equal potential for achieving celestial glory. We delight in the scripture, "All are called according to the gifts of God unto them."[1]

The policy for inclusive language approved by the First Presidency in 1978 and since reflected in our hymn texts and other church publications was a beginning to fuller recognition of the equality of women. The major breakthrough occurred, though, in 1984 with the approval of Section 156 of the Doctrine and Covenants which sanctioned the ordination of women to priesthood responsibility. These two events have heralded the dawn of a new age for men and women of the church and ultimately for the world. Unfortunately, they have not been received with equal enthusiasm by all members of the church. In an effort to understand and perhaps clarify the situation for myself, I have attempted to discover if our belief in the masculinity of God is truly valid.

Sexuality is necessary for the procreation of the human race and is part of our earthly life. It seems that it would be inappropriate to attribute sexuality to the Divine. The attributes of God by which we attempt to define him/her for our understanding include omniscience, justice, omnipotence, love, and so forth. These qualities could be applied to those of either sex. Furthermore, maleness has meaning only in relation to its opposite, femaleness. "For there must be an opposition in all things."[2] To say that God is male implies that there must be a female counterpart. This could mean male and female combined in one Supreme Being, or it could be a separate entity such as a goddess.

Indeed, until the ancient Judean patriarchs arrived on the scene, most previous civilizations did worship the goddess. This was natural for them because, in their experience, only the female could produce new life from within her body. For centuries primitive people did not understand the role of the male in procreation. Those early civilizations were mainly agricultural, and the women were the ones who gathered the food for the tribe. The female was not only the producer, but also the sustainer of life. This led to a matriarchal society in which kinship was traced through the mother. In their quest for the ultimate source of life, people worshiped not only their ancestors, but their primal ancestor or original mother, whom they deified as the Divine Ancestress.

Archaeologists have discovered in every area of the Near and Middle East, small female figurines representing this "great mother" goddess, dating from the Upper Paeolithic period (approximately 25,000 B.C.) and extending right up to about A.D. 500. At this time the church managed to stamp out goddess worship, but only by replacing it with the veneration of the Virgin Mary. The Great Goddess was regarded as changeless, immortal, and omnipotent. The worship of the Goddess was widespread and very influential. According to Marija Gimbutas in her essay "Women and Culture in Goddess Oriented Old Europe"

There were, in my opinion two primary aspects of the Goddess (not necessarily two goddesses) presented by the effigies. The first is "She Who is the Giver of All"—giver of life, of moisture, of food, of happiness—and "Taker of All", i.e., death. The second aspect of the Goddess is her association with the periodic awakening of nature: She is springtime, the new moon, rebirth, regeneration, and metamorphosis.[3]

The Semitic peoples who were the forerunners of the Jews worshiped such a goddess as a direct result of their custom of ancestor worship and their mother kinship system. The goddess figure has been found in Abraham's ancestral city of Ur, which would indicate that she was probably known to Abraham and his progenitors.

The essence of all theological thought is the search for the ultimate source of life. These ancient people naturally assumed that the ultimate source would be similar to the known source, i.e., the female. This is not to suggest that God is female, just that it would be natural for these

primitive people, living in a matriarchal society to assume so.

The next question to arise then is "When and why did society, and particularly the Jews, change to a patriarchy?" There seems to be a little evidence to answer this question with authority. It is known, however, that the goddess eventually acquired a male counterpart, sometimes a brother and sometimes a son, who became her consort. They were known in various cultures as Baal and Ashtoreth, Isia and Osiris, or Apsu and Tiamat.

Where did this male god come from? Apparently not all early civilizations were agricultural as were those of the fertile crescent. Northern tribes were pastoral with an economy based on stock trading. They lived in small clans, grazing large herds over immense areas of land. The primary tasks of these pastoralists were undertaken by men, horsemen and warriors who became dominant in their culture. Between 4500 and 3000 B.C. these northern tribes executed a series of invasions in which they eventually conquered the southern matriarchal civilizations. Their supreme father-god was a young warrior. It is thought that the amalgamation of these two religions resulted in the appearance of the male counterpart of the goddess.

When Abraham and Lot came on the scene, about 1800 B.C., they were nomadic herdsmen, if not before they left Ur, at least from that time onward. As part of a patriarchal society it would have been natural for them to assume God to be male. That is not to suggest that God is male—just that it would be natural for these early patriarchs to assume so. For at least six centuries the Jews were equally at home in worshiping both the god and the goddess. The temples to Ashtoreth stood next to those of Yahweh. After the Jewish patriarchs finally succeeded in destroying goddess worship, women came to be treated as chattel. Women lost their original high status as creator and sustainer of life and with it their independence. The same story is repeated in culture after culture with the introduction of male worshiping religions.

Knowledge of paternity is essential to a patrilinear system. It is also difficult to ascertain.

In the ancient struggle waged by men to shift matrifocal social structures to a new focus on property rights, male gods were invented to legitimize a system whereby a female's labour and reproductive capacity belonged exclusively to one man.[4]

This resulted in the devising of laws which would ensure the bondage of women. These laws, conceived three thousand years ago to support this patriarchal system, still exist today. They affect not only our legal system, but also our attitudes. Moreover, they form the basis of most of today's problems. Merlin Stone, in her essay entitled "The Three Faces of Goddess Spirituality" explains the relationship between Old Testament laws and many of the problems of today's society, including rape, divorce, prostitution, incest, pornography, abortion, and war. The absence of women from the decision-making levels of church and state ensures that these laws retain their authority and explains why the aforementioned problems are so difficult to eradicate from our society.

The text of the Bible, as we now have it, clearly assumes that the Deity is male. As a general principle, there is no obvious reason why a metaphysical Supreme Power should be endowed with sex or gender at all. On the other hand, if God is to be credited with such attributes, one would expect that these would somehow combine both male and female qualities. Is there anything in the Bible which would indicate that God possesses female as well as male qualities? Other than references to wisdom being personified as a woman which is commonly accepted, one might think not. However, in the book entitled *The Divine Feminine* by Virginia Ramey Mollenkott, one finds multiple references to the feminine imagery used to describe the Divine.

More pervasive than any other Biblical image of God as female is the image of a maternal deity. Not only is the creator depicted as carrying in the womb or birthing the creation, but also Christ and the Holy Spirit are depicted in similar roles . . . Isaiah 42:14 uses a simile of Yahweh's experiencing labour pains . . . "now I will cry like a travailing woman." A more serene, transcendent image of God the Mother occurs in Acts 17:28 . . . God is the one who has given life and breath to everyone . . . for it is in God that we live, and move, and exist. Although the apostle (Paul) does not specifically name the womb, at no other time in human experience do we exist within another person.[5]

Job 38:28, 29 gives an image of both father and mother: "Hath the rain a father? . . . Out of whose womb came the ice?" Jesus in John 16:21 compared his suffering on the cross to bring forth a New Humanity to a woman's labour in bringing to birth new life. Paul used a similar image in Galatians 4:19: "I travail in birth again until Christ be formed in you."

Jesus spoke of the Holy Spirit as mother in John 3:6: "That which is born of the flesh is flesh; and that which is born of the Spirit, is spirit." To be born of the flesh is to emerge from a human mother; to be born of the Spirit is to emerge from the divine Mother.[6]

Without taking the time and space to duplicate the work of Ms. Mollenkott in this essay, I would like to indicate that she has found feminine images of the Divine in the Bible to compare God to a nursing mother (Isaiah 49:15), God as midwife (Isaiah 66:9), God as mother bear (Hosea 13:8), God as female homemaker (Psalm 123:2), God as female beloved (Romans 8:35-39), God as a bakerwoman (Matthew 13:32), God as mother eagle (Deuteronomy 32:11, 12), God as mother hen (Luke 13:35), and as mentioned earlier, God as Dame Wisdom (Proverbs 1:20-33).

I have employed only a few of the numerous biblical images of God as feminine. That these seem new to us is because we have been conditioned to think of God as masculine. It is time now to open our minds to this feminine imagery of God found in our scriptures and to see the implications for a better society based on equality and justice.

If we are able to accept the feminine aspects of God, we are then faced with two other dilemmas. One is the attitude of the Apostle Paul toward women as recorded in the New Testament. The other is the problem of Eve.

I have chosen to address the issue of Paul first. Since he is one of the principal theologians of the New Testament, many are fond of quoting him to indicate his support for the repression of women. Biblical scholars, by comparing the works commonly attributed to Paul, have divided them into two categories: those definitely believed to be Paul's and those which are obviously written by someone else, designated by scholars as the pseudo-Pauline writer. The well-known passages which demand subservience and silence from Christian women "have been identified. . .as either certainly or very probably not from the hand of Paul."[7] Galatians 3:28 which concerns the equality of male and female is Paul's writing, and is consistent with his doctrine that Christ was the second Adam: "As all were lost by Adam's transgression, all are now redeemed by the faithfulness unto death of the second Adam."[8] The significance of Christ's death and resurrection is the equality and unity of all who are in Christ. "There can henceforth be no distinction between Jew and Greek, slave and free—and male and female."[9]

There is evidence that this equality and unity did exist for a few centuries in the early Christian church but eventually succumbed to the conservative opposition who could not abide so revolutionary a vision and instead enforced the "terms of the old order, demanding silence and submission from women believers and leaving them to work out their salvation in married or celibate discipline."[10] These forces, no doubt patriarchal, are responsible for women's inferior position in the Christian church and should not be attributed to Paul who is "the only certain and consistent spokesman for the liberation and equality of women in the New Testament."[11]

Let us now examine the problem of Eve. Traditionally Eve has been held responsible for the original sin. This has reflected on all subsequent women and has supposedly rendered them inferior to men. The story of Eve is part of the creation story and is told in both chapters one and two of the book of Genesis. It is necessary to note there that there were two oral traditions from which two different writers took their stories to be written down and included in the canon of scripture. The writers were called Elohist and Yahwist after the names they preferred to use for God. This explains why there is more than one version of some of the stories in the Old Testament and why they do not always agree. This is the case with the creation story, even in the Inspired Version. The Elohist version of Eve's creation, recorded in chapter one, differs from the Yahwist version in chapter two. John A. Phillips explains it this way:

In the first chapter of Genesis, God creates "mankind" in his image. As if to stress that the creation of "mankind" includes the female of the species, the writer repeats: "In the image of God he created him, male and female he created them." The direct consequence of creation in God's image is the governance of the earth and all its creatures; therefore the simultaneous creation of the sexes is significant. If the woman is created at the same time as the man, it follows that she shares equally in the work of governance. The contradition between this story and the account of the creation of the first human pair in Chapter 2 of Genesis has long been troublesome to commentators. In the second story, God forms Adam, (a single representative being) out of adamah (a clod of earth) and animates him with the breath of life . . . God . . . forms the first woman out of a rib of the sleeping man, and presents her to him. . . . The implication of the story is clear: Created after the man, out of his substance and especially for him, her purposes are subordinate to his.[12]

Faced with a choice between these two interpretations of Eve's creation, why does that in chapter two usually predominate? The reason takes us back to the old argument about the patriarchal society. It seems to be human nature to create a scapegoat so that we, in blaming another, can judge ourselves to be good. As Mary Daly points out, this was "an exclusively male effort in a male dominated society"[13] and "it succeeded primarily in reflecting the social arrangements of the time."[14] In choosing the Yahwist version, men laid the blame for original sin on the female even though she may not have been more guilty than they.

What does it mean to be created in the image of God? Surely it does not mean a physical image. We would not dare to limit God to the physical components of a body—either male or female. If the term "God" brings to mind a male image, perhaps we need to look for another word for the Divine. What better place to look than at the term God himself used. In instructing Moses what to call him he said, "I am that I am."[15] Perhaps the word "Being" would be a better name for God if we could still retain the idea of the personal God we have come to know and love. "God is Be-ing."[16] In this Be-ing we live and move and have our being. Mary Daly declares, "It is the creative potential itself in human beings that is in the image of God."[17] This is compatible with Hymn No. 69 in *Hymns of the Saints* from which we sing, "From God's own image being comes, in human form, female and male."[18] The members of both sexes must reach out toward becoming complete human beings. Many will best be able to do this by reaching out toward an androgenous God. It will not matter then if we refer to God as "him," as I have had to do in this article, or as "her" which may be more meaningful to some. What matters is that we cease to attempt to make God conform to a male image, that we cease to look on women as less worthy than men, and that men and women work together to accomplish "the work intrusted to all,"[19] the building of the kingdom of God here on earth.

The Roman historian Virgil was quite accurate when he said, "We make our destinies by our choice of gods."[20] Our destiny lies ahead of us. Let us choose wisely. Mary Daly has said that the prophetic function is to point beyond to what has never been but can become. That we have a prophet who has done this attests to his divine authority, and is the source of rejoicing among thinking Latter Day Saints.

Notes

1. Doctrine and Covenants, enlarged and improved edition (Independence, Missouri: Herald house, 1978) Section 119:8.
2. Book of Mormon (Independence, Missouri: Herald House, 1966), II Nephi 1:81.
3. Charlene Spretnak, ed., *The Politics of Women's Spirituality* (New York: Anchor Press, 1982), 27.
4. Ibid., 499.
5. Virginia Ramey Mollenkott, *The Divine Feminine* (New York: Crossroad, 1983), 15.
6. Ibid., 18.
7. John A. Phillips, *Eve: the History of an Idea* (San Francisco: Harper and Row, 1984), 121.
8. Ibid., 121.
9. Ibid., 121.
10. Ibid., 122.
11. Ibid.
12. Ibid., 27.
13. Mary Daly, *Beyond God the Father* (Boston: Beacon Press, 1973), 45.
14. Ibid., 45.
15. The Holy Scriptures, Inspired Version, Exodus 3:14.
16. Daly, 33.
17. Ibid., 29.
18. *Hymns of the Saints* (Independence, Missouri: Herald House, 1981), Hymn No. 69.
19. Doctrine and Covenants: 119:8.
20. Spretnak, 561.

CHANGING SEXUAL ROLES: A SCRIPTURAL PERSPECTIVE FOR TODAY'S PROBLEMS

Donald J. Breckon

Sexual Teachings in the Old Testament

In the beginning, God created humankind, both male and female. Significantly, human beings were created as sexual beings, with the same basic reproductive system as the rest of the animal kingdom. Additionally, God specifically told the people to use their reproductive systems, to be fruitful and multiply, and fill the earth (Genesis 1:30). However, humans, with greater intellectual capacity, did not function sexually as mere animals. Instead, each civilization that evolved placed various limits on the kinds of sexual expression that were socially acceptable.

The early history of the Hebrews as reported in the Old Testament suggests that the male was either created as the more dominant of the two sexes, or quickly evolved into that position. The physical strength and endurance needed to survive in that agricultural society which was plagued by frequent wars, favored the development of the patriarchal system, with its concommitant male dominance.

Women were regarded as property. They were classed with goods, servants, and animals as valuable property, but still property. The people were commanded "Thou shalt not covet thy neighbor's house, thou shalt not covet thy neighbor's wife, nor his man servant, nor his maid servant, nor his ox, nor his ass, nor anything that is thy neighbor's" (Exodus 20:17). Note that the priority suggested in this commandment valued real estate over wives, wives over servants, man servants over maid servants, and all servants over animals.

The Old Testament repeatedly makes it clear that women's value was dependent on their ability to bear children, preferably male children, who could in turn become agricultural workers or soldiers. Thus, Sarah and Rachel, who were barren, gave their handmaidens to their husbands Abraham and Jacob hoping they might father male children (Genesis 16 and 30). Many years later, David even took it as a measure of God's greatness that God could make a sterile woman fertile (Psalm 113:9).

The male's penis or "phallus" became a symbol of power. Statues of the phallic symbol were carved from bones or shaped from clay and displayed in prominent places, including the temples.

The rite of circumcision initially was a sacrificial act. It involved giving up of the foreskin of the penis, thought to be the most valued part of the anatomy, as a part of a covenant made with God.

A universal custom of the times was for a man to place his hand on his own penis or the penis of another person when making a vow or entering into a contractual relationship (Genesis 24:2 K.J. version). Biblical translators of subsequent generations have substituted the words "under the thigh," but support the concept.

This intermingling of religious and sexual roles is further illustrated by the exclusion from the Lord's congregation of men who had their genitals injured or cut off (Deuteronomy 23:1). Further, it was declared sinful to waste the seminal fluid containing "man's precious seed." This is graphically illustrated by the story of Onan. Onan had an older brother who was married to a woman whose name was Tamar. The older brother died, leaving Tamar a childless widow. According to Jewish law it was the duty of the younger brother to have sexual intercourse with his brother's widow in order that she might have a child and continue the dead brother's family line. In the act of sexual intercourse with Tamar, Onan decided that he did not want to father a child that would not bear his own name. He, therefore, withdrew at sexual climax and spilled his semen on the ground. The scriptures indicate that he was immediately killed by God for this sin (Genesis 38:1-26 K.J.).

If readers were to stop at this point in the story, they could draw all sorts of conclusions from it such as the Roman Catholics have done in their statements suggesting that sex is only for procreation, and therefore the use of contraceptives is sinful. The story continues, however, and tells how Tamar, still childless, veiled herself as a prostitute and sat by the road and enticed her father-in-law, Judah, to have sexual intercourse with her. Tamar became with child, and averted the horrible stigma which Judaism placed on dying childless. Many believe that the major point of the story is the untiring efforts to which Tamar would go to have a child carry on her dead husband's family line, thus illustrating a woman's major role in life.

During much of Old Testament times it was considered sinful to abstain from marriage, because the Lord wanted the earth filled with people. The need and the commandment to increase the population of the earth undoubtedly were used to rationalize the widespread acceptance of polygamy and the use of concubines. (Interestingly, the need and the commandment to populate a desert area was again used to rationalize polygamy in the Mormon church.)

Jewish religion had a continuing problem in keeping pagan fertility rites and temple prostitution purged from their religion. I Kings, II Kings, and Hosea speak of temple prostitution having been incorporated into religious rites. The practice was condemned by the prophets, and Judaism primarily followed the laws of Deuteronomy which forbade prostitution (Deuteronomy 23:17-18).

The Old Testament affirms that sexuality is God's creation, and that sexual intercourse is not a sin. Adam and Eve did not repent of their sexual activity. The sin of Adam and Eve was in desiring to "know good from evil" which is best interpreted to mean that they wanted to be like God or even to be God (Genesis 3:10). Significantly, people were commanded to be sexually active, as a natural part of life.

The Old Testament also affirms that the appropriate place for sexual activity is between husband and wife. There are many exceptions, as the biblical writers described actual practices of the day. But even with this honesty, the principle remained, that the proper place for sex is within the marriage relationship, and any sexual activity outside of marriage was strongly condemned (II Samuel 11-12). For adultery there were severe penalties that included death by stoning (Leviticus 20).

Sexual Teachings in the New Testament

The teachings of the Old Testament evolved somewhat during the teachings of Jesus. Jesus did not marry, and said very little about sex, thus apparently accepting the Jewish teachings on this issue. He did support marriage as an institution (Matthew 19:3-11). He used a marriage feast to illustrate the joys of the kingdom of God (Matthew 22). He spoke of feasting banquets, a woman adorned for her husband, and a bride and groom going into the marriage chamber (Matthew 25). It is also interesting to note that he did not spend his time denouncing women or sex. He did not demand abstinence. He did forgive harlots, and he intervened in the stoning of a harlot on one occasion. His concepts of marriage and sex were apparently the same as the Jewish society of which he was a product.

Significantly, Jesus discussed religious truths with women, and defended the right of Mary of Bethany to discuss the meaning of life with him. He accepted women as colleagues and friends, and was accompanied on journeys by women disciples. Interestingly, it was the women disciples who stood by Jesus on the cross, who discovered the empty tomb, and who carried the news of the Resurrection to the apostles.

The attitude of Christianity toward women in the years immediately following the life of Christ are varied, and today's Christians can find scriptural support for whatever position they prefer. The most prolific writer of the time was Paul, so the attitude of the church is usually inferred from his writings. Paul traveled widely and wrote to many congregations, so, not surprisingly, his writings contain apparently conflicting perspectives.

Paul is most commonly thought to be sexist. He was himself unmarried. He taught that "the husband is the head of the wife" (Ephesians 5:23) and that "man was created in the image and glory of God while woman was the glory of man"

(I Corinthians 11:7). He advised that "women were to learn silence and subjection," not speaking in church, and asking questions of their husbands later (I Corinthians 14:34).

These teachings of Paul may have reflected his orthodox Jewish background, or may have reflected a position held in an early part of his ministry. Paul states the reason for much of his beliefs was his conviction that the second coming of Christ was imminent, and that people needed to prepare for the end of time. He stated, "The appointed time has grown short, and from now on let those who have wives live as though they had none" (I Corinthians 7:29). "The unmarried man is anxious about the affairs of the Lord, how to please the Lord, but the married man is anxious about worldly affairs, and how to please his wife" (I Corinthians 7:32-33). Paul seems to believe that it was best not to marry, but if someone wanted or needed sex, then marriage was preferable to sex outside of marriage (I Corinthians 7:9).

Other scholars stress other dimensions of Paul's attitudes toward women. He accepted women as ministers. Women assisted Paul, and were instrumental in founding and supporting new churches. The names of Priscilla, Lydia, and Phoebe are but three of such women who played major leadership roles during the time. Controversy exists on whether women were actually ordained during the time. Romans 16:1, 2 is particularly noteworthy in that it refers to Phoebe as a deacon in the church. Other nonscriptural writings of the time support the concept that Phoebe and other women were indeed ordained ministers.

Paul did stress that "There is neither bond nor free, male nor female; for ye are all one in Christ Jesus" (Galatians 3:28). Such a statement seems in conflict with other statements he made about women keeping silent in church. Scholars have suggested that such statements may have been added to the text after Paul's death. Others have suggested that that statement may have been directed to specific women in a specific congregation where women may have become a dominating and disruptive force. If either of these positions is accepted, or if one accepts the premise that Paul's beliefs on the matter changed over time, it is not appropriate to take such statements out of context, or to generalize to all people for all time.

Paul's beliefs about women's role in the church seem to be best summarized in Galatians 3:27 "there is neither male nor female." His beliefs about sex, marriage, and procreation seem, at least on the surface, to be atypical of that generation and of the majority of the generations before and since. It may be that Paul's views on sex and marriage were influenced more by circumstances of his own day, by his chronic illness, and perhaps even by personal psychological inadequacies than by either the teachings of Judaism or Jesus.

Sexual Teachings of Other Early Christian Leaders

Beginning with Paul's writings and continuing for several centuries, the church denounced sexual relations as evil, especially for men who were involved in the ministry of the church. Women came to be despised. Tertullian, an early bishop, proclaimed, "Woman you are the devil's doorway. It is your fault the son of God had to die; you should go in mourning and rags."*

St. Chrystostom said, "Among all savage beasts there is none found so harmful as woman."** Johnson and Belzer also point out that Pope Gregory officially imposed celibacy on the priesthood in 1075, declaring that sexual intercourse even within marriage was sinful. Married priests that resisted were tortured until they recanted, or were killed.

In the year 1250, St. Thomas Aquinas preached that marriage without sex is more holy than marriage with sexual intercourse. Thus, certain days of the week were set up as unfit for coitus: Thursday in memory of Christ's arrest, Friday in memory of his death, Saturday in memory of the Virgin Mary, and Monday in commemoration of the departed. Sex was also forbidden during Lent and on the hundred or so "Saint's Days" which occurred throughout the year.***

During the Protestant Reformation many views on sexuality were changed. Martin Luther, among others, spoke out against the inconsistencies of the teachings, and the deviation from the teachings of Christ. He viewed the new teachings on sex and marriage as part of the apostasy.

Still later, the Puritans sought to return to the fundamental teachings of the early Christian church and the Old Testament. They came to America from around the world, seeking religious freedom. They wrote many of their beliefs into law in the new country, during the sixteenth, seventeenth, and eighteenth centuries. Many vestiges of these laws remain today in laws on obscenity, pornography, adultery, fornication, contraception, abortion, and sex education. Sex was considered indecent. People didn't talk about it,

*Warren R. Johnson and Elwin G. Belzer, *Human Sexual Behavior and Sex Education* (Ann Arbor: Books Demand BMI in Philadelphia: Lea and Febiger, 1963), 101.

**Ibid.

***Kenneth Latourette, *A History of Christianity* (New York: Harper & Row), 525f.

teachers didn't teach it, and preachers didn't preach about it. As a result, some contemporary liberals remarked that America would be better off if instead of the Pilgrims landing on Plymouth Rock, that Plymouth Rock had landed on the Pilgrims.

The rigid, puritanistic laws were obeyed by many, but increasingly with the passage of time, began to be openly ignored and subsequently repealed. The pendulum appears to have moved to the other extreme. Sexuality appears not only to be emphasized in today's society, but openly exploited. It is valued and devalued, bought and sold, discussed and taught, and, at times, seems to dominate other aspects of culture.

However, in recent months, there seems to be a shift back to a more moderate position. Movements are occurring to modify overly permissive laws on obscenity, pornography, abortion, and other things. The overly proscriptive, sexist, teachings of the past appear to have disappeared from the laws of the country and the teachings of most churches. Similarly, an overpermissive attitude does not appear to be acceptable to the majority of Christian people, resulting in Christian political action groups dedicated to changing such laws. In short, the concepts of sexuality, and indeed sexual roles themselves, continue to be fluid, changing from person to person, group to group, place to place, and time to time.

An Evolving Position for Today's Church

It is little wonder that society as a whole, and more specifically, the church, continues to struggle with changing sexual roles, Given the overriding biological, historical, cultural, theological, and political factors that are often contradictory, ambivalence is to be expected. Indeed, individual and social ambivalence is always characteristic of major social change.

Change occurs at differing rates, and acceptance of change occurs at even more disparate rates. Such circumstances are especially true in a church where many people are conditioned to wait for God to direct the church. Many people appear unable or unwilling to differentiate between policy and doctrine, even at times blurring the distinction between resolutions and revelations.

The First Presidency has, however, exerted major leadership roles by calling for continued study of the issues surrounding human sexuality. (See Appendix for list of studies.) Dialogue on issues helps clarify the dimensions of an evolving position, and helps create a climate in which change can occur and can be accepted. Dialogue helps individuals and the church as a whole arrive at policy that is rational, coherent, and acceptable to at least half the membership.

In this spirit of inquiry, the church has repeatedly studied the issues surrounding the role of women in the church for the last decade, with at least two formal committees reporting. Similarly the church has studied the issue of marriage and divorce. Committees have also reported the results of their deliberations on abortion. In yet another report, the entire issue of human sexuality was examined, including, but not limited to, homosexuality and fornication.

The results of these studies have been printed, distributed, and summarized in the Herald. A variety of reactions and resolutions subsequently evolved and have been introduced at World Conference with varying results. Some resolutions reaffirm past practice and belief, others call for more study, while yet others call for immediate change. People of both conservative and liberal persuasion find scriptural support for their personal beliefs, and lobby for adoption of their beliefs as church policy, believing that uniformity of beliefs is essential to unity of purpose. This situation occasionally creates the impression that the church is schizophrenic and does not agree on doctrine or policy. A broader perspective suggests that it has always been that way, and perhaps always will be.

Of course, while the dialogue occurs many members remain unaware. Others choose to ignore controversy, thus not having to clarify an unsubstantiated personal view. Some prefer to wait for a revelation from God, while others refuse to accept such revelation.

The question can be raised of the significance of a prophetic church not "leading the way" on such issues. The federal government demanded equal treatment of women and eliminated barriers and forms of discrimination long before the church did. Other churches arrived much earlier at a similiar position. Similarly, those members more conservatively oriented ask if the church is not simply following secular bodies into apostasy.

No final resolution of these issues is apparent; however, the World Church has evolved guidelines regarding sexual roles. They have not as yet been summarized in a single document, nor widely understood by the membership. They appear to this author to be sound, consistent, in harmony with federal law, and accepted by the majority of the membership.

The following list of currently acccepted and practiced guidelines is not official, nor even direct quotes from documents. Rather, it represents this author's attempt to outline in a coherent fashion the current church policy on sexual roles. It draws heavily on committee reports, resolutions, and so on, but is paraphrased and organized within the framework of the perspective of the author.

Church policy and practice at the present time is to emphasize the following:

—Sexuality is a God-given expression that is part of human wholeness.

—Marriage is ordained of God, and is a sacred Christian covenant.

—Monogamy is the basis of Christian marriage.

—The church has an obligation to affect attitudes toward sexuality and marriage, and should encourage open discussion of it in family and church groups.

—Ministerial counseling should be directed at preparing individuals for mutually fulfilling marriage.

—Sexual expression is a normative part of married life. A variety of sexual expressions are acceptable if entered into voluntarily by both parties and are mutually fulfilling. Persons should not be intimidated or coerced into sexual expressions that are offensive to them.

—Ministerial counseling should be available to individuals that find marriage unsatisfactory. Marital counseling should stress healing and reconciling ministries.

—The church should provide caring ministries rather than render judgment when legal or moral grounds result in dissolution of a marriage.

—Remarriage of divorced parties should be approached with the same preparation and consideration appropriate for every marriage, but should also include exploration of factors that led to the dissolution of the former marriage.

—Abortion counseling should be available to a woman, her companion, and others involved, and should include consideration of alternatives, and a deep appreciation for the worth of human life.

—A woman has the right to make her own decision to continue or terminate a pregnancy. Counseling should explore a full range of moral, medical, legal, financial, and cultural factors.

—Simplistic positions that regard all abortions as murder or all abortions as a simple medical procedure without moral significance should be avoided.

—The church should provide acceptance and extended supporting ministries to individuals who consider abortion and choose to either continue a pregnancy or abort it.

—Sexuality can be given a variety of acceptable expressions outside of marriage. Overly simplistic views are usually a matter of personal values and should not be imposed on others.

—All sexual expressions should be guided by love rather than exploitation. Sadism and rape should not be tolerated.

—Sexual acts involving others must be between consenting adults, and must be out of sight and sound of unwilling observers.

—Those who engage in sexual relationships must be prepared to accept responsibility for physical and emotional conditions that may result, either in the short term or long term.

—Overly simplistic positions on homosexuality and heterosexuality inhibit change, tend to reinforce stereotypes, and should not be imposed on others.

—The church must admit that it doesn't know a whole lot about sexuality, and will have to evidence its faith in the Creator not by rendering judgment, but by receiving and loving those who engage in sexual practices currently considered deviant.

—The church should become a significant influence to help create conditions in which sexuality will be seen as part of the abundant life which God seeks for humanity.

—The church reaffirms that no one should be excluded from church roles merely because of God-given sexuality, or expressions of that sexuality.

Appendix

Chronological Order of Reports of Studies

Committee Report on Induced Abortion (1974). First Presidency, RLDS Church, Independence, Missouri.

Committee Report: Task Force on Single Life-Style (1978). First Presidency, RLDS church.

Summary Report of the Committee on Human Sexuality (1979). First Presidency, RLDS church.

Report on the Study of the Ordination of Women (1984). First Presidency, RLDS church.

Ham, Wayne. "Neither Male nor Female," *Saints Herald*, July 1984.

The Roman Letter: An Occasion to Reflect on "Joseph Smith's New Translation of the Bible"

Dale E. Luffman

Without a doubt, Romans is Paul's greatest work. Martin Luther characterized the letter as "rightly the chief part of the New Testament and the clearest gospel of all."[1] Unfortunately, this has not always been the perception of the church as expressed in the Reorganization of the Restoration movement. Rather than being "the clearest gospel of all," Romans has often been seen as one of the most confusing of the New Testament documents. Perhaps this is because the text itself possesses "a central concern and a remarkable inner logic that may no longer be entirely comprehensible to us."[2] Further, many of our contemporary situations and problems are not posed in the New Testament. This requires the development of a proclamation of the gospel in relation to the scripture itself[3]—not vice versa. Understanding Romans may necessitate our allowing the letter itself to be developed in relation to the situation in which the letter actually is.[4]

The General Character of the Letter

Romans is the longest of the Pauline letters. The content of the Christian faith is critically shaped by its writing, with only Matthew and John as possible equals.[5]

The letter to the Roman saints holds a unique position in the Pauline Corpus inasmuch as it is the only letter written to a congregation which had not been founded or visited by Paul himself. Accordingly, he does not refer to previous visits, nor to events that took place after his departure, as is found in the other authentic letters.

He does not pursue his dealings with the church inasmuch as such dealings simply did not exist previous to the writing of the letter. From the post-apostolic period to the present, Paul has been considered the undisputed author of Romans. Romans appeared in Marcion's list of epistles and in the Muratorian Canon. Although it originally followed the Corinthian correspondence, by the fourth century Romans stood at the head of the Pauline letters.

As a composition, Romans is a coherent letter with a unique thrust and development of ideas written primarily in Jewish terminology and addressed to Gentile Christians.[6] Although it appears to be a "systematic, well-organized, and thoroughly throught-out statement of Paul's theology,"[7] it would be a mistake to treat Romans as the compendium or essence of Paul's thought. It is a situational and particular letter, written from the city of Corinth (Acts 20:1-4), after Paul's long stay at Ephesus. (It was at Ephesus that he had previously written Philippians from prison.) The date of the composition is most likely the winter of A.D. 55-56,[8] although others place the dating as late as A.D. 58.

Why is Paul writing to the Christians in Rome?

Since I no longer have any room for work in these regions, and since I have longed for many years to come to you, I hope to see you in passing as I go to Spain, and to be sped on my journey there by you, once I have enjoyed your company for a little. At present, however, I am going to Jerusalem with aid for the saints.—Romans 15:23-25

197

The Roman letter is contingent in character; its motivation is not only in Paul's own unique situation, but specifically in the situation among the Christians in Rome. The church in Rome was a mixed congregation made up of Jews and Gentiles who had become Christians. Although the letter appears to be a treatise of the gospel, it should be observed that a combination of structural coherence and temporal contingency occurs in Romans. The occasion of the letter has profound consequences of Paul's theology as represented in Romans, as he makes the gospel a word on target.

The Quest for the "Core" of Paul's Thought

Since Philipp Melanchthon wrote that Romans was a "compendium doctrinae"[9] there has been a tendency to view the Roman letter as a systematic and comprehensive document, a "dogmatics in outline," which summarizes the essence of the apostle's thought.[10] But,

it is a methodological error to view Romans as a theological structure developed in a vacuum—a view that portrays Paul as engaged with himself in thought, wrestling with the perennial truth of the gospel. The hermeneutical advantage of "timelessness" cannot silence the historical illegitimacy and impossibility of this procedure.[11]

To impose a premise on the basis of an unexamined presupposition poses critical problems for responsible exegesis in Romans as well as in all scripture. Such is the present dilemma facing Roman Catholicism in dealing with the established canon of scripture in light of its tradition, thereby continuing to corrupt the interpretation of scripture by imposing the primacy of tradition.[12] In an equally and perhaps more crucial sense the "dispensational" understanding of the scriptures (a product of the nineteenth century, and significantly influenced by the notation system of the Schofield Bible) has im-

posed a whole set of unexamined presuppositions on biblical texts providing for spurious understandings of the scriptures. This view has had significant influence on biblical interpretation, particularly among the evangelical churches.

We, as members of the Reorganized Church of Jesus Christ of Latter Day Saints, face a similarly crucial issue in light of our tradition with respect to our heavy reliance on Joseph Smith's New Translation of the Bible. In searching for the core of Paul's thought in Romans, one encounters a significantly different text in the New Translation, particularly chapter seven.

Richard P. Howard's writings are particularly helpful at this point.[13] Howard proposes that

even though many of the early Mormon people were conditioned to think of the revision (of the Bible) as a restoration of original, lost texts, it seems clear from serious textual analysis that such a proposition is not warranted.[14]

Howard notes that it is helpful to reflect on the conceptualization of the use of the term "New Translation" to describe the meaning of this work for Joseph Smith, Jr. It is apparent that the terms *translate* and *revelation* are used interchangeably by Joseph Smith, Jr. "'Translation' for Smith was neither a scholarly nor a linguistic exercise, but rather an *intuitive* one."[15]

The "translation" process

was an oracular process whereby God spoke, Smith listened and repeated what he heard, and the scribe wrote the text. . . . One may have a picture of how Smith proceeded on Romans. He intently and prayerfully read from the SCB [Smith-Cowdery Bible], and where he had a strong impression or intuition ("burning of the bosom"?) that a particular word or phrase or verse needed correction, he marked the SCB [Smith-Cowdery Bible] accordingly and then dictated the word, words, phrases, or verses to the scribes.[16]

Howard notes that "Smith later reworked some of his earlier revisions, either emending between the lines or attaching later revisions written on scraps of paper to the MS sheets."[17]

Apparently, later RLDS editors had some conceptual difficulty with the use of the term "translation" as it related to biblical revision. Howard points out that the 1867 publication committee chose to modify Smith's term "New Translation," substituting instead "Translated and Corrected by the Spirit of Revelation." This was a very curious and significant modification which led toward a tradition of inerrancy which would surround Joseph Smith's revision of the Bible. In the 1930s a decision was made to describe the work as "An Inspired Revision." Accordingly the "Inspired Version," has become the short title used by most RLDS people to describe Joseph Smith's "New Translation." Unfortunately, it breathes a pejorative aspersion toward other versions of the Bible, thereby inhibiting the use of other versions which could be of great value in scripture study.[18]

Howard further indicates that it is difficult to show just what Joseph Smith perceived Paul to have written in Romans.[19] He writes,

due to the largely stylistic nature of Smith's alterations of the SCB text, and due to the fact that he brought as much (in terms of personal philosophy, theology, and opinion) to the "translation" experience as he garnered from it, the effort at exegesis [is] destined to suffer.[20]

The essential character of Joseph Smith's "translation" process prevents one from discovering "the thought of Paul" inasmuch as no consistent and clarifying hermeneutic is apparent in Joseph Smith's "translation" of Romans. This is especially true as consideration is given to Romans seven. We do not discover any formal writings or teachings by Joseph Smith, Jr., which would help in this venture either. It seems apparent that

there is to be found in the "New Translation" a set of premises which are based on unexaminable presuppositions that pose critical problems for responsible exegesis in Romans. Accordingly, the "insights" which are to be found in the New Translation can be more responsibly viewed as Joseph Smith's commentary on the Authorized King James Version of the Bible in the exegesis of the letter to Romans, if responsible exegesis is to occur. As we allow the letter itself to be developed in relation to its situation we must also use the best texts available.

The Specific Occasion of Romans

The occasion for Romans lies in Paul's argument with the Roman Christians.[21] "The letter is not only written from a specific situation but also addressed to a specific situation; therefore, its arguments and structural form are dictated by specific needs and circumstances."[22] It is not a summa theologea or a treatise which summarizes the other writings of Paul into this one great synthesis, nor is it "the testament of Paul."[23] It is not just a curious letter designed to introduce Paul to the church in Rome, although the letter does effect such an introduction. As William D. Russell points out, Paul "felt that he had something to contribute to the Roman saints' understanding of the gospel."[24] So Paul wrote to identify some very specific points in this letter as he utilized a form quite different from that found in the other authentic letters of Paul.

Paul utilized a different polemic style than was utilized in the other authentic letters to make an apologetically persuasive argument which focused on the church as the one people of God—Jew and Gentile.[25] God's salvation-historical plan is central to the writing of Romans (Romans 1:16, 17). But beyond this, several convergent factors stand behind the composition of this occasional and yet systematic letter.[26]

Convergent Factors

1. First, Paul was in *a new situation* when he wrote to the Romans. It appears that Paul saw a specific connection between his mission and Spain. The Roman Christians represented a link in the apostolic mission which was to all the Gentile world. Apparently Paul anticipated support from the Romans for his Spanish mission having written that it was his desire "to be sped on my journey there by you" (Romans 15:24). In the missionary task Rome was to be utilized (Romans 15:16-24). This provides one significant reason for the composition of the letter.

2. Second, *the journey to Jerusalem seems to upstage Paul's mission to Spain*. He writes: "At present, however, I am going to Jerusalem with the aid for the saints."[27] He appeals for Rome's active intercession in his behalf:

> I appeal to you . . . to strive together with me in your prayers to God on my behalf, that I may be delivered from the unbelievers in Judea, and that my service for Jerusalem may be acceptable to the saints, so that by God's will I may come to you with joy and be refreshed in your company. —Romans 15:30-32

It should be remembered that the "collection" visit is the fulfillment of Paul's commitment to the apostolic council in Jerusalem (Galatians 2:10). However, the meaning of the collection—the "contribution for the poor among the saints at Jerusalem" (Romans 15:26)—transcended the need for the economic support for the saints. For Paul it represented the blessing of salvation for all Israel, demonstrating the ingathering of the Gentiles as the eschatological unity of the church (Romans 15:26-28). Such a unity of Jews and Gentiles would fulfill the purposes of God and Paul's apostolic mission. Beker writes:

The collection is a decisive step on the way to the eschatological hour and the beginning of what soon will come to pass. What deserves our attention is that it not only symbolizes the unity and equality of Jew and Gentile in the one church of God but also expresses the salvation-historical priority of Israel and the Jewish community over the Gentiles.[28]

Here the theme of the letter is brought into a specific focus, integrating the particularism of the collection and the universalism that is identified in the letter itself as it expresses the gospel: "The power of God for salvation to every one who has faith, to the Jew first and also the Greek" (Romans 1:16).

It seems apparent that the "collection" provides Paul an opportunity to appeal to the Romans for support (Romans 15:30-32). It therefore provides Paul with an opportunity to develop a "hidden letter" to the Jerusalem saints,[29] thereby rehearsing with the church in Rome his upcoming dialogue with the Jerusalem contingent. Fear and anxiety are evident (Romans 15:30). But why?

3. The third convergent factor may provide an answer. In the first letter of Paul to the Corinthians, the church in Galatia is mentioned as a major contributor to the collection (I Corinthians 16:1). However, a review of the list of contributing churches in Romans evidences a conspicuous absence of the Galatian churches (Romans 15:26). Only Macedonia and Achaia are named.

Apparently the agreement made at the apostolic council (Galatians 2:9) had not worked out as well as Paul had anticipated. The case at Antioch is evidence of such potential ongoing disagreement (Galatians 2:11-14) and tension regarding the social and religious status of Judaism in Christianity. Further, the words of "greeting" by James and the elders in Jerusalem are of significant merit for our understanding the basis of Paul's anxiety. Apparently his anxieties were well founded:

And they said to him, "You see, brother, how many thousands there are among the Jews of those who have believed; they are all zealous for the law, and they have been told about you that you teach all the Jews who are among the Gentiles to forsake Moses, telling them not to circumcise their children or observe the customs."—Acts 21:20-21

Although Paul had written to the Galatian churches regarding the true function of the Mosaic law and its relation to God's grace manifested in Christ, it is apparent that Paul had lost his case. He did not want to lose another! Beker suggests that the omission of Galatia in the list found in Romans could indicate that, just prior to the writing of the Roman letter, Paul had received word that despite his apostolic letter to the Galatians he had lost his case with the Galatian churches. No doubt this contributed to the heightening tensions between Paul and Jerusalem inasmuch as Paul's response to the Galatian crisis had most likely created the impression that the position of the Jew in salvation history was a negative one at best.[30]

Accordingly, in light of such tensions and Paul's related anxiety regarding the urgency of the situation, Paul wrote Romans to discuss, among other things, *the "Jewish question."* Perhaps part of his intent was that he would be able to diffuse the fiery Galatian letter and thereby reduce the hostility of the "brethren" in Jerusalem and perhaps even Rome. Here, as an authoritative interpreter of the gospel, Paul gives an orderly intelligible account of God's act in Christ to a specific and particularly needful situation, making the gospel a word on target for the particular needs of the Gentile mission as it interfaced the Jewish Christian community.

4. The fourth convergent factor behind the composition of the Roman letter is to be found in *the tension between the weak and the strong* (Romans 14 and 15). Here is found Paul's concerns regarding the relationships between the Jewish Christians and the Gentile Christians.

It is my conviction that Paul was not as ignorant of the Roman church as many commentators seem to suggest. Paul had many associates and friends who had been associated with the Roman congregation.[31] He was apparently aware, as a result of ongoing contacts and communications with these associates, that the issues he had faced in Galatia, and would yet face in Jerusalem, were to be faced in Rome. Accordingly, Rome represented an opportunity for Paul's apostolic mission to the West, or on the other hand, a closed door to such an apostolic venture. The future of his apostolic ministry perhaps hung in the balance. Beker indicates that Paul's basic apostolic effort of bringing both Gentile and Jew into the one church is jeopardized in Rome.[32] Disunity is represented in the "weak" and "strong" factions found in Rome. Such disunity, a dismembering of the body of Christ, was seen by Paul as a disobedience to the gospel. It arose out of a fundamental misinterpretation and misunderstanding of the gospel both in Rome (Romans 14 and 15) and in Jerusalem (Romans 15:30-32). Paul the apostle was therefore obligated (the mission of the church according to his understanding depended on such exposition and apostolic proclamation) to write specifically what the meaning of the gospel was as it related to the basic equality of both Jew and Gentile. Making the gospel a word on target, he declared the oneness of Jew and Gentile as the people of God within a unity which also preserved the salvation-historical priority of Israel. This was the result of the fact that the "gospel" was "the power of God for salvation to every one who has faith, to the Jew first and also the Greek. For in it the righteousness of God is revealed through faith for faith" (Romans 1:16, 17). "The end of the law" (Romans 10:4) had been brought about by the righteousness of God ratifying God's promises to Israel. Apostolic witness had declared this gospel to Gentile and Jew alike. Paul therefore proclaims his understanding of God's promises to Israel in his opening statement—a statement which opens his address and permeates the rest of the letter:

Paul, a servant of Jesus Christ, called to be an apostle, set apart for the gospel by God which he promised beforehand through his prophets in the holy scriptures.[33]

As all people, "both Jews and Greeks, are under the power of sin,"[34] only Christ alone (the unifying factor) can bring about the possibility of new life through the forgiveness of sins, bringing "about the obedience of faith for the sake of his name among all the nations" (Romans 1:5). Inasmuch as "the righteousness of God has been manifested apart from the law,"[35] both Jew and Gentile alike are called to live solely by faith (sola fide) and solely by grace (sola gratia) in "the righteousness of God through faith in Jesus Christ" (Romans 3:22).

Summary

The key to understanding Paul's letter to the Romans is primarily a situational one. As the apostle to the Gentiles[36] he candidly declared a gospel which was free from "works of the law" (Galatians 2:16). By doing so he created suspicion and distrust among the Jewish Christians. They apparently felt that Paul wanted to overthrow Judaism and the scriptural roots of the gospel. No doubt Paul's fiery letter to the Galatians further aggravated the already existing situation. In a very real sense Paul's apostleship had succeeded only too well (particularly after the fall of Jerusalem in A.D. 70 when the church became almost synonymous with Gentile Christianity).

The main thrust of the Roman letter confronts Judaism head-on.[37] This aspect of the letter, unfortunately, has been overlooked. Many commentators, perhaps in light of premises based on other presuppositions, have directed their exegesis toward a Gentile church. This is an unfortunate error. Kümmel states the problem succinctly:

Romans manifests a double character: it is essentially a debate between the Pauline gospel and Judaism, so that the conclusion seems obvious that the readers were Jewish Christians. Yet the letter contains statements which indicate specifically that the community was Gentile-Christian.[38]

As a "dialogue" with the Jews,

the convergence of causes that motivate the letter indicates Paul's need, at this particular point of his career, to develop and clarify the fundamental issue behind his apostolate, the question of Israel's function in the gospel.[39]

Although Romans may appear to be a "dogmatics in outline" it is more appropriate to consider the letter not as a timeless theological product but as an orderly and intelligible account of God's act in Christ. This makes the gospel a word on target addressed to specific problems and situations, developing and clarifying the fundamental issues behind Paul's apostolate and the question of Israel's function in the gospel of God. Under the pressure of the need for theological clarification Romans is written. Such hermeneutical understanding may enable the reader of Romans to appreciate deeply the need to relate to Paul's text in light of Paul's own setting-in-life, taking care in utilizing "translations" which impose other hermeneutical understandings which were not a part of the situation itself.

Notes

1. J. Christiaan Beker's lecture on Romans at Princeton Theological Seminary, March 5, 1980.
2. Ernst Käsemann, *Commentary on Romans* (Grand Rapids, Michigan: Wm. B. Eerdmans, 1980), viii.
3. Helmut Thielicke, *The Evangelical Faith* vol. 3 (Grand Rapids, Michigan: Wm. B. Eerdmans, 1982), 138.
4. Because of this fact a conscious decision was made by the author to use the most reliable text available for the Roman letter. The Revised Standard Version has been utilized as the most responsible English language translation available at this time. As will be discovered, Joseph Smith's revisions of chapter 7 of the Roman letter seem to impose a hermeneutical understanding of the letter which was not a part of the situation itself. Perhaps confusion among the membership of the church over the message of Romans is attributable in part to the textual revisions of Joseph Smith's New Translation of the New Testament of the Bible.
5. J. Christiaan Beker lecture.
6. Ibid.
7. William D. Russell, *Treasure in Earthen Vessels* (Independence, Missouri: Herald House, 1966), 102.
8. J. Christiaan Beker.
9. J. Christiaan Beker, *Paul the Apostle: The Triumph of God in Life and Thought* (Philadelphia: Fortress Press, 1980), 59.
10. Even Karl Barth and Anders Nygren exemplify this tendency in their writings. Both bypass critical historical issues, depriving their interpretations of the hermeneutical spice of the Roman letter.
11. Beker, *Paul the Apostle*, 65-66.
12. Thielicke, *The Evangelical Faith*, vol. 3, pp. 127-139. It should be noted, however, that Karl Rahner, Hans Kung, Edward Schillebeeckx, and David Tracy have to varying degrees been successful in calling this position into question.
13. Richard P. Howard, "Some Observations on Joseph Smith, Junior's Revision of Romans 3:21-8:31," unpublished paper (used by permission).
14. Ibid., 4.
15. Ibid., 5.
16. Ibid., 5 (SCB is a designation for the Smith-Cowdery Bible used for the translation process. The reader may also want to refer to Richard P. Howard's excellent study, *Restoration Scriptures: A Study of Their Textual Development* (Independence, Missouri: Herald House, 1969), ch. 9, pp. 150-161.
17. Ibid., 5.
18. Ibid., 5-6.
19. Ibid., 6.
20. Ibid., 6.
21. Beker, *Paul the Apostle*, 69-70.
22. Ibid., 70.
23. Werner Georg Kümmel, *Introduction to the New Testament*, rev. ed. (Nashville: Abingdon Press, 1975), 312 ff.
24. Russell, 112.
25. Romans 3:21-30; 5:18-21; 10:12; 11:32; 15:8-12.
26. Beker, *Paul the Apostle*, 71-74.
27. Romans 15:25 (cf: Galatians 2:1-10; I Corinthians 16:1-4).
28. Beker, *Paul the Apostle*, 72 (cf: Romans 15:27, 28).
29. Beker, *Paul the Apostle*, page 72 (cf: Willi Marxsen, *Introduction to the New Testament*, Philadelphia: Fortress Press, 1968, page 95. Marxsen states: "In writing this letter Paul has in certain respects the problems at Jerusalem in mind.").
30. Beker, *Paul the Apostle*, 73 (cf: Willi Marxsen, *Introduction to the New Testament*, 94).
31. Romans 16:3, 7, 11, 21 (Acts 18:1, 2).
32. Beker, *Paul the Apostle*, 74.
33. Romans 1:1, 2 (cf: Romans 4:1-12; 15:8).
34. Romans 3:9 (cf: Romans 3:23).
35. Romans 3:21 (cf: Romans 3:21-26).
36. Galatians 1:15; Romans 1:5, 13, 14; 11:13; 15:16.
37. Beker, *Paul the Apostle*, 75 (cf: Romans 2:1-11, 17-29; 3:1-20; 4:1; 6:1-15; 7:1, 4-6; 9:1-11:36).
38. Kümmel, 309.
39. Beker, *Paul the Apostle*, 77.

MORMONISM AND THE LIMITS OF GRACE

Clare D. Vlahos

There has never been a secure place for a doctrine of grace in mainstream Latter Day Saint thought. Instead of undeserved salvation, Mormonism has offered alternatives of perfectability and merit by obedience to a new law. This paper will argue that this omission has not been accidental. Mormonism's theological anthropology is incompatible with grace as Paul, Augustine, or Luther understood it. In this paper I would like to examine the metaphysical pluralism identified in Mormon thought by Sterling M. McMurrin[1] and Paul M. Edwards.[2] I will then relate this pluralism to the place of grace in Mormonism and to other traditional explanations of evil.

The core of the doctrine of grace in Galatians and the third chapter of Romans is that righteousness is an imputed righteousness. It is the faith of Christ that God declares adequate for humanity which meets the standard defined by the Mosaic law. Because the law itself could never be kept, the law only condemned those who attempted to live by it. Luther emphasized the Pauline imagery of a judicial declaration of human justification within the act of faith. Humanity finds the condition of faith in the declared righteousness as elusive as perfect obedience to the law. Therefore, Luther claimed one need only accept an imputed faith as well as an imputed righteousness. Such acceptance means basically that one no longer tries to justify himself or herself by obedience to the law.

That the omission of grace from Mormon mainstream thought has not been accidental is indicated by occasional writings within Reorganized church publications. For many years into this century, the Reorganized church has frequently treated the areas of sin and salvation within the framework of the "new law."[3] At times, the New Testament gospel and at other times the message of Joseph Smith, Jr., were regarded as new and more accurate information or existential truths requiring individual obedience. While the new law was a means to salvation, sin was a barrier to salvation. Being obedient to the new truths ended in certain modifications of behavior. Sin, however, was specific acts in which the new truths were not obeyed. Sin could thus be overcome by the right knowledge and a strong will to act on that knowledge.

Some later authors within the Reorganized church looked for an alternative framework with which to discuss sin and salvation. Noting the rigidity and frustrations of the legal framework as well as drawing on neo-orthodox thought, these authors attempted to introduce a concept of grace into discussions of sin and salvation. In the alternative framework sin was regarded not as specific acts but as a characteristic of the human condition. For example, "sin is not 'good in the making.' It does not call for improvement but rather for destruction. Sin is not 'ignorance' which can be eradicated by education."[4] Nevertheless the doctrine of grace that emerged did not find a place for imputed righteousness or faith. What emerged had more in common with a Thomistic doctrine of implanted supernatural graces within the human personality or an Eastern Orthodox conception of human quickening, and redirecting by the Holy Spirit.[5]

Most recently within the RLDS church has emerged a publication and program emphasis toward a "wholeness" theme.[6] This framework like the new law is at a loss to find a place for grace. Sin is, however, not specific acts or a characteristic of the human condition. Sin is viewed more as imbalance in the person or as a negative but transformably social condition. There is evidence of a return to liberal theology's themes of human freedom, improvement, and a narrower divine-human distance. There is also at times a return to the new law's conception of salvation by right knowledge and technique.[7]

This somewhat chronological review of three frameworks in which RLDS authors have treated salvation and sin indicates that there has been some effort to include grace within the discussion. We should note three things: Grace was so peripheral to RLDS thought that the new law framework could easily ignore the subject. On the other hand, the RLDS neo-orthodox framework did not find a place for Pauline grace with its imputed righteousness and faith. Finally, the wholeness framework has found even a modified Pauline grace more peripheral than that right knowledge of human problems and techniques for correcting them can transform humanity.

The preceding example is pertinent to Mormon thought in general. Because theology always operates within a system comprising many doctrines, one can never change even part of an implicit system such as Mormonism by fiat without suffering consequences elsewhere. This paper will argue that Mormon thought cannot easily incorporate grace into its implicit system because of the nature of other doctrines. Because these other doctrines are very central to the heart of Mormonism, I will argue that not only does Mormon thought resist grace, Mormon thought is incompatible with Pauline grace.

The theological umbrella of which grace is a dependent part is the doctrine of evil. In Luther the prominence of grace makes the influence of evil on grace a more reciprocal one. In Mormonism grace is so peripheral that evil is determinative for the understanding of grace. We thus must investigate Mormon grace by the secondary question of how Mormon evil compares to other understandings of evil in which grace finds a hospitable home.

Theological systems by individual theologians might be said to apply specific theological principles to the traditional religious doctrines. The main traditions for treating evil are much too broad to speak, for example, of the Mormon or the Reformation theological principle. Instead let us look at three guiding images that have been widely used for the formulation of theological principles by individual theologians in discussing evil. The three images are evil as a fall, evil as development, and evil involving struggle.

The fall image is the most pervasive in Western Christianity. Drawing its basic insights from Paul, this image guided Augustine, Aquinas, Luther, and Barth in their discussions of evil. The image narrative claims that humanity was created good and free, humanity chose the lesser good for itself, and humanity is presently imprisoned in its choice. Redemption to humanity's ultimate good can come about by God's unmerited gift of salvation alone.

The fall image is concerned to justify a monistic universe in which God's omnipotence is challenged neither by an opposing evil power nor human freedom. An evil power God did not control would deny God's omnipotence. The fall image places current responsibility for human sin on humanity's prior free choice of the lesser good. Thus, humanity is responsible; God's goodness is not denied by a divine creation of evil, and an uncontrolled evil is replaced by a wrong human choice for a lesser good. But the problem remains of how good humanity in a good evironment could choose wrongly if God did not create evil. The answer for some, such as Calvin, was predestination.[8] That is, God predesinted some of undeserving humanity to salvation and some to condemnation. The implicit responsibility for human sin thus becomes God's for the predestinarians. It was felt better by these theologians to question God's goodness rather than God's omnipotence.

Pauline grace as earlier described derives primarily from the fall image. Human nature is morally corrupt. It is not free to choose salvation either through obedience to the Mosaic law nor through faith to implement Christ's righteousness. Divine grace thus is correlate with divine omnipotence, human corruption, and divine control over evil in some form. If humanity was not corrupt there either would be no need for salvation or humanity could achieve salvation on its own. If evil were a real competing power, divine grace against such an uncontrolled evil would have the ring of metal washers. We might summarize by saying grace is one form of human salvation in a universe of divine omnipotence.

A second monistic image has been elaborated by John Hick.[9] This second or development image also attempts to justify divine omnipotence. The development image changes the context of evil from the consequences of a past human choice to a transitory arena for creating persons in the likeness of God.[10] There is no question of a real evil challenging divine omnipotence. God is completely responsible for evil.[11] God's goodness, however, is justified because an overriding future good turns present evil to a tool for good.[12] The fall image had to retrieve God's omnipotence at the expense of divine goodness when the question was raised of the inexplicable emergence of evil in a good world. The development image compromises God's omnipotence in suggesting a necessity outside divine control: that a saving free human personhood can only be created in a certain way, a way that involves pain and suffering.[13]

Grace is not immediately pertinent to the development image. While there is divinely created evil, there also exists human freedom which is gradually achieving salvation. Divine omnipotence is asserted at the beginning of the salvation process when God chose to make current freedom and future personhood available to humanity. Having set this process for achieving salvation, God cannot give salvation to humanity except as humanity is transformed through the maturing process.[14] Because there is a necessity in the way to personhood, God cannot even change the rules and declare humanity justified.

The third image we will consider, divine-human struggle against evil, is pluralistic. Sterling McMurrin and Paul Edwards claim the metaphysical pluralism of this image is characteristic of Mormonism.[15] It can further be argued that the struggle image is a natural form for pluralism in the discussion of evil and that Mormonism has held this image as the dominant one.

The struggle image conceives evil

206

through the picture of an independent uncontrolled force against which God and humanity contend for the salvation of humanity. The image is pluralistic not only because God's omnipotence is compromised by an uncontrolled evil. In Mormonism both evil and humanity as well as "all primary being is original and uncreated."[16] There is not then a question of human freedom, the reality of evil, or of God's goodness since evil was not created. But the divine omnipotence is sacrificed.

The development image employed a form of the divine self-limitation argument to reconcile divine omnipotence with divine goodness, human freedom, and the reality of evil.[17] The struggle image discards divine omnipotence and retains uncompromised goodness, freedom, and evil. That there is no divine omnipotence means God cannot deliver unmerited salvation should there be need of it. However, there is no need of grace with this image, only divine assistance in humanity's struggle. The divine-human struggle for salvation values the efficacy of human action and the freedom of human choice. There is not the value placed on the necessity of the developing process itself as the only way of maturing humanity into salvation. The necessity lies in the fact of struggle against uncontrolled evil which must be defeated if salvation is to be achieved. The creature's freedom is of paramount importance.[18] Divine aid in the struggle comes more as an augmenting of humanity's effort.[19] Failure is possible if the human effort is shallow. Because evil is an externally opposing and uncontrolled force, human sin is not so much a condition of the human will. Sin occurs if external evil is not opposed properly. In other words, sin becomes equated to specific acts. If sin were a condition of the will as in the fall image there would be no struggle possible involving humanity.

The Mormon explanation of evil is not identical to the struggle image framework. Like any religious movement whose thought is a combination of various influences, Mormonism has found usable features in all these images we have discussed. What is characteristic of Mormon thought, however, is the dominance of the struggle image in its doctrine of evil. The effect of this dominance has meant several things. It has meant an underlying theological pluralism in the Utah church's thought and an unwillingness in the Reorganized church to carry out its monistic vocabulary in all its doctrines. Further, the struggle image acts as a limitation on the tendencies of other images in Mormon thought. For example, Mormonism finds the salvation process of the development image agreeable, but the dominant struggle image's pluralism in Mormonism will not permit evil to be the divine creation. Finally, in place of the centrality of a monistic universe or divine omnipotence, the struggle image elevates human freedom and the efficacy of human action to a place of value. In this image human freedom is to be preferred to divine omnipotence.

In contrast, the fall image, when dominant, precludes pluralism and the efficacy of human action. The fall image accepts a historical human freedom that vanished after it made the fall possible. Likewise, the development image precludes pluralism but accepts the efficacy of human action in the salvation process. The future salvation of humanity pictured by the development image brings it closer to the future orientation of the struggle image.

The presence of subordinate images in Mormon thought colors the character of its dominant image. The presence of multiple images in a doctrine of evil has meant the confusions of logically contradictory positions. We noted earlier

McMurrin's claim that Mormonism refuses to consistently carry through its finitism because of the emotional appeal of an absolute God in worship. Likewise, the RLDS experiments in new law, neo-orthodox grace, and wholeness are possible when competing images have crowded but not trespassed the boundaries of the dominant image.

Specifically we can note that the subordinate fall image within Mormonism has legitimized the vocabulary of a fall and an absolute monistic God. But the struggle image has drawn the line at questioning the efficacy of human action or providing a place for unmerited grace. In turn, the development image has reinforced the tendency toward a future good in Mormonism and has helped deemphasize unmerited grace in a process that requires human freedom. But the development image's monism also has been blocked by the dominant struggle image.

Let us summarize by reiterating the necessary presuppositions for a doctrine of grace. Grace is a product of the fall image. Unmerited grace requires a monistic metaphysics or in theological terms: God is omnipotent. Grace also requires divine goodness to save humanity from its just condemnation. Likewise, grace cannot be given if humanity is free or can perform efficacious acts that contribute to its salvation. Finally, grace is not only posssible but may be required in a monistic system. Only in monism is there need to claim human responsibility for evil to preserve the divine goodness from a similar responsibility. Humanity's responsibility has made it impotent to self-transformation. Thus grace is necessary to make salvation a possibility.

Mormon thought is incompatible with a doctrine of grace. Because Mormonism holds an underlying pluralism within the struggle image of evil, God is not endangered with responsibility for evil. Humanity is free and can perform efficacious acts to achieve salvation. This means unmerited grace is not a possibility. And, finally, God is not omnipotent and therefore is incapable of saving humanity against uncontrolled evil. As an old Presbyterian preacher once remarked, "There is no grace for Latter Day Saints in this world or the next."

Notes

1. Sterling M. McMurrin, *The Theological Foundations of the Mormon Religion* (Salt Lake City: University of Utah Press, 1965).
2. Paul M. Edwards, *The Credibility of Existence,* Philosophy of Religion and the RLDS church, unpublished, 1975.
3. This framework is still found in current treatments of salvation and sin, especially in the discussion of stewardship and finances. See Presiding Bishopric, "'I, the Lord God, Make You Free'," *Saints Herald,* vol. 126, no. 3 (Feb. 1, 1979): 9.
4. F. Henry Edwards, *The Divine Purpose in Us* (Independence, Missouri: Herald Publishing House, 1963), 102.
5. Ibid., 116; Clifford A. Cole, *The Revelation in Christ* (Independence, Missouri: Herald Publishing House, 1963), 304.
6. Some themes of this most recent emphasis are also found in earlier writings such as Roy Cheville, *Spiritual Health* (Independence, Missouri: Herald Publishing House, 1966).
7. "We were created to be divinely energized. This is one way to view grace," Charles E. Mader "God or Nothingness," *Saints Herald,* vol. 126, no. 3 (February 1, 1979): 12.

"Over and over again I have seen lives transformed as a result of self-help programs. . . . Perhaps it is because they contain the basic principles of spiritual health and reconciliation." Merlene Miller, "Twelve Steps to Spiritual Wholeness," *Saints*

Herald, vol. 126, no. 1 (January 1, 1979): 7.

"The emphasis here is on those aspects of life which, when interrelated properly and in consort, bring about a condition of wholeness. Persons so in process are penetrated by and responsibly committed to the Holy Spirit . . ." Roy Schaefer, "Church Life-Style, A Wholistic Approach," *Saints Herald* vol. 125, no. 3 (March 1978): 23.

8. John Hick, *The Center of Christianity* (San Francisco: Harper & Row, Publishers, 1978), 90.
9. John Hick, *Evil and the God of Love* (Cleveland: Collins & World, 1966). Some writings within this image are Irenaeus, Schleiermacher, and liberal theology.
10. Hick, *Center,* 86.
11. Ibid., 90.
12. Ibid., 83.
13. Hick, *Evil,* 291, 293.
14. Ibid.
15. See McMurrin, *Theological,* 8-9.

While Paul Edwards attributes pluralism to Utah Mormons he denies RLDS thought has a pluralistic theological anthropology (see *Credibility,* 72). In disagreement with Edwards, I believe McMurrin's comment that Mormon theologians have moved ambiguously between the emotionally satisfying absolutism of traditional theism and the finitism logically demanded by their denial of creation" (*Theological,* 29) is also true of RLDS thought. Later in this paper I will attempt to take note of this theological ambiguity by suggesting the Mormon doctrine of evil is informed by the struggle image as dominant but that the fall and development images are subordinate images.

Besides Mormonism, Origen, William James, and some idealists employ this image.

16. McMurrin, *Theological,* 49-59; Edwards, *Credibility* 72.
17. By "divine self-limitation argument" I mean the position that divine omnipotence is preserved if God chooses not to activate a potential divine power. The weakness of the development image is the suggestion that there may be only one salvation process— which uses divinely created evil—that God cannot alter if salvation is to take place.
18. McMurrin, *Theological,* 96.
19. God quickens graces in humanity of love, joy, peace, and mercy. Graces are already present by creation but are made valid by Christ (Edwards, *Credibility,* 73).

AN RLDS REFORMATION?
Construing the Task of RLDS Theology
Larry W. Conrad and Paul Shupe

A slightly modified version of this paper appeared in Dialogue: A Journal of Mormon Thought, *Vol. 18, No. 2 (Summer 1985): 92-103.*

The last twenty-five years have seen Reorganized Latter Day Saints struggling to discover what it means to be the body of Christ in the modern world. Clifford A. Cole, in "The World Church: Our Mission in the 1980s," explains that the RLDS church entered a new era in the early 1960s when the First Presidency sent Charles D. Neff and D. Blair Jensen as missionaries to the Orient.[1] The mission marked the beginning of a remarkable period of intense, critical examination of the basic beliefs and purpose of the church. Such periods of reformation do not occur in churches without considerable controversy and disappointment; the RLDS church proved no exception. Much progress was made, but not without some anguish and deep searching.

The Orient mission itself raised several issues. Cole reports that Neff, in the course of his work in Japan, noticed how very little was printed in the church's tracts about the basics of Christian faith. Consequently, Neff wrote the Basic Beliefs Committee and asked if the church had anything to help him in missionary work. All he could find was material explaining how the RLDS church differed from other Christian denominations. This literature was of little help in Japan, where only 3 percent of the population was Christian.[2] Cole summarizes the Joint Council's reaction: "That confrontation forced us immediately to recognize that we are called primarily to teach the basic faith rather than the ways we are different from some other Christian people."[3]

Thus church leaders sought to uncover and clarify just exactly what that basic faith entailed. Helpful but nonetheless unsettling information poured in from two major areas: history and biblical criticism. Although many examples could be cited from these areas, we shall note only a few. The results of historical research conflicted with the church's traditional view of its history. In a 1962 *Saints' Herald* article, James E. Lancaster challenged traditional accounts of the Book of Mormon translation. Testimonies from Emma Smith, David Whitmer, Oliver Cowdery, and other eyewitnesses clearly indicated that Smith "translated" by means of a small seer stone placed in his hat. Thus Lancaster concluded that the "translation" process should be understood as conceptual, not literal.[4] In 1965, Robert Flanders' *Nauvoo: Kingdom on the Mississippi* presented startling revelations about the excesses of the Nauvoo era, particularly with regard to Smith's involvement in politics and theological speculation.[5] The church learned of the fruits of biblical criticism as RLDS ministers attended theological schools and Protestant seminaries. Contrary to traditional RLDS teaching, most scholars hold that the New Testament contains no definite prescription for church organization. In fact, Jesus did not found a church. Rather, the loose-knit community of his followers gradually evolved into the church. Biblical criticism also questioned the RLDS notion of the kingdom of God, as well as the view that the gospel is a set of propositions or principles.

These and other internal developments, coupled with the changes in American society in the 1960s and 1970s forced many in the church to admit the failure of traditional teachings to respond creatively to the new situation. Church leaders thus recognized the need to do theology. The papers prepared by the Religious Education Department in 1967 and 1968,[6] the First Presidency's 1979 papers,[7] and other individuals and committees commissioned to write RLDS theology have each attempted to make RLDSism more coherent and consistent internally, and more relevant and palatable to those outside the church. Yet while this flurry of theological thinking and writing has occurred, we are unaware of any theological discussion of how Reorganized Latter Day Saints ought to understand the task of doing theology. The church has recognized that it must do theology and has, at least in a tentative way, committed itself to doing theology. But a discussion of how the task of doing theology ought to be construed from an RLDS perspective has never appeared in print. It is just such a discussion that this essay hopes to initiate.

We are convinced that the questions and crises of the last two and a half decades remain with the church in the 1980s, and that the roots of the problem are theological. Having briefly outlined the characteristics and causes of the period of RLDS reformation, we shall proceed to evaluate three current the-ological trends. Each of these trends attempts to address those developments which led to the shaking of the foundations of RLDSism. Space limitations prevent us from developing an exhaustive typology of the ways that theology is presently understood and written in the church. The categories we employ below and the examples cited should be regarded only as representative of general trends. In our analysis of the three trends, we will attempt to illumine the price paid for and the benefits gained by the way in which each construes the task of theology. We refer to these construals as RLDS fundamentalism, theology as history, and the transliteration of Protestant thought. In conclusion, we issue a call for dialogue and elaborate our own model for doing theology from an RLDS perspective.

RLDS Fundamentalism

The first alternative comes from RLDS fundamentalists.[8] The fundamentalists correctly charge that the church has changed. They, however, do not like the changes. Perhaps the most systematic exposition of the fundamentalist position is Richard Price's *The Saints at the Crossroads*. Price identifies nine "fundamental Restoration distinctives" which, he asserts, set RLDSism apart from other Christian churches.[9] These nine may be summarized in three basic claims. First, Jesus Christ founded a specific church organization which later departed from the truths of the gospel and thereby lost the authority to represent God and administer the sacraments. After centuries of dark apostasy, light again burst forth as God intervened to restore the true church through Joseph Smith, Jr. This Restoration is preserved in the Reorganization. Second, the church enjoys and possesses a sacred deposit of modern, infallible revelations given through the founder and his successors in the prophetic office. The Inspired Version, Book of Mormon, and Doctrine and Covenants contain the words of God as dictated to the prophets. Third, the church's chief mission is to participate in God's redeeming activity by building Zion, the literal city of God, at Independence, Missouri.

What kind of task is theology if one begins with these fundamentals? Strictly speaking, theology in the classic sense has no role at all. Fundamentalists regard openness to the various theological trends of the larger Christian community as evidence of "apostasy."[10] Especially fearful of ecumenical influences and tendencies, they decry the results of the RLDS period of reevaluation and propose a return to the previous teachings of the church. They understand what we would call the theological task almost exclusively in terms of telling the "story of the Restoration," supported by vigorous proof-texting from the three standard books. The greatness of RLDS tradition lies in the scriptures as seen through the lens of the Restoration. The present crisis can be ended by obeying the command to teach all nations the distinctive RLDS gospel and abandoning the present ill-fated flirtation with the vain "theologies of men."

We see three key insights in the fundamentalist position. First, although the fundamentalist alternative represents an antiquated way of understanding scripture and the divine activity in the world, we must acknowledge that such a world view dominated the thinking of most church members for many decades and, to a certain extent, still does. Second, although fundamentalism fails to ask and answer the questions of our age, its insistence on the importance of the identity of the RLDS church as a particular historical community seems to us an important facet of the answer a responsible RLDS theology should include. We are

convinced—and we will develop this point more fully below—that a theology can be truly RLDS only when it takes our particular (and, yes, peculiar) history seriously. Third, fundamentalist writings reflect a strong fervor for what they regard as the truth. The best theologians approach their task with a determined passion to search out and express the truths of the Christian message, yet with humble recognition that their feeble attempts ever fail to capture those truths.

Yet fundamentalism does not represent a viable option. This is so precisely because it is so completely inflexible and insistent on its own infallible apprehension of gospel truths that at best it has difficulty listening, and at its worst becomes arrogant and idolatrous, in effect worshiping itself. Reflecting on the theological task, Paul Tillich observed that a theological system should satisfy two basic needs:

the statement of the truth of the Christian message and the interpretation of this truth for every new generation. Theology moves back and forth between two poles, the eternal truth of its foundation and the temporal situation in which the eternal truth must be received.[11]

Few systems achieve an acceptable balance between the two poles and either sacrifice elements of the Christian truth or fail to address the contemporary situation. Others, wrote Tillich, like American fundamentalists, fail on both counts. Tillich continues:

Afraid of missing the eternal truth, they identify it with some previous theological work, with traditional concepts and solutions, and try to impose these on a new, different situation. They confuse eternal truth with a temporal expression of this truth.[12]

RLDS fundamentalists are equally guilty.

Rather than seriously face conclusions necessitated by developments in twentieth-century biblical scholarship, physics, psychology, and history, RLDS fundamentalists resort to old arguments and clichés which are no longer convincing. Price, for example, in his chapter on "The Church Misinterpreted," assails the "Position Papers" for claiming that "there was no divinely established structure" for the first century church.[13] Obviously, then, the RLDS claim to be the restoration of that church is erroneous. The Papers further argued, to Price's dismay, that no single organization may rightfully claim to be the only true church.[14] In our view, the author(s) of this "position paper" is on solid ground here on the basis of New Testament and historical scholarship. Price's rebuttal, however, merely restates the age-old RLDS position with sixteen proof-text references to the three standard books in one and a half pages.[15] Nowhere does Price even consider the complexities of the New Testament data.

In the final analysis, RLDS fundamentalists have chosen to represent remnants of a nineteenth-century worldview. They attempt to respond to twentieth-century questions with nineteenth-century answers, often refusing to acknowledge the legitimacy of the questions. They unstintingly reject all attempts at revision and modernization of the church's message.[16] Unfortunately then, the fundamentalists, in their desire to remain faithful to the RLDS tradition, have foreclosed all possibilities for the creative transformation of that tradition.

Theology As History

RLDSism is first and foremost a historical faith. It is the story of a people who believe themselves to be called to a unique mission, who were persecuted and driven into the wilderness. The heart of the faith is centered on key events: Joseph Smith, Jr.'s vision in the grove, the appearance of the Book of Mormon, the several attempted gatherings, the martrydom of its founder, the Reor-

ganization. RLDS doctrine evolved alongside these events, and the one is not separable from the other. The two are locked together, and depend on each other.

Given this fact, it is not surprising that in the past the church has done its theology by retelling its version of how and why these events occurred. When a later generation of the church comes to believe that doctrines taught and practiced by a previous one are no longer true, it is likely to dissent, not from the doctrine itself in a straightforward theological manner (thereby admitting the fallibility of past formulations) but rather by arguing that the true church never believed or practiced that doctrine. Thus, for example, the church ascribes the system of temple rituals to a post-Nauvoo Brigham Young, moves the command to baptize for the dead to an "appendix" in its canon, and most recently, in a paper by the church historian, admit that yes, Joseph Smith, Jr., was at least close to the appearance of polygamy, but that it was taught only as an "accident of history," as a thing out of Smith's control.[17]

It is not our intent to lump the work of Richard P. Howard into the same category with the first two examples of this trend as though there is no qualitative difference between them. Historical research has come a long way from the parade of "story of the church" volumes.[18] Indeed, it is only when historical scholarship has reached its present level of competency that the inadequacy of this method for doing theology appears.[19] Thus, when we say that RLDS theology cannot be done this way, we do not impugn the work of the present generation of historians. Rather, we argue only that the tools of the historian are not those of the theologian, and that church members ought to stop both expecting church historians to do theology, and berating them when their work cannot solve the church's *theological* difficulties. A closer look at Howard's paper will better reveal the point.

In the first half of his essay, Howard draws out clearly the connection between the church's insistence that Joseph Smith, Jr., did not teach polygamy and Joseph Smith III's repulsion over believing that his father could be connected in any way with such a practice. We are grateful for this insight, for it goes a long way toward explaining the sensibilities of the Reorganization as a church molded in the image of Joseph Smith III.

In the second half, despite the fact that he draws only on RLDS sources, he concludes that Smith was in fact closely related to and responsible for the initiation of the chain of events that led to the practice of polygamy. He stops just short of putting the teaching in Smith's hands, but does not seem to deny that polygamy was the logical extension of doctrines that he did promulgate. Even this modest conclusion[20] places the RLDS reader in an awkward spot. Traditionally, the RLDS church has taught that polygamy is immoral. The question then emerges: What ought the church do with a prophet who made the error of starting this chain of events? Howard, *as a historian*, can only give a historical answer. He focuses on Smith's "repentance" from his connection with the doctrine as evidence that his teachings and his doubts were overpowered by impersonal forces of history. This may or may not be a satisfactory *historical* answer. Imogene Goodyear has her doubts.[21] But regardless of its historical success or failure, it merely shifts the ground of our *theological* question which now becomes: How can a man who misread his historical context this badly rightly be called a prophet of God? And another follows this one: What gives authority to the church he founded?

Howard cannot answer these questions regardless of how good his scholarship is. The difficulty simply is that the tools of history are inappropriate to the task. He and other RLDS historians are placed in the unenviable position of having to raise painful theological questions in the course of their historical work that they cannot answer there.[22] The RLDS theologian owes a great debt to the present generation of historians. Had they not begun their work twenty to thirty years ago, there would not now be a call for the study of theology. But the church can no longer expect its historians to define and defend the faith. Theologies must be found that adequately consider the historical character of RLDS faith and can use the work being done by RLDS historians without being confined to the methods of history for the advance of the theological enterprise. An RLDS theology depends on the church's history and the creative, interpretive work of its historians, but must never be simply determined by that history.

The Transliteration of Protestant Thought

We have seen that while RLDS fundamentalism and theology as history both contain certain insights into how the RLDS church has understood, and continues to understand, and identify itself, neither can be followed exclusively. Indeed, neither can be accurately considered theology as the term is generally understood in the broader Christian community. The third trend, however, seeks to be theology in just this sense. This type of theology is promoted by persons who comprise what might be called the first generation of RLDS theologians. As there are no RLDS seminaries, and almost no published RLDS theological writing of interest to non-RLDS readers, these persons have learned their craft in Protestant seminaries that are largely unaware of RLDSism. Hence, what they have learned is mostly Protestant theology, which seldom fits neatly alongside the traditional RLDS language used almost universally throughout the church. One should not be surprised, therefore, to find these first RLDS theologians struggling to find RLDS names for the exciting, even intoxicating, ideas of a Tillich, a Bonhoeffer, or a Whitehead.

This is exactly what we see in Geoffrey F. Spencer's essay, "Revelation and the Restoration Principle."[23] Spencer rightly thinks that the church could benefit from Paul Tillich's concept of the Protestant Principle. The Protestant Principle refers to Tillich's understanding of ultimate concern and idolatry. He understands idolatry as the elevation of proximate, preliminary matters to the level of ultimate concern.[24] Idolatry often occurs in churches, for instance, when persons come to identify the particular finite forms through which the ultimate finds expression as being the ultimate itself.[25] The Protestant Principle is the ongoing, critical protest against such idolatries. Protestantism, which began as an attempt to embody the principle, often fails to remain faithful to it. But the principle continues to beckon and stand in judgment on the church.

For theologians, the principle is a simultaneous "yes and no" to all theological statements. Tillich reminds us that all theological formulations are merely finite, fallible, historically conditioned attempts to express the inexpressible. This profound insight serves to prevent our absolutizing past statements and thus inevitably propels us toward the future and ever new interpretations. The Protestant Principle is therefore implicitly eschatological, always pressing forward to more accurate and relevant formulations of the truth.

Impressed by this insight, Spencer sees

clearly that RLDS theology must either embrace this principle or drift on toward complete irrelevance. But because naming this "yes and no" the *Protestant* Principle seems less than ideal for a church that has never regarded itself as Protestant (*or* Catholic), he is wont to describe the truth of the principle in explicit RLDS language. So, after explaining Tillich's concept, Spencer proceeds to formulate a *Restoration* Principle and consider its possible implications for the RLDS movement. In our view, this Restoration Principle is little more than a transliteration of the Protestant Principle: a Protestant idea with an RLDS name. He explains that, "Customarily, to some extent, the Restoration has been seen essentially as the reintroduction of certain realities which existed in a form of purity or completeness in a former era but were lost."[26] Realizing that historical research puts such a notion in grave danger, he wants the Restoration Principle to aid the church by informing or changing the way it understands the concept of restoration, making restoration anticipatory rather than reactionary.

Spencer's attempt to relate the best of Protestant theology to RLDSism is laudable. But his construal of *RLDS* theology as the transliteration of Protestant thought into RLDS categories, fails to fully consider or appreciate the RLDS heritage as a particular people with a particular history. Most importantly, his use of the term *restoration* is problematical. All denotative and connotative meanings of the term point backward, toward the recovery of something lost. *Restoration* refers to a return to a former or original state. For example, to restore a painting means to return it to its former state. Spencer, however, wishes to interpret *restoration* to mean just the opposite: "Restoration exemplifies the readiness to live in the spirit and expectancy of the future in respectful and honest appreciation of our past rather than in bondage to it."[27] Or again: "The readiness to hold our contingent forms, structures, and doctrines up for further interpretation may be one important way in which we manifest what 'restoration' is."[28] Yet the fact remains that the entire essence of the church's understanding of restoration has been to look back and recover just those past forms, structures, and doctrines. The very word *restoration* designates such attempts.

Moreover, to say that "to some extent"[29] "Restoration" has meant bringing back the old-time religion is to seriously underestimate the enduring influence of this view and to ignore its particular history in RLDSism. If Spencer wants to use Tillich's insight, he ought to simply call it the Protestant Principle or find some other way to express the idea to RLDS audiences.[30] One is not free to define RLDS symbols and images as one would like. They have specific meanings and histories which must be admitted and dealt with, even if it means abandoning the symbol as irretrievable. We regard *restoration* as simply incapable of undergoing such a radical and unprecedented reversal of meaning. It is not susceptible to this kind of reinterpretation; thus a Restoration Principle can never mean what Tillich meant by Protestant Principle.

Spencer's method of thinking theologically does offer some important advantages. The most striking aspect of this essay is its openness. It frees the RLDS theologian to utilize the work of past and present Protestant and Catholic theologians. Second, the method recognizes the need for dialogue between RLDS symbols and history and the broader Christian community. Third, it recognizes the need to modify and reinterpret church tradition. It can no longer claim to infallibly possess the truth. "The vulnerable church," he correctly writes, "is the one which has closed down the canon, set the limits of belief, claimed infallibility and finality for its pronouncements, and believes it can weather the storm."[31] Finally, it exemplifies the courage required to make what may be unpopular stands in a church still suspicious of the theologian.

Conclusion

We began this essay by making three basic claims. First, we suggested that the RLDS church is presently involved in a genuine struggle to discover what it means to be the body of Christ in the modern world. This struggle has created a near crisis of identity and authority. Second, the roots of this struggle are theological. And third, this struggle prompted the church to do theology. To these we now add a fourth claim: theology never emerges in a vacuum. Each way of construing the task of theology grows out of and reflects some particular facet of the theologian's situation and church—in this case, the struggle of RLDSism to embody Christ in the world. Thus, from the way each particular theology is done, one may obtain clues to the nature and character of the present situation of RLDSism.

What then can be learned from the three trends discussed above? From fundamentalism, theologians ought to learn that RLDSism has been and continues to be a church with a particular history and a particular matrix of symbols, stories, and events. This history and these symbols each manifest a certain historical and institutional momentum. In addition, each demonstrates greater or lesser degrees of persuasive and religious power. From RLDS historians should be learned the fact that RLDSism tends to claim infallibility for many of its teachings and practices. This tendency is destructive as well as false and erroneous. Finally, the first RLDS theolgians recognize that the church has a certain, though not yet fully defined, kinship with the wider Christian community and seeks to discern the parameters and depth of that relationship.

Each of these three trends we have examined fails as a way of construing the task of RLDS theology precisely because each grows out of only one facet of the church's present situation, and focuses its attention on that one problem. Consequently, they ignore, or seem to, other dimensions of the present situation. Fundamentalism, determined to protect the particularity of RLDSism, asserts the infallibility and unsurpassability of the RLDS gospel and ignores the wider Christian community. Historians correctly criticize the church's misguided, unwarranted claims of infallibility, but lack the methodological tools to answer questions about the enduring value of a movement which possesses no exclusive claim to truth. Historians are unequipped to answer theological questions about what divine authority may inhere in a church which is as fallible and historically conditioned as any other. Theologians transliterating Protestant thought into RLDS categories see the proper relationship between RLDSism and Protestant and Catholic forms of Christianity, but fail to appreciate the enduring influence of RLDS symbols and stories. Viewing RLDSism as but one Christian church among many prevents claims of infallibility, but often gives little hint as to what truth, if any, RLDSism might uniquely contain.

The several successes and failures of these ways of construing the task of RLDS theology point out yet again the urgent, critical need to do RLDS theology. Clearly, new models are needed, models that build upon the insights of preceding models and respond more fully to the present situation of RLDSism. Again, space limitations prevent us from elaborating a fully developed model. We can, however, offer a few suggestions which may serve as catalysts for further inquiry and discussion.

In our judgment, a truly RLDS theology will be governed by or characterized by integration. First, an RLDS theology must come to terms with what RLDSism is as well as where it came from (its history) and that toward which it moves (its telos). The work of the RLDS theologian therefore requires historical research, participation in the church as a worshiping community, and internal dialogue. Second, RLDS theology must understand the complexity and diversity of the broader Christian community. Helpful activities include the study of Protestant and Catholic theology, membership in ecumenical organizations, and the active cultivation of friendships with Christians of all traditions. Finally, such a theology must be attuned to the demands and challenges of the modern world. Awareness of the modern situation may emerge from the study of the natural and social sciences, the exercise of Christian discipleship, and attempts to dwell within the same global village with various cultures and religions.

Authentic RLDS theologies will hold each of these elements of the present situation in tension with one another, learning from each, using the insights of one to critique the limited understandings of the others. Such theologies are undergirded by the faith conviction that God is at work in and through all three. Continual application of the "yes and no" of Tillich's Protestant Principle ensures that theologians appreciate the value of tradition, but never rest content with mere repetition of the past for its own sake. Critical but never aimlessly destructive, authentic RLDS theologies will require constant dialogue, dialogue which will prohibit claims of infallible apprehension of Christian truth.

To understand the task of RLDS theology in this way offers one additional advantage: it opens the theological enterprise to all church members, and in fact depends upon the unique participation of each. Theology so conceived is not primarily a task for the church as an institution to do, nor is it the domain of a few academicians. Rather, it should be done primarily by and for the community of individual RLDS Christians confronted with the daily call to be the hands and heart of God in the world. Those who lack the time and means to read Whitehead or Tillich, or to attend ecumenical conferences, or to labor in a Latin American barrio may still be involved in the theological enterprise by reflecting on and seeking the presence of God in their own communities and aligning their life choices, vocational, educational, devotional, economic, with that at once loving, abiding, and chastizing Presence.

Notes

1. Clifford A. Cole, The World Church: Our Mission in the 1980s," *Commission* (September 1979): 42.
2. Ibid.
3. Ibid.
4. James E. Lanceaster, "'By the Gift and Power of God': The Method of Translation of the Book of Mormon," *Saints' Herald* 109 (November 15, 1962): 798-802, 806, 817.
5. Robert Bruce Flanders, *Nauvoo: Kingdom on the Mississippi* (Urbana, Illinois: University of Illinois Press, 1965). See especially pp. 179-341.
6. Reference here is to the series of papers written by persons in the RLDS Department of Religious Education in 1967 and 1968 as study papers for the Curriculum Consultation Committee. Whether or not the term "position papers" accurately describes the nature and intent of the papers, they became widely known as the "Position Papers." In some ways, the papers represent the climax of the RLDS period of reformation. They admirably attempt a serious examination of the implications of the new historical, biblical, and theological findings. A small book containing slightly marked photocopies of the papers is available from Cumorah Books in Independence, Missouri. For details on the development of the papers and the subsequent controversy over them, see William J. Knapp, "Professionalizing Religious Education in the Church: The 'New Curriculum Controversy,'" *The John Whitmer Historical Association Journal* 2 (1982): 47-59.
7. The First Presidency presented a series of six papers to church officials and companions at meetings on January 9 and 10, 1979, in Independence, Missouri.
8. For examples of RLDS fundamentalist literature, see: Merva Bird, "Women's Ordination? No!" (Independence, Missouri: Cumorah Books, 1980); Richard Price, "Decision Time" (Independence, Missouri: Cumorah Books, 1975); and Richard Price, *The Saints at the Crossroads* (Independence, Missouri: Cumorah Books, 1975).
9. Price, 232-233.
10. Ibid., 20-32.
11. Paul Tillich, *Systematic Theology*, 3 vols. (Chicago: University of Chicago Press, 1951-1963), 1:3.
12. Ibid.
13. Price, 115.
14. *Position Papers*, 50.
15. Price, 117-118.
16. For example, see Price, 1-6.
17. Richard P. Howard, "The Changing RLDS Response to Mormon Polygamy: A Preliminary Analysis," *The John Whitmer Historical Association Journal* 3 (1983): 14-29. Also Section III, *Restoration Studies III*.
18. Works in this tradition include Joseph Luff, *The Old Jerusalem Gospel;* Inez Smith Davis, *The Story of the Church;* William H. Kelley, *Presidency and Priesthood;* and W. J. Haworth, *The Fall of Babylon.*
19. We are not here claiming that Howard set

out to write a theological treatise or that he regards his work as doing RLDS theology. We are saying that his essay indicates that he is aware of and concerned about the theological issues raised by his research.

20. We know of no non-RLDS historian who has stopped at this point. Certainly no LDS scholar will, and in what may be the definitive biography of Smith, *No Man Knows My History*, Fawn M. Brodie (an "outsider") is certain that Smith taught the doctrine. (Editor's note: Fawn Brodie is a former Mormon and is related to members of the LDS church hierarchy.)

21. Imogene Goodyear, "Joseph Smith and Polygamy: An Alternative View," *The John Whitmer Historical Association Journal* 3 (1984): 16-21. This paper was originally developed as a response to Howard's "The Changing RLDS Response."

22. The fine historical work of William D. Russell exhibits this same quandary. For example, his essay "A Further Inquiry into the Historicity of the Book of Mormon," *Sunstone*, September-October 1982, 20-27, casts serious doubts on the traditional church belief about the historicity of the book, yet he concludes the essay with the claim that the book can still be regarded and used as scripture. We find this conclusion interesting and perhaps somewhat surprising. But the conclusion cannot fully address the theological issues at stake. For example, if Russell's account is correct, and we think that it is, then what ought the church do about its claim to have a prophet who claimed to possess gold plates which he translated with the Urim and Thummim?

23. Geoffrey F. Spencer, "Revelation and the Restoration Principle," *Restoration Studies II*, ed., Maurice L. Draper (Independence, Missouri: Herald House, 1983), 182-192. Other RLDS thinkers have read and profited from Protestant theology. For example, see Peter A. Judd and Clifford A. Cole, *Distinctives: Yesterday and Today* (Independence, Missouri: Herald House, 1983), and Peter A. Judd and A. Bruce Lindgren, *An Introduction to the Saints' Church* (Independence, Missouri: Herald House, 1976). Spencer alone, however, seeks to deal with this theology on its own terms, and makes his debts to particular theologians explicit.

24. Paul Tillich, *Dynamics of Faith* (New York: Harper and Row, 1957), 28-29. For further explanation of Tillich's Protestant Principle, consult Tillich, *Systematic Theology*, 1:227, 3:244-245 and Tillich, *The Protestant Era* (Chicago: University of Chicago Press, 1957), v-xxv.

25. Tillich, *Dynamics of Faith*, 96-98.

26. Spencer, 188.

27. Ibid., 189.

28. Ibid.

29. Ibid., 188.

30. Spencer might simply challenge the church to respond to and embody the Protestant Principle. Relabeling the Protestant Principle as the Restoration Principle may be regarded as an unnecessary concession to the RLDS fear of Protestant and Catholic theology. By now, the church as a whole ought to be willing to openly acknowledge and accept insights from Protestant and Catholic circles. The Protestant Principle is one such insight.

31. Spencer, 191.

The Method of Translation of the Book of Mormon

James E. Lancaster

(Reprinted by permission from the *John Whitmer Historical Association Journal*, vol. 3)

It is a principle of history that the further we are in time from a historical event, the more we see this event through the haze of the intervening years. This is true of the history of the church. Our concept of events that transpired from 1820 to 1844 tends to become idealized. In the latter half of the previous century, eyewitnesses to the early events of the Restoration were still living. These eyewitnesses on numerous occasions left testimonies describing things that transpired in their day. Their accounts may surprise and sometimes even disturb us. They are often at variance with our own cherished views. This is particularly true with regard to the process by which the Book of Mormon was translated. We can best understand the method used by the prophet Joseph Smith in his translation of the Book of Mormon if we look at this event through the first-hand accounts of the early witnesses. And from such a viewpoint we may find it possible to place a broader interpretation on the nature of the Book of Mormon record itself.

Any consideration of the method of translation of the Book of Mormon must begin with the testimony of its translator, Joseph Smith, Jr. The prophet testified on numerous occasions regarding the coming forth of the Book of Mormon. A record exists of what transpired on one of the first occasions where Joseph Smith was publicly asked about the translation of the book. A conference of the church was held at Orange, Cuyahoga County, Ohio, on October 25, 1831; twelve high priests, seventeen elders, four priests, three teachers, four deacons, and a large congregation attended.[1] At this conference, several of the brethren took occasion to testify to the truth of the Book of Mormon.

> Brother Hyrum Smith said that he thought best that the information of the coming forth of the Book of Mormon be related by Joseph himself to the elders present, that all might know for themselves.
>
> Brother Joseph Smith, Jr., said that it was not intended to tell the world all the particulars of the coming forth of the Book of Mormon; and also said it was not expedient for him to relate these things.[2]

One week later these words appeared in a revelation given through the prophet at a special conference of the church meeting at Hiram, Portage County, Ohio: ". . .and after having received the record of the Nephites, yea, even my servant Joseph Smith, Jr., might have power to translate, through the mercy of God, by the power of God, the Book of Mormon."[3] This was the pattern that Joseph Smith was to follow throughout his life when asked regarding the Book of Mormon. Never at any point did he reveal any of the details of the method of translation. He did, however, stress the divine aspects of this translation.

Joseph's earliest published testimony concerning the translation appears in the *Elders' Journal* of July 1838. He wrote:

> Moroni, the person who deposited the plates, from whence the Book of Mormon was translated,

in a hill in Manchester, Ontario County, New York, being dead, and raised again therefrom, appeared unto me, and told me where they were, and gave me directions how to obtain them. I obtained them, and the Urim and Thummim with them, by the means of which, I translated the plates and thus came the Book of Mormon.[4]

In March 1842, in response to a letter from John Wentworth, editor of the *Chicago Democrat,* Joseph Smith printed in the *Times and Seasons* a brief statement of belief as well as a short history of the Mormon movement.

With the records was found a curious instrument which the ancients called "Urim and Thummim," which consisted of two transparent stones set in the rim of a bow fastened to a breastplate.

Through the medium of the Urim and Thummim I translated the record by the gift and power of God.[5]

In the next issue of the *Times and Seasons,* Joseph Smith began the publication of his biography. Though first published in 1842 it states that the writing was begun in 1838. Regarding the translation of the Book of Mormon, Joseph Smith wrote:

By this timely aid was I enabled to reach the place of my destination in Pennsylvania, and immediately after my arrival there I commenced copying the characters of the plates. I copied a considerable number of them, and by means of the Urim and Thummim I translated some of them, which I did between the time I arrived at the house of my wife's father in the month of December, and the February following.[6]

What is possibly the prophet's last published statement regarding the translation was made in a letter to N. E. Seaton, a newspaper publisher, which was printed in the *Times and Seasons:*

The Book of Mormon is a record of the forefathers of our western tribes of Indians, having been found through the ministrations of an holy angel, and translated into our own language by the gift and power of God, after having been hid up in the earth for the last fourteen hundred years, containing the word of God which was delivered unto them.[7]

As the foregoing quotations demon-strate, the statements of Joseph Smith give no detailed information regarding the translation of the Book of Mormon. Rather, that it was "by the gift and power of God" that the record of the Nephites was made available to the world.

Emma Smith Bidamon was interviewed late in her life by her son Joseph Smith III regarding her knowledge of the important events which transpired in the early church. This interview took place in February 1879, in the presence of Major Lewis C. Bidamon, her husband. At one point in the interview Emma stated the following:

A. In writing for your father I frequently wrote day after day, often sitting at the table close by him, he sitting with his face buried in his hat, with the stone in it, and dictating hour after hour with nothing between us.

Q. Had he not a book or manuscript from which he read or dictated to you?

A. He had neither manuscript nor book to read from.

Q. Could he not have had, and you not know it?

A. If he had had anything of the kind, he could not have concealed it from me.

Q. Are you sure that he had the plates at the time you were writing for him?

A. The plates often lay on the table without any attempt at concealment, wrapped in a small linen tablecloth, which I had given him to fold them in . . .

Q. Where did Father and Oliver Cowdery write?

A. Oliver Cowdery and your father wrote in the room where I was at work.[8]

Many are familiar with this testimony but have seemingly overlooked that the wife of the prophet claims Joseph Smith translated the Book of Mormon sitting with his face in his hat with a stone placed in the hat. He did not even look at the plates which were nearby, wrapped up in a small tablecloth.

A similar testimony is borne out by another witness to the translation, David Whitmer. In 1887 he published a booklet entitled *An Address to All Believers in*

Christ. This booklet is a summary of his beliefs regarding the Restoration and the role he played in the movement. He states:

I will now give you a description of the manner in which the Book of Mormon was translated. Joseph Smith would put the seer stone into a hat, and put his face in the hat, drawing it closely around his face to exclude the light; and in the darkness the spiritual light would shine. A piece of something resembling parchment would appear, and on that appeared the writing. One character at a time would appear, and under it was the interpretation in English. Brother Joseph would read off the English to Oliver Cowdery, who was his principal scribe, and when it was written down and repeated to Brother Joseph to see if it was correct, then it would disappear, and another character with the interpretation would appear. Thus the Book of Mormon was translated by the gift and power of God, and not by any power of man.[9]

How can the testimonies of Emma Smith and David Whitmer, describing the translation of the Book of Mormon with a seer stone, be reconciled with the traditional account that the Book of Mormon was translated by the "interpreters" found in the stone box with the plates?

Fortunately there is additional testimony by Emma Smith Bidamon on this important issue. Sometime in the early part of 1870, Emma S. Pilgrim, the wife of the pastor of the RLDS church in Independence, Missouri, wrote to Emma Bidamon, requesting information about the translation of the Book of Mormon. Emma Bidamon replied in a letter written from Nauvoo, Illinois, March 27, 1870. Her letter states in part:

Now the first that my husband translated was translated by the use of the Urim and Thummim, and that was the part that Martin Harris lost, after that he used a small stone, not exactly black, but was rather a dark color. I cannot tell whether that account in the *Times and Seasons* is correct or not because someone stole all my books and I have none to refer to at present, if I can find one that has that account I will tell you what is true and what is not.[10]

Emma's letter indicates that at first the Book of Mormon was translated by the Urim and Thummim. She refers to the instrument found with the plates. However, this first method was used only for the portion written on the 116 pages of foolscap which Martin Harris later lost. After that, the translation was undertaken with the seer stone. Emma's testimony is corroborated by David Whitmer in an interview appearing in the *Chicago Inter-Ocean*, October 17, 1886.

The first 116 pages when completed were by permission of the prophet intrusted to the hands of Martin Harris, who carried them home to his incredulous relatives in triumph, hoping by the exhibition to convert his family and kinfolk from their uncompromising hostility to the religious premises he had adopted. Upon retiring at night he locked up the precious pages in a bureau drawer, along with his money and other valuables. In the morning he was shocked to find that they had been stolen, while his money had been left untouched. They were never found and were never replaced, so that the Book of Mormon is today minus just 116 pages of the original matter, which would increase the volume fully one-fourth of its present size. This unpardonable carelessness evoked the stormiest kind of chastisement from the Lord, who took from the prophet the Urim and Thummim and otherwise expressed his condemnation. By fervent prayer and by otherwise humbling himself, the prophet, however, again found favor, and was presented with a strange, oval-shaped, chocolate-colored stone, about the size of an egg, only more flat, which, it was promised, should serve the same purpose as the missing Urim and Thummim (the latter was a pair of transparent stones set in a bow-shaped frame and very much resembled a pair of spectacles). With this stone all of the present Book of Mormon was translated.[11]

A consistent account appears in a later interview with Whitmer.[12]

Indications that there were two methods of translation also appear very early in anti-Mormon works. In a book published in 1834, *Mormonism Unvailed*, by Eber D. Howe, the following statement appears:

Now, whether the two methods for translation, one by a pair of stone spectacles "set in the rims of a bow," and the other by one stone, were provided against accident, we cannot determine—perhaps they were limited in their appropriate uses—at all events the plan meets our approbation.

We are informed that Smith used a stone in a hat, for the purpose of translating the plates. The spectacles and plates were found together, but were taken from him and hid up again before he had translated one word, and he has never seen them since—this is Smith's own story.[13]

D. P. Hurlburt, in the latter part of 1833 collected information from the townsfolk in Palmyra, regarding the translation of the Book of Mormon. This material was later used by Howe in his book. From this it must be concluded that at an early date both the prophet's friends and antagonists knew two methods were involved in the translation process.

David Whitmer was interviewed numerous times in his later years by newspaper correspondents seeking information about the early days in the church from one of its founders. The resulting newspaper accounts do not always agree in detail. This may be due in part to Whitmer's age, but it may also be a result of the reporters' misunderstanding or carelessness. On numerous occasions he issued corrections to statements he was purported to have made. However, there are two statements by David Whitmer that do not come to us through this medium. The most important is his own booklet *An Address to All Believers in Christ,* previously quoted. The other is a statement he made to a member of the Reorganized Church, J. L. Traughber, Jr., in October 1879, and printed in *Saints' Herald.* In connection with this latter testimony it should be pointed out that David Whitmer did not meet Joseph Smith until June 1829.[14] According to the testimony of Emma Smith and David Whitmer, the angel took the Urim and Thummim from Joseph Smith at the time of the loss of the 116 pages. This was June 1828, one year before David became involved with the work of translation.[15] David Whitmer

could never have been present when the Urim and Thummim were used. He clearly states in his testimony to Traughber:

> With the sanction of David Whitmer, and by his authority, I now state that he does not say that Joseph Smith ever translated in his presence by aid of Urim and Thummim; but by means of one dark colored, opaque stone, called a "Seer Stone," which was placed in the crown of a hat, into which Joseph put his face so as to exclude the external light. Then, a spiritual light would shine forth, and parchment would appear before Joseph, upon which was a line of characters from the plates, and under it, the translation in English; at least, so Joseph said.[16]

One of the earliest interviews with Whitmer appears in the *Chicago Times,* August 7, 1875. Chicago papers also printed at least two other similar articles. One appeared on December 18, 1885, in the *Chicago Tribune.*[17] A corrected summary of this later article appeared in the same paper on January 24, 1888, on the occasion of Whitmer's death.[18] In 1881 David Whitmer made a statement to the *Kansas City Journal* which appeared in that paper on June 5.

> I, as well as all of my father's family, Smith's wife, Oliver Cowdery, and Martin Harris were present during the translation. The translation was by Smith, and the manner as follows: He had two small stones of a chocolate color, nearly egg shaped and perfectly smooth, but not transparent, called interpreters, which were given him with the plates. He did not use the plates in the translation, but would hold the interpreters to his eyes and cover his face with a hat, excluding all light.[19]

In reading the various accounts given by David Whitmer it should be remembered that by his own testimony he was not an eyewitness to any method of translation other than that of the "seer stone." It is possible his accounts of the translation ·by use of the Urim and Thummim are a result of conversation with Emma Smith or Martin Harris, who were Joseph's scribes at that earlier time.

The testimony of Oliver Cowdery, Joseph's principal scribe, is similar to the prophet's own, for it gives little detailed information about the method of translation. There are three published statements of Oliver Cowdery regarding his work in assisting Joseph Smith in the translation of the Book of Mormon:

These were days never to be forgotten—to sit under the sound of a voice dictated by the inspiration of heaven, awakened the utmost gratitude of this bosom! Day after day I continued, uninterrupted, to write from his mouth, as he translated, with the Urim and Thummim, or, as the Nephites would have said, "Interpreters," the history, or record, called "The Book of Mormon."[20]

Still, although favored of God as a chosen witness to bear testimony to the divine authority of the Book of Mormon, and honored of the Lord in being permitted, without money and without price, to serve as scribe during the translation of the Book of Mormon, I have sometimes had seasons of skepticism, in which I did seriously wonder whether the Prophet and I were men in our sober senses when he would be translating from plates through "the Urim and Thummim" and the plates not be in sight at all.

But I believed both in the Seer and in the "Seer Stone," and what the First Elder announced as revelation from God, I accepted as such, and committed to paper with a glad mind and happy heart and swift pen; for I believed him to be the soul of honor and truth, a young man who would die before he would lie.[21]

* * *

I wrote, with my own pen, the entire Book of Mormon (save a few pages), as it fell from the lips of the Prophet Joseph Smith, as he translated it by the gift and power of God, by the means of the Urim and Thummim, or, as it is called by that book, "holy interpreters." *I beheld with my eyes, and handled with my hands the gold plates from which it was translated.* I also saw with my eyes and handled with my hands the "holy interpreters." That book is *true.* Sidney Rigdon did not write it. Mr. Spaulding did not write it. I wrote it myself as it fell from the lips of the Prophet.[22]

It is interesting to note that Oliver Cowdery refers to the use of the "seer stone" but in such a way as to make it synonymous with the Urim and Thummim and the interpreters. He further states that Joseph translated with the plates out of sight. This generally supports the accounts previously examined.

The remaining key witness, Martin Harris, provided only one reliable statement. It came from his later years when he resided in Utah. It is reprinted below.

Martin Harris related an incident that occurred during the time that he wrote that portion of the translation of the Book of Mormon which he was favored to write direct from the mouth of the Prophet Joseph Smith. He said that the Prophet possessed a seer stone, by which he was enabled to translate as well as from the Urim and Thummim, and for convenience he then used the seer stone. Martin explained the translation as follows: By aid of the seer stone, sentences would appear and were read by the Prophet and written by Martin, and when finished he would say, "Written," and if correctly written that sentence would disappear and another appear in its place, but if not written correctly it remained until corrected, so that the translation was just as it was engraved on the plates, precisely in the language then used.

Martin said further that the seer stone differed in appearance entirely from the Urim and Thummim that was obtained with the plates, which were two clear stones set in two rims, very much resembling spectacles, only were larger. Martin said there were not many pages translated while he wrote, after which Oliver Cowdery and others did the writing.[23]

Martin Harris also claims that the prophet, Joseph Smith, used two methods of translation. Harris very clearly distinguishes the Urim and Thummim which "was obtained with the plates" from the seer stone. Interestingly enough, Martin Harris does not tell us why Joseph Smith used the seer stone. According to other witnesses the stone's use was due to Martin Harris's own indiscretion. Harris merely said that for "convenience" the prophet used the seer stone.

One other witness to the events that transpired in the Whitmer home has left an account of the translation of the Book of Mormon. Michael Morse who was married to Trial Hale, a sister of Emma Smith, was present at the time of the translation. In an 1879 interview with W. W. Blair of the Reorganized Church, Mr. Morse described the method of translation of the

Book of Mormon. The pertinent parts of his testimony are related by Blair:

He further states that when Joseph was translating the Book of Mormon, he [Morse] had occasion more than once to go into his immediate presence, and saw him engaged at his work of translation.

The mode of procedure consisted of Joseph's placing the Seer Stone in the crown of a hat, then putting his face into the hat, so as to entirely cover his face, resting his elbows upon his knees, and then dictating, word after word, while the scribe— Emma, John Whitmer, O. Cowdery, or some other, wrote it down.[24]

Isaac Hale, Emma's father, provided additional information about the translation of the Book of Mormon. His testimony first appeared in 1834, fairly early in the history of the church. Isaac Hale was obviously antagonistic toward Joseph Smith and the Mormon movement. He stated:

The manner in which he pretended to read and interpret, was the same as when he looked for the money-diggers, with the stone in his hat, and his hat over his face, while the Book of Plates were at the same time hid in the woods![25]

The same source also contains the statement of Alva Hale, one of Isaac Hale's sons. Alva's account is similar to his father's.

William Smith, younger brother of the prophet, is an often quoted source about the translation method. Since he was not a resident of Harmony, Pennsylvania, where the translation took place, we cannot be certain he was an eyewitness. Therefore, his testimony may be secondhand. In 1883 William published a small book of his experiences in the church. In regard to his brother's translation of the Book of Mormon he wrote:

In consequence of his vision, and his having the golden plates and refusing to show them, a great persecution arose against the whole family, and he was compelled to remove to Pennsylvania with the plates, where he translated them by means of the Urim and Thummim (which he obtained with the plates), and the power of God. The manner in

which this was done was by looking into the Urim and Thummim, which was placed in a hat to exclude the light (the plates lying nearby covered up), and reading off the translation, which appeared in the stone by the power of God.[26]

In a sermon preached in the Saints' Chapel at Deloit, Iowa, June 8, 1884, William said:

When Joseph received the plates he also received the Urim and Thummim, which he would place in a hat to exclude all light, and with the plates by his side he translated the characters, which were cut into the plates with some sharp instrument, into English. And thus, letter by letter, word by word, sentence by sentence, the whole book was translated.[27]

In July 1891 William Smith was interviewed by J. W. Peterson and W. S. Pender of the Reorganized Church. This interview was published in 1924, thirty years after William's death.

The Urim and Thummim were set in a double silver bow which was twisted into the shape of the figure eight, and the two stones were placed literally between the two rims of the bow. At one end was attached a rod which was connected with the outer edge of the right shoulder of the breastplate. By pressing the head a little forward, the rod held the Urim and Thummim before the eyes much like a pair of spectacles. A pocket was prepared in the breastplate on the left side, immediately over the heart. When not in use the Urim and Thummim was placed in the pocket, the rod being of just the right length to allow it to be so deposited. This instrument could, however, be detached from the breastplate, and his brother said that Joseph often wore it detached when away from home, but always used it in connection with the breastplate when receiving official communications, and usually so when translating, as it permitted him to have both hands free to hold the plates.

In answer to our query, William informed us that he had, himself, by Joseph's direction, put the Urim and Thummim before his eyes, but could see nothing, as he did not have the gift of Seer. He also informed us that the instruments were too wide for his eyes, as also for Joseph's, and must have been used by much larger men. The instrument caused a strain on Joseph's eyes, and he sometimes resorted to the plan of covering his eyes with a hat to exclude the light in part.[28]

This statement described two methods

of translation. In the first method a rod affixed to the Urim and Thummim was inserted into a breastplate. The prophet's second method was to cover his eyes with a hat. William further reports that the first method was "usually" employed when translating and the second method was "sometimes" used to avoid eye strain. This seems inconsistent with William's earlier statements that mention only the second, supposedly less frequent, method.

An examination of the eyewitness testimony produces the following consensus on the method of translation of the Book of Mormon: (1) Nephite interpreters often called "Urim and Thummim" were found with the plates on Hill Cumorah; (2) these interpreters were used first in the translation of the plates; (3) the portion translated by use of the interpreters was copied onto 116 pages of foolscap and later lost by Martin Harris; (4) because of the indiscretion of Martin and Joseph, the Nephite interpreters were permanently removed; (5) the Book of Mormon that we have today was translated by use of the seer stone; (6) Joseph Smith translated by placing the seer stone in his hat and covering his face with his hat to darken his eyes; (7) the plates were not used in the translating process and often were not even in sight during the translation; (8) other persons were sometimes in the room while Joseph Smith dictated to his scribe; (9) all witnesses to the translation agree to these facts.

In August 1829, a newspaper in Palmyra, New York, the *Palmyra Freeman*, printed the earliest known reference to the Book of Mormon. Although the original issue of the *Freeman* has been lost, fortunately, the article was republished by the *Rochester Advertiser and Telegraph* of August 31, 1829. This latter newspaper is still available in the Reynolds Library in Rochester, New York. The article is noteworthy because it attempts to explain the method of translation of the Book of Mormon prior to its publication.

The *Palmyra Freeman* says—The greatest piece of superstition that has come within our knowledge now occupies the attention of a few individuals of this quarter. It is generally known and spoken of as the "Golden Bible." Its proselytes give the following account of it.

In the fall of 1827, a person by the name of Joseph Smith, of Manchester, Ontario Co., reported that he had been visited in a dream by the spirit of the Almighty and informed that in a certain hill in that town was deposited this golden Bible, containing an ancient record of a divine nature and origin. After having been thrice visited, as he states, he proceeded to the spot, and after penetrating "mother earth" a short distance the Bible was found, together with a huge pair of spectacles. He had been directed, however, not to let any mortal examine them, "under no less penalty than instant death." They were therefore nicely wrapped up and excluded from the "vulgar gaze of poor wicked mortals." It was said that the leaves of the Bible were plates of gold, about eight inches thick on which were engraved characters of hyroglyphics. By placing the spectacles in a hat, and looking into it, Smith could (he said so at least) interpret these characters.

Another extant article was printed in the *Rochester Gem* of September 5, 1829. Both early newspaper accounts conform generally to the statements witnesses later made regarding the method of translation.

The testimony of the eyewitnesses seems to conflict with the prophet where he states that "with the records was found a curious instrument which the ancients called Urim and Thummim which consisted of two transparent stones set in the rim of a bow fastened to a breastplate. Through the medium of the Urim and Thummim I translated the record." Joseph Smith's account, however, can be reconciled with the seer stone testimony of Emma Smith and the witnesses. First it must be recognized that the translation of the Book of Mormon took place at the very beginning of Joseph's ministry. At that stage in his understanding of his prophetic role and his relationship with God he evidently had need for a physical symbol of God's power to assist in the translation. Regardless of the physical media used, the essential quality of the translation stressed by the prophet was that of revelation or inspiration from God. In a statement to William H. Kelley and G. A. Blakeslee, dated September 15, 1882, David Whitmer said the following regarding the inspirational nature of the translation of the Book of Mormon.

He had to trust God. He could not translate unless he was humble and possessed the right feelings toward everyone. To illustrate so you can see: One morning when he was getting ready to continue the translation, something went wrong about the house and he was put out about it. Something that Emma, his wife, had done. Oliver and I went upstairs and Joseph came up soon after to continue the translation but he could not translate a single syllable. He went downtairs, out into the orchard, and made supplication to the Lord; was gone about an hour—came back to the house, and asked Emma's forgiveness and then came upstairs where we were and then the translation went on all right. He could do nothing save he was humble and faithful.[29]

Soon after Oliver Cowdery became scribe for the prophet, he began to desire the power himself to translate the records. Oliver was given a promise of this power and an explanation of it in a revelation through Joseph Smith in April 1829.

Oliver, verily, verily I say unto you, that assuredly as the Lord liveth, which is your God and your Redeemer, even so sure shall you receive a knowledge of whatsoever things you shall ask in faith, with an honest heart, believing that you shall receive a knowledge concerning the engravings of old records, which are ancient, which contain those parts of my scripture of which have been spoken, by the manifestation of my Spirit; yea, behold, I will tell you in your mind and in your heart by the Holy Ghost, which shall come upon you, and which shall dwell in your heart....Ask that you may know the mysteries of God, and that you may translate all those ancient records which have been hid up, which are sacred, and according to your faith shall it be done unto you.[30]

Oliver Cowdery attempted to translate, acting upon the revelation given, but because of his own misunderstanding was unsuccessful. In answer to Oliver's problem another revelation was received by Joseph Smith a few days later.

Behold, you have not understood, you have supposed that I would give it unto you, when you took no thought, save it was to ask me; but, behold, I say unto you, that you must study it out in your mind; then you must ask me if it be right, and if it is right, I will cause that your bosom shall burn within you; therefore, you shall feel that it is right; but if it be not right, you shall have no such feelings, but you shall have a stupor of thought, that shall cause you to forget the thing which is wrong; therefore, you can not write that which is sacred save it be given you from me.

Now if you had known this, you could have translated: nevertheless, it is not expedient that you should translate now.[31]

From the statement of David Whitmer and from the revelations to Oliver, we understand that Joseph Smith did not regard the process of translation as mechanical. The power to translate resided not in the material device used, but involved the heart and mind of the translator. It would appear that the inspiration received by the prophet in these circumstances involved general concepts rather than literal information. As such the translation was one of revelation. It was necessary for Joseph Smith to express in his own words and phrases the inspired concepts that passed through his mind. Supporting this view is the fact that Joseph Smith did not hesitate to change the wording of the 1830 Palmyra edition of the Book of Mormon. In preparing the 1837 Kirtland edition, the prophet made several hundred changes in the original so that the language there would more adequately express his inspiration.

That the use of the seer stone involved a process of inspiration is also borne out by the manner in which the early revelations were given. During the time that the Book of Mormon was being translated

Joseph Smith received revelations through what he later in his history in the *Times and Seasons* referred to as the Urim and Thummim. In this period "Urim and Thummim" can only pertain to the seer stone. From the *Times and Seasons* it is evident that revelations given up to June 1829, and later recorded in the *Book of Commandments*, were received through the seer stone. When these revelations were republished in 1835 in the Doctrine and Covenants the prophet authorized numerous changes in both their wording and content.

By the time of the organization of the church, Joseph Smith's concept of the process of inspiration had progressed to the point where he was able to dispense with the use of any material instrument in receiving revelation. It is recorded by David Whitmer that

after the translation of the Book of Mormon was finished, early in the spring of 1830, before April 6th, Joseph gave the stone to Oliver Cowdery and told me as well as the rest that he was through with it, and he did not use the stone any more. He said he was through the work that God had given him the gift to perform, except to preach the gospel. He told us that we would all have to depend on the Holy Ghost hereafter to be guided into truth and obtain the will of the Lord. The revelations after this came through Joseph as "mouth piece;" that is, he would enquire of the Lord, pray and ask concerning a matter, and speak out the revelation, which he thought to be a revelation from the Lord.[32]

It is obvious that Joseph Smith felt he had grown beyond the use of the earlier media of translation. He established the policy that the newly founded church would depend solely on the Holy Spirit for revelations.

Many of the Saints at first did not understand what Joseph regarded as a more profound principle of revelation. We have noted Oliver Cowdery's difficulties in this area. Some of Joseph's early followers never grew beyond an almost magical belief in the seer stone. David

Whitmer was to make a statement near the end of his life that all the revelations given by the prophet after he had discarded the seer stone were not of God but were words of the man, Joseph Smith.[33] Possibly as a result of these ideas a revelation was given to the church through Joseph Smith at Fayette on April 6, 1830. This document stresses that revelation comes to the prophet by the Comforter.

Wherefore, meaning the church, thou shalt give heed unto all his words, and commandments, which he shall give unto you, as he receiveth them, walking in all holiness before me; for his word ye shall receive, as if from mine own mouth, in all patience and faith . . .

For behold, I will bless all those who labor in my vineyard, with a mighty blessing, and they shall believe on his words, which are given him through me, by the Comforter.[34]

Yet, some members of the church still clung to a belief in a more mechanical method of revelation through a seer stone. Hiram Page, who had married David Whitmer's sister, Catherine, possessed a stone, apparently the seer stone obtained from Oliver Cowdery. With this stone Page claimed that he was receiving revelations. The Whitmer family, which by marriage included Hiram Page and later Oliver Cowdery, believed many of the things supposedly coming forth from the stone. Accordingly, at a conference of the church convened September 26, 1830, a revelation was given to Oliver Cowdery through Joseph Smith. It emphasizes again the role of the Comforter.

Behold, I say unto you, Oliver, that it shall be given unto thee that thou shalt be heard by the church, in all things whatsoever thou shalt teach them by the Comforter, concerning the revelations and commandments which I have given.

But, behold, verily, verily I say unto you, no one shall be appointed to receive commandments and revelations in this church, excepting my servant Joseph, for he receiveth them even as Moses . . .

And if thou art led at any time by the Comforter to speak or teach, or at all times by the way of commandment unto the church, thou mayest do it . . .

And again, thou shalt take thy brother Hiram between him and thee alone, and tell him that those things which he hath written from that stone are not of me, and that Satan deceiveth him;

For, behold, these things have not been appointed unto him.[35]

The church was plunged into dissension again on this point in 1837.[36] Ultimately many of the early believers were expelled from the church.

These events help us understand Joseph Smith's later reluctance to discuss the details of the translation of the Book of Mormon. By 1838, when he wrote his biography, he chose not to describe the translation in such a way that it would perpetuate the mechanical view of revelation. Instead, Joseph Smith, when pressed regarding the method of translation, very carefully stated that it was done by "the gift and power of God." Beyond this he would never elaborate.

In keeping with this decision, Joseph Smith apparently used the term "Urim and Thummim" to cover all instruments used to translate or determine the will of God.

It is obvious that Joseph Smith did not use the type of instrument referred to in the Old Testament as Urim and Thummim. Modern biblical scholarship is virtually unanimous in concluding that the ancient Urim and Thummim was a device for casting lots used by Hebrews to determine the will of God. It appears that the identification of the Nephite Interpreters with the biblical Urim and Thummim was made only gradually. The words "Urim and Thummim" are never mentioned in the Book of Mormon, the *Book of Commandments*, or early newspaper accounts. They first appear in the *Evening and the Morning Star* and the *Messenger and Advocate* in 1833 and 1834[37] when it is suggested that Joseph may have used a Urim and Thummim. By 1835 this

identification had been given official sanction by the incorporation of "Urim and Thummim" into the pertinent revelations in the Doctrine and Covenants.[38] Thereafter, in discussing his history, Joseph Smith used the term "Urim and Thummim" to include both the Nephite Interpreters and the seer stone.[39]

It is possible that today when reading the testimony of the witnesses some may become too concerned with the seer stone and forget that the important ingredient for Joseph in the translation was the "gift and power of God." The witnesses had no such concerns. Joseph Smith, Emma Smith, Oliver Cowdery, David Whitmer, and Martin Harris were unwavering to the end of their lives in their belief in the divine origin of the book. In the very same testimony in which Emma Smith describes the method of translation of the Book of Mormon, she reaffirms her faith in it.

And, though I was an active participant in the scenes that transpired, and was present during the translation of the plates, and had cognizance of things as they transpired, it is marvelous to me, "a marvel and a wonder," as much as to any one else . . .

My belief is that the Book of Mormon is of divine authenticity—I have not the slightest doubt of it. I am satisfied that no man could have dictated the writing of the manuscripts unless he was inspired.[40]

Oliver Cowdery's last words as he lay dying in David Whitmer's home were these: "Brother David, be true to your testimony to the Book of Mormon."[41] David Whitmer, who all through his life testified to the authenticity of the book, requested before his death that there be engraved these words on his tombstone: "The record of the Jews and the record of the Nephites are one, truth is eternal." None of the witnesses to the Book of Mormon who had seen the process of translation and received divine testimony of it ever denied their belief that the book was the work of God.

Notes

1. *Times and Seasons* 5 (April 1, 1844): 482.
2. *Far West Record*, vol. 1 of *History of the Church of Jesus Christ of Latter-day Saints* (Salt Lake City): 219n.
3. Doctrine and Covenants, 1835 ed. (Kirtland, Ohio): Sec. 1, para. 5.
4. *Elders' Journal* 1 (July 1838): 43.
5. *Times and Seasons* 3 (March 1, 1842): 707. Also in I. Daniel Rupp, *Religious Denominations*, 1844, 405, 406.
6. *Times and Seasons* 3 (May 2, 1842): 772.
7. Written January 4, 1833, from Kirtland, it appears in *Times and Seasons* 5 (November 15, 1844): 707.
8. *Saints' Herald* 26 (October 1, 1879): 289, 290; vol. 3 of *History of the Reorganized Church of Jesus Christ of Latter Day Saints* (Independence, Missouri: Herald House, 1952): 356.
9. David Whitmer, *An Address to All Believers in Christ* (Richmond, Missouri: 1887): 13.
10. RLDS Church Archives, Independence, Missouri. For the circumstances surrounding this letter, see vol. 4, no. 12 of *The Return* (Davis City, Iowa, July 15, 1895), 2. This letter is also mentionend in Fawn M. Brodie, *No Man Knows My History* (New York: Alfred A. Knopf, 1945): 20.
11. *Chicago Inter-Ocean*, October 17, 1886. Reprinted in *Saints' Herald* 33 (November 13, 1886): 706, 707.
12. *Richmond Democrat*, January 26, 1888, from *Plattsburg Democrat*, reprinted in *Saints' Herald* 35 (February 11, 1888): 94, 95.
13. Eber D. Howe, *Mormonism Unvailed* (Painesville, Ohio, 1834): 77.
14. *Times and Seasons* 3 (August 15, 1842): 884.
15. *Times and Seasons* 3 (May 16, 1842): 785.
16. *Saints' Herald* 26 (November 15, 1879): 341.
17. Also reprinted in *Saints' Herald* 33 (January 2, 1886): 12, 13.
18. Also reprinted in *Saints' Herald* 35 (February 4, 1888): 67.
19. As quoted in *Saints' Herald* 28 (July 1, 1881): 198.
20. *Messenger and Advocate* 1 (October, 1834): 14. (From a letter written by Oliver Cowdery to W. W. Phelps, September 7, 1834.)
21. Oliver Cowdery, *Defence in a Rehearsal of My Grounds for Separating Myself from the Latter Day Saints* (Norton, Ohio, 1839). Reprinted in *Saints' Herald* 54 (March 20, 1907): 229, 230. The authenticity of this document has been questioned, mainly on the grounds that apparently no copy of the original 1839 printing has ever been found.
22. *Deseret News*, April 13, 1859.
23. *Millennial Star* 44 (February 6, 1882): 86, 87.
24. *Saints' Herald* 26 (June 15, 1879): 190, 191.
25. Howe, 265. See also the *Susquehanna Register*, May 1, 1834. Joseph Smith defended himself against the money-digger charge in *Times and Seasons* 3 (May 2, 1842): 772. See also *Times and Seasons* 4 (March 1, 1843): 118.
26. William Smith, *William Smith on Mormonism* (Lamoni, Iowa, 1883): 10-12.
27. *Saints' Herald* 31 (October 4, 1884): 644.
28. *Rod of Iron*, Zion's Religio-Literary Society, Independence, Mo., vol. 1, no. 3, p. 6, February 1924.
29. Clark Braden and E. L. Kelley, *Public Discussion of the Issues Between the Reorganized Church of Jesus Christ of Latter-day Saints and the Church of Christ, Disciples, Held in Kirtland, Ohio*, St. Louis, 1884, 186.
30. *Book of Commandments*, 1833, ch. 7, p. 19, 20. Later revised and reprinted in 1835 in Doctrine and Covenants, Sec. 34.
31. *Book of Commandments*, ch. 8, p. 20, 21; 1835 Doctrine and Covenants, Sec. 35.
32. David Whitmer, 32.
33. Ibid.
34. *Book of Commandments*, ch. 22, paras., 4-5, 10; 1835 Doctrine and Covenants, Sec. 46.
35. *Book of Commandments*, ch. 30; 1835 Doctrine and Covenants, Sec. 51.
36. Lucy Smith, *Biographical Sketches of Joseph Smith the Prophet and His Progeni-*

tors for Many Generations, Liverpool, 1853, 211-213.

37. The *Evening and the Morning Star* 1 (January 1833): 2; *Messenger and Advocate* 1 (October 1834): 14.

38. Compare 1835 Doctrine and Covenants, Sec. 36 with *Book of Commandments*, ch. 9.

39. After Oliver Cowdery's death, the seer stone was given by his wife, Elizabeth, to Phineas Young, who took it to Utah. See David Whitmer, 32. It was exhibited by the Church leaders in Utah and viewed by many. As late as 1930 it was still in the archives of the LDS church. See B. H. Roberts, *Comprehensive History of the Church* (1930), vol. 6, 230-31.

40. *Saints' Herald* 26 (October 1, 1879): 289, 290.

41. David Whitmer, 8.

BIBLICAL MESSIANISM AND THE BOOK OF MORMON

Bruce W. Clavey

The concept of a "messiah" in Israel was not born with all the values attributed to it today. Rather, it was a metamorphosis of belief over the course of hundreds of years of history. Though certain writings ascribe a full knowledge of Christ to ages as far past as the days of Adam, the known development of messianism cannot be traced much further back than the first millenium B.C.[1] My purpose here is not to present an exhaustive history of this theme, but to acquire a larger sense of the many values present as it is unfolded in the Bible and the Book of Mormon.

Messianic Kingship

The literal interpretation of the word *messiah* is "anointed." The expression first appears in connection with the consecration of the descendants of Aaron to their priestly office.[2] Later, when the government of Israel became a monarchy the rite of anointment expanded to include the setting apart of the king. Just as the anointment conferred holy authority when administered by the priests, it sealed upon the king a special relationship with Yahweh when confirmed under the hands of his prophet. In *Messianic Theology and Christian Faith*, George A. Riggan states:

The broad powers of the king derived from the idea that he was Yahweh's son. . . . He is not begotten of God in the process of his physical origin, but precisely in the event of his enthronement; he is a son not by right of birth but by adoption. He is therefore not a god (cf. II Kings 5:7). Especially is he not Yahweh masquerading in the form of a man. He is

emphatically and precisely a man who, in his royal functions and by divine appointment, is also Yahweh's son.[3]

As the earthly arm of Yahweh's judgment the king was an intermediary in close relationship with his prophet, who was the transmitter of the divine word. His domain was to exceed the physical boundaries of Israel: "Ask of me, and I shall give thee the heathen for thine inheritance, and the uttermost parts of the earth for thy possession."[4] Consequently, the king was empowered to rule the nations.

The reign of David appears to have been a pivotal point in the development of the messianic theme. Many scholars agree that Israel's reflection on this period as being the pinnacle of their history grew out of its contrast to later, more turbulent, times.[5] David was indeed a powerful figure, mounting the throne and guiding the nation through a troubled era. In the years following his death, however, the morale of Israel suffered and it became easier to see David's Jerusalem as a kingdom worthy of renewal.[6]

The humanity of several post-Davidic kings became highlighted against the backdrop of adverse political activity; the kingdom of Israel had come into the subservience of other nations, and its tribes now stood divided against themselves. The event of royal anointment no longer connoted a bestowal of divinity upon the king in the eyes of the people of Israel. It was reduced to a reminder that the royal calling (if not responsibility) was to renew the kingdom and to usher in the world-wide reign of Yahweh.[7] In this environment a hope was born that a monarch would rise in the future and assume the mantle of "world-ruler." Fashioned by the words of the prophets and the desires of the nation, the ideal king gained definition as *the* Messiah of Israel.[8]

Increasingly, Israel began to look at the Messiah in an eschatological way.[9] Not only would he come to govern Israel and exalt it above the nations, he would bring the end times: "Let the floods clap their hands; let the hills be joyful together before the Lord; for he cometh to judge the earth" (Psalm 98:8-9). All previous observances relative to the Messiah became a type or shadow of Yahweh's great work to come.

There was much latitude offered as to what image the great Messiah might take. According to one modern author

some expected him to be a human being who would emerge from the Jewish people, perhaps the long-expected ruler from the Davidic line. Others believed the origin of the Messiah to be cloaked in mystery. Some texts suggest the expectations of a divine being who would descend from heaven and lead the righteous to a transformed life in the kingdom of heaven....But most Jews agreed that the Messiah's coming would mark the beginning of God's victory over the powers of evil.[10]

The Book of Mormon opens on the eve of the Babylonian conquest of Jerusalem. It mentions Zedekiah who was installed king of Israel by Nebuchadnezzar of Babylon following the revolt of Judah. Zedekiah was permitted to retain the royal office as long as he demonstrated his subservience to Babylon. Not many years hence, though, he proved rebellious, forcing the hand of Nebuchadnezzar. Riggan notes:

Finally, his patience exhausted, the emperor obliterated the towns of Judah and in 587 B.C. destroyed Jerusalem and the Temple. Zedekiah's sons were slain before his eyes; he was then

blinded and taken with most of the remaining populace into exile. So ended messianic royalism as an effective political force in Judah.[11]

It is at the close of Israel's sacral kingship that Book of Mormon history bears off and resumes on another continent. The story line does not indicate that there is any royalty among the members of Lehi's party fleeing Jerusalem. It does, however, refer to Nephi's "reign and ministry." Since the record notes his capabilities as a lawgiver and a sage, he may have rendered informal service as both prophet and king. Our first reference to a legitimate succession of royal authority is just prior to Nephi's death. As a function of his prophetic calling, Nephi "anointed a man to be a king and a ruler over his people now, according to the reigns of the kings." Each ruler in succession for a few hundred years is renamed Second Nephi, Third Nephi, and so on.[12] We should remember that the term *anoint* recalls the most basic meaning of Messianic kingship. The ceremony of the new king's consecration and the bestowal of his title, we presume, reminds him that his calling is to renew the kingdom that was experienced during the reign of Nephi.

As Nephite history progresses, a surprise awaits the reader: the kingline from Israel is alive and well in the Book of Mormon. Zedekiah's sons were not all indeed killed by Nebuchadnezzar, but one, Mulek, escaped and traveled over the seas with a small colony to reside in the new land. Were Mulek and his lineal heirs considered possible messiahs? When discovered by the party of Mosiah, the descendants of Mulek's people "denied the being of their Creator." Yet the Book of Mormon does award his seed an unusual eminence. Note that Zarahemla, of the line of Mulek, was leader of his people at Mosiah's coming, and that the name of the land was after his own. Furthermore, his genealogy was of such import that it was reported in Mosiah's sacred records. Nearly six hundred years after Lehi left Jerusalem, the lineage of Zedekiah is still of remarkability among the people of Nephi.[13] Though the king line has been long since dormant, there appears to be a patient vigil, a watch for someone to appear from the seed of the ancient king. This never happens.

Following the reign of Nephi, whose link with heaven was pronounced through angelic visitations, the Book of Mormon grows silent as to how closely Nephite people associated their kings with Deity. Not until the reign of Benjamin do we discover an esteem so strong that a portion of his address was devoted to "demythologizing" the king:

"I have not commanded you to come up here that you should fear me, or that you should think that I, of myself, am more than a mortal man. For I am like yourselves, subject to all manner of infirmities in body and mind."—Mosiah 1:40-41

Mosiah II ruled with a benevolence equaling that of his father Benjamin, and at the close of his reign, he unfolds to his people "all the trials and troubles of a righteous king." Undaunted by his best efforts to humanize himself, "they waxed strong in love toward Mosiah; they esteemed him more than any other man . . . they esteemed him exceedingly, beyond measure" (Mosiah 13:58, 61).

Nevertheless, in spite of some similarities, it is difficult to prove that Israelite kingship had a strong influence on Nephite monarchy. Yet messianism was not a concept fixed in kingship alone, but one which was continually developed by the prophets.

Prophetic Motifs

Though strong in spiritual heritage, the House of Israel was weak in political strength. Nestled in an area central to three Old World powers—Egypt, Assyria, and Babylon—Israel became a prize to warring nations seeking to enlarge their domain. In their history, Jews of the sixth century B.C. could only recall national bondage—they had suffered enslavement in brick pits, seen half of their total nation carried away to live as transplanted vassals in a foreign land, and now faced the threat of annihilation under new lordship. The desire to be free was transferred to the shoulders of the Messiah. Isaiah presents the image of an "Anointed Conqueror" who rises to heal the woes of Israel. At his coming, "the adversaries of Judah shall be cut off" and he "shall assemble the outcasts from Israel and gather together the dispersed from Judah."[14]

Biblical historians suggest that the hope for a messiah became coupled with a strong sense of national calling. As a result, prophets offered distinct motifs of the being who was to come to redeem Israel. One image was the "Son of Man," an expression coined in the visions of Daniel, and later echoed by Jesus. The "judgment scene" in the seventh chapter of Daniel is the fount from which John the Revelator draws the imagery of his message, and is of importance here. It records the dissolution of the hostile dominions of the world and the inheritance of a kingdom of "all people, nations, and languages" by the Son of Man.[15]

Although the seers of Israel acknowledged the gross sin in the nation, their utterances revealed the patient forbearance of the Lord and his continuing covenant with that people. An image offered by the prophet Jeremiah foretells "a Branch" that would rise up and see the salvation of Israel. Zechariah added that this personage would construct a temple unto Yahweh and take his place upon the throne therein. These ideas build a motif of the messiah later sacred to Israel.[16]

Through certain passages in the book of Isaiah the people of Israel corporately assume the calling as a chosen "Servant" of Yahweh. "But, thou, Israel, art my servant, Jacob whom I have chosen, the seed of Abraham my friend." The mission was to be a witness to the nations: "I the Lord have called thee . . . and give thee for a covenant of the people, for a light of the Gentiles." In yet other references, the servant seems to be a human personage with a mission "to raise up the tribes of Jacob, and to restore the preserved of Israel."[17] Scholars probing the past for a servant-type have proposed a series of figures who, according to Bernhard Anderson, range from Moses to Isaiah himself. Others, however, "believing that no historic person of ancient Israel fits the picture, propose that the figure is one who appears on the horizon of God's future—that is, the Messiah."[18]

Isaiah's servant is remembered as a "man of sorrows, acquainted with grief." His mission is not established through any exquisite "form or comeliness," but rather through his oppression and affliction at the hand of God. "It pleased the Lord to bruise him; he hath put him to grief." However, the pleasure of the Lord is only in the servant's vicarious death:

Surely he hath borne our griefs, and carried our sorrows. . . . He was wounded for our transgressions, he was bruised for our iniquities; the chastisement of our peace was upon him; and with his stripes we are healed.—Isaiah 53:4, 5

The unique way in which the Book of Mormon treats these various images deserves our attention. In each instance, it is equally as important to consider what is not said as it is to value what is said. An analysis of the "Son of Man" influence illustrates this point. The Book of Mormon is not only devoid of the concept of the messiah's inheritance in the eternal world; there is absolutely no reference to the term *Son of Man* in the entire text. The absence of this metaphor may be understandable in the context of how the biblical writings emerged. Scholars now believe that the book of Daniel may have been compiled from ancient sources as late as the first century B.C., which would have placed it beyond accessibility to the people of the Book of Mormon.[19]

Early leaders of the Book of Mormon seemed aware of the presence of the branch symbolism in their word of scripture. We find passages quoted from Isaiah which predict the coming of "a rod out of the stem of Jesse" and a "branch shall grow out of his roots."[20] However, before many years of Nephite history pass, the context of the branch shifts notably, as shown in the words of Lehi:

"Joseph truly saw our day. And he obtained a promise of the Lord, that out of the fruit of his loins the Lord God would raise up a righteous branch to the house of Israel; not the Messiah, but a branch which was to be broken off . . . that the Messiah should be made manifest to them in the latter days."—II Nephi 2:6-9

Although the messiah is mentioned here simply to avoid a confusion of images, the passage does indicate a messianic use of the branch. Later the parable of Zenos illustrates the people of Israel as an olive tree, and the branch becomes a byword to signify limbs which had been removed and planted in other places of the Lord's vineyard.[21] The phrase is never again equated by Nephite prophets with the coming messiah.

The servant motif receives the most attention by Nephite prophets. To be certain, they have selected the choicest of Isaiah's passages and interpreted them in the widest messianic sense possible; yet with the servant images, they are applied with an unusual accuracy.[22] In addition, new passages appear to plumb even greater depths:

And the world, because of their iniquity, shall judge him to be a thing of nought; wherefore, they will scourge him, and he will suffer it; and they will smite him, and he will suffer it.—I Nephi 5:237

"'For, behold, blood cometh from every pore, so great shall be his anguish for the wickedness and the abominations of his people'."—Mosiah 1:101

"'He will take upon him the pains and the sicknesses of his people; and he will take upon him death, that he may loose the bands of death which bind his people. And he will take upon him their infirmities that his bowels may be filled with mercy, according to the flesh, that he may know according to the flesh how to succor his people according to their infirmities'."—Alma 5:21-22

Here, as in Isaiah, the greater meaning of the servant is not bound up in his trial and execution, but in the humiliation he faces as he rises to meet his mission. When the raw facts are stripped away, we see revealed the intense anguish and willing submission of the messiah as he takes the yoke of punishment which rightfully belongs to the people of the Lord.

Of the suffering servant, Isaiah said, "His visage was so marred more than any man, and his form more than the sons of men." When Jesus appears at the temple in Book of Mormon's Bountiful, he quotes this passage in full context.[23] In his subsequent commentary he carefully extracts certain characteristics of the servant out of the Isaiah text and insists that they are not fulfilled in the messiah, but in a prophet yet to come:

Behold, the life of my servant shall be in my hand; therefore they shall not hurt him, although he shall be marred because of them. Yet I will heal him, for I will show them that my wisdom is greater than the cunning of the devil.—III Nephi 9:96-97

This servant shall declare a "great and marvelous work" with such success that "kings shall shut their mouths."

Out of the servant imagery in the Book of Mormon springs an altered form of the conqueror. Although the text nowhere indicates that the destruction of Gentile adversaries is the direct work of the messiah, in the aforementioned section of Jesus' exhortations, he names himself the moving force behind the potential actions of Israel's remant:

"Thy hand shall be lifted up upon thine adversaries, and all thine enemies shall be cut off....And thou shalt beat in pieces many people; and I will consecrate their gain to the Lord, and their substance to the Lord of the whole earth. And, behold, I am he who doeth it."—III Nephi 9:53, 55

Hence, Israel becomes the arm of the conqueror. The new mission occurs in the last days, and takes the form of a warning:

Therefore it shall come to pass that whosoever will not believe in my words—who am Jesus Christ—which the Father shall cause him [the servant] to bring forth to the Gentiles...shall be cut off from among my people who are of the covenant. And my people who are a remnant of Jacob shall be among the Gentiles, in the midst of them as a lion among the beasts of the forest, as a young lion among the flocks of sheep, who, if he go through, both treadeth down and teareth in pieces, and none can deliver.—III Nephi 9:98-99

So important seems this promise that it is repeated twice by Jesus, and again by Mormon near the close of Nephite history.

Eschatological Prophets and Antitypes

The dissonance in the several identities listed helps to illustrate the uncertainty surrounding an attempt to imbue one personage with all the traits of all the messianic figures so early in Israelite history. In addition, it opens the concept that there may have been more than one figure expected to rise in Israel in the last days. Howard M. Teeple discusses this possibility in his book, *The Mosaic Eschatological Prophet:*

Jewish views differed as to the identity, number, and role of the eschatological persons. The three chief offices in Israel—those of king, priest, and prophet—appeared in eschatological thought and, as in actual history, often overlapped. Our literary sources do not give us a full picture and ideas existed of which we can catch only a glimpse.[24]

An "eschatological prophet" may refer to

the messiah, or to a forerunner of the messiah, or to an assistant that may accompany the messiah when he comes.[25] In addition, it was fully expected that any one of these roles might be fulfilled in the return of a heroic figure from Israel's past.

Teeple presents the prophet Elijah as a personage who was expected to reappear and assume the calling of the messiah or his counterpart. The story of his miraculous departure in a heavenly chariot and consequent escape from death foreshadowed his ultimate return to continue the Lord's work in the House of Israel. The impact of this belief was seen in the people's response to the bold deeds of both Jesus and John the Baptist: "Art thou that Elias who was to restore all things?"[26] Later, expectations rose to include the coming of Moses with Elijah. Hence, we are not surprised at the account of Mark 9, in which both prophets appear transfigured before Jesus and divulge to him the final course his life.[27]

In all of the passages of the Book of Mormon foretelling the coming of eschatological personages, only one insinuates the reappearance of a revered prophet. In Jesus' quote of Malachi he promises, "I will send you Elijah, the prophet, before the coming of the great and dreadful day of the Lord." Elijah's calling to reunite the family of Israel loses its messianic sense, however, when foretold by Christ himself.[28]

The coming of Moses into the role of latter-day prophet is due in part to controversy over how his mortal life closed: did he die a natural death, or was there an assumption of his soul into heaven with a promise of return?[29] The Book of Mormon touches on this dilemma in this section on the disappearance of Alma:

The saying went abroad in the church that he was taken up by the Spirit, or buried by the hand of the Lord, even as Moses. But behold, the scripture says the Lord took Moses to himself; and we sup-

pose that he has also received Alma in the spirit, to himself. —Alma 21:21-22

This Book of Mormon author equates the mysterious departure of Alma with the ancient riddle of Moses' death. If the question of Moses' return to Israel is also opened before the people of Nephi, we might expect the same to be true of Alma. On this matter, however, the text is silent.

Some of the familiar Book of Mormon motifs qualify well as eschatological prophets. The marred servant, previously noted as a minister of the last day, is shadowed in the words of the resurrected Jesus. A second, more unusual, circumstance arises out of Jesus' visit in which three Nephite disciples receive an exciting endowment:

Blessed are ye, for ye shall never taste of death, but ye shall live to behold all the doings of the Father to the children of men, even until all things shall be fulfilled according to the will of the Father, when I shall come in my glory with the powers of heaven. —III Nephi 13:18

Instead of a foreshortened life with a promise of imminent return, the lives of the three Nephites are immortalized so as to extend their earthly ministries into the latter days. Four hundred years later, Moroni records that "my father and I have seen them, and they have ministered to us" (Mormon 4:13). The influence of this passage, however, has far exceeded the Book of Mormon; throughout the history of the Restoration many Saints have demonstrated a belief in the ongoing work of these men.

One of the clearest images of an end times prophet is cast by Lehi in his blessing on his youngest son Joseph. Lehi recalls an extra-biblical promise uttered by Joseph, son of Jacob, that a seer would be raised up from his own lineage. The work of the seer presupposes the coming of Moses, the delivery from Egypt, and the collapse of the House of Israel:

"And he shall be great like Moses, whom I have

said I would raise up to you . . . and unto him will I give power to bring forth my word unto the seed of thy loins . . . to the convincing them of my word. . . . Out of weakness he shall be made strong, in that day when my work shall commence among all my people, to the restoring thee, O house of Israel," saith the Lord—II Nephi 2:15, 17, 18, 24

Lehi promises that this prophet will rise as a descendant of his son Joseph. It appears that he will be exalted out of weakness; the glory of his work will contrast the rudeness of his upbringing. In addition, he shall be powerless to do anything but that to which he has been called, and his life shall not be destroyed at the contrivance of his enemies.

A major problem of this prophecy is in the identification of who is speaking; the text lists Lehi, Joseph, and the Lord as contributors at various points. Most of it may be ironed out through careful consideration, but the following passage presents special difficulties: "His name shall be called after me; and it shall be after the name of his father. He shall be like me" (II Nephi 2:29-30). For all the effort to portray a clear image, one mystery remains: will this prophet be named Joseph or Lehi? The answer lies in the identity of the speaker in this passage.[30] Whichever it be, the prophet will stand up in the likeness of the speaker with a mission to fulfill among a remnant of Israel.

Many of the beliefs and theories relating to the eschatological prophet were drawn from an older facet of messianism: the concept of "antitypes." This early hypothesis suggested that all apocalyptic figures and events paralleled a framework of historic "types and shadows" from the past. As stated before, the work of the messiah had been defined in terms of Israelite heritage: he would restore a kingdom rivaling the fame and prosperity of 1000 B.C. Jerusalem. Even so, the Messiah himself was understood by the Israelites as an extension of other biblical

personalities. J. A. Motyer states that

the faithfulness and self-consistency of their God provided them with a key to the future, on so far as it was necessary for faith to discern things to come. God had acted "typically" and characteristically in certain great persons and events in the past, and, because God does not change, He will so act again. Three such persons of the past were specially woven into the messianic pattern: Adam, Moses, and David.[31]

Adam, the "firstborn," was the source of life. He is remembered in relation to the peace and prosperity of Eden, and was granted "dominion over the earth" until his fall. Moses was immortalized an originator of law, and mediator of covenant. In this, he is set apart from the prophets, who were seen as preachers and propagators of the same. Furthermore, he was the mighty deliverer of Israel from bondage. An understanding of David as an antitype is derived from the Psalms. "There are certain Psalms which centre round the king," Motyer states, "and, limiting inquiry to those psalms which are indisputably royal, they depict a very precise character and career." He cites references to victory over world opposition, establishing world rule under Yahweh, and Zion as the basis for an everlasting rule and a peaceful and prosperous kingdom.[32]

The response to these personalities in the Book of Mormon draws our attention. Moses' esteem has already been noted with regard to his status as an eschatological prophet. However, he also appears in the record as an antitype to the messiah:

"The Lord will surely prepare a way for his people, to the fulfilling of the words of Moses, which he spake, saying: 'A prophet shall the Lord your God raise up to you, like me; him shall ye hear in all things whatsoever he shall say to you'."—I Nephi 7:43-44

Adam's status as an antitype is preserved in a refreshing treatise on earthly life and eternal life:

"Adam fell, that men might be; and men are, that they might have joy. And the Messiah will come in the fullness of time, that he may redeem the children of men from the fall."—II Nephi 1:115-116

The early Nephite writers, however, do not recall David in a positive vein. With the exception of the extracts from the writings of Isaiah, David is remembered solely for his "many wives and concubines, which thing was abominable" (Jacob 2:33).

The Book of Mormon submits an additional antitype for the consideration of its readers, in the personage of the prophet Abinadi. Raised up during the days of wicked King Noah, Abinadi speaks out against the riotous living of the royal family, and is imprisoned to be executed. Note that many characteristics of the passion story are loosely present: the delivery of Abinadi into the hands of the king by the chief priests, the cross-examination, the outrage at the prophet's message about the coming of God and the demand that he recall his words, Abinadi's admission that he goes willingly to his death but insistence that his blood would be innocently shed, the wavering of the king, and his final resolve to permit the death at the compulsion of the priests. As Abinadi speaks, he unfolds the Book of Mormon's most sublime address regarding the identity of the messiah, noting that he "suffereth himself to be mocked, and scourged, and cast out" and that he shall be "led, crucified and slain" by his own people. Then, like Moses, Abinadi offers himself as a similitude, saying ". . . this much I tell you: What you do with me . . . shall be as a type and a shadow of things which are to come."[33] When finished Abinadi is removed from the court by Noah's priests to be put to death. The resonance of his prophecy and death is recorded in several generations to follow.

The concept of multiple eschatological figures reached an extreme perhaps in the beliefs of the Essene sect of ancient Judaism. A fuller concept of their approach has unfolded in recent years with the appearance of the Dead Sea Scrolls. The Essenes differed from the Pharisees and Sadducees in their expectation that the last days of judgment would be ushered in, not by one, but by two messiahs. They were referred to as the messiah of Aaron and the messiah of Israel. Geza Vermes, a pioneer in the field of Qumran Essene studies, outlines the distinct responsibilities that each figure was to fulfill:

The respective tasks of the two Messiahs can be determined with relative ease. The Davidic Prince was to lead the people to triumph, to defeat the Gentiles, and to bring into being the Kingdom of God. In matters of doctrine he was to obey the Priests. . . . The Messiah of Aaron, on the other hand, is represented as the High Priest of the Kingdom. He was to conduct the liturgy during the battle against the ultimate foe, and as the final Interpreter of the Law he was to reveal the significance of the Scriptures and their relevance to the events of the Messianic age and to the endless time of eternal bliss.[34]

The Book of Mormon reflects no development of thought that resembles "multiple messianism." As noted before, many characteristics unique to the Israelite messiah are often reassigned in the Nephite record, but never to a person worthy of being referred to as another messiah. Nephi establishes the stance of the new culture through his commentary on Isaiah's servant text: "For there is but one Messiah spoken of by the prophets, and that Messiah is he who should be rejected of the Jews" (II Nephi 11:34).

Textual Contrasts

The Book of Mormon details a "cloned" civilization—one that had, at its origin, the characteristics of Hebrew thought and culture. However, because it was removed from the presence and influence of Israel and was transplanted, we should expect to find variations in their expectations and beliefs. With regard to their values of messianism, we are not dis-

239

appointed. A close look at the words of the Nephite prophets reveals that their concept of Christ does not appear full-blown at the outset of their history, but is an entity that develops over the course of their first few decades. Nevertheless, it appears to incorporate the same systematic metamorphosis of belief that was mirrored hundreds of years later, thousands of miles away, by a people with a largely different heritage and history.

The first highlight in the messianic theme appears in the theophany of Lehi, wherein a vision of God upon his throne is subtly equated with a foreseen appearance of the messiah. This inspiration paved the course for the Book of Mormon's primary theme: that the messiah and the Lord God were the very same being.[35] Nephi's vision (as related in the Palmyra edition of 1830) follows closely, and refers to the coming of the messiah as the "condescension of God."[36]

That the messiah would come in the kingly character of God's Son was not treated in detail until several years of Nephite history had passed. Jacob, younger brother to Nephi, opens the door in a discourse that reflects the relationship of God's great works to men in "the flesh."[37] By chapter 11 of II Nephi, the messiah is thought of in his human mode, and here receives development as the Son.[38]

Abinadi is the first to address the dual nature of the messiah's personality in its largest sense, reasoning that the messiah was at once to be both God, and the Son of God:

"I would that you should understand that God himself shall come down among the children of men and shall redeem his people. And because he dwells in flesh, he shall be called the Son of God."—Mosiah 8:28-29

Abinadi foresees the presence of the eternal God in the human body of Jesus.

The prophet does not suggest that God forsakes his abode in the eternal world, but that, as the Father, he is the spirit of the human Son. Jesus is

"the Father because he was conceived by the power of God; and the Son because of the flesh; thus becoming the Father and the Son—they are one God, the very eternal Father of heaven and of earth."—Mosiah 8:30-31

The messiah personifies the power of redemption and the struggle of agency even in the shadow of death:

"Thus the flesh becoming subject to the Spirit, or the Son to the Father, being one God, suffers temptation, and yields not to the temptation, but suffers himself to be mocked, and scourged, and cast out, and disowned by his people."—Mosiah 8:32

The Book of Mormon clarifies the Godship of the messiah as a critical theme. Nephi states that the same God of Abraham, Isaac, and Jacob who delivered the Israelites from bondage would be taken by them and crucified. When Jesus appears in the Book of Mormon, he calls on the Nephites to step forward and test his wounds, "that ye may know that I am the God of Israel, and the God of the whole earth" (III Nephi 5:14). Finally a great biblical promise is made contingent upon this union:

"But, behold, thus says the Lord God: 'When the day cometh that they shall believe in me, that I am Christ, then have I covenanted with their fathers that they shall be restored in the flesh, upon the earth, to the lands of their inheritance.'"—II Nephi 7:12

To make certain that the matter doesn't rest there, a prophecy exhorts the "Gentiles" of our day to realize that it is just as important for them to be convinced that Jesus is the eternal God, as it is for the Jews to believe that he is Christ. Mormon summarizes that the purpose of his writing is "that the Jews, the covenant people of the Lord, shall have other witnesses besides him whom they saw and heard, that

Jesus whom they slew was the very Christ and the very God" (Mormon 1:88).

The nomenclature used to identify the messiah in the Book of Mormon draws from the entire spectrum of the Judaeo-Christian concept of divinity. In addition to the characteristics mentioned before, Nephi adds the proper nouns "Lamb" and "Only Begotten," the use of which is reserved for the New Testament in Bible history. It is interesting to note that the expressions *Redeemer* and *Holy One of Israel* are also used among the Nephites to denote the messiah. These are metaphors which, in biblical writings, are never clearly established in reference to either the messiah or to Jesus. Though the expressions *Holy Ghost* and *Spirit of God* never appear synonymous to Jesus or the messiah in the Book of Mormon, the text coins the term *Spirit of Christ*.

Readers of the Book of Mormon should be aware that it contrasts the Old Testament when it speaks so clearly of Jesus of Nazareth. Where the Israelite prophets render general images of the messiah's calling, Nephi sages append facts about the life of the personage that fulfilled the role. In addition to the knowledge of his trial and death on the cross noted earlier, we are informed that he was to come as a babe, would be born "at Jerusalem" to a virgin named Mary, was to be named Jesus, would be preceded in his ministry by a prophet who baptized him in water, and that the Holy Spirit would descend as a dove to consummate his baptism. Furthermore, he would perform acts of healing and casting out of devils, and would be followed by twelve men who would stand up in the ministry he inaugurated. Lehi's "600-year prophecy" prescribes the very date upon which the messiah is to be born.[39] Book of Mormon prophets reflected such a clarity of foreknowledge, that they spoke about the atonement as if it was an event of the past. "Now if Christ had not come into the world, speaking of things to come as though they had already come, there could have been no redemption" (Mosiah 8:79). At this, the air of mystery so central to the character of the Israelite messiah dissipates among the Nephites.

Conclusions

In terms of biblical messianism, we have treated the surface values outlined in volumes of scholarly works. The hope of the Israelite tribes was deeply rooted in the network of their social, political, and religious environments. Their belief that a messiah was forthcoming took on new meaning with every turn in their history; the promise of his deliverance was a constant reminder of their dependence on God's word. To construe their patterns of thought to be simply a foreknowledge of Jesus' ministries is to misrepresent them. We are reminded that the execution of Jesus was largely grounded in his defiance to accept many of the current messianic labels esteemed by his countrymen.

The field of Book of Mormon messianism is also broad, but largely unexplored. It is evident that the work commands a working knowledge of several facets of Old Testament belief. In addition, the text outlines a hope that is congruous with the peculiar circumstances of Nephite history. Yet it is also apparent that it diverges from the mainstream of contemporary Israelite thought and accelerates into Pauline concepts from the Christian era. The system that required a millennium to ferment among the "Gentiles" of the New Testament was unfolded within a few short years to the people of Nephi. The Book of Mormon message of the first-century Jesus is developed so fully that it cannot be exhausted in terms of messianic studies alone. Where that leaves off, we must begin to look at it in terms of its

Christology. Perhaps one day more detailed studies may further explore the complex approach to the messiah presented in the Book of Mormon.

Notes

1. The Restoration concept that Christianity was revealed to the generation of Adam is rooted in the enhanced passages of Genesis chapters 1 through 8 in the Inspired Version. This study will present developments occurring in the Messiah theme only during the last several centuries before Christ.
2. Raphael Patai, *The Messiah Texts* (New York: Avon Books), 1979, xxi–xxii.
3. George A. Riggan, *Messianic Theology and Christian Faith* (Philadelphia: Westminster Press, 1967), 25.
4. Ibid., and Psalm 2:8. Biblical references in this study are from the Inspired Version (Independence, Missouri: Herald House).
5. Bernard W. Anderson, *Understanding the Old Testament*, 3rd ed. (New Jersey: Prentice-Hall, 1975), 186.
6. Ibid., 187–188.
7. Riggan, 25.
8. Anderson, 482.
9. J. A. Motyer, "Messiah," in *The New Bible Dictionary*, ed. J. D. Douglas (Grand Rapids: Wm. B. Eerdmans Publishing Co., 1975), 812. The term *eschatology* is used to denote a system of beliefs that the world and its civilizations will come to a dramatic close in the fulfillment of a divine purpose. The expression *apocalyptic* is closely enjoined, and shadows events real and/or symbolic to occur when God's will and power are revealed.
10. Howard Clark Kee, Franklin W. Young, and Karlfried Froehlich, *Understanding the New Testament*, 3rd ed. (New Jersey: Prentice-Hall, 1973), 52.
11. Riggan, 34. See also II Kings 25:1.
12. Jacob 1:9, 11. All quotations are from the RLDS authorized edition of the Book of Mormon (Independence, Missouri: Herald House, 1966).
13. Omni 1:31–34, Helaman 3:57. That Mulok (mentioned as the forefather of Zarahemla in Mosiah 11:78) and Mulek are the same person can be deduced in comparing the situa-

tions referenced in Omni 1:26 and Helaman 2:129.
14. Motyer, 816.
15. Ibid., 817–818.
16. Ibid., 816–817; Anderson, 481–482.
17. Isaiah 41:8, 42:6, 49:6.
18. Anderson, 460.
19. Patai, xxiv.
20. Isaiah 11:1, II Nephi 9:116.
21. Jacob 3 reflects the prophecy of Zenos as recorded in the ancient brass plates. Therefore, the Book of Mormon insinuates that the conflict in the use of the term *branch* predates Nephite history.
22. See the use of Isaiah 53 in Mosiah 8:16–27.
23. Isaiah 52:14, in III Nephi 9:82.
24. Howard M. Teeple, *The Mosaic Eschatological Prophet*, Journal of Biblical Literature Monograph Series, vol. 10 (Ann Arbor, Michigan: Cushing-Malloy, 1957), 1.
25. Ibid.
26. Paraphrased from John 1:20–22; Teeple, 3. See also Matthew 16:14–15.
27. Teeple, 9. Jeremiah, Joshua, and Enoch were other historic figures who, in some communities of faith, were expected to return in the last days (pp. 3, 11).
28. III Nephi 11:26, Malachi 4:5.
29. Teeple, 41–43.
30. The traditional interpretation names Joseph of Egypt as the speaker in this passage. This is buoyed up by the presence of a parallel reference to the words of Joseph in Genesis 50 (Inspired Version only). On the basis of internal evidences, however, it appears that Lehi is the speaker here, foretelling a prophet to rise in his name and likeness. That it refers to the fruit of "thy loins" instead of "my loins" (2:27) suggests that it is Lehi addressing his son. See Jim Snell, *An Open Book*, No. 19 (Kansas City, Kansas: Snell Printing, 1975).
31. Motyer, 812.
32. Ibid., 814. This is a rather crude paraphrase of Motyer's excellent outline of the use of Psalms in Cultic Israelite worship.

33. The capture, trial and execution of Abinadi are found in Mosiah, chapters 7-9. An objection may be raised that Mormon later refers to the Lamanite slaying of the people of Amulon as the fulfillment of the "type and shadow" of Abinadi's death (Alma 14:68-69). The reader should note that Abinadi thrice relates his death in similitude of some future event (Mosiah 7:50, 7:110, 9:24). There is no mystery in the way the first reference relates to the death by fire of King Noah, or that the third reference is fulfilled in the death of the Amulonites. But that Abinadi's death could be a "type or shadow" of the death of Noah or his priests (as Mormon suggests in the Alma passage) may be beyond the range of typology. Biblical typology, according to one author, "is developmental rather than prefigurative and predictive," and is related with the "great ideas and events of the history of salvation." This would suggest that the omen of Mosiah 7:110 is related more to the death of Christ (a great event in the history of salvation), than to the priests' or to Noah's (which are extremely predictive). The burden of the correctness of this application rests with Mormon as abridger of the record. See John L. McKenzie, "Type, typology," in *Dictionary of the Bible* (Milwaukee: Bruce Publishing, 1965), 904.

34. G. Vermes, *The Dead Sea Scrolls in English*, 2nd ed. (New York: Penguin Books, 1975), 49.

35. I Nephi 1:5-13. Verse 20 entwines the events of Lehi's vision and insists that they "manifested plainly of the coming of a Messiah."

36. The key phrases relating to the messiah in Nephi's vision (I Nephi 3:58, 62, 86, 192-193) appear in the 1830 edition of the Book of Mormon without the term "Son of" previous to the names "God," "Eternal Father," and "everlasting Father." Both the original and printer's manuscript agree with the printed volume. The expression "Son of" was inserted into these passages prior to the 1837 edition of the book and appears in current versions.

37. II Nephi 6.

38. Previous to II Nephi 11, the only references to the Son appear in I Nephi 3. Many of those occurrences may be eliminated per discussion in footnote 36, and the few remaining can easily be understood as Nephi's anachronistic terminology as he recalls his vision in writing after several years.

39. Alma 5:19, II Nephi 15:5, and I Nephi 3:4, 72-85. The "600-year prophecy" was tested by the infidels in III Nephi 1:9.

ORDINATION AND MINISTRY IN THE BOOK OF MORMON
G. St. John Stott

"All are called according to the gifts of God unto them," Joseph Smith III told the 1887 General Conference of the Reorganized Church of Jesus Christ of Latter Day Saints (hereafter referred to as RLDS church). The appointee and the ordinary member (by implication both the self-sustaining minister and the unordained) were called alike to "labor together with God for the accomplishment of the work intrusted to all" (Doctrine and Covenants 119:8b). In the hundred years since no one has equaled the formulation "all are called" for either concision of inclusiveness, and so, not surprisingly, recent discussion of the status of the ministry of the unordained—a category which, even after the recent provisions for the ordination of women are acted upon, will include most RLDS[1]—has taken President Smith's words as its starting point. But to start with Joseph Smith III involves the risk of ignoring, or forgetting, or never finding out what earlier understandings of the place of the unordained in the church had been. The result has been the neglect of insight brought to the church by Joseph Smith, Jr., particularly in the Book of Mormon—even though the Book of Mormon provides a context in which God's call to each church member (as affirmed in Doctrine and Covenants 119) makes compelling sense.

At first glance the Book of Mormon seems to suggest two models for a call into God's service.[2] On the one hand there is a clear presumption that revelation given to an ecclesiastical superior will direct an individual's call to a specific priesthood office. Thus we read in Mosiah 11:17-19, "Now Alma was their high priest...and none received authority to preach or to teach except it were by him from God." The authority to minister within the church is given—by inspiration—by the church's presiding high priest. This is a familiar enough position for Latter Day Saints: no one taking the honor of priesthood upon self without being "called of God, as was Aaron" (Hebrews 5:4, KJV), and Aaron being called to minister in the priest's office by God's revelation to Moses (Exodus 28:1). Or as Joseph Smith, Jr., wrote in the "Wentworth letter": "We beleive that a man must be called of God by 'prophesy, and by laying on of hands' by those who are in authority to preach the gospel and administer in the ordinances thereof."[3]

On the other hand, the Book of Mormon also reports the ministry of those who were unordained, or merely ordained by those who are clearly without authority themselves, without any doubts as to its legitimacy. The most notable example is the ministry of Abinadi. One of Noah's people, Abinadi "went forth among them and began to prophesy, saying, 'Behold, thus saith the Lord, and thus has he commanded me, saying, Go forth'" (Mosiah 7:28-30). No doubt because the Nephite church of the day was blind to the spirit of revelation "because of the wickedness of their king and priests" (Mosiah 7:27), this ministry was given in opposition to both church and state, and without the benefit of an ecclesiastical call. So was that of Abinadi's disciple, Alma I.

One of Noah's court priesthood, Alma fled the court after failing to influence the king, and began a clandestine teaching and baptizing ministry at the waters of Mormon without being called to the work by an ecclesiastical superior. His call—like that of Abinadi—was unmediated; it came directly from God.

These two accounts of how God calls individuals into service could hardly be more different. The one involves a direct, unmediated call: a private vocation which has nothing to do with the church. The other describes a public call, given through the church, in which there is no necessity for a sense of vocation on the individual's part. An although one could hypothesize that the two models are complementary rather than contradictory since, ideally speaking, any individual called to a priesthood office would receive a personal witness to the rightness of the church's call, such a hypothesis cannot be educed from the Book of Mormon. No Nephite (or Jaredite) is reported as viewing his vocation as a legitimation of an ecclesiastical call. The two callings were always seen as distinct.

As it happens, early Latter Day Saint thought distinguished between God's *modus operandi* in calling a prophet, and the means whereby he calls the priesthood of an organized church. He was thought to speak directly to the prophet, calling him to gather and organize a church, but indirectly (through the prophet—the church's presiding high priest) to those who are to serve in its priesthood. The unmediated call was thus something exceptional: part of the prophet's experience, but not known to the rest of the church since they were called through him. "No man can administer salvation . . . except he is authorized from God by revelation, or by being ordained by some one whom God hath sent by revelation," Joseph Smith, Jr., wrote in 1839,[4]

clearly distinguishing between the unmediated call of the man directly authorized from God by revelation, or by being ordained by some one whom God hath sent by revelation," Joseph Smith, Jr., wrote in 1839,[4] clearly distinguishing between the unmediated call of the man directly authorized by God and the ecclesiastical calls of those ordained by him (or by those sent out by him) under the spirit of revelation. But for all its attractiveness this model of the relationship between the two calls cannot be applied to those described in the Book of Mormon.

The problem is not that unmediated calls do not occur in times of apostasy, when a church needed to be organized or reorganized, and a religious elite bypassed because they rejected the spirit of revelation. They obviously do. The cases of Alma and Abinadi have been noted, and other examples can easily be found in both Nephite and Jaredite history. Thus during the period of corrupt religiosity which marked the beginning of Benjamin's reign, prophets suddenly appeared "among his people" in Zarahemla, proclaiming the word of God "with power and with authority" (Words of Mormon 1:25-26). And unlike the priests which Benjamin later appoints (Mosiah 4:4), the prophets derived their authority from their vocation, not from any ecclesiastical call. Similarly, among the Jaredites, during the reign of Shule,

there came prophets among the people, who were sent from the Lord, prophesying that the wickedness and idolatry of the people were bringing a curse upon the land, and they should be destroyed if they did not repent.—Ether 3:61

Shule protected these prophets (Ether 3:63), but they were not his to command. They were "sent from the Lord," not commissioned by the king.

Such unmediated calls, however, did not occur only in times of apostasy. Even when the church was faithful and responsive to the Spirit, the Book of Mormon reports, God would sometimes speak directly to an individual rather than through the church's high priest. The story of Ammon provides a case in point. One of the sons of Mosiah II was, like his brothers and Alma the younger (the son of the high priest), an "unbeliever" who rejected the faith of his father and was not a member of the Zarahemla church. He, his brothers, and Alma II are converted, however, when God sends an angel to them; and immediately following their commitment to Christ they begin a lifetime of service to the church:

[They] traveled round about through all the land, publishing to all the people the things which they had heard and seen, and preaching the word of God in much tribulation, being greatly persecuted by those who were unbelievers, being smitten by many of them. But notwithstanding all this, they imparted much consolation to the church, confirming their faith, and exhorting them with longsuffering and much travail, to keep the commandments of God.—Mosiah 11:201-2

Thus they bring to a persecuted, but still faithful, church a full-time revival ministry of preaching and exhorting—without the benefit of an ecclesiastical call.

Of course it could be argued that there was such a call, never recorded as part of the Book of Mosiah (or, if recorded, edited out by Mormon). Such a call could have come before the conversion with Alma telling the incredulous rebels that God had a work for them to do—but they not believing him until they were born again. Or again it could have come after the conversion, as part of the church's recognition that "they were instruments in the hands of God" (Mosiah 11:206). In either case the fact that the call has gone unmentioned points to its unimportance for the author or redactor of Mosiah; and it is not hard to see why. A pre-conversion call from the church would pale into insignificance beside the discovery of God's love—or at least that was to be Mormon's experience. At the age of ten he had been called by Ammoron to be the Nephite record keeper (and, by implication, the religious leader of his people), and instructed to take up his responsibilities when he was twenty-four years old (Mormon 1:1-5). But then, at the age of fifteen, he was "visited of the Lord, and tasted, and knew of the goodness of Jesus" (Mormon 1:16)—and it was this experience rather than the call from Ammoron that he was to remember when he justified his work on the Book of Mormon plates. "I am a disciple of Jesus Christ, the Son of God," he wrote. "I have been called of him to declare his word among his people, that they might have everlasting life" (III Nephi 2:97). The ecclesiastical call was forgotten; the only call that mattered for Mormon was the unmediated one from Christ. We must suppose that it would have been the same for Ammon, or the historian of his conversion. As for a post-conversion call, it too would seem to be redundant when it was so evident that God was working in the lives of Ammon and the others.

It is perhaps significant in this context that not only is there no mention of an ecclesiastical call for Ammon, there is also no mention of a baptism. Since baptism, according to II Nephi 3:69, was to serve "as a witness and a testimony before God and to the people that [those baptized] had repented and received a remission of their sins,"[5] it was probably unnecessary for Ammon and his companions to be baptized. They had, after all, provided that witness straightway after their conversion in the most public of circumstances. ("I have repented of my sins, and have been redeemed of the Lord; behold, I am born of the Spirit," Alma testified [Mosiah 11:186].) If that were so, and the self-evident fact of being born again made the ritual of a baptismal witness to the new birth unnecessary—and the comparable

246

instance of there being no baptisms when all of Benjamin's people were converted, leaving no one to witness to by the ordinance, suggests that it could be (Mosiah 3:1-9; 4:1, 2)—then it is not impossible that a self-evident vocation could make the church's call and ordination without any point.

Be that as it may, some better explanation for the silence on the question of an ecclesiastical call for Ammon and the others is needed than that the author of the Book of Mosiah forgot. The narrative of the Book of Mormon is usually full of detail, with even "unimportant" events included. Thus, although Ammoron's call had little importance for Mormon by the time he wrote his history, it was still mentioned. And when Alma II succeeded his father as high priest it is duly recorded how he had that office "conferred... upon him" (Mosiah 13:63), even though the mere fact of his succession was all that the narrative needed at that point. But nothing is said about Ammon and his brothers. Common sense suggests that, given the copiousness of the Book of Mormon, if no call was mentioned then, for one reason or another, there was no call.

This commonsense assumption seems to be born out by Ammon's own testimony before Lamoni's court. Required to defend his authority to teach the gospel, he made no mention of an ecclesiastical call. "Are you sent from God?" Lamoni asked him, and he replied, not with a reference to a commisssioning and sending forth by Alma I and the Zarahemla church, but with a testimony of his vocation: "I am called by his Holy Spirit to teach these things" (Alma 12:111-12). Presumably the vocation was all there was—and that being so it is impossible to see an ecclesiastical call and a subsequent ordination as *sine qua non* for ministry in an organized church.

Nothing is known of how Abinadi was called (except that it was by an unmediated call), but Alma I, Alma II, the sons of Mosiah, and Mormon all received their vocation with their conversion. Conversion— the discovery of salvation in Christ—created in them a desire to serve that was nonexistent before. Before they were saved Alma the elder was content with his status as a priest in the corrupt priesthood of Noah's court, his son and the sons of Mosiah were unbelievers, and even Mormon was no more than "a sober child." After conversion—indeed, immediately after conversion—they move from a concern for personal salvation to a desire to minister to others. The first Alma gathers a church around him at the waters of Mormon; the second Alma, together with Ammon and his brothers, sets off on a preaching tour of the Nephite churches, and Mormon endeavors to preach to his people, until the Lord stops his mouth. In each case the new birth brings a desire to bring others to "the knowledge of the truth, and to the knowledge of their Redeemer" (Mosiah 11:206). The Holy Spirit which effects the conversion also brings the call.

The operation of the Spirit was different in each case, of course. Alma I was touched by its power as he listened to Abinadi's preaching; Mormon was overwhelmed by its witness when alone; Alma II, together with the sons of Mosiah, was subdued by its power revealed in the ministry of an angel. But not too much should be made of the differences, and what is peculiar to each call. Although, for example, there was an angel speaking "as it were with a voice of thunder, which caused the earth to shake" (Mosiah 11:163), it was neither the personality of the angel nor the voice of thunder which won Alma and his companions to Christ. What they responded to was "the power of God" (Mosiah 11:170)—the power which, in the Book of Mormon, lies behind all conversions (cf. Mosiah 1:120). The angel was thus by the way:[6] what was important was the Holy Spirit's transformation of five unbelievers into servants of God. This transformation was what the younger Alma's experience had in common with his father's, or with that of Mormon, or (by implication) with all other conversions.

The idea that conversion brought a transformation of character, and that a person's call to give ministry came with his or her conversion was a theological commonplace of the world addressed by the Book of Mormon. It had entered American theological thinking with the assumption of Jonathan Edwards that sin was selfishness and virtue disinterested benevolence,[7] and though most of Edwards's system was to suffer from neglect in the nineteenth century, this idea did not. Joseph Bellamy's definition of conversion in his *True Religion Delineated* (1750), a definition elaborated from Edwards's ideas, could thus serve the needs of the revivalists of the Second Great Awakening (an awakening which touched Palmyra and the young Joseph Smith) as well as summarize the lesson to be drawn from the first:

Conversion [Bellamy wrote] consists in our being recovered from the sinful state we are in, by nature, to a real conformity to the divine law; that is, in our being recovered from a disposition to love ourselves supremely, live to ourselves ultimately, and love that which is not God wholly, and a practice agreeable to this disposition; to a disposition to love God supremely, to live in him ultimately, and to delight in him superlatively, and to love our neighbors as ourselves; and a practice agreeable thereto; . . .[8]

This view of conversion lies behind Charles Grandison Finney's reflection that "convicted, repentant, renewed sinners" would have "their love to men renewed . . . and be filled with a tender and burning love for souls"[9] and it parallels the understanding of conversion to be found in the Book of Mormon.

Alma II, for example, follows a pattern almost exactly like that described by Bellamy, moving from selfishness and alienation from God to a Christ-centered life of service. He was at first "a very wicked and idolatrous man" (Mosiah 11:159), but after his conversion he passed through the stages of conviction: "I remembered all my sins and iniquities for which I was tormented with the pains of hell" (Alma 17:10); repentance, "O Jesus, thou Son of God, have mercy on me" (Alma 17:16); and renewal, "I was harrowed up by the memory of my sins no more . . . [and] my soul was filled with joy" (Alma 17:17, 18). His life then became one of ministry to others.

From that time even until now, I have labored without ceasing that I might bring souls to repentance, that I might bring them to taste of the exceeding joy of which I tasted, that they might also be born of God and be filled with the Holy Ghost. —Alma 17:22

A similar description is given of the conversion of Ammon and his brothers. They were "the very vilest of sinners" whom the Lord "saw fit in his infinite mercy to spare" (Mosiah 12:7-8). "The Spirit of the Lord [worked] upon them" (Mosiah 12:7) and brought them to know "much anguish of soul because of their iniquities" (Mosiah 12:8) before bringing them to salvation. "They were desirous that salvation should be declared to every creature, for they could not bear that any human soul should perish" (Mosiah 12:5). Since these individual conversions follow a pattern that was thought normative in the religious culture in which Smith had grown up,[10] he would have felt no need, either as author or as translator of the Book of Mormon, to make explicit to a contemporary audience that what happened to Alma II and the sons of Mosiah was typical rather than exceptional.[11] Almost certainly Smith would have taken for granted, and presumed that his readers would have done the same, that in the world of the Book of Mormon as well as in the America of his day, every conversion marked the convert's call to ministry.

The relationship between the ecclesiastical call and the vocation is thus the opposite of the first of the hypotheses mentioned above. The two calls *are* complementary—but it is the vocation which is primary, not the ecclesiastical call. The vocation, as we have seen, is the desire to minister to the needs of others which comes with new birth. It begins as an unfocused and unchanneled concern for others and is only later given direction as personal (unmediated) revelation prevents inappropriate service and indicates the ministry that is desired. (Although this ongoing revelation is obviously part of the call, the call begins with the gift of the desire to serve, and it is this initial vocation which concerns us here.)

The ecclesiastical call enters the picture when the ministry desired by God is that belonging to an office in the priesthood. Under some circumstances the ecclesiastical call provides a specific context in which the vocation could be lived out—a relationship between the two very different from that in which the vocation was merely supposed to validate the priesthood call.

As it happened, few were called to the priesthood of the Nephite church, presumably because all church members were thought to be called by virtue of their conversion to the church's basic ministries of caring and witnessing. No one needed a call through the church to undertake them. Those whom Alma I baptized in Mormon, for example, having accepted his message of "repentance, and redemption, and faith on the Lord" (Mosiah 9:37), were expected

to bear one another's burdens that they may be light, and . . . to mourn with those that mourn, and comfort those that stand in need of comfort, and to stand as witnesses of God at all times, and in all things, and in all places . . . even until death. —Mosiah 9:39-40

Only a minority of Alma's converts—one out of every fifty (Mosiah 9:51) —were ordained ministers, and even these few were given an ecclesiastical call only because certain ministries within a congregation or group needed to be entrusted to a single individual.

At its most elaborate, Nephite polity envisaged two ordained ministers serving a congregation—the priest and the teacher. The nomenclature is perhaps confusing because the priest's responsibility was to teach. They were "to preach to [their congregations], and to teach them concerning the things pertaining to the kingdom of God" (Mosiah 9:51). The teacher, though he could teach, was primarily to govern the congregation (Mosiah 11:98).

Few other details are given, but evidently Smith had anticipated no confusion over the nature of these offices and he felt no need to gloss his text. Nephite congregations must have reminded him of something he knew well—perhaps Methodism, with its governing class leaders, and the teaching ministry given to the preacher or exhorter[12] or the classical Presbyterian polity of pastor and teacher respectively charged with teaching and governing under the direction of a presiding elder,[13] except that the Nephite church probably had no presiding elders on the congregational level. Certainly something along those lines can be imagined as being the case in Zarahemla—perhaps even something similar to the early LDS church (its deacons excepted)[14] with the priests called "to preach, teach, expound, exhort" and the teachers "to watch over the church always" (Doctrine and Covenants 17:10a, 11a).

It takes less imagination to see why priests and teachers were needed in the Nephite church than to imagine what that church was like. Without these ministers, individual churches would have risked doctrinal anarchy and the breakdown of discipline. Not everyone could be *the* expounder of doctrine, or *the* governor of a church. If conflict was to be avoided there needed to be an authoritative source of doctrine or church government. Further, in order that those who were to preach, teach, and govern could be seen to minister with the authority of the church (even by those blind to the inherent spiritual authority of their ministry—for which, see below) it was necessary that their call be mediated through the church. Otherwise they would be open to the charge, and perhaps even the temptation, of raising up churches to themselves.[15] and yet for all the undisputed importance of the priesthood, it should be obvious that those who served in other ways—without an ecclesiastical call were no less "called" than those whose ministry required a public, mediated call and ordination. In the one case, revelation to the church's presiding high priest called an individual to ministeral office. In the other, unmediated revelation to the individual gave direction to his or her desire to serve. The one revelation was hardly superior to the other.

Neither was the authority of the priesthood greater than that of the unordained. In the one case, to be sure, the ecclesiastical call had been followed by what was variously described as appointment, consecration, or ordination. ("Appointment" was a term used to refer to the whole process of calling, installing and perhaps even ordaining. "Consecration" had reference to the installation of a new minister in a congregation. "Ordination," however, usually only referred to the laying on of hands to set an individual apart to a priesthood office.) But though the ritual of consecration and ordination could mark an individual as the one God wanted to perform a certain kind of ministry and though no one not so consecrated and ordained could rightly perform that ministry in a faithful church, the legitimacy of specific acts of ministry was not deducible from the fact of ordination. The authority of a person's ministry was discovered in the witness of the Holy Spirit. This witness was not reserved for the ministry of the ordained.

Those whom Alma I ordained priests were supposed, by God's grace, to "wax strong in the Spirit...that they might teach with power and authority from God" (Mosiah 9:59), but they were not the only ones. All who ministered for God were supposed to be empowered by his Spirit, and their ministry was to reveal their empowerment. Since God worked "by power" (Moroni 10:7) any ministry inspired by God had to be a revelation of that power. The revelation was not necessarily dramatic, though it could be, as when the power of God prostrated Lamoni's court (Alma 12:151), but it was sensible. A person could recognize the inspiration of an authentic act of ministry by the presence of the Spirit in its performance. If a minister acted in the power of the Spirit, his ministry was authoritative; if he acted without the Spirit, his ministry had no authority at all.[16] The same was true of the ministry of the unordained: if blessed by the Spirit's witness it was as authoritative as could be desired; if not it was the absence of the Spirit and not the lack of ordination which made the act human rather than godly.

The scruples shown by Ammon (not the son of Mosiah, but a descendant of Zarahemla) when urged to organize a church among the people of Lehi-Nephi illustrate this point. Although Limhi and many of his people desired baptism,

Ammon felt that no one in the land, himself included, "had authority from God" (Mosiah 9:176). He suggested, therefore, that they not immediately organize a church but wait instead for God to supply their needs. So they waited not for a minister to be sent from Zarahmela to baptize them but for the Spirit to come upon them so that they could, with perfect authority, "form themselves into a church" (Mosiah 9:177). As it happened Limhi and his people left Lehi-Nephi for Zarahemla before any such endowment occurred, and in Zarahemla they were baptized by Alma I. But Alma's authority was hardly greater than, or even different from, that awaited by Ammon. Alma claimed no authority on the basis of his ordination to Noah's court priesthood; instead he dated it from an outpouring of the Spirit at the waters of Mormon (Mosiah 9:44—that is, from just such a cleansing endowment as Ammon had looked for.

Although the Book of Mormon does not rule that authoritative ministry is signaled by the presence of the Spirit and by nothing else, we would hardly expect such explicitness from a history, not a theological textbook, unless its latter-day readership needed instruction on that point. They did not. Ever since the first Great Awakening, "New Light" preachers had been teaching Americans to value the witness of the Spirit above seminary training and a certificate of ordination. Not surprisingly, Smith felt no need to elaborate on his text. A figure such as Alma—authorized in his ministry by the Holy Spirit rather than by his ordination to the priesthood of a corrupt, established church—would have seemed no more controversial in 1830 than did John Wesley. Wesley, Methodists argued (and most evangelicals would have agreed), derived his authority as a reformer from God's call and empowerment, and not from his Anglican priesthood. As Nathan Bangs expressed it,

it was not...the credentials which he received from the archbishop of Canterbury which gave him either his qualifications or his commission; but it was most evidently his other endowments, his designation to this work by the Head of the Church, and the influence of the Holy Spirit. These were his credentials. On these his claims rested. [17]

When Bangs pointed to an unmediated call from Christ and an endowment of the Spirit as Wesley's qualifications for ministry he was not seeing the founder of Methodism as a special case. Any minister who was not called, directed, and empowered by the Holy Spirit was, for Bangs, but a "blind leader of the blind," and completely without spiritual authority. [18] This attitude was widespread. As a result, congregations expected the Spirit to "apply the truth [of a sermon] with demonstrative power to the heart," and thereby validate a minister's words; [19] and, in general, looked for the "awakening, convincing" power of the Spirit to act as the "seal" to any ministry. [20] Smith consequently hardly needed to enlarge on the theme of authority when working on the Book of Mormon. In this respect the work brought to its first readers a message that they were well prepared to accept when it showed ministers looking to the Spirit of God and not to their ecclesiastical call and ordination as the source of their legitimation.

A lack of ordination, therefore, did not mark a man or woman [21] as "uncalled" or unempowered in the world of the Book of Mormon. As already noted those charged with priesthood ministries in the Nephite church were given by their ordination an unquestionable ecclesiastical authority. But the presence of the Holy Spirit, the sign of divine power rather than church status, served to confirm the comforting and witnessing ministry of the unordained (even preaching, teaching, and exhorting, as long as it did not usurp the magisterium of the priesthood) as well as the teaching, governing, and, by extension, sacramental[22] ministries of the church's leaders. The ecclesiastical call that preceded ordination was not an exceptional call—even for the ordinand. Revelation to the church, through the presiding high priest, merely complemented and gave fresh direction to the unmediated call that had come with conversion to every member of the church. As they discovered salvation and came to feel, in the words of Alma II, "to sing . . . redeeming love" (Alma 3:46) all were indeed called into the service of God.

Notes

1. In 1982, the last year for which the total number of RLDS priesthood has been published, there was one ordained member for approximately every twelve unordained (11.97, to be precise). These figures make no allowance for inactivity, but taking that factor into account still makes the priesthood a minority in the church. See *World Conference Bulletin* (1984): 111, and (1982): 158.

2. There is a conscious naïvete here. The Book of Mormon doesn't suggest: either its pre-Columbian authors do, or Joseph Smith, Jr., does; the Book of Mormon does not. However, as I wish to sidestep the issue of authorship and concentrate on the content of the Book of Mormon I deliberately attribute the suggestion to the book itself. As it will be immediately obvious I do not see this device of attribution as a means to gloss over real or apparent internal differences of doctrine.

3. Dean C. Jesse, *The Personal Writings of Joseph Smith* (Salt Lake City: Deseret Book, 1984), 219.

4. Ibid., 421.

5. The same view of baptism can be found in Doctrine and Covenants 17:7. Although II Nephi 13:7-9 treats baptism as mandatory, Book of Mormon history does not show this view of baptism to have been generally held. II Nephi 13 differs in other areas of doctrine from the Book of Mormon norm, and should be used only with caution. A consideration of possible reasons for this contamination lies outside the scope of this paper.

6. "Angels speak by the power of the Holy Ghost," but then, after receiving the gift of the Holy Ghost, so can men and women (II Nephi 14:2-3). The messenger was relatively unusual, but not the force of his message.

7. Edwards was following Shaftesbury and Frances Hutcheson in this, but he insisted that human beings had no natural impulse to benevolence but stood in need of grace.

8. *The Works of Joseph Bellamy, D.D., First Pastor of the Church at Bethlehem, Conn., with A Memoir of his Life and Character*, 2 vols. (Boston: Doctrinal Tract and Book Society, 1853), 1:163.

9. *Lectures on Revivals of Religion* (1835), rev. enl. ed. (Oberlin, Ohio: E. J. Goodrich, 1868), 15.

10. Jesse, 6.

11. For a discussion of emendations clarifying and elaborating on the meaning of the Book of Mormon text, see Stan Larson, "Changes in the Early Texts of the Book of Mormon," *The Ensign*, September 1976, 77-83.

12. Smith was possibly a member of a Methodist probationary class while in his teens (Pomeroy Tucker, *Origin, Rise, and Progress of Mormonism* [New York D. Appleton, 1862] 18), and is reported to have attended the Methodist church in Harmony, Pennsylvania, while working on the Book of Mormon (*Amboy Journal*, April 30, and June 11, 1879). In 1838 Smith was to report that prior to his first vision he had become "somewhat partial to the Methodist sect" (Jesse, 198).

13. Presbyterian polity is discussed in Charles Augustus Briggs, *American Presbyterianism: Its Origins and Early History* (New York: Scribner's, 1885), 96; the Smith family's involvement in Presbyterianism is outlined in Milton V. Backman, Jr., *Joseph Smith's First Vision: The First Vision in Its Historical Context* (Salt Lake City: Bookcraft, 1971), 67-69.

14. Smith's failure to define a deacon's calling, and the omission of any reference to the deacon in lists of priesthood office in the earliest text of "the Articles and Covenants of the Church of Christ" (i.e. ch. XXIV of the Book of Commandments) suggests that the office of deacon was an afterthought.

15. Raising up churches to oneself is described in IV Nephi 1:28f and prophesied in Mormon 4:42.

16. When "the Spirit of the Lord is grieved and...has withdrawn" from an individual, Smith wrote to the church on March 20, 1839, "amen to the priesthood or the authority of that man" (Jesse, 401). The connection between authentic ministry and the Holy Spirit can also be seen in Doctrine and Covenants 83:3c, though the idea that ordinances are a necessary preliminary to theophany is foreign to the Book of Mormon.

17. Nathan Bangs, *An Original Church of Christ; or, A Scriptural Vindication of the Orders and Powers of the Ministry of the Methodist Episcopal Church* (New York: G. Lane, 1837), 299.

18. Ibid., 298.

19. James Bradley Finley, *Sketches of Western Methodism: Biographical, Historical, and Miscellaneous, Illustrative of Pioneer Life*, ed. W. P. Strickland (Cincinnati: J. B. Finley, 1854), 209.

20. *The Autobiography of Peter Cartwright, the Backwoods Preacher*, ed. W. P. Strickland (Cincinnati: Swomstedt and Poe, 1860), 456.

21. Although the women of the Nephite church did not receive ecclesiastical calls to be a congregation's priest or teacher they were, by their conversion, as much called to give ministry as the men. Presumably the implied ban on women teaching and governing was, like that in the New Testament or Smith's own day, a reflection of contemporary cultural standards. (See Ramsay MacMullen, "Women in Public in the Roman Empire," *Historia*, 29:2 [1980], 208-19, for a valuable discussion of socially acceptable roles for women at the time Paul was writing. Amanda Porterfield provides a useful starting point for understanding the place of women in the churches of the early nineteenth century in *Female Spirituality in America: From Sarah Edwards to Martha Graham* [Philadelphia: Temple University Press, 1980].) As cultural understandings of women's social roles changed it became possible for women to serve in new ways within their congregations. But, from the perspective of the Book of Mormon, Doctrine and Covenants 156:9 has not made women ministers when they were not before. Revelation has enlarged the scope of their ministry, but it has not promised either a call or an empowerment which women, in common with unordained men, did not already have as "children of Christ" (IV Nephi 1:20).

22. In organized churches, ordination, baptism, laying on hands for the gift of the Holy Ghost, and "administering the flesh and blood of Christ" were ministries performed by elders and priests (Moroni, chapters 1-6). Elders were formerly called disciples (Moroni 3:1) after the twelve disciples chosen by Jesus in his New World ministry (III Nephi 5:18-22; cf. III Nephi 2:97, and Doctrine and Covenants 17:8b: "an apostle is an elder..."). Prior to Christ's appearance in Bountiful the ministry of a disciple (sc. elder/apostle) was given under the Old Testament title of high priest. Outside of organized churches—and in times of apostasy—baptism could be performed by the unordained, and those baptized could organize themselves into a church (sc. congregation). Unity between the various congregations came from their accepting the leadership of the presiding high priest or disciple.

REINTERPRETING THE INSPIRED VERSION

C. Robert Mesle

Traditionally, Latter Day Saints have thought of the Inspired Version (Joseph Smith's "New Translation") of the Bible as a restoration of the original biblical texts. Since Joseph's lifetime, however, there has been an explosion in knowledge of the Bible comparable to the explosion of scientific knowledge in many other fields. In the last century and a half scholars have discovered older and better copies of the biblical texts and have greatly expanded their knowledge of biblical languages and history. These discoveries, if considered honestly, lead to a reinterpretation of the Inspired Version.

Older Texts

In the 1800s the oldest text of Isaiah available to scholars was only about 800 years old, having been copied about A.D. 1000. In 1947 the Dead Sea Scrolls were found; these included copies of the book of Isaiah dating from about 150 B.C.—1,150 years closer to the original! This is only one case of many in which recent discoveries have provided older and better texts of the books of the Bible. Though no *original* texts of biblical books are extant today, there are literally thousands of ancient copies of them, and they do not support the traditional view of Joseph's work as being a restoration of the original texts.

Two Creation Stories

Joseph shared the usual belief that Moses was the author of the Pentateuch—the first five books of the Bible. Consequently, he rewrote the early chapters of Genesis as if God were speaking directly to Moses. In doing so, he apparently recognized that there are actually two separate accounts of creation in Genesis 1 and Genesis 2. He tried to solve this problem by inserting in Genesis 2:5 the suggestion that God created all things spiritually before creating them naturally. Latter Day Saints should be aware that when Joseph produced the Book of Abraham he once again presented the creation story as if God were recounting it. But there Joseph replaced the phrase "I, God, said," with "They, the gods, said." This evidence suggests that these works represent his own theological speculations.

Over the past 150 years biblical scholars have reached virtually universal agreement that Moses did not write the Pentateuch. It is the product of at least four major strands of oral tradition which were written down and edited together by different people over a span of centuries.[1] For convenience scholars have designated these four strands with the letters J, E, D, and P. The J strand was probably committed to writing about 1000 B.C. and begins with the creation story which now appears in Genesis 2. The E strand was written down a century or two later. Deuteronomy, written between 700 and 550 B.C., provides the bulk of D though D includes some other material as well. The P document was produced by Hebrew priests about 500-400 B.C., during or shortly after the Exile, when they were trying to emphasize the central role of the priests in Israel in the absence of any polit-

J (c. 1000 B.C.)

Then the Lord said to Moses,
"Pharaoh's heart is hardened,
he refuses to let the people
go. Go to Pharaoh in the
morning.

And you shall say to him,
'The Lord, the God of the
Hebrews, sent me to you
saying, "Let my people go,
that they may serve me in
the wilderness; and behold,
you have not yet obeyed.
Thus says the Lord, By this
you shall know that I am the Lord."

the fish in the Nile shall
die, and the Nile shall become
foul, and the Egyptians will
loathe to drink water from the Nile.'"

And the fish in the Nile
died; and the Nile became
foul, so that the Egyptians
could not drink water from the Nile;

And all the Egyptians dug
round about the Nile for
water to drink, for they
could not drink the water
of the Nile.

E (c. 750 B.C.)

Go to Pharaoh in the
morning; wait for him by the
river's brink, and take in your
hand the rod which was turned
into a serpent.
And you shall say to him,

"I will strike the water that
is in the Nile with the rod
that is in my hand, and it
shall be turned to blood."

and in the sight of Pharaoh
and in the sight of his servants,
he lifted up the rod and struck
the water that was in the Nile, and
all the water that was in the Nile
turned to blood.

(But) Pharaoh turned and went
into his house and did not lay
even this to heart.

P (c. 400 B.C.)

And the Lord said to Moses,
"Say to Aaron, 'Take your
rod and stretch out your
hand over the waters of Egypt,
over their rivers, their canals,
and their ponds and all their
pools of water, that they may
become blood; and there shall be
blood throughout all the land of
Egypt, both in vessels of wood and
in vessels of stone.'"
Moses and Aaron did as the Lord
commanded.

the magicians of Egypt did
the same by their secret
arts; so Pharaoh's heart
remained hardened, and he
would not listen to them;
as the Lord had said.

ical leadership. P begins with the creation story of Genesis 1. Each tradition tells and expands Israel's faith stories with its own theological concerns.

An excellent example of the ways in which these strands were woven together is found in the accounts of the Exodus. To best appreciate the example given here, carefully read Exodus 7:14-24. Try to keep track of who actually performs the miracle, and what the miracle actually is. Difficulties will gradually emerge. Then see how the apparently unified account can be "unwoven" into three distinct stories with different miracles and different major actors.

Notice that in J, God performs the miracles directly. J consistently presents God as the major actor, while Moses serves as spokesperson. E always emphasizes the importance of Moses. Thus Moses performs the miracle (with God's power) by wielding the rod. The priests (P), however, went to establish their own authority on the example of Aaron, so they insert him into the story and present him as the user of the rod.

There is also a marked growth of the miraculous. In the earliest account (J), God kills the fish so that the water becomes foul. In E, Moses turns (only) the Nile to blood. (Good editing creates the impression that this killed the fish.) In the account furthest from the event—as would be expected—the miracle is most spectacular. Aaron turns not only the Nile but all the water in Egypt into blood (compare verses 19 and 24).

This is a small but striking example of what scholars have found running throughout the Pentateuch. Such evidence overwhelmingly supports the view that it is a product of many hands over many centuries and not a single document produced by Moses as it was dictated by God. It also accounts for the presence of two creation stories. Genesis 1 fits the theology of P, while Genesis 2 fits the style and concerns of J. There is no need to posit distinct spiritual and natural creations.

It is important to stress that during Joseph's lifetime modern biblical scholarship had not yet really emerged as a fruitful discipline. Scholars had not yet recognized the four strands of tradition in the Pentateuch. Thus Joseph's recognition of the problem and his attempt at a creative solution can be appreciated, but that appreciation should not negate 150 years of learning by scholars around the world.

Hardening Pharaoh's Heart

The account of the Exodus provides another fine example of the Inspired Version as Joseph's theological commentary on the Bible. In chapters 7-14 there are ten places where the text indicates that God hardened Pharaoh's heart (7:3, 13; 9:12; 10:1, 20, 27; 11:10; 14:4, 8, 17). In other places the text more ambiguously reads simply that Pharaoh's heart was hardened. It is the priestly account which asserts clearly that God caused the stubbornness, and it dominates the story.

In every place where P indicates that *God* hardened Pharaoh's heart, Joseph changed the text to say that *Pharaoh* hardened his own heart. It is easy to understand and sympathize with the motives for this change. It is repugnant to suppose that a loving God would intentionally make persons unloving and rebellious. Our main concern, however, is with the intent of the original author.

The perspective of P is clearly stated in the Jerusalem Bible translation of Exodus 10:1-2.

Then Yahweh said to Moses, "Go to Pharaoh, for it is I who have made his heart and his courtiers stubborn, so that I could work these signs of mine among them; so that you can tell your sons and your grandsons how I made fools of the Egyptians and what signs I performed among them, to let you know that I am Yahweh."

While this thesis is stated throughout the story, it is clearest and most inescapable—even in the Inspired Version—in chapter 14, where the account climaxes at the Red Sea. Moses is directed to trick Pharaoh into thinking that the Israelites have foolishly trapped themselves against the sea. God then promises:

I for my part will make the heart of the Egyptians so stubborn that they will follow them. So shall I win myself glory at the expense of Pharaoh, of all his army, his chariots, his horsemen. And when I have won glory for myself, at the expense of Pharaoh and his chariots and his army, the Egyptians will learn that I am Yahweh.—Exodus 14:16-18, JB. See also 14:1-4, 8.

This plan, of course, succeeds in convincing both Egyptians and Hebrews that the God of Israel is sovereign.

If any doubt remains about the intent of the original biblical author, it should be removed by Romans 9:15-18 RSV, a section in which Paul indicated his reading of Exodus and in which Joseph made no changes:

For [God] says to Moses, "I will have mercy on whom I have mercy, and I will have compassion on whom I have compassion." So it depends not upon man's will or exertion, but upon God's mercy. For the scripture says to Pharaoh, "I have raised you up for the very purpose of showing my power in you, so that my name may be proclaimed in all the earth." So then he has mercy upon whomever he wills, and he hardens the heart of whomever he wills.

Clearly Paul understood in Exodus that God hardened Pharaoh's heart, which decisively establishes that the scriptures available to Paul read basically as they appear in the King James Version and modern translations, not as Joseph changed them to read. (Someone might argue that the "errors" crept into the text even before Paul's time. But if God directed Joseph to make such corrections, why not Paul?) It seems clear that Joseph's changes, regardless of whether they are theologically preferable, reflect his *own* theology and not that of the *original* biblical author.

The Coming of the Kingdom

The value of understanding the Inspired Version as commentary may also be shown in Joseph's treatment of New Testament texts predicting the imminent coming of the kingdom. Here again one encounters a virtually universal agreement among biblical scholars—that most early Christians expected Jesus to return in their own immediate future. For example:

And [Jesus] said to them, "Truly, I say to you, there are some standing here who will not taste death before they see the kingdom of God come with power."—Mark 9:1 RSV; 8:44 IV

And he [Christ] said to me, "These words are trustworthy and true.... Behold, I am coming soon...for the time is near.... Behold I am coming soon."—Revelation 22:6, 12 RSV

Joseph did not change these passages. Other important passages he left unchanged include Mark 1:14-15; Matthew 16:27 (IV 16:31); I Corinthians 15:51-52; Matthew 10:5-7, 23 (IV 3-6, 20); I John 2:18; and Revelation 1:1; 3; 14:7.

Obviously for the early Christians to have been mistaken on such a central issue is distressing to many modern Christians. Joseph apparently recognized many passages in which the belief in Christ's imminent return was clearly stated and changed them to allow for a more futuristic interpretation. Compare the following passages as they appear in the Inspired Version and other Bibles: Mark 13:24-30; I Thessalonians 4:13ff; I Corinthians 7:26-31; 10:11. Notice that Paul includes himself and his original readers among those who will be alive when Jesus returns. This belief so permeated the thought of Paul and other New Testament authors that it could not be eliminated by simply amending a few lines. Here again, Joseph offered a theological commentary rather than restoring the original texts.

Conclusion

The Inspired Version is a valuable resource for understanding the thoughts of Joseph Smith, Jr., regarding certain scriptural passages. It can be a helpful resource for persons seeking to reflect on the relationship between the Bible and their own theology. Sometimes Joseph's insights were historically sound.[2] But Saints do both Joseph and themselves a serious injustice if they view his work as a restoration of the original texts of the Bible, and an even more grave injury if they refuse to use other versions of the Bible for not being "inspired."

Restricting use to the Inspired Version, as if it were a perfect translation, closes one off from the insights of centuries of dedicated biblical scholars. Modern versions such as the Revised Standard and Jerusalem Bible represent the best available knowledge of the original biblical texts and their meanings. They should be used also by any who wish to fully honor Joseph's deep passion to understand the scriptures.

1. Interested readers should review Walter Johnson's excellent article, "Background of Bible History" Part I, in the *Saints Herald*, August 1980.
2. With so many changes made, it is not surprising that some turn out to be historically correct as well as theologically interesting. One good example is given in Angela Crowell's responsible article, "Joseph Smith's Translation of the Lord's Prayer," in the *Saints Herald*, July 1983.

V
BIOGRAPHY

BIOGRAPHY

Editor's Note:

Nathan James Weate, Ph.D. (social studies education), teaches at the Junior-Senior High School in Lamoni, Iowa. He has degrees also in liberal studies and in professional writing. Co-author F. Carl Mesle, B.A., has been involved for many years in civic and community affairs in Independence, Missouri, where he has served in various ministerial roles for the Reorganized church.

The article by Thomas J. Morain, Ph.D. (history), is the presidential address delivered at the 1982 annual meeting of the John Whitmer Historical Association and it appeared in Volume 3 (1983) of the association's *Journal*. He is research historian for Living History Farms at Des Moines, Iowa, and a grandson of John F. Garver of whom he writes.

JOHN KALER
MISSIONARY AND MOLDER
Nathan James Weate with the assistance of F. Carl Mesle

We never know the legacy we will leave. John Kaler didn't know, but his persistent efforts resulted in some significant dividends to both the church and the community.

John Kaler's daughter Edna Royster taught in the Raytown, Missouri, schools for over thirty years and was highly acclaimed both as an educator and a contributor to charitable causes.[1] An older son Elmer served the church faithfully for nearly eighty years, and was remembered by the Saints in the Kansas City Stake as a spiritual counselor and a tireless cook at camps and reunions.[2] A younger son Asa Hiram ("Al") built up a nationwide mail-order business which he generously transferred to his loyal employees at retirement time.[3]

What caused Edna, Elmer, and Al to do these things? The answer can be found partly in the quality and type of life that John Kaler lived. He molded the outlook and attitudes of his children just as definitely as he served as a missionary. His assignment to Australia provides the best insight into this unusual man.

John Kaler was born in 1866 in Ohio, the son of poor, immigrant, German Catholic parents, and was the only son born this side of the Atlantic.[4] All his brothers died early. His father and two brothers died during an epidemic of typhoid fever in Ohio during the 1870s. John and two sisters lived to adulthood.[5]

While still quite young John was "bound out," since his parents could not provide for the family, but John had the

mettle to survive his days of indenture. He learned to farm, and he learned carpentry and cement skills. He worked diligently for his overseer and was confident he was being prepared for a greater work.[6] He read his Bible and later stated that as he read his boyhood religion became unsatisfactory to him.[7] He searched many Protestant denominations and finally chose, at age twenty, to affiliate with the Congregational church in Ohio. By this time he was a slender, six-foot-tall, stern, but kind, young man.[8]

A short time after his conversion to the Congregational church, John journeyed to Knob Noster, Missouri, where he encountered the Restoration and was baptized March 14, 1888.[9] In rapid succession, he was ordained a priest (May 26, 1889), undertook full-time ministry (spring, 1890, to the Independence, Missouri, District), assumed elder's responsibilities (April 14, 1891), and accepted the work of a seventy (April 14, 1892).[10] Shortly after his ordination to the office of seventy, John was assigned by World Conference action to the Australasian mission and left for that assignment, only to receive word from the First Presidency when he reached Denver to proceed no farther until additional instructions were sent.[11]

John's report of his Denver activities states: "I have preached 92 times, baptized 8, blessed 13 children, administered to the sick 100 times, and ordained one deacon."[12] That delay of a little more than one year influenced more than his relationship with the church: he married a young widow, Mrs. Mary (Babbitt) Healy, on June 13, 1893. His journey to Australia was resumed with her at his side.[13]

Perhaps companionship provided their only earthly solace in those next few weeks for the trip on that turn-of-the-century vessel, the S.S. *Australia,* proved demanding for both of them. They spent from July 6 to July 13 going to Honolulu. Leaving Honolulu July 29, they arrived August 5 in Apia, Samoa, and then sailed on to Auckland, New Zealand, arriving at Sydney, Australia, on August 15.[14] The little ship pitched and tossed, rolled and slid, causing John and Mary seemingly endless days and nights of seasickness, although one of the sailors told John it was a remarkably smooth voyage. For the rest of his life, John had an aversion to sailing.[15]

After arriving in Australia, John lost little time becoming engaged in missionary duties. He and Mary stayed for a while at the home of George Lewis.[16] John "labored," he writes in his diary, by preaching on the street and in private homes.[17] Very early in his Australian assignment he encountered an old-time RLDS family, the Flood family (grandparents of Bishop Frank Flood).[18]

After nearly a year, on August 2, 1894, his diary entry states: "Obtained house of Bro. Wright . . . put in some garden in front and back yard."[19] He wrote,

Mary fixed up the house quite lovely by spending some over £10—of her own and I also sent some household goods from Sydney including a nice New Home Sewing Machine [with which Mary] earned considerable by sewing.[20]

Three weeks later on August 23 John had secured the agency for New Home Sewing Machines.[21] This tendency to be engaged in various entrepreneurial activities—carpentry, sales, cement and masonry, landscaping—persisted throughout John's life. But an interesting aside is the involvement of Mary in the sewing machine agency.

Mary, the daughter of Ira and Rachel (Nowell) Babbitt, was born February 11, 1863, in Doniphan County, Kansas, across the Missouri River from St. Joseph, Missouri. Mary's mother, Rachel, was the daughter of Mormon parents, Silas and Nancy (Hatch) Nowell. They were sturdy stock: Mary's grandmother, Nancy, was born February 28, 1805, and lived until 1902.[22] Mary Salvina Babbitt married John Timothy Healy, a railroad section foreman, and they had two children, John and Will, before John Healy died in 1884 of a railroad accident on the Lexington branch line of the Missouri Pacific.[23] In order to provide for these two young sons, Mary and her parents agreed that Mary would move from Napoleon (Lafayette County), Missouri, to nearby metropolitan Kansas City where she could earn good wages as a dressmaker in a shop near Tenth and Baltimore. John and Will went to live with Mary's parents on a farm near Caney, Kansas. Mary forwarded a substantial portion of her weekly earnings to her parents, providing not only for her sons, but supporting her parents as well. By the time Mary remarried her sons were nearly raised, so she went to Australia willingly, although her parents felt more than a bit of consternation since her contribution to their finances was significant, and was now being cut off.

Mary's ability as a seamstress must have been one reason John Kaler obtained the sewing machine agency.[24] With her helping with the family finances, John could spend additional time in ministry. Of course, he must have already been very much occupied with missionary labors because his diary entry of January 1, 1895, contains this General Conference report for 1894: "Preached 68 times, baptized 2, Confirmed 7, Adm. to Sick 26 times and blessed 10 children. Traveled 1925 miles." He gave the breakdown of those miles into 396 by water, 268 on trains, 1060 by wagon, and 200 on foot (note the one mile discrepancy).[25] Whether one journey of that year was recorded as on foot or by wagon is unknown.

John traveled with Gomer Wells. After ministering in the home of a Brother Rodgers, they left Laurieton for Nambucca, about 110 miles away, only to be misdirected. They

had 25 miles rough bush road only saw one settler dark and rain came on us and we lost our way but after many miles of careful traveling we happily came to the main road.... [Some distance down the main road, they found an empty house.]

Oh, how tired I was for I had walked about 12 miles befor* the trap** to chose the road, for Gomer to drive in for it was dark with dense forest on either side, for the last few miles I had sharp pains in my back & chest & I prayed my heavenly father to protect us from sickness during this unavoidable exposure. I went to the creek near and drew up water in a bottle with a part of the harness line and prayed the lord to bless it to my good that it might be both food and drink to me.... so we traveled about 52 miles or more, 25 over hilly and sometimes rough and muddy roads with no accommodation for night.... At midnight we laid down on the porch of the old house and I slept for couple hours and felt better, but G [Gomer Wells] slept little. At 4 AM Wed. May 2 we hitched up and by help of the rising new moon, we continued our journey one of us walking ahead. At 6 o clock we came to ferry and crossed road good but hilly. 9 AM at "Bowra" small village, at 11 at Argents hill P.O. and were welcomed at the very nice, comfortable, home of old bro and Sr. Argent whose house is on hillside faceing river bottom, ... We came about 110 miles in little over two days.[26]

Increasingly, John traveled by foot. He wrote on January 10, 1895, to the *Saints' Herald*:

I have determined ere now to travel and preach, money or no money. And this can be done by carrying a tent, blankets for bed, food, etc. I have

---

* The underlines, spellings, and grammar in all quotations are unchanged from the original.
** A "trap" is a small, horse-drawn carriage.

found this way of traveling to work splendidly, as the climate here is well suited to "camping" nearly all the year.[27]

Such dedication on his part matched natural events of equal determination, since the Australian winter of 1895 from about April or May through August was the "coldest and dryest ever known" with "bush fires rageing everywhere." John reflected that the elements worked hardships on all.[28]

Gomer Wells worked with John in Sydney during that winter. A terrible summer followed the cold, dry winter, and on January 25, 1896, Gomer wrote to the *Saints' Herald* that "the heat of this summer is unparalleled in the history of this country. Mercury has registered 108° here in Sydney, while farther inland 116 to 120 has been reached—all in the shade."[29] The results of such climatic fluctuations were most felt on agriculture, not only in Australia, but around the world, for that was a year of unseasonable weather everywhere.[30]

The Kaler family soon experienced another change, about as momentous as going to Australia, for on July 8, 1896, their first child, Elmer, was born.[31] But, other things were also aborning for which John could take partial credit. The Hamilton church building in Newcastle, New South Wales, had been completed toward the end of 1895.[32] Also, things were moving fast in Sydney. C. A. Butterworth, the seventy appointee minister who was in charge of the work in Australia, purchased a building site in Balmain (Sydney, New South Wales) for $390. A church member from Tuncurry who owned a sawmill promised fifty dollars' worth of lumber. Three of the local members who were carpenters and builders donated their time.[33] By the end of the year, progress on the Sydney building was good.[34]

John was also engaged in other things.

Since Cornelius Butterworth enjoyed good seafood, the two of them fished and oystered to obtain those delicacies.[35] On August 24, 1897, he wrote that he had been "getting out timber to build me a house there [Sydney] on church lot."[36] Gomer Wells had helped John learn some of the finer points of carpentry work such as hanging doors, installing window sashes, and building cabinets.[37] At this time, John's work seems to shift from the stage of "getting acquainted" into "maturity." This may have been partly due to changes in John's outlook and attitude, but much of it was the natural growth of the church groups, societal changes, and Australian movement from several colonies toward a nation-state.

To be sure, John and his co-workers had preached the gospel in many places. Those first few years of reports of John's ministry carry the names of Wallsend, Tuncurry, Nambucca, Newcastle, Hamilton, Balmain, and Sydney in New South Wales, Queensferry in Victoria, and Adelaide in South Australia.[38] The church in Australia grew from 362 at the beginning of 1893 to 588 at the end of 1897, an increase of 62 percent in just five years.[39] Such an increase, accompanied by the construction of two buildings and the expansion of programs, was now followed by a period of consolidation and stabilization of efforts. As preparation for a new era of church work in Australia, the Victoria District and New South Wales District conferences each made requests through official motions to the General Conference asking that a member of the Twelve be assigned to the "Land Down Under."[40] Such an assignment would provide not only a more powerful missionary thrust to the work in the island continent, but also a stronger administrative voice to the work both in Australia and at the World Church level.

The move into their new home marks the beginning of the second phase of John and Mary's assignment to Australia. The move from the Wright house to Sydney was by boat and began on September 27, 1897. John wrote: "We got our goods all ready to move to Sydney...and we went by S. S. *Express*...had splendid journey. Elmer didn't get sick, but Mary & I did." The move wasn't a one-step achievement: "From Oct 7 to 31st Bro. Ellis & I got the house ready for use by 10 days help from W. Ellis—I worked hard against odds for we had to move our goods 3 times in one month and I had hard work to obtain." Then on November 1, "We moved into our new cottage on church lot 65 Nelson Street Balmain West."[41]

As 1898 unfolded, John continued to be very active. On April 13, he assumed ownership of a bicycle agency. The bicycles he handled were a unique, chainless type that had a worm gear and driveshaft mechanism. They were not successful, and he had overspent on advertising, but the next month he sold some bicycles, which was amazing since Australia was moving into the winter season.[42]

By the end of 1898, John could write with satisfaction about three items: spiritual blessings, temporal prosperity, and family growth.

I have been blessed in delivering the word, we also have prospered temporally as well as in Spirit so that the Cottage is paid for and I am also out of debt and have the necessities of life. Our Baby girl [Edna] born Oct 9th has prospered nicely and is a lovely child. The year closes and all is well with us, thank God.[43]

The year 1898 was also significant to the church. Gomer Wells began relying greatly on a bicycle (probably purchased from John Kaler) for missionary travel, thus promising greater mobility and speed.[44] Another advantage to the church came from an article in the *Town and Country Journal*, a Sydney weekly publication which was decidedly the largest of its type in Australia. A picture of the three appointees—Butterworth, Kaler, and Wells—and another of the Sydney elders was printed along with an article outlining the church's statement of faith and commenting on the distinction between the Utah and Independence groups. A series of debates between John and a Christadelphian provided even more publicity.[45] Baptisms did not follow from this intense effort, however, nor did they the following year even though Butterworth, Wells, and Kaler were joined by another appointee, Walter Haworth.

During 1899, John seems to have prospered even more, since he was able to purchase a "new chainless cycle" which he took to a conference at Newcastle. He was unable to use it, however, because of wet weather and decided to cancel a missionary trip up the coast due to wet and cold weather. He indicated he was particularly pleased, in spite of the cold, since he had sufficient work to earn money which allowed him "to buy me good winter clothes—Good all wool undershirts proved a blessing that I never enjoyed before but I expect to wear them in the future."[46]

One item of significance to the church during 1899 was that publication began on the *Australian Ensign*. This may have been premature since the *Saints' Herald* carried a plea early in 1900 for American subscribers so that costs could be covered, but even this request was insufficient since the *Ensign* suspended publication during 1900.[47]

Gomer Wells returned to the United States early in 1900 after seven years in the "Land Down Under."[48] John and Gomer had become popular ministers during their tenure together. For one thing, they only charged £3 ($15) to perform a marriage ceremony whereas ministers of other churches charged £5 ($25).[49] Walter Haworth became John's

missionary companion and the two of them traveled by bicycle throughout the countryside of New South Wales. Argent's Hill, Tuncurry, Krambach, and Rozelle are all mentioned in his report book as meeting places.[50] It appeared that John would soon find his work accelerating. Then, in June 1900, he recorded: "Wife very bad with what seemed nervous prostration and pain in head so was unable to do any work at all for a time."[51] While Mary showed slight improvement from time to time, this undiagnosed illness plagued her until she died in 1949. Another change occurred. John's explanation is not clear, but for some reason the Kaler family moved, on August 8, 1900, from the cottage next to the church into a house at 128 Evans Street, Balmain West.[52]

The Australian membership had increased little between 1897 and 1900—from 588 to 608.[53] But 1901 was a different year. First of all, much progress was made on the Wallsend building in Newcastle.[54] Second, a new complexion was given to the entire country since on January 1, 1901, Australia's status in the British Commonwealth shifted from that of several independent colonies to a federation of states.[55] The Kaler family experienced growth through the birth of a third child (the second son), Asa Hiram, on April 24.[56] Missionary efforts were boosted by the return of Gomer Wells in October.[57] John retained an interest in what was happening to the broader church movement, showing his concern by writing: "I am pleased to learn that Graceland College is receiving substantial aid, and hope all indebtedness will soon be cancelled forever."[58] And, on still another front, John recorded that on November 1, "I opened the work at Brisbane Queensland and continued to baptize till I had baptized & confirmed 28—27 of these were Brighamites. I organized a branch there." The group, calling themselves the South Brisbane Branch, included, within seven weeks of the time John arrived, two elders, one priest, one teacher, and one deacon.[59] Also, during the year, John recorded yet another time when he experienced contact with Bishop Frank Flood's grandparents, writing: "I went to Parramatta, visited Bro. [John] Flood."[60] By year's end, the membership in Australia had grown to 697, a 15 percent increase in just one year.[61]

But even 1901 was not as eventful as 1902. For one thing, the long-sought-after ministry of an apostle was granted by General Conference action. Apostle J. W. Wight, who had previously labored in Australia as a missionary elder, was returned in his new office; in addition, Seventy C. A. Butterworth was called to the Council of Twelve and his assignment continued in Australia.[62] What had been unavailable previously to the Australian Saints was now granted in duplicate. Such ministry along with the growing momentum of the Australian Mission resulted in another surge of membership from 697 to 803.[63] John was not present for part of this expansion, however, since he and his wife and family returned midyear to the United States.[64] In his last letter to the *Saints' Herald* before leaving Australia he wrote the following:

One of the worst drouths ever known here has been raging the past six months and in some parts there is no food or water for man or beast.

Here in Sydney, vegetables are scarce and high and the outlook for winter is very gloomy, for poor people. Butter forty cents and steadily advancing, they expect it to be sixty-two cents during winter. Milk is ten cents a quart, and everything higher than I have seen it for eight years. Most of the Saints live near the coast where the drought is not near so severe, but yet all classes will be more or less effected by the great ruin wrought by months of dry neather [sic], heat, and fire inland.

All efforts to eradicate the bubonic plague here have failed; it continues in a mild form. "Change and decay in all around I see."

Wife's health is very poor and I trust the change back to her native clime will revive her health.[65]

On May 13, 1902, John, Mary, Elmer (nearly six years old), Edna (three and one-half years old), and Al (just thirteen months) set sail from Sydney on the S. S. *Sierra*. If the trip over had seemed rough, this trip back would make them wish the good times would return. Waves went clear over the ship. For two days, the ocean was so rough that cooks couldn't prepare food and none was served. After the worst had passed, soup was served to the passengers in jars so that the top could be removed, a quick sip taken, and the top clapped on again before the next pitch or roll. Had it been a less stout ship, all might have been lost, but the S. S. *Sierra* survived these South Pacific turmoils and continued in service through World War II.[66]

John's ministry was missed by the Australian Saints. In a letter dated July 31, John's long-time missionary friend, Gomer Wells, wrote, "We have . . . *lost* much in the returning of Elder Kaler. He is a long-headed fellow and wisdom is not absent from his deliberations, and we haven't any of such workers to spare."[67]

John was not to lose any time, on his return to the United States, finding additional opportunities to labor in the ways Gomer Wells knew him to work—he simply changed one pasture for another. In the next several years, he served the church in the Spring River (1902-1903), Northeastern Missouri (1903-1905), Central Oregon (1906-1907), and Eastern Oregon (1906-1907) districts, and Independence Stake (1905-1906, 1907-1911).[68]

Those years were extremely busy ones for John. Mary's illness plagued her more after their return from Australia.[69] John took her frequently to Eldorado Springs for mineral water treatment. The Kalers usually visited the home of Roy S. Budd, who was later to be an apostle, which undoubtedly provided a spiritual uplift for John. On one of those trips Mary became hysterical because the bright sunlight hurt her eyes so much. Her head was completely covered, and at the next train stop she was placed on a straight chair and two or three men carried her from the station down the street to a hotel, up a narrow, outside staircase to a second floor room. After staying in the room for the night, Mary was able to resume the trip.[70]

Because of Mary's prolonged illness, John assumed many household and gardening duties which, in that day, were typically the wife's responsibility. While their home at 1221 E. Walnut in Independence, Missouri, which still stands today, had a small back lot, John had the space filled with such produce as Kentucky Wonder beans, sweet corn, radishes, and green vegetables. Neighbors and church friends provided other vegetables as well as fruits in abundance which John promptly canned if they could not be used immediately.[71]

John continued his ministry in America although Mary's illness increased in severity. He was frequently seen street preaching in downtown Kansas City during the evening. The street vagrants and derelicts would heckle and taunt him with questions which, to many, seemed ridiculous, but John answered each question with patience, indicating his conviction that God loves each one and wants to show each the way.[72] John's patience was not just a sham. His children remembered him as stern but extremely kind. He didn't often threaten them with a whipping, one child recalled, but even if John said he was going to administer "laying on of hands," he could be talked out of it.[73] His attitudes seemed, in many ways, advanced for the age in which he lived. He weighed matters carefully and made decisions on the basis of what he deemed

right and true rather than by prevailing attitudes. As an example, he permitted his children to attend movies, which was unusual for that day. He would reach in his pocket, remove one dime for each child's admission, then say he had better give them each another dime since he was sure they would want popcorn.[74]

In 1905, the church yielded to John's request that he be assigned to the Pacific Northwest. It was John's firm hope that the change in climate would improve Mary's condition. If anything, her condition worsened after one year in Castle Rock, Washington, and Montavilla, Oregon, so John requested reassignment to the Independence, Missouri, area so Mary could be close to the medical facilities of the Sanitarium.[75]

After returning from the West Coast, John labored under many constraints, partly (perhaps largely) due to his wife's continued illness. He recorded in 1908 that he was "Very much tied at home."[76] This bothered him, since he strongly desired to minister to the church, its people, and those to whom he could take the gospel. His entries for 1908 contain this explanation:

Wife in dark room all year with little change over last year, part of year I hired housework done and worked out to make up balances   rest of time I did the work myself   preached Sundays Some in Kan. C and suburbs, But was the poorest record I have made since I entered into missionary work nearly 20 year ago.[77]

That poorest record in twenty years amounted to attendance at 200 services, preaching 35 times, 3 baptisms, in charge 12 times, and 1 marriage.[78] John gives some insight into one of the major problems which beset appointees of that day. He explains that he "worked out to make up balances" since appointees typically were not given sufficient elders' and family expenses to provide for needs.[79] With Mary's illness complicating matters, John had to work for pay more than most appointees and had more household duties to do.

John's entries for just one month in his Ministerial Labor Report Booklet, the month of August 1909, give some insight into the various tasks he did with no complaints. This booklet was not a diary, so should not be compared with what one would expect to find in a diary. Each page was only 3½ inches by 6½ inches. Pages were ruled into thirty-one lines for the days of the month plus several lines for monthly summaries and fifteen to twenty columns to enter such items as number of times preached, number of people baptized, and other ministerial functions. John kept all of his records on these sheets, then wrote small entries on each day, telling of events and thoughts. For August, 1909, he recounts the following:

Home feeling dull from hard work
Put in sewer   2.50
So. Side people to build Ch.
Tent work   Ind—Mo.
Canned green beans 13 qts.
spoke on 'Watch the Way'
spoke in tent on Divine Healing
made tomato and apple butter and canned some
canned 14 qts corn   wash day
very hot of late, made jam
Alex. S. died last week   Buried Sunday
work on st. curbing last three days
Doing all home work again   Canned apples

John had a strong interest in world events. Partisan politics did not normally catch his eye, but matters dealing with the weather, exploration, discovery, production, conflict, and social conditions had strong appeal. Two of John's entries from September 1909, are fascinating:

Dr. Cook claims to have reached North Pole a year ago last April

. . . .

Commander Peary wires that he reached Pole last April, discredits Cooks claim

Such interests seem to be outmatched only by his desire to serve the church and by his love of family.

Throughout his writings he refers to something a family member did or something he did for a family member. Examples:

October, 1909 Got suits for boys Mtgomery Wards Spent $25.00
January 15, 1910 Took Ma Sanitarium 1 P.M.
February 17, 1910 Ma a month in Sanitarium
February 28, 1910 To K.C. got. . .suit for Elmer
April 24, 1910 Asa Sick Staid at Home
April 25, 1910 Asa 9 yesterday
April 30, 1910 Grandad Babbit came to see us
May 2, 1910 to Sanitarium with Grandpa
October 6, 1910 repairing house so mama can come home
February, 1911 Came home 8 P.M. Mama not well, hurt herself worked at home with house work   children were all tired doing it all

There are repeated entries about canning, washing, housework, adding to or reconstructing their home, working for others as a handyman, visiting Mary in the Sanitarium, writing for church publications, and going on missionary trips.

Several things stand out about John Kaler: First is his love for people. He constantly served others. He had unbelievable stamina, doing carpentry, masonry, landscaping, and plumbing tasks while a full-time minister. One of his children commented, "Dad worked from morning 'til night." The molding of lives occurred by force of personality and example. His three children, although only fifteen, thirteen, and ten years old when he died, exemplified those same qualities seen in their father.

To the end of his life, John Kaler was also a missionary. In fact, he was planning a series for Fort Scott, Kansas, when he became ill in early September of 1911. He had drunk milk from a cow that had drunk water from a stream condemned because of typhus bacteria. His temperature soared several times to 108° F.[80] He entered the Independence Sanitarium and Hospital, worsened quickly, and died on September 12.[81] I. N. White said during funeral obsequies that John Kaler's kindness and prayerfulness, his reliance on God, his strong testimony to the divinity of the work, and his zeal in vindication of the truth were remarkable.[82] Doctor Joseph Luff commented that he loved John Kaler because of his integrity and love of the gospel work, and that he was always to be depended on.[83] A necrology printed in the *Journal of History* stated: "He was ever faithful and true and was fully relied upon, by the church, to act well his part."[84] A *Zion's Ensign* article affirmed the following:

Bro. Kaler was diligent and faithful in his work. He was an efficient laborer as a minister, the secrets of his success being humility before God, and his disposition to study. He bore his burdens cheerfully and without complaining, being always ready to help in any good work. He was untiringly devoted to his family through the long and trying affliction of his companion, because of which he was compelled to remain at home the greater part of the last few years, but whenever opportunity was afforded he was busy in his calling as a minister.[85]

And in *Church History* was recorded this: "Brother Kaler was remembered for his integrity and kindness and for his excellent primary pioneering ministry in Australia where he served for nine years."[86]

Mary lived for almost forty years after John's death. She suffered from the same health problems which began in Australia until the time of her death, described in her obituary in the following terms: "While in Australia, she began to have trouble with her eyes, and in later years she had to spend much of her time in darkened rooms."[87]

Regarding the church's work in Australia, much progress has been made.[88] This progress is most evident in the number of congregations and their locations. More than forty church groups provide ministry in New South Wales, Victoria, Queensland, South Australia, West Australia, and Australian Capital Territory.[89]

John Kaler converted people to the Restoration message, but he did more than that: he shaped the lives of people with whom he associated and never forgot his duties to family. The result is that he left a legacy in the form of children who have benefited church and community. John Kaler was an unusual man— a devoted father and husband, a capable and tireless workman, a committed Christian—because he knew how to be both a missionary and a molder.

Notes

1. *Kansas City Star* (about 1965). Article titled "Party Expresses Pupil Gratitude."
2. Comments made to writers by friends of Elmer Kaler.
3. *Kansas City Star*, Monday, February 8, 1982, 8A.
4. *Saints' Herald* (January 3, 1891): 10.
5. Conversation with Al Kaler, January 1984.
6. Conversation with Les Kaler, December 1983.
7. *Saints' Herald* (January 3, 1891): 10.
8. *Saints' Herald* (January 3, 1891): 19; conversation with Al Kaler, January 1984.
9. Pearl Wilcox, *Saints of the Reorganization in Missouri* (Independence, Missouri: published by the author, 1974), 164-165, 401.
10. John Kaler, "Minister's Diary," John Kaler Journals and Papers, RLDS Library and Archives, Independence, Missouri, inside front cover.
11. *General Conference Minutes*, 1892, 83.
12. *General Conference Minutes*, 1893, 24.
13. John Kaler, "Minister's Diary," 21.
14. Ibid., 21.
15. Conversation with Al Kaler, January 1984.
16. John Kaler, "Minister's Diary," 23.
17. Ibid., 25.
18. John Kaler, "Personal Journal," John Kaler Journals and Papers, RLDS Library and Archives, 33.
19. John Kaler, "Minister's Diary," 27.
20. Ibid., 26 (side notes to p. 27).
21. Ibid., 27.
22. Biographical sheet in John Kaler Journals and Papers, RLDS Library and Archives.
23. Conversation with Al Kaler, January 1984.

24. Conversations with Les Kaler (December 1983) and Al Kaler (January 1984).

25. John Kaler, "Minister's Diary," 28.

26. John Kaler, "Personal Journal," 36-37.

27. *Saints' Herald* (February 27, 1895): 136.

28. John Kaler, "Minister's Diary," 32 and 33.

29. *Saints' Herald* (March 11, 1896): 168.

30. *The History of the Reorganized Church of Jesus Christ of Latter Day Saints* (Independence, Missouri: Herald House, 1969), vol. 5, 369.

31. John Kaler, "Minister's diary," 41.

32. *RLDS Church History*, vol. 5, 369.

33. *Saints' Herald* (December 16, 1896): 322.

34. *RLDS Church History*, vol. 5, 369.

35. John Kaler, "Minister's Diary," 40.

36. *Saints' Herald* (October 6, 1897): 631.

37. Conversation with Al Kaler, January 1984.

38. John Kaler, "Minister's Diary."

39. *RLDS Church History*, vol. 5, Appendix D, Statistical Summaries, 645.

40. Ibid., vol. 5, 413.

41. John Kaler, "Minister's Diary," 53.

42. Ibid., 58, 61; conversation with Al Kaler, January 1984.

43. John Kaler, "Minister's Diary," 65.

44. *RLDS Church History*, vol. 5, 451; *Saints' Herald* (December 28, 1898): 828.

45. *RLDS Church History*, vol. 5, 451-452; *Saints' Herald* (April 20, 1898): 246-247.

46. John Kaler, "Minister's Diary," 66-68.

47. John Kaler (*Saints' Herald*, July 11, 1900): 452-453; *RLDS Church History*, vol. 5, 476; "Minister's Diary," 75.

48. *RLDS Church History*, vol. 5, 509; *Saints' Herald* (March 21, 1900): 178-179.

49. Conversation with Al Kaler, January 1984.

50. John Kaler, "Minister's Diary."

51. Ibid., 79.

52. Ibid., 81.

53. *RLDS Church History*, vol. 5, Appendix D, Statistical Summaries, 645.

54. Ibid., vol. 5, 510.

55. Ibid., vol. 5, 519.

56. John Kaler, "Minister's Diary," 85.

57. *RLDS Church History*, vol. 5, 519.

58. *Saints' Herald* (December 18, 1901): 1020.

59. John Kaler, "Minister's Diary," 87.

60. Ibid. (January 1, 1900 to December 31, 1901), entry for March 1, 1901.

61. *RLDS Church History*, vol. 5, Appendix D, Statistical Summaries, 645.

62. Ibid., vol. 5, 589-590.

63. Ibid., vol. 5, Appendix D, Statistical Summaries, 645.

64. Ibid., vol. 5, 590.

65. *Saints' Herald* (May 21, 1902): 516.

66. John Kaler, "Minister's Diary" (January 3, 1902 to May 28, 1905), entry for May 13, 1902.

67. *Saints' Herald* (September 3, 1902): 859.

68. *RLDS Church History*, vol. 5, 575; vol. 6, 58, 99, 145, 181, 242, 286, 333, 370, 400.

69. John Kaler, "Minister's Diary" (January 1, 1902 to May 28, 1905); *Ministerial Labor Report Booklet* (January 3, 1908 to December 32, 1911). This booklet is privately owned by Les Kaler.

70. Conversation with Al Kaler, January 1984.

71. *Ministerial Labor Report Booklet;* conversation with Al Kaler, January 1984.

72.-75. Conversation with Al Kaler, January 1984.

76. *Ministerial Labor Report Booklet.*

77. Ibid.

78. Ibid.

79. Ibid.

80. Conversation with Al Kaler, January 1984.

81. *Zion's Ensign* (September 21, 1911), p. 2 and (September 28, 1911), pp. 4 and 5.

82. *Saints' Herald* (September 27, 1911): 927.

83. *Saints' Herald* (September 27, 1911): 927.

84. *Journal of History* (Lamoni, Iowa: Board of Publication, Reorganized Church of Jesus Christ of Latter Day Saints), January 1912, 124-125.

85. *Zion's Ensign* (September 21, 1911): 1.

86. *RLDS Church History*, vol. 6, 415.

87. *Saints' Herald* (November 5, 1951): 1078.

88. Conversation with Al Kaler, January 1984.

89. *Church Directory* (Independence, Missouri: Herald House, 1984), 5-7.

Addendum

1. *Ministerial Labor Report Booklet* was graciously loaned to Jim Weate by Les Kaler. It has since been returned.

2. All of John Kaler's personal accounts other than his *Ministerial Labor Report Booklet* which were used in preparation for this article were on file in John Kaler Journals and Papers, Accession 5277, Library and Archives, the Auditorium, Reorganized Church of Jesus Christ of Latter Day Saints, Independence, Missouri.

A FANTASIA ON THE DIARIES OF JOHN GARVER

Thomas J. Morain

(Reprinted by permission from *John Whitmer Historical Association Journal*, Vol. 3.)

Neither side of my family tolerates profanity in normal conversation, but most of them accept it when there is no other way to say something quite so effectively. I say this to put in perspective one of my grandfather's favorite stories. John Garver was on a preaching mission somewhere staying all night with a family when a young boy in the house felt called upon to defend his father. With all the conviction he could muster, the boy emphatically insisted: "Any man who says he doesn't like my dad is a damned liar." I don't know how Apostle John Garver reacted to that piece of information, but I rather believe that the boy escaped serious censure for his word choice.

It has been my observation of the Garver family that the little boy's dictum would also express the feelings of Garver's own three daughters toward their father and that that opinion is generally shared throughout wide circles in the church. "Any man who says he didn't like John Garver is a damned liar." I was two years old when my grandfather John Garver died, and I have no personal recollection of him. I think I missed something.

I do not plan to present a biography of Garver. You may be convinced that this paper certainly doesn't tell everything there is to tell about the man, and you will be right. But please remember, I warned you that biography is not my intention. Granted, we do need to know something about the author of the diaries, but the questions they have raised for me in the past two years are not necessarily answered by knowing more about the man who wrote them.

I have chosen as my title "A Fantasia on the Diaries of John Garver." In music, a fantasia is "a composition of no fixed form with a structure determined by the composer's fancy." I could think of no better description of this paper. Not only did I need something that could stretch a little to let me include some different approaches to the material, but it is a good reminder of the way I have lived with the diaries. I have found in them a springboard to wonder, to frustration, to contemplation. This paper is less an account of Garver than it is an exposé of its composer's fancy, but, at least for its author, it has been a very rewarding experience.

I needed a title that permitted me the freedom to deal with the diary in two ways. On one hand, I want to discuss the historic value of the diaries—what they tell us about life in Lamoni seventy years ago, the routine of a young RLDS appointee, the theological and administrative concerns of the church at the time. On the other hand, however, I need the freedom to explore some of the larger questions which I found myself confronting as I lived with the diaries. On several occasions, a daily entry chronicles how God played a direct role in the events recorded: healings, revelations, prophecies. This is not the stuff with which historians feel most comfortable, but I want to deal with the material as honestly and as completely as I can. Can historians be believers? Must we pretend that we do not believe things like that to be good historians? If we accept one account of divine intervention as historic fact, must we accept all accounts? Or shall we validate only the weirdos we like? In short, I found myself asking: how should historians deal with Divinity? It is the question which a serious student of Mormon history must confront at some time. However, I want it clearly understood that I do not regard what I am about to present as an encyclical binding on all John Whitmer members. It comes in the form of a very personal progress report, where I am floundering at the present time.

Therefore, the queasiness you may be feeling by this point is entirely justified, for what follows I would not inflict on any other group of which I am a member. Like it or not, this paper is very much a product of my love affair with the entire John Whitmer Historical Association which for the past nine years has been for me a very important source of intellectual, social, and spiritual nourishment.

While there have been many high points, three moments from past Whitmer meetings are so much a part of this paper that I must cite them directly. The first was a prayer at Park College by Alma Blair in which he begged that we never treat the sacred facts of our history as footnotes with which to pad our professional careers.

The second was what I consider to be my conversional experience in Mormon history. It was at Nauvoo at the first annual Whitmer meeting. Jan Shipps read a paper on the psychological orientation of Joseph Smith, and suddenly I saw things in a whole new way. At the time, my religious heritage seemed increasingly to be offering two dead-end options: (1) to embrace a tradition which required me to put my intellectual training

on the shelf and to accept a rather preposterous story on the grounds that some good people had accepted it before me, or (2) to reject that tradition and then decide whether to edge out of the church slowly or to stay and sit quietly so that I would not disturb the believers. But Jan's paper changed all that. She posed alternatives which had never occurred to me and dived in after answers with all the intellectual rigor she could bring to the subject. A whole new world opened up for me that afternoon. Before that, faith required a suspension of critical thought. After that, faith encouraged the best critical thought I could bring to it. Since the first Whitmer meeting, I have never attended a conference where I did not find the thrill of stretching in search of better answers and still better questions, or where I did not feel the joy of sharing with good friends who were there for the same reason and with the same expectations. For nine very good years, John Whitmer, I thank you.

At a Whitmer meeting in the chapel of Park College, Velma Ruch presented a slide lecture on English churches and the changing style of crosses. In a beautifully illustrated slide series, she gave examples of people whose lives were changed because they felt they had been touched by God and given a mission. It was not until about a year ago that I put together her theme with what H. Richard Niebuhr had observed about his own studies in American religious history. He wrote a book entitled *The Social Sources of Denominationalism* to argue that American churches were better explained by economic, political, and social forces than by theological concerns. But in later years, he recanted a bit. While such forces could account for the way churches developed, economics or politics did not adequately explain what he termed "the religious impulse," what Ruch was calling "the way of the cross." The banks of a stream guide its course but they don't explain its origin. Historians chart the course of the stream, Niebuhr was suggesting; they don't account for its source.

At World Conference in the spring of 1978, my mother and her two sisters, Mrs. Verna Smith and Mrs. Bertha Johnson, were at Aunt Bertha's with assorted cousins up and down the generational line. John and Mynn Garver's daughters grew up in Lamoni as part of a clan of thirteen cousins within a one-block area on North Silver Street, under the water tower. In the middle of the afternoon, Aunt Bertha pulled out some items which she had stored from grandmother's apartment since the latter's death in 1959. Among them was a small locked tin box which had never been opened because no one had the key. However, a cousin from Des Moines was there who, fortunately, had married a professional safecracker. (He owns Strauss Lock Company.) With a few simple tools and thirty minutes reprieve from the running narrative update on his in-laws' family and friends, Uncle Bud picked the lock and opened the box.

No one had paid much attention to the box before because Grandmother had said there was nothing important in it. To her, that was probably true. There were just some old papers, the kind that are hard to throw away because of their sentimental value but useless to keep around. There were several of Grandpa's themes from his freshman English course at Graceland, and a description of their wedding service from a 1907 *Lamoni Chronicle*.

There were also three small books, Grandpa's diaries from 1908 to 1912. The largest book held the first three years and proved to be the best. The latter two books had been printed to be diaries, with the day of the year printed at the top of each page, thus prescribing how much space to devote to each day's events. The pages in the first book, however, were originally blank, and in it Grandpa's entries for some days extended several pages while others lasted only one short line.

In the summer and fall of 1979, I read the first two years of tiny script into a dictaphone, and a secretary transcribed them. She was not a church member, and the original typed copy spelled "Lamoni Steak" as if it were a euphemism for chuck roast. She also typed out "Ladder Day Saints," probably thinking the term referred to the church's upward aspirations. The diaries and *revised* transcripts today are in the permanent collection of the RLDS Archives available to anyone who wishes to see them.

The diaries are not the meditations of John Garver. Only rarely does he record his personal thoughts or feelings in them. They are a chronicle of his church activities, in fact, a carefully composed chronicle of his conduct. There is a clue to the nature of the writings in the very first entry, January 1, 1908.

According to promise made to High Council of Lamoni Stake and the Stake Conference May and October respectively, I was to take up the work of the Lamoni Stake January 1 as a counselor to John Smith, President, to devote my entire time therein. So, on January 10, I left the employ of the Herald Publishing House where I had labored as mailing clerk and entered actively into the ministry.

Red flag. In his January first entry, he discusses what happened January tenth, ten days later. There is nothing illegal about this, of course; you can do in your own diary whatever you darn well choose. But it is obvious from this and several other references that while there may be daily entries, they were not put there on a daily basis.

In fact, we must wonder how long it was after the events until they were finally written down in the diary. In an extreme example, his entry of January 20, 1909, has the benefit of several months of hindsight. He and O. B. Thomas had been conducting a preaching series at Lone Rock and decided to close:

The Lord blessed in these meetings most abundantly. A good many people came from time to time to hear and though there seemed no immediate results, a number of baptisms *the following spring* evidenced the fact that God had been with us even to a greater extent than we had at first thought. I spent the night at the J. M. Holloways. (Emphasis added.)

January 20, and he knows what happens "the following spring."

He tips his hand in September of that year. There are only twelve entries for the entire month, when normally there is an entry for each day. However, he explains that the "items from the 4th to the 30th inclusive accidentally burned before being transferred." In other words, he made notes of his activities on separate sheets before he transferred a block of them into his dairy as a permanent record.

Wondering what the diaries were to John Garver is another way of asking the question: why were the diaries written? Why did he go to the trouble of making two records of his daily activity, one temporary and one permanent? He does not ever tell us directly but I think we can make a reasonable guess by exploring two additional questions: (1) who wrote the diaries? and (2) to whom were they written? If we knew this information, perhaps we would gain a better perspective on their content.

Therefore, the first question: Who wrote the diaries? Since their discovery in the spring of 1978, there have developed two completely separate theories of their origin. One school of thought, advanced by Garver critics, is that they were written by Solomon Spaulding very late in his life, stolen by Garver and hidden away in a tin box which he planned to dig up later. A second position, and I must admit that I find this far more likely, is that John Garver himself actually wrote them and that they are indeed what they claim to be, a record of his ministry in the Americas, primarily in Decatur County, Iowa.

However, believing that they were written by Garver tells us little until we know who Garver was at the time. Again, the first entry tells us something. In 1908 he was beginning full-time church appointment as counselor to the Lamoni Stake president, coming to that job from a previous position as mail clerk in the Herald Publishing House. Having been born in 1878, he would turn thirty years old that year.

Beyond this, what do we know about the man? Garver had not been raised in the church. Neither of his parents would ever join. His father's family were of a Mennonite tradition, though how strong in that faith his father was is unclear. A Hans Jacob Garber was a Mennonite convert in Switzerland in the early 1700s who fled to America in the face of religious persecution. On the ship *Hope* Garber landed in Philadelphia in 1733 and made a homestead in Lancaster County, Pennsylvania.

Three generations later, Albert Garver was born and married a red-haired Irish woman. Lillian McGaw was Scotch Irish. Scotch Irish was what Protestant Irish called themselves to distinguish themselves from Irish Catholics. The McGaws were members of the Dunkards, German pietists, similar to the Mennonites. Lillian had several brothers who were Dunkard ministers and, according to her son in later years, she always wanted one of her sons to become a minister also. The son who would fulfill that wish, John Garver, was born in 1878 in a small house near Goshen, Indiana. As a young child, he attended worship services wearing a little cap characteristic of his mother's tradition.

Albert Garver was a railroad section man by profession. He helped keep the track in good repair. The family grew and continued to move westward, often living in rough towns on the midwestern railroad frontier. In later years, the elder Garvers would identify with the Methodist church in Kansas and Nebraska. As the oldest of what would eventually become a family of seven children, John was forced to move out of the home at the age of twelve when the family was living in Kansas because the parents could not feed that many mouths. He would tell the story of walking down the lane with his small bundle of things tied up in a handkerchief. He remembered looking back and seeing his mother crying in the doorway waving good-bye. His parents were not sending him into the world to starve. A healthy twelve-year-old had little difficulty getting work on nearby farms, and he kept in touch with his family. But he grew up quickly.

Finding his own positions, he gradually worked his way into southwest Iowa and into the employment of a family who were members of the Reorganized church. They took him to a preaching series. He was converted and baptized in 1897 and immediately made known his intention to get to Graceland College somehow. Graceland was only two years old at the time. I have no idea who or what instilled in a nineteen-year-old farm hand, the son of a railroad worker, the burning desire to improve himself with a college education, but someone or something did. For five more years John Garver saved his money to attend Graceland and finally went to Lamoni in the fall of 1902. He had been ordained a priest in 1901.

He often told the story of his first night in Lamoni. He spent it in the hotel because he knew no one he could ask for a room. He was up very early the next morning, shining his shoes and getting ready for the day. In fact, he was up so early that the squeaking of his freshly shined shoes earned him a sharp reprimand from the hotel owner. Between that and his natural anxiety, his ordeal with higher education was not off to a good start and he claims that if there had been a train leaving town before his first appointment, he would have taken it. He was not prepared to begin college work. He was twenty-three years old but had not begun even high school work. His formal education had been in a one-room country school, and he knew he had a lot of work ahead of him.

(Another story he loved to tell about himself was that he had written some official at Graceland, explaining his background and his desire to serve the church and asking what courses he ought to take. The letter came back, as he tells it, stating: "I have read your letter and strongly suggest that you study composition.")

Garver was a student at Graceland for five years, going to class part time and working at any jobs he could get. His work on the farm and his full physical maturity stood him in good stead on the football field, a violent sport indeed at the turn of the century. He was captain of the first Graceland team and won the first varsity letter the school awarded. He did odd jobs at Liberty Home for the Joseph Smith family where he is reported to have been a favorite. He did farm work for church families. He was an editor of the *Lamoni Chronicle* for two years before getting a job in the mailing room at the Herald Printing Company. On Saturday morning, January 5, 1907, the Herald Printing and Bindery Plant was entirely destroyed by fire. It was John Garver who sounded the alarm at 7:40 A.M.

Finishing his work at Graceland in the spring of 1907, Garver was approached by the Lamoni Stake High Council with a call to be a counselor to the stake president, and he accepted. He had been ordained an elder in 1906 and a high priest in 1907. He went under full-time appointment for the Reorganized church in January of 1908 and was active in the ministry until his death in 1949. His final position was a member of the First Presidency with Israel A. Smith and F. Henry Edwards. He had remained a favorite of the Smith family. He was the only person outside the immediate family present in the hospital room at the death of President Frederick M. Smith in 1946, and it was John Garver whom the family asked to offer prayer at that moment.

What we must not do, however, is to read back into the 1908 diary the apostle or president John Garver who appeared in later years. This was a young man, thirty years old. In the summer of 1907, he had married Mynn Hayer, the oldest of four sisters. The Hayers were not part of the high councils of the church; they had only recently moved there from Illinois. Another Hayer daughter, Audie, would marry James Kelley, Jr., son of the president of the Council of Twelve and nephew of the presiding bishop.

I include this background to sketch a picture of a man who wrote the diaries. He had established a name for himself as a promising talent, popular with his superiors and his peers. While he kept touch with the Garvers, his world had become the church, and any vocational ambitions he had must have been in the context of the world of the church. In answer to the question of who authored the diaries, I suggest that it was a young man who sincerely believed that the Restoration was the cutting edge of God's interaction with the world, who had committed himself to the church, and who was taking his first assignment as an appointee.

This assessment of the author then suggests a direction for the second question: To whom were the diaries written? The books are the details of his church activity. Whoever reads them will see Garver's account of himself in full-time ministry. He recorded his sermon topics and his evaluation of how well the services went, at which services he presided, to whom he administered in times of sickness, how the work was going in outlying branches, and occasionally, how he accounted for his time when not engaged in formal ministerial duties. In other words, I suggest that he was writing to the church, perhaps more specifically to the church leaders whom he was anxious to please.

This, of course, helps answer our original question: Why were the diaries written? I think the answer is that he wanted to give a good account of himself, to show himself approved, and his diaries are his record. Even if he never expected or intended anyone else to read them, he was trying to see himself through the eyes of those who were in a position to supervise his work. He was trying to understand his activities as they would understand them. In no way was he pandering to church officials or himself, puffing himself up in the diaries to look more important. He was simply reporting his activity, laying the record on the table. But what he chose to record is what they would be interested in, that is, his performance in his first ministerial assignment.

Of course, a reader seventy years later finds interest in items Garver considered commonplace. One of the fascinations of the diary for me is its window on daily life in a small Iowa town. For example, I was impressed again and again with the amount and severity of sickness. In December of 1908, the couple's infant daughter Verna developed whooping cough and a warning placard was placed in the window. Grandmother came down with a painful sore throat which developed into quinsy. Since I did not even know what quinsy was, I had to ask and once I knew, I wished I hadn't asked. Quinsy is a severe infection inside the throat which develops very painful boils. If they are too deep to be lanced by a physician, one must wait for the body to fight them naturally which means waiting several days for them to come to a head and break through to drain. For four days, Grandmother was miserable with quinsy while the baby had whooping cough. Grandmother had been sick for over a month with the infection. During that time, the community became excited over an outbreak of smallpox.

On February 2, the whooping cough sign was removed, and both mother and daughter were much better. Still, three weeks later, Verna was threatened with pneumonia. Whooping cough, quinsy, smallpox, pneumonia—many families today go through their entire lives untroubled by any of them, but the Garvers lived in fear of each in a span of two months. Granted, that was a banner two months for germs, but the diaries are full of requests for administration from those suffering from these and other killers of the past. (On March 8, 1908, for example, Garver had been called to the little coal camp of Cleveland to administer to a three-year-old girl. Her name was Tessie Morgan.) Many today-all-but-forgotten diseases were then a part of everyday life.

In June of 1909, Garver himself was sick for a couple of weeks with German measles. When he recovered, he fumigated the room, which probably meant that he closed the doors and windows and burned formaldehyde candles for a day to kill any lingering traces of the disease.

Or, for others of you who may want to look back at Lamoni only through the soft haze of lilac blossoms or apple harvests, consider transportation. Last year in his presidential address, Grant McMurray urged Whitmer historians to "travel the dusty roads of Lamoni" in search of our social history. Yet, what every native of southern Iowa knows at least by his or her second or third birthday is that Decatur County roads are dusty only at their best. At their worst, they are mud. On Wednesday, February 17, 1909, John Garver and L. G. Holloway boarded a morning train for Grant City and from there walked eight miles in an Iowa February to Allendale for a preaching series. They carried their books and satchels with them. It was already muddy, but a slight thaw and more snow the following day made things worse. By Sunday, the weather was very bad and the mud was "shoe-top deep." Garver wrote:

Owing to the mud which made walking all but impossible, we had been puzzled what to do. Interest was fair despite prejudice, but at close of the meeting, we felt directed to close and so announced, leaving a good feeling. I, however, felt depressed over the condition of the work at Allendale. Outlook very poor.

With the series ended, they had no reason to remain in Allendale. Therefore, despite the unpleasant weather, they made plans to head for home.

February 22, 1909. The weather was threatening rain, mud so teams could not be out, no prospects getting to Grant City and railroad soon, so, our work done, we shouldered our books and sachels and struck out across the country, our faces turned homeward, intending to spend a few days at Pawnee, where we had a branch, if it should freeze up. Johnathan Holloway had rode a horse so we took turns, one riding while the others walked. About 2 miles out of Allendale, it began to rain and continued worse until we reached Hatfield, 10 miles on the way. Here we dried out clothing by a store stove, ate the cheese and crackers a Christian brother had given us at Allendale, and trudged on. John H. went on home with the horse and L. G. Holloway and I switched off at the home of Charles Jones, having walked about 16 miles in mud and rain. Were warmly welcomed, stayed night.

The next day.
Foggy and muddy. L. G. and I shouldered again

our luggage and trudged on to his father's where we had dinner walking on home p.m., reaching there at six. Found baby sick, pneumonia threatening. D. A. Anderson and I administered to her. She was revived.

Nor was mud a problem only in the spring thaw. On July 11, 1909, Garver and Brother Traxler had three Sunday preaching assignments. After preaching at New Buda, they left by buggy for a 3:30 service at Downey, and then went to Andover for an evening worship. In the Grand River bottoms, they got stuck in the mud so firmly that they broke the crossbar on the buggy trying to get out. Garver walked barefoot a quarter of a mile, rode horseback to Downey where they borrowed another buggy from a church family to continue on their way.

But there were pleasant moments also. In August, he and Mynn took the baby to the chautauqua series in Lamoni. One night they watched an artist and another night heard the Jubilee Singers. Perhaps the wit for which Garver would become famous had already surfaced for he was selected by the chautauqua committee to introduce Dr. H. W. Sears, who was billed on the program as a humorist. A year later, he attended the Graceland College oratorical contest in which Leslie Wight won a scholarship for his performance. In December, John and Mynn and her younger sister went "sled riding" in the morning.

The diaries also show a domestic side to life in the Garver family. When he was not absent on a preaching series, Garver often helped his wife with the washing on Mondays. Hauling the water to the stove and then to the washtubs and hauling heavy baskets of clean clothes to the line was strenuous work and usually took most of the day. In the summer, he spent several days at work in his large garden, an activity he enjoyed immensely. Two days in June he spent picking cherries at

his wife's parents' farm, and he might have spent some pleasant hours in the evening helping Mynn pit and can the fruit. In August, he and Mynn were peeling apples.

On December 11, 1909, the diary notes that "Leonard Midgorden came to board with us while attending college." The last three entries for the year report that "Len and I sawed wood PM," "chopped and sawed, Len helped," "chopped, Len helping me saw." What made those entries special to my wife and me was that until about a year ago Leonard Midgorden lived in Ames, our hometown, where he and his wife had been pillars of the congregation and foster parents to decades of Iowa State students. We made a special time during Sunday school one morning and read those diary passages to the congregation when Leonard could be present. Then we gave him a very special invitation to come out and saw wood for us any time he wanted.

Garver occasionally pitched in when there was farm work to do for the church. On March 30, 1909, he hauled hay to the Saints Home. In another month, he and Father Hayer sowed oats at Liberty Home and moved some hogs there. In August, he was back at the Saints Home stacking hay. Besides farm work, he hauled cement blocks and coal to Liberty Home, spent three days laying carpet in the church and mended tent for some outdoor meetings. He sounds like a handy man to have had around.

On July 16, 1909, just over a year after their first child had been born, Garver while way on a preaching series received a letter from his wife with some information about a lot they had been eyeing as a future residence. He wrote back to Mynn immediately, also "to Sister Gaulter who owned the lot we wanted, and to G. W. Blair and C. Danielson [an uncle of his wife] to see about borrowing if necessary, also to my father." Among family and friends, they were successful in putting together the necessary financing.

The rest of the month and on into November finds him busily hauling rock and sand, digging the basement, making and hauling cement blocks and working on the lot. The house was eventually finished and became their home on North Silver Street for almost forty years.

The main focus of the diaries, however, is John Garver, counselor to the Lamoni Stake president. It is on this subject that he spends the most time and effort. He lists his sermon topics and scriptural texts. He reports what role he played in administrations and whom he visited on his travels around the stake. He sometimes emphasizes the purpose of the visits by noting that they were "official visits" to the homes of the Saints. On occasion on these official visits, he even notes that he "prayed officially," perhaps to keep us from thinking that he just slipped one in before anyone could stop him. He helped with funeral arrangements, most notably for Alexander Smith, a son of Joseph the Prophet and brother of President Joseph Smith III. Alexander died in Nauvoo on August 12, 1909, but was buried in Lamoni. Garver drove some of the many visiting relatives to the cemetery following the Sunday afternoon funeral service.

As an official representative of the Lamoni Stake Presidency, he had to deal with touchy problems in the branches. We watch him learning an artful touch in church administration. He counseled caution in the calling of several new priesthood members when there seemed to be no urgent need nor divine initiative in the matter. At the small Graceland Branch (not to be confused with Graceland College; this was a coal camp some distance northeast of Lamoni), he negotiated the transfer of responsibility from the neighboring Lucas congregation to Lamoni Stake.

December 7, 1908: Jonathan R. Evans, president of the branch, came out from Lucas to attend business meeting 7:30. Under our mutual director, Brother Evans was released from responsibility and the branch placed under responsibility of Stake president. I presided at this meeting.

According to F. Henry Edwards, who worked closely with Garver for over twenty-five years in the Joint Council, Garver's training in Lamoni Stake gave him an intimate working knowledge of the dynamics of congregational life and invaluable insights into how to deal with people on church matters. I got a sense of that development as I read the diaries. Garver would move into a congregation for a week during a series, visiting the members through the day, preaching in the evening, and then going home with a family for the night. While he was there, he became part of that congregation but never lost sight of his responsibilities as a representative of the larger jurisdiction. That indeed must have been valuable training, as Edwards suggests.

In September of 1908, Garver was called to his parents' home in Nebraska where his mother was dying of cancer. He met one of his brothers in St. Joseph and together they arrived at Superior, Nebraska, a train station eighteen miles from home. They rented a livery, drove out, and found their mother near death and suffering greatly. Even though the diary entry was recorded some time later, it captures how he felt as he sat at his mother's bedside.

September 30, 1908: Remained up all night of arrival. Brother Norman had largely had the care of mother and was, with the rest of the family, well worn out. So Lon and I stayed by mother continuously, relieving them. Toward evening Mother seems to lose consciousness, grew rapidly more critical, labored for breath and as night came on, the end seemed immediately inevitable. However,

279

she rallied from her inaction from time to time and continued to suffer on during the night. She took her last nourishment or stimulant in the morning of this day; the muscles of her throat seemed to become paralyzed so she could not swallow what was placed in her mouth and would strangle badly making the giving of anything impossible. She continued seemingly unconscious and labored for breath until the end. During the silent and heartbreaking watches of this night I experienced a bitterness and a feeling of rebellion such as never came to me before, and please God may never come to me again. It had been the hope and prayer of my gospel life to be able someday to carry the message of truth to my people. Here was my mother passing away, and my ambition so far as she were concerned shattered. When once I became reconciled for her to go, I became anxious for her suffering to end; but she suffered on the most pitiful sight one could behold. As I sat beside her after having repeatedly gone apart alone and pleaded with God for her release and saw her suffer on and on and the family consequently distressed beyond the power to express, remembering how fervently I had prayed and how long and consciously I had labored to make myself competent to represent and interpret the truth to her and to others, and how I had been insistently pleading with God to take her—to liberate her from the excruciation of her pain and the family from their distress as a consequence of her suffering, and how the very heavens in this hour of my direct need seemed as if of stone, and God would not even recognize my cry, no feeling that he was even inclined to listen, my soul became gradually as the painful hours wore on, filled with a bitterness and a rebellion against heaven that I am utterly unable to express. But finally as morning waned, and when I had been left with mother for a time alone, God by the sweet influence of his spirit touched my soul, and there came in place of bitterness and rebellion a sweetness and a resignation at once comforting and humiliating; and I seemed to ask these questions: Had not suffering and sorrow come into the world as a result of the weakness of men? Must not your family meets its portion? Should your mother simply because she is your mother, escape her portion; or your family simply because it is your family escape your portion? Why should God answer your prayers any more than the prayers of any other man unless in his divine wisdom the good of your mother and the good of your family could thus be best conserved? Was not your mother a good and noble woman in life? Will her lot not be among those entitled to the gospel message in the

spirit world? If you remain faithful to your calling, may you not yet in that spirit world minister the word of eternal life to your mother? As each of these questions were presented, unmistakably by the good spirit and each received its proper answer the spirit rested upon me in an abundance I have rarely experienced. After the darkness of bitterness and rebellion, though through God's mercy, the morning broke, and as the light of the dawning day flooded in through the windows of the chamber the light of God's divine influence flooded my very being; and the spirit of resignation that possessed my soul then has remained until this day.

His mother lingered on through the following day and passed away at 9:30 in the evening. The funeral was held on Sunday at the Methodist Church in Mt. Clair, Nebraska. Garver wrote:

And at these services a great many who had been helped in times of distress and sickness and need came to pay their respects to the dead and the living. Burial was in the Nelson Cemetery, Nelson, NE.

He remained with his family the following week, taking care of family business to relieve his father and working on a railroad section crew to earn money for his passage home. With that money and a free pass on a train carrying cattle east, Garver records that he "was able very nearly to meet the expense of my trip home and back."

On several occasions, the diaries record instances of divine intervention, and these intrigue me. On June 21, 1908, he was finishing a preaching series at Lucas and staying in the home of J. R. Evans. The previous evening had been a very successful service. He wrote:

Went home night before and retired as usual grateful for the power of the spirit felt in the evenings work. But could not sleep. This condition continued, and I became much disturbed in mind, continuing until quite distressing until about 2 a.m. when I dropped off into a fitful slumber, awakening again, however, before break of day, and could sleep no more. I arose early and seemed to realize that something had occurred and felt that I would not be able to continue my effort at Lucas. At 4:45 a.m. a messenger stepped on the porch and handed me a telegram from Father Hayer stating: "Come home. Minnie sick." Message had been started 8 p.m. night before. By immediate action I reached a phone, secured a livery man and was soon on the way to Chariton to catch 10 a.m. train for Togo. Train left station two minutes late and I swung on with car in motion, reaching Togo on time. Was met by Father Hayer. In answer to my anxious inquiry "How is Minnie," he replied "She is all right, and so is the girl." Baby born <u>2 a.m.</u>!

Two a.m. was precisely the time he had dropped off into a fitful slumber. To make sure no one would miss that point, he underlined "2 a.m." in the diary. Later, with the record of another birth in town, we would learn that "being sick" was understood as "going into labor." It was their first child, Verna Winifred.

Earlier that spring, he had preached a series at Hiteman which had ended with several baptisms. It was a good series.

March 8: I was in the spirit a great part of the night previous and much during the day of this date. God seemed very near, and granted unto me the assurance of my calling in the Stake work and of my acceptance with him. I was given to know and so stated to the branch that if the Saints were faithful, the Lord would add to their numbers and that the work at Hiteman would soon be strengthened. I bid farewell to the Saints with warm feeling toward them and with the assurance that this feeling was returned.

The following September, after another good series in Hiteman, Garver proudly recorded the following:

The meetings at Hiteman were a feast and a delight to the Saints. The persons named were added to the church, and hundreds heard the truth with prejudice being removed as a result. In this and by several others being added by baptism during preceding months, and by a great many additions by letter from the Cleveland and Lucas branches, and by the recognition of the Lord in the sending of his Holy Spirit to the edification, union, and building up of the Saints was seen and demonstrated the fulfillment of that which had been shown me by the spirit in March previous, as already stated. My heart was made glad by these experiences.

And one final instance. In January of 1909, Garver had finished a series in Lone Rock. The weather was bad, but he

was asked by the priesthood to remain with them for a Sunday afternoon meeting to discuss some priesthood calls. He agreed. At the conclusion of the meeting, he was anxious to return home.

January 21 1909: After meeting, at the suggestion of James Martin, Jr., I took one of his horses and went on [to Lamoni] reaching here at 6:40. Mud was very bad and the horse had had no exercise for considerable time and when I reached Father Hayer's farm, the horse was sick. He grew rapidly worse. Dr. More, vet, was out of town so I secured brother M. C. Luse, retired vet. Father Hayer and [Luse] went to town for medicine. The horse by this time being in dreadful agony. Everything seemed to indicate that by the time the medicine was secured, he would be beyond help. I was in a plight. A borrowed and a valuable horse, horse's death staring me in the face; value at least $200 and not a cent to restore the loss. I went down on my knees in stall next to the horse, presented the situation to God, pled for his help and a manifestation of his divine power in behalf of the needs of his children. Shortly after I arose, the horse also arose, shook himself, began chopping at the hay before him, and when the men returned, they were surprised to see him improved. The [medicine] was given, and I remained with the horse until 12:15, when I left him and went home to bed.

I have read and reread the passage about the healing of the horse so often that I could almost cite it from memory. I took it as the test case. How can I deal with that information honestly as a historian, bringing to bear on it what I have been taught about objectivity without sacrificing the real meaning of the passage? How can I know what *really* happened in that stall? How can I know if the horse was *really* sick when it lay down? Perhaps it was just winded and had a sore throat. How can I know if it *really* got up as Garver described it? Can I simply take the word of one who so very much wanted to believe in himself as a divinely ordained minister authorized to perform such administrations?

The believer in me sneered, "You spineless academic worm, slithering away from admitting you believe in divine healing because it would make you sound funny." But the historian stuck to his guns, and the debate ground on and on. We went over and over the same old arguments until we were sick of them. But then, out of the ashes, a new thought began to formulate. Is this the most inspired question that we can ask—was the horse really sick? Does the answer to that really tell me anything significant about John Garver or about anything else? Does anything in his subsequent career change one iota if the horse wasn't really sick?

The new questions were like a wave washing away yesterday's worries, and I wondered how I ever could have spent so much effort on them. The historian in me finally accepted that by historical methods I can never know if or how God healed that horse. Historical methods can no more validate Divinity than litmus paper can tell you whether creamy peanut butter tastes better than chunk-style. (I wrote this part at the kitchen table.) Even people present at the same event will differ in their interpretations of what happened. We do not see God directly in history, but only second-hand, through the accounts of people who claim to have experienced God directly.

Then how should a historian approach an instance like Garver in the barn? I believe that the best question the historian can ask is what difference did Garver's belief that he encountered God on his knees beside that horse make on John Garver? I am absolutely convinced that he believed God healed that horse. What difference did that event make in his life? Now there is a question much more suited to the methods and tools available to the historian.

Working through the episode in the barn gave me a new insight on some other things. Before I struggled with the diaries, I, too, was concerned with that old haunting bugaboo of Mormons and Mormon-haters alike, that gnawing question that keeps more people coming to Whitmer meetings than all the stamps Betty Winholtz has ever licked: were there *really* golden plates? I can honestly say that today, I don't care very much. It would be interesting to know, but I don't ever expect to know and I can live without knowing for sure one way or the other. It certainly *was* important when I sat there listening to Jan Shipps's paper nine years ago. Once, knowing whether there were or were not plates was what Mormon history was *all* about. What is important to me today is the difference belief made in the lives of those who believed it. That's what Mormon history is. That's what any religious history is. For while we're on the subject, historical methods aren't going to prove whether that crucified body did or did not rise on Easter morning. But there seems to be a pretty good case that some people believed it did and that in their lives, it made a difference.

But, asks the believer, isn't that a cop-out? You're dodging the central issue. Does God or does God not intervene in human history?

I'm not dodging, replies the historian, but you can't prove it by me.

Then what good is history if it won't give you the answers?

Isn't that obvious, you myoptic turtle? It teaches us the questions. The essence of the Restoration is that each individual can experience God directly. We do not have to base our faith on the experiences of the past. We have a right to expect our own confirmations. We do not need our history to reassure us. We need our history to frustrate us, to make us want to know if what they claim happened to them could happen to us, to force us to seek our own experiences *because* we cannot find adequate proof secondhand through the experiences of others.

My favorite story in the Bible is Moses at the burning bush. He had all the right instincts of a first-rate historian. He could have made tenure in three years. He didn't publish one big book. He divided it into five books and published them separately, giving him five publications instead of just one. Confronted with a voice coming out of a blazing plant, Moses starts in on an oral history, a biography. "Whom shall I say sent me?" What was he after? References?

But think of the trouble we could have been spared in the past five thousand years if God had been a little less stingy with his vita. "I am that I am." Now I ask you, what kind of an answer is that? Do you know where a smart-aleck answer like that would get him today? A computer would take that, he'd be listed as "Am, I" and stored away on a disk between Allen and Amsberry. And we'd think, good, we know who he is. We've got it on computer.

Moses came down out of the mountain not knowing much more than he did before he went up except that *something* up there burned and that he had a rather frightening task ahead of him. What should a historian ask about that experience? Did the bush *really* burn without being consumed? Is there a possibility that the light at that time of day might have reflected against a rock and given the illusion of fire? Could Moses have been high from sniffing royal embalming fluid? Does it *really* matter whether the bush burned or not? It would be comforting to be able to prove conclusively that the bush burned without being consumed—the weight of the plant before and after, the number of BTUs generated. But we can't take those readings. All we really know is that Moses came down from the mountain believing that he had just encountered God, and *that* is what makes the event historically significant.

I do not believe that I shall ever know what happened in that stall in a Lamoni barn in 1908, or whether the bush really burned in front of Moses. But I think I've got a better grasp on some things because I've taken the time to wonder about them. Robert Frost said it much better in far fewer words.

O Star, the fairest one in sight,
We grant your loftiness the right
To some obscurity of cloud.
It will not do to speak of night
Since dark is what brings out your light.
Some mystery becomes the proud
But to be wholly taciturn in your reserve
Is not allowed.
Say something to us we can learn by heart
And when alone repeat.
Say something. And it says, "I burn."
But say with what degree of heat.
Talk Fahrenheit! Talk Centigrade!
Use language we can comprehend.
Tell us what elements you blend.
It gives us strangely little aid
But does tell something in the end.
And steadfast as Keats' Eremite,
Not even stooping from its height,
It asks a little something of us here.
It asks of us a certain height.
So when at times the mob is swayed
To carry praise or blame too far,
We may choose something like a star
To stay our minds on.
And be stayed.

For nine very good years, John Whitmer, I thank you.

VI
ZIONIC COMMUNITY

ZIONIC COMMUNITY

Editor's Note:

Ronald L. Romig, M.A., is a draftsman for the firm of Bremson Photo Industries in Kansas City, Missouri. Co-author John H. Siebert, Ed.Sp., is editor of External Communications for the engineering firm of Black and Veatch in Kansas City, Missouri. Both authors are residents of the Harvest Hills community in eastern Jackson County, Missouri.

A resident of Palmdale, California, John E. Thompson is adjunct instructor in religion at Chapman Residence Education Center in Lancaster, California. After receiving the B.A. in history, *magna cum laude,* he earned a master of arts degree in Old Testament studies and the master of divinity, cum laude, at Trinity Evangelical Divinity School in Deerfield, Illinois.

Roger D. Launius, Ph.D. (history), resides in Utah, where he is chief of the Office of History, Ogden Air Logistics Center, Hill Air Force Base, Utah. Part of his article appeared as "The Mormon Quest for a Perfect Society at Lamoni, Iowa, 1870-1890," in *Annals of Iowa,* 47 (Spring 1984): 325-42. The author expresses appreciation to Christie Dailey and Katherine Scott Sturtevant for their editorial assistance.

JACKSON COUNTY, 1831-1833: A LOOK AT THE DEVELOPMENT OF ZION

Ronald E. Romig and John H. Siebert

In the early 1830s there appears to have been an evolving, changing plan regarding the development of Zion in Jackson County, Missouri.

If a snapshot had been taken in 1832 or early 1833 which stopped (in freeze frame fashion) the activity of the members who had gathered to Jackson County, it would be revealing. The members were trying to implement the call to establish Zion by following the guidelines and principles of development available to them. There were two sources for these directions: the church authorities, and their own interpretations of the revelations concerning the building up of Zion.

Such a snapshot would reveal a plan with these elements:

1. City of Zion is to be located in Jackson County, Missouri. Independence is the Center Place.
2. The temple is to be located westward on a lot which is not far from the courthouse.
3. Church leaders were to purchase the land, every tract lying westward, even unto the line running directly between Jew and Gentile, and every tract bordering by the prairies.
4. Zion and the temple were commanded to be built by a gathered people obeying the Law of Consecration.[1]

After May or June 1833, a view of the plan for developing Zion had more elements in addition to the earlier ones:

1. City of Zion is to be located in Jackson County, Missouri. Independence is the Center Place.
2. There are now twenty-four temples to be located in the center of the city of Zion, which is westward on two lots which are not far from the courthouse. (See Proposed Plat of City of Zion p. 293.)

3. Church leaders were to purchase the land, every tract lying westward, even unto the line running directly between Jew and Gentile, and every tract bordering the prairies, and some lands to the east if necessary for agricultural purposes to support the city.
4. Zion and the temples were to be built by a gathered people obeying the commandments, especially the Law of Consecration and, "yea, let it [first temple] be built speedily by the tithing of my people."[2]

At first look there seems to be quite a bit of difference between these two pictures.

Traditionally, present-day members of the church have accepted a static view of experiences of the early church members in Jackson County. Somehow, a "snapshot" containing only *some* of the elements of the early development of Zion has been accepted by the present-day church. Because Joseph Smith, Jr., remained in Kirtland, and the period was so short, the early settlement of Jackson County is often seen as a transition period between Kirtland and Far West. Each month of each year, however, in that early period presented a changing picture of the building process.

There are many elements to be viewed in the development of Zion in that early period. The most commonly accepted image of how it was to transpire is closely associated with Joseph's first visit to Jackson County in the summer of 1831.

Joseph arrived in Jackson County about the middle of July.[3] Enough had been revealed about the probable location of Zion that ten teams of missionaries, including Edward Partridge, W. W. Phelps,

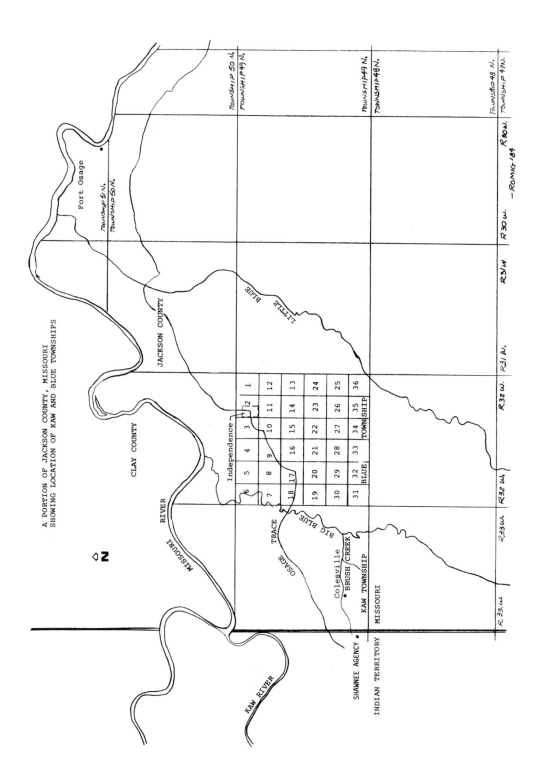

A PORTION OF JACKSON COUNTY, MISSOURI
SHOWING LOCATION OF KAW AND BLUE TOWNSHIPS

N

Fort Osage

JACKSON COUNTY

CLAY COUNTY

MISSOURI RIVER

Independence

BLUE

LITTLE

Township 51 N.
Township 50 N.

Township 50 N.
Township 49 N.

Township 49 N.
Township 48 N.

Township 48 N.
Township 47 N.

—ROMIG 184

R. 29 W.
R. 30 W.

R. 31 W.
R. 32 W.

R. 32 W.

R. 33 W.

R. 33 W.

6	5	4	3	2	1
7	8	9	10	11	12
18	17	16	15	14	13
19	20	21	22	23	24
30	29	28	27	26	25
31	32	33	34	35	36

BLUE TOWNSHIP

TRACE

OSAGE

BIG BLUE

Colesville
BRUSH CREEK
KAW TOWNSHIP
MISSOURI

SHAWNEE AGENCY

INDIAN TERRITORY

KAW RIVER

287

A. S. Gilbert and his wife, Joseph Coe, Sidney Rigdon, and the Colesville members had set out on this mission.[4] Although Zion was an unspecified destination they all converged at Independence, Missouri. There they met Oliver Cowdery, Ziba Peterson, Peter Whitmer, Jr., and F. G. Williams, who, except for Parley P. Pratt, comprised the first missionary team to the Indians which were referred to as Lamanites.[5]

Some adjustment in emphasis apparently occurred during this western mission. Ezra Booth, a member of the team, claimed that revelation had indicated that the Lamanite mission would be instrumental in locating Zion *among* the Lamanites.[6] Direct access to the Indians, however, had been denied to these earlier missionaries. Indian Agent Richard Cummins wrote to Gen. William Clark, the superintendent of Indian Affairs at St. Louis, and related the following about the missionaries' visit to the Indian Territory in February 1831:

I A few days ago three men all strangers to me went among the Indians preaching to and instructing them in religious matters...I have refused to let them stay, or go among the Indians unless they first obtain permission from you...If you refuse then they will go to the Rocky Mountains, but what they will be with the Indians.[7]

Oliver Cowdery applied to Clark[8] but apparently did not receive a reply. They stayed in Jackson County until the western mission teams arrived. During this visit, Joseph and the others somehow visited the Indian Territory and preached to the Indians.[9] Before Joseph ended his visit to Jackson County, arrangements were made to expose the Indians to the gospel.

Let my servant Sidney Gilbert obtain a license (behold, here is wisdom, and whoso readeth let him understand), that he may send goods also unto the people, even by whom he will as clerks, employed in his service, and thus...my gospel may be preached unto [them].[10]

As a result of this western mission, Zion was now clearly to be located "on the *borders* by the Lamanites."[11]

The revelation further designates Independence as the Center Place and the site for the temple.[12] During the missionaries' first visit to Jackson County, much of the time was probably spent in exploring the land. Reynolds Cahoon, one of the missionaries who arrived in Independence on August 4, recorded the following:

I found some of the brethren, and there my mortal eyes beheld great and marvelous things such as I had not even expected to see in this world.... After tarrying in Independence a number of days, engaged in exploring that region of the country, the Lord commanded us to return to our families in the east. We left Independence August 9.[13]

Even before Joseph's arrival in Jackson County, the manner of application of the Law of Consecration as he had originally envisioned it was being tested. Newell Knight, a member of the Colesville, New York, branch recorded the following:

On our arrival [to the Kirtland area] it was advised that the Colesville branch remain together, and go to a neighboring town called Thompson, as a man by the name of Copely had a considerable tract of land there which he offered to let the Saints occupy. Consequently a contract was agreed upon, and we commenced work in good faith. But in a short time [approximately five weeks] Copely broke the engagement.[14]

When Copley refused to consecrate, he became disaffected and sued in the Geauga County Court to remove the church members from his property. He won the suit.[15] The Colesville members were counseled to remove to Zion and Bishop Partridge was sent to Missouri to administer the economic development of Zion.[16] Hence the short-lived Thompson experiment served as a school for the new bishop, giving him a pattern for future implementation of Zionic principles.[17] To control Missouri consecrations, Partridge developed a consecration agreement and inheritance lease form. These procedural

—Courtesy LDS Church Historical Department

The conditions faced by the church members and leaders in Jackson County were extremely difficult. As the temporal and spiritual leader in Zion, Bishop Partridge was responsible for the total welfare of the members who gathered there. His concern included not only the food, clothing, and housing for the members but also the nurturing of their spiritual condition that would augment the developing of a Zionic city. As he began implementing his understanding of the Law of Consecration, he realized adjustments were needed and frequently solicited advice from Joseph and the leaders in Kirtland.

Joseph arrived by stage in Independence on his second visit, April 24, 1832. Councils were called, the church was further organized, and economic conditions were discussed. As a result, an additional dimension of the Law of Consecration was agreed upon and implemented as the United Firm.[19] This was seen as a means of generating cash and needed capital for the church and the development of Zion.[20]

A problem of cash flow is hinted at in Joseph's response to W. W. Phelps: "You complain that there have already to many deciples arive there for the means."[21] The prophet evidently felt that the cash problem might be solved if all the members who removed to Missouri would do a better job of complying with the Law of Consecration. A document referred to as the "Olive Leaf" was sent to Zion offering solutions to this problem. As a result meetings were called, and the members were encouraged to participate. David Pettigrew related, "Bishop Partridge appointed a solemn assembly in all the branches, which was held as a day of confession and repentance."[22] In a letter to friends in Fulton County, Missouri, Salmon Sherwood stated that he attended the solemn assembly held at

modifications (i.e., drawing up legal contracts) theoretically provided the church civil protection from potential suits.

An element of Partridge's personality is revealed in a letter he sent to his wife prior to her joining him in Missouri:

You know I stand in an important station, and as I am occasionally chastened I sometimes fear my station is above what I can perform to the acceptance of my Heavenly Father. I hope you and I may conduct ourselves as at last to land our souls in the heaven of eternal rest. Pray that I may not fall.[18]

This suggests a lack of self-confidence in his abilities to satisfactorily perform such an important task. It also suggests that he was inclined to do as he was told by Joseph. It is probable that what we see of Partridge's administration of the Law of Consecration in Missouri reflects his best understanding of Joseph's intentions for its operation.

No 1.

BE IT KNOWN, THAT I, *Titus Billings*

Of Jackson county, and state of Missouri, having become a member of the church of Christ, organized according to law, and established by the revelations of the Lord, on the 6th day of April, 1830, do, of my own free will and accord, having first paid my just debts, grant and hereby give unto *Edward Partridge* of Jackson county, and state of Missouri, bishop of said church, the following described property, viz:— *Sundry articles of furniture valued fifty five dollars twenty seven cents,— also two beds, bedding and extra clothing valued seventy three dollars twenty five cents,— also farming utensils valued forty one dollars,— also one horse, two waggons two cows and two calves valued one hundred forty seven dollars*

in Jackson county Mo,

For the purpose of purchasing lands, and building up the New Jerusalem, even Zion, and for relieving the wants of the poor and needy. For which I the said *Titus Billings* do covenant and bind myself and my heirs forever, to release all my right and interest to the above described property, unto him the said *Edward Partridge* bishop of said church. And I the said *Edward Partridge* — bishop of said church, having received the above described property, of the said *Titus Billings* do bind myself, that I will cause the same to be expended for the above-mentioned purposes of the said *Titus Billings* to the satisfaction of said church; and in case I should be removed from the office of bishop of said church, by death or otherwise, I hereby bind myself and my heirs forever, to make over to my successor in office, for the benefit of said church, all of the above described property, which may then be in my possession.

In testimony whereof, WE have hereunto set our hands and seals this ———— day of ———— in the year of our Lord, one thousand eight hundred and thirty ————

IN PRESENCE OF ————

[SEAL.]

[SEAL.]

Seal

—Courtesy LDS Church Historical Department

No 2

BE IT KNOWN, THAT I, *Edward Partridge*

Of Jackson county, and state of Missouri, bishop of the church of Christ, organized according to law, and established by the revelations of the Lord, on the 6th day of April, 1830, have leased, and by these presents do lease unto

Titus Billings of Jackson county, and state of Missouri, a member of said church,

the following described piece or parcel of land, being a part of section No. *three* township No. *forty nine* range No. *thirty two* situated in Jackson county, and state of Missouri, and is bounded as follows, viz:— *beginning eighty rods E. from the S. W. corner of s'd sec, thence N. one hundred and sixty rods, thence E. twenty seven rods 25L, thence S. one hundred and sixty rods thence W. twenty seven rods 25L, to the place of beginning containing twenty seven & ½ acres be the same more or less subject to roads and highways*

And also have loaned the following described property, viz:— *Sundry articles of furniture valued fifty five dollars twenty seven cents, — also two beds, bedding and clothing valued seventy three dollars twenty five cents, — also sundry farming utensils valued forty one dollars, — also one horse, two cows, two calves and two waggons valued one hundred and forty seven dollars*

TO HAVE AND TO HOLD the above described property, by him the said *Titus Billings* to be used and occupied as to him shall seem meet and proper. And as a consideration for the use of the above described property, I the said *Titus Billings* do bind myself to pay the taxes, and also to pay yearly unto the said *Edward Partridge* bishop of said church, or his successor in office, for the benefit of said church, all that I shall make or accumulate more than is needful for the support and comfort of myself and family. And it is agreed by the parties, that this lease and loan shall be binding during the life of the said *Titus Billings* unless he transgress, and is not deemed worthy by the authority of the church, according to its laws, to belong to the church. And in that case I the said *Titus Billings* do acknowledge that I forfeit all claim to the above described leased and loaned property, and hereby bind myself to give back the leased, and also pay an equivalent for the loaned, for the benefit of said church, unto the said *Edward Partridge* bishop of said church, or his successor in office. And further, in case of said *Titus Billings* or family's inability in consequence of infirmity or old age, to provide for themselves while members of this church, I the said *Edward Partridge* bishop of said church, do bind myself to administer to their necessities out of any funds in my hands appropriated for that purpose, not otherwise disposed of, to the satisfaction of the church. And further, in case of the death of the said *Titus Billings* his wife or widow, being at the time a member of said church, has claim upon the above described leased and loaned property, upon precisely the same conditions that her said husband had them, as above described; and the children of the said *Titus Billings* in case of the death of both their parents, also have claim upon the above described property, for their support, until they shall become of age, and no longer; subject to the same conditions yearly that their parents were: provided however, should the parents not be members of said church, and in possession of the above described property at the time of their deaths, the claim of the children as above described, is null and void. **In testimony whereof, WE** have hereunto set our hands and seals this _____ day of _____ in the year of our Lord, one thousand eight hundred and thirty _____

IN PRESENCE OF ——

[SEAL.]

[SEAL.]

—Courtesy LDS Church Historical Department

Independence, and that all present entered into a covenant to obey the Law of Consecration and consecrate all their property to the bishop. He also indicated that there were "provisions aplenty but can not be purchased by those who have no money."[23]

After this series of solemn assemblies many of the members agreed to participate in the economic order provided for by the commandments. However, many (if not most) of these members were poor.[24] Even after they consecrated their money and personal property to the church, most of them received all of these consecrated items back, and they also received church-purchased land for their inheritance. (See Titus Billings' agreement forms, pp. 290, 291.)

In the midst of these economic difficulties,

One Bates from New London, Ohio, subscribed fifty dollars for the purpose of purchasing lands, and the necessaries for the saints, after his arrival here, sued Edward Partridge and obtained a judgement for the same. Bates shortly after denied the faith and run away on Sunday, leaving debts unpaid.[25]

Possibly as a result of this newly discovered legal weakness, Joseph's implementation of the law appears to have been changed again.[26]

"Concerning inheritances," he [Joseph] explained, "you are bound by the law of the Lord to give a deed, securing to him who receives inheritances, his inheritance for an everlasting inheritance, or in other words, to be his individual property, his private stewardship."

He further taught that if an individual transgressed and left the church, the inheritance still belonged to him.[27]

The forms used in the consecration agreements were changed somewhat during this time. The term *lease*, however, still appeared on the form.[28] Perhaps Partridge and Phelps were planning yet another change in the forms, as indicated in John Taylor's testimony in the

Temple Lot case. He said that they promised everyone deeds, but he never got his.[29] Also W. W. Phelps, in an editorial for the next to last issue of *The Evening and the Morning Star* to be published in Independence, stated,

and when they are gathered, instead of becoming a common stock family, as has been said, . . . each man receives a warranty deed securing to himself and heirs, his inheritance in fee simple forever.[30]

The ensuing civil disruption, in all likelihood, prevented the development of any new forms.

Partridge seems to have followed the prophet's guidance as much as possible regarding the physical development of Zion, as he had done in the economic sector. Most of the missionaries who had accompanied Joseph to Missouri on that first trip returned to their homes and families in Kirtland. Partridge, however, stayed in Jackson County and started bringing the plans into reality. He began acquiring the designated sites as well as other lands in Blue and Kaw townships, purchasing first the lands surrounding the Colesville settlement.[31] It would appear that he lived somewhere near these early purchases for a while because when he purchased city lots in Independence (Blue Township) in August of 1832 a Jackson County land record states his residence as "Edward Partridge, of Kaw Township."[32] "From his comfortable setting in Painesville, Ohio, he and his family were now on foot in western Missouri living with several other families in an open and unfinished cabin."[33] He also purchased the $63\frac{43}{160}$ acres west of town that encompassed the temple site.[34] Hyrum Rathbun, in his testimony during the Temple Lot case, explained his understanding of the extent of this area to be used for the temple

I have it in my mind that there were about three acres set apart for the temple lot . . . and the rest of it was for the purpose of settling saints on it, for the

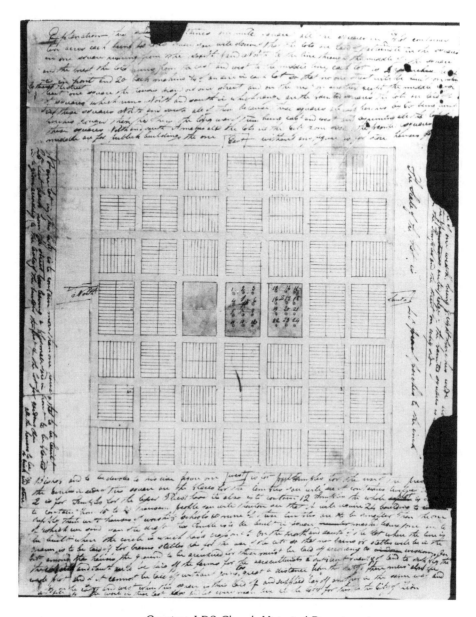

—Courtesy LDS Church Historical Department

homes of saints ultimately, and they concluded to buy more lands than that, and settle homeless saints on it. That was the idea of the church authorities at that time.[35]

This statement indicates that there was an understanding that a small portion of the sixty-three acres Partridge had purchased was for the building of the temple. Accordingly Partridge built his own home, as well as an adjacent schoolhouse that also served as a meeting house in bad weather, on a portion of this larger tract.[36] John Corrill, counselor to the bishop, lived on the temple tract[37] and Partridge may have begun establishing other members on portions of this acreage as well. Titus Billings' inheritance was part of eighty acres Partridge had purchased. This allotment was west of the acreage surrounding the temple site. This land presently contains the Sanitarium and land south of it. By 1833, due to the skillful

293

and dedicated guidance of Partridge and the industry of the members, the conditions in Zion were gradually improving. Also, tensions between Zion and the church leaders in Kirtland, caused by Joseph's reluctance to move to Missouri, seemed to be lessening.[38]

Kirtland was beginning to develop into a sizable church community too. Joseph probably realized that there should be a better plan for guiding its growth. He may have concurrently envisioned a need for more magnificent dimensions for developing the city of Zion.

The church leaders in Kirtland discussed the newly forming aspects of the plan for Zion. It had been decided, in October 1831, that the apostles "would be ordained and sent forth from the land of Zion."[39] This enlarged plan may have been seen as a necessary step in preparing the way for this to take place. On June 25, 1833, Joseph Smith, Jr., Sidney Rigdon, and F. G. Williams wrote from Kirtland to W. W. Phelps and others in Zion. Along with other instructions was included a draft of the city commonly designated since as the "Mile Square City."

We send by this mail, a draft of the city of Zion, with explanations, and a draft of the house to be built immediately in Zion, for the Presidency, as well as for all purposes of religion and instruction.... Should you not understand the explanations sent with the drafts, you will inform us, so that you may have a proper understanding, for it is meet that all things should be done according to the pattern.[40]

Because of the slow mail the members in Jackson County probably did not receive these for a month or more.

Accompanying the draft was a directive from the First Presidency to the brethren in Zion to commence immediately to build a house of the Lord.

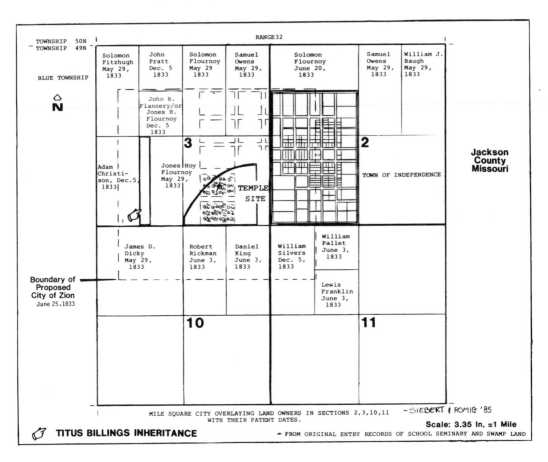

MILE SQUARE CITY OVERLAYING LAND OWNERS IN SECTIONS 2,3,10,11 WITH THEIR PATENT DATES.

—SIEBERT & ROMIG '85

Scale: 3.35 In. =1 Mile

TITUS BILLINGS INHERITANCE

← FROM ORIGINAL ENTRY RECORDS OF SCHOOL SEMINARY AND SWAMP LAND

On August 2, 1833, the prophet received divine sanction from the Lord for the above directive, and the inhabitants of Zion were informed, "that it is my will that a house should be built unto me in the land of Zion, like unto the pattern which I have given you. Yea, let it be built speedily, by the tithing of my people." . . . Upon receiving this revelation, the leaders in Zion met in council and discussed the tithing of the people and laid plans for the erection of the Lord's house. But there the matter rested.[41]

No attempt was made to record this proposed "plot" plan into the local land records, as was typically done with town plats. Later, the Kirtland plat was recorded in the Geauga County land records. Since the Independence plat was not recorded, it remained open for modification.

About the time this plan for the city of Zion arrived in Jackson County, trouble erupted. A contributing factor may have been this comprehensive plan for the land surrounding Independence. The non-member citizens of the county decided to remove the Mormons from Jackson County. On July 20, 1833, they met and agreed that the church's printing establishment should be closed and the members be required to move from the county.[42]

These nonmember residents proceeded to carry out their plans, and the two-story brick home of W. W. Phelps, which housed the press on the second floor, was attacked and razed.[43] Orson Hyde had been sent from Kirtland to deliver communications from Joseph Smith. While in Independence he witnessed these events: "I saw the office of the Evening and Morning Star lying in a pile of ruins. I saw Mr. Gilbert's brick house lying prostrate, or at least part of it, and the inmates flying there from. I also saw the doors of Mr. Gilbert's store split down, and the windows of many of our dwellings broken in."[44] Edward Partridge and Charles Allen were tarred and feathered on the county courthouse lawn.[45]

The timing of the mailing of the plan to the members in Jackson County seems to suggest that Joseph had no understanding of the impending difficulties facing those who had gathered to Zion. By November the members were being expelled from Jackson County and were in no position to implement the plan.

The plan does raise some interesting questions: How well did the plan match the geographic situation and settlement conditions in the Independence area? What problems are suggested if the plan had been implemented?

The plat for the city of Zion has some unique facets—the most salient being the introduction of a provision for twenty-four temples in the center of the city on two fifteen-acre blocks. An additional fifteen acres were designated for storehouses. These forty-five acres of the temple complex were oriented on a north-south axis. Another interesting feature was that all residents of Zion—farmer, tradesman, and merchant alike—would live in the city so they would have equal cultural benefits. This aspect of the plan called for barns and stables to be to the north and south of the plat area. "On the north and south are to be laid the farm for the agriculturalist, and sufficient quantity of land to supply the whole plot; and if it cannot be laid off without going too great a distance from the city, there must also be some laid off on the east and west."[46] Also of interest are the planned 135-foot-wide streets and houses arranged on alternate streets so they would not face one another.

The church did own some of the property included in the proposed city's boundaries. Since Partridge had already settled some members on their inheritances within these boundaries what would have happened to these members and their lands? Titus Billings is a good example because of the existence of his

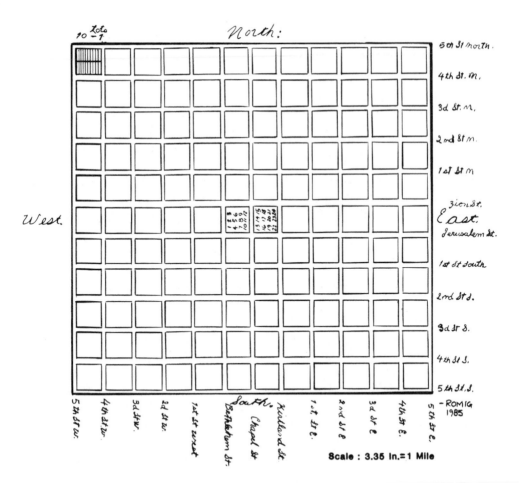

REVISED PLAT OF CITY

August 1833   Romig/Siebert

Overlay of scale "Mile Square City" over Temple Lot and the town of Independence. Contains elements of Partridge's pre-June 1831 plan for the development of Zion

consecration forms which have the legal description of his property. Was it likely that Billings would be given other property outside the city of Zion since he was a farmer, and the church would develop his inheritance into half-acre lots, as the plan for the city proposed? Or had farmer Billings suddenly become a real estate developer with the right to develop whatever lots fell into his land holdings?

Was the plan for the city of Zion an idea that would in time be molded around the existing development that Partridge had established and the large quantities of land owned by nonmember Jackson County citizens, or was it to be built at a later period—after the existing order was swept away as a result of the promised millennial cleansing that was indicated by revelations?[47]

If the plan called for an immediate reordering, how might Partridge have felt about altering many of the things which he had worked to establish over the previous two years?

The physical layout of the mile-square city interfered with the existing plat of Independence. Was Joseph aware of how Independence was platted when he proposed the plan for the city of Zion?

—Courtesy LDS Church Historical Department

297

Jackson County had been organized in 1827, as had been Independence, the county seat. City lots first went on sale on July 9, 10, and 11, 1827. Of the seventy-eight lots available for purchase on the west side of town, thirty-two or nearly half of them—were purchased in those first three days. The cost of an average unimproved town lot was $10.00, with much larger lots going to $35.00. In regard to purchasing the public lands which surrounded Independence, the intended purchaser applied for the land he wanted at the closest U.S. Land Office where he would have to meet certain requirements before being issued a certificate of ownership. Some original entries (patent lands) for Jackson County were recorded in Boonville, Missouri, before the land office was opened in Lexington, Missouri, but the issuance of the certificates was often delayed several months. Although the town of Independence had been surveyed, boundaries set, lots laid out, and a plat drawn up for the July 1827 sale, the U.S. Certificate was not acquired by the county until after the sale. Land patents (paper) took much longer to obtain and many owners did not wait to receive them before selling all or part of their approved acquisition. The certificate was proof of ownership. Therefore, under these circumstances, it is likely that in 1833 an official plat map of Jackson County which showed ownership of all acquired land was not available for viewing at the courthouse in Independence.[48]

The site Joseph designated for the first temple lay west beyond the west edge of the platted town of Independence. Perhaps the lots comprising the western portion of the town were largely unoccupied and, even though owned by others, were thought to be easily purchasable.

Related experience would indicate that Joseph had little concern about the existing situation in regard to land ownership.

On August 3, 1831, the temple site was dedicated and a corner marked with a stone: however, the church did not yet own the land.

A similar instance at a later period relates to the revision of existing plans for city development. Joseph proposed a revision to the Phelps/Whitmer plat of Far West. The original mile-square city of Far West had been divided into half-acre lots, Joseph's proposal, which was implemented, increased the size to two square miles and lots were to be one acre in size. This transpired after many members were already settled and living on lots according to the earlier plat.[49]

Closer examinations reveals the draft of the city of Zion and its explanations detail an area that is clearly not a mile square. It measures larger than a mile, and the sides from east to west are twenty rods longer than from north to south. There also seems to be some question concerning the number of residents the city could hold.

An evaluation of the plan was prepared by F. Y. Fox. . . . The 40 x 60 blocks are drawn with 32 lots

William W. Phelps

—Courtesy LDS Church Historical Department

each, obviously unintentional, since each lot is to contain one half acre. One wonders how 15 or 20 thousand people, which the plan indicates, are to reside on the square with the limitations of one house to a lot. If all the public buildings and storehouses are confined to the reserved squares, there are provided 960 lots. There would be that many residences, no more. Five to a family and one family to a residence would give a population of 4,800.[50]

The site for the first temple, marked with a cross, is at the heart of the plan. If we assume that the cross indicates the same site which was dedicated for a temple in 1831, we can then superimpose the draft of the city of Zion over a scaled map of the area and demonstrate the dimensions of the city. (See scaled illustrations.)

W. W. Phelps was present at the dedication of the temple site. In 1864 he wrote an account of that event which is in some variance with the traditionally accepted perspective of the event: "We planted a stone at the southeast corner of the ten acres for the first temple."[51]

This remembrance seems to combine some of both the early and later dimensions of the development of Zion. The reference to "ten acres" seems to be similar to what Rathbun remembered; a portion of the land was understood to be for the actual temple site and the rest which surrounded it was for members' inheritances. The reference to the *first* temple seems to relate to the later dimension of the plan which called for twenty-four temples to be built in the city for worship and public use. A better explanation of Phelps' remembrance may be that it is based on yet another, later revision of the plan.

Note: there is to be a belfry on the east end of the house sufficient to contain and support a large bell.

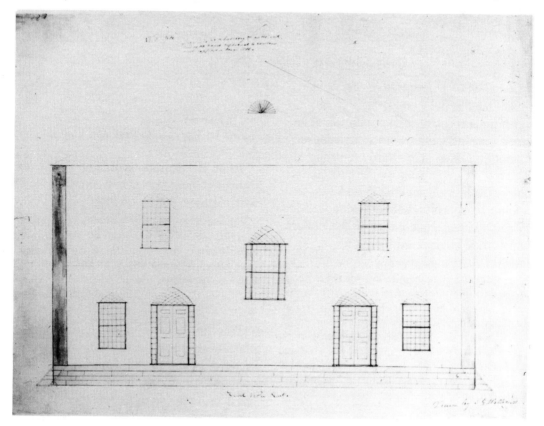

299

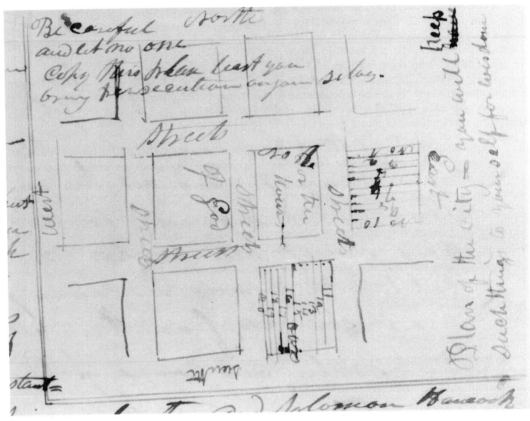

Corner of Phelps' letter to his wife Sally. The letter is dated June 2, 1835.

—Courtesty LDS Church Historical Department

Perhaps because of the outbreak of violence against the Saints in Jackson County, Oliver Cowdery returned to Kirtland in early August. On August 6, before his arrival, the First Presidency sent a letter to church leaders in Missouri detailing additional elements of the pattern which they envisioned for Zion:

"The revelation respecting the two houses to be built in Kirtland in addition to the one we are now building for the presidency and the other for the printing are also binding upon you that is you at Zion have to build two houses as well as the one of which we have sent the pattern . . . they are to be of the same size in the inner court of the one of which you have received the pattern they will therefore be larger than the ones we are to build in Kirtland you are to print an Edition of the schriptures there at the same time we do here . . . the two last mentioned houses are to be built as soon after the other as means can be obtained so to do. The pattern of the last mentioned houses as yet to be given . . ." Signed by Rigdon, Williams and Joseph Smith, Jr.[52]

After deliberating with the First Presidency, Oliver prepared another letter which stated the following:

Those patterns previously sent you, per mail, by our brethren, were incorrect in some respects, being drawn in great haste. We send you another. I have found since my arrival [in Kirtland] that our brethren here have spared no pains or labor to assist us in Zion in all things, as fast as they had understanding communicated to them.[53]

This new plan changed the proposed plat in a number of dramatic respects. It increased the total number of lots, changed the temple blocks from fifteen to ten acres, removed the reserved block for storehouses, and changed the temple block complex orientation from a north/

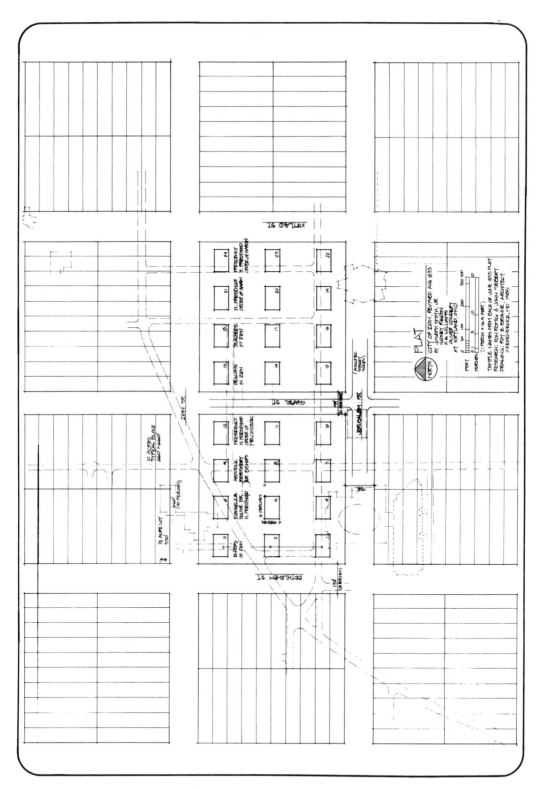

Scale drawing of temple location as per the August 1833 revision superimposed over present-day landmarks.

Roy Browne—Architect

Siebert/Romig

south axis to an east/west axis.[54] This change may have been prompted by concern about the total population capacity of the first plan. Applying Fox's formula to the revised plat, the city could now hold more than 13,000 (2,600 lots x 5 per family = 13,000 total population). At any rate, the reserved area at the heart of the plan was reduced by more than half. Changes affecting the first temple pattern were also sent. The size of the structure was enlarged, and there were to be nine windows on each side.[55]

W. W. Phelps' later remembrance of ten acres for the temple seems to be more in harmony with this revised version of the plan. In 1835 Phelps included a little drawing on the corner of a letter to his wife, Sally, who was in northern Missouri. This drawing suggests that the actual location of the Phelps' inheritance had been indicated to him. Even though this is a rough characterization of the later plan the letters which appear to spell "ours" are located on what is numbered "16,"

near the temple complex. This suggests that individual inheritances may have been allocated as the plan continued to evolve. The admonition, "Keep such things to yourself," accompanies this sketch.[56] Such information was perhaps not for the general membership at that time. Further research may reveal additional inheritances based on this later version of the plan.

In light of the changing nature of the early church's plan for the development of Zion, no one view, or snapshot, of the correct or precise physical and scriptural method of developing Zion is comprehensive. The period was not as static as has been previously portrayed. It was a time of rapid change and much revision. The people who were part of the Zion-building process 150 years ago had to follow the instructions of their leaders to know what direction the church was taking on a daily basis. Even at that they didn't always succeed in reaching their objective.

Notes

1. Doctrine and Covenants (Independence, Missouri: Herald House, 1978) Section 27; Joseph's use of the term *City* in Section 27 synonymously with Zion, gives an early picture of his conception of Zion; Doctrine and Covenants, 57.
2. William E. Bennet and Alma P. Burton, eds., *Readings in LDS Church History from Original Manuscripts.* 3 vols. (Salt Lake City: Deseret, 1953-1958) vol. I, fold-out illustration of Plat of Zion; Doctrine and Covenants, 94:3.
3. B. H. Roberts, ed. *History of the Church of Jesus Christ of Latter-day Saints.* 7 vols., 2nd ed., rev. (Salt Lake City: The Church of Jesus Christ of Latter-day Saints, 1978) vol. I, 188.
4. Heman C. Smith, ed. *History of the Reorganized Church of Jesus Christ of Latter Day Saints,* 8 vols. (Independence, Missouri: Herald Publishing House, 1967) vol I, 196-204. Note the error on p. 204. Rigdon's wife did not go on this trip: see *History of the Church of Jesus Christ of Latter-day Saints,* vol. 1, 188.
5. Ivan J. Barrett, *Joseph Smith and the Restoration* (Provo: Brigham Young University Press, 1973), 188.
6. E. D. Howe, *Mormonism Unveiled* (Salt Lake City, Utah: Modern Microfilm Company), 212.
7. Clark 1831 Letterbook. Reproduction on display, LDS Visitors Center, Independence, Missouri. Original at Kansas State Historical Society, Topeka, Kansas.
8. Ibid.
9. LDS History, vol. 1, 190-191; F. Collier, *The Unpublished Revelations of Joseph*

Smith (Salt Lake City, Utah: Collier Publishing, 1979), 57; Letter from W. W. Phelps to B. Young dated August 12, 1861.

10. Doctrine and Covenants, 57:4b; Bob and Doroles Young, *ZION: Application of the Celestial Law* (Independence, Missouri: published by the authors, 1983), 50; quote from Kirtland Revelation Book, 90.

11. Doctrine and Covenants, 27:3d.

12. Doctrine and Covenants, 57; Larry C. Porter, "Joseph Knight Jr.,—Incidents from History," *BYU Studies* (Spring 1970): 380, 318; Dean Jesse, "Joseph Knight's Recollections of Early Mormon History" *BYU Studies* (Autumn 1976): 39. "Joseph at this time looked out the country and found the place for the city and temple and set a mark."

13. *Journal History of the Church* (Salt Lake City: Church Historical Department) Reynolds Cahoon Journal Entries for June 9, 1831, and August 13, 1831. Reynolds was probably referring to the beautiful aspects of the prairies which Joseph also described in glorious terms.

14. *Scraps of Biography, 10th Book in Faith-Promoting Series* (Salt Lake City: Juvenile Instructors Office, Church of Jesus Christ of Latter-day Saints, 1883), 69-70; Doctrine and Covenants, 56, preface.

15. Leonard J. Arrington, Feramoz Y. Fox, Dean L. May, *Building the City of God* (Salt Lake City: Deseret, 1976), 21.

16. Doctrine and Covenants, 54:2; Doctrine and Covenants, 52:9.

17. D. Brent Collette, "In Search of Zion: A Description of Early Mormon Millennial Utopianism as Revealed Through the Life of Edward Partridge" (master's thesis, Brigham Young University, 1977), 33.

18. Collette, 42.

19. Donald Q. Cannon, Lyndon W. Cook, eds., *Far West Record: Minutes of the Church of Jesus Christ of Latter-day Saints* 1830-1833 (Salt Lake City: Deseret, 1984), 45-48.

20. Joseph A. Geddes, *The United Order Among the Mormons (Missouri Phase): An Unfinished Experiment in Economic Organization* (Salt Lake City: Deseret, 1924), 70.

21. Dean C. Jesse, compiler and ed., *The Personal Writings of Joseph Smith* (Salt Lake City: Deseret, 1984), letter of July 31, 1832, p. 247.

22. *Far West Record*, 61. Quote from David Pettigrew Journal.

23. Newspaper Reports on Mormonism File.

RLDS Library and Archives.

24. *Building the City of God*, 372-3. Chart on page 372 shows extant copies of consecration and stewardship forms. Chart on page 373 delineates income property and personal property of the seven extant consecrations. The total amount consecrated by the seven families was $1,210.97, or a mean of $173.00 each.

25. *Evening and Morning Star*, vol. 2, no. 14 (July, 1833).

26. Warren A. Jennings, "Zion Is Fled" (Doctoral diss. University of Florida), 94-5.

27. Milton B. Backman, Jr., *The Heavens Resound: A History of the Latter Day Saints in Ohio, 1830-1838* (Salt Lake City: Deseret, 1983), 74-5; Joseph Smith, Jr., to Edward Partridge, May 2, 1833, Edward Partridge papers, cited in O. F. Whitney, "The Aaronic Priesthood," *Contributor* 6 (October 1884): 6-7.

28. *Building the City of God*, 26-27.

29. *The Reorganized Church of Jesus Christ of Latter Day Saints vs. The Church of Christ* (Lamoni, Iowa: Herald Publishing House and Bindery, 1893), 189.

30. *Evening and Morning Star*, vol. II, no. 13, July 1833.

31. Record of Original Entries to Lands in Jackson County Missouri, Jackson County Courthouse Annex, Independence, Missouri.

32. By permission of Pauline Siegfried Fowler, based on original research.

33. Collette, 44.

34. Jackson County, Missouri Land Records, Book B, 1.

35. *RLDS Church vs. Church of Christ*, 230.

36. H. S. Salisbury, "History of Education in the Church," *Journal of History*, vol. 15 (July 1922): 259.

37. *The Life and Testimony of Mary Lightner & Mary E. Lightner's Life History* (Salt Lake City, Utah: Kraut's Pioneer Press), 7.

38. Doctrine and Covenants, 87:8.

39. L. W. Cook, *The Revelations of the Prophet Joseph Smith* (Provo, Utah: Seventy's Mission Bookstore, 1981), 327.

40. LDS History, vol. 1, 363-64.

41. Barrett, *Joseph Smith and the Restoration*, 238.

42. *RLDS History*, vol. I, 315.

43. R. Etzenhouser, *From Palmyra, New York, 1830 to Independence, Missouri, 1894.* (Independence, Missouri: Ensign Publishing

House, 1894), 322-25. "Kansas City Journal," cited in *Herald*, June 15, 1881. The article features an interview with Col. Thomas Pitcher, a leader of the county militia that participated in driving the Saints from Independence.

44. *Evening and Morning Star*, vol. II, no. 15, December 1833.

45. *RLDS Church vs. Church of Christ*, 250. Testimony of Robert Weston, son of Samuel Weston, famed Independence blacksmith, and eyewitness to the razing of the *Star* building.

46. *LDS History*, vol. I, 358.

47. Doctrine and Covenants, 45:4-10.

48. By permission of Pauline Siegfried Fowler, based on original research.

49. *Far West Record*, 119-121.

50. Julius C. Billeter, *The Temple of Promise: Jackson County, Missouri* (Independence, Missouri: Zion's Printing and Publishing Co., 1946), 56.

51. *LDS History*, vol. I, 358; *Journal History*, August 3, 1831.

52. Cook, 196, 323.

53. Alvin R. Dyer, *The Refiner's Fire: Historical Highlights of Missouri* (Salt Lake City: Deseret, 1980), 106.

54. Manuscript History, 1805-1844, Reel 8, Book A2, 203.

55. Mormon Visitors Center, Independence, Missouri.

56. W. W. Phelps to Sally, June 2, 1835, Joseph Smith Collection Microfilm, LDS Church Archives, Register No. 1.

THE INITIAL SURVEY COMMITTEE SELECTED TO APPOINT LANDS FOR GATHERING IN DAVIESS COUNTY, MISSOURI (1837-1838)

John E. Thompson

On April 26, 1838, the prophet Joseph Smith, Jr., received a revelation in Far West, Caldwell County, Missouri, which stated:

> And again, verily I say unto you, it is my will that the city of Far West should be built up speedily by the gathering of my saints; and also that other places should be appointed for stakes in the regions round about, as they shall be manifested unto my servant Joseph, from time to time.[1]

With a determination to fulfill this commission, a group led by the prophet went north to the vicinity of the Grand River in Daviess County, Missouri. On May 19, 1838, they visited a mound which Smith named Tower Hill in honor of a "Nephite tower or altar" at the top.[2] Later that same day, Smith visited an area about half a mile to the north of Tower Hill which he named Spring Hill (later to be renamed by revelation Adam-ondi-Ahman).[3] Then, soon after, he commenced the process of laying out a city plat which continued into the month of June.[4]

When the prophet's party arrived at Tower Hill for the first time, they met there the family of Lyman Wight (whose residence had been in that vicinity already for about one year).[5] Lyman Wight had not only been, at an earlier date, a member of the Far West High Council, but he also had been appointed to an earlier church survey committee to appoint lands in the north (Daviess County) for gathering. The history of this first survey committee, then, will also help us to obtain a fuller understanding of the ecclesiastical controversy between the First Presidency of the church, the Zion Presidency, and the Far West High Council in that same period, the latter part of 1837 and the beginning of 1838.

Lyman Wight

Lyman Wight was an early convert to the church who, soon afterwards, took up residence in Jackson County, Missouri. In September 1833, he was appointed one of ten high priests who were to watch over the branches in Zion.[6] Naturally, he became active in the defense of the Saints there.[7]

After the expulsion of the Saints from Jackson County in the winter of 1833, Wight went with Parley P. Pratt to Kirtland, Ohio. There he was instructed by revelation to raise companies for the redemption of Zion.[8] He did as he was instructed and on June 8, 1834, he was made General of the Zion's Camp expedition under the leadership of Joseph Smith.[9]

When the expedition to Missouri failed to redeem Zion, Lyman Wight was one who chose to "stay in the region round about" (LDS Doctrine and Covenants 105:20). Settling in Clay County, he was tried in August of 1834 by the High Council for a doctrinal error. President David Whitmer, of the Presidency of Zion, oversaw the trial and decided against him.[10]

In 1835, Wight returned to Kirtland and stayed there for some time. While there, on December 29, 1835, Lyman was blessed by the patriarch, Joseph Smith, Sr., who declared him "to be of the lineage of Joseph who was sold into Egypt without mixture of blood."[11] He also received his endowment "from on high in Kirtland," just as the "voice of the Spirit through Br. Joseph Smith jr." had promised.[12] By July 1836, however, he had returned to Clay County, Missouri.[13]

In December 1836, the Missouri Legislature formed the twin counties of Caldwell and Daviess in northern Missouri. Many Missourians believed that Caldwell County had been created expressly as a home for the Mormon people and that they had agreed to stay within its bounds. There is no evidence that the Mormons ever, explicitly or otherwise, agreed to such a deal and it seems unlikely that they would have. At any rate, the Missourians' faith in such an agreement and the Mormons "breaking" the agreement, later proved to be a source of conflict between them.

Among the first to disregard the intentions and understanding of the Missourians was none other than Lyman Wight. In the spring of 1837, he moved his family to a relatively unpopulated area near a bend of the Grand River in Daviess County.[14] He first moved into a house that had been built by Justice of the Peace Adam Black in 1835.[15] That very summer, Wight and a few other Saints who had joined him were warned by Daviess County citizens to leave the county or expect trouble. Nobody left, the date passed and nothing happened, at least not then, but it was a haunting precursor of the conflict that took place the following year. The next year, Wight built himself a house nearby, which, according to his son's description, was about fifty yards distant from the first house, "on higher ground but not on top" of a hill that the prophet later named Tower Hill.[16] The foundation stones of this second house are still visible.

While settling in Daviess County, Wight remained active in the affairs of his brethren in nearby Caldwell County to the south. The record shows that on April 24, 1837, he was again charged with erroneous doctrine, this time by Apostle David W. Patten, and convicted by the Far West High Council.[17] Though the record is not that clear on the disposition of his case, Wight probably repented and was forgiven for soon after he became a member of that very same High Council, a place of honor, and the name Lyman Wight appears repeatedly in the minutes of that council until February 5, 1838.[18] He was also involved in a leather store in Far West as early as May or June of 1837.[19] Probably because his home was already in Daviess County, Lyman Wight was selected to be a part of a committee to survey lands in that place for gathering in the fall of 1837.

The Appointment of the Initial Survey Committee and Their Labors in Daviess County

Interestingly, the initial actions which resulted in the appointment of the survey committee took place, not in Missouri, but in Kirtland, Ohio, at that time the headquarters of the church, on September 17, 1837.[20] The prophet had then addressed a conference of elders on the subject of the gathering doctrine of the Saints. The perception of the elders was that the sites currently approved for gathering were full to overflowing and that other stakes needed to be appointed. According to the History of the Church (LDS)

it was moved, seconded and voted unanimously that President Joseph Smith, Junr., and Sidney Rigdon be requested by this conference to go and appoint other stakes, or places of gathering, and that they receive a certificate of their appointment, signed by the clerk of the Church.[21]

The next day, Bishop Newel K. Whitney issued a memorial from Kirtland which urged the Saints to build up Zion by the tithe (predating the revelation of July 8, 1838, by almost a year).[22] The memorial also made clear that the ultimate destination of Smith and Rigdon's upcoming journey was Missouri:

The church of Kirtland has, therefore, required at the hand of our beloved brethren Joseph Smith jun. and Sidney Rigdon; (men who have not thought their lives dear unto them, in order that the cause of God might be established,) Presidents, whom God has appointed to preside over the whole church, and the persons to whom this work belongs, that they should go forth, and lay off other stakes of Zion or places of gathering, so that the poor may have a place of refuge, or places of refuge, in the day of tribulation which is coming swiftly on the earth.

All these things will be attended with expense.[23]

The prophet and his counselor wasted no time in beginning their journey to carry out this commission. Only ten days after the elders had voted in favor of the establishment of other stakes, they departed for Missouri.[24] By October 13, they had already reached Terre Haute, Indiana.[25] From there Sidney Rigdon wrote a letter describing the Indiana real estate. But he made clear that the eyes of the travelers were still on their goal, that small piece of real estate known as Far West, Caldwell County, Missouri, Zion in exile.[26]

Rigdon and Smith apparently arrived in Far West about November 6.[27] We have an account of what transpired there in the prophet's own words:

The High Council was immediately called and many difficulties adjusted, and the object of our mission was laid before them, after which the propriety of the Saints gathering to the city Far West, was taken into consideration, after a lengthy discussion upon the subject, it was voted, that the work of gathering to that place be continued, and that there is a plenty of provisions in the upper counties for the support of the place, and also the emigration of the Saints; also voted that other

stakes appointed in the regions thereabout, therefore, a committee was appointed to locate the same; consisting of Oliver Cowdery, David Whitmer, John Corril, and Lyman Wight; who started on their mission before we left.[28]

The prophet continued:

It was also voted that the Saints be directed to those men for instruction concerning those places; and it may be expected that all the information necessary will be had from them concerning the location of those places, roads &c. Now we would recommend to the Saints scattered abroad, that they make all possible exertions to gather themselves together unto those places; as peace, verily thus saith the Lord, peace shall soon be taken from the earth, and it has already began to be taken; for a lying spirit has gone out upon all the face of the earth and shall perplex the nations, and shall stir them up to anger against one another: for behold saith the Lord, very fierce and terrible war is near at hand, even at your doors, therefore, make haste saith the Lord O ye my people, and gather yourselves together and be at peace among yourselves, or there shall be no safty for you.[29]

The committee diligently set out to do their work as soon as possible, even before Smith left Far West for Kirtland. By the first of December, they were prepared to make a preliminary oral report before the Far West High Council.[30] It is obvious that the High Council was favorably impressed with what was said. They accepted provisionally the committee's report even while waiting for the "bills of the surveys."[31] It is unclear whether these bills were ever drawn up, but the committee continued to function.

During the first month, the survey committee apparently spent a good deal of time noting promising locations in the north of Far West, most likely in Daviess County and possibly other areas farther north along the shores of the Grand River. Oliver Cowdery described his labors surveying in a letter dated January 21, 1838, which he sent to Joseph Smith in Kirtland:

I was absent, when North, some twenty days, and should not have returned there but for the failure of Col. Wight to forward provisions as he agreed. I labored incessantly every day except one,—rain, snow or frost. I lay on the cold damp earth; had but little to eat, and that in different; but explored a great and precious country. I ran many lines with compass and chain, found a great many of the finest millsites I have seen in the western country and made between forty and fifty choice locations.[32]

Cowdery's letter demonstrates both the extent and the detail of the survey effort. The fact that he "explored a great and precious country" and made as many as fifty locations for possible gathering sites suggests that the initial survey covered a much larger area than the area which would later be called Tower Hill and Spring Hill (Adam-ondi-Ahman). The survey ranged all up and down the Grand River and its tributaries. At the same time, a formal survey was also carried out in a few locations, since Cowdery speaks of running lines "with compass and chain." In both respects, it was similar to the later survey conducted by the prophet and his assistants in May and June 1838.[33]

Though it is not clear what actions the survey committee made after the December meeting of the High Council, the committee did continue to function. David Whitmer, the president of Zion, apparently was too busy with his other obligations to continue the surveying work, so the High Council replaced him in December with Frederick Granger Williams.[34] Williams, ironically, had himself been removed from the First Presidency of the church only a short time earlier as the result of a complaint lodged by none other than Lyman Wight.[35] Whether this affected their working relationship on the survey committee is unknown.

Oliver Cowdery had been ill for six weeks prior to the date of his January 21, 1838, letter to the prophet. However, he had not given up the work of surveying. He wrote, "Notwithstanding the feeble state of my health, I had previously made preparations, and yet espect to start to morrow morning (Monday) to view still east of where I previously went."[36]

Whether or not Cowdery was able to make a second trip to Daviess County at that time, the survey committee was still in existence as late as April 12, 1838.[37] It is quite possible that whatever papers the initial survey committee prepared were later taken over by the First Presidency of the church. Thus, the work of the initial survey committee as well as the advice of one of its members, Lyman Wight, clearly influenced the direction that the later survey, in May and June of 1838, traveled as well.

Ecclesiastical Warfare, Dissenting, and the Survey Committee's Fate

In late 1837 and early 1838, the church's internal problems dramatically climaxed. As the initial survey committee was beginning its labors in Missouri, the church in Ohio was threatened with dissolution brought about by internal strife.[38] Missouri Saints and their local leaders were having problems of their own. As early as 1835, the Presidency of Zion, headed by David Whitmer, John Whitmer, and William W. Phelps, were in some degree of conflict with the Saints in Zion.[39] These problems came to a head in this period as well.

On November 6, 1837, the Far West High Council (in the same meeting in which the survey committee may have been appointed) a number of "difficulties" were brought up and reportedly resolved.[40] Cowdery, from his perspective, had a different view of what had taken place: "You will see by the conference minutes from this place that we had a judge when S. & R. were here."[41]

Part of the problem was that the Zion Presidency was somewhat independent, and the First Presidency did not feel comfortable about that. The next day, therefore, a general assembly of the Saints in Far West voted Joseph Smith, Jr., "the first President of the whole Church to preside over the same."[42] Of course, not until the dissenting members of the Zion Presidency were excommunicated was the problem fully solved, but this initial step was necessary as a means of lessening the opposition's ability to resist the First Presidency.

Therefore, to understand the fate of that initial survey committee, it must be realized that of the original five members of the committee two were also members of the Presidency of Zion (David and John Whitmer) and a third was their scribe (Oliver Cowdery). All three of these men, who had been witnesses to the Book of Mormon, were excommunicated in March and April of 1838.[43] A fourth member, Bishop John Corrill, was also a dissenter from the policies of the church in this period, although he did not actually leave the church until sometime later.[44] Only Lyman Wight remained firm in support of the First Presidency of the church throughout this period. And, when David Whitmer stepped down from the survey committee in December 1837, he was replaced by Frederick G. Williams, who probably was also a dissenter during this period.[45]

By January of 1838, Oliver Cowdery was already viewing the survey committee as far more than a mere means of locating gathering sites. Aware of his rapidly deteriorating personal relationship with the prophet, which had apparently been aggravated by the Fanny Alger matter,[46] Cowdery had come to see Daviess County as a place of refuge from the prophet for dissenters like himself. He wrote his brothers in Kirtland:

It is expected that Smith and Rigdon will come here to live, and it will be my endeavor to seek a location for myself and friends somewhere else. I am delighted with the county North, and now think we shall all find it to our interest to locate there. It will shortly be ahead of this county. The timber is better and more plenty, besides Grand River which

is navigable for steam boats passes through its centre. Evidently if *they* come *here* that is the place for *us*. My object in going North now is to secure, if possible, a place in that county and on my return shall write you more fully.[47]

Cowdery's plans, however, were never realized. Time had run out for him and for the Zion Presidency. Though Cowdery could not know it, even as he was writing this letter, the prophet and Rigdon had left Kirtland, Ohio, and were on the road to Far West to take up residence there. There was no time for Cowdery to make his move to Grand River. The entire Zion Presidency and Cowdery himself were caught up in the midst of an ecclesiastical power struggle and were destined to end up on the losing end.

Again, though Cowdery did not know it, the day before he optimistically wrote his brothers in Kirtland, a group of conspirators had met at a "social meeting" in the home of Apostle Thomas B. Marsh in Far West. Marsh, in company with Apostle David W. Patten and seven members of the Far West High Council, discussed "the proceeding of the Presidents in this place."[48] Even at this point in time, their evident goal was to pull down the presidents of Zion altogether (and Oliver Cowdery with them).

On January 26, 1838, a committee reported that the Zion Presidency ought to be removed from their office. The council resolved that the entire church (in Missouri) should vote on the matter.[49] The vote against retaining them in their office was overwhelming.[50] After this event, their excommunications were almost an anticlimax. John Whitmer and W. W. Phelps were the first to go, on March 10, 1838.[51] On April 12, 1838, Oliver Cowdery was excommunicated from the church and removed from the "committee to select locations for the gathering of the Saints."[52] The next day, David Whitmer, former president of Zion, was likewise excommunicated.[53] Thus ended not only the history of the Zion Presidency, but the initial survey committee as well.

Instead of becoming a haven for the Zion Presidency and other dissenters, the area around Grand River, in the vicinity of Lyman Wight's home, was afterwards named Adam-ondi-Ahman by the prophet himself. It became a stake of Zion with the prophet's own uncle, John Smith, as president. Ironically, instead of being far enough from Far West to be isolated from Smith and Rigdon, as Cowdery had envisioned, it proved to be so close to Far West that all three members of the First Presidency preempted land for their own use there. In fact, it could also be easily shown that the First Presidency were often in Daviess County on a somewhat regular basis in the period between May 19, 1838, and their arrest by the militia in Far West later in the year. Instead of a haven for dissenters, Adam-ondi-Ahman became a home for the faithful.

The Revelation

Since the Zion Presidency had, in the prophet, already authorized a survey committee to locate gathering sites in the Grand River area, it is perhaps not clear at first glance why the revelation of April 26, 1838, was needed to authorize a second survey of the same area.

Since the material in the revelation which deals with the building up of Far West and the arranging of stakes in the neighboring area is not new, it seems likely that one of the reasons for the second survey (and the revelation), beyond the practical need to formalize the land survey for preemption claims, may

have been an attempt, conscious or otherwise, to minimize the role of the dissenting Zion Presidency in the establishment of this new Zion in northern Missouri. The revelation of April 26, 1838, combined with the second survey of Daviess County in May and June, conveniently redirected the attention of the church from the unfaithful Zion Presidency to the true leadership of the church. In time, then, their role would be effectively obliterated from the collective memory of the Saints.

This state of affairs parallels developments in the history of the planning of the Far West temple. The Zion church had selected a committee "to assist the Presidency [Zion Presidency] to build the house of the Lord" in Shoal Creek on November 15, 1836.[54] In April 1837 their authority to do so was challenged and the work lapsed.[55] Then, on August 5, 1837, the Zion Presidency and the Far West High Council voted to resume the work at a moderate pace.[56] Yet, on November 6, 1837, apparently at the instigation of the First Presidency of the church, it was voted to postpone the Far West temple "till the Lord shall reveal it to be his will to be commenced."[57]

On April 26, 1838, the prophet, by revelation, authorized the construction of a temple in Far West.[58] The defunct Zion Presidency, suspect in orthodoxy, had been stopped in their plans, only to have the prophet freshly authorize the work under his own leadership. From this fact, Thomas B. Marsh concluded "Thus we see that the Lord is more wise than men, for Phelps and Whitmer thought to commence it long before this, but it was not the Lord's time, therefore, he overthrew it, and has appointed his own time."[59]

310

Notes

1. An extract of the April 26, 1838, revelation appeared in *Elders' Journal of the Church of Jesus Christ of Latter Day Saints* (henceforth called *Elders' Journal*) 1 (August 1838): 52-53. See also *Elders' Journal* 1:34. For an earlier manuscript copy of the entire revelation, see "The Scriptory Book of Joseph Smith Jr - President of the Church of Jesus Christ, of Latterday Saints In All the World. Far West April 12th 1838," (henceforth called "Scriptory Book"), entry of April 26, 1838, 32-34, microfilm of holograph, Library-Archives, The Church of Jesus Christ of Latter-day Saints (henceforth called LDS Archives). (For a typescript edition of the "Scriptory Book," see H. Michael Marquardt, ed., *Joseph Smith's 1838-1839 Diaries*, Salt Lake City: Modern Microfilm Co., 1982.) A letter of April 30, 1838, from Thomas B. Marsh to Wilford Woodruff (typed copy in LDS Archives) also gives a summation of the contents of the revelation. This letter was also printed in *Elders' Journal* 1 (July 1838): 36-38. In LDS editions of the Doctrine and Covenants, see Section 115:17-18. This revelation is not printed in the Doctrine and Covenants of the Reorganized Church of Jesus Christ of Latter Day Saints (Independence, Missouri). The text, however can be found in *The History of the Reorganized Church of Jesus Christ of Latter Day Saints*, vol. 2 (Independence, Missouri: Herald House, 1896), 151-152.

2. "Scriptory Book," May 19, 1838, 43-44. A later and considerably modified version of this appears in "Manuscript History of the Church of Jesus Christ of Latter-day Saints," Book B-1, Willard Richards (scribe), 791-792, microfilm of holograph, Special Collections, Brigham Young University. Book B-1 is the immediate ancestor of Joseph Smith, *History of the Church of Jesus Christ of Latter-day Saints*, vol. 3, B. H. Roberts, ed. (Salt Lake City: Deseret Book Company, 1974), 34-36. Tower Hill itself is the site of an Indian burial mound, which may be an explanation for this comment about the Nephite tower or altar.

3. "Scriptory Book," May 19, 1838, 43-44. For a discussion of the chronology of the naming of Spring Hill Adam-ondi-Ahman, see John E. Thompson, "Spring Hill and Adam-ondi-Ahman: A Reconsideration of the Date of Doctrine and Covenants 116," a paper read at the sixteenth annual meeting of the Mormon History Association, Rexburg, Idaho, May 2, 1981. See also Lyndon W. Cook, *The Revelations of the Prophet Joseph Smith* (Provo, Utah: Seventy's Mission Bookstore 1981), 333-334.

4. This survey was apparently the basis of the plat map of Adam-ondi-Ahman drawn by Bishop Alanson Ripley, which is reproduced in Alvin R. Dyer, *The Refiner's Fire: The Significance of Events Transpiring in Missouri* (Salt Lake City: Deseret Book Company, 1978), 166. Probably also a result of this survey is a list of land claims drawn up by George W. Robinson, the recorder for the church. See "Record Book A.: Adam-ondi-Ahman Mo," microfilm of holograph, the H. G. Sherwood Papers, LDS Archives.

5. Leland Homer Gentry, "A History of the Latter-day Saints in Northern Missouri from 1836 to 1839," Ph.D. disser., Brigham Young University, 1965, 224-225. See also Leland Homer Gentry, "Adam-ondi-Ahman: A Brief Historical Survey," *BYU Studies* 13 (Summer 1973): 554. Gentry cited in support of his understanding *Times and Seasons* 1 (March 1840): 65. Further evidence of this understanding is in the fact that this July 7, 1837, letter of W. W. Phelps was actually printed three years earlier than the *Times and Seasons* version in the *Latter Day Saints' Messenger and Advocate* 3 (July 1837): 529. From this I conclude that Gentry was absolutely right in his assertion that Wight was in Adam-ondi-Ahman by 1837. Lyman Wight and other Saints in Daviess were, according to Phelps, warned to leave Daviess County by August 1, 1837, or suffer the consequences. Apparently, the warnings were ignored and the date passed without incident. Thus, Philip A. Wightman ("Lyman Wight," M.A. thesis, Brigham Young University, 1970, 33) is clearly wrong in arguing that Wight did not move to Tower Hill, Daviess County, until February 1838.

6. "The Conference Minutes and Record Book of Christ's Church of Latter-day Saints, belonging to the High Council of Said Church or their Successors in Office, Caldwell County, Missouri, Far West: April 6, 1838," September 11, 1833, p. 36, LDS Archives. (Since this document is normally referred to as the Far West Record, henceforth, we shall abbreviate it to *FWR*.) See also Donald Q.

Cannon and Lyndon W. Cook (eds.), *The Far West Record* (Salt Lake City: Deseret Book Company, 1983) under date.

7. *History of the Church*, 1:433.

8. Doctrine and Covenants 103:30 (LDS editions only). This revelation was not published until the 1844 edition of the Doctrine and Covenants. At that time, the text printed only the secret name Baurak Ale with no indication that Joseph Smith was intended by it. Earlier manuscripts, however, had the name Joseph Smith with no mention of Baurak Ale. Finally, some time after the death of the prophet, the solution was devised to print the secret name with the name of the prophet in brackets. Most recently of all, however, LDS editions have deleted the secret name from the text.

9. *History of the Church* 2:88.

10. FWR, August 21, 1834, 63-64. Apparently Wight had said: "All disease in this church is of the Devil and that medicine administered to the sick is of the Devil, for the sick in the church ought to live by faith." In the wake of the cholera cases that were among the faithful of Zion's Camp, President David Whitmer ruled that Wight's optimistic teaching was unacceptable.

11. Lyman Wight, quoted in Wightman, 28.

12. FWR, June 23, 1834, 41-42.

13. *History of the Church* 2:453.

14. Gentry, "Northern Missouri," 226.

15. Letter of Orange Lysander Wight, 1903, 3-4, typescript copy located in Special Collections Library, Brigham Young University.

16. Orange Lysander Wight, "Adam-ondi-Ahman," photocopy of 1903 original, LDS Archives. (This map was discovered among some papers in the St. George Temple in Utah by Tom Truitt and Lauritz G. Peterson in 1977).

17. FWR, April 24, 1837, 74. Part of Wight's error was reportedly believing that the Doctrine and Covenants edition of 1835 was only a "telestial law," the Book of Commandments constituting a "celestial law." David W. Patten was later killed at the Battle of Crooked River in the fall of 1838.

18. FWR, April 24, 1837-February 5, 1838, 74-99.

19. FWR, no date, 76.

20. *History of the Church*, 2:514.

21. Ibid.

22. *Messenger and Advocate* 3 (September 1837): 562. A later version of this same document is printed in *History of the Church* 2:516. The July 8, 1838, revelation on tithing is now printed as LDS Doctrine and Covenants 119:5.

23. *Messenger and Advocate* 3 (September 1837): 562.

24. *History of the Church* 2:517.

25. Ibid.

26. Letter of Sidney Rigdon as printed in *Elders' Journal* 1 (October 1837): 5-6.

27. *History of the Church* 2:521. This material is apparently based on *Elders' Journal* 1 (November 1837): 27-29.

28. *Elders' Journal* (November 1837): 27.

29. Ibid.

30. FWR, December 7, 1837, 92. See also Gentry, "Adam-ondi-Ahman," 554.

31. FWR, December 7, 1837, 92.

32. Letter of Oliver Cowdery, Far West, Mo., to Warren A. Cowdery, January 21, 1838, containing a copy of a letter of the same date by Oliver Cowdery to Mr. Joseph Smith, Jr. Original in the Huntington Library, San Marino, California. Copy in the RLDS Library and Archives, Independence, Missouri. Microfilm of document in LDS Archives.

33. *History of the Church* 3:34-40.

34. FWR, December 7, 1837, 92.

35. Ibid., 82-83.

36. Letter of Cowdery to Joseph Smith, January 21, 1838.

37. "Scriptory Book, April 12, 1838, 31.

38. James B. Allen and Glen M. Leonard, *The Story of the Latter-day Saints* (Salt Lake City: Deseret Book Company, 1976), 114.

39. See Letters of W. W. Phelps, microfilm of holograph, Genealogical Society, Salt Lake City, Utah. An undated missive of Phelps in this collection, believed to have been written about July 20, 1835, states: "The three Presidents of Zion act for his good, whether in Zion, Kirtland, or England, and have a right to assist in regulating the affairs of her stakes: Therefore, when anyone attempts to meedle with her affairs, he will be held to an account before God. As ever. W. W. Phelps."

40. FWR, November 6, 1837, 80-82.

41. Letter of O. Cowdery to Cowdery, January 21, 1838.

42. FWR, November 7, 1837, 82.

43. W. W. Phelps and John Whitmer (along with Marcellus Cowdery) were excommunicated by the Far West High Council on March 10,

1838. (*FWR*, 104-108, under date.) Oliver Cowdery was removed on April 12, 1838. (*FWR*, 118-126, under date. See also "Scriptory Book," April 12, 1838, 31.) And former President David Whitmer on April 13, 1838. (*FWR*, 131-133, under date.) All of these excommunications are briefly mentioned in *History of the Church* , vol. 3, as well. See also *History of the Reorganized Church* 2:143-151.

44. John Corrill, *A Brief History of the Church of Christ of Latter Day Saints* (St. Louis: John Corrill, 1839). (A reprint of this work is available from Modern Microfilm Company, Salt Lake City.)

45. Since Apostles T. B. Marsh and David W. Patten were prime movers in the removal of the Presidency of Zion and other dissenters such as Oliver Cowdery at that time in Missouri, it is worthy of note that it was T. B. Marsh who played a key role in having F. G. Williams removed from the First Presidency. *FWR*, November 7, 1837. See also *History of the Reorganized Church* 2:117-120. That Williams' dissent was more serious than has generally been recognized is also indicated by the fact that he apparently left the church entirely sometime within the next few months. The proof of that assertion is found in *History of the Reorganized Church* 2:167.

46. In his January 21, 1838, letter to his brother Warren, Oliver Cowdery called the prophet's relationship with Fanny Alger "a nasty, dirty affair." It may well be that this was the very matter discussed in the Far West High Council on November 6, 1837. (See *FWR*, November 6, 1837, 81-82.) Cowdery's charges themselves became a charge against him at his excommunication on April 12, 1838, for which see *FWR* under date, 118-126. Curious confirmation of Cowdery's understanding of what took place between Joseph and Alger may be found in a letter from William E. McLellin (formerly of the Twelve) to Joseph Smith III, dated July 1872, RLDS Library and Archives. In the letter McLellin reported a conversation that he had had with Emma Smith, the prophet's wife, in Nauvoo, Illinois, in the year 1847:

"Again I told her [Emma] that I heard that one night she missed Joseph and Fanny Alger. She went to the barn and saw him and Fanny in the barn together alone. She looked through a crack and saw the transaction!!! She told me this story too was verily true."

47. Letter from O. Cowdery to W. Cowdery, January 21, 1838.

48. *FWR*, January 20, 1838, 94.

49. *FWR*, January 26, 1838, 95-96.

50. *FWR*, February 5-9, 1838, 99. On February 10, 1838, the Council also took from Oliver Cowdery, W. W. Phelps, and John Whitmer the right to sign licenses. Thomas B. Marsh and David W. Patten were made presidents pro tempore over the church in Zion the same day. The *coup* was complete.

51. *History of the Church* 3:6-8.

52. "Scriptory Book," April 12, 1838, 31. The material mentioning the survey committee is not found in *FWR*, April 12, 1838, 126. However, the "Scriptory Book" is itself such an early witness that we may assume safely that Cowdery's membership on the survey committee was indeed discussed on that occasion. Since *History of the Church* 3:18 was indirectly derived from the "Scriptory Book" text as it was altered later by the scribes of "Manuscript History of the Church," the lack of any mention of the survey committee in the decision recorded in that later source has no bearing at all on the historicity of the "Scriptory Book" version here. Indeed, the scribal tendency to remove this mention of the survey committee as unimportant should be viewed as part of a larger conscious or unconscious desire to forget about it and its accomplishments because of the source from which those accomplishments came: the Presidency of Zion.

53. *History of the Church* 3:18.

54. *FWR*, November 15, 1836, 68.

55. *FWR*, April 3, 1837, 72.

56. *FWR*, August 5, 1837, 79-80.

57. *FWR*, November 6, 1837, 81.

58. LDS Doctrine and Covenants 115:8-16. See also *History of the Reorganized Church* 2:151-152.

59. Letter of Thomas B. Marsh to Wilford Woodruff, typed copy, LDS Archives. This letter was also published in *Elders' Journal* 1 (July 1838): 38. It should, of course, be stated that Marsh's interpretation of the Lord's time for building the Far West Temple, from the benefit of hindsight, was not by revelation and is not necessarily historically accurate, since the Temple was never built beyond laying of four cornerstones, which are still visible in Far West on the site.

QUEST FOR ZION: JOSEPH SMITH III AND COMMUNITY-BUILDING IN THE REORGANIZATION, 1860-1900

Roger D. Launius

(Part of this article appeared as "The Mormon Quest for a Perfect Society at Lamoni, Iowa, 1870–1890," Annals of Iowa, 47 (Spring 1984): 325–42. I wish to express appreciation to Christie Dailey and Katherine Scott Sturtevant for their editorial assistance.)

I

Perhaps the single abiding objective of the members of the Church of Jesus Christ of Latter Day Saints during the lifetime of Joseph Smith, Jr., was the establishment of a viable Utopian community on the earth, a place to which the righteous might gather for protection from the evils of the world and the sanctuary from which the gospel might be carried to the nations of the globe. Ultimately this society would serve as the vehicle for the establishment of an earthly kingdom of God and as the catalyst for the millennium. In pursuit of this vision, the Mormons had established settlements at Kirtland, Ohio; Independence and Far West, Missouri; and Nauvoo, Illinois, but in each case the vision had dissolved in failure and disillusionment. The reasons for failure were complex, but essentially rested on the unwillingness of the Saints to live under the strict laws of the community established by the prophet and on persecution by non-Mormons.[1]

Although a mob murdered Joseph Smith, Jr., the Mormon prophet, on June 27, 1844, neither the movement he had founded nor the aspirations of his followers for a physical Zion died with him. Numerous groups arose after Smith's death to claim a portion of the Mormon legacy, each adopting in some measure its Zion-building ideal. Brigham Young headed the largest and most important of these groups, establishing his church's headquarters in Salt lake City, Utah, and presiding over the creation of numerous religiously-oriented communities in the Great Basin of the Rocky Mountains.[2] But Young's organization was not alone in its community-building mission, for other sects claiming the heritage of Joseph Smith, Jr., also believed that part of their religious commitment included the formation of Zionic societies on the earth.[3] During the 1850s several of these lesser Mormon factions coalesced into the Reorganized Church of Jesus Christ of Latter Day Saints, having its headquarters and most of its membership in the Midwest. This group was composed largely of conservative Mormons who exemplified the most cherished virtues of American Christianity, but nonetheless clung to a vision of a perfect community to be established by the Saints.[4]

By the time the Reorganized church had emerged during the 1850s under Jason W. Briggs and Zenas H. Gurley, Sr., Many Saints had been forced to re-evaluate the church's visions of Zion and the gathering of the righteous in relationship to past failure, but few rejected the belief outright. Undoubtedly, the majority of the Saints looked with great longing toward the day when the prophet would call them to gather at a selected place and establish Zion on earth. But Briggs and Gurley believed they had no authority to dictate policy regarding the question of Zion and the gathering, and, consequently, they persuaded the Reorganization's General Conference of 1852 to adopt a very mild statement on the subject. The resolution stated: "that in the opinion of this conference there is no [place] to which the Saints on this continent are commanded to gather at the present time." The conference did not reject the "sacred goal of bringing forth Zion in America," but it adopted a cautious policy that asked the Saints to wait until a more opportune time before beginning a settlement. The policy proposed that the Saints be satisfied for the present "to turn their hearts and their gazes towards Zion, and supplicate the Lord God for such deliverance." This statement underscored the uncertainty of the new Mormon organization during the 1850s, but it also accented the longing of the church to implement the quest for a physical Utopian community.[5]

II

When twenty-seven-year-old Joseph Smith III, son of the Mormon founder, assumed leadership over the Reorganized church on April 6, 1860, the organization achieved the status of an important Mormon faction second only to Young's sect in the Great Basin, The younger Smith dealt with many serious questions during his first years as president of the Reorganized church, but his policy regarding the Utopian society envisioned by his father was one of the most important issues of his administration.[6] Immediately on his acceptance of the church's presidency, Smith's followers believed that he would begin the long anticipated gathering of the Saints for the building of a Zionic society. But the young leader's impressions about the nature of the movement's Zionic mission was somewhat different from that of many of his followers. While convinced that his father's approach toward organizing righteous communities was basically correct, Smith realized that the early Mormons had tried to accomplish too much too quickly. He believed that neither the early church members nor the non-Mormons had been sufficiently prepared to overcome their fundamentally selfish human nature and accept an all-sharing Zionic lifestyle. Smith noted that besides selfishness, the Saints had never exhibited the respect for each other that made possible a communitarian society, nor had they shown the personal piety and striving for perfection crucial to the successful establishment of such a Christian Utopia. Non-Mormons, on the other hand, did not understand the significance of such a society to the Mormon movement's millennialism and oftentimes castigated it and in some cases sought to destroy it.[7]

Smith soon came to believe that the Reorganization's Zion-building effort should be more liberal and all-encompassing than it had been during his father's lifetime. For the younger Smith the millennial kingdom of God could be initiated only through personal righteousness and moral perfection, and would reach full fruition only if the righteous destroyed evil in society. Joseph Smith's hope that the Saints would purify themselves and at the same time become moral crusaders in the world became a corollary to his father's Zionic program under which early Mormons had retreated from secular society to create their Utopia away from outside influences. Therefore, the logical conclusion of

Smith's philosophy was an emphasis on the spiritual nature of Zion rather than its physical, community-building aspects.[8]

As a result of Smith's personal emphasis on the inner purity of the Saints and the necessity of working to change the world for the better, the young leader immersed himself in humanitarian reform movements and urged his followers to do the same. In the mid-1860s, for instance, he published an editorial in the church's official newspaper, the *True Latter Day Saints' Herald*, that succinctly stated his beliefs: "The church should begin to take a high moral ground in regard to the very many abuses in society, which can only be reached, to correction, by a strong setting upon them of the current of public opinion."[9] He called for a churchwide crusade to eliminate sin, the primary barrier to the establishment of Zion, and for the Saints to move out as reformers to a world filled with all manner of evil. The effort might take decades, even centuries, but Smith believed the church would ultimately triumph if it moved in a cautious, steady, and unified manner. Therefore, Smith agitated in both political and social spheres for the reform of American society.[10]

Joseph Smith's concern with the spiritual aspects of the kingdom of God did not mean that he totally neglected the church's desire to build a righteous community. He insisted only that this particular quest take a less important role than it had during the early years of the church's existence. As evidence of his commitment to the creation of a Zionic center for the church Smith considered very early in his career establishing a religious community at Independence, Missouri. Prodded not only by church members who longed for the beginning of a Utopian experiment and expected the prophet to act, but also by a Quincy, Illinois, lawyer named Godfrey who saw the prospect of a lucrative legal fee for his services, Smith in mid-1860 explored the possibility of pressing claims for damages suffered by the church in 1833 when the early Saints had been expelled from their property in western Missouri. Considering the prospect of founding a church-sponsored community in Missouri using reparations gained from the legal settlement, Smith sent Godfrey to Independence to research the land records at the courthouse and bring back information about the feasibility of a civil suit in Jackson County.

Anticipating victory in such a lawsuit, Smith sent his stepfather, Lewis Crum Bidamon, to Independence to scout the area for property that the church might purchase for a Mormon settlement. Bidamon had been there for only a few days, however, when he realized that the Saints had virtually no chance of obtaining a favorable settlement in the courts. First, the Reorganization possessed no deeds to the church's 1833 property for which it sought payment and, consequently, had only the most tentative of claims based on the continuation of the movement and young Joseph Smith's personal status as the son of the early Mormon prophet. Second, many of the Missourians who had expelled the Mormons in 1833 were still living in the vicinity and were still strongly opposed to the church. The Missouri courts which would decide the case almost certainly would reflect their hostility. Third, even if the Reorganization could have won the case, the movement into the area would have aroused hostility and might well have forced another violent reaction.[11]

Rather than return to Joseph Smith III in Nauvoo with this discouraging news, Bidamon decided to scout for an alternate location for the anticipated Reorganized church community. He worked his way northward into Iowa looking at land as he went. Everywhere he found land promoters and speculators anxious to sell him large tracts for the proposed community. Although Bidamon could make no final arrangements, he informed potential sellers that his stepson would be able to close any business deals. As a result, land promoters from Missouri and Iowa began to inundate Joseph Smith with offers of land for sale, proposing attractive packages with little money down and liberal credit terms.

Young Smith was flabbergasted that his stepfather had overstepped his authority so extravagantly, and by the time Bidamon returned to Nauvoo Joseph had built up weeks of anger which he vented on him. He told his stepfather that he had been wrong in looking for land outside Jackson County, that the Reorganization had no concrete plans for the formation of a community of any type, and that Bidamon should inform all the promoters that the church had no interest in buying land at that time. Bidamon apologized for his poor judgment and made amends as best he could. In spite of Bidamon's actions, however, his report about the impossibility of a lawsuit proved valuable and Smith based his decision to halt plans for it on his stepfather's realistic assessment.[12]

Apparently Bidamon's excursion into Iowa reached many more people than just the land promoters to whom he talked during the trip. Soon thereafter Smith began receiving letters from ambitious promoters all over the United States offering to sell their land at very reasonable prices. Most of the offers, such as the one made by the former territorial Chief Justice of Utah, John F. Kinney, were quickly disposed of by Smith, who replied that the Reorganization had no plans for the establishment of a church settlement anywhere in the immediate future.[13]

Other offers were not so easily dismissed. Some were made by old members of the church or friends of Smith's father. Not long after his ordination as president of the church, for example, Smith received an offer from James Arlington Bennett, the debonair proprietor of the Arlington House educational institution on Long Island, New York. Bennett had been a friend of Joseph's father during the 1840s, and may have joined the church just before the prophet's death. In his letter Bennett reminisced about his friendship with the prophet and applauded young Joseph's acceptance of leadership in the Reorganization. Bennett noted that as a small token of the esteem in which he held the church and the Smith family he was willing to help Joseph establish a Utopian community for the Saints that would be as important as anything his father had achieved. Smith read this proposal with particular interest. "I am not aware of what property you have in Nauvoo," he said,

but if it were necessary & meet to form a nucleus around which the Saints might congregate I have 160 acres of land in Livingston County, Illinois most admirably located between the Grait R. Roads that I would give for the purpose. Here immense numbers of the Saints could repair from all parts of the U.S. including Utah. Where under your plan their respectability and power would soon be felt.

Smith considered this offer for a time, but ultimately turned it down. Smith's mother may have influenced him to disregard Bennett's proposal, for she disliked and distrusted him, on one occasion even calling him an "old arch hypocrite."[14]

Smith also received a letter from another Bennett not long thereafter, John Cook Bennett, a man whom the Saints had expelled from the church in 1842 on charges that included attempted murder of the prophet. In June 1860 Bennett wrote the Reorganization leader from

Polk City, Iowa, a small town north of Des Moines, where he was raising chickens for the commercial market. He told Smith that he owned many acres of prime land that he would gladly make available for the church's use as a communal gathering center. As they discussed the possibilities, however, Bennett asked that Smith keep their correspondence secret and that he send him a fictitious name and address so they could communicate in strictest confidence. Smith recalled his reply to Bennett in his memoirs, "I immediately wrote him that any communication addressed to Joseph Smith, Box 60, Hancock County, Illinois, would reach me and be given proper and due consideration," adding that he "had but one name and address for the communications of either friend or foe." After this harsh reply Smith never heard from Bennett again.[15]

The aborted lawsuit, the questionable offers from friends of the Saints, and Smith's natural inclination to pursue spiritual purity rather than physical community-building, prompted the Reorganization leader to deemphasize for the immediate period any communal experiment on the part of the Saints. This decision was reinforced during the late summer and early fall of 1860 when religious persecution arose in Hancock County over a misinterpretation of Smith's beliefs concerning the community-building aspects of the Mormon religion. On July 1, 1860, Smith had written a letter to a longtime friend, George F. Edmunds, Jr., a lawyer at the county seat of Carthage, that stated that the young prophet had decided to remain in Nauvoo for at least five years, managing his religious affairs from his home.[16] The letter was soon made public and although everyone in the community ever having dealt with Joseph Smith III recognized that he was an honest, upstanding citizen, many residents could still remember the

difficulties that had arisen because of the Saints' settlement at Nauvoo during the 1840s. They had seen Smith's father turn a frontier topsy-turvy in less than five years, and they had no desire to see a second generation prophet do the same.

Most residents of the county were relatively unconcerned with the situation, but some outspoken non-Mormons proclaimed on the basis of a misreading of the letter that Smith intended to revive his father's dream of a Mormon commonwealth in the county and demanded action to stop such a move.[17] The misunderstanding reached large proportions within a few weeks after the letter had been made public, and by the first of August dissident elements in Hancock County began to act against Smith and his followers. On August 21, more than one hundred Carthage residents met at the county courthouse and passed resolutions prohibiting Smith from practicing his religion anywhere in the region. Other towns soon followed suit, passing their proscriptions on to Smith who ignored them.[18]

The most forceful opposition to Smith came from residents of Nauvoo, and was led by Mayor Robert W. McKinney. McKinney cared little about Smith's religion, but he feared that the young church leader, who was a candidate for mayor and had a sizable following, could oust him from office in the election scheduled for the fall of 1860. Consequently, McKinney used the religious issue as a means of discrediting Smith's candidacy. Under his leadership the townsmen held a rally and passed a series of resolutions prohibiting Smith's religion in Nauvoo, sending a young lawyer in the town, J. Bernard Risse, to deliver the resolutions to Smith at his office. Risse, who knew Smith through his capacity as a Nauvoo Justice of the Peace, gave him the resolutions and stood awaiting a reply. The young Reorganization president noted immediately that no one had signed the document and it was, therefore, nothing more than an anonymous complaint. He called this to Risse's attention, telling him to have the leaders in charge of the meeting sign the resolutions. Risse refused, prompting Smith to ask

Who is responsible for this move, and for this document? Who authorized it, or who had sought in this manner to suppress me in the free expression of any religion? Is this public opinion expressed in this manner? If so, to whom may I look for the enforcement of the interdiction contained therein?

Risse refused to answer these questions and left Smith's office quickly. The prophet never heard any more about these resolutions; however, he made it clear to the citizens of Nauvoo that should they be presented with signatures he would bring suit on grounds of freedom of religion.[19]

Throughout the summer and fall of 1860 Smith received a few more demands that he stop practicing "Mormonism" or leave the county, but he ignored them and nothing more happened. The anti-Mormons were never well organized, and since neither Smith nor his church posed an immediate threat to the community few people were so concerned about his activities actually to take direct action. In addition, some members of the county came to Smith's support. George Edmunds, to whom the letter had originally been addressed, stood up in his behalf, claiming that he had committed no wrong, that he was entitled to basic civil liberties, and that his intentions concerning the use of Nauvoo as a church gathering center had been misinterpreted. Thomas C. Sharp, one of the foremost anti-Mormons of the 1840s, also spoke on Smith's behalf, telling the people of the county that he believed Joseph to be an entirely different type of man from his father and that the younger

Smith had no intentions of founding a Mormon Utopian citadel in Nauvoo. Moreover, Sharp said he had survived one Mormon conflict and had no wish to become involved in another. Writers from the *Chicago Journal* and *New York Times* also commented that the opposition to Smith in Hancock County was misguided, and that anyone who took direct action against the new Mormon leader would find that Smith had many supporters not only in the county but also nationwide.[20]

Aided by such opposition from outside elements as well as his own inclinations, by the fall of 1860 Joseph Smith had decided to avoid possible conflict with the non-Mormon community by announcing an exceptionally cautious policy regarding the Zionic experiments that many church members expected. In an epistle to the Reorganization he stated his policy. Smith told his followers, "there is no command to gather . . . at any given locality." Before any such gathering could take place, be continued, "there are many obstacles to be met by us, which are to be overcome, not the least of which is . . . prejudice." He counseled the Saints to remain in their present homes and to demonstrate their Christian faith there. But while most Latter Day Saints accepted this policy as undeniably logical, evidence indicates that most also considered it only temporary and looked forward to the time when their prophet would announce the gathering of the Saints to a Zionic center.[21]

III

While Smith managed to ignore the members' calls for the beginning of a communal experiment during the first few years of the 1860s, pressure from his followers mounted throughout the remainder of the decade. An 1863 article in the church newspaper summarized the general belief of the Saints about the quest for Zion. The author wrote that members live "daily as strangers and pilgrims on the earth, who look for 'a city which hath foundations, whose builder and maker is God.'" It was only the prophet's movement to Plano, Illinois, in early 1866 and the location of most of the church's officials and offices there that curtailed much of the membership's demands for the establishment of a separate Utopian settlement. For a time, at least, Plano satisfied the Saints communal expectations because with its large church population, proportionate percentage of important church officials, and numerous supporting institutions—its printing office, administrative offices, and religious educational activities—it served as an official gathering location for the movement.[22]

Plano did not satiate the membership's desires for long, however, and increasing pressure forced Joseph Smith to respond to the demands that the church begin its "Zion-building mission." He wrote in the *True Latter Day Saints' Herald* in 1868 that he heard from every quarter the constant cry for community building but told the church that it had not yet accomplished the self-purification necessary before it could succeed in establishing such a society. "Strife and contention, with disobedience," he chided, "are sure fruit that the gospel, the great witness, had not wrought in us the work of peace, and without peace in our hearts we predict that *no perfectness will come in Zion.*" He claimed that only when the Saints cease "evil of any and every kind, [and] become champions of truth, [then] there will be no want of definite action or policy" in forming a Utopian society.[23] A little over a year later Smith suggested that those who wished to engage in gathering together to establish a Zionic community should informally settle with others of like mind without waiting for an official pronouncement by the church leadership about a specific project.[24]

Although officially silent about the gathering of the Saints during this period, Smith wrestled with the question. He believed in the ultimate Zionic mission perhaps as strongly as anyone in the church, but his caution and emphasis on the spiritual made him act more hesitantly. In late 1869 Smith began to perceive a way to undertake a form of the old community-building issue accepted by most church members without violating the spirit of his more idealistic approach. Smith and other church officials of similar beliefs called for the Reorganization to establish not a full-fledged communal experiment, but a less ambitious joint-stock company that would make land available to Latter Day Saints on terms equitable to both the company and the settlers. In so doing the church would indirectly sponsor a settlement of church members and satisfy the repeated pleadings of many Saints to undertake such an experiment, but it would have neither official church management nor the millenarian overtones of similar settlements established by the Saints in Missouri and Nauvoo during the 1830s and 1840s. In essence, Smith could publicly emphasize the spiritual aspects of Zion while the joint stock company would satisfy the membership's demands for a physical settlement.

The movement toward the founding of this corporation and a settlement for the Saints began at the Reorganization's General Conference in October 1869. During this meeting representatives from throughout the movement were informed by Joseph Smith about the prospects of beginning a company to establish a religious community. He made it clear that he did not intend the experiment to be the final Zion-building enterprise. Rather, as he told the conference, "it is given as a means to an end, not as the end itself."

Nonetheless, Smith called the organization of a corporation whose express purpose was to establish a Latter Day Saint community a step toward the full realization of the church's Zionic mission. The proposal received enthusiastic support from the conference body, and with this approval Smith moved quickly toward organization of the company.[25]

Immediately after the conference Smith appointed Bishop Israel L. Rogers, the church's chief financial officer, to take charge of the company. During the winter of 1869-70 Rogers and a carefully selected group of associates prepared a proposed constitution for the corporation. The Order of Enoch, as they titled the new company (the name was the same used by Joseph Smith, Jr., for the organization that managed the Mormon communal experiment in Independence, Missouri, between 1831 and 1833), was a legally constituted organization empowered to buy and sell land and securities, construct buildings, manufacture machinery, lease assets, and make contracts. The proposed constitution stated the company's purpose:

The general business and object of this corporation shall be the associating together of men and capital and those skilled in labor and mechanics, belonging to the church . . . for the purpose of settling, developing and improving new tracts of land, . . . to take cognizance of the wants of worthy and industrious poor men, who shall apply therefore, and provide them with labor and the means for securing homes and a livelihood; and to develop the energies and resources of the people who may seek those respective localities for settlement.

Rogers and his committee recommended that the Order of Enoch's charter specify a twenty-year existence, at which time the shareholders could either renew the charter for another twenty years or dissolve the company.[26]

With the details of the Order of Enoch's government drafted, Rogers was ready to begin soliciting support and financial com-

mitments from the church membership. In February 1870 he sent a printed circular to each congregation of the movement explaining in detail the purpose and organizational structure of the new corporation and asking for investments from the Saints. The members responded rapidly, and by May 1870 the Order of Enoch had received pledges of $28,000 with the prospect of even more coming in thereafter. Rogers wrote in the church newspaper that this financial response came because the Saints believed "that the *First Order of Enoch* is but the beginning of the prosperity of Zion."[27]

On May 15, 1870, Rogers addressed an open communication to the church commending them on their generous pledges to the Order of Enoch and announcing the formal organization of the company in the fall of 1870. He asked that as many subscribers as possible attend the first meeting of the corporation, to be held in conjunction with the church's General Conference in September at Council Bluffs, Iowa. At this meeting, he added, the subscribers were to approve formally the company's constitution and by-laws and elect a board of directors. Joseph Smith was present but took no part in the proceedings when the subscribers met on September 19, 1870, following the church's semi-annual conference. At the meeting those present ratified the Order's constitution as presented by Israel Rogers. They also chose a board of directors consisting of seven faithful Saints; and elected Elijah Banta, a giant, amiable man from Sandwich, Illinois, president and Rogers treasurer of the company.[28]

They then moved on to what many thought the most important and historic event of the meeting, an appointment of a committee to seek "a suitable location for the purchase of land & the operation of said company." Elijah Banta; David Dancer, a wealthy businessman from Wilton Center, Illinois; Israel Rogers; and Phineas Cadwell of Magnolia, Harrison County, Iowa, a future member of the Iowa state legislature, assumed this responsibility. Smith and Rogers believed, as Rogers had written in May 1870, "we feel assured that the committee will be directed in the search for a location by that Spirit which had charged the affairs of God's people . . . [and] that a step toward the redemption of Zion may be taken, and taken now." As the first annual meeting of the Order of Enoch came to an end the Saints believed that their dreams of a physical community would soon be realized.[29]

IV

The committee on location began work immediately after the fall conference looking for the ideal land for settlement. Banta became their prime field operative, and he began traveling throughout Illinois, Iowa, and Missouri in search of inexpensive but productive land. He stumbled across a large tract of land in Decatur County, Iowa, quite by accident but immediately found that it was exactly what he had been looking for. The Reorganized church had a strong, active congregation of approximately fifty members at Pleasanton, Iowa, a few miles east of this land, and Banta had gone there to visit some of the members. Ebenezer Robinson, one of the congregational leaders, told Banta that he had experienced a vision in which he had been told that the Latter Day Saints were to gather in large numbers on either side of the state line west of Pleasanton. In this supposed vision, Robinson had heard the voices of angels singing this verse:

> Give us room that we may dwell!
>   Zion's children cry aloud:
> See their numbers—how they swell!
> How they gather, like a cloud!

As a result of Robinson's testimony Banta decided to investigate the prospects of purchasing land immediately west of Pleasanton.[30]

Between October 3 and November 24, 1870, Banta made several visits to Decatur County to look over the land and make arrangements for its purchase. One of its most attractive features, he found, was that a large part of Fayette Township could be purchased on liberal credit terms for as little as eight dollars an acre. In addition, the prospects of a railroad being built through a town site there were excellent. After reviewing all its attractions, the committee on location decided to purchase the property as soon as the board of directors could meet and give its approval. By April 5, 1871, the board had met, with Joseph Smith present as a matter of courtesy, and sanctioned the purchase. Shortly thereafter Banta contracted on behalf of the Order of Enoch for the purchase of 2,680 acres in one large tract and several smaller parcels in southern Decatur County for the sum of $21,768.84.[31]

Soon after purchase the Order of Enoch's directors began planning for the land's development. Banta dispatched surveyors to the newly acquired property during the summer of 1871; the team divided it into eighty-acre and 160-acre parcels. Meantime, other company officials prepared for the Saints to establish homes on the property, developing priorities for choosing the first colonists and formulating policies for governing the community. With these activities still under way the first settlers arrived in covered wagons from Wisconsin during early July 1871. These settlers, the families of Samuel Ackerly and Robert K. Ross, had waited years to "gather" with the Saints and were heartened by the beginning of the Order of Enoch experiment. Soon other settlers followed, and the handful of families on the property began building homes, breaking land, and making other improvements.

Most of these first settlers' farms were purchased outright from the Order of Enoch, but Elijah Banta and the other members of the board offered rental or rental-purchase arrangements to settlers with less money. As a result the Order of Enoch often built one-and-a-half-story homes and assorted outbuildings on eighty-acre tracts and rented them to the settlers; the Order collected one-third of the crops for the use of the property. For a larger proportion of the crop yield, however, the Order of Enoch would allow a settler to acquire title to the farm. In this way the Order's directors made it possible for families to raise their standard of living and eventually purchase their farms.[32]

When Israel Rogers made his first secretary's report to the Order of Enoch shareholders on September 1, 1871, he enumerated the successes of the company's first year. Most important, Rogers reported that the company was financially secure. After the purchase of the Decatur County property the Order had operating capital amounting to $22,731.16, money sufficient to continue developing the Decatur County property. Rogers also reported that the company's settlers were industriously improving the property. He added that many had already completed "spacious accommodations," and that the Order had erected twelve homes at the cost of $7,678.40 for property renters. Additionally, Order of Enoch employees and settlers had worked together to break the sod of 1,600 acres, plant acres of nursery plants, and make other improvements.[33]

From the community's inception, the Latter Day Saints settling there considered religious fellowship its most important advantage. Virtually all of the colonists took part in the Reorganized church congregations nearest their farms.

In November 1871, however, fifteen settlers who had been attending the Little River congregation of the church, located in the western part of the county, organized a new group that met on the Order's property. This group became known as the Lamoni Branch, after a benevolent king in the Book of Mormon. In time this group built a building (24 by 36 feet) to meet in which they called the "sheepshed," partly because they considered themselves sheep of the fold of Jesus Christ but also because one unimpressed church member upon seeing the structure remarked, "Humph! It looks like a sheepshed."[34]

After the initial flurry of activity the directors of the Order of Enoch allowed the settlement in Decatur County to develop independently and by 1874 it had grown into a modest farming community. It had a population of about 150, most of whom were Reorganized church members. It boasted a general store, a blacksmith shop, a few homes near these shops, and ranging farms. During this time the settlers asked the directors of the Order to begin the incorporation of the community as the town of Lamoni to further city development, but little progress was made at the time. The directors did not forcefully manage the experiment during the mid-1870s, and the colony operated virtually autonomously under what might be called a policy of "benign neglect."[35]

V

Joseph Smith III, who had no official role in the Order of Enoch, watched the development of the Lamoni experiment from his church administrative offices in Plano. The community's establishment had been a boon to the church, giving the members hope for an expression of the best intentions of the movement. But he had wanted the Order of Enoch to serve as a crucible out of which might arise a people with the spiritual unity and moral integrity needed to begin the establishment of a physical Zion. He was disappointed, therefore, that the Order's leadership seemed to allow affairs at its colony to drift aimlessly. As a result, he quietly prodded its leaders to act more responsibly by encouraging them at every opportunity and by intimating that in time the church headquarters would be located in Lamoni.[36]

Smith's efforts to promote more forceful leadership from among the directors of the Order of Enoch were only moderately successful, for these men acted lethargically in all to many cases, as in their hesitancy to take advantage of an opportunity broached by a railroad in 1875 to allow it to pass through the company's land. This move would have ensured the settlement's easy access to the outside world and provided a focus for the establishment of an important town. Instead it came to nothing. Seeking to goad the Order's directors still further, Joseph Smith persuaded the General Conference of April 1875 to designate a special committee of removal separate from the Order of Enoch to "arrange for and effect the purchase of lands, locate a town site, and perform such other acts as are consistent with the making of such locations" of gathering. Smith's skills as a politician were shown in this maneuver, for he realized that if all else failed the threat of removal of church support from the Order of Enoch and of placing it elsewhere would be a powerful lever in influencing its leaders. Smith could either use the church-authorized committee to support the Order's work or pursue an independent experiment in community-building under direct church control.[37]

Apparently Joseph Smith had no real intention of withdrawing church support from the Order of Enoch, but the conference action served the purpose he had intended. The Order of Enoch leaders had perceived the new committee as a threat to the welfare of the Lamoni settlement. This perception was compounded by Smith's apparent willingness to consider other gathering locations. For instance, during the 1870s he met with the town fathers of Nauvoo to discuss the city's proposal that the Reorganization make its headquarters there and encouraged the efforts of Saints moving into Independence, Missouri. As a result, the Order's leaders met with Smith and other church officials on May 11, 1875, to discuss the situation. After obtaining these directors' promise to act more responsibly, Smith pledged the church's support for the Lamoni community. Later, on June 6, 1875, Smith privately told the Order's leaders that he and several close associates had investigated the possibility of moving the church's headquarters from Plano to Lamoni. As a result, Smith asked David Dancer; W. W. Blair, the prophet's closest advisor; and John Scott, a well-respected church member, to oversee the removal of the church's assets—administrative offices, publishing house, and religious education facilities—to Lamoni as soon as practicable. He cautioned that this committee should not act hastily, and that the move should take several years at least. Nonetheless, this decision meant that Smith and the church looked forward to a bright future in Lamoni.[38]

Following this meeting, the directors of the Order began to manage the Lamoni settlement more forcefully; so much so that at the General Conference of 1877 the body endorsed officially the movement of the church headquarters to Lamoni. When Joseph smith visited the settlement in August 1877 he was favorably impressed. He said, "the country where the Order of Enoch has located the scene of their operations has been frequently described, but we found a changed land to that we visited and rode over some six years ago." He continued:

Then, a wilderness of arable land, untouched by the plow, and dotted only here and there by a farm or a grove, greeted the eye; now, a cheerful scene of busy farm-life, a wide spread of growing corn and wheat and rye and oats and waving grass was seen everywhere, broken now and then by an interval of untilled land, showing the places yet open to the settler, where the cattle roamed freely the occupants, literally, of a "thousand hills" It was rightly called a rolling country; very fair to look upon, and giving to the careful and industrious husbandman a just reward for his labor.[39]

Following Smith's visit the Order's leaders continued to improve conditions at the Decatur County settlement, but little out of the ordinary happened until 1879, when plans for a railroad through the Order of Enoch property hastened the selection of a formal townsite. The Leon and Mt. Ayr branch of the Chicago and Burlington Railroad was being constructed in early 1879, but the plans dictated that the tracks be laid several miles north of the Latter Day Saint property on a nearly straight line between Leon and Mt. Ayr. Elijah Banta, representing the Order of Enoch, and several influential residents of the settlement met with the railroad officials and agreed to furnish certain concessions to the company in return for laying its tracks through the Order's property. Specifically, the Order agreed to plat a town on the railroad line, obtain a charter from the state legislature, and provide 200 acres of land for the town. Order of Enoch officials carried out these stipulations during the spring of 1879, and by the end of the year the railroad had been completed through the property; the first passenger train passed through the townsite on December 25, 1879.[40]

VI

In spite of the favorable activity there, Joseph Smith held off on a presidential announcement about when the church headquarters would be moving to Lamoni until 1880, commenting only that it would be soon. Smith had often received letters from church members seeking advice about where to move to be with other Saints, and he had usually replied by asking them to remain where they were but if they had to move Plano was a good location. By mid-1879, however, he was telling them not to go to Plano under any circumstances because of the poor economic situation. He wrote one prospective settler in the later part of 1879, "I would not like to encourage you to come, and then have you no chance to maintain yourself." Instead Smith began advising the Saints to move to Lamoni.[41]

Conditions in Plano worsened during 1880, even as they brightened in Lamoni, and the hard times there led Smith to make the final step toward moving church headquarters to Lamoni. He wrote to his closest advisor, W. W. Blair, explaining that Plano was becoming a ghost town and the church had to move its administrative offices soon or poor economic conditions in Plano might make property sales impossible:

The bottom is out of the Plano real estate market. Deering is removing, car by car, all he has. The lumber yard is about empty, and the men are being discharged, one by one. Many are making removal to Chicago, and some are going elsewhere; and Plano will soon be a dismally dull business place.

He finally concluded, "I agree with you, *move at once.*"[42]

It did not take the Saints living in Plano long to leave after the official word came that all church administrative offices were beginning the move to Lamoni. By early 1881 most of the church's membership had moved away—the bulk of them settling in the Lamoni area—and most of those left in Plano were packing. A last General Conference met in Plano in April 1881, and most of the Saints approached it with both a feeling of sorrow at leaving

325

and a hope for a better future in Iowa. Joseph Smith struck the general mood of the Reorganization during these months in a letter to a close friend. "There is now an opportunity to make a striking step forward in our work," he wrote in March 1881. "I believe that we should take that step. I have made the matter one of constant study and prayer; and have that assurance that makes me bold to go forward."[43]

When it first became apparent that the church would move its headquarters Joseph Smith had purchased for $1,000 sixty acres of relatively poor land in southern Decatur County, a few miles from Lamoni, from a church member named Moses A. Meader. David Dancer, one of the driving forces behind the Order of Enoch, believed that Smith's property would be unacceptable for the prophet's use and arranged on October 21, 1879, to trade Smith forty acres of rich farmland about a mile west of Lamoni for his other property. Dancer also agreed to purchase the remaining twenty acres of Smith's property, thereby allowing him to realize a small profit on the transaction.[44] Thereafter, Joseph Smith built on this acreage a twenty-room Victorian farmhouse, which he named Liberty Hall. Constructed of Michigan lumber by Thomas Jacobs, an itinerant carpenter who lived with the Smiths for years thereafter, work on Liberty Hall began during the summer of 1881 and by late fall it was ready for occupancy.[45]

When Smith and his family received word that Liberty Hall was nearly completed they packed their household goods for the trip to Lamoni. During the first part of October 1881 Smith contracted for the shipment of their possessions to the new home. The household goods were accompanied by Smith's wife, Bertha, and their children—a group that included four girls and four boys at the time. Joseph, on the other hand, remained in Plano for several days after the departure of his family to complete some business affairs. When Bertha arrived in Lamoni with the children, however, she found that the house was not yet ready for occupancy and had to find other lodging for a few days until work could be completed.[46]

In spite of this tentative start, the family quickly learned to love Liberty Hall and the house began to take on something of the character of its inhabitants. It had a well-used formal parlor for special occasions, a less formal living room filled with plants and the furniture most used by the family. Liberty Hall also had an office for Joseph's use, complete with bookshelves from floor to ceiling on three walls to shelve his extensive library. Additionally, the family enjoyed a well-planned, modern kitchen, a lavish dining room, and upstairs suites of rooms for the boys, girls, parents, and guests. Outside, the Smiths planted an extensive orchard and vineyard that eventually rivaled any in the community. Finally, Joseph fenced the remainder of the forty acres, farmed some of it, had cattle in a small pasture, and enjoyed a well-used fishing lake on another part.[47]

The move of the Smith family signaled the official demise of Plano as a Reorganized church religious center and ushered in the reign of Lamoni as the church's stronghold. Before leaving Plano, however, the Smith family received a warm send-off from the town. The local newspaper reported the farewell celebration:

The citizens of Plano presented Elder Joseph Smith with a magnificent gold-headed cane on Wednesday evening. J. H. Jenks presented it in a fine speech. The ladies of Plano presented Mrs. Joseph Smith with an elegant silver cake basket. As these were presented by those outside the [Reorganized] church, the speaker being a Methodist, it speaks well for the standing of Elder Smith in particular, and the Mormon people in general.

By November 1881 nearly all of the church institutions had been relocated in Lamoni and the little church settlement grew in activity.[48]

The most important Reorganized church institution to be reestablished in Lamoni, after the office of president itself, was the publishing house. The Herald Publishing House office had been located in Plano since 1863, and had risen to almost legendary status in the church. On October 15, 1881, Joseph Smith, the director of the establishment, announced in the *Saints' Herald* that the printing office was moving and that the next issue of the *Herald* would appear on November 1 as scheduled from Lamoni, Iowa. Once moved, the *Herald* office set up temporary quarters in a frame building in Lamoni and later moved to a fine brick office in the heart of the town.[49]

VII

As the church headquarters relocated in Lamoni the town appeared to take on even more vitality and charisma. Physically it changed because of the large influx of people into the community and the building their arrival required. For instance, in 1881 the population of Lamoni stood at approximately 300; it had expanded to 490 by 1885, to 1,133 by 1895, and by 1900 the community had 1,540 residents. With this increase came a broadening of businesses and manufacturing concerns located in Lamoni. In 1896 the retail businesses on Lamoni's main business district included three general stores, a dry goods store, three men's clothing stores, two drug stores, two jewelry stores, two banks, three millinary shops, four restaurants, a shoe shop, three butcher shops, two hotels, two buggy dealers, a grain elevator, and several other stores. It numbered as manufacturers one tailor shop, two furniture building establishments, four blacksmith shops, two machine shops, a gristmill, two lumberyards, three printing plants, and other assorted small factories.[50]

Lamoni was a busy town in which to live not just economically, for the Saints inhabiting the community sought to take advantage of the social aspects of their close proximity as well. After all, the fostering of a righteous community of believers was critical to the concept of Zion so long cherished by the Saints. Lamoni's residents organized a Chautauqua Society for intellectual study and advancement, the Civil War veterans in the community established a chapter of the Grand Army of the Republic for fellowship, others organized Odd Fellows and Masonic lodges, and many more became involved in other social organizations. One important group, organized on April 12, 1883, was the Ladies Union Mites Society which encouraged a multitude of worthwhile civic projects. For others the Lamoni Silver Band and the Mandolin Band or community-sponsored baseball and football teams occupied leisure time.[51]

The gathering of these Saints in one location logically meant that the community suddenly became a powerful political force in the county. The Reorganization had discouraged its numbers in local areas to elect church members to office or to influence the opinions of non-Mormon officials in the past. In 1876 a statement was printed in the *Saints' Herald:* "No subject is of less importance to the Saints than politics." With the rise of Lamoni after 1880, however, the issue became unavoidable.[52] As naturally happened in an area with many people of like mind, a voting block quickly and informally developed that ran counter to the established party system. Between 1875 and 1885, for instance, the Saints at Lamoni radically shifted their voting pattern six times, and in every case the shift was toward a Saint or proven friend of the church who was a candidate for office. A typical example came in 1883 when Elijah Banta ran for the Iowa legislature as the Democratic nominee from Decatur County. The Lamoni vote was two to one in favor of Republican candidates for all other races during this election, but reversed itself to a two to one majority for Democrat Banta. This election brought a highly critical reaction from a local newspaper, the *Decatur County Journal*, published in Leon, the county seat:

One word to our Republican Mormon friends. If you were told we opposed Mr. Banta because he is a Mormon, it was a falsehood. We had no objection to his religion. We opposed him as a political trickster, and a man of intemperance habits; but most of our Republican Mormon friends supported him because he is a member of their church. To this we solemnly protest, and declare we do not wish to mix politics and religion.[53]

If these political activities antagonized the non-Mormons in Decatur County, it did not push them so far that they ever undertook violence to rid the countryside of the sect, as had been the case with the early Mormon church. Neither did the Reorganized church members pay much attention to these outside influences, for the religious life of the community was of paramount importance. The Saints living in Lamoni considered themselves richly blessed by the community experience. A homogeneous society of politically conservative, morally upright, and economically compatible people, the town developed something of a family atmosphere where the residents cared for the needs of each other. Perhaps Joseph Smith III was the epitome of this, for he enjoyed living there so much that he balked, but finally consented, when asked to relocate in 1906 to Independence, Missouri. He particularly cherished worshiping in a relatively large congregation of Saints of like mind, interacting with his followers virtually every day on the streets, and being intimately involved in

their lives. He took great delight in the pastoral ministry of the flock of Saints in the town. Because of this satisfying experience Smith came to believe during the 1880s that Lamoni was serving its purpose well. It had become a Reorganized Mormon mecca; a center for gathering for the Saints, and a stable, religious, and conservative society in which all enjoyed a measure of the blessings inherent in such a communal experience.[54]

But Smith's contentment with life in Lamoni did not mean that he became complacent or parochial in his view of Zion. His commitments were still to the spiritual perfection of his people and the eventual building of an ideal society in Independence, the traditional Center Place of Zion in Mormon thought. As the ultimate location of the church headquarters, Smith believed it necessary to encourage the Saints living in Independence to push even further in their demonstration of a Zionic lifestyle by serving as Christian examples to their neighbors. He encouraged the community of Saints in Independence, which had been growing since the 1870s, to build up the area as the ultimate "Center Place of Zion," adding that if they worked cautiously and with forethought the time would come when the church headquarters would be moved there. This was not an inconsistent position, however; Joseph Smith III had long interpreted the Lamoni experience as a mere stopping point in the journey toward Zion.[55]

Such a position, coupled with the genuine success of the settlement at Lamoni, fostered definite action when the time came for the Order of Enoch's charter to expire in 1890. Joseph Smith III asserted that no further purpose would be served in continuing the corporation for another twenty years. The company's shareholders largely agreed with Smith's conclusion that the Order had served its purpose in providing a place where the Saints could live together in relative peace and harmony and asked its board of directors to cease operations and divide the assets among the shareholders. They did so not with remorse, for they were pleased with the success of the experiment and fully convinced that the Lamoni settlement had helped give the Saints strength to move toward the eventual building of a spiritual kingdom of God on earth.[56]

After the dissolution of the United Order of Enoch the church took no part formally in the creation of a second Zionic experiment until 1909 when another United Order of Enoch was organized in Independence, Missouri. Lamoni continued to be the most important location for the Reorganized church membership for many years. An indication of its importance was the creation there in 1896 of the sect's only institution of higher learning, Graceland College. Even so, with the demise of the Order of Enoch,

Lamoni began to lose some of the uniqueness that had set it apart. This situation was accelerated in 1906 when Joseph Smith, by then an old man, moved his family to Independence, Missouri. Furthermore, within a decade many of the church's other administrative officers had moved there as well and by the end of the 1920s the Reorganized church had formally established its headquarters in Independence.[57] In essence, the communal experimentation within the Reorganized church during the nineteenth century was an outgrowth and evolution of the Zionic ideal of early Mormonism. It emerged in the minds of the Saints after the long experience of the Order of Enoch, more reasoned and perhaps more mature. That Zionic ideal, moreover, has continued to evolve since that time taking on new dimensions as the church's perspectives and understandings have changed.[58]

Notes

1. The best analyses of early Mormonism's quest for an earthly Zion can be found in Mario S. DePillis, "The Development of Mormon Communitarianism, 1826-1846" (Ph.D. disser., Yale University, 1960); Leonard J. Arrington, Feramorz Y. Fox, and Dean L. May, *Building the City of God: Community and Cooperation Among the Mormons* (Salt Lake City, Utah: Deseret Book Co., 1976), 15-40; Klaus J. Hansen, *Quest for Empire: The Political Kingdom of God and the Council of Fifty in Mormon History* (Lincoln, NB: Bison Books, 1967), 3-71; Leonard J. Arrington, "Early Mormon Communitarianism: The Law of Consecration and Stewardship," *Western Humanities Review,* 7 (Autumn 1953): 34-69; Joseph A. Geddes, *The United Order Among the Mormons (Missouri Phase)* (New York: Columbia University Press, 1922).
2. Arrington, Fox, and May, *Building the City of God,* 41-321, *passim.*

3. The great diversity and unique religious beliefs of these movements have been discussed in Steven L. Shields, *Divergent Paths of the Restoration* (Bountiful, Utah: Restoration Research, 1982).
4. Alma R. Blair, "The Reorganized Church of Jesus Christ of Latter Day Saints: Moderate Mormons," F. Mark McKiernan, Alma R. Blair, and Paul M. Edwards, eds., *The Restoration Movement: Essays in Mormon History* (Lawrence, Kansas: Coronado Press, 1973), 207-30; Joseph Smith III and Heman C. Smith, *The History of the Reorganized Church of Jesus Christ of Latter Day Saints* (Independence, Missouri: Herald Publishing House, 1971 ed.), vol. 3; Inez Smith Davis, *The Story of the Church* (Independence, Missouri: Herald Publishing House, 1969 ed.), 390-441.
5. Early Reorganization minutes, Book A, June 13, 1853, RLDS Library Archives, Independence, Missouri.

6. Richard P. Howard, "Images of Zion in the Reorganization," in David Premoe, ed., *Zion: The Growing Symbol* (Independence, Missouri: Herald Publishing House, 1980), 45-49.

7. Joseph Smith III to J. J. Pressley, March 31, 1880, JSLB 3, RLDS Library Archives; Doctrine and Covenants (Independence, Missouri: Herald Publishing House, 1970), Sections 42, 57, 77, 81; "The Location of Zion," *True Latter Day Saints' Herald*, 3 (October 1862): 74; "Questions and Answers," *Saints' Herald*, 38 (September 26, 1891): 616; John Zahnd, "Room in Zion," *Saints' Herald*, 56 (July 7, 1909): 638.

8. Joseph Smith III to Alfred Hart, May 9, 1880, JSLB 3; Joseph Smith III to William H. Kelley, March 22, 1871, William H. Kelley Papers, RLDS Library Archives.

9. Joseph Smith III, "Editorial," *True Latter Day Saints' Herald* 8 (September 1, 1865): 67.

10. Joseph Smith III, "Editorial," *True Latter Day Saints' Herald* 29 (February 18, 1880): 49; *True Latter Day Saints' Herald* 27 (September 18, 1880): 284; Joseph Smith III to Rev. F. Wilson, September 23, 1878, JSLB 2, RLDS Library Archives; Joseph Smith III to David R. Ramsey, August 6, 1879, JSLB 2; *Weekly Argus* (Sandwich, Illinois), July 16, 1881; *Kendall County Record* (Yorkville, Illinois), December 8, 1875, April 4, 1878.

11. Joseph Smith III, "Autobiography," in Edward W. Tullidge, *The Life of Joseph the Prophet* (Plano, Illinois: Herald Publishing House, 1880), 775-76; *Amboy* (Illinois) *Times*, March 17, 1864; *Complainant's Abstract of Pleading and Evidence in the Circuit Court of the United States, Western District of Missouri, Western Division, at Kansas City, the Reorganized Church of Jesus Christ of Latter Day Saints vs. the Church of Christ at Independence, et. al.* (Lamoni, Iowa: Herald Publishing House, 1893), 275-78; Joseph Smith III, "Editorial," *Saints' Herald* 24 (January 15, 1877): 25.

12. Smith, "Autobiography," in Tullidge, *Life of Joseph,* 775-76.

13. Joseph Smith III, "The Memoirs of President Joseph Smith (1832-1914)," *Saints' Herald,* 82 (April 16, 1935): 495.

14. James Arlington Bennett to Joseph Smith III, May 6, 1860, Joseph Smith III Papers, RLDS Library Archives; Emma Bidamon to Joseph Smith III, January 21, 1870, Mormon Collection, Chicago Historical Society, Chicago, Illinois.

15. Smith, "Memoirs," *Herald* 82 (January 8, 1935): 49-50; Robert Bruce Flanders, *Nauvoo: Kingdom on the Mississippi* (Urbana: University of Illinois Press, 1965), 93-96, 242-77.

16. Joseph Smith III to George F. Edmunds, Jr., July 1, 1860, Joseph Smith III Papers; Thomas Gregg, *History of Hancock County, Illinois* (Chicago: Charles C. Chapman and Co., 1880), 376-77.

17. Smith to Edmunds, July 18, 1860; Smith, "Autobiography," in Tullidge, *Life of Joseph,* 777.

18. *Carthage Republican,* August 23, 1860, August 24, 1860.

19. Ibid., July 10-November 26, 1860; Smith, "Memoirs," *Herald* 82 (March 19, 1935): 370; (March 26, 1935): 399-400.

20. Joseph Smith III to D. C. Murdock, January 6, 1894, JSLB 5 RLDS Library Archives; Joseph Smith III to D. A. Alvord, July 15, 1896, JSLB 7, RLDS Library Archives; *New York Times,* August 29, 1860; *Chicago Journal,* August 24, 1860.

21. Joseph Smith III, "An Address to the Saints," *True Latter Day Saints' Herald* 1 (November 1860): 254-56; Gregg, *History of Hancock County,* 376-77.

22. "The Location of Zion, No. 4," *True Latter Day Saints' Herald* 3 (April 1863): 138; Smith, "Memoirs," *Herald* 82 (June 25, 1935): 817-18; (July 2, 1935): 848-50.

23. Joseph Smith III, "Pleasant Chat," *True Latter Day Saints' Herald* 13 (June 1, 1868): 168-69.

24. *True Latter Day Saints' Herald* 16 (August 1, 1869): 81, 16 (September 1, 1869): 146.

25. Joseph Smith III, "What Shall it be Called?" *True Latter Day Saints' Herald* 17 (March 1, 1870): 144-48.

26. "Proposed Constitution of the First United Order of Enoch," *True Latter Day Saints Herald* 17 (February 15, 1870): 126.

27. Israel L. Rogers to Samuel Powers, February 10, 1870, Miscellaneous Letters and Papers, RLDS Library Archives.

28. Israel L. Rogers, "To the Saints," *True Latter Day Saints' Herald* 17 (May 15, 1870): 289-90; "The Order," *True Latter Day Saints' Herald* 17 (October 1, 1870): 595; Jason W. Briggs, "A Condensed Account of the Rise and Progress of the Reorganization

of the Church of Latter Day Saints," M. H. Forscutt-H. A. Stebbins Letterbook, RLDS Library Archives.

29. Order of Enoch, Minutes 1870-1882, 7, RLDS Library Archives; "To the Saints," 290; Joseph Smith III, "The Movement," *True Latter Day Saints' Herald* 17 (July 15, 1870): 435.

30. "Report of the Board of Directors to the Stockholders of the First United Order of Enoch," *True Latter Day Saints' Herald Supplement* 18 (June 17, 1871): 1-4; Frederick W. Blair, comp., *The Memoirs of President W. W. Blair* (Lamoni, Iowa: Herald Publishing House, 1908), 174-75; *The Saints' Harp* Plano, Illinois: Herald Publishing House, 1870), Hymn No. 939.

31. Elijah Banta, Journal, Book B, 157-58, Mormon History Manuscripts Collection, Frederick Madison Smith Library, Graceland College, Lamoni, Iowa; Order of Enoch Minutes 1870-1882, 7-12.

32. Pearl Wilcox, "The First United Order of Enoch and the Founding of Lamoni, Part 1," *Restoration Trail Forum* 6 (February 1980): 4.

33. Israel L. Rogers, "Report of the Secretary of the Order of Enoch," September 1, 1871, RLDS Library Archives.

34. Asa S. Cochran, "The Founding of Lamoni and the Work of the Order of Enoch," *Saints' Herald* 54 (January 22, 1908): 80-83; Order of Enoch Minutes 1870-1882, 7-12; Larry E. Hunt, *Frederick Madison Smith: Saint as Reformer*, 2 vols. (Independence, Missouri: Herald House, 1982); Wilcox, "The First United Order of Enoch, and the Founding of Lamoni, Part 2," *Restoration Trail Forum* 6 (May 1980): 3.

35. Order of Enoch Minutes 1870-1882, 38-48; *History of Ringold and Decatur Counties, Iowa* (Chicago: Lewis Publishing Co., 1887), 782-88; Smith and Smith, *History of Reorganized Church*, 4:120.

36. Smith, "The Movement," 435; Joseph Smith III to David Dancer, November 26, 1877, JSLB 1, RLDS Library Archives; W. W. Blair, "The Gathering," *True Latter Day Saints' Herald* 23 (September 1, 1876): 513; Blair, comp., *Memoirs of W. W. Blair*, 187-88.

37. *True Latter Day Saints' Herald* 22 (May 15, 1875): 299-300; Joseph Smith III to Bro. Hendrick, January 4, 1877, Joseph Smith to J. W. Brackenbury, March 6, 1877, Joseph

Smith III to William H. Kelley, March 22, 1877, Joseph Smith III to Charles Derry, June 9, 1876, all in JSLB 1; Smith, "Memoirs," *Herald* 82 (November 5, 1935): 1424; Joseph Smith III, Diary, December 18, 1877, RLDS Library Archives; *Carthage (Illinois) Gazette*, December 26, 1877; *Plano (Illinois) Mirror*, June 22, 1876.

38. Joseph Smith III to Phineas Cadwell, December 8, 1877, Joseph Smith III to Lars Peterson, January 9, 1878, Joseph Smith III to David Dancer, July 15, 1878, all in JSLB 1; Joseph Smith III to David Dancer, February 18, 1879, March 10, 1879, JSLB 2; Order of Enoch Minutes 1870-1882, 49-60; Blair, comp., *Memoirs of W. W. Blair*, 191-92.

39. Smith and Smith, *History of Reorganized Church* 4:186; *Saints' Herald* 25 (January 15, 1878): 24.

40. Joseph Smith III, "Editorial," *Saints' Herald* 26 (October 15, 1879): 312; T. J. Andrews, "Impression on Visiting Decatur County," *Saints' Herald* 26 (August 1, 1879): 228-31; Joseph Smith III, "An Order of Enoch," *Saints' Herald* 26 (July 15, 1879): 218-19; "Editorial Items," *Saints' Herald* 26 (September 1, 1879): 263; Order of Enoch, Minutes 1870-1881, 61-62.

41. Joseph Smith III to Henry Bach, November 26, 1879, JSLB 2.

42. Joseph Smith III to W. W. Blair, October 30, 1880, JSLB 3.

43. Joseph Smith III, "Editorial," *Saints' Herald* 27 (October 15, 1880): 322; *Weekly Argus*, May 15, 1880; *Plano Mirror*, April 14, 1881; Joseph Smith III to David Dancer, March 26, 1881, JSLB 3.

44. Land Records, Book 33, p. 277, Recorder's Office, Decatur County Courthouse, Leon, Iowa.

45. Smith, "Memoirs," *Herald* 82 (March 5, 1935): 303; (December 10, 1935): 1588, (December 17, 1935): 1615.

46. *Kendall County Record*, October 13, 1881; Joseph Smith III, "Editorial," *Saints' Herald* 28 (November 1, 1881): 332; Clara B. Stebbins, "My Neighbor, Joseph Smith," in Mary Audentia Anderson, ed., *Joseph Smith, 1832-1914: A Centennial Tribute* (Independence, Missouri: Herald Publishing House, 1932), 50; Smith, "Memoirs," *Herald* 82 (December 17, 1935): 1615.

47. Smith, "Memoirs," *Herald* 82 (December 17, 1935): 1615-16; *Herald* 84 (May 22,

1937): 656-57; Interview with Alma R. Blair, January 14, 1976; Alma R. Blair, "Liberty Hall Taking Shape," *Restoration Trail Forum* 2 (February 1976): 1, 8; Alma R. Blair, "Liberty Hall Lives Again," *Restoration Trail Forum* 4 (August 1978): 7-8.

48. Smith, "Memoirs," *Herald* 82 (December 17, 1935): 1615-16; Joseph Smith III, "Editorial," *Saints' Herald* 28 (November 1, 1881): 322; *Weekly Argus*, September 17, 1881.

49. Joseph Smith III, "Editorial," *Saints' Herald* 28 (October 15, 1881): 322.

50. James C. Reneau, "A History of Lamoni, Iowa, 1879-1920;; (M.A. Thesis, University of Iowa, 1953), 72.

51. Alma R. Blair, "Lamoni, Iowa—Way Stop on Return Road to Zion," *Restoration Trail Forum* 4 (August 1978): 4; Smith, "Memoirs," *Herald* 82 (December 10, 1935): 1587-88; (December 17, 1935): 1615-16; Joseph Smith III to Israel A. Smith, December 26, 1898, March 31, 1899, September 20, 1904, August 15, 1905 June 5, 1906, Miscellaneous Letters and Papers, RLDS Library Archives.

52. *True Latter Day Saints' Herald* 23 (November 15, 1876): 262.

53. *Decatur County Journal* (Leon, Iowa), July 6, 1882, October 11, 1883, October 18, 1883; *Saints' Herald* 29 (May 15, 1882): 152; *Saints' Herald* 31 (December 27, 1884): 825-27; *Saints' Herald* 32 (May 23, 1885): 333; *Saints' Herald* 38 (September 25, 1886): 593; Alma R. Blair, "A Loss of Nerve," *Courage: A Journal of History, Thought, and Action* 1 (September 1970): 29-36.

54. Joseph Smith III to Audentia Anderson, January 27, 1897, Miscellaneous Letters and Papers; Davis, *Story of the Church,* 559-64; Smith and Smith, *History of Reorganized Church,* 3:582-84, 598, 616, 4:274; Alma R. Blair, "Lamoni—A Hundred Years," May 26, 1979, Address presented at the Annual Meeting of the Mormon History Association, Graceland College, Lamoni, Iowa.

55. Joseph Smith III to F. C. Warrity and the Saints at Independence, Missouri, April 22, 1880, Joseph Smith III to Joseph Luff, February 22, 1881, both in JSLB 3; Joseph Smith III, "Editorial," *Saints' Herald* 24 (January 15, 1877): 25; Joseph Smith III to D. S. Mills, July 17, 1883, Joseph Smith III to Samuel Brannan, July 17, 1883, both in JSLB 4, RLDS Library Archives.

56. Smith and Smith, *History of Reorganized Church,* 3:582-84, 598, 616, 4:274.

57. Davis, *Story of the Church,* 573-75.

58. Useful resources pointing the direction the image of Zion has taken, together with the currently accepted approaches within the Reorganization, can be found in Premoe, ed., *Zion: The Growing Symbol;* Clifford A. Cole and Peter Judd, *Distinctives: Yesterday and Today* (Independence, Missouri: Herald Publishing House, 1984); Peter Judd and A. Bruce Lindgren, *Introduction to the Saints' Church* (Independence, Missouri: Herald Publishing House, 1976).

VII
SPECIAL FEATURES

SPECIAL FEATURES

Editor's Note:

Barbara J. Higdon, Ph.D. (English and speech), delivered her inaugural address as president of Graceland College, Lamoni, Iowa, on September 24, 1984. She came to the office of president of Graceland after serving several years as dean of faculty and academic affairs at Park College, Parkville, Missouri.

David B. Carmichael, Jr., M.D., is a rear admiral (retired) in the United States Naval Reserve. He is internationally renowned as a cardiologist and surgeon. His article was the commencement address on May 19, 1985, at Graceland College.

Velma Ruch (see section II—Priesthood) in "The Church and the College" presents a testimonial statement about the relationships between education and religion.

In his essay on poetry, Paul M. Edwards, Ph.D. (history) shares some insights in a piece first published in *Dialogue,* vol. 16, No. 4 (Winter 1983). He is president of Temple School for leadership education and training of the Reorganized Church in Independence, Missouri.

THE PRESENT TIME OF PAST THINGS

Barbara J. Higdon

September 26, 1984

Colleagues who are students, faculty, administrators, trustees, representatives of the RLDS church, and friends of Graceland College, fellow presidents and representatives, friends of higher education and my family, I am deeply grateful and profoundly awed by this gathering. Your presence here today does not so much honor an individual as it does Graceland College and the educational enterprise which many of us serve. I would like very much to direct our attention to where it properly belongs, to the nature and importance of our task so that we may all go from this celebration renewed in spirit to continue the important work we are called to do in behalf of the development of the human spirit.

Saint Augustine wrote, "The present time of past things is our memory; the present time of present things is our sight; and the present time of future things is our expectation." Memory, sight, expectation—the three elements that compose our scholarship, our teaching and learning and our experience as human beings.

Higher education in the United States has had a remarkable past. It has served our nation well, and our society depends on it to a degree not fully acknowledged publicly. Colleges and universities have become so important that they have replaced in this secular age the influence on human development that was once exerted by organized religion. Although we may regret this shift, we believe, with good experiential evidence, that an education does often make an important

difference in the life of a person—may even stimulate her rebirth. It is an article of our faith that higher education assists many men and women to cope more successfully with life in a complex industrial society. Those of us who work within the framework of a liberal arts institution believe that a liberal education fosters the formation of rigorous and able minds, that it invests the lives of many who are touched by it with a sense of their own importance, and that it enables persons to humanize everything they touch in life; that it, to invert Max Weber's phrase, creates specialists with Spirit. And on a practical level it should also be noted that private higher education in this country offers this priceless experience to one-fourth of the nation's undergraduate population at little or no cost to the taxpayer.

Liberal arts education, indeed all education, is a moral odyssey, beginning and ending as do all meaningful human endeavors, in the human spirit. Liberal education ties people together within the bonds of their cultural tradition while at the same time calling their attention to the richness and variety of God's creation. The values of education: respect for the pursuit of truth and the power of ideas, belief that truth is always partial and dependent on other truths for its own validity, recognition of the piety and playfulness, to use Richard Hofstetter's phrase, with which ideas should be engaged, intellectual competency—these values protect our lives from quiet desperation. Liberal study holds up the best of human behavior: justice, compassion, humility, loyalty, courage, and virtue. The basic purpose of a liberal arts college is spiritual, offering its students the personal and social coherence, without which, as Walter Lippmann observed, "modern persons are haunted by a feeling of being lost and adrift, without purpose and meaning in the conduct of their lives."

I hope I will be forgiven for a moment if I take a brief and somewhat anecdotal look at the proud record of Graceland College. The sons and daughters of this institution have demonstrated the excellence with which Graceland has fulfilled its humanizing and educating mission. The success of its graduates goes far beyond the level its size and financial balance sheet might suggest were possible. Generations of self-sustaining ministers and general officers of the RLDS church, competent men and women practicing the important careers of our society, responsible parents and concerned citizens, an Olympic decathlon winner and a Pulitzer prize winner, a 95 percent acceptance record to law schools, and 85 percent acceptance record to medical schools, documented recognition by employers that not only are Graceland College men and women well-trained but they also have the value added behaviors of integrity, which marks the successful professional in any pursuit. Now for the anecdotes. This is a quotation from a letter of a recent Graceland graduate in nursing: "I many times think of the instructors who encouraged me to feel I could make an impact on high-quality health care in the nursing field. I can tell you that when I came from Graceland I felt that I was a special kind of nurse with lots to offer the profession. I thank my Graceland instructors for the invaluable encouragement and confidence they gave me as a new graduate and professional." I attended a conference for college presidents this summer sponsored by the American Council for Education. Dr. Robert Corrigan, Chancellor of the University of Massachusetts Boston Harbor campus, spotted the name Graceland on my name tag. He said to me: "For a long time I've been waiting to say this to someone from Graceland. The best three students I ever had came from your school—how do you explain that? What are you doing at Graceland?"

In this present time of past things, our memory reminds us that we are beneficiaries of an important and proud heritage that has called forth the best expressions of our humanness.

Everyone in this room knows that we face a difficult present. The changing demography in this country and its resulting financial impact on our institutions, high interest rates, uncertainty about energy costs, unemployment, lack of growth, the competition of vocational postsecondary education, increasingly complex governance arrangements resulting in critical problems of institutional morale in a no-growth or even retrenchment mode, increased need to meet government regulations, all combine to challenge our ability to continue the tradition of the past. I am reminded almost daily of a comment made by a graduate professor of mine who loved to tell us about how he had risen at 3:00 A.M. for four years to milk cows in order to pay his undergraduate college bills—in the good old days when students could still pay all of their costs through their own efforts. And he would always end the story by saying that he was assured that the experience built character. "But," he would add, "I felt I could do with a little more money and a little less character." My sentiments exactly. Since we may not be able to opt for more money, we need to acknowledge that we may well be confronted with an unparalleled opportunity to strengthen institutional character by reviewing and redefining the essential nature of what we do. In a more affluent and permissive time we may have succumbed in part at least to the lure of the inessential and the inconsequential and may have confused it with excellence in education. The realities of our present time of present things challenge us. Today only about 18 percent of the total adult population 25 years or older hold four-year or graduate degrees. About 71 percent hold high school diplomas. Even before the National Committee on Excellence in Education's 1983 publication of *A Nation at Risk, The Imperatives for Education Reform,* college people knew what had happened to competence in basic skills in this country among high school graduates. Eighty-four percent of American institutions of higher education report that entering freshmen have serious problems in the basic skills. Obviously the amount of educational work to be done is enormous. Plenty of uneducated people are available and the various handicaps associated with primary and secondary school educational deprivation can be corrected. Higher education must not become an elitist opportunity where only the richest, brightest are given the privilege.

Graceland College needs in this present time of administrative transition for us to focus our thought and creativity on our expectation of future things. I would first like to suggest an appropriate methodology for that process. A liberal arts institution to be true to itself must practice the habits of a liberal arts education in thinking about its future as an institution as surely as its graduates must practice those same habits in thinking about their individual futures. Those habits include research and analysis, logic and creativity, hard work and integrity. The entire college community must reaffirm its commitment to the teaching and learning enterprise.

We must also reevaluate the quality of our scholarly fellowship. Sherman Paul has pointed out that a community of scholars no longer able or willing to communicate with each other is no longer a community. Many faculty have become psychologically and intellectually strangers to one another. This must not happen at Graceland. We must resist the temptation to be more concerned about ourselves than about our profession and our institution. We must find again if we have lost it, the willingness to give our lives to our task. It is that important.

If these remarks seem especially directed to faculty and students, it is because your relationships are at the heart of the teaching/learning process. The rest of us provide support systems. All of us need to reflect occasionally on the nature of that activity. The professional educator practices and models the qualities of restraint, strives continually to define reality and accepts the obligation of the educated to serve society. The quality of restraint reminds us that the authority and competence of a professor invites a student's trust. We cannot tolerate the betrayal of that trust. Second, the quest for truth and the quest for reality are the same. The professional educator discovers, interprets, and conveys. Finally, education should not merely confer competence, it also offers an obligation of service to society. Faculty and administrators are still role models of this behavior.

We also need to remind each other that interaction with students outside the classroom is just as important to the development of the student's potential, as the structured relationships in lecture hall and laboratory. Professor Henri Nouwen writes, "My whole life I have been complaining that my work was constantly interrupted, until I discovered that my interruptions were my work." Much more difficult, since it contradicts a dearly held belief, we need to accept the challenge of the student whom Lloyd Averill prefers to call the unpracticed rather than the disadvantaged or underprepared. We need to refuse to believe that academically deprived students are lost to intellectual accomplishments at the college level. There are ways to bridge the gap. Consider, for example, Elementary School No. 27 in Indianapolis which has a chess club called the Masters of Disaster, so named because it has so many losing seasons, that won the National Elementary School Chess Championship over the Hunter College Elementary School. CAEL News reported that "the children of New York City's intelligentsia had lost to the inner city kids of Indianapolis." In a test of skill in intellectual gamesmanship, exceptional teaching in an exceptional learning environment has produced determination and serious purpose. Our goal for the future should be to open higher education not only to persons who measure high in the narrow tests of verbal and mathematical aptitude, but also to open it to those with the qualities of the Masters of Disaster. Teachers should become more concerned with making subject matter a vehicle for growth in students: informational, intellectual, and applied growth. In other words, the knowledge of a given course should be usable for human purpose. Our students should become active practitioners.

The recently published book by Sherry Turkle entitled *The Second Self: Computers and the Human Spirit* illustrates the immediacy of the old challenge to the liberal arts to humanize its students. A psychologist and sociologist at MIT, Turkle has become aware in the last ten years of a growing trend among persons who work with computers to define their reality in machine-like terms. She reports that one young computer programmer with marital problems accused his wife of

being a "lousy peripheral" and another believed that when a computer becomes sufficiently intelligent, it will displace a human body as some immortal soul's "receptacle" in this universe. Increasing technology on every front challenges liberal arts education to continue to define the human vis-à-vis the technological while at the same time teaching the technical skills that careers demand. Related to that, of course, is the need to differentiate between a vocation and an occupation, between a calling and having a job. At stake here is nothing less than the nurture of the human soul.

I describe here an institution of the future where students perceive their tasks as larger than earning a degree and getting a job; where faculty see their task as larger than teaching their discipline; where administrators see themselves not as functionaries but as creative and sensitive planners and executors. Otherwise, even though there are many excellent and successful parts, the parts sum will be less than the whole which is somehow dull and undernourished.

As we look toward a difficult and precarious future our expectation should be that, supported by the wisdom and skills of the combined community represented here today, Graceland College and the other excellent institutions of higher education in this country will discover that fine balance between external pressures and their own souls. To do that we may well have to follow Morris Keaton's advice: "Safety for colleges in the future lies in greater risks—not thoughtless gambling, but deliberate chancing of socially important and hitherto unmet responsibilities. Often the vitality of a college can be traced to a critical risk, often a distinctive moral commitment. Colleges must break with our myths and imitative habits and hazard those ventures in purpose."

Dr. Gleazer has spoken here of a widening circle, of awareness, analysis, and action. Emerson summarizes the substance of our celebration as he speaks of widening circles:

Our life is an apprenticeship to the truth . . . around every circle another can be drawn . . . there is no end in nature, but every end is a beginning . . . there is always another dawn risen on mid-neon, and under every deep a lower deep opens.

My commitment here today to friends and colleagues is best expressed in the affirmation:

> We shall not cease from exploration
> And the end of all our exploring
> Will be to arrive at where we started
> And know the place for the first time

"KNOWLEDGE COMES BUT WISDOM LINGERS"

David B. Carmichael, Jr.

Dr. Higdon, members of the 1985 graduating class of Graceland College, family and friends of the graduates, ladies, and gentlemen. I am humbled and honored to return to this campus on this signally important day, and join the graduates, their family, friends, and faculty in acknowledging publically their achievement. The diploma you graduates receive today is simply a formal way of attesting to a whole series of accomplishments. For these you deserve congratulations from us all.

But, in addition, your family and other supporters share in the significance of this day. When your choice was crystallized and you declared your intent to attend a private college, you and your family assumed financial burdens that would have been less onerous if you had made some other selection. Tuition is expensive at this and all private colleges and universities, and in spite of this, times have been so difficult that some fine private institutions have had to close their doors.

Striking even closer to the Graceland student are other facets of your choice. Many of you come from great distances, adding significant travel cost. You have been isolated from large population centers where lucrative part-time jobs are readily available. For those of you who come from families whose livelihood has stemmed from farming and its allied occupations, this has been a particularly difficult time. When *U.S. News & World Report* chose to analyze the plight of the farm community, the editors chose nearby Mt. Ayr, Iowa, for their in-depth study.

In many ways, therefore, your diploma carries the inference of a greater level of effort and sacrifice than did mine, and I applaud you and your supporters for your choice of Graceland College. No matter where your next challenges may lead you, my personal experience tells me that, again and again, you will realize that your time here in southern Iowa, on this beautiful campus, has been a unique preparation that will serve you well.

Written history has the peculiar ability to focus information, and it is not difficult to reflect, at least in a general way, on the world earlier Graceland students entered.

A decade ago, the Vietnam War ended and some of the uncertainties a Graceland graduate might have had about the morality of that conflict were resolved. Two decades ago, the graduate might have been caught up in what Norman Cantor described as "The Era of Permanent Protest." The student rebellion at Columbia University was yet to occur, but it was a time of confusion and uncertainty. Haight-Ashbury, the black liberation movement, the disturbing pronouncements of Timothy Leary, and the love generation with its hippy communities reflected the restlessness of youth. Draft cards were burned for the first time in 1965.

Thirty years ago the divisions between a free society and communism were being defined, and the residue of that period remains with us today. At Panmunjon in Korea, the 38th parallel had been defined as the line of hegemony of the Communists north of the line, and the United Nations forces to the south. The so-called "truce teams" that followed the bitter fighting up and down the Korean land mass were still arguing over such minutia as the shape of the table where the negotiations would occur. Did an oblong table with a "head" and a "foot" give a subtle advantage to one side over another?

Forty years ago the graduate received his or her diploma just as a cataclysmic world war was ending. At this distance it is hard to invoke the uncertainty of that era. It was a time of heavy daily casualty lists being published in our papers, as well as the imposition of rationing of such things that we think of as commonplace; shoes, sugar, meat, gasoline, oil. Travel of almost any sort was suspended by the need of the military to shuffle men, women, and materiel back and forth across our country to support both European and Asian theaters of war. At graduation, the job market and the universities were glutted by virtue of the needs of returning soldiers, sailors, and marines.

The uncertainty of those times, however, was eclipsed by the situation facing the graduate of a half century ago. In the mid-1930s the Graceland graduate emerged into a grinding worldwide depression. For all practical purposes there were no jobs, and it is a tribute to the power of oratory and effective communication that the national will was rallied by an almost faceless voice, that of President Franklin D. Roosevelt delivering inspiring messages he called "fireside chats," by radio to a tense and depressed people.

I am not prescient enough to even speculate about the view historians will have of the world of 1985. I suspect—and I sincerely hope—that you are entering a time that will be remembered both for a slow, cautious reduction in world tensions as well as for unbelievable technological advances.

Who the instruments of my optimistic view of world politics will be, I have no realistic idea. Toynbee, Spengler, and other historians have plotted the cycles civilization seems to follow. We have had indescribable world tension for so long that my hunch, driven by my fervent hope, is that the worst is over and there are better days in the immediate future.

As to technological achievement, the prospects boggle the rational mind. When I was a premedical student at Graceland College, if someone had told me that poliomyelitis and rheumatic fever would become medical curiosities; that every sanatorium for the treatment of tuberculosis would be closed; that scarlet fever would be cured by a single injection of the newly discovered penicillin; that major joints would be implanted into humans with superb clinical effectiveness; that we would operate safely inside of the open heart in a nearly bloodless field while a pump-oxygenator did the work of both heart and lungs; that electronic pacemakers with a battery life exceeding ten years would totally change the outlook of the patient immobilized with complete heart block—I would have thought the individual was either an idle dreamer, or, as the English might say, had "gone round the bend."

This was all epitomized for me two weeks ago. My wife and I were walking along a beach in Maui. A plastic container had washed up and was caught in some rocks and I picked it up to discard it properly. I noted that it had contained concentrated material for use in kidney dialysis. Suddenly all of the technological change that led to my being on that beach at that moment occupied my thoughts.

My aircraft ticket and seat selection had been generated by a computer. My trip to Hawaii had been accomplished in a jet aircraft operating at more than 500 knots per hour and at an altitude of 37,000 feet. The very clothes I had worn on the trip were synthetic materials. The plastic container raised the whole issue of sustaining life in the face of an otherwise 100 percent fatal kidney failure. I would leave the beach and spend the evening watching a telecast of a Boston orchestra transmitted via satellite to a television receiver in my condominium.

Literally *none*, that is *none* of those phenomena existed when I reached Graceland. There were no jet aircraft. Television was only a theoretical possibility. Data processing was largely manual, and the computer that dominates our lives today did not exist. We were in the very infancy of the science of plastics and synthetic fibers. Aircraft pressurization was just developing. A trip to Hawaii was at sixteen knots per hour by ocean liner, and the artificial kidney was more than a decade away.

Given these examples of technological progress in the relatively short time since I was a Graceland student, you can let your minds wander to the very outer edge of your imagination and I doubt if you will even touch the hem of the garment that is your future over a similar span of time.

As I said, I am not prescient enough to even attempt to define the rate of progress, but I do want to address what I would like to call "The Alchemy Factor."

In fact, when I was given this gracious invitation to address you, that was the title—The Alchemy Factor—that I initially chose. But please, for a moment, put yourself into my position. Every time one goes to the bookstore or scans the newsstand during an airport visit, one sees such titles as *The China Syndrome*, *The Parsifal Mosaic*, *The Odessa File*, *The Gemini Contenders*, *The French Connection*. These books are written by enormously successful writers and, here and there, the content is provocative—in fact, very often provocative, but I allude to intellectual content and not prurience.

I don't know how each of you view your college chief executive, but by virtue of her scholarly attainments, her administrative capacity, her reputation as a leader, I find Dr. Higdon to be a particularly impressive woman. More than that, I suspected and hoped that my fellow Graceland student, Dr. Velma Ruch, might be in the audience. With these two penetrating intellects scrutinizing the results of their choice of commencement speaker, I was afraid "The Alchemy Factor" might evoke thoughts of Robert Ludlum, Frederick Forsyth, and John D. MacDonald, and I would begin this task facing some iconoclasm in the minds of these respected critics.

With this conundrum in mind, I did, as I have so often since I was introduced to his writings in my early youth, turn to Alfred, Lord Tennyson. I was, after all, talking to you graduates about your future, and Tennyson was preoccupied not only with the past but indulged himself in some remarkably accurate speculation about things yet to come. In *Locksley Hall* he wrote:

> For I dipt into the future,
> Far as human eye could see.
> Saw the vision of the world
> And all the wonder that would be.
>
> Saw the heavens fill with commerce
> Argosies of magic sails,
> And the pilots of the purple twilight,
> Dropping down with costly bales.
>
> Heard the heavens fill with shouting,
> And there rained a ghastly dew
> From the nations' airy navies
> Grappling in the central blue.

Perhaps later in this same poem is where my more or less optimistic view of your future stated earlier in this address had its inception, for Tennyson also wrote in the same work

Till the war-drum throbbed no longer,
And the battle-flags were furled
In the Parliament of Man,
The federation of the world.

There the common sense of most
Shall hold a fretful realm in awe
And the kindly world shall slumber,
Lapt in universal law.

And so I chose yet another line from the same poem for my title:

"Knowledge comes, but wisdom lingers."

And I defend it because I firmly believe that knowledge—like the alchemy factor which is my final point—is transmuted, changed into wisdom by the alert and thoughtful student prepared in a college of this quality, and exposed to the ideals of this faculty and administration.

But a moment more about the alchemy factor. You will recall that the alchemists are best known because these ancient and medieval scientists and mystics believed that with the proper formulae, they could change base metals into noble metals. It was clearly an attractive hypothesis to believe that one could take a dull lump of lead and transmute it into glistening, valuable gold.

In taking this limited view of alchemy, however, we do these ancient scholars an injustice. Not only did they foster for the first time the experimental method, but they laid the foundation for much of modern chemistry and pharmacology.

Aristotle had enunciated his belief that all material objects were made up of varying quantities of four phenomena: heat, cold, moisture, and dryness. These combine to make the four elements of the world Aristotle saw. Therefore, heat plus moisture resulted in air; heat plus dryness resulted in fire; cold plus dryness resulted in earth; and cold plus moisture resulted in water. More than this, Moslem scientists who worked with metals in ancient times believed that they were all one spe-

cies and could be transmuted one into another. Independently in China, Tao scholars arrived at similar conclusions.

Mystical philosophers were much concerned with the search for perfection and they found the work of the alchemists—in their desire to take something base and make it noble—to be a great allegorical truth. For complex reasons, gold has been associated with value and perfection since before recorded history. Spengler attributes this more to the yellow color and metallic glint than to gold's other physical properties, but suffice it to say that in both the ancient and modern worlds, its primacy has been maintained. The term "gold standard" attests to its continuous inference of perfection.

Superior alchemists, and there were many, notably metallurgists and chemists from Egypt and ancient Islam, scoffed at the perception that they were merely trying to create wealth by vulgar alteration of metal. They felt that within the metal, as within the human personality, were factors that could be uncovered or changed—transmuted—to satisfy their desire to attain perfection.

As a consequence, two varieties of science emerged from their efforts. The first was the experimental method which fostered chemistry, pharmacology, metallurgy, and contributed to physics. The second was less precise and laden with mysticism and allegory, but also contributed to the sciences of psychology, human behavior, and philosophy. These developments led to such diverse results that on the one hand Libanius, in 1597, wrote *Alchymia* which was the first systematic treatise on scientific chemistry; while on the other Ben Jonson wrote his play *The Alchemist* which, with its character Sir Epicure Mammon, was a deadly satire of the mystical and larcenous traits that had entered the less precise aspects of the field of alchemy. Centuries later we continue to confront the dichotomy of "pure" or "exact" science as it is perceived to differ from "social" or "behavioral" science.

In the Western world, the experimental method was first defined by Roger Bacon in late medieval times when he wrote, "Of the three ways that men think they acquire a knowledge of things: authority, reasoning, and experience, only the last is effective and able to bring peace to the intellect."

It took an obscure Austrian monk, Gregor Mendel, to take a simple evocation of the experimental method, the careful charting of the attributes of garden peas, to found that whole science of genetics. He was able to prove what Darwin had speculated in his *Origin of Species*, and all of the immaculate series of discoveries of gene structure as well as the chemistry of nucleic acid have evolved from Mendel's careful work.

Those of you who have studied psychology, heredity, human intelligence, and anthropology may have had exposure to Sir Francis Galton. He did many things, but he was early in the introduction of exact measurements and statistical analysis into studies of human heredity and intelligence. His famous "Law of Regression" opened the whole field of dysgenics and led, in the arena of measurement of intelligence, to wide differences with equally imposing scholars such as Professor Arthur R. Jensen and Professor Lewis M. Terman.

As with the split of alchemy into hard, verifiable physical science, behaviorists have had greater difficulty forming unimpeachable laws to explain intelligence, emotion, personality, maturity. Truths become "statistical truths," as we apply the concept of the "moving average," "randomness," "multivariate analysis," and the "trend line" to form laws elucidating human behavior.

And here is where my metaphor—the alchemy factor—finally takes shape. The alchemists proved to be right; elements can undergo transmutation. It took until the twentieth century for this to occur and be validated by the experimental method. Now isotopes of elements, transmuted elements if you will, pervade all science. The stimulus of war led to the Manhattan Project, and its product, nuclear fission, validated the alchemists and brought the two branches, scientific and philosophical, into a unitarian position.

Each of you graduates has been exposed to your own version of the alchemy factor. You came to this campus bringing inherited traits, personality, a level of physical and emotional maturity, a desire to educate yourself—in short, a "trend line." Here on this campus the alchemists, your faculty and your friends, the courses you have taken, the books you have read, the concepts to which you have been introduced, the whole "Graceland Core Curriculum," have evoked a change. For most of you, time will show that your personal "trend line" had a steeper ascent during your Graceland experience.

The two titles for this discourse suddenly come together. The alchemy factor of this campus will always help you transmute the knowledge which you have gained here and of which Tennyson speaks, into the wisdom we all seek and can serve us well throughout productive lives.

THE CHURCH AND THE COLLEGE

Velma Ruch

Presentation to Executive Committee—
Commitment to Excellence Fund Drive
November 19, 1983

In 1995 Graceland will celebrate its centennial. It will be a celebration of a venture of faith by a church and a college and a recognition of the ongoing need of each for the other. While many other colleges sponsored by religious denominations have drifted away from their primary roots, Graceland and the church have maintained a creative relationship in which each recognizes the other as integral to its mission.

I have appreciated over the months reading and hearing President Smith's statements about the college, particularly regarding its importance to the church. Today was no exception. If I can speak for the college, President Smith, we value your acute perception of the educational process and your recognition of the dependence of the church on such a process. Likewise, we recognize our dependence on the church. Through it we find a center for our learning and a reason for being.

Every president of the Reorganization has been actively involved in planning for or supporting the work of the college. Graceland, as Roy Cheville writes of it, came into being after "a quarter of a century of dreaming and advocating, of discussing and debating, of planning and remaking plans, of delaying and starting over again." It developed from a fledgling church which from the very beginning had taken education seriously. One of the first buildings erected in Independence in 1831 was a log schoolhouse. Underlying the efforts to establish a college was the belief that a church that had as its creed "All Truth" should support any effort to open the doors of discovery. For that reason the founders, contrary to the practice of the majority of denominational colleges of the time, desired that the college should be "nonsectarian." Again the words of Dr. Cheville, "liberally spiritual without dogmatic restraints, religiously appealing without creedal compulsion." The wonder of it all was that it worked.

The eleven students, three faculty members, one dean and one janitor who met on September 17, 1895, to open a college did a very venturesome thing. I am certain they came with courage and great hopes, but it must have been somewhat lonely and perhaps even frightening for that little handful to realize they were responsible for translating the educational dreams of a whole church into actuality.

Mark Forscutt, the dean of the college, must have showed some of those hopes and fears as he prayed the dedicatory prayer. "Oh," the account goes, "how he prayed for the college that was and the college that was to be." That prayer, I believe, is part of our heritage. Not only did it bless that little group on September 17, it was operative in the growth of a struggling college, and I wouldn't be surprised if its power is not still with us.

From the time I was a student, it has been part of my faith that this was a college called into being by God and the place for the working out of his purposes in the lives of many. At no time was I more convinced of that than the year I served as acting president. The sudden call to an unlooked for kind of leadership could have been a very stressful experience. It was not. I came to recognize very clearly that a power that was not from me could nevertheless work through me and that for the sake of those gathered on this hill inadequacies could be overcome and potential stumbling blocks surmounted. In the thirty-seven years I have been on the staff of the college we have had a series of crises—some of them of significant proportion—but I have been humbled time and time again when I have seen our mistakes and our human proclivity for creating chaos turned around, and we have again become strong. Because I have seen this happen so often, temporary upheavals can no longer disturb me as they once did. Instead, they present the kind of challenge that always comes from a crisis experience—to be the best that we can be.

It was Frederick M. Smith, Graceland's first graduate, who selected the motto for the college: *Prudens Futuri.* For a long time we did not know where it came from and then one of our language teachers, Christy Christenson, found it in one of the Odes of Horace.

Prudens futuri temporis exitum calignosa nocte premit deus.

The wise god covers with the darkness of night the issues of the future.

No one knows what was in President Smith's mind when he chose that phrase, but it is interesting to speculate. I once wrote an analysis of my thoughts on the matter. To me the words suggest an institution that stands on the border between the light and the dark, the known and the unknown; a college that daily discovers what it means to exist on the threshold of otherness and the point of intersection of the finite and the infinite; a college that faces the challenge of the yet uncreated and whose search for identity, never complete, is always in process of discovery.

Through the years I have served on one committee after another charged with stating the mission of the college, its relationship to the church, and its aims and objectives. A couple of days ago I read through some of my accumulated notes and I realized no statement was definitive. We did in a sense have to reinvent the wheel every so often because persons changed, situations changed, and we had to make our mission relevant to the contemporary situation. Nevertheless, I found one statement that I think incorporates much of my own feeling about our mission. As a college "we should be a center of highest intellectual competence where learning can take place in a setting that recognizes the world as spiritual." In such a setting knowledge may be translated to wisdom and education be supported by a fellowship of love in Christ.

Behind all those words lies our only reason for being and our most significant contribution to the work of the church: the transformation of persons. The acquisition of knowledge for its own sake serves very little purpose. If the question *how* is not also accompanied by the question *why* we remain restless and incomplete. We "learn and learn and never come to a knowledge of the truth." *How* is a technique of investigation. *Why* is our reason for being, the center that gives coherence to all our study. Though we cannot provide that center for students—it must be a personal acquisition—we can create an awareness of calling, of vocation, and assist students to that holy juncture where calling is transformed into response. We can support and sustain those who seek and share the testimonial conviction that even through periods of darkness they may find that which undergirds life and discover the answer to the why of education and the purpose of their being.

I have recognized in these past thirty-seven years the privilege and responsibility of being a teacher at Graceland and have given considerable thought to what it means to be a Christian teacher of literature or of any discipline. Very briefly let me share with you the ideals such a teacher, I believe, should strive toward.

First, the Christian teacher must have intellectual integrity and scholarly competence. Inadequate or slip-shod scholarship has no place.

Second, the Christian teacher must be open to insights from various sources. The experiential should be enlarged by the conceptual and the conceptual by the experiential.

Third, a Christian teacher must reflect the Spirit of Christ. The life of scholarship expressed through teaching cannot be compartmentalized or separated from what the scholar is in the deepest recesses of being. Earl McGrath once said, "I've always felt that a person's life and character, his personality and developing ideas are shaped more by people and personality than by cognitive learning." That is indirect teaching, but it is potent.

Fourth, a Christian teacher's relationship with students should be permeated by love and the humility of great vision. It is important to combine scholarship with compassion. As we think great thoughts we must feel with one another. In a technological society it separates us from the machine.

Finally, a Christian teacher has a sense of commission, a recognition of the One who has called and what the response requires. As teachers we do what we do not because we should but because we must. Our teaching is a gift to the One who has called us and we are concerned that the gift be worthy.

Someone has said, "To give to a cause in which you believe is a beautiful experience." All of you are here today because you know that to be true. In the work that lies before us in the next few months we will all have the opportunity to invite others to share in the joy of that experience. Our goal—though on the surface financial—is more than that. It is the giving of our lives so that the places we occupy may shine as Zion, the redeemed of the Lord.

MOONBEAMS FROM A LARGER LUNACY: POETRY IN THE REORGANIZATION

Paul M. Edwards

(Reprinted by permission from *Dialogue,* vol. 16, no. 4)

It was Stefan Kanfer, I believe, who suggested that "inside every man there is a poet who died young." Many in the Restoration have felt this urge to express an emotion, to describe a scene, or to acknowledge a love, and have done so in verse—some perhaps even in poetry. Within the Mormon movement the attempt to express one's feelings has produced hundreds of pieces of poetry. Even when limiting our view to the Reorganization, there has been a significant amount of work done, though this has not necessarily produced any significant poetry.

This study addresses poetry within the Reorganized Church of Jesus Christ of Latter Day Saints, and defines an RLDS poet as someone who belongs to the RLDS church and who has published poetry in some form or other. While these may appear to be large parameters, they include a rather select—if not necessarily superior—group of persons. In defining poetry I shall revert to the words of an old first sergeant: "It is what they say it is!" Thus, if something has been published as poetry I have not chosen to argue. These definitions are both too inclusive and too exclusive, but the simple fact of determining that there is an RLDS literary tradition of some kind makes any other definition awesome.[1]

While any generalization I might make about style would be unfair to some authors and too kind to others, a major difficulty with most RLDS poetry is that it is poor poetry. The critic, as most of you know, is like the eunuchs in a harem; they know how it is done, they've seen it done every day, but they are unable to do it themselves. While feeling this impotence, I nevertheless remember John Ciardi's definition of a bad poem as one that "either misplaces its human sympathies" or has such gross "technical incompetencies" as to be unacceptable. Herein lies the problem. Some of our poetry is technically well done, or is at least experimentally interesting. Some makes a significant effort to deal with the human empathy. But in the main, it has failed to do either.

Most is written in traditional verse forms, often in syllabic rhyme with emphasis on visual rather than assonantal schemes, as this poem by Joseph Dewsnup, Sr., shows:

Help my rejoicing soul to reach
  The bliss of her supreme desire
To know and tell thy wonderous love
  'Tis human hearts with joy shall move.

I feel myself unworthy, Lord
  Of thy dear love and sacred trust;
Yet, as thy holy breath and word
  Called man immortal from the dust.[2]

RLDS authors, like the majority of English-speaking authors, have formalized the two-ascent foot and produced what is often an adulterated iambic octameter, pentameter, tetrameter, or trimeter—often in the same poem. David Smith, one of the more formal and technically correct of the RLDS poets, wrote primarily in iambic octameter as did his son and fellow poet, Elbert A. Smith. Briefly in the 1940s unmetaphoric forays into Imagism were popular. Most post-1960 poetry is in iambic octameter, pentameter, or blank verse even though there have been some experiments in haiku, li, and other specialized forms. What is often identified as blank verse by authors and editors is usually free verse having no meter whatsoever.

False rhyme schemes are quite common and have little of the musical quality that I would prefer. There was (and is) a great respect in the later years for short pithy poems with very uncomplicated subjects; longer and more complicated attempts, when found, lack the thematic structure one finds in much great poetry. There are few attempts at more classical forms; and only occasional use of blank verse with little experimental work of the "word jazz" variety.

The primary exception to these comments appeared during the 1960s in *Stride,* a magazine for youth, where some excellent beginning poetry was published. This medium ceased publication in the 1970s, cutting off an important outlet.

On the other hand, RLDS poetry does not generally identify with Ciardi's human sympathies. This may be a case of the blackness of the kettle irritating the pot. Yet, I feel words—so often chosen for the sake of the implicit message—are without muscle or history and as such stand stark, embarrassed by their simplicity. Note this 1954 poem from *Saints' Herald:*

There was no chancel for the white-robed choir;
No cushioned pews nor windows of stained glass;
But angels sang an anthem from the skies
To wondering shepherds seated on the grass.

There was no bassinet with bows of blue,
No silken pillow for his small dark head;
But Mary wrapped a king in swaddling clothes
And laid him gently in a manger bed.[3]

Words are used both rhetorically, in order to avoid passion; and reflectively, in order to create relationships between the fact and the image. We limit the ability of the language to speak when the overtones of association fail to be developed by the factual, rather than the intuitional, nature of their use.

Symbols in RLDS poetry rarely get beyond their own static presentation to achieve a new emphasis, particularly when they are measured to fit into lines or to accomplish a rhyme, and are full of weak adverbs and adjectives or, as is often the case, completed with accents designed to create instant dialect for the sake of meter. They reflect the tendency to perform in poetry rather than to relate through it.

Most of us use metaphor fairly routinely to define and express our feelings. Such use creates a bridge between two unlike, yet related, aspects of the metaphor itself. This is the essence of what is often called Platonic love. The tension created allows us to inject something new into what was understood separately before, and in doing so, to acknowledge something which was not before. More than this, the metaphor is a statement about our understanding of our existing world, our immediate environment. It is, as well, the mark of our willingness to venture away from the ultimate, the concrete, for (as Ann-Janini Morey-Gaines states in her beautiful review of *Gyn/Ecology*) "metaphor is the language of invention and process, not finality and ultimate destination. We rehearse our alternatives in story and myth, and our stories are our conversations about our choices, not only what we desire but also what we fear; the things before and the things behind. Without our stories, metaphors are the critical continuities with which we explore experience."[4]

For what is apparent in this attempt to

expand on understanding, to go more than one way at a time in our thinking, is that the point from which we speak metaphorically is over-defined. There is no reaching out in the sense that Morey-Gaines has suggested; the vast majority of our metaphoric usage is limited to comparison. There is no new comprehension for either the reader or for the poet, no point at which we can read back into the metaphor a new understanding of the place from which we left. Often what we write is superior verse; but lacking this metaphoric sense, it is not good poetry.

I suspect there are many excellent and practicing poets who will serve as living proof of the limitations of my comments. But I accept Paul Valery's assumption that one line of a poem is given to the poet by God, or by nature, or even by experience, but the rest he/she has to discover alone. Most RLDS poetry in publication reads as if the authors wanted to write a poem, not that they had a poem—or a line—to be written. They do not acknowledge the image before the thought, failing to recognize that in the writing we must live our "way through the imaged experience of all these ideas."[5] Such an experience in writing poetry requires an abstraction, an imagination. But more than that, it requires a life-time of watching, of waiting, of seeing normally unseen things and hearing in the silence of one's wondering the words that not only recall but regenerate the experience. It requires that the poet be the kind of person who sees and feels simultaneously so that he/she might think with his/her body and feel with his/her mind.

Much of the poetry of the RLDS does not reflect this sort of poet. Much of the problem can be attributed to the amateur nature of both poets and editors. Every poetic effort appears to be accepted as a valid one. Certainly a poet must practice, but I am leery of the tendency to publish

every exercise. These practice efforts are often clever, sometimes amusing, and once in awhile edifying and true. But they leave nothing for the limitless world of consideration. The vast majority of published authors within the RLDS tradition have had fewer than five works published, with the largest percentage having only one. Thus, many of the published works are first poems—often only poems—without the selectivity that is brought about by experience, critics, competition, and a literary tradition.

One reason for this, I believe, is the "presentational nature" of what is written. I refer to the emotional shorthand used to describe an event, recapture a mood, or celebrate an occasion. Note this response to the opening of a new church building.

> A church is more than wood and brick,
> block and mortar, steel and stone . . .
> they are the shell but not the soul
> a church is more than these alone.
>
> Mute walls cannot respond to prayers
> of dedication; neither can
> they take the good news to the world
> of God's enduring love for man.
>
> So let this dedication be
> of mind and sinew, heart and nerve
> of all who enter—that each one
> may come to worship . . .leave to serve.[6]

This "light verse turned sober" tends to be very limited in scope, it has as a theme something pragmatic rather than abstract, it has few if any timeless or enduring qualities, and more than not it is limited to the existence of an emotion, not a response to the emotion. Often it is simply what Emma Lou Thayne has called "metered moralizing."[7]

Writing prose is often more testimonial, of the prayer meeting variety, composed of an outpouring of the warm consideration of the grace of God and the love of the Saints. But writing poetry is more than testimonial, it involves a great deal of hard work, and it hinges on the author's willingness to risk self-exposure in an effort to expose the reader. It is hard to read poetry, and I would venture that most poetry printed by the RLDS is not read, primarily because it says nothing new and its rewards are not worth the effort of understanding.

The other side of this, of course, is that poets are not used. Many promising poets whose work appeared at one time in *Stride* have failed to continue writing, or at least to submit work for publication.[8] Some have gone on to become accomplished poets but few either write about, or for, the Reorganization. This is true in part because neither the reader nor the editors have been able to grow with the poet's professionalism.

Thus there are few RLDS markets for insightful and demanding poetry. In the first place there are not enough knowledgeable readers to create a demand. In the second place the market has been greatly restricted by both editorial and official reaction as to what poetry should be.[9] It has not been used by committed and concerned people, by leaders or dissenters, for inquiry, for dissent, or for a means to push on the frontiers of our beings. Once again we seem to present poetry to fill empty spaces, not empty hearts and minds.

II

The majority of RLDS poetry, particularly since 1900, does not relate to the Reorganization, the Restoration, or to the institutional church. Certainly it does not characterize the unique nature of the movement or any of its peculiar beliefs. For a quick quantitative look at this point I surveyed four major works in the RLDS tradition and issues of *Stride* from 1957 to 1969.

Poetic Voices of the Restoration[10] published 244 poems by RLDS authors covering over ninety years and yet only twenty-one of these dealt with distinc-tively RLDS topics. In *Hesperis*, written by the theologically minded David H. Smith and Elbert A. Smith,[11] fewer than twenty of the approximately fifty poems dealt with the church, its history, or theology. *Discovery*, a small work by Naomi Russell, produced only two RLDS verses of the forty-eight. *That Ye Love*,[12] a collection of works by Evelyn Maples, deals with distinctive RLDS concepts in only eight or so of her ninety-four poems. In *Stride*, which during the editorship of William D. Russell published a large amount of poetry written by youth, fewer than thirty of the more than 150 pieces had anything to do with the special nature of the movement.

I imagine there are many reasons for this, the most obvious being that there is very little about the RLDS movement distinctly unique, and what there is, is more historical and scriptural and does not seem to inspire poetic commentary. This is not to suggest that the church does not have a significant heritage and message, but only to point out that it is not being stated in published poetry. A second reason is the "autobiographical and confessional" nature of our literature.[13] This might be illustrated by the fairly common topic and style shown in the following poem published in the *Herald* in 1945.

> I chanced to meet a friend one day
> As I was going on my way.
> In our exchange of thoughts and views
> I had a chance to speak the news
> Of gospel truth brought back to earth
> To give to men the soul's rebirth,
> To tell him how God speaks once more
> Just as he did in days of yore;
> But no—I just forgot to say
> The words I should have said that day.[14]

The Mormon movement as a whole is prone to such poetic lapses since the nature of our story is told in the lives of those who have sensed the message and lived the life. It is easier—perhaps for our purposes better—to explain the nature of the life so affected than it is to try and capture the effect.

One of the more enlightening works on Mormon literature is Eugene England's essay, "The Dawning of a Brighter Day."[15] In it he states that most literature has missed the Mormon view of the search for self. While I think the pragmatic nature of this search is far less significant for the RLDS than the LDS, I would agree with him that the search is most often an individual one, often associated with God but rarely with the institutional church. This may or may not be a significant factor, but it does explain a good deal about the lack of passion that is found for exemplifying the church through poetry.

In identifying what this means about our people, however, wisdom suggests that I be guided by the words of David H. Smith, early RLDS leader, who wrote of his craft in "The Poet's Story":

> And do not think that he has passed
> through every scene he pictures forth
> think of the poet least and last
> and take his song for what 'tis worth.[16]

It is my contention that so far the singer is more expressive than the song.

In a second comment made by England, this time in his review of Cracroft and Lambert's *A Believing People*, he states that America's great literature "has almost invariably grown out of the religious failure of a group. . . ." Thus, he suggests, we ought perhaps to be "pleased to have been spared such greatness."[17] Surely he writes in jest. There is always a chance that the LDS may have missed such problems; but for the RLDS, failure is not unknown and we are not pleased by our inability to find expression in poetry, nor—as he suggests for the LDS—have we "been too busy doing more important things."[18] If he is even reasonably serious, then I feel he has miscalculated the significance of poetry in the religious expressions of a people. I would think this would be even more true within the LDS tradition because of its uniqueness, while the RLDS find some of their literary expression in the larger and less unique field of Christian and Protestant literature.

Whatever the reason, however, it is observable that RLDS poetry—either officially or privately published—has, as a rule, not reflected the doctrine, theology, or history of the movement.

III

At the risk of sounding over dramatic let me suggest that the poetry of the RLDS tradition is too free from discomfort and/or joy. I am reluctant to use the word tragedy, as some suggest, and I do not want to argue that poetry is only born out of the pain of human existence. There is a point at which a people, however, have been blessed (or damned) with an abundance of mediocrity. We have not had the advantage of harassment, for relatively small attacks have befallen the Reorganization; we have not had the advantage of wilderness, for it is our effort which has placed us in the mainstream of Christianity; we have suffered neither isolation nor persecution as did our forefathers in the Restoration. We have not even had the advantages that our Utah friends had of exile, for we rarely separate ourselves physically or psychologically from midlands America that is our home. And few great periods of joy, limited mountaintop experiences, or comtemporary miracles are around to inspire.

Lack of institutional awareness of either the joy or pain of humankind leaves us unrepresentative of the people to whom we speak. Not that we have not ourselves suffered our own personal difficulties or that in the framework of the church we do not feel broken and alone, but there is no continuing instutional assumption of the essential nature of human suffering. More and more as we reach out to other countries, as we become aware of the pain and suffering of the less fortunate, when we are willing to die our deaths on the crosses of other persons' needs, we may begin the understanding of instutional expression.

In the meantime we have not really learned ourselves. We have not paid the price of knowing where our hearts are. We have not dealt with the existential loneliness we feel, or feel we should feel, as a peculiar people. While I believe that many of our people have become existentially sound as persons, they still have not been willing to view the dark side of religious experience. While they revel in the conversion they do not understand the loss that each conversion recalls. Religious poetry suggests aid in the lonely struggle (or undertakes to explain the death of loneliness through God), the togetherness of our human struggle, or the details of our partnership with God. We are reluctant to express the dark side of the church—as David Smith did the dark side of his soul[19]—and in so doing identify only the progression and the power. But as such we have provided nothing equal to a "Hound of Heaven."

I need to state a bias here, for I feel there is something within the nature of the movement which makes poetic expression difficult, if not nearly impossible. I start by affirming that our poetry is, to quote Gabriel Marcel, "not in tune with the deepest notes of our personal experience."[20] He suggests an "ontological hunger" which reflects on our ability to express ourselves about our experience. Karl Keller touched on it when he suggested that we have denied ourselves a literature because "we have learned to love the Word of God but not the words of Joseph Smith."[21] This is unlike the Jews for whom the words of the prophets produced a love of the words themselves, and thus a lively literary tradition.

But it goes deeper than this. The RLDS tradition, as well as its theological implications, give rise to a literature—at least a poetry—of narration rather than expression. This is a public rather than a private response. The paradox of the sacred and profane worlds has been well stated by others and needs no comment here. But the implications of this conflict within the RLDS community can be seen in the restrictive nature of a poetry that is public rather than private.

The immediate experience of sacred power in the life of a person is vastly different from the commitment of one who finds dedication in a religious community through the process of socialization. Often our most definitive character is formed in the social process of our religious understanding. But that is not where the power of our conversion lies. The assumption that our religious expression is the narration of this social process is a key to explaining the lack of animation in RLDS poetry. It lacks the power expressed by one who, making a sacred and personal decision, has literally been trapped in the meaningfulness of this pivotal communication with the divine.

As a generalization I believe that RLDS poetry lacks evidence of phenomenological reverberations from experience. To produce religious poetry—or any poetry for that matter—one must go beyond the sentimental vibrations that one feels. These repercussions must be allowed to spread out, mingling immediate experience with universal experience to create reverberations. The human capacity for reflection is the ability to transform information into knowledge, to alter understanding from "the sphere of being" into the "sphere of coming into being."[22] In the vibrations our literary efforts mimic experience. But in the reverberations such experience becomes our own. RLDS poetry often appears to have bounced off the authors, but the work never seems to have possessed the authors.

Readers, even less involved and looking for the warm verification of previous convictions, will have found the collected works perhaps more easily identifiable but no more rewarding.

IV

Finally, I would suggest that our poetry has generally provided neither "an escape from dullness" nor "freedom from the known." The first term, borrowed from Ezra Pound, suggests that poetry must begin with the call to experience, but that such a call must create unaccustomed understanding, must uncover the non-discovered, must live with the spontaneity of a new affection. The partial power of poetry is that it calls us to see again that which has grown old with recognition, to find in metaphor a resemblance that is new, in allegory a new tale from an old story, in simile a new identification for a familiar form, in imagery a total sensory suggestion, and in symbolism a look in several directions at once. Can anyone avoid the freshness aroused in Wadsworth's description of a painting:

I held unconscious intercourse with beauty
Old as creation . . .[23]

or wonder at the motivation of another poet who observes the obvious:

We see the wintertime draw near
The harvest fields are white.[24]

I have gone to Krishnamurti for my comment about "freedom from the known."[25] In reading RLDS poetry I call to mind the failure to remove it from the restriction of old emotions. There is a point, I believe, when the dictates of our search as persons, as well as our presentation of our thoughts about persons, call us to ask questions and to stand silently awaiting answers. These answers come not in observation but in the maturation of persons confronting their world. I have always called this frame of mind philosophical; others call it poetic. Both recognize that life is often lived in a manner which does not include that thing which makes it significant. It is that thing we search for, both in cognition and in expression. We call it God and love and peace. But we do not know enough of what it is to speak about it, or to it, other than in the language of our intellects. Those that know me know that I am not speaking against reason, or scholarship, or even logic, but against the assumption that all that is to be known is cognitive. Our poetry is evidence of our limited ability to share what we seek, and what we feel about what we have found.

Is it possible to find what we seek, or is it like the breeze that we crave on a hot summer evening? We cannot provide it, but we can open the window of our lives for it to enter. Such "waiting," if that is what it is, is not passive, it is passionate, passionate in the sense of urgency and intensity. It is also frightening. Such passion will lead us to places that we have not been before. If we are to seek what has not been found, then we must discover how to leave what we have. This is what we seek though we do not know it or like it. This freedom from the known then is the passion, not of knowledge, but of rejection, of moving away, of cutting off the limitations of yesterday's sensations. It is the openness to new sounds that makes us listen, like the love of love makes us loving. We seek to be silent and to love, yet if we achieve both we are not aware of being either.

To suggest that the poetry of the RLDS movement lacks passion, then, is to suggest that it is too conscious of what it is. It is not risk, it is not the leap from that which is known to accept without recognition that which is unknown. The idea of losing one's life in order to have life has been pronounced theologically, religiously and philosophically, with little avail to most of us. But it is the nature of poetry in its most meaningful form. It is the point at which poetry and religion become as one. The weakness of our poetry is the weakness of our poets. They feel passionate about what they have learned but have yet to learn to be passionate about their awesomeness. The concern is there, the love is there, the interest in expression and perhaps the gnawing desire to express is there, but we have not yet been good enough listeners.

Notes

1. It should be noted that I have not considered the rather large body of unpublished materials that I personally know exists among some RLDS authors.
2. Jasper Dewsnup, Sr., "Prayer," *Autumn Leaves* 1 (January 1888): 68.
3. Berde Rooney, "Royalty," *Saints' Herald* 101 (December 20, 1954): 16.
4. Ann-Janini Morey-Gaines, review of Mary Daly, *Gyn/Ecology: The Matathesis of Radical Feminism* (Boston: Beacon Press, 1978), in *Soundings* 65 (1982): 340-351. For the reader interested in the use of metaphor as cultural tool this is a very significant article. This should not overshadow, however, the impact of Mary Daly's work on the nature of feminism.
5. Paul Valery, *The Art of Poetry* (New York: Vintage Book, 1916), 41.
6. Naomi Russell, *Discovery: A Collection of Poetry* (Independence: Russell, 1976), 73.
7. Emma Lou Thayne, "The Chiaroscuro of Poetry" in Thomas Alexander, ed., *The Mormon People: Their Character and Tradition*, Charles Redd Monographs in Western History No. 10 (Provo: BYU Press, 1980), 34.
8. There were a dozen or so showing great promise: Twyla Jones, Gary Wick, Elaine Cook, Gaye West, Beth Higdon, Vere Jamison (Evan Shute), Pam Lents, Rosemary Yankers, Barbara Hiles, Billi Jo Maples, and Bruce Koehler, to name but a few.
9. William Russell in his response to this paper in its original form provided an excellent illustration to this point when he reported that an RLDS poet had sent a poem to the *Herald* only to be told by the then-managing editor that it was a good poem, but "can't you write it in prose?"
10. Frances Hartman, *Poetic Voices of the Restoration* (Independence: Herald House, 1960).
11. David H. Smith and Elbert A. Smith, *Hesperis or Poems by Father and Son* (Lamoni, Iowa: Herald Publishing House, 1911).
12. Evelyn Maples, *That Ye Love* (Independence: Herald Publishing House, 1971).
13. Suggested by Eugene England in his review of Richard Cracraft and Neal Lambert, *A Believing People: Literature of the Latter-day Saints* (Salt Lake City: Bookcraft, 1974) in *BYU Studies* 15, no. 3 (1975).
14. Melvin Knussmann, "Last Opportunity," *Saints' Herald* 92 (December 1, 1945): 2.
15. Eugene England, "The Dawning of a Brighter Day: Mormon: Literature after 150 years," *BYU Studies* 22 (Spring 1982): 131.
16. David H. Smith, *Hesperis*, 99.
17. England, *A Believing People*, 365.
18. Ibid., 367.
19. David H. Smith wrote the following in the midst of his early trouble with mental illness:
    I turn unto my task with weary hands,
      Grieving with sadness, knowing not the cause;
    Before my face a desert path expands,
      I will not falter in the toil, nor pause;
    Only, my spirit somehow understands
      This mournful truth—I am not what I was.
    Hesperis, 102-103.
20. Gabriel Marcel, quoted in Ralph Harper, *Nostalgia* (Baltimore: John Hopkins Press, 1965), 31.
21. Karl Keller, "On Words and the Word of God: The Delusions of Mormon Literature," *Dialogue: A Journal of Mormon Thought* 4 (Autumn 1969): 13.
22. These terms are not mine but result from a source read so long ago that I cannot identify it. To the author I express my gratitude.
23. Ernest de Selincourt, ed., *The Prelude* (Oxford: Clarendon Press, 1959), 1:562.
24. Minnie McBain, "The Gospel's Autumn," *Poetic Voices of the Restoration*, 126.
25. J. Krishnamurti, *Freedom from the Known* (New York: Harper and Row Publishers, 1969).